Goals for American Education

NINTH SYMPOSIUM
OF THE
CONFERENCE ON SCIENCE,
PHILOSOPHY AND RELIGION

THE PAPERS included in this volume were prepared for the ninth meeting of the Conference on Science, Philosophy and Religion in Their Relation to the Democratic Way of Life, which was held at The Men's Faculty Club of Columbia University on September 7, 8, 9, and 10, 1948. Each paper represents only the opinion of the individual author.

GOALS for AMERICAN EDUCATION

Ninth Symposium

Edited by

LYMAN BRYSON
PROFESSOR OF EDUCATION
TEACHERS COLLEGE, COLUMBIA UNIVERSITY

LOUIS FINKELSTEIN
PRESIDENT, THE JEWISH THEOLOGICAL SEMINARY OF AMERICA

R. M. MACIVER
LIEBER PROFESSOR OF POLITICAL PHILOSOPHY AND SOCIOLOGY
COLUMBIA UNIVERSITY

PUBLISHED BY THE
CONFERENCE ON SCIENCE, PHILOSOPHY AND RELIGION
IN THEIR RELATION TO THE DEMOCRATIC WAY OF LIFE, INC.
NEW YORK
1950

DISTRIBUTED BY
HARPER & BROTHERS
NEW YORK AND LONDON

All rights reserved including the
right of reproduction in whole or
in part in any form.

Second Printing, January, 1951

COPYRIGHT, 1950
BY THE CONFERENCE ON SCIENCE, PHILOSOPHY AND RELIGION
IN THEIR RELATION TO THE DEMOCRATIC WAY OF LIFE, INC.
3080 BROADWAY, NEW YORK CITY
Printed in the United States of America

Preface

These papers were prepared for and discussed at the Ninth Conference on Science, Philosophy and Religion, held in New York City in September, 1948.

In their invitation the program committee asked for contributions on the subject, "What Should Be the Goals For Education," defining it arbitrarily as that above the secondary school level. Each writer was requested to discuss the issue from the special point of view of his own background and experience, bearing "in mind that we are approaching the whole question from the standpoint of a conference in which science, philosophy and religion are all represented, and which seeks to integrate the training and experience of a great variety of intellectual and spiritual disciplines."

The oral proceedings of the sessions were recorded, and although it has not been possible thus far to arrange for their publication, the stenotype report is available at the Conference offices to qualified students.

Owing to their diversity in subject matter and approach, these papers follow no uniform pattern or procedure. Further, a major change in Conference technique begun in the Sixth Symposium, *Approaches to Group Understanding,* has been followed in the subsequent volumes. The invitation for the Ninth Conference, concluded with the following:

> Thus the editors will use each paper as a basis for a chapter, not necessarily following the original form in every detail, but rather editing in the sense of clarifying the relationship between the various chapters that will make up the volume. Each author will, of course, be free to use his paper in its original form elsewhere, indicating the purpose for which it was prepared.

The papers in this volume were edited in accordance with this plan, and the comments edited and placed as footnotes (alphabetical series) to the relevant parts of the texts. In the table of contents the folio number indicates only the first comment by that author in the chapter concerned. Due to the editing, the comments printed do not necessarily give each writer's complete discussion of the paper in question, or his total position on the subject concerned. A number of the comments which were very helpful in preparation for the September sessions but which did not add appreciably to the written record, have been omitted from the book for the sake of brevity.

A paper entitled "The Higher Learning Versus The Higher Education" by Professor W. H. Cowley was circulated with the others for study before September, 1948. The paper has been omitted at the request of the author, who was unable to rewrite the article as he wished.

This year the editors of the symposium have again sought a greater measure of integration through the use of cross references. Editorial notes are indicated by brackets.

Now that the Conference has published nine volumes, it seems appropriate to list in this preface the preceding eight:

Science, Philosophy and Religion, A Symposium, 1941. (The papers prepared for the meetings held in New York City on September 9, 10, and 11, 1940.) Out of print.

Science, Philosophy and Religion, Second Symposium, 1942. (The papers prepared for the meetings held in New York City on September 8, 9, 10, and 11, 1941.)

Science, Philosophy and Religion, Third Symposium, 1943. (The papers prepared for the meetings held in New York City on August 27, 28, 29, 30, and 31, 1942.) Out of print.

Approaches to World Peace, Fourth Symposium, 1944. (The papers prepared for the meetings held in New York City on September 9, 10, 11, 12, and 13, 1943.) Out of print.

Approaches to National Unity, Fifth Symposium, 1945. (The papers prepared for the meetings held in New York City on September 7, 8, 9, 10, and 11, 1944.) Out of print.

Approaches to Group Understanding, Sixth Symposium, 1947. (The papers prepared for the meetings held in New York City on August 23, 24, 25, 26, and 27, 1945.)

Conflicts of Power in Modern Culture, Seventh Symposium, 1947. (The papers prepared for the meetings held in Chicago on September 9, 10, and 11, 1946.)

Learning and World Peace, Eighth Symposium, 1948. (The papers prepared for the meetings held in Philadelphia on September 7, 8, 9, and 10, 1947.)

Preface

The group that met at Amherst in 1944 and at Lake Mohonk in 1946 and 1948, again assembled there in June, 1949, for discussion of a number of suggestions that had been submitted to the Council of the Conference of which Doctor Harlow Shapley has served as chairman. The Council will meet again for further discussion in the autumn of 1949. Other proposals and criticisms of the activities of the Conference generally will be welcome.

The editors express their deep gratitude to all who participated in the Conference program, to those who attended the sessions, to the authors of comments, and above all to the original writers, whose work formed the basis of the Conference meetings and of this volume. In particular, they record their indebtedness to the officers of Columbia University, who made possible the meeting at the Harkness Academic Theater, and to the officers and staff of the Men's Faculty Club where the working sessions were held. They again wish to thank Miss Jessica Feingold for her indispensable help in every phase of the Conference program. They wish to thank Mr. Roger L. Shinn, who was again entrusted with the task of preparing the papers and comments for this edition.

As noted in its previous publications, the Conference on Science, Philosophy and Religion has not regarded itself as a permanent institution, but as existing from year to year, so long as those who participate in it believe it worthwhile to renew their meetings. The membership of the Conference, the participants in the meetings of 1948, and the authors of papers and comments are listed on pages 525 ff.

At the close of the Ninth Conference, a meeting of the members was held, and the following Board of Directors was elected:

William F. Albright
Van Wyck Brooks
Lyman Bryson
W. G. Constable
Henry S. Dennison
Louis Finkelstein
Lawrence K. Frank
Philipp Frank
Theodore M. Greene

C. P. Haskins
Robert J. Havighurst
Charles W. Hendel
F. Ernest Johnson
Harold D. Lasswell
David E. Lilienthal
Alain L. Locke
Robert H. Lowie
R. M. MacIver

Richard P. McKeon
John C. Murray, S.J.
John U. Nef
F. S. C. Northrop
Harry A. Overstreet
Wilhelm Pauck
Anton C. Pegis
Gerald B. Phelan
Roy W. Sellars

Harlow Shapley
George N. Shuster
Donald C. Stone
George F. Thomas
Harold C. Urey
Gerald G. Walsh, S.J.
Luther A. Weigle
M. L. Wilson
Louis Wirth

Doctor Louis Finkelstein was re-elected President of the Conference; Doctor Lyman Bryson was elected First Vice-President; Professor Robert H. Lowie, Professor Roy W. Sellars, and Doctor George N. Shuster were re-elected Vice-Presidents; Doctor Harlow Shapley was elected President of the Council; and Miss Jessica Feingold, Executive Secretary.

It was voted that during the period before the Tenth Conference a committee, headed by Dean Harry J. Carman, should consider plans for reorganization of the Conference, possibly looking toward its establishment on a permanent basis. Dean Carman is to report to the group at the next business meeting in September, 1949.

Table of Contents

PAPERS

I On the Rise and Decline of Higher Education, *Robert Ulich* — 1
   COMMENTS BY:
      John LaFarge, S.J. — 8
      B. Othanel Smith — 9
      Rowland W. Dunham — 11
      Louis J. A. Mercier — 13
      Paul L. Essert — 14
      John D. Wild — 14
      Thurston N. Davis, S.J. — 15
      Clem C. Linnenberg, Jr. — 15
      Swami Akhilananda — 16

II Higher Education in a Time of Change, *Lyman Bryson* — 19
   COMMENTS BY:
      Harold Taylor — 21
      George N. Shuster — 21
      C. P. Haskins — 23
      Herman Finer — 23
      Christian Gauss — 24
      Louis J. A. Mercier — 25
      Alain L. Locke — 27
      Swami Akhilananda — 29
      Scott Buchanan — 30

III The Axiological Orientation of (Higher) Education, *T. V. Smith* — 31
   COMMENTS BY:
      Paul L. Essert — 33
      Herman Finer — 33

	John LaFarge, S.J.	34
	Quincy Wright	40
	John D. Wild	40
	Louis J. A. Mercier	40
	Gerald B. Phelan	47
	George B. de Huszar	49
	Louis W. Norris	51
	Thurston N. Davis, S.J.	52
IV	Higher Education and the Unity of Knowledge, *Karl W. Deutsch*	55
	COMMENTS BY:	
	Herman Finer	56
	Louis J. A. Mercier	73
	David Bidney	73
	Henry Margenau	102
	Philipp Frank	131
	C. P. Haskins	132
V	The Unity of Knowledge, *Scott Buchanan*	141
	COMMENTS BY:	
	Louis W. Norris	146
	Alexander Meiklejohn	147
	John D. Wild	148
VI	The Contemporary Devaluation of Intelligence, *John Courtney Murray, S.J.*	153
VII	Education and Politics: The Problem of Responsibility, *Charles W. Hendel*	163
VIII	The Need for a New Organon in Education, *Alain L. Locke*	201
IX	Education and One World, *Howard Mumford Jones*	213
	COMMENTS BY:	
	Herman Finer	217
	Paul L. Essert	225

Table of Contents xi

Louis W. Norris	225
Swami Nikhilananda	225
Clem C. Linnenberg, Jr.	225
John D. Wild	227
Swami Akhilananda	229
Ruth Strang	232
I. L. Kandel	232
Louis J. A. Mercier	232

X The Function of the University in a Free Society, *Donald C. Stone* 235
    COMMENTS BY:
    Quincy Wright 238
    Clem C. Linnenberg, Jr. 241

XI The Goal of American Education, *John U. Nef* 243
    COMMENTS BY:
    George B. de Huszar 249
    Louis J. A. Mercier 252
    John D. Wild 254
    Paul L. Essert 259
    Ruth Strang 259
    Harold Taylor 260

XII What Should Be the Goals of Education Above the Secondary School Level, *Louis J. A. Mercier* 261
    COMMENTS BY:
    John LaFarge, S.J. 264
    Paul L. Essert 275
    John D. Wild 278
    Louis W. Norris 282

XIII The Need for Normative Unity in Higher Education, *Mordecai M. Kaplan* 293
    COMMENTS BY:
    Herman Finer 299
    Gerald B. Phelan 300

Ruth Strang		303
John LaFarge, S.J.		321
John D. Wild		325
Thurston N. Davis, S.J.		326
B. Othanel Smith		327
I. L. Kandel		328
David Bidney		330
Clem C. Linnenberg, Jr.		336
Paul L. Essert		338
Louis J. A. Mercier		339

XIV Prolegomena to a Future Centered Education, *Theodore Brameld* 341

COMMENTS BY:
Harry B. Friedgood	341
Quincy Wright	344
B. Othanel Smith	347
John D. Wild	357
Rowland W. Dunham	363
E. V. Sayers	364
Gerald B. Phelan	365
Louis J. A. Mercier	367
Harry Slochower	369
I. L. Kandel	370
Ronald B. Levy	370

XV The Administration of a Municipal College, *George N. Shuster* 373

COMMENTS BY:
Louis J. A. Mercier	380
John D. Wild	381

XVI The Goals of Higher Education, *Earl J. McGrath* 385

COMMENTS BY:
Louis J. A. Mercier	386
Norman Foerster	392

	B. Othanel Smith	402
	Harry B. Friedgood	403
XVII	The Role of Objectives in Higher Education, *Ordway Tead*	405
	COMMENTS BY:	
	Rowland W. Dunham	416
	Louis W. Norris	417
	B. Othanel Smith	424
	Paul L. Essert	426
	Louis J. A. Mercier	426
	Swami Akhilananda	427
XVIII	Education as Experiment, *Harold Taylor*	429
	COMMENTS BY:	
	I. L. Kandel	430
	John LaFarge, S.J.	432
	B. Othanel Smith	440
	John D. Wild	441
	Max C. Otto	441
	Thurston N. Davis, S.J.	443
	Paul L. Essert	444
	Mason W. Gross	446
	Louis J. A. Mercier	447
XIX	Guiding the Emotions, *Rowland W. Dunham*	449
	COMMENTS BY:	
	Harry B. Friedgood	449
	Archibald Davison	460
	Louis J. A. Mercier	467
	John D. Wild	468
Appendix I	Light on the Goals of Education from Preceding Conference Sessions and Publications, *F. Ernest Johnson*	471

Appendix II	What Should Be the Goals for Education?	
	1. *Lyman Bryson*	485
	2. *R. M. MacIver*	492
Appendix III	COMMENT BY:	
	Quincy Wright	501
	I. L. Kandel	508
	Harry J. Carman	512
	George B. de Huszar	516
	Louis J. A. Mercier	520
	Ruth Strang	522

Contributors to "Goals for American Education" — 525

PROGRAM

Ninth Conference on Science, Philosophy and Religion, September 7, 8, 9, and 10, 1948 — 529

Index — 539

CHAPTER I

On the Rise and Decline of Higher Education

By ROBERT ULICH

*Professor of Education, Graduate School of Education,
Harvard University*

I

DURING THE PAST two decades much has been written on general problems of the college and the university, about their aims, social responsibilities, curricula, and the relationship between liberal and applied education, but few, if any, of these writings try to connect sufficiently the problems of the present with those of the past. Consequently, an attempt to understand and judge the role of higher education in our civilization by means of the historical approach may be useful.

As did the French rationalists and Gibbon in the era of the Enlightenment, and Lamprecht, Spengler, and Toynbee in our times, so here we also consider pragmatically the causes of rise and decline of human institutions. Specifically we are trying to discover the conditions, set by the inception of the university in the period of Scholasticism, which have caused the schools for higher education to grow or disintegrate. And since the degree of achievement cannot be judged without knowledge of the tasks to be accomplished, we have to combine our discussion with an account of the purposes the universities were expected to discharge in their various periods of existence.

There are certain rather obvious answers. First: the university has always been expected to provide for intelligent youth an education which would prepare them for doing so-called "professional work" and to make them fit with respect not only to the knowledge required, but also to desirable qualities of character and general maturity. This function is to be understood not only from the point of view of youth who wish to develop and apply their talents and initiative, but also from the point of view of society whose existence may depend on the full utilization of its intellectual capacity. No doubt, the almost unique ascendence of medieval higher learning from the time of Abelard (*c.* 1100) to the time of Albertus Magnus and Thomas Aquinas (*c.* 1250) was largely due to the fact that it provided a channel for the long pent up stream of intellectual curiosity at a period when, in consequence of political and economic changes, there existed also a definite need for men of systematic training. Disintegration began in the fourteenth century when the Scholastic university no longer satisfied the intellectual curiosity of its students, partly because the republic of scholars housed too many complacent, ignorant, and lazy men, and partly because the Scholastic ways of thinking no longer pointed forward but went in circles without new and challenging goals appearing clearly enough on the horizon.

Thus, at the beginning of the sixteenth century the *Epistolae Virorum Obscurorum* could create universal laughter at the brutishness of the academic teachers, which would not have been possible if the exaggerations of this satire had not contained a good kernel of truth; Erasmus of Rotterdam ridiculed the academic class in his *Encomion Moriae;* and Louis Vives, a faithful son of the Catholic Church who had no reason to picture things worse than they really were, wrote in *De Causis Corruptarum Artium* about the venality of the professors:

> One may show me any candidate whom they have rejected during the past two hundred years, provided he had been long enough in school and paid the necessary amount of money whatever were his age, his estate, his talent, his experience, and his mores. If one does not believe it, he may, throughout France, inspect all kinds of craftsmen, sausage makers, cooks, carters, sailors, smiths, and worse than these, loafers and bandits, who are masters or bachelors of arts. Nor are this type of people missing in Germany, or in Italy, and if one cannot find them otherwise, he may inquire for them in Rome.[1]

However, the causes of decay lay only partly within the orbit of the university, as had been the conditions which brought about its rise. For whereas the twelfth and thirteenth centuries witnessed the flowering of medieval feudalism and the guild system, the following centuries witnessed their gradual transformation into the absolutist society with all

---

[1] Translated by the author from *Tomus* VI, p. 73 of *Johannis Ludovici Vivis Valentini Opera Omnia, Valentiae Edetanorum.* In officia Benedicti Monfort, MDCCLXXXII.

the maladies and birth pangs characteristic of periods of change. Whereas during the thirteenth century Paris and Bologna could not produce enough scholars, already in the fourteenth century they produced too many. The problem of employment of the learned class appeared, and with it the first academic proletariat, the Vagantes.[2] These were social critics and declassés who hurled their versified invectives against the rich potentates and moneymakers of the church.

It would be easy to prove a similar relationship between intellectual satisfaction of the individual student, social prestige of the universities, conditions of employment, and the general economic and political situation found in every other critical period in higher education.

Closely connected with the function of the university to provide intellectual satisfaction is its task to develop methodical thinking and research. The stupendous rise of Scholasticism from the primitive forms of contrast in Abelard's *Sic et Non* to the highly developed dialectic in Thomas Aquinas' *Summa Theologiae,* resulted from the introduction of Aristotelian logic; the decay came when the imitators of Aristotle refused to modify their deductive form of thinking in favor of a combination of inductive and deductive methods of research.[3]

But we should not always quote the Scholastic universities as an example of failure of adjustment of the mind to new and more creative methods: the Protestant universities of the sixteenth and seventeenth centuries were just as defective or even worse. In their initial period they rejected even the works of Aristotle in favor of a mere inspirational form of thinking, with the result that already some years after the beginning of the Reformation Melanchthon repentingly admonished his academic colleagues at Wittenberg to readmit the Greek philosopher to the intellectual Pantheon.[4]

But even so, the onesided emphasis on the philological interpretation of the Bible, or The Word, resulted in a continuation of Scholasticism in a Protestant framework and made seventeenth and eighteenth cen-

---

[2]See Robert Ulich, *Vagantenlieder* (Carmina Burana) Jena, Eugen Diederichs, 1927
[3]See Paul Oskar Kristeller; "Humanism and Scholasticism in the Italian Renaissance," *Byzantion*, XVII, pp. 346–374.
[4]Compare Melanchthon's *Adhortatio ad Christianae Doctrinae, per Paulum proditae, Studium* of the year 1520 where he calls Greek philosophy *"hircissantem anum"* (*Corpus Reformatorum*, XI, 1843, p. 38) with his *Oratio de Vita Aristotelis* of the year 1537 (*ibid.*, p. 342), where he says: *"hoc doctrinae genus, quod tradidit Aristoteles, summo studio conservandum est."*

tury Protestant theology one of the most barren events in Western thought, incapable of holding its stand against pietist and romantic individualism on the one hand, and rationalist intellectualism on the other.

The third, also rather obvious, criterion of a healthy situation of higher education lies in the problem of control and financing, or, what Sir William Hamilton and President James B. Conant of Harvard call the problem of patronage.[5] The questions to be raised in this connection are primarily these: Is the spirit of the protectors of the university one of genuine respect for the tasks and goals of higher education, or is it extraneous to them and consequently perpetuating universities more as media of social power than as instruments of truth? Within our Western civilization this has always meant: does the university, in its search for means of support and subsistence, become increasingly dependent on denominations which have lost contact with the deeper sources of the Spirit and are, consequently, distrustful of the free development of thought? Or does higher education submit to the dominance of governments which are afraid of losing their role in society to more progressive forces and, consequently, wish to use education for propaganda rather than for truth and enlightenment?

It was the great fortune of the Scholastic university in the period of its flowering that, after initial, and essentially justified, distrust of the newly discovered works of Aristotle, the medieval church embraced the great universities of the thirteenth century as its beloved children. Their glory was at the same time the glory of Christianity. And since the church then represented a universal principle, claiming to serve both the *summum bonum* as well as the *summum verum,* it was able to provide for the universities a form of protectorate that conformed with their moral as well as their intellectual principles.

It was also an understanding form of patronage which made possible the ascendency of the German universities from the foundation of the universities of Halle (1694), Goettingen (1737), and Berlin (1809). Through the nineteenth century the enlightened bureaucracy was sufficiently educated to sympathize with the specific life conditions of scholarship. There were reactionary episodes, such as that of the

[5] Sir William Hamilton, *Discussions on Philosophy and Literature, Education and University Reform,* 2nd ed., Longman, Brown, Green and Longman, London, 1853; James B. Conant, *Academical Patronage and Superintendence,* Harvard University, Graduate School of Education, Cambridge, 1938.

Goettinger Sieben, Bismarck's *Kulturkampf,* and the *Sozialisten-Gesetz,* but measured against the usual shortcomings of all political institutions and the conditions in other nations, the German university professor enjoyed a very comfortable position. Perhaps he was too much pampered by the various territorial governments during the fifty years before the rise of totalitarianism; so he forgot that a scholar needs not only the freedom and leisure for thought but also the courage to fight for these precious values.

In contrast to the periods of flowering, the periods of crisis and decay in higher education are always those of conflicting principles between the controlling body and the immanent idea of higher education. Thus, at the end of the Middle Ages up to the French Revolution and the times of Napoleon the once glorious University of Paris was caught in the struggle between the diverging power of the Church, on which it was dependent, and the power of the State, on which it was also dependent. Against these two conflicting forces it was unable to assert its own inherent obligations.

Oxford and Cambridge, under the deceiving protection of a political oligarchy in alliance with the established church, were in danger of inbreeding and degenerating into fashionable country clubs until the fresh wind of nineteenth century liberalism and of scientific ideas blew even through their gates and made again great institutions out of them. The fate of the German universities under Hitler's tyranny needs only brief mention in order to evoke in us the memory of one of the greatest catastrophies of Western intellectual life.

But now a question arises: the three conditions just mentioned, namely, satisfaction of intellectual standards, development of methods of research, and finding adequate forms of patronage, have been discharged successfully also by institutions other than the universities, for example, by the scholarly academies of the Renaissance, and by special professional schools as already proposed and instituted during the eighteenth century and richly developed during the nineteenth and twentieth centuries.[6] Why, nevertheless, have we a distinctive feeling that they never could, nor should, replace the university? And why, actually, did they never succeed in doing so even when, as during and after the French Revolution, they were expected to do so and supported

---

[6]One may think especially of the French Institut Pasteur, of the German Kaiser Wilhelm Institute, and the many research institutes now financed by industrial corporations.

by governments? Is it simply habit that we want to preserve our various *almae matres,* or is there a deeper reason behind it?

I believe there is. It is only the university in the form as it has developed from the thirteenth century onward that has brought about a certain universality and unity of knowledge which must not be confused with a mere compound of specialties. This development has much to do with the tradition of the *septem artes liberales* as it sprang from the Hellenic *Egkyklia Paideia* and, in more modern times, from the rise of the Philosophical Faculty.[7]

Our present concern with the preservation of the liberal arts, or with general education, is a new upsurge of the idea that special knowledge receives its final worth and dignity not only from itself, but from its being part of a greater unity. So we believe also that the specialist, in spite of all devotion to his particular calling, should not be just a specialist, but remind us at least to a degree of the older idea of the *uomo universale.*

It is, of course, an historical error to believe that any institution of higher education ever flowered merely as a center of *études désintéressés.* This would deny the very basic psychological fact that man wants to live a life of purpose and receives much of his necessary self-respect from his service within the community. But true it is that periods which we admire for their cultural richness appreciated not only the usefulness of a person but also his sensitiveness to the deeper, namely, the moral, esthetic, and inspirational, dimensions of culture. This sensitiveness is not just a gift of nature, but an acquisition by which man realizes the beauty and comfort that spring from the experience of a deeper unity and harmony in the variety of appearances. This is exactly a value which special institutions can hardly provide; therefore the best of our Institutes of Technology, which decades ago were nothing but technical schools, now want their students to attend courses outside the narrow professional path.

With the function of the university to provide a degree of universality, or unity in variety, is closely connected its task of guaranteeing the continuity of the civilization it is expected to serve.

The relation between tradition and change is one of the basic prob-

---

[7] See P. Abelson, *The Seven Liberal Arts,* Contributions to Education No. 11, Teachers College, Columbia University, New York, 1906. See Immanuel Kant, *Der Streit der Fakultaeten,* Nicolovius, Koenigsberg, 1798.

lems in every civilization. Never in history has the danger of reaction been effectively met by a sudden break with the past. Where and when this was tried it ended in a sort of counter-revolution, as in the restoration after the Cromwellian era, in the Napoleonic dictatorship, and the regime of the Bourbons after the French Revolution. Later historians will perhaps tell their contemporaries that also the Stalinist system is not so much a continuation of Lenin's revolution as a constantly stiffening orthodoxy that is afraid of new developments. The university is the place where, in close connection with its ideal of universality and its task of a liberal and general education, the sense for the subtle dialectic of historical retardation and progress should be sharpened. The academic man should know that the responsibility for the future involves the responsibility for the past.

But the deeper meanings of both universality and continuity cannot be realized if facts and parts of knowledge are related to each other merely on a horizontal level. If this is done, width of scholarship does not end in depth, but in encyclopedism or historicism. And, by necessity, both result sooner or later in unconvincing eclecticism, or in relativism. In order to make knowledge the instrument of a universal and continuous culture, the vertical direction of thought is just as much, perhaps even more, needed than expansion on the surface. In other words, unification of parts can never come from the parts themselves, but only from a principle that unites them, and this, in turn, is not only a principle in the sense of a method, but it is a mode of thinking which ultimately springs from the power of a conviction.

In all great periods of higher learning there worked, explicitly or silently, an integrating philosophy behind the various scholarly activities: Christian Scholasticism behind the great universities of the Middle Ages, rationalist idealism behind the universities which flowered during the last decades of the eighteenth and the first decades of the nineteenth century, and scientific optimism behind the universities of the second half of the nineteenth century and the first decades of the twentieth century. If this scientific optimism, extending from science into various pragmatic and empiricist philosophies did not always provide a *Weltanschauung* in the most comprehensive sense because the latter requires a metaphysics, it procured at least an effective stimulation and the contact of the modern universities with the greatest power of the present, industrial production. The future will show whether there lies at the same time an immense peril.[a]

II

Before applying the results of our historical analysis as criteria for a judgment on the present university, let us first summarize them. We discovered three more or less obvious conditions requisite to a healthy state of higher education.

1. The universities must satisfy the intellectual and professional ambitions of a period, in other words, fulfil the function of intellectual leadership.
2. They must be helpful in the development of methods of thinking and research.
3. They must live under a system of patronage sympathetic to the idea of *libertas philosophandi*.

But in the progress of our deliberations we discovered that the university discharges its specific mission in society only when also some other and less tangible requisites are fulfilled. Therefore we continue:

4. The university must be the symbol of the universality of knowledge.
5. It must be the symbol of the continuity of culture.
6. It must fulfil the function of *Sinndeutung,* or philosophical interpretation of the civilization in which it operates.

In spite of the validity of these criteria, their practical application is difficult because of the many facets which higher education presents to the observer. Anyone's judgment, therefore, will depend to a degree on his personal impressions and inclinations, and, in consequence of this, have only partial value.

However, some tentative answers, restricted to the situation in the United States, will be offered for consideration.

Our first question, that which is concerned with the intellectual

---

[a]Comment by John LaFarge, S.J.:

The "peril," if I may add my own interpretation, is not merely in making people so content with this world as to make them lose consciousness (and the conscience that goes with that consciousness) of that ultimate world for which this world is the seed-ground, the laboratory, and the anticipation; not merely in that—but also of losing *even this world,* with all that it has of liberty and joy.

[Cf. the Discussion of medieval and Renaissance education in Chapter V by Scott Buchanan, Chapter VII by Charles W. Hendel, Chapter IX by Howard Mumford Jones, and Chapter XII by Louis J. A. Mercier.]

leadership of the university, should with respect to the United States be divided into two parts, one related to the undergraduate college, the other to the graduate level. Nevertheless, if one looks into the writings of Abraham Flexner, Theodore M. Greene, R. M. Hutchins, H. M. Jones,[8] and the various reform programs of our colleges and universities, one is confronted with a very critical attitude toward American higher education as a whole. This attitude is critical to such a degree that one may ask the question whether much of what we call today "higher education" bears merely the institutional label because it has to do with young men and women after eighteen, but has neither the desirable spirit nor the desirable quality. If one examines our typical undergraduate colleges he finds them busy with many subjects which, at least before the First World War, a European boy learned in his secondary school.[b]

The majority of the instructors in the smaller so-called liberal arts colleges have given up any ambition to be productive scholars; often the smallness of the college library, the smallness of income, and the burden of instruction make it barely possible for a professor to keep

[b]Comment by B. Othanel Smith:
One may be forgiven, I hope, for entertaining the notion that the practice of crowding boys through studies advanced for their years is not unrelated to the social debacle of Europe. We are learning from studies of human development that when the growth pattern of the individual is coerced by social pressure, primitivization of behavior results. The individual exhibits all sorts of irrational behavior toward his fellows. Surely European society has manifested enough of this sort of conduct during the past half century to make one wary of its educational practices. It is difficult for me to separate the educational ideals and practices of a people from the status of their social sanity. Our own sanity is nothing of which to boast. But I fail to see how it can be improved by recourse to the practices of those who have done no better.

Professor Ulich's reply:
Professor Smith fails to convince me by his reference to "the social debacle of Europe." Unwittingly, he proves my own point of view. For the catastrophe of Europe, especially that of Germany, coincides chronologically with, and was partially caused by, the abandonment and gradual loss of the requisites and standards of education as I have advocated them in my paper.

[8]Abraham Flexner, see especially *Universities, American, English, German*, Oxford University Press, New York, 1930.
Theodore M. Greene, Chairman of Committee appointed by American Council of Learned Societies, *Liberal Education Re-examined*, Harper & Brothers, New York, 1943.
Robert M. Hutchins, see especially *The Higher Learning in America*, Yale University Press, New Haven, 1936.
Howard Mumford Jones, *Education and World Tragedy*, Harvard University Press, Cambridge, 1946.

up with the progress in his field of teaching. President Jordan of Radcliffe drew my attention to an article in the *American Historical Review* of October, 1927,[9] according to which less than twenty-five per cent of the persons equipped with the Ph.D. in history continued to write and publish anything. We certainly should not overestimate the value which lies in the writing of books and articles. Nevertheless, how can one be a productive teacher who for forty years of an assumedly scholarly career does not feel the urge to wrestle independently and creatively with a problem of thought?

In the meantime the Graduate Schools seem to insist on confusing a somewhat advanced technical training with true professional education, which always should be much more than merely technical. As a result the quality of scholarly production in the United States, with its 1,500 colleges and universities, is low in comparison with the creativeness of the university professors of much smaller countries.

The whole problem of the relationship between quality and quantity will increase in difficulty when the plans, laid down in the Report of the President's Commission on Higher Education, come true. According to them the number of students "enrolled in non-profit institutions for education beyond the traditional twelfth grade" in this country should increase from 2,354,000 in 1947 to 4,600,000 in 1960.[10]

The question, then, should not only be to what degree sufficiently gifted young men and women will have an opportunity for higher education. We should also ask ourselves to what degree the American colleges can offer young men and women the kind of intellectual stimulation which makes it worthwhile for them to neglect the chances offered in practical life and devote four or more precious years to theoretical studies. Furthermore, we should ask the question as to what degree American society will be able to use people with such an extended education in positions that give them satisfaction and a guarantee for further development. These questions are not merely of academic

---

[9]Marcus W. Jernegan, "Productivity of Doctors of Philosophy in History," *American Historical Review*, October, 1927. Though this article has been written more than twenty years ago, it is probably still valid. In all likelihood, the percentage would be smaller in 1948 than in 1927.

[10]See *Higher Education for American Democracy,* Report of the President's Commission on Higher Education, Harper & Brothers, New York, 1948, p. 39, and Seymour E. Harris, *How Shall We Pay for Education?* Harper & Brothers, New York, 1948.

and psychological importance, they are of decisive significance for the future of this country. Will it consist of men and women who remember their education as something meaningful and formative for their whole life, and consequently carry over from their school period into their adulthood a spirit of joyful initiative? Or will the nation consist of a population a considerable part of which runs around with the finest of their life expectations partly or completely unfilled? Of men with such an attitude consisted the vanguard of most of our modern negative revolutions; even the United States may no longer have an expanding frontier for its academic class.[11] We will have more and more people with academic degrees; it will cost parents more and more to educate their children; and yet, with the increasing number of bearers of doctorate titles running around, the prestige will decrease from year to year, and so will the practical reward for all the prolonged effort.[c]

With the foregoing question is closely related our second point, namely, the creativeness of the university with respect to scholarly methods. In all likelihood, in most of the typical American colleges, which are generally satisfied with the mere transmittal of knowledge, not much will happen in this respect. The responsibility will lie primarily in the score of institutions which are penetrated by the idea of scholarly research and which appoint their professors primarily according to this criterion. Even there a tendency seems to develop among

[c]Comment by Rowland W. Dunham:
I find many college teachers are wondering about some phases of mass college education as proposed in the President's Commission Report. If we are facing a critical shortage of teachers for the secondary schools in the immediate future, the situation would appear likely to be equally desperate in the colleges. Many of us have experienced an extreme shortage at present. Whether an improvement in the future can keep pace with increased enrollment is certainly doubtful.

The matter of student aptitudes is also to be considered. Lowered standards are not to be considered. Increased vocational offerings with as strong a general education requirement as possible may be one answer granting the probability of a larger percentage of students with lower mentalities. The whole situation is one that challenges higher education in the days to come.

[For further discussion of the report of the President's Commission, see Louis J. A. Mercier's comment on Chapter II by Lyman Bryson, Chapter IV by Karl W. Deutsch, Chapter VII by Charles W. Hendel, Chapter XIII by Mordecai M. Kaplan, and Chapter XVI by Ordway Tead.]

[11]See Harris, *op. cit.,* pp. 61 ff.

the most creative scholars to shift the emphasis of their work toward the graduate level, unless the reform movement connected with the idea of a general education changes this trend.

There emerges, however, a dangerous rival on the horizon, namely, the organization of scientific research on a grand scale of big industrial corporations and government institutions. Something like "Five Year Plans" begin to emerge everywhere, not only in Russia. No doubt, in times such as ours, when much of all mental effort serves the purpose of competition between more or less hostile nations, the criterion of quick, practical, and coordinated efficiency will be decisive. Yet, should this development go further and further, it may not only lead toward a further desiccation of the humanities, which cannot prove their immediate cash value to the heads of universities, business corporations, and state departments, it may also cause people to prefer specialization in mammoth laboratories to the quiet and comprehensive thinking of the scholar—with the result that eventually even the big laboratories will vainly look for creative ideas. But most of all, the whole trend will end in an attitude that regards the professor no longer as a trustee of the Spirit and a searcher for Truth, but as one of the hundreds of thousands of technical appointees apparently needed for the survival of modern competitive societies.

It is almost unnecessary to point out how closely the situation just described is linked to our third problem, that of patronage. The time has come even in the United States when fewer and fewer institutions will be capable of retaining their independence in view of the ever widening tasks of highly expensive research with a more and more tax ridden economy. I personally do not believe that the problem of the advisability of federal support, now so ardently discussed in political and educational circles, can be solved on merely administrative grounds. Rather it should be formulated in terms of the following alternatives. As long as the spirit in the American institutions of higher learning is healthy, *i.e.,* as long as professors, trustees, and presidents are willing to defend the principle of academic freedom against any interference from outside, there will be no danger in accepting government money, especially if it is not used for appointments, but exclusively for buildings, libraries, and equipment. In contrast, if the spirit of freedom is gone, and the professor and his trustees are venable, it will not make any difference whether minds are bought by private or by public money. The demon of decay will walk over the campus anyhow.

Still more open to an inevitable subjectivity of judgment than the first three problems just discussed are the last of our three questions concerning the rise or decline of higher education, namely, whether it helps to provide unity and continuity of thought and the degree of philosophical self-interpretation which every culture needs to avoid superficiality. Since the three functions are closely interrelated, the attempt can perhaps be made to answer all three at once.

No doubt there is at stake in our higher education—and in this respect it is but a reflection of our whole civilization—the question of our ability to combine the horizontal with the vertical movement of thought.[d] In other words: will it be possible to relate the ever expanding sphere of descriptive-experimental knowledge and research to a deeper dimension of thought from which, first, all our mental endeavor receives an inner unity, in spite of its manifoldness, which, second, allows us to link new ideas to the great chain of thought and thus gives us that feeling of historical continuity without which change becomes chaos, and which, third, gives us assurance that humanity is not just a whim of an inscrutable creator but a meaningful part of a meaningful whole?[e]

There is no hope, perhaps we should not even cherish such hope, that modern man will ever achieve the sense of unity and continuity as part of a dogmatic and authoritative *Weltanschauung* that we believe to have existed in the Middle Ages—though probably medieval man felt the conflicts and dissensions within his narrower realm of thought just as intensely as we now feel the clefts in our more expanded intellectual and spiritual world. But the matter we are discussing here is not one of a universal doctrine of thought; rather it refers to a

[d]Comment by Louis J. A. Mercier:

This has long been a favorite thought of mine. The prospector in search of a gold mine works horizontally, but once he has found the mine, he works vertically. The search for the mine may give more easily the romantic sense of a common adventure, but only the digging into the mine yields results. And if the mine is a real mine, the nuggets are orthodox nuggets, in conformity with the objective truth about nuggets [See Professor Ulich's next paragraph]. What is the use of conferences about science, philosophy, and religion, if we do not recognize them all as shafts of truth, and dig into them to bring up their special orthodoxies?

[e][Cf. Comment by I. L. Kandel, in Appendix III.]

psychological state which we might call the "feeling of intellectual meaningfulness." Perhaps this feeling never exists completely in highly developed civilizations, because in them there is always some reason for non-conformity. So, how exactly can we expect to have our peace of mind presented on a silver platter? But what the students on the higher level of education could expect and should be confronted with is the philosophical endeavor of the mind that pierces the fleeting surface of reality in order to reach into the deeper sources of existence. Certainly, not every student can become a trained philosopher; however, he should be allowed to participate in the struggle of trained human reason to understand the place of man within the universe.[f] Fortunately, there can be a unity in spirit and endeavor, and a discipline of tolerance, that bind the searching individual minds more closely together and connect them all more intensely with a source of inspiration than the orthodoxy of conformism.[g] Courage of thinking to the degree

[f]Comment by Paul L. Essert:
Should this participation be academic or should it be directed toward the active participation of the student in community life where man's place within the universe is being studied in reality? Or should it be in both—the active participation in community *and* the withdrawal of the student to viewpoints of perspective?
I am increasingly intrigued by the movement of the university into the community, not in the interests of perfecting technical equipment of the student but in the recognition that the university has an obligation to take its resources to all men. Could it be that this concept of "mission" in the improvement of community life might become the *Weltanschauung* of the late twentieth century?

[g]Comment by John D. Wild:
On the basis of Professor Ulich's very enlightening historical analysis, our Western universities have never recovered the health and vitality they once enjoyed under religious auspices in the twelfth and thirteenth centuries. Granted that modern man will never "achieve the sense of unity and continuity as part of such a dogmatic and authoritative *Weltanschauung* as we believe to have existed in the Middle Ages," might it not be possible for him to recapture this sense of unity at least at the philosophical and metaphysical level, without dogmatic religious assumptions? Such a program, difficult as it is, would seem to fit more naturally with Professor Ulich's historical analysis than the rather vague and indeterminate "unity in spirit and endeavor" which he would seem to recommend. How does this differ, after all, from that vague "scientific optimism" which, as he correctly points out, has already proved its inadequacy?

Comment by Louis J. A. Mercier:
Why should men be so afraid of the "orthodoxy of conformism?" We conform to an orthodoxy as soon as we believe that we know anything. Knowledge attained necessarily sets up an orthodoxy. It is orthodox to believe that arsenic is a poison. The medical profession puts "a claim of property" on that finding. As soon as we know, we put in such a claim and we lose our own freedom of thought. What we really ask for is freedom of research, and the goal of freedom of research is to put an end to freedom of thought.

On the Rise and Decline of Higher Education

of dissension has never been an impediment to cultural vitality; such impediment has arisen much more from the intention of finite men and institutions to declare their infallibility and thus to change the idea of truth as an obligation and direction into a claim of property—which is the deepest heresy against the Spirit man can commit.[h] The other heresy is the tendency we can observe in so many modern scholars who are proud of their "scientific" attitude, which often is nothing but a tendency to exclude from one's intellectual conscience questions which relate man to the great and universal problems of life and which, for this very reason, cannot be subjected to relatively simple experimental forms of verification.[i] But exactly these questions and their answers, however tentative, are those from which man receives his sense of dignity, his measures to find out what in human life is important and what is unimportant, and his urge for responsibility to himself and his fellow men.[j]

The baby who has swallowed pepper has lost his freedom of thought about pepper through his research. He henceforth will conform to the common orthodoxy about red pepper.

The only question is whether there are other means of research than experimental verification. Professor Ulich seems to think that there are. Well, if there are, and they are worth anything, they will yield truth, and issue necessarily in an orthodoxy, philosophical or religious.

[h]Comment by Thurston N. Davis, S.J.:

I feel that the impression of monolithic conformism which is here given to the greatest work of the medieval Scholastics would scarcely be confirmed by a careful reading of the history of St. Thomas Aquinas's life and thought. Aquinas was a revolutionary in his own age. The synthesis which resulted from his daring introduction of Aristotle into respectable Christian circles, was not the work of a moment nor the result of some ecclesiastical decree. It would be enlightening for those who speak too glibly of authoritarianism to explore the intellectual tensions and unresolved differences of viewpoint which characterized the age of Aquinas, as they still characterize (on the philosophic level) the minds of those who put their unqualified faith in the same body of revealed Truth.

Comment by Clem C. Linnenberg, Jr.:

Is there an inescapable and harmful conflict between the two, within and among cultures, and hence in educational goals? Much of the excitement over this issue comes from an unspoken premise that unity is the same thing as conformism. The confusion of the two comes alike from unity's friends, such as the neo-Thomists, and its foes. Professor Ulich has sought, very tellingly, to dispel this confusion.

[i][Cf. Comment by Quincy Wright, in Appendix III.]

[j]Comment by Thurston N. Davis, S.J.:

Dr. Ulich attempts to create a position midway between the "heresy" of conformism and authoritarianism and the "heresy" of the rigidly scientific attitude. Here Dr. Ulich's paper seems less satisfying than elsewhere. For will not such a unity of tensions be merely verbal so long as certain fundamental issues (God, human soul, immortality, dignity of person, meaning of truth, etc.) remain unsettled? Surely it is obvious that no "discipline

Only if modern higher education comprises these transcending tasks within the orbit of its duties to the younger generation and to civilization as a whole, will the university survive as a meeting place of minds; if it does not, it will disintegrate into a number of advanced vocational schools which will have to leave the deepest concerns of man to other agencies of civilization.[k]

---

of tolerance" could ever succeed in giving that "feeling of intellectual meaningfulness" to a mind confronted with a *mélange* of ideas compounded out of Dewey and Maritain, or, to bring the matter closer to home, out of President Hutchins and Professor T. V. Smith. [Cf. Chapter III by T. V. Smith.]

[k]Comment by Swami Akhilananda:

We are thoroughly convinced that so long as a sound philosophy is not adopted by a civilization, there cannot be any such hope as Professor Ulich and most of us are entertaining at this critical period of history. So we suggest that the administrations as well as the faculties of the universities should fully realize their responsibility when they are propagating a culture that will overemphasize hedonism as the primary objective of life. This type of attitude in a culture would inevitably create the problems that we are facing in our industrial society and in the competitive systems of thought such as the so-called capitalistic and communistic groups.

Some may misconstrue these remarks by supposing that we are thinking of civilization which negates life in the world. So we want to make it clear that our intention is not to advocate that scientific investigation and use of the results for human society be stopped. What we mean to say is that the pursuit of pleasure should be subordinated to the higher principle of knowing the Reality or God and feeling His presence in us and in our fellow beings. Until and unless we focus our minds on this as the supreme objective of life, there is hardly any possibility of individually and collectively removing the causes of conflict in human society. It is true that the social scientists of the industrial civilization are no doubt trying to solve psychological, economic, and social problems, but in spite of their honest effort they cannot remove mental conflict, tension, and frustration in individuals and groups, unless their efforts are based on the understanding and realization of the basic unity of man and his goal.

Comment by B. Othanel Smith:

Professor Ulich's analysis is interesting and stimulating. But I am puzzled when he claims that his criteria of a university are valid. Historical validation of criteria leaves much to be desired. In order to accept the thesis that what universities have done historically they should now do, certain conditions must be satisfied. First, we must know what the role of the universities was in the earlier period or periods. Second, we must know that the social circumstances today are the same in all essential respects as those of the earlier historical period taken as a standard. Third, we must know that what the universities did at that time was what they ought to have done. Professor Ulich deals only with the first of these conditions.

Knowledge about the past is not given. It is constructed. There is no way of checking this constructed past against an actual past. Although it is not the purpose here to deny the historical accuracy of Professor Ulich's criteria, it is desirable to recognize that one can hardly claim that they are the last word on the subject.

Assuming that what one proposes to do should be related to actual conditions, it is relevant to ask that the pertinent social facts existing today be shown to conform to those which by supposition existed during the historical period in question. Unless this is done we cannot know that the criteria proposed have any relevance to the period in which we now live. But even if this requirement were met, we would still be uncertain about the validity of the proposed criteria. For how do we know that the universities operating according to these criteria in the historical periods mentioned by Professor Ulich should have conducted themselves by these criteria? It seems safe to say that no amount of historical fact and reasoning can meet the third requirement for the application of knowledge about the past to current affairs. It is not easy to escape the belief that Professor Ulich came to his historical analysis with certain convictions about the goals of higher education which he did not tell us about, and that had he come with a different outlook he would have recited a different history.

Professor Ulich's paper reflects an obvious fear, on the one hand, that too many people will go through our universities without getting an "education," and, on the other hand, that if they are properly educated they will find nothing to do with it and will hence become social misfits and sources of disturbance. Both of these fears are coupled with a preconception of what a university education is and should be, without regard to the character and aspirations of the people. In this nation we may yet raise the level of public intelligence higher than anyone has yet dreamed of, without wrecking ourselves on the shoals which Professor Ulich sees ahead. I suspect that if this high level of public intelligence is to be achieved, however, it will be necessary to define the goals of higher education more in terms of the conditions required for healthy personalities in an age of social transformation than in terms of the "lessons" of history.

Professor Ulich's reply to Professor Smith:

Professor Smith seems to belong to the group of people who are afraid that emphasis on high standards violates the principles of democracy. I personally believe with Jefferson that the two depend upon each other. The principles of democracy and justice would be violated only if selection meant giving privileges to a few and neglecting the others: but that is not necessary.

What Professor Smith says about a subtle interdependence between personal convictions and criteria of historical evaluation is admitted by all critical philosophers of history. However, if a scholar uses history surreptitiously, or merely in order to prove his subjective opinions, then he makes himself guilty of a lack of intellectual honesty and methodological self-criticism. *Errare humanum est,* but I may at least claim to be aware of the danger.

Finally, with respect to Professor Smith's remarks about the general value of historical studies, I am much afraid that those who refuse to learn from history will have to repeat its detours and errors. Unfortunately, not only they, but also their contemporaries have to suffer the consequences.

Professor Ulich's reply to other comments:

In complementing or carrying further some of my ideas according to their own systems of thought, several commentators have given me a welcome opportunity to clarify further my own standpoint. The area of agreement seems to lie in the emphasis on a universal *Sinndeutung,* as one of the obligations of higher education. But, apparently, some of my critics would prefer a higher degree of conformity in terms of a specific religious and theistic metaphysics to the more pluralistic search for the meaning of life, as I advocate it.

In order to clarify this point we should distinguish between the individual teacher and the learned republic as a whole. Though the mind of the individual teacher should be sensitive to new and enriching insights and not even afraid of revealing intellectual conflict to the students, it cannot be pluralistic. Here as so often, the extremes meet. The display of agnosticism and relativist thought, experimenting without aim and direction, have the same effect on the intelligent student as narrow dogmatism; they throw him into doubt and suspicion as to the meaning and capacity of human reason. It is the duty of the academic teacher to understand various answers to a problem and make them understandable for the student, but he should be able to tell the student in what he himself really believes.

In contrast, the modern university as a whole can only be pluralistic. Whatever our answer may be with respect to the desirability of a united and uniting *Weltanschauung,* our present cultural and intellectual situation is not yet ripe for it, or too ripe for it, or not yet again ripe for it.

But despite my cautious attitude, too cautious for some of my friends, I hope to have made this clear: unless there exists, besides all the merely horizontal and social relations, a vertical line of thought which connects the manifold interests of humanity with a deeper level of inspiration, there cannot be a stable and at the same time progressive civilization, nor a healthy university. Without these conditions, learning becomes inevitably accumulative, encyclopedic, and an analytical affair.

Of course, in the expression of the ultimate, the fragmentary instrument of our conceptual thinking will always be insufficient and, in the best case, approximating. All search for final unity contains by necessity a "meta"-physical and, if one wants to say so, "mystical" element, symbolic of cosmic laws and energies which the human mind can but imagine. This is the curse, but it is also the beauty of the language by which man converses with the universe. That which remains as the last and most precious result is a profound sense of reverence.

CHAPTER II

Higher Education in a Time of Change

By LYMAN BRYSON

Professor of Education, Teachers College, Columbia University, Counsellor on Public Affairs, Columbia Broadcasting System

HISTORIANS HAVE BEEN carrying on a long dispute about the nature and chief purpose of the higher education of the past, of those institutions and folkways out of which our own amorphous higher educational institutions have sprouted. We may some day get valuable guidance out of their findings if they ever agree, but whatever the old pattern may have been, we have new patterns now and must use them. We cannot wait to find out what our ancestors intended before we decide what we intend for ourselves. It seems to be clear enough, in any case, that higher education, thought of as the elite of youth growing up in intimate intellectual association with the greatest minds of their time, is impossible on a large democratic scale. Even in a democracy there are not enough great minds to go around. We cannot accept either the educational ideal of liberalizing the minds of gentlemen, or the ideal of training a ruling class, as long as we maintain, as our dominant ideals, equality of opportunity and equality of responsibility for sharing in government.

I agree with those who believe that the old structure has been damaged beyond repair and that the new forms have not yet clearly emerged. Without mourning the old, it is still possible to be dissatisfied with the tentative new. But I do not agree that the mere intrusion of numbers, or of vocational training—the favorite villains—are entirely to blame. The ideal of equality requires of us that we do the best we can with numbers and make excellence of the highest sort accessible to all our youth. And the ideal of freedom requires of us that we imbue all training, for whatever human interest or occupation, with the sense of public responsibility.

My purpose here is to offer three theses which can serve, I believe, as a beginning toward locating the specific problems to be solved. The solutions will require more experience and obviously more wisdom than anyone has now. These propositions have to do with the method by which a modern university or college, accepting, as it evidently must, the task of training men and women for practical life, will accomplish also the task of training them for liberal living and responsibility to their time and their culture. Citizenship may be, in this connection, too narrow a word. It is certainly not mere national responsibility that we mean, since a nation can be narrowly served. Nor is it the mere enlargement of the national ideal to a multiple chauvinism which substitutes an acceptance of a combination of all narrow nationalisms as something higher than naive patriotism. Leaving the problems raised by those sentiments aside, we can address ourselves rather to the more difficult work of devising ways in which "educated" citizens can be loyal to the higher values of all civilization, regardless of national or international affairs. It would be a wonderful era in the world's history if we could get all citizens, in all nations, to think without suspicion and strive without violence in international affairs. But there are even greater things in the world than peace and education should maintain them.

How does an institution, committed by egalitarian ideals to a great breadth of vocational training, achieve also its larger task? The Chicago and St. John's plans would provide a way for students, both in college and in adult groups afterward, to keep alive the traditions of their culture and the highest challenges to the human spirit. I have no quarrel with that method, as far as it goes. But it cannot succeed, even in its own narrow terms with its own restricted clients, unless it is based on a popular culture far more thoughtful and serious than we seem to have now. I would go further and say that if these reforms, of which I can suggest only the beginnings here, could actually be instituted in our higher education, more people would read and discuss great books and the ideas would cut deeper into their lives. The great books idea would then be, I think, a little less extraneous, a little less of an exhilarating hobby than it is now.[a]

[a] [For further discussion of the "Chicago Plan," see Chapter III by T. V. Smith, Chapter VIII by Alain L. Locke, Chapter IX by Howard Mumford Jones, Chapter XI by John U. Nef, Chapter XIII by Mordecai M. Kaplan, Chapter XV by George N. Shuster, Chapter

The first thesis is that we have gone wrong in substituting stimulation for education. It is my own practical observation, which must agree with the experience of most men who have anything to do with college graduates, that the markets are now overrun with eager, able, admirable young men and women who are big with purpose but have nothing else to offer.[b]

It is difficult to explain to them that there are only a few ways in which one can be useful to the world and to the best things in it. One is in humble service, doing the daily work of business and home. They have generally been taught to reject this as not good enough for their training and their powers. They have been stimulated beyond any such humility by the educational processes which were designed in the beginning to be sure we did not bring up a generation of complacent and slothful materialists but which appear to endanger us with generations of high-minded incompetents.[c] Another of the evidently avail-

---

XVI by Earl J. McGrath, Chapter XVII by Ordway Tead, and George B. de Huszar's comment in Appendix III.]

[b]Comment by Harold Taylor:

This thesis needs a lot of work on it before it could turn out to be true. Most colleges do not stimulate intellectual interest or moral interest. They acknowledge it when they see it, but do very little to bring it on. The life around the college stimulates the student to want to be successful easily, and in conventional terms. The colleges, for the most part, encourage that attitude to success, and stimulate the students to build a record for the college year book—to make a fat and pretentious paragraph of the triumphs of college life—membership in clubs, office holding in associations, fraternities, sports, and success in the game of getting grades. I do not feel that colleges have stimulated purposes. They have given tacit approval to stimuli already present in American society, and have encouraged young people to think about life and success as a series of little victories over other people.

On the other hand, I agree with Mr. Bryson that the young who graduate from college are for the most part eager, anxious to do what is right, and usually unable to present anything very employable to an employer. In a technical aspect, most useful pieces of knowledge do little to educate the student liberally. Yet we should not therefore conclude that the things which are useful, either for getting things done, or for increasing technical skill, have no liberal values in them. In college education, ability to state one's own position about American foreign policy is one aspect of a technical or vocational skill. The other skills necessary for fulfilling the purposes and functions of life in America can be taught without interfering with the ultimate humanism to which the college must be devoted.

[c]Comment by George N. Shuster:

What concerns me is just what Mr. Bryson has put his finger on: the prevalent feeling that everybody owes the college graduate not merely a living but a vice presidency. [Cf. Chapter IX by Howard Mumford Jones.] Have we not gone along assuming that training designed for the relatively academic professions could be extended to very large numbers of people without creating a vast army of displaced academicians? It is

able ways of serving your community and the world is to put at their service some special gift with which you are endowed. If you are not thus endowed, alas, no amount of idealism will make you useful and this also is a lesson that education does not teach our youth. When experience of practical affairs teaches this lesson, it is effective but it hurts much more.

The third way of service, the way in which an education ought to launch the eager and intelligent young, is the old way of "success." I do not mean the pursuit of any lowborn materialistic goddess of competition. I mean rather to reassert the dignity of ambition, temperate and liberal and honest, but seeking its achievements nevertheless in the ordinary business of the world. Whether the young idealists and their teachers like it or not, the world will always listen, in the discussion of the great questions, to those who have earned prestige by real achievement. This may not be the wisest leadership for the world to follow

---

all very well to say, as we are often in danger of saying, that a world which has trained too many lawyers must proceed to create reasons why there should be more lawyers. Perhaps, but the bill comes high.

Bricklayers in New York City are currently being paid $27 a day because there are so few bricklayers, and because the building trades are efficiently organized. If one of these gentlemen were to toil for three hundred days, his salary would of course be $8,100—a tidy sum, which I do not begrudge him. He need not belong to a club or a learned society, and his everyday wardrobe is not an extensive one. He does not need to employ a nurse, as does a dentist, and the library requirements for the art of bricklaying are modest. Meanwhile the average young Ph.D. has, if he lived frugally and abstained from all the little emptiness of love, paid about $5,000 for his postgraduate education, and has signed up for a teaching job at a salary of about $3,000, made possible in many instances only by the financial windfall produced by the Bill of Rights designed especially for G.I. consumption.

The tragedy of American culture is that the bricklayer, with sixteen hours to kill every day plus weekends, senses no kinship between himself and education, while the college graduate fails to realize that bricklaying is an honorable profession. Extending educational opportunities means nothing unless this gap can be bridged over. I do not know how to do it, and Mr. Bryson probably does not either. But he deserves the heartiest kind of applause for seeing that the gap is right in front of our collective noses.

It is possibly sinful, but I do not see how everybody is going to be given the benefits of a college education unless somebody is willing later on to work in a garage, spray trees, mix concrete, and take dictation. And be happy while doing these things—or at least as happy as a human being ought decently to permit himself to be.

[Cf. the discussion of the place of vocational preparation in the goals of education in Chapter III by T. V. Smith, Chapter IX by Howard Mumford Jones, Chapter XV by George N. Shuster, Chapter XVI by Earl J. McGrath (including comment by Louis J. A. Mercier), Chapter XVIII by Harold Taylor (including comments by Mason W. Gross and Dr. Mercier), and comment by George B. de Huszar in Appendix III.]

but it seems quite likely that it will still be followed for a long time and youth should be prepared to achieve their ideal good in a world of that sort. It may also be said in passing that the sudden eruption of charismatic leaders into the affairs of any nation has not, in most cases, been an improvement on the old habit of listening to those who have shown good judgment in their own careers. Examples are Mussolini and Hitler. The world may not be led swiftly forward by its successful people who are apt to be stodgy and too slow; it has generally been led into disaster by its suddenly elevated failures like those just named.

Whichever of these three ways of service may be followed by the young idealist he needs skills; he needs to know how to make a place for himself. Except for the second path which is reserved for the very few, those not self-selected but marked by stigmatic destiny, he needs to know how to get on in and with the world as it is. I do not know how many idealists we are now losing because they are frustrated by being stimulated beyond their capacity and inspired beyond their practical skill.[d]

This would indicate that vocational training is still the basis of service to the world, even in high and great things, and I would not shrink from that conclusion.[e] Not mere vocational training however. Not mere

[d]Comment by C. P. Haskins:
There are few more bitter experiences for youth than to emerge into the world bursting with idealism and the desire to do good in society, only to find that society is not prepared to open avenues to do good to one who is not equipped to render a specialized and useful service. The reaction is apt to be both violent and hostile. I thoroughly agree with Lyman Bryson's description of the difficulty of convincing young people that there are only a few roads (such as the three which he has so cogently set out) by which practical good can be done in the world. These are not the roads for which young idealism seeks, unless that idealism has been tempered with a measure of preparation and of realism in pregraduation days.

[e]Comment by Herman Finer:
I take Dr. Bryson's point well—that we must make vocational education our main focus. However, I do not think that what the world now needs is to be obtained by centering our higher educational effort upon this axis. Are we concerned principally with the making of citizens of a democratic state and of the world, or not? I would regard it as destructive of the cultivation of contributory citizenship to fall back into vocationalism. All that so many other of the Conference papers warn against is to be suffered, if we return to what cannot but be narrow, segmented, introverted, self-centered, necessarily blinded to the wider issues because made so dazzlingly brilliant in the narrower ones.

It seems to me that if we want self-governing but creative citizens, simultaneously with vocational competence, then a time must be set for the former, and a time for the latter. Therefore, cut down the undergraduate years from four to three, and make the students work harder, more earnestly, with severer standards of application and attain-

equipment for success. Not even primarily that, but that surely as instrumental to being able to speak for your ideals and be heard.

The second of the three propositions is that we fail to teach our young people, in the process of their higher education, the difference between the function and the purpose of their own public activity. By public activity I mean their work because the work by which one earns a living has always a public aspect.

By purpose, I mean the driving force of personal ambition, to make a living, to support a family, to educate children and protect the old, to be admired or famous or rich or great. And by function I mean the use to society of what you get done in achieving your purposes. A homely and precise illustration would be the work of a real estate agent. His purpose is to make a living and compete with rivals in his own world for the prizes they all desire. His function is to help families find homes and business enterprises to get housing and cities to grow in decency and health. The purpose and the function are not the same thing. They should not be in conflict; in a perfect society no man's proper purpose could be in conflict with his appropriate function. An educated man is aware of the function he is fitted to fulfil and does not allow his purposes to defeat the social usefulness he is capable of. An educated man cannot be content to be a destructive and selfish business man or an incompetent professional worker, letting his purposes override his function, and then think to make up for that by activities as a public figure. If all functions are fulfilled the role of the public figure is greatly diminished and it might well be argued that the dangerous aspects of the welfare state that we seem now to be establishing are largely in the attempt to care for the public interest by public actions that would be private actions if this ideal were lived up to. I cannot now defend the proposition that the welfare state is in itself a confession of educational failure, in both quality and distribution, but I think it could be argued.[f]

---

ment, than now. Keep these three years for their induction into their duties and rights as Americans and cosmopolitans. Then, afterwards, let them spend as much time on their professional education as they wish, and at some stage in the vocational years give them some further insights into the relationship of their work to their worth.

[f] Comment by Christian Gauss:

I cannot share Lyman Bryson's fear of the "welfare state." Political systems are justified in proportion as they minister to human welfare. Our democracy sees human welfare in terms of two major and, in practice, conflicting goods. The Declaration lists them as freedom and equality; the Constitution as the "blessings of liberty" and "the general welfare." These concepts are not coordinate and coextensive. Each limits the other and

The third proposition may not seem to follow logically from what has been said up to here. I have been urging that the institutions of higher education accept the vocational role and liberalize man's practical activities by making educated men and women so effective in the world that their ideals may be better realized and that vocations be liberalized by inculcating in all workers the highest possible ideal of service on the job.[g] The first thesis can be advanced only if one can

---

their balance is being continually upset in our time, by research in science and technology. As I see it, one of the major functions of higher education in our democracy today, is to make clearer to potential candidates their responsibility toward maintaining the balance between these two antinomial conceptions. The discredit into which "the welfare state" has fallen in the day of the atom bomb indicates the urgency of our problem.

Comment by Herman Finer:
Dr. Bryson thinks, apparently, that the establishment by the state of the social services (including education), of social insurance, of measures for the raising of the standard of living, productionally; of the credit agencies of the government; of the monopoly-regulating institutions of the government—that all of these or some of them might be private actions if we were better educated. If this is what he means, I believe it contains a serious fallacy about the nature of the state and the economy, and a serious one about the efficacy of education. The welfare state is no caprice; it is the deliberate creation of the human mind. It is, indeed, the product of education, not of its failure. I doubt whether there was ever a time for education for benevolent anarchy. Every statesman, every political philosopher, every church admits the value of education for social living, indeed, relies on it heavily—but relies on other measures, such as hedonism, natural human sympathy, and at the margins compulsion, for some welfare purposes that would be neglected without it, or if sought by education alone would require so great an expense of energy and spirit and manpower on education (one educator standing over each hesitant, grudging, malingering citizen responsible for a welfare duty), that many other values would be lost in the meanwhile. And, let it be remembered, that it needs the failure of not all, but only of a few among all, to do their social duty, to spoil the effect of a nationwide voluntary social activity: hence the problem if there were not government to do the things, would be to have a master standing over each citizen, who otherwise might be a backslider: the Egyptian taskmaster over the brickmaking Israelite, but instead of a flail in his hand, a berating text, or a lesson from the priests.
[Cf. Chapter IV by Karl W. Deutsch and Dr. Finer's comment (note d) thereto.]
[g]Comment by Louis J. A. Mercier:
Professor Bryson would "liberalize all vocations by inculcating in all workers the highest possible ideal of service on the job." Good, that was the ideal of the craftsman in hierarchical societies: to do a good job, to pass the craft from father to son, in fact to be proud of his social condition; Paul Revere, metal worker. But now? What about the highest possible ideal of service in garbage collecting? In fact, the question may be raised: How can we have a society at all if we are to have an intellectually equalitarian society? Who will wash the dishes?
Are we not planning against nature? And is it not nature that is saving us in spite of ourselves? Men are still born and will continue to be born with different capacities, a good many without the capacity and therefore without the will for a higher education,

continue to hope that young idealists may become reasonably effective in the world as it is, without losing their ideals just as they get the power to express them. The second proposition depends on the hope that workers can learn that their own success must always be subordinated to their public usefulness. The third proposition is based on the hope that the forced vocationalism of our colleges and universities will not only be liberalized but that it will also be kept in its own subordination to the needs of the spirit.

I want vocationalism liberalized because of the likelihood that many young people will be interested so much in that aspect of their continued education that the liberal ideas that they get can reach them best in that association. But this cannot mean—if we are brave and wise enough to keep our civilization—this must not mean that the higher and richer experiences of the mind and soul shall be denied to those who are preparing to work, or that anything shall happen to prevent the dedication of some of our best to the service of these higher experiences. Work has its rights and its honor. One of its highest honors is to keep the world going as peacefully and prosperously as possible so that beauty and truth may be served by gifted disciples and be open freely to all.

It is evidently difficult to maintain a place for the contemplative life in a society based on egalitarian ideals. It may be too much to expect that all men, given an opportunity to enjoy the fruits of contemplation and the creations of the highest artistic or scientific or re-

---

and so quite content to do the manual work of the world. Even the President's Commission does not credit more than forty-nine per cent as capable of completing fourteen years of schooling, and finds only thirty-two per cent with the mental ability to complete an advanced liberal or specialized education.

Are we not getting our equalitarian society quite otherwise? As the cost of manual work goes up, the intellectual worker has to take on manual work. The professor now must prepare for his class and also wash the dishes. The bourgeoisie was born when the dining room was taken out of the kitchen. The bourgeoisie is dying as the dining room is going back into the kitchen under the name of breakfast-nook.

Is not the most we can ask that everyone gets the education of which he is capable? Why then not fully realize that when we look for salvation through higher education we are talking out in terms of thirty-two per cent?

This also raises the question: Should we not discuss the question of a moral education of which all normal men are capable, as opposed to an intellectual education beyond the reach of so many?

[For further discussion of the report of the President's Commission, see Chapter I by Robert Ulich (including comment by Rowland W. Dunham), Chapter IV by Karl W. Deutsch, Chapter VII by Charles W. Hendel, Chapter XIII by Mordecai M. Kaplan, and Chapter XVII by Ordway Tead.]

ligious or philosophic gifts, will care to enjoy them. But democracy can do no less than keep those opportunities alive. And whether or not all men understand their own needs in the highest reaches of their possible development, it is nevertheless the business of higher education to maintain and protect the contemplative life, the life of knowledge for its own sake and creation of the best.

The vocational demand is a natural human demand and cannot be denied. The basic purpose of education is to make men great to the limit of their natural powers, by teaching them to want and strive for things they would otherwise ignore. So it is the business of higher education in a country like ours, and in a time like this, to meet the challenge of vocationalism by making vocations instrumental to ideals, to liberalize the practical purpose by setting it in the framework of the larger good, and it is also necessary to make those whose vocations are practical, as most must always be, see that devotion to the things of the spirit is also a vocation. In a basic sense it is the business of all education to give each person an ideal of himself toward which he can struggle. Education cannot determine the setting in which the struggle will be made but it can help to provide the weapons of mind and character and set the goal.[h]

My three propositions grow better out of one another than may appear. A higher education in which it was insisted that ideals have to have trained and properly placed power behind them, that made every practitioner of business or profession watchfully conscious of his duty to the larger purposes of his culture in all that he worked at, and that kept also some of its best minds and most devoted spirits for the highest things regardless of use, such an education would have at least these three of the basic virtues possible to what we have now—an ancient aristocratic education for the elite changed into an egalitarian opportunity open to a democratic multitude. My own guess is that if these very difficult things could be accomplished most of the other needed virtues would follow.[i]

[h] [Cf. Comment by George B. de Huszar, in Appendix III.]
[i] Comment by Alain L. Locke:
  Laudably incisive as is Professor Bryson's diagnosis of the situation, I am not at all sure that his remedial prescriptions are sufficient, or that his somewhat overoptimistic prognosis is warranted. His prescription, if I rightly understand it, is a formula of individual enterprise success properly subordinated and moderated to public usefulness. The somewhat wishful prognosis is that this can and will take place within the tra-

ditional incentives and code of present day American democratic life and living. I seriously doubt that any such large scale transformation of education can take place successfully without a drastic change of emphasis in values, especially with respect to what constitutes "success," and without quite fundamental reconstruction of educational objectives, incentives, and controls.

In the first place, so democratically extended a program of higher education, though obviously socially desirable, promises to alter quite radically the educational *status quo*, first in relation to supply and demand, then with respect to rewards and incentives, and finally with regard to the main objectives or "uses" of education. As the old motivations of individual success become progressively unattainable with the rapid enlargement of educational competence, other goals and incentives will have to be provided. And, since education is never independent of its social order, I can only envision that as leading away from a competitive order in the very direction of a "service state," which Professor Bryson regards as so democratically unpromising and stultifying. The state will sooner or later have to exact its *quid pro quo,* especially since the democratic extension of higher education must rest more and more upon the use of public tax funds, both directly and indirectly. That would involve curtailing considerably both the self-selection and the self-distribution of its trainees. Quotaed supply, based on objective criteria of selection and publicly distributed product seem to be in the cards; with considerably more of a planned educational economy to match an increasingly planned social order.

But with the abandonment of traditional educational *laissez faire,* not all "freedoms" in this field will necessarily vanish, shift though they must. The new scope for the individual use and enjoyment of education may well be found in the future, not in the vocational but in the cultural aspects of living. For it will be recognized fully, as it is beginning to be now, that education at public expense for the proper discharge of citizenship responsibilities and the proper and socially desirable use of leisure is a necessary democratic investment. For if our type of civilization survives its atomic crisis, an almost undreamed of increase of leisure will be an inevitable development. Education for living in that way supersede in primary place the seemingly more utilitarian education for livelihood skills, and in a typically democratic way, and for democratic objectives.

Comment by Christian Gauss:

I cannot agree that we have "new patterns now and must use them," in the sense which Lyman Bryson implies. We must of course deal with numbers and with "vocational education," of which more later. If, however, by pattern we mean the aims of higher education, I still feel we are on safer ground if we accept a very old Greek definition of democracy as "a competition in all forms of excellence." We must make it clearer that this competition must be opened to all on the same terms, as at present ours is not, and that moneymaking, and "vocational education" which ministers to it, are not forms of excellence which education can consider. Higher education is concerned with the financially disinterested pursuit of "the true, the beautiful, and the good." It is one of the merciful dispensations of nature (or divine ordinance) that, excluding idiots, all men can achieve moral excellence. In this field the janitor with only a modest I.Q. can outdo the president of his corporation or his college. All education should encourage competition in this high form of excellence. In this respect there is, however, no difference between the aims of kindergarten and graduate schools. Education becomes higher when it also devotes itself to the pursuit of truth and beauty. These are restricted forms of competition and since the supply of great minds for teaching is limited, the possible number of candidates must be limited also. This is not undemocratic. The son of Polish immigrants or native born Negroes feels he is a member of a truly democratic community when he finds that he is privileged to represent his school by proving only that he is a better musician or debater or athlete than the sons of more socially prominent families. School life as organized by school boys is at present more effectively democratic than school curricula which attempt to meet the problem of numbers by eliminating standards of accomplishment and therefore standards of competition. To bring into schools the teaching of "vocational" subjects which can be more effectively taught by experts in those vocations outside of school or school hours, does not make our education either higher or more democratic.

This confusion will probably not disappear until we recognize with Whitehead, for instance, that *all education is vocational*. Its aim is moral; it is education in view of conduct. To those interested in higher education, the particular vocation pursued by a pupil is less important than the spirit in which all vocations are pursued.

Comment by Harold Taylor:

Agreeing with so much of the specific in Mr. Bryson's three propositions, I would like to go beneath them to some assorted implications which lurk there.

The total implication is that the good man in contemporary American society is one who is successful in regular American terms, has an "achievement" to his credit, and is able to conform suitably to the variety of public demands put upon him. After he has done all this, he is entitled to speak for liberalism and for truth in ringing voice, because he has position and weight.

I do not think that this is the way such things go. As James said, "Our undisciplinables are our proudest product . . . the university most worthy of rational admiration is one in which your lonely thinker can feel himself least lonely, most positively furthered, and most richly fed." If we wait until we have a right to speak, if we prepare our defenses instead of making raids, we gradually postpone the time of speaking out until we have scarcely anything to say. This proposition which Mr. Bryson recommends for the young, who I believe should be eager and impulsive, is too safe.

Mr. Bryson also uses the term "welfare state" in a pejorative sense. I am not sure what he means by a welfare state, but I am very much afraid he can only mean a state where medical, social, educational, and economic facilities are available to the individual without charge, and that the welfare of each is guaranteed, thus preventing him from the game of showing his true talent by gaining these things for himself. This may not be what Mr. Bryson means, but the trend of the argument puts this into my head as the implication of the successful man in the welfare state. The implication also remains that the carriers of culture, and the contemplative ones, should somehow be excused from tedious work and achievement to give freely to the rest of us the fruits of their contemplation.

It is difficult to see how this could be arranged, except by accident, if what our colleges should do is to liberalize vocations; one escape might be, of course, simply to announce contemplation as a vocation and hire people for that purpose. If this were not done as "welfare," it is difficult to see the source of financial support available from private enterprise, since contemplation has never appealed to business people as a profit making occupation.

However, one can agree with the suggestion that colleges must take closer account of their relation to the contemporary world, and that students should be taught things which are useful for living and working. I would prefer that students also took with them from college a set of ideals to which society might be made to fit, rather than a tendency to adapt themselves to existing situations. This usually makes it difficult for employers and for the young, but it seems to me to be the only way in which anything exciting may be expected to happen, both in personal and public action.

Comment by Swami Akhilananda:

Professor Bryson seems to feel that "an educated man cannot be content to be a destructive and selfish business man" in a perfect society. We fully agree. But present society unfortunately shows the symptoms of imperfection, as most of the highly educated persons in most of the countries are devoting their energy to destructive purposes. Chancellor Hutchins and some of the scientists of the University of Chicago have definitely indicated their unwillingness that atomic energy be used for wholesale destruction. On the other hand, many outstanding educationalists, including presidents of well known universities, have promoted the discovery and use of many destructive weapons. We do not hereby suggest that these particular individuals only are to blame for the conflict between the purpose and function of man's work. This situation would arise whenever education is taken as the training of the intellect only, ignoring the development of the total personality, namely, the integration of emotions, thought, and will.

So we suggest that in the perfect society man's purpose and function in life—in other words, his pursuit of happiness and the attainment of the spiritual ideal—must be harmonized. Destructive tendencies can be removed from human behavior and aspiration only when he inspires himself with the knowledge of the higher self and control of the empirical self and its inordinate tendencies.

Education to us is the attainment of the perfection that is already inherent in man. A perfect man is he whose ideal and action are in harmony. Every educated man, no matter how much of a misfit he may be in society, knows the highest truths taught by his own religious discipline. Yet he cannot carry them out because of his inability to control his inordinate tendencies. Moreover, because of his intellectual awakening he will rationalize all his destructive tendencies, as we found during World War II, in the name of "nationalism," "democracy," "freedom," and the like. An educational system should see this and help to bring out perfection in man. One may not be highly efficient in technical or vocational training, yet one must have sufficient mental equipment to be an integrated person and in harmony with his fellow beings. We do not hereby minimize the importance of vocational training, but we do emphasize that even the highest scientific training will make one a misfit and a destructive force, if one is not properly integrated.

Comment by Scott Buchanan:

Mr. Bryson has raised the original question of this Conference: How do we find the unity of life and knowledge that we seek? He says that we can find it by withdrawing from the ultimate metaphysical, theological, or academic question, and seeking the materials and forms as they are presented or could be presented in the practice of the useful arts. I agree that we must withdraw from the immediate attack on the ultimate question, and that such a withdrawal would involve falling back on the skills and routines of the useful arts. Modern education has certainly been a withdrawal, and it has failed to keep even the skills. My suggestion is that the liberalizing dimension that Mr. Bryson seeks is to be found in the collective participation in the political arts. Government is the master useful art, and in a self-governing community it invites participation by everybody. It also puts all knowledge to work, harnessing the liberal arts to the common task of persuasion and deliberation. The good government that might result from our full participation might emancipate the vocations from their present servitude to mere private purpose and allow them to discover their public functions. David E. Lilienthal has recently proposed that each citizen take four years off from his private business and give himself for this period to public service in the government. I pass this on as my recommendation to the individual members of this Conference. Participation in government was originally the vocation of the men of liberal education; government might well become for us the liberal education of everybody. [Cf. Chapter V by Scott Buchanan.]

CHAPTER III

The Axiological Orientation of (Higher) Education

By T. V. SMITH
Professor of Philosophy, Maxwell School, Syracuse University

Apology to Philosophers

SKIRTING TRIVIALITIES and surmounting technicalities, education has to do with the *practical,* the *possible,* and the *impossible.* This order of enumeration is intended, uninvidiously, to graduate progression from the beginning of formal education to its end. Since it is human education that is in question, we are privileged to seek, indeed are required to exploit, leeway as between educational teleology and pedagogical mechanism: that is, between "goals," which pull us, and "drives," which push us. There is the question—though we shall not make it our question—as to whether "goals" are projected by desire in order temporarily to *end* desire, or whether they are objectively imbedded in nature, perhaps planted there by deity, in order, through grounding finite purpose, to fulfil a purpose more than finite. As for our present intent, we hold that men are both discoverers and creators, and that education has to do with either and each, depending upon the point of view.

It is clear that "introverts" will *create* objects of fixation and will project them as goals in order to escape from loneliness. "Extroverts" will *discover* goals and will use them as devices to escape from reflection. And since, by assumption, this bifurcation is made to include all human beings, a certain strategic obfuscation of the difference will enable us to take both sides and thus to exploit as the golden mean of pedagogy what is common to both human types—what indeed enables the two to understand themselves and to tolerate and, God willing, to enjoy the difference between them.

Taking Sides with the Introverts

While I mean, as warned, to work both sides of the *subjective-objective* street, I shall, from congenital commitment, keep my base on the side of the subject. Here, then, I stand with the introverts. The honest way of avowing this stand is to state the question now from this point of view. Since it is human education that is in question, let us then approach the problem of "objectives" from the *subjective* experience of man and the *social* experience of mankind. In this "mode" the goals would seem to be: to develop, to discipline, and to enhance man's chief qualities. These qualities I take to be (1) man's drive to do, (2) his desire to know, and (3) his prepotency to appreciate.

Attention Educators!

In this order and with this emphasis, then, I approach the subject itself in the thought that Imagination is more important in education, as in life, than is either Reason or Will. More important, but not itself all important.

As Action is inevitable (men being continuous with the mammals), it is incumbent on educators to dedicate themselves to Skill of Performance as an honorable goal. This is the Will element. It is a high mission of education to sublimate and civilize it, but to do so by exploiting it. As Science is indispensable to life (with anything like the quantity of life which present populational taste requires), it behooves us to count better and better knowing as a major goal of education. ("Know-how" is, after all, one half *know,* and that the harder half.) The interthreading of Imagination with each of these, like a warp common to all woofs, will prepare us through amplification of the other two goals, to climax their utility with its "worth," a climax unique among human experiences and so paramount among the goals of education. This order of value is suggested also as the likely temporal order in the educative process: the "practical" for primary education, the domain of Will; the "possible" for the secondary, the domain of Reason; and the "impossible" for higher education, the domain of Imagination. These three stages, being continuous and relative to one another, are supposed not to mark exclusive occupancy but to indicate emphasis within the total orientation. Anything I hazard as to content for the stages and as to seasons for the succession is meant to be only suggestive, leaving wholly to experts, in research upon each period, to determine its proper curricular content and to date the transitions in biographical terms.[a]

Deference to the Theologians

While fraternization with the theologians is not among my motives in promoting this trinity as our hierarchy of goals, one may gladly welcome consequences not intended, if only they be good. Among the unearned increments of this triune axiology—"practical—possible—impossible"—is the privileged access it furnishes theologians into our pedagogical midst. I am not among those who would dismiss theology from *higher* learning, not even in this climate of opinion superinduced by a Marxist age. Rather I would put it just there, where it belongs: among high discussions of glorious "impossibilities." And I would keep it away from where it does not belong: away, for instance, from primary and secondary education, where its introduction tends to foredoom virtues that *are* possible to diminishing returns when later it is discovered how purely hypothetical are the speculative terms in which

---

[a]Comment by Paul L. Essert:

While I recognize that it would be a mistake to try to package these goals in distinct and separate forms for the different levels, as you clearly point out, I am nevertheless, convinced that they roughly represent different stages and possibly ages in educational growth. Wouldn't you say, however, that the movement from the vocational to the possible and the possible to the imaginative is very roughly drawn, in fact, a rather zigzag course? We have found many times, for example, that a learner is motivated to master the skills by having a brief encounter with the possibilities. The mastery of the skills then takes on new meaning and new purpose. Or again does one drive his imaginative stakes out a distance from the possible and then for a while keep coming back to the possible?

Comment by Herman Finer:

Without for the moment accepting the three orders of value, the "practical," the "possible," and the "impossible"; or the highly ambiguous terminology, especially the distinction between "possible" and "impossible," I strongly dissent from the suggestion that they can be, ever are, or have been, in "likely temporal order in the educative process." I suggest that the three values are of simultaneous significance and impact upon the mind, whether the pupil gets formal education or not. Do you mean to tell me that the domain of the Will is not always, from babyhood, instinct with the visitation of Reason? For example, that if he is being taught democratic living, it can be done without, as Rousseau taught in *Emile,* learning quite early the confession of the Savoyard Vicar—that is, in learning what Smith calls the impossible (God, Society, the nature of Sovereignty, Tolerance, and Intolerance, etc.).

[Cf. Comment by Quincy Wright, in Appendix III.]

moral validity has been proclaimed.[b] To concentrate man's claim of perfection into some monopolistic emphasis is inevitably to breed fanaticism which, by conceiving the impossible as possible and by treating the merely possible as practical, makes impossible both the practical and the possible. There is no monopoly upon the impossible. Science and art and politics partake of it, and so are agencies of the spiritual life. Theology seems to differ in that it has no other aspect. This distinction is later to be argued. We are for the moment but welcoming the theologians to our discussion, asking only that they park at the door their dogmaloaded guns, alongside those of the systematic philosophers. We mean like Santayana, to glorify their role by promoting them to the domain of imagination; but experience has taught us prudence even in our desire to glorify such as seek and accept glory as a main motive. Glory as imagination easily becomes vainglory of action. We only add here the constructive note: that to pluralize the will to perfection is our one available method so far discovered of saving it from the poison with which its own will to power is tainted.

Shaking Hands before the Fray

Being all together now, gathered in the name of Truth, Beauty, Goodness, and their like, let us proceed to argue with those who come as our equals (bringing thus the precondition of all honest argument) and to fight with such as smuggle superiority into our midst through

---

[b]Comment by John LaFarge, S.J.:

I am somewhat confused by this apparent unwillingness to grant that "theology"—*i.e.*, any idea as to the ultimate meaning of reality and of the universe—can have a place in the early stages of education. I can readily see that early education is not the place for abstract ideas, technical formulations of doctrine, or its finer and more subtle implications and applications. But even very small children can profoundly sense and experience the transcendent, and their intuition of certain broad aspects of transcendental truths can put the more sophisticated adult to shame, so much so that for "little children" is rendered particularly easy the entrance into the Kingdom of God. Even if the child cannot differentiate, it can certainly apprehend in a broad way that there *are* certain great girders which uphold the structure of the universe, that there is a certain Holy One to whom reverence should be paid, etc. If theology were simply a set of abstract proposals, I could see better the point in his difficulty; but not when it is a question of the young becoming aware of some of the great outlines in the total course of man's history. On the contrary, I believe that in the early stages of education the young are peculiarly ready to assimilate a certain historical sense; that they can be conscious of a great world tale that is told, in which God, man, and nature all play a dynamic part. Professor Mercier's paper [Chapter XII] is relevant here.

The Axiological Orientation of (Higher) Education

claiming some esoteric access to educational norms. The best we equals can expect is to have to accept as curricular pabulum only what the majority can agree upon through sustained discussion. The best our would be superiors can be allowed to make away with is to treasure in private (corporate privacy of the like-minded or individual privacy of pure introversion) whatever they claim above the (Heaven knows) low enough common denominator of our aforesaid rational agreement. We equalitarians are always at a disadvantage with the superior ones unless we can keep them separated from their guns. We do now, however, have the Supreme Court on our side, to protect us from sectarian sidearms, at least upon our own educational premises. If I, or any other one, prove unprepared to abide this judicial intervention, our common arbiter, all democratic anathemas be upon me—or him!

I. *The Goal of the Practical*

Since I have relegated the practical primarily to early education, this goal (or constellation of goals) protrudes into our discussion of higher education only incidentally. Let me make clear what the incidence is upon our present emphasis. It becomes relevant, in a word, through the *theory* of practice, or more concretely through the *feel* of action. Since admittedly goals of the various educational levels are not purely discrete (the life intended through all stages being an organic unity), we must at each level make clear who is to specialize at another level upon the goals which we ourselves as specialists neglect. There are those, for example, who anathematize vocationalism in education. We are not among them, nor are we sympathetic with them. But we need not ourselves specialize on (though we must not disdain) vocational skills at the higher educational level, provided they have been adequately emphasized as a precondition of advancement to higher education. Happy are we if we can take them for granted, only brightening them through our stage with imaginative "shine." If they have been neglected before, we must emphasize them in higher education; for man does not live on cake alone. Precious as thought is, thinking alone is not enough to make a man. As men cannot live without the concrete fruits of humble skills, so man the individual cannot live well without the integrative role of skill itself.

The Indispensability of Skill

Learning how to do something well is the precondition of learning how to do anything better; and is, for a fact, the ground condition of learning anything at all. Spirit unembodied is disembodied, and is full of flightiness. The coordinations first of tactual muscles, then of eye muscles with grosser ones, presently of ideals (high purposes) with muscular effort, and finally of the investment of the whole enterprise with imaginative wholeness—this is a process which, beginning humbly at birth or before, ends only with death or thereafter. In kindergarten then, the key word becomes skill; and that key we can never afford to throw away. We only learn to use it so well that it operates, as whatever operates best, subconsciously throughout the whole range of our intellectual sojourning. To learn to do something so well as to enjoy doing it for its own sake is the *sine qua non* of both Bentham's "felicity" and Spinoza's "blessedness." Incentives that are not felt in the process of doing are not available for the process of growing. Action based on motives imported, is adventitious action; and adventitious action begets only externalism. As education is initially the process of making action, whether muscular or mental, self-priming, so education must begin at the pump, not at some abstract periphery all but off the reservation altogether. This is the true indictment of intellectualism: it is extrinsic. Until it becomes intrinsic to function, it cannot become self-supporting. It becomes truly self-supporting when Reason is transformed into Imagination. To make life psychologically self-supporting, this is the summary goal of all our separate goals of education.

Self-support spells self-reward. The intellectual who is steady in his role and happy in its discharge is he who has made of his life a vocation. Life cannot become a "vocation" without its subject having a *vocation*. Intellectual pursuit may itself become that vocation, indeed had better become it, if thinking be one's job; but such high vocation must itself rest upon lowly skills that have been learned, and learned in the only way that learning "takes"—by attention to the humble job of training.[c]

[c] [Cf. the discussion of the place of vocational preparation in the goals of education in Chapter II by Lyman Bryson (including comment by George N. Shuster), Chapter IX by Howard Mumford Jones, Chapter XV by Dr. Shuster, Chapter XVI by Earl J. McGrath (including comment by Louis J. A. Mercier), Chapter XVIII by Harold Taylor (including comments by Mason W. Gross and Dr. Mercier), and comment by George B. de Huszar in Appendix III.]

The more this job is got over with in the early educational process, the more later stages can rely upon it for adventure into what is not yet actual, but is possible, or at least is not impossible. The intellectual who adventures forth muscularly unequipped is risking mental disaster and inviting moral cynicism. Helplessness is not holiness; indeed adult helplessness is hopelessness.

The realm of the first cluster of goals is, then, the practical: right down on the ground where things are and are what they are. Whoever has watched a crawling baby learn to explore cracks in the floor first with fumbling fingers, and then with intent curiosity maturing to hold, to examine, to taste, and even to swallow, he has looked in upon the essence of education. Nor will his subsequent exploring of the planets or exercising himself in "the intellectual love of God" wholly escape continuity with that dim dawn when the heaven of factuality first lay open to infantile inspection. Since eventually every justifiable process must become self-justifying, why not *now?* "Now" is the moment of "skill," whenever mind and muscle enter into the first careless rapture of their strange hymen.

Not to treasure this majestic moment is blind. Not to utilize this possession is prodigal. Not to esteem this rapture is to be suicidally imprudent. It was to this continuity of growth that Aristotle alluded in tempering the demand of accuracy to the potentiality of each stage of learning: mathematics requires what rhetoric does permit; and rhetoric permits a leeway too large for statistics. It was, furthermore, to the other crucial point—clarity as to the levels—that Aristotle pointed in advising against teaching ethics (as an intellectual discipline) to the young. They are fitted only for the practical, or at most progressively for the possible; and the effort to jump the guns upon their maturity leads only to moral disaster. (What the pseudo-Aristotelians of our time need is a little tincture of pure Aristotelianism!)

Starting then with what we have in infancy, we can build around the humble center of *projecting* an expanding but self-supporting life of mind. Spell the "practical," as unitary activity, out into as many goals as seem desirable, and you have the proper pluralization of the purpose of primary education. All the while the humble center of skill is expanding through skilful*ness* into larger and larger incidences of mind. This brings us then, through a discussion of the *theory* of practice, to a proper place to reconnoiter for our advance into the possible.

II. *The Goal of the Possible*

Building upon the practical, now modestly assessed, secondary education advances into the realm of the possible. The "possible" spells what is not yet but may become. Since imagination is but a name for importing the future, as memory is but a name for accumulating the past, the yet-to-be equalizes the proportion of mind and body. Such equalization is required in the education of an animal who is also spirit. The *practical* (*i.e.,* the already-is) gives a heavy disproportion to muscle; the *impossible* (*i.e.,* the never-to-be) reverses the disproportion, yielding the majority to mind. It is the *possible* (*i.e.,* the may-be but not-yet) which, to repeat, equalizes the proportion: it builds upon the practical, starting but not stopping with it; and it utilizes the visionary, stopping though not starting with it. The possible becomes practical only through reliance upon skill, a reliance achieved in dealing with the real, in order to make some of the irreal actual.

It is difficult at all times and in all matters to get the proper balance. The resilience of youth comes in handy here. Even in anger, the balance comes hard, as Aristotle says. Of course to get angry is easy enough. But it is an achievement to know whom to get angry at, when to get angry, how angry to get, and what to do about it all. In the totality of an animal nature which is also spiritual perhaps the best we can hope for is a sort of statistical balance. The first ecstatic taste of the visionary unbalances the best, and so we may allow at the onset of adolescence an exuberance of impracticality not expected, or permitted, at the end of secondary education.

Let us illustrate in the social field. Radicalism is but an *over* devotion to ideas; reaction, an *over* devotion to habits; conservatism (substitute "liberalism," as you will, reforming then the whole to fit the name chosen for the part) is *right* devotion to both idea (the not-yet-real) and habit (the already-made-actual). Proper induction into the art of making this mixture come right is the essence of education for the possible. It may be far from unwholesome, may indeed be inevitable, that men learn how much they can take of the elixir of ideality through "hangovers" from episodic over indulgence in it. Enthusiasm is natural, and fanaticism not strange, in youth. He who is not radical in his youth is a fool; he who is radical after youth is an ass.

What teacher has not seen the torrent, and ridden with it, the torrent of high moral impulse (without any means at hand at all) which was to sweep share-cropping, industrial feudalism, discrimination against color and class from the earth in a single season, or at least from one's homeland in two seasons at most? It is a rhetorical question so far as I am concerned; for how pensively do I recall an early oration of mine entitled, "Omnipotence Unbound!" The theme was that we are *as yet* bound by "time" and "space" and "sex" and "doubt." "As yet," I said. "These obstacles," I went on, "we are rapidly overcoming through science, psychoanalysis, and high religion. When we finish that—and the end is near!—we'll enter forthrightly into our human heritage: Omnipotence, *unbound!*"—and will live happy ever afterwards. The presumption of fabricating a "World Constitution" and the pathos of building a "World Government" out of thin air and usually, alas, upon the foundation of disgust with the best mankind has yet been able to achieve—these are the similar pieces today of arrested adolescence. Behold men who were as youths encouraged to debate the undebatable before they were well grounded in the factuality of efficient habits and solid patriotism!

On this latter point of patriotism we cannot be too emphatic today. Our Supreme Court has made it clear that American citizenship, an object of longing throughout the world, carries heavy responsibilities. It disallowed to Professor D. C. Macintosh, of the Yale University Divinity School, his petition for citizenship because he put private conscience above patriotism. "When he speaks of putting his allegiance to the will of God above his allegiance to the government, it is evident," says Justice Sutherland for the majority, "that he means to make *his own interpretation* of the will of God the decisive test which shall conclude the government and stay its hand." Though "we are a Christian people," as the Justice allows, "we are (also) a Nation with the duty to survive," he adds. We must, therefore, as the Justice concludes, "go forward upon the assumption and safely can proceed upon no other, that unqualified allegiance to the Nation and submission and obedience to the laws of the land, as well those made for war as those made for peace, are not inconsistent with the will of God." No man can therefore be "morally justified" in substituting his own will, or his notion of the will of God, for what the Court calls "the wisdom of Congress," that is, if one wishes to put it so, for what Congress regards as the will of God for citizens.[d] This is no time to encourage confusion upon this highly important matter, not even in the name of education. Education must be practical before it can specialize upon the possible, as it must sanely assess the possible before it can claim even for conscience public license to enjoy the liberty of what is perfectionistically "impossible."

Induction into what is possible, at our second level of education, (spell out the pluralized goals as you will) has, then, to do with utilizing the skill bequeathed from below, sensitizing to the best ideas of change which the race has produced, accommodating the two to each other under careful hands guided by eyes watchful over the delicate process of spirit's bold fraternization with flesh. The "possible" is an advance beyond the actual through steady strategy as touching the means at hand. He who learns well this sly business of mixing (Plato called it "the art of mensuration") is the statesman of the future: statesman all the

[d]Comment by Quincy Wright:
I would raise a question on T. V. Smith's apparent endorsement of Mr. Justice Sutherland's opinion, that loyalty to the State requires that Congress in its solemn enactments always be above the individual conscience. Such a view is particularly objectionable in a democracy which recognizes that the State is for man.

Comment by John D. Wild:
I should not myself care to question that loyalty to one's country and its traditions embodies most important values, but Mr. Smith's rather unqualified statement of the matter calls forth certain doubts in my mind. He would seem to imply that there is no higher practical value than "unqualified allegiance to the Nation," and no higher court of appeal to which we have access than "the wisdom of Congress." But surely such unqualified tribal loyalties have been directed to monstrous ends, for instance, in Nazi Germany. Is it not the duty of any citizen still retaining any traces of rationality to rebel against such social corruption, on the basis of an appeal to some higher authority? If not, what then becomes of the right of revolution so zealously cherished wherever democratic thought is alive? What defense is there against the ever present dangers of nationalistic Fascism?

Comment by Louis J. A. Mercier:
Professor Smith exults because Mr. Justice Sutherland disallowed the petition of Professor D. C. Macintosh because "he put his allegiance to the will of God above his allegiance to government." Well, another justice said just the opposite, stressing that it is the very essence of freedom that the citizen and the government "render to Caesar what belongeth to Caesar and to God what belongeth to God," both being under the natural law. And it is the very essence of tyranny to leave it to the government or the majority to make any decree against the moral law. There is no guarantee that what the Court calls, "the wisdom of Congress," is any sounder than the wisdom of Hitler in determining the will of God for citizens. That is where the authoritative theologian comes in, as he explains the moral system of the Ten Commandments and of the Gospels.

way from marriage in which "I is *not* de one," on up to a world government grown out of the sad soil of the governments of this world. Democratic education at the secondary level is not, then, indoctrination into high ideals, of which the youth is already chock-full. It is accepting the necessary under the guidance of the possible. The youth is later to learn what theory is yet good for after he has discovered that it is good for nothing, practically speaking. He is at this level to learn—and it can be learned only from those who themselves have learned it—what ideals are *not* good for. While learning this, he must also learn how to take it without cynicism, so as not to reap adult ulcers from adolescent illusions. What socially he has to learn, in short, is Reinhold Niebuhr's broadened dictum: that politics of our kind is but "proximate solutions of insoluble problems."

Success at this level requires sensitivity to ends, good judgment as to means, skill in articulating both men and measures—and patience. Above all, patience—which is the hardest if not the highest of democratic virtues. It is hard for the obvious reason, and for a philosophical reason not perhaps so obvious. The obvious difficulty arises from the incidence of need upon the adolescence of man. When we most require patience, we lack it most. Still under the youthful dominance of action— old drives reinforced by new glandular pressures—not yet a good judge of ideals though subjected to their glittering seduction, still unseasoned in the application of already developed skills, the overgrown child but underdone man has to learn patience to the tune of impetuosity. Harder still it is to learn because its full mastery requires from the operative base of the *actual* an adventure into the never-never land of the impossible. The lower patience consists in awaiting the fruits of action; the higher and harder patience is of passion, not of action. The patience required to do nothing is harder for man, and far more necessary for his higher reach, than the patience "to do something for God's sake"—*i.e.,* to act regardless.

There is a presupposition—cosmic, if you will—which undergirds all our processes, even those of the loftiest rationality. To wait on that is the over-condition of all successful reform; and to wait on that is the under-condition of education for the *impossible*. But before passing to the impossible as such, let us see something of its incidence upon the possible, as we have remarked already the incidence of the possible upon the actual.

An example is better here than exposition. Look at Abraham Lincoln. Concentrate first upon his general attitude toward life. That was, according to his intimate friend Swett, to "regard the whole world" as a "question of cause and effect." "He did not believe," continues Swett, "the results could be materially hastened or impeded." And so, concludes his friend: "His tactics were to get himself in the right place and remain there still, until events would find him in that place." Emotionally, this Spinozistic attitude was generalized by Lincoln in these words: "What I deal with is too vast for malice." So much for the general.

As to the more specific, take this case: Lincoln's attitude toward slavery. He hated it; but he would not abolish it by federal power, as of course he could not by state power. He sympathized with the slaves, but he would return to their masters every fugitive from thralldom that could be caught. What he did about slavery, as he immortally declared to Greeley, he did with reference to another subject, an abstract one, indeed almost a metaphysical if not mystic one: "the Union." And he, in explanation of all this, perpetrates at Cooper Union this final paradox of natural piety as touching so monumental an evil: "Wrong as we think slavery is, we can yet afford to let it alone where it is, because that much is due to the necessity arising from its actual presence in the nation."

Paradoxical that is indeed. But more paradoxical is this: that a child begotten of man and born of woman, upborne after birth by an animal body, pulled down by his own passions, is yet spirit, lifting his heart ever toward, and living constantly with his head in, the realm of the impossible: that realm visible to the mind's eye but untouchable by the body's hands. Education is also for that realm, or what is imagination for—and how achieve magnanimity!

III. *The Goal of the Impossible*

When a man has become as skilled as he can, when he has become as accommodating in society as is possible, and when, rolling these together, he has made himself into the best cooperant in action, social and political, which it is in him to become—what then? Only more of the same? "More of the same," certainly—but not *only*. There is the third dimension of human life: there is the *impossible,* the vast and majestic realm touched to glory by "the light that never was on land or sea."

> The clouds that gather round the setting sun
> Do take a sober coloring from an eye
> That hath kept watch o'er man's mortality;
> Another race hath been, and other palms are won.

How stands man related to those "other palms"—*e.g.,* the fronded palms of poetry? That he stands in relation to the purely imaginative is not to be denied. What led him from the practical to the possible points farther. What of the theoretically possible proves not practical after his best effort (and so proves "impossible" for him), testifies to the same high end. But the final testimony is just here: in the ideals, norms, laws, and principles that are what they are because they are not possible of any further realization through any available action.

Justice no man has seen, nor shall see. Yet what is man's political life without it? The useless becomes the worthful. *Beauty* no man has seen, nor shall see. Yet what is man's whole artistic aspiration without it? The useless becomes the worthful. *Truth* no man has seen, nor shall see. Yet what is science without it? The useless becomes the worthful. *Holiness* no man hath seen, nor shall see. Yet where is religion without it? The useless becomes the worthful. Descending, no man has seen or shall see "Average." Yet what is statistical investigation without it? So far are we from *seeing* such a norm (save with the mind's eye) that discernment of its infinite distance becomes the soul of wit, as when (Mauldin's) Willy said to Johnny, the bullets whistling all around them—"I feel like a fugitive from the law of averages." The natural law no man has seen or shall see. Yet what is the history of thought without it? And where is democratic theory[e] without the ideal of *Equality?*— an ideal which is surely incapable of being made objectively to describe any two human beings in any of their determinative relations to each other. The impractical which is also not possible remains the supremely worthful. Shall not a man, merely because he is man, rise to con-

[e] Comment by Herman Finer:
 Is not democracy an "impossible?" If not, what is it? If it is, is its teaching to be deferred to the age of seventeen or eighteen; or is something about it to be taught earlier, and if so, what? Are not all social rights and obligations "impossibles"—that is, incorporeal attestations of the mind that there are values above matter? Are they, or not? If they are, are they incommunicable, or if communicated, unassimilable by youths well under university age?

templation and to the appreciation of what he contemplates, whether he "discover" it with Plato or "create" it with John Dewey? Shall not a man also "enjoy God," as the creed so earnestly enjoins?

It is "the *principles* of things" which, because they *are* principles, are not those things, nor become necessarily things-in-themselves, just this type of "irreality" (ideality if you insist upon positivity) it is that furnishes major preoccupation for the true life of the spirit. This is philosophy to which we now come, but come because we must. Not actual in the sense of the "practical"; not realizable, moreover, in the sense to which we have assigned the "possible";—this *tertium quid* is important, highly important, over and above the call of action. Even for action it is important, if action is to be understood as well as perpetuated. And if we were to insist that this *tertium quid* for education is completely "useless" (as it is in the easiest meaning of the term), it would remain worthful, and might indeed come through inner discipline to be the supremely worthwhile. There is a surplusage to each and every high ideal, which is over, above, and beyond all that is realizable in action. It is not that any ideal belongs wholly to the "impossible," but rather than any and every ideal that is available for action has a disproportion of itself that remains over and above what can be done in its name. This surplusage of every ideal is the glory of life, wherever located and however described.

The apprehension and appreciation of that disproportion must, therefore, be the goal of goals in the strategy of education. Too abstract by far to be set as a goal for the young (note the obsolescence of grammar in early education, because grammar is the pure *principle* of language); too unchallenging to action to be counted as goal for young men and women riding strong the high tide of animal spirits (we wisely disallow the vote until maturity has brought other motives to the fore than that of reform); this surplus of value is too indispensable and too worthful not to be accounted high guerdon for education. There is left for its assignment, a stage less naive than childhood and less impetuous than youth. Indeed, at the age and from the stage that men possess experience enough to discern the role of principle (for though not wholly dependent upon experience, principle is at first discerned *in* experience) on to the end of life these "impossibles" are the goals set by nature to be appropriated by man. Their creation, if they be created by man, represents his most

The Axiological Orientation of (Higher) Education 45

Olympian achievement. Their discovery, if they be not created by man, represents his most divine seizure.

Before returning to our colleagues for an assessment of their contributions, we must now summarize. Then we shall attend to the theologians, as ambivalent custodians of the Impossible, and to the philosophers, who ought to be neutral custodians, and to all others in turn who serve in their own way the spiritual life. The moral, meantime, of all that we have been saying is threefold: (1) that the problematic is soluble, when it is, because of and by means of what is not problematic; (2) that many problems which cannot be "solved," can yet be "resolved" through identification with the situation in which they arise; (3) that when we can neither *solve* the problems nor *resolve* the situation, we may still, finally, through deepening self-mastery, *absolve* ourselves from a sense of guilt and so escape useless repinings over what is not within our power. The over-goal of education, then, for men who know that they are not God, is to prepare through solution of problems that are soluble, through resolution of problems that are predicaments—to prepare, I repeat, for spiritual absolution of self from what is too much for us but what nevertheless is always with us. The soul thus matured always "finds somebody at home when he calls upon himself." Moreover, whoever else calls upon him finds the Somebody for whom he has long been looking, a somebody educated in all dimensions of his being. His it is to garner the wealth of the world as harvest of a quiet eye.

At this juncture, then, we may now welcome at the front door—some of whom we earlier let go out the back door—all our pedagogical collaborators; and at their head troop the theologians. We welcome them now, and trust them here, as in primary and secondary education we distrusted them. Our new amity rests on two grounds: (1) our students now know most of what is practical and a good deal of what is possible. Though they may not yet fully understand the pathos of Justice Holmes's dictum that "to think great thoughts you must be heroes as well as idealists," still they will have dependable inklings of what Holmes, the wise American, confided to Pollack, the wise Englishman: "The business of making a new world is longer, tougher, and less pleasant than even the most prudent of us foresaw." Knowing that much, they will no longer be so easily misled, not even from the pulpit on Sunday, in their social practice, by that Ideal Justice which is "surplus" to all political practice. Communism with its romanticism will not so easily cripple liberals with such realism. (2) The theologians, too, have meantime got their bearing better. They have overgrown, perhaps in fortunate cases have outgrown, the primal but insidious undertow of "realism": the impetuous attribution of full reality only to what is purely ideal and so is truly impossible. This corruption of categories is a first, if not the final, sin against the holy spirit of logic. The best of their group will have surmounted the ontological temptation without losing its precious axiological increment.

If God be defined as "a being than Whom no more perfect can be conceived," they will smile now, though with appropriate wistfulness, at the further notion that this implies *existence;* for they now know that perfection increases in proportion to the distance of its object from the existent. The higher the ideal—to paraphrase Nicolai Hartmann—the weaker it is to work its way; the lower, the stronger. Practice is informed of the practical, not of the perfect. Moreover, the theologians have learned, or are learning, that what is possible beyond the present practical leaves all but undiminished the realm of the impossibly perfect.

Let George Santayana speak now for our theologians—Catholic, Jewish, Protestant—and bespeak an honorable level of elevation for those still attaining but not yet attained: "I knew," confesses he, "that my parents regarded all religion as a work of human imagination, and I agreed, and still agree, with them there. But this carried an implication in their minds against which every instinct in me rebelled, namely that the works of human imagination are bad. No, said I to myself even as a boy, they are good, they alone are good; and the whole real world— is ashes in the mouth."[f]

He who knows not of himself, what Santayana elsewhere proclaims, that "religion is the fairy tale of morality," is yet caught in the toils

---

[f]Comment by Louis J. A. Mercier:

The perfect attainment of objectives, not only in education, but in morals and religion, is impossible. We did not need Santayana to tell us so. St. Paul and St. Thomas did. To call further for continuing with "the possible" to be tested by trial and error, and to keep out ultimates till after adolescence, is to continue to revamp Rousseau. But the latter is to run counter to human nature. The child, the primitive, wants to know who made the world. To add that even the adult can never get beyond imagining as to ultimates, is more serious. At least we should know what the philosopher and the mystic did to reach them as realities. We also need to know how it came about that the theologian stepped in with his assurances.

of ethical provincialism. His postgraduate work lies ahead. There is such a thing, as Santayana also declares, as being "all the truer for not professing to be true."

Such apprehending of the "impossible" for what it is will sustain, might even swell, what truly is possible, and will not decay the practical. Such a *vision* of the divine no longer leaves men adrift morally because in passing from their youth to manhood they have outgrown some dogma of sacerdotalism.

Come the Philosophers

Trooping just behind the theologians, if not even arm in arm with them, come the philosophers. Let Santayana speak for them, too. This immortal modern out-Platos Plato, the father of all who treasure imagination. Plato promoted his ideally "just" society (of course the *Republic* portrays the most horrible totalitarianism) beyond the realm of the practical, without permitting it to achieve full citizenship in the realm of principle: impractical he made it, but not yet fully impossible.

"Perhaps in heaven," he equivocates, "there is laid up a pattern of it for him who wishes to behold it, and, beholding, to organize himself accordingly. And the question of its present or future existence on earth is quite unimportant. For in any case he will adopt the practices of such a city to the exclusion of those of every other" (*Republic* 594).

Dangling there, the ideal was left by the Greek to gnaw at the vitals of animal urgency until it seduced even Plato into "a little gentle violence" for the subjects' own good, as it has always driven lesser minds, to ruin all chances the ideal has of becoming possible by forcing it into the narrow molds of what is practicable: (1) intolerance in art, (2) censorship of theology, (3) limitation of citizenship, and (4) proselytism in religion with his final fanaticism against atheism (which in the *Laws* Plato identifies with what literally came to be Christian theism).[g]

All this, as Santayana clearly sees, because Plato confused the goal of higher education with the goals of the lower. Plato wanted *to do*

---

[g]Comment by Gerald B. Phelan:
   I find it curious that at one moment Mr. Smith seems to advocate the totalitarian (if I were a leftist I would say "fascist") dogma of the "unqualified allegiance" of a citizen to the law of the land (many persons are being condemned to death or imprisonment at Nuremberg and elsewhere, by courts presided over by Americans, for their allegiance to that dogma), and at another moment criticizes Plato for advocating in *The Laws* a "restriction of citizenship."

something about the purely perfect. This is not permitted, not permitted by the very nature of the perfect. He wanted to impregnate power with it, and succeeds only in poisoning it with power. Only the powerless can be perfectly pure. In a larger purview, Plato conceived "the spiritual life" to be "intoxication with value." Now, the spiritual life lies in the other direction, in the direction marked by Santayana as "disintoxication from value." Thus the philosopher is saved from the belittlement usually wreaked by impetuosity, as the theologian may be saved from the pusillanimity of proselytism (the will to power so illy disguised), by getting clear at last, and firmly grasping, the "impossible" as the final goal of education.[h]

It is not as a philosophical disciple of Santayana that I speak thus, but only as making him a sort of axiological engineer. I do not myself follow him, but only use him to make brevity compatible with effective exposition. Negatively, Santayana does help to clear the brush away: skepticism yields catharsis to animal urgency. Positively, he is truly clairvoyant: "give me the luxuries and I'll not grieve for the necessities." (When I, in the ensignia of a conquering army, sought in Italy to help this philosopher, offering food, drink, and clothing—all of which he somewhat needed—he would avail himself of "power" only to further on its way to publication and influence his, at that moment, latest contribution to spirit, *The Idea of Christ in the Gospels, or God in Man*.)

Santayana is trebly rewarding as an example, for he not only brings back to us the theologians and the philosophers, at last properly briefed, but he also presents to our cause the *litterateurs* and the scientists. As for the latter, since "knowing is not eating," the "laws of nature," the

[h]Comment by John D. Wild:
 I think that Mr. Smith is right in distinguishing the values of practical action from those of detached "imagination" and "contemplation," but I am somewhat confused as to what he says of the relation between the two. On the one hand he seems to say that impractical contemplation is important for action, so far as action needs to be understood. This would indicate a close dependence of the one upon the other. And yet on the other hand by describing the objects of contemplation as "impossible," he would seem to suggest a complete divorce between the two, and a complete irrelevance of the one to the other. In my opinion the former alternative is preferable. Is it not true that a practical goal must first be imagined and understood before it can be desired and realized in practice? If this is so, the objects of pure contemplation, including values, so far as they are really grounded in the nature of things, must guide all sound action, and therefore have a tremendous practical importance. But I hardly think that Mr. Smith would agree with this, as it would not seem to fit very well with his emphasis on contemplation *à la* Santayana as "disintoxication from value," and more especially with his view that the objects of contemplation are created rather than discovered by man.

"principles of science" are *for* but neither *in* nor *of* the practices of the laboratory or of the legislature. And as for the former, the poets are under the domain of his matchless insight, left free to roam wherever they will, across all boundaries of Being, and to share whatever they will from the place and level where they find it:

> . . . whether all to me the vision come
> Or break in many beams,
> The pageant ever shifts and Being's sum
> Is but the sum of dreams.

If all this but seems to boil down to Spinozism, then let all "god-intoxicated" ones make the most of it. Let, especially, in American education, the pseudo-Aristotelians make the most of it. But why not give to our meaning its chosen habitation and its proper name? Sophisticated by Aristotle's spread but not chastened by either his patriotism or his skill, President Hutchins of Chicago, and his acolytes, confuse all realms, making for themselves a shrill vocation of "anti-vocationalism," and depriving as far as they can the young of skill, without which they can neither support themselves (save on more talk about talk) or rise to a full view of the glorious "impossible."[1]

---

[1] Comment by George B. de Huszar:

In so far as I know, Professor Smith is the first educator who explicitly refers to Mr. Hutchins's theories as pseudo-Aristotelian. For a long time I have been wondering why this has not been pointed out more often and more explicitly. Almost all the critics have assumed that Mr. Hutchins stood for Aristotle and Catholicism and then they have proceeded to attack him in the name of science and positivism.

But Mr. Hutchins rejects theology and wishes to substitute metaphysics as a unifying principle. He has retreated down the corridor of the ages and taken refuge in the monastic cell of Thomas Aquinas only to find that he was at a place where Thomas Aquinas had never been. I am surprised that Catholic scholars have not been more explicit in pointing out that Mr. Hutchins's position is simply untenable, that without theology one cannot talk of Saint Thomas, or of Catholic thought. However, I am aware of at least one such scholar, William J. McGucken, S.J., who in *The Philosophy of Catholic Education* states that "When he [Mr. Hutchins] quotes Aquinas, he quotes an Aquinas that never existed."

Mr. Hutchins has stated "We have excluded body building and character building. We have excluded the social graces" (*The Higher Learning in America*). He has further stated, in *No Friendly Voice,* that the university "should relax its desire to train them [students] in the moral virtues." However, Aristotle recognized that moral insight is not a function of the intellect only, but depends partly on careful training in good habits applied to minds of good natural disposition. He maintains that knowledge is less stable, and consequently less valuable than character, and in the *Nichomachean Ethics* states: "Choice cannot exist either without reason and intellect or without a moral state; for good action and its opposite cannot exist without a combination of intellect and character."

Men shut themselves out from "the intellectual love of God" who have neglected at the proper stages to learn the emotional love of fellow men and the enkindling pride which skill gives to vocation. Abou Ben Adhem, thy tribe doth not increase under such auspices! If these abortive intellectuals ever, like Spinoza, ground lenses or made a living at any other honorable skill save talk, their cleverness at spilling laryngeal liquidity might well come to have other consequences—for "ideas have consequences"—than to proclaim "the good news of damnation" hurled by Hutchins against the humble goods illustrated in democratic politics of the "possible" and against the disinterestedness of high secularity[j] more sacred to spirit than is dialectical sacerdotalism.

Fascinated as this group is by "the medieval grace of iron clothing," few of them will ever don the institutional discipline which their preachments reinforce in its insidious sabotage of our most beneficent constitutional separation of church and state. Protestant anxiety over Neo-Thomistic certitudes is not the stuff of which educational statesmanship is made. It lacks the resolution required for loyalty to its own tradition of liberty; and it lacks the courage to become proselyte to the opposing tradition of authority. Of sterner stuff than this is "the intellectual love of God." Spinoza's nobility of spirit is not to be divorced from hands skilled at the bench and a heart humbled with cosmic piety. But then Spinoza knew that presumption is poor propaedeutic to perfection.

[Cf. Mr. de Huszar's comment on Chapter XI by John U. Nef, and his general comment in Appendix III. For further discussion of the "Chicago Plan," see Chapter II by Lyman Bryson, Chapter VIII by Alain L. Locke, Chapter IX by Howard Mumford Jones, Chapter XI by John U. Nef, Chapter XIII by Mordecai M. Kaplan, Chapter XV by George N. Shuster, Chapter XVI by Earl J. McGrath, and Chapter XVII by Ordway Tead.]

[j]Comment by John LaFarge, S.J.:

Is not Professor Smith a bit of a theologian himself? "High secularity," as he expresses it, is a pronouncement in the forum of theology; and if high secularity has been assumed as a dogma by higher education, its influence *as a dogma* will infallibly be sensed in education's earlier stages. After all, children's minds and attitudes are formed not by artificially classified curricula, but by persons apprehended as a totality; and the secularist, quite like the philosopher or the religiously minded teacher, brings his world philosophy with him as an inseparable part of his personality. The theologian is told that he should keep away from the marketplace. But is only the highest secularist to have unlimited access to the same arena, where our lives and our liberties are at stake?

The Axiological Orientation of (Higher) Education

A Closing Word with a Backward Glance

Perfection, never doubt, *is* the goal of education. Practicality is, however, no enemy of perfection. It *is* perfection at the level of organic action. Skill is the mode through which perfection comes to pass in the realm of body. It is the channel for imagination headed *downward*. "Downward" indeed, as the poet well has it,

> Downward the voices of duty call,
> Downward to toil and be mixed with the main.

Nor is patriotism an enemy of perfection. It *is* perfection at the highest point of social effort as yet dependably organized by man. Moral virtue, political skill, is the mode through which perfection comes to pass in collective life. It is the channel for imagination working its magic *laterally*. Patience is the bridge for progress from the actual toward the Impossible through what is possible, moving by discernable means *from where we are, with what we've got*.

Modally plural, perfection is more than action, individual or collective; more than integration, organic or cultural. Perfection is orientation toward what is impossible of implementation, but toward what in contemplation, is fully self-rewarding.

Whoever has discerned the *essence* of action has acted so well as to transcend action even while indulging it, reaping in action the harvest of a quiet spirit. Such persons are "confronted and controlled by a profound recollection," as Santayana so clairvoyantly describes the *feel* of action, "in which laughter and tears pulse together like the stars in a polar sky, each indelibly bright, and all infinitely distant." Whoever, indeed, has made his own the principles of things has promoted himself, without demoting anybody or depreciating anything, into the realm of spirit. *Will* has helped him, and deserves reward. *Reason* has helped him, and deserves reward. Both indeed are already largely compensated by the mantle which all the while at every level overspreads them. That itself is man's own final reward, to and through whatever goals: the *Mantle of Imagination*.[k]

[k]Comment by Louis W. Norris:
  Professor Smith's views of the "impossible" raise serious problems. First, reservation of concern, or at least of study, about the "impossibles," *i.e.,* ideal goods, for higher education is to abandon primary and secondary students to the will of the times. It is to rid

their actions of norms which could and should be testing the ways they take. In fact, one reason instruction in moral and esthetic themes in college is so difficult is that these subjects have been allowed to go by default.

In the second place, Professor Smith takes a fatalistic view of the college student's relation to human affairs. To be sure there are absolutes, *e.g.*, beauty, holiness, justice, the complete nature of which man never appropriates. But he embodies them in his life in remarkable degrees, and it is just for this that we have honored a Jesus, a Beethoven, or a Lincoln. Studies by Hartshorne, Dimock, Fahs, and others have shown that these ideas *do* motivate the lives of secondary students. The history of religion shows that the great values have not been mere "impossibilities" to contemplate, but they have been "powers that make for righteousness."

Thirdly, science points more and more to a world of organic process. Whitehead's view of a reality that is at every point interrelated to every other has greater support from science than Santayana's scheme of discrete realms of being to which abstract rational analysis can bring us. Whitehead adds that the ideal possibilities (Smith's "impossibilities") lure man esthetically toward greater actualities.

And it might be added, that this musing upon the ideal "impossibilities" which Santayana and Smith take to be the ultimate consummation of philosophy, and therefore of education, is what has given philosophy a bad name in American schools. Thales fell into the well while stargazing, and most American students think he got what he deserved. But there is no reason why our youth should not be taught to look into the wellsprings of human action with stars in their eyes!

Comment by Quincy Wright:

I would like to underline T. V. Smith's suggestion from George Santayana, which I would interpret to mean that even if man makes God in his own image, God is not necessarily bad. In fact, God might continually become better through association with men gradually becoming civilized.

However, I would rather state his trilogy, not as "the practical," "the possible," and "the impossible," but as "the factual," "the probable," and "the possible," thus bringing it into contact with Charles E. Peirce's three types of reality, "what is," "what is likely to be," and "what may be." I would prefer to call T. V. Smith's "possible" the "probable" because that word emphasizes differences in degree. Is it not the task of reason to distinguish the varying degrees of probability that the non-existent will come into existence in the future? I think T. V. Smith's word, "possible," tends to throw all the varying degrees of probability into a single basket of "the possible." I also have some objection to classifying all norms and ideals as "the impossible," unless one clearly recognizes that by the "impossible" we mean a line asymptotic to "the possible." I would rather carry the idea by the word "possible," meaning something which is improbable in very high degree but which may be closely approached if not in fact achieved. Another advantage of this terminology is that it permits the genuinely "impossible," the fairy stories recognized as impossible, to accompany all stages of education as a relaxation, and a recognition that the imagination can travel beyond the actual, the probable, and the possible to the realm of fancy.

Comment by Thurston N. Davis, S.J.:

In *The Jacobins,* Professor Crane Brinton has assembled a mass of evidence to show that when the Revolution of 1789 attempted to destroy traditional Christianity, the Jacobins immediately set up in its place a religion of civic virtue which duplicated—down to the tiniest details—the very thing its founders had vowed themselves to kill. It seems to me that Dr. Smith's paper falls into this general pattern. He declares himself opposed to the dogmas and indoctrinations of "sacerdotalism" and bids the theologian divest himself of his authoritarian "sidearms" before entering the arena of debate; yet, strange as it may seem, Dr. Smith, having made his declarations and demands, is himself armed to the teeth. Quite candidly, I find his paper surcharged with assumptions, decretals, syllabi of errors, and infallibilities.

First of all, his essay makes it clear that Dr. Smith wants nothing to do with religious "indoctrination" of the young in primary or secondary education. The question of religion is to be postponed until the student is ready for "postgraduate work" in the things which are "all the truer for not professing to be true." Surely he sees that this program, with all its assumptions, is as thoroughgoing an indoctrination as any which he opposes.

Secondly, the dogmas implied in Dr. Smith's division ("practical—possible—impossible") are too numerous to count. Nor does he stop at dogma; there is a genuinely "mystical" flavor about such phrases as the "disinterestedness of high secularity."

No democratic, secularist "church" can be expected to endure without Fathers and Doctors. Hence we find here the Santayanas, the Deweys, and the Holmeses of Professor Smith's highly selective canonizing. Surely traditional Christianity never cited its Fathers with more reliant docility than does Dr. Smith when he bids Santayana utter in the name of "Catholic, Jewish, and Protestant theologians" the great revelation that religion is the "work of human imagination," "the fairy tale of morality."

Comment by Gerald B. Phelan:
Mr. Smith's insistence on the "Practical" and the "Possible" on the one hand, and his enthusiastic advocacy of the contemplation of the "Impossible," threw my mind back to the sixth century when St. Benedict composed his famous "Rule." It is indeed paradoxical to find in Mr. Smith's paper a Spinozistic Intellectualism, a Santayanian Platonism, and a Deweyite Pragmatism, linked with an ill disguised atheism which advocates many of the educational ideals that St. Benedict of Nursia proposed in the sixth century of our era. Maybe Mr. Smith would have different views if *he talked it over* with a "theologian."

[Cf. Chapter XIV by Theodore Brameld for a discussion advocating "utopianism" and goals conceived in terms of the "impossible." Cf. also the discussion of education for contemporary life in Chapter IX by Howard Mumford Jones and Chapter XVIII by Harold Taylor.]

CHAPTER IV

Higher Education and the Unity of Knowledge
An Operational Approach to the History of Thought

By KARL W. DEUTSCH

Associate Professor of History, Massachusetts Institute of Technology

---

I. The Purpose of This Paper
II. The Unity of Man
III. The Transfer of Knowledge and the Transformation of Society
IV. Technological Growth and Crises in the Unity of Knowledge
V. The Industrial Revolution in the Field of Knowledge Today
VI. Some Tasks for Universities: Education for Coherence
    1. Reason in History: Some Technical and Social Aspects for a Basic Course in the History of Thought and Science
    2. Research on the Role of Models in the Natural and Social Sciences
    3. Research on Key Concepts
    4. Some Specialized Courses and a Tentative Curriculum
VII. Some Possible Results of This Curriculum

I. *The Purpose of This Paper*

THE MAIN THOUGHTS of this paper can be summed up briefly. The production and reproduction of knowledge may be looked upon as a part of the production and reproduction of actual human life, supplementing the reproduction of human beings and the production of goods and services. Under certain conditions in history, each of these functions has been disrupted by crises: crises in the community's ability to absorb an increase in population, or a greater flow of goods, or a greater flow of diversified knowledge. Each of these special crises was connected with conditions in the other fields. But to the extent that it was resolved at all, each crisis had also to be overcome by appropriate adjustments in the social practices bearing directly on its specific difficulties.

Today we are facing a crisis in thought and education, side by side with the world's critical problems in politics and economics. Our specific intellectual dangers include incoherence in the minds of individuals and mutual incomprehension between different scientific fields, national traditions, or philosophical or religious systems of value.

An attack on this particular crisis should start from four realities:

1. Our growing awareness of the interdependence of human minds, both with their social and cultural surroundings, and with their technological equipment.

2. The growing need of modern technology, and the growing demand of masses of individuals, for a very large increase in the numbers of persons with higher education, so as to challenge the previous status of higher learning as the privilege of an *élite*.

3. The historical connection between general technological growth and recurrent crises in the unity of knowledge.

4. The current industrial revolution in the production and treatment of knowledge, which has produced machines performing some limited functions of thought, promised to change the future of many "white-collar" occupations, and make possible new insights into the nature of thinking.

Under these conditions higher education in our democracy is being driven toward major changes by social pressures from below and by inner technical necessities. If our universities are to provide in this situation a more systematic education for coherence, they will need a more adequate development of the philosophy of science and thought. As possible approaches toward developing such equipment, this paper will discuss tentative examples for a basic course, some research projects, and an undergraduate curriculum, in the hope to provoke further and better contributions toward such an enterprise.

References in this paper to some data from the natural sciences cannot endow it with the accuracy of these more mature disciplines. No attempt is made to borrow their prestige. If the social sciences are to become some day in much of their work as accurate as some natural sciences are now, they will have to develop more effective techniques of observation and measurement, and more clearly specified concepts and methods of reasoning, leading through precisely described steps to results which can be tested through adequately specified operations.[a]

[a]Comment by Herman Finer:
 Query: which natural sciences? accurate to what degree and in what comprehension? and

II. *The Unity of Man*

Are human minds interdependent? The answer may be fundamental to our problem.

If human minds are interdependent, then they are not separated from each other by unbridgeable differences in some mental qualities, or by a supposedly "ineffable" character of a "spirit" which defies communication. Even though the range of human experiences may be beyond the range of a particular technique of communication at a particular time, we may then still assume that these experiences are not incommunicable or unintelligible in principle, and that we can explore matters of the mind by the methods of science and reason.

Interdependence of minds means also that they can change and can be changed. Men's minds, in that case, cannot be treated in isolation from each other, from the society in which they live, or from the technology they work with. Society and technology are not a mere external environment for an individual's mind, but they interact with its innermost structure. "Human nature," then, is no more narrowly "unchangeable" than these, and society and culture in turn are no more narrowly unchangeable than the outcome of the ever new interplay of men's minds with their environment and history.

To call human minds unintelligible or unchangeable looks like a tempting shortcut to defend threatened values or preserve genuinely cherished aspects of our heritage against the challenges of our time. It may remind us not to confuse the few things which we already know and can communicate with the number of things which some of us "know" (*i.e.,* recognize) but cannot yet communicate wholly or in part, and the vast number of things which we do not yet know at all. But any broad denial of mental communication might blind us to the meaning of the farreaching changes in present day science and research. And spiritually,

---

when? I deny that the essential controlling power of mind is measurable and predictable, and this for essential reasons. Any study of the nature of history and philosophy will yield the reason, which I need not repeat; and no amount of natural science analogies will make the slightest impression on such well founded reasoning. Omit spirit, and social science is muck.

the very defense of values by means of the ineffable and the irrational would involve the ruthless sacrifice of a major tradition of Western civilization.

The interdependence of individual human minds has long been accepted in that tradition as a fact, though described differently by different observers. Aristotle called man "a political animal," Descartes and Leibnitz taught that rational thought necessarily involved data common to different individuals. Kant saw in the "categories" a standardized inborn mental equipment common to all rational human beings who by means of this identical basic equipment are capable of communicating thought to each other with results valid for all. It was this community of mental structure, given prior to each individual's experience, according to Kant and some of his school, which made man a social being and his mind a social mind, with society thinking in the mind of every individual.[1]

The poet Coleridge spoke of "the all in each of all minds."[2] A modern biologist, Julian Huxley, lists the possession of a common "tradition" among the unique biological characteristics of man, alongside of his possession of a "switchboard" mind capable of both choice and inner conflict, unlike the simple reflex arcs in the poorer nervous systems of insects and other lower forms of life.[3] Similarly, common traditions and conceptual thought are identified with man's nature in a recent report by a committee of one of America's outstanding universities: "[The] abilities . . . to think effectively, to communicate thought, to discern relevance, and to discriminate between values . . . are not powers adventitious to man but 'his glassy essence.' . . . In their integration, they are his being and his end. He is his endeavor to grow in them. As this endeavor flags or is frustrated the less human he becomes."[4]

What is the upshot of these views? Do they suggest some common underlying notion?

Perhaps it is this: a concept of man as the *learning species*—with an

---

[1] Cf. R. Mueller-Freienfels, *The Evolution of Modern Psychology*, Yale University Press, New Haven, 1935, pp. 395-400; M. Adler, *Wegweiser*, Hess, Wien-Leipzig, 1931, p. 73; etc.
[2] Cited in *General Education in Free Society, Report of the Harvard Committee*, Harvard University Press, Cambridge, 1945, p. 206. (Henceforth cited as *General Education*.)
[3] J. S. Huxley, *Man Stands Alone*, Harper & Brothers, New York, 1941, pp. 1-33.
[4] *General Education*, pp. 249-250.

equal stress on both of these words. Man, in this light, appears distinguished by his ability to learn widely and quickly *as a species,* far beyond the lifetime or capacities of any individual. Such learning as a species, through the persons of individuals but progressing beyond them, requires greatly superior facilities for storing information and puts a heavy premium on the unity of the tradition and on the unity of the whole living species which does the learning.

Biologically, man differs from all other dominant species in the history of evolution by his continued ability for fertile interbreeding throughout all the varieties and races of mankind, instead of developing into sharply differentiated subspecies incapable of producing fertile offspring. If the genealogy of every other dominant life form in the history of this planet has resembled a fan with lines of descent radiating ever more widely apart, man's genealogy looks like a net, with lines receding from each other only to come together again.[5] Not only in the invisible network of learning, but in the living network of our descent there seems illustrated the unity of our common heritage, nature, and function.

How does this common learning come about? And what preserves its unity?

III. *The Transfer of Knowledge and the Transformation of Society*

Education is a vital part in the learning process of the species. If it degenerates into the simple reproduction of the knowledge, habits, or preferences of any older generation or existing society, then it loses most of its share in that process of *new* learning which gives it life—that "instability forward" in which Jan Christiaan Smuts and A. J. Toynbee have seen the secret of growth.[6]

Education involves the reproduction of man's "tradition" which helps to make him man—but it includes the growing and dynamic aspects of that broad heritage, as the indispensable setting for the uniqueness and peculiarity of each particular local and historical culture in which any concrete education must go on.

Within these qualifications, education involves decisively the trans-

---

[5]Huxley, *loc. cit.*
[6]A. J. Toynbee, *A Study of History*, 2nd ed., Oxford University Press, London, 1945, III, pp. 112–127.

fer of knowledge. The kinds of knowledge transferred can be grouped under two headings:

1. the transfer of information
2. the transfer of learned behavior, including the learned coordination of unlearned behavior, or "instincts."

Such transfers involve the *products* of specific cultures of a particular place and time—including knowledge motivating, stimulating, and aiding producers of *more* knowledge among those to whom the transfer has been made. But the transfer of these invisible products of a particular culture or society does not necessarily involve the accurate reproduction of that society itself.

On the contrary, a major trend seems now at work in the educational thought of industrialized nations the world over, which in its implications seems to aim at the emergence of a new society different from any other men have ever known.

The Quantitative Expansion of Higher Education

The underlying aim of this worldwide trend in educational thinking seems to be the gradual end of all monopolies of knowledge, the end of the scarcity economy in education.

But how could an economy of abundance in knowledge and education be imagined, even as a long run aim?

Abundance, like scarcity, is relative. Abundance of educational opportunity would mean, first of all, such a supply of opportunities as would keep ahead of all demand of more than critical urgency. It would mean, secondly, a supply of such opportunities and of trained specialists of all kinds as to dilute, and finally abolish, most of the present scarcity value of trained skill, and hence abolish most of the chances of preferred access to social and economic privilege which such scarce skills command today.

This would require eventually the training of abundant numbers of specialists in all relevant fields, the development of abundant social and economic opportunities for the application of their skill,[7] and the development of efficient methods for the transfer of knowledge (both

[7] The crucial importance of ample material and social opportunities for applying these skills is elaborated in this author's "The Value of Freedom," *The American Scholar*, Spring, 1948, pp. 150–160.

of information and learned habits) to new candidates and to such helpers as might be needed for its applicants.

Such a society, obviously, has not yet been achieved. But that responsible leaders of education are envisaging such a long range aim seems evident from such titles as *Education for a Classless Society* by Mr. James B. Conant,[8] President of Harvard University; from the announced intention—from a quite different economic and political system—of the Soviet government to abolish gradually through economic and educational expansion the differences between town and country, and between mental and manual labor;[9] and from the considered judgment of a representative group of America's educational and religious leaders in the recent *Report of President Truman's Commission on Higher Education*,[b] calling for the abolition of social, economic, regional, or racial differences in educational opportunities in the United States.

"The only possible solution" they report, "is, as rapidly as possible, to raise economic and cultural levels in our less advanced areas, and in the meantime to provide outside assistance . . . At least forty-nine per cent of our population has the mental ability to complete fourteen years of schooling. . . . *At least thirty-two per cent of our population has the mental ability to complete an advanced liberal or specialized professional education* . . . The American people should set as their ultimate goal an educational system in which at no level—high school, college, graduate school or professional school—will a qualified individual in any part of the country encounter an insuperable barrier to the attainment of the kind of education suited to his aptitude, and interests. . . . High school education . . . should be provided for all normal youth. . . . The time has come to make education through the fourteenth grade available in the same way that high school education is now available. . . . The time has come to provide financial

---

[b] [For further discussion of the report of the President's Commission, see Chapter I by Robert Ulich (including comment by Rowland W. Dunham), Louis J. A. Mercier's comment on Chapter II by Lyman Bryson, Chapter VII by Charles W. Hendel, Chapter XIII by Mordecai M. Kaplan, Chapter XVII by Ordway Tead.]

[8] J. B. Conant and F. T. Spaulding, *Education for a Classless Society*, Harvard University, Graduate School of Education, Cambridge, 1940.

[9] V. M. Molotov, *The Soviet Union in 1942: The Third Five-Year Plan*, New York Workers Library, 1939, pp. 61, 67.

assistance to competent students in the tenth through fourteenth grades...."[10]

These aims speak for themselves. Their substantial achievement, wherever it should be approached, should go far to abolish the class forming function of knowledge.

Are they meant to be achieved? We live in an age of worldwide pressure for social change. In politics everywhere, such pressure puts a premium on promises. Yet, the new aims for education seem rooted, beyond expediency, in a deeper process: in the industrial revolution in the gaining and use of knowledge which has come to pass in our day.

IV. *Technological Growth and Crises in the Unity of Knowledge*

Ever since the Stone Age, knowledge has grown together with man's productive equipment. In some times and fields, it has lagged behind his practical arts; in other times and problems, it has led the way. The bond between the two has often been stretched. But it could not be broken. Produced by the allocation of efforts and resources, knowledge grew as invisible capital side by side with the visible capital of man's tools and buildings: it functioned as a "general" or as a "specific" factor of production, according to whether it could or could not be readily transferred from one combination of resources to another.[11]

Technological growth involved growth in the division of labor and in the specialization of knowledge. This specialization, however, raised three dangers: first, the danger of *immobility* of specialized knowledge, leaving its possessors insecure in the face of changes; second, the danger of intellectual *incoherence* for individuals and whole communities, stifling cooperation between different fields or kinds of knowledge, and rendering important social problems so obscure as to breed irrationalism and despair in the victims of social maladjustments; and third, the danger of men's *moral blindness* to the actual challenges before them, and to the consequences of their own actions for the welfare of others and for the inner life of their own minds.

---

[10]"Excerpts from the First Reports of the President's Commission on Higher Education," *New York Times,* December 16, 1947, p. 44, italics supplied.

[11]For these terms, cf. G. V. Haberler, *The Theory of International Trade,* The Macmillan Company, New York, 1937, pp. 182 ff.

Higher Education and the Unity of Knowledge

Since Socrates's insight that "no man errs willingly," Western man has been aware of the essential connection between ignorance and evil, and between the will to goodness and the will to truth. Certainly, our tradition has also needed intuition, emotion, and will, but the search for rational truth has remained one of its foundations.

In the history of knowledge, then, the problem posed by a growing technology has been how to combine a growth in specialization with an increase in mobility. In the moral and spiritual history of man the problem at such times has been to prevent ignorance or incoherence from growing instead of shrinking with the growth in men's powers, and from putting their additional formidable obstacles in the way of men's moral action.

This problem has arisen several times in the past and has been solved to some extent at levels appropriate to each.

When Greek merchants brought together the bewildering diversity of specialized knowledge and experience from Egypt, Babylon, the Phoenicians, the people around the Mediterranean, and the various Greek city states themselves, they faced the problem of developing a kind of mobile knowledge applicable to a wide range of specialized situations. The Greeks achieved a partial solution to this problem between 600 and 300 B.C. by developing new techniques: in reporting through Solon and Herodotus; in generalized thinking through Ionian science; in mathematics through Thales and the Pythagoreans; and in logic through Zeno and the Sophists, and later Aristotle; and in teaching methods through the Sophists, Socrates, the Academy of Plato, and Aristotle's Lyceum.[12]

A similar combination of advances in generalized science and philosophy, mathematical techniques, and better teaching methods, was at work in the resolution of the next great crisis in the problem of specialization and mobility of knowledge. That second crisis in the West was brought on between 1200 and 1600 A.D. by the growing volume of specialized knowledge available from the productive activities of an ever growing number of crafts and guilds, from merchant ventures first in the Mediterranean and then beyond, from the Crusades and the

[12] Cf. Werner Jaeger, *Paidea*, Oxford University Press, New York, 1945, I, pp. 101–114, 150–184, 298–321; Charles Singer, *A Short History of Science*, Oxford University Press, London, 1940, pp. 5 ff.; W. T. Sedgwick, H. W. Tyler, and R. P. Bigelow, *A Short History of Science*, The Macmillan Company, New York, 1939, pp. 37, 44; G. Childe, *What Happened in History*, Pelican Books, New York, 1946, pp. 198–223, etc.

reception of Arab techniques and learning, from ever growing laws and patterns of administration, ecclesiastical and profane, and from a web of ever more complex commercial and financial transactions.

On the technical level of the transfer of knowledge, the log jam was broken again by the development of systems of generalized rational thought and methods of logic, first by the Scholastics and later by the Humanists; by the new mathematical techniques of Arab numerals, algorithms, algebra, the decimal system, modern bookkeeping and computation; by the new concepts and models such as "equilibrium" and "mechanism"; and by the new methods of teaching developed by the cathedral schools, the guilds, and by the universities.[13]

The science of Galileo and Newton, the later "Age of Reason," the American and French Revolutions, and the Industrial Revolution, all worked with this new intellectual equipment. They brought out its latent powers, and they finally carried it beyond its original frame in the nineteenth century thought of Hegel, Marx, and Darwin, in a search for intellectual synthesis which foreshadowed many problems of today.

V. The Industrial Revolution in the Field of Knowledge Today

Today, and at least for the past fifty years, we have again been in the throes of a major crisis of knowledge and intellectual coordination—the third such crisis in Western history. It has been a crisis in our mere capacity to store, order, and recall the items of information pouring into our minds and libraries from all fields of science and practical experience. It has become harder to survey data from different fields, to discern their mutual relevance, and to recombine them across departmental boundaries to fruitful new concepts.

It has also been a crisis in our ability to transfer our learned behavior from problem to problem; and so it has robbed us of our sense of security and familiarity in a world which seemingly we can no longer "explain," that is to say, in which we no longer know how to behave in new fields or unfamiliar situations, or what to expect from a future of which we suspect only that it will differ greatly from our past.

[13] Cf. Singer, *op. cit.*; Sedgwick-Tyler-Bigelow, *op. cit.*; E. Rosenstock-Huessy, *Out of Revolution: Autobiography of Western Man*, William Morrow & Company, New York, 1938, pp. 453–561.

Higher Education and the Unity of Knowledge

Of course, those fifty years have been years of political and economic crises, wars, and revolutions. They brought enough changes and struggles for change to bewilder almost anyone. But the generations which emerged from the wars and revolutions of the age of Cromwell and the Thirty Years' War, or from the age of Jefferson and Bonaparte—these generations do not seem to have been quite as perplexed with the sheer difficulty of thinking coherently, of comprehending what was going on. One of the peculiar traits of our time seems to be the coming together of a wave of rapid technological and social change with the climax of a crisis in our obsolescent mental equipment.

All possible improvement in our mental tools will only, therefore, solve at best a small part of our problems. The world's ills cry out for action, and it is action which must deal with them. But in this multitude of needed actions, thought must play its part.[e] What has been done to develop better tools of thought?

The Search for a Science of Science

The past fifty years have paralleled, as it were, on a much larger scale, many of the efforts at solution of Greece and of the late Middle Ages. They have seen extended search for more generalized methods of rational thought through a new understanding of logic, semantics, and mathematical and scientific method; through new studies of society and of the sociology of knowledge; through new studies of psychology, the learning process, and new teaching methods; and through a vast

[e]Comment by Herman Finer:
  The brief history of knowledge and its transmission is extremely dubious. Admittedly, it is difficult to be explicit in such a short span. But calling the troubles of mankind a "crisis of knowledge and intellectual coordination" only, over the ages to our time, is to emphasize again the major omission in the paper: the spiritual struggles over what was and is Right or Wrong. The paper omits the problems discussed by the Grand Inquisitor in the *Brothers Karamazov*. If the bulk of the world's "ills" cry out for action, does Dr. Deutsch think that the identification of what is *ill*, is simply a problem of knowledge and intellectual coordination?

Dr. Deutsch's reply:
  I agree with Dr. Finer about the crucial importance of the questions of what is *Right or Wrong*. I believe that it can be answered in general terms, and specific answers found for each particular time and place, by an analysis of the probable consequences of each alternative course of action or inaction. These consequences are not only external ones, for other persons or the outside world, but also internal consequences for the inner health or disintegration of the personality of the doer.

expansion of teaching facilities and mass training programs in all major countries of the world.

The new industrial scale of these efforts has put its mark on their nature. The flood of publications on "Semantics," "Theory of Signs," "Metascience," "Symbolic Logic," and "Heuristics," is not accident. What is being developed under all these labels is the beginning of a science of science, something which seems related to particular fields of knowledge as machine tools—*i.e.*, machines that make machines—are related to any particular type of machinery.[14]

All these approaches aim at analyzing the processes of scientific thought into clearly labeled *elements* suitable for separate manipulation; and at standardizing basic concepts, the rules for their combination, and the translation of recognizable patterns, so as to transform more and more of them into "interchangeable parts" which can be transferred to different *recombinations* from worker to worker and from field to field.

This analysis and reorganization of thought processes is not limited to the management of knowledge which has already been acquired, or to the transfer of existing techniques from their old field to a new one.[15] Rather, as in G. Polya's "Heuristics" or in J. B. Conant's and J. D. Bernal's notions of the "Strategy of Science," it is attempting to give new insight and power to our advances into the unknown, which so far largely have been guided by the unanalyzed mental processes labeled "intuition."

[14] Early suggestions along these lines were made by Descartes, Leibnitz, Engels, Bolzano and others. For a few samples of contemporary work, cf. Bertrand Russell and Alfred M. Whitehead, *Principia Mathematica*, Cambridge University Press, London, 1914; P. W. Bridgman, *The Logic of Modern Physics*, The Macmillan Company, New York, 1927; R. Carnap, *The Logical Syntax of Language*, Harcourt Brace & Company, Inc., New York, 1937; Charles Morris, *Foundations of the Theory of Signs*, Monograph No. 2, *International Encyclopedia of Unified Science*, University of Chicago Press, Chicago, 1938; Philipp Frank, *Foundations of Physics*, University of Chicago Press, Chicago, 1946; and other monographs in the *International Encyclopedia of Unified Science*; G. Polya, *How to Solve It*, Princeton University Press, Princeton, 1944; A. Tarski, *Introduction to Logic and to the Methodology of the Deductive Sciences*, Oxford University Press, New York, 1941; etc., etc.

[15] E.g., in J. V. Neumann and O. Morgensterne, *Theory of Games and Economic Behavior*, Princeton University Press, Princeton, 1944.

The Industrialization of Memory

The search for sharper and more manageable tools has been paralleled, if not outpaced, by a vast growth of material equipment. Industry has produced new "sense organs" and devices for subtler discrimination between different events in nature: radar, electron microscopes, radioactive isotopes, etc. It has developed impersonal and often automatic recording devices—cameras, microphones and phonographs, television cells, Geiger counters, and all the rest—in such quantities that Hume's and Berkeley's simple image of none but human "observers" struggling with none but personal "sensations," seems clearly contradicted by the facts.

Industry has done more. It has developed devices serving three basic functions of memory: the storage, recall, and association of large numbers of items of knowledge. Information is *stored* in libraries, on cards, filing systems, photographs, films, and microfilms; on phonograph records, sound film, and magnetized wire; on punched cards and punched tape. It is *recalled* with the help of code numbers, classification systems, catalogs, bibliographies, index cards, file folders, index tabs, accession sheets, routing slips, and other document control devices, or by the automatic mechanism of the Hollerith machines. Many of the devices for recall fulfil already some of the basic functions of *association*: past and future information may be associated by file folders, library classifications, or routing slips. I.B.M. machines can be set to recall facts in particular patterns of association: such as the names of physicists with at least one year of radar experience, male, under thirty-five years old, with a knowledge of Spanish and German. Further improvements believed attainable within the next ten years have been described by Dr. Vannevar Bush in a paper which has attracted wide attention. Dr. Bush foresees machines which can scan information, recognize pattern, reduce spoken dictation to writing, and retain "associative trails" within their coded microfiling systems.[16]

This growth of memory devices is one aspect of the growth of communications and control engineering. In terms of quantity, the share of communications and control equipment in each million dollars

---

[16]Vannevar Bush, "That Men May Think," *Atlantic Monthly*, 176, July, 1945, pp. 105–108; reprinted in *The Atlantic Reader*, Pocket Book Ed., New York.

spent on capital investments in the United States has risen significantly in recent years.[17] In terms of quality or performance we now have in operation devices which follow and take account of their own "mistakes," from the domestic thermostat to the automatic airplane pilot; devices which calculate and predict, such as differential analyzers, electronic computers, and the various automatic predicting and calculating devices directing anti-aircraft batteries; devices which discriminate between desired and undesired information, such as wave filters which separate "messages" from "noise"; and devices which make decisions between different possible paths according to previously established operating priorities (or "values") and "hunt" for possible alternative pathways, if the usual ones are blocked—as do automatic telephone switchboards. All these devices are in a very real sense advances in the acquiring, storing, transmission, and recombination of knowledge.[18]

During the Second World War things were carried further. Machines took over some of the specific tasks of analysis, comparison, and combination of data which are characteristic of *thought,* advancing toward a new level the old intellectual partnership between man and the work of his hands. Scientists of the Antisubmarine Warfare Operations Research Group developed the concept of the "search rate, or numbers of square miles which a given craft can search over in an hour. . . . It was soon realized that the situation must be described in terms of probability. . . . From this probability of sighting would be computed . . . the effective search rate. Operational data were punched on I.B.M. cards and then analyzed by machine methods. On the basis of a sighting probability curve, obtained from operational data, different aircraft search plans could be compared in efficiency, and the best plan found."[19]

In this partnership between men and machines in the business of thinking, the number of skilled men needed does not necessarily go down. There arises a new demand for men skilled to set up the more complex problems by new mathematical techniques, and to organize the raw data so that they can be put on the punched cards of the I.B.M. machine, or on the punched tape of the electronic calculator, in such

---

[17] Minneapolis-Honeywell Corporation, Report to Stockholders, 1947, *New York Times,* December 31, 1947.

[18] Cf. Norbert Wiener, *Cybernetics,* Herrmann et Cie., Paris; John Wiley & Sons, Inc., New York, 1948, pp. 53–56.

[19] J. Ph. Baxter, 3rd, *Scientists Against Time,* Little Brown & Company, Boston, 1946, pp. 405–406.

Higher Education and the Unity of Knowledge

a manner that the machinemade solutions shall have significance.[20] The gain is not primarily in the saving of men, but in the new range of analysis, correlations, and predictions, which men and machines can work out in cooperation.

The Mobilization of Personnel

The mobilization of intellectual techniques and engineering devices has been paralleled by the mobilization of men.

One aspect of this mobilization can be observed in the long rise of industrial research laboratories associated with such names as Thomas A. Edison and Charles F. Kettering. Under peacetime schedules of preference, where time is usually valued less highly and money more than in war, these laboratories first developed techniques for the efficient combinations of men and facilities in the organization of thought and the industrialization of invention.[21]

The great wartime organizations of science, such as the Office of Scientific Research and Development, or the "Manhattan Project," continued this trend. But with the growth in the scale of their activities they brought a change in kind. One lesson of the "operational research" developed during World War II has been the discovery "that scientists were very much more interchangeable than their specialized training would have led us to expect, and that, particularly in the new brands of scientific war work which was Operational Research, scientists trained in all subject could make equally significant contributions. . . . War experience has already taught us the need to keep our scientific manpower flexible by avoiding over-specialization and inculcating general scientific method into teaching."[22]

The *general* value of certain special scientific skills over a wide variety of applications was stressed by "the father of operations research," Professor P. S. M. Blackett, who became in 1942 Chief Adviser on Operational Research to the First Sea Lord of the British Ad-

[20] Wiener, *op. cit.*, p. 154.
[21] Cf. C. C. Furnas, *Research in Industry*, D. Van Nostrand Company, Inc., New York, 1948, pp. 1–55, 182–193, 295–307; J. G. Crowther, *The Social Relations of Science*, The Macmillan Company, New York, 1941, pp. 464–490; H. R. Bartlett, "The Development of Industrial Research in the United States," in National Resources Planning Board, *Research—A National Resource, II: Industrial Research*, Washington, D.C., 1941, pp. 19–77.
[22] J. D. Bernal, "Lessons of the War for Science," Discourse at the Royal Institution, November, 1945, multigraphed excerpts, M.I.T., Ec. 21; 1947; p. 10.

miralty, and Nobel Laureate in Physics in 1948. "Many war operations involve considerations with which scientists are specially trained to compete. . . . This is especially the case with all those aspects of operations into which probability considerations and the theory of error enter . . . the scientist can encourage numerical thinking on operational matters, and so can help avoid running the war by gusts of emotion . . ."[23]

The experience of American war research confirmed the unexpected importance of transferring and recombining specialized scientific information and personnel for the solution of new tasks: "In the U Chemistry Division a great effort was made for many months to avoid the development of central laboratories, (but) . . . the benefits to be derived from teamwork of sizable groups were too great to be neglected . . . When the organic chemist works in a central laboratory he is in constant contact with other men with special skills in other portions of the field, and out of the resultant pooling of knowledge and techniques great gains are derived. . . . However versatile or broadly trained the academic scientists might be, most of them now found themselves working on problems of which they had previously known little or nothing."[24]

The outcome was summed up by the Coordinator of Research and Development, Rear Admiral Julius A. Furer, in a letter to Dr. Vannevar Bush: "That your group would contribute brilliant ideas and achievements to the war effort was expected, but that you would be so versatile . . . was unexpected by many."[25]

The trend of our technology has been toward more machines per worker, more communication and transportation per consumer, more undertakings hitherto impossible (such as rapid weather forecasting, or nuclear engineering), more automatic equipment, flowline production, process industries, and systematic search for new discoveries. It has included the growing mechanization of some of the simple elements of thinking, and the probable future mechanization of some of the more repetitive types of intellectual labor. With such a trend, we shall need in our labor force not a smaller but an ever larger proportion

[23]Cited in Baxter, *op. cit.*, p. 404; cf. also Sir Charles Goodeve, "Operational Research," *Nature*, London, March 13, 1948, pp. 377-384.
[24]Baxter, *op. cit.*, pp. 20-22.
[25]*Ibid.*, p. 25; cf. also pp. 122, 404-410.

of skilled personnel, including scientists. The large scale mobilization of such personnel for peacetime and wartime research, and the versatility of their skills, have demonstrated the need and the possibilities of meeting it. The quantitative manpower goals of President Truman's Commission on Higher Education may well be in line with these realities.

As to their quality, the needed new skills differ from the old crafts of artisans by their greater precision, generality, ease of analysis, transfer and recombination for new tasks—that is, precisely by their greater resemblance to the general skills taught by higher education.

This qualitative change is perhaps already visible in a field of critical importance: the skills of communication and coordination. During the past few decades, the practical need for coordination and coherence has been met in part by a series of applied new sciences or practical arts, each arising from a set of particular problems. Traffic jams have led to traffic engineering, congested cities to town planning, distressed or backward areas to regional development. A science of logistics, and specialized "logisticians," were forced on the United States Navy by the experience of the war.[26] The growing rise of private corporations has led to a large literature on problems of management, sometimes even called "scientific management." In the field of public economic policy, planning has been attacked in theory by some, only to be accepted or imitated by many. There was planning of industrial priorities in the American war effort, and there are allocation problems in the "Marshall Plan," or European Recovery Program, in American postwar foreign policy. Russia is operating under her Fourth Five Year Plan. Britain saw the Prime Minister's *Economic Survey for 1947* open with a section on "How the Plan is Made."[27] Publications on the history, theory, and practice of planning in the various countries are legion. And, since public opinion in most industrial countries now holds that full employment, social security, and educational opportunity are necessities of life, and must be provided by government if private efforts should lag or fail, there seems little doubt that we are heading, in the long

---

[26]Duncan Ballantine, *U.S. Naval Logistics in the Second World War,* Princeton University Press, Princeton, 1947, pp. 1-8, 101-131, 181-204, 273-282, 289-296.

[27]Cmd. 7046. *Economic Survey for 1947. Presented by the Prime Minister to Parliament,* etc., February, 1947, His Majesty's Stationery Office, London, 1947, pp. 4-9.

run, for more rather than less "programming," "balancing," and planning.[d]

What about the men who must control these problems? With the growing flow of goods, services, and information there is a growing need for human "traffic junctions," "literate drivers," "traffic officers," and "traffic engineers." Where can these men be trained? And what is it that they need to learn?

VI. *Some Tasks for Universities: Education for Cohesion*

It is as places for such training that universities are needed. Some individuals may be trained elsewhere; and some, perhaps many, will graduate as specialists in some particular profession with little interest in the coherence and coordination of many specialized professions other than their own. But the common root in the words, "unity" and "university," is not merely a matter of etymology. From their early beginnings, universities have cared for the unity of knowledge as a condition for the ultimate unity of the society in which they functioned. An understanding of this unity and coherence of knowledge is becoming a necessity for the long run effectiveness of any specialized professional training. What is more, for an increasing number of persons the very arts and sciences of coherence and coordination themselves are becoming important specialties to be acquired in the course of a university education.

[d]Comment by Herman Finer:
There is a contradiction of no little importance between Dr. Deutsch and Lyman Bryson [Cf. Chapter II]. Dr. Deutsch thinks there is little *planning* doubt, that we are heading for more rather than less "programming," "balancing," and "planning." Dr. Bryson seems to deplore the fact that a want of education has led us into the state's concern for welfare—that is, welfare planned by the state. Which is wrong, or which is right: Dr. Bryson's belief that education has failed because planning by authority has been found necessary, or Dr. Deutsch's deduction from all history that it is necessary, and that education should lead to, and not away from, planning? Evidently, their reading of history, that is, the development of the place of mind in society, does not tally; and it would seem that their judgments about the human will must differ; which means that they differ regarding what can be achieved by education. But that problem, namely, at what point education is of no avail, has, I think, not been tackled by any of the papers in the series, with the possible exception of T. V. Smith's, and then not directly and fully—yet it is essential to know what are education's limits, for then other social means must be employed. See, for example, John Stuart Mill's wrestling with this problem in his *Essay on Liberty,* and the attention he was compelled to pay to this in *Utilitarianism.*

Indoctrination or Communication?

It might here be objected that a major task of a university should be indoctrination in the loyalties approved by those who control it. In the view of the Harvard Report, "the impulse to rear students to a received idea of the good is in fact necessary to education. . . . Our society, like any society, rests on common beliefs and . . . a major task of education is to perpetuate them."[28] But no university could perpetuate a belief regardless of its truth. *Amicus Plato, magis amica veritas.* If we need agreement on common loyalties, it is vital to know which loyalties by their very nature can be agreed upon. No university can enforce agreement on those ultimate values which belong to the realms of religion or philosophy. Nor could it enforce agreements on points of fact in opposition to the fact finding methods of science without destroying science at its roots.[e]

What then are the loyalties—the relatively stable preferences in thought and action—on which men can agree in a democracy? Are they not to be found on the intermediate level, between the facts of accurate experience and the ultimate values projected by groups and individuals into the unknown? That is to say, can they not be sought on the level of the common methods and processes by which facts are found, probable consequences may be estimated, and the practical compatibility of values be tested?[f] Perhaps we may trust men's freedom to choose

[e]Comment by Louis J. A. Mercier:
It seems to me that the university does enforce agreement. At least all the professors do on the matters they consider true, else the student gets zero. There is no more assurance that the professor of science has the truth than others. In fact assurance is less easy than in metaphysics. The science of today is not that of yesterday, whereas a whole continues to be greater than a part.

[f]Comment by David Bidney:
Dr. Deutsch has here raised a fundamental problem which is of especial concern to the cultural anthropologist and educator. On the one hand, every sociocultural system, in so far as it is an integrated whole, must have its common values, beliefs, assumptions or cultural "universals." On the other hand, the perpetuating of traditional beliefs, regardless of their truth value, is incompatible with our modern scientific approach and to the idea of cultural progress. The question then arises whether it is possible to have cultural values or common beliefs which may be compatible with the data of science and serve as a focus of integration for our contemporary culture.

Dr. Deutsch tends to assume uncritically and dogmatically that no universities can "enforce agreement" on the ultimate values of religion and philosophy and that the only common basis of agreement is to be found in the acceptance of the methods and processes

[28]*General Education*, p. 46.

values so long as they will accept the obligation to seek and face the truth about the *consequences* of these values in the world of fact.

Such an obligation is more easily accepted than fulfilled, but the wider dissemination of the skills needed for its fulfilment may prove increasingly important for the survival of freedom.

---

of science. Of course, there is no logical method of "enforcing agreement" in the sense that all minds alike will accept a given formulation on ultimate values; in matters of theory it is notoriously difficult to obtain unanimity among highly trained scholars, as these Conferences have amply demonstrated. This, however, need not prevent us from seeking such agreement nor inhibit our educators from attempting to indicate to their students the basic values and presuppositions of our cultural heritage. After all, one of the functions of higher education is to prepare men for citizenship in a given community, and how is one to obtain this sense of community without a critical appreciation of the common values upon which our sociocultural life is based? It is difficult to see how agreement on "common methods and processes" of science can achieve anything more than a purely formal and empty consensus which may then be utilized for the most inhuman purposes. We need but remind ourselves that the Nazi doctors who experimented on their human victims were thoroughly acquainted with the common methods of scientific procedure.

Dr. Deutsch's reply:

I can only regret that I did not succeed in making sufficiently clear the distinction which could have avoided our misunderstanding. The point is in the difference between *ultimate* values projected beyond our experience into the unknown, and *basic* assumptions or values—that is, preferences in thought or action—which are part of our common experience of living. The distinction between the two kinds is not sharp, but it is real.

Recognition of some rational faculties in all normal adult human beings, or of their need for love and some degree of freedom, or belief in the desirability of doing to others as we would be done by—all these might well come within the field of basic values or loyalties on the intermediate level, on which agreement can be sought, reached, and maintained, both in daily life and by the body of our universities. The ultimate purpose of human life or of the universe, the specific attributes of ultimate reality or of God—these are ultimate values which cannot be uniformly or conclusively imposed by an educational system without destructive and interminable conflicts with independent critical thought or individual belief.

Comment by Louis J. A. Mercier:

The university must encourage "such critical appreciation of the common values on which our sociocultural life is based," but it should be possible for it to bring out that our sociocultural life is all wrong. That is what needed to be done under the Nazis. We have therefore to develop a critical apparatus of values transcendent to one particular sociocultural life. We must get to universal principles. The study of the history of the whole cultural heritage of the race is one means of doing so, at least it can help us to discover the constants of human nature. However, we cannot hope that the study of this heritage will give us only moral constants. It will reveal many immoral ones. We still shall have the problem of distinguishing the moral from the immoral, and in universal terms, not in the terms of succeeding given sociocultural modes of life.

How can these skills be taught in universities, and how can this manner of thinking be communicated? There seem to be four promising approaches which might be utilized in combination:

1. A unifying course of study in the actual development of knowledge in the History of Science and Thought.
2. A study of the role of models, such as "mechanism" or "organism" in past and present thought in both the physical and social sciences, as well as in other fields of culture, leading to a critical understanding of the traditional models inherited from the past and to their possible supplementing by new and more useful ones.
3. Research on key concepts which are used over a wide range of different sciences.
4. More specific research and training in relevant special subjects such as mathematics, logic, and the theory of communication.

The first of these three approaches is historical and deals with actual experience. The second and third approaches deal with specific comparisons of more narrowly correlated data and the search for new, specific tools of thought. The fourth approach deals with basic theories and specific techniques helpful for the carrying out of some of the tasks implied in the others.

1. Reason in History: Some Technical and Social Aspects for a Basic Course in the History of Thought and Science

Such a course could also be called a course in the History of Knowledge. It would be based on the notion of the unity of knowledge, the observable interdependence in every epoch and culture, of "scientific" and "non-scientific" ways of thinking, and in particular of "natural" and "social" science.

The main purpose of this course would be to unite the integrating approach of the history of men and movements with the technical approach of an analysis of concepts and ideas. It would be an attempt to see ideas and intellectual operations in their connections and setting, but to try to analyze each of these operations so as to know more accurately what they are, how they function, and what they imply, and in particular to judge how they might function if transferred to another time or to another setting.

Only the sketchiest of samples can be given in the paragraphs that follow. At best they will be samples of how one man might attack such a problem, rather than how other men with other backgrounds should attack it. With this reservation, the samples may indicate some of the problems that might be studied in the course of a half year's work, covering some key problems in the history of knowledge from classical Greece to the new departure of the High Middle Ages.[29]

Since it would deal with science as with one particular way of acquiring and transferring knowledge, the course might start with a brief discussion of the concept of knowledge as both information and learned behavior, that is, both "know what" and "know how," and the acquisition of knowledge through operations from which *traces* or *symbols* are derived which ultimately are stored in the mind of the individual, or induce change in some association between some traces stored there already. Such effective traces of operations may be said to constitute "experience."

Abstraction and Symbols

Abstraction begins in the body of each individual. Traces are automatically abstracted by each sense organ through its peculiar way of interacting with the outside world. Stored in the organism they usually preserve invariant some pattern of nervous activity analogous to some pattern of relations among the external events from which they were derived. In the case of vision, "the eye receives its most intense impression at boundaries, and . . . every visual image in fact has something of the nature of a line drawing."[30] It is these outline patterns of sight, sound, and other sense impressions, which permit recognition, cumulative experience about "similar" events, and social agreement that one outline represents the "same" object which each individual sees in a slightly different private manner. "Abstractive seeing is the foundation of our rationality . . ."[31] Thought is just this abstracting, storing, and recombining of symbols, and their reapplication to action, and "mind" is a general name we may apply to any set of facilities, organic, electric, or social, to the extent that they fulfil these functions. ["Mind,"

---

[29]Readers not interested in this sample may well skip the rest of this section, and proceed directly to the next.

[30]Wiener, *op. cit.*, p. 159.

[31]Susanne K. Langer, *Philosophy in a New Key,* Harvard University Press, Cambridge, 1942; Penguin Books, Inc., New York, 1948, pp. 56–59.

thus understood, cannot exist without "body," but differs from it. If a man retains his brain tissue but becomes unable to abstract, store, or recombine information, we say he has "lost his mind."]

Historically, thought has grown through the social processes of work and speech, and for the symbols we call "words" the social character of speech has implied, even among primitive peoples, some further degree of abstract generality—usually the greater the larger the circle of speakers and the more complex the division of labor among them.[32] According to Franz Boas, Indian tribes which lacked unmodified common names or words for Platonic universals, such as "house," could "easily be taught to isolate the term 'house' out of expressions meaning 'that-house-yonder,' 'my-house-here,' and 'the-house-made-of-wood'. . . . Once they have been made to feel the intellectual need for the bare term 'house,' they will accept the usage and thus push the language ahead a thousand years in one generation."[33] With the growth of society, words thus become *concepts,* that is, symbols for *classes* of things or operations, or of partial, isolated aspects of things or operations, potentially suitable for effective transmission, recall, and recombination.

Intuition and Mimesis

But transmission of simple information can occur quickly without abstract words, by pointing; and learned behavior often can be transferred most rapidly not by symbols but by *mimesis,* that is, by unanalyzed imitation of someone else's behavior pattern as a whole, as in a mob or a panic. Similarly, recall or recombination of information deeply stored in memory or obscured by later associations could conceivably be carried out much faster and over a wider range of items not by deliberate effort to think of each item, but by *vision* or *intuition,* that is, by an unanalyzed, wholesale mental process, with no internal labels attached to its constituent steps, and hence with the appearance of a complete experience or apparition even to the mind which produced it. Not only has the deliberate search for, and utilization of, such visions for the mobilization of an individual's past experience and the

---

[32]Cf. Childe, *op. cit.,* p. 6; M. Schlauch, *The Gift of Tongues,* Modern Age Press, New York, 1942, pp. 286–287.
[33]Schlauch, *loc. cit.*

guidance of his decisions been described by anthropologists in several primitive cultures,[34] but we find similar patterns in religious experiences and even in serious discussions of sources of scientific insight in our own civilization.[35]

Visions may synthesize new knowledge from elements of the past, while mimesis transmits learned behavior which already exists in the human models of imitation.[36] But since both vision and mimesis are types of unanalyzed behavior, even the results of vision can only be transmitted to others by mimesis. The innovating repercussions of any particular vision thus tend to grind to a stop since they can only be transmitted by conservative, non-innovating imitation. In theory, continued change in a society might be maintained by a steady flow of innovating visions, but in actual history it seems that every society gaining and transmitting its knowledge exclusively or mainly by non-analytical methods—from primitive hunters to the vast river civilizations of the Orient—has eventually fallen into stagnation. In the long run, mimesis and intuition could not serve as foundations of science. What other method, then, could be developed that might perhaps lack the short run convenience of vision or mimesis but also its long run limitations?

Reason: Concepts, Rules, and Trails

Recurrent sequences of experiences were remembered and communicated. Standardized by social usage, they could form the beginnings of "reason" which has linked separate abstract concepts and symbols of operations by organizing them in the manner of a step-by-step trail, permitting the knower to retrace each of his steps, and others to repeat for themselves what he had done. Trails are familiar to primitive hunters tracking their quarry and to settlers marking paths. Myth and

---

[34] Ruth Benedict, *Patterns of Culture*, Pelican Books, New York, 1947, pp. 35–39.

[35] Cf. William James, "Mysticism," in *Varieties of Religious Experience*, Modern Library, Inc., New York, n.d., pp. 370–413; Walter B. Cannon, "The Role of Hunches," in *The Way of an Investigator*, W. W. Norton & Company, Inc., New York, 1945, pp. 57–67; Polya, "Bright Idea," in *op. cit.*, pp. 56–58; cf. also B. Russell, "Plotinus," in *A History of Western Philosophy*, Simon and Schuster, New York, 1945, pp. 289–290; and Joshua Rossett, *The Mechanism of Thought, Imagery, and Hallucination*, Columbia University Press, New York, 1939, *passim*.

[36] For a general discussion of mimesis by a historian, see Toynbee, *op. cit.*, I, pp. 191–195; III, pp. 245–248.

folklore have left us the image of the retraceable manmade trail of knowledge in the pebbles of Hansel and Gretel and in the thread of Ariadne.

Finally, both unanalyzed perception and repeatable analysis become possible in the case of pictures which thus could also become starting points for science. A process of retracing and verifying information seems possible for the beholder of the "magical" but anatomically accurate neolithic cave drawings which show the exact spot where an arrow will pierce a buffalo's heart.[37]

Every social process of deriving words and concepts, and of linking them in some patterns, retraceable or not, involves at least an implicit *"conceptual scheme,"* as Dr. Conant calls it, that is, an implicit set of decisions and preferences as to which aspects of experience to abstract separately, which ones to class together under a common concept, which ones to look for, and which ones to ignore.[38] Such a scheme may have been derived in part by intuition. It may be taught by custom and learned by mimesis. It may be based on magic, that is, on human social behavior projected into non-human nature and gaining such practical results as it does from ununderstood actions applied to unanalyzed processes.[39] And it may be almost unchangeable, embedded in the traditional culture of the community.

Yet with the division of labor between agriculture and towns in the first great river civilizations and the rise of different social strata within them, with the rise of elaborate structures of government, with the development of the division of labor between craftsman and priest into the rise of organized priesthoods, temples serving as repositories of wealth and knowledge (*e.g.,* astronomical observations), with the rise of pictorial writing, as in Egypt and Babylon—with all these there arises the *organization* of that which is known, corresponding, so to speak, to the organization of the knowers. The *conceptual schemes become explicit*. They may be as inflexible as the society which gave them birth, but they are now available for diffusion and change if they should become accessible to other groups less rigidly bound by tradition. And

---

[37] Singer, *op. cit.,* p. 3.

[38] Cf. J. B. Conant, *On Understanding Science,* Yale University Press, New Haven, 1947, pp. 24, 102, 137–138.

[39] ". . . one of the most striking of Dobuan beliefs is that no result in any field of existence is possible without magic. . . . Yams cannot grow without their incantations . . . no wind blows unless it is magically called. . . ." Benedict, *op. cit.,* pp. 131–132.

such groups may be at hand among the merchants at the fringes of the traditional society.

Merchants are neither priests nor craftsmen. They have to be more practical and adaptable than the first, and more skilled in abstract thought than the second. Measure and number are the tools of their trade, from the counting of cattle and the weighing of metal to the changing of coins. If they command skills of transportation and belong to regions and peoples outside the great irrigation civilizations, they may succeed in trading with more than one of them, unfettered by the tradition of any, and sifting what they will accept from each against the background of their own needs and culture. Here, perhaps, is a clue to the greatness of Greece and Israel: growing in their own image, they became at the same time foci of the culture of almost the whole Mediterranean and Near East.

The mobilization, sifting, transporting, comparing, and accepting of goods involves the mobilization, abstraction, analysis, and recombination of symbols. The invention of small silver coins was reinforced by that of alphabetic writing and the introduction of iron tools which made metal work and metal arms widely available. Then fell the bronze age monopoly of metal weapons, as well as the monopoly of gold coins and the monopoly of writing. Recombination of separate elements became a practical experience on a larger scale than ever before.

Recombination of words and symbols is as old as thought. But now, in Israel and Greece, recombination began to show its power to derive *new* patterns from the past and to project them into the future. The very name of Prometheus signifies "forethought" and its legendary bearer was said to have rebelled against the gods, stolen from them their secret knowledge, and taught men all useful arts. If the combination of wings and a horse yielded the symbol of Pegasus for poets, the combination of wings and men yielded the image of Daedalus and Icarus, and with it an undying inspiration for the possibility of human flight as a fruit not of magic but of knowledge and labor.

Trade calls for *law,* once it emerges beyond piracy. Goods are exchanged more conveniently if there are some general rules of peace and confidence at the market place and there is a measure of equality in reading agreement. Weights, measures, coins, require agreement as to accurate standards, and as to the rules of their exchange or combination. These rules are explicit but abstract, binding anyone in the market.

The experience of accurate general standards of measure and of explicit but impersonal rules for social action was matched by the development of interest in *accurate standardized concepts* and in *explicit general rules for their recombination*—that is to say, in the patterns of *generalized* thought or *reason,* which is one of the two basic pillars of science.

When the rules for the recombination of symbols become explicit they provide the basis for the rise of conscious generalized thought or "*reason.*" All reasoning involves the combination of memories for prediction and eventual action—the ability "to achieve ends clearly conceived in advance"—[40] but it involves essentially *combinations which are themselves remembered like a marked trail, and which are retraceable, step by step,* both by the individual himself and by others. It is in this sense, we speak of reasoning as "demonstrative." But what rules of recombination will be selected, what kind of trails marked out, what degree of success achieved in the actual prediction and control of external events in society or nature, and what importance or unimportance assigned to such success—these are not questions of the abstract nature of reasoning in general but of the concrete, historical culture and society in which that reasoning is taking place.[41]

Matching, Logic, Proof, and Culture

There are, of course, general statements that will be found to apply to most or all kinds of "reasoning." Reasoning generally implies the operation of *matching,* that is, of putting different physical objects side by side—or recalling together sets of remembered symbols—and noting their relative similarity or difference. From this operation of matching things or symbols, or things and recorded or remembered symbols with each other, can be derived the operation of *recognition;* the "judgment of sameness," in which P. W. Bridgman has seen the basis of "identity,"[42] and perhaps the notion of *"quality"* which would mean the application or even creation of a new recognition pattern either through

---

[40]R. G. Collingwood, *The Idea of History,* Clarendon Press, Oxford, 1946, pp. 46, 21.

[41]Cf. Benedict, *op. cit., passim;* Clyde Kluckhohn and W. H. Kelly, "The Concept of Culture," in *The Science of Man in the World Crisis,* R. Linton, ed.: for Columbia University Press, New York, 1945, pp. 78–106; for the rise of generalized scholastic reasoning in different cultures, cf. G. Sarton, *Introduction to the History of Science,* Williams and Wilkins Company, Baltimore, 1927, I, pp. 26–29.

[42]Bridgman, *op. cit.,* p. 92.

new abstraction from outside events or through new recombination of symbols already stored. From these operations could then be derived the notion of quantitative comparison, the notion of "more" or "larger," derived from matching undivided objects or their images and noting the part sticking out, or matching several discrete objects or images and noting the objects left over. There could be further derived the concept of *quantity;* the operation of ordered matching or "counting"; and the concepts of number ("matchability") and of particular numbers (*e.g.,* "four," "fourness," etc.).

These, and many similar operations and concepts—such as the general concept of measurement—would follow from the general characteristics of the operations of separately labeled, retraceable remembering, comparing, matching, abstraction, and recombination, which together we call reasoning. The generality of these basic operations implies that they could be performed, in principle, not only by all normal human beings, but even by machines using television screens, photoelectric cells, and other devices now in use. What classes of objects will be lumped together as "identical," what criteria will be singled out for recognition, would depend on the structure and possibly the past of each such machine. But whether and to what extent living men will actually carry out such operations in their minds, how much time and attention they will devote to them, what purposes, if any, they will seek, and what kind of results they will achieve—that will depend on the actual lives which they live and in which they have grown up, on their history, society, and culture.

In this sense we can trace to the rise of towns in Mesopotamia, Egypt, and India, the replacement of the personal measures of the span and the forearm by standardized social measures; the drawing up of multiplication tables by the Sumerians before 2500 B.C.; and the development of ideographic and phonetic scripts.[43]

But for more widely generalized standards and explicit rules of recombination we must wait for the sea girding commerce of the Greeks. For generalized proof we need a society complex enough to know argument, but with a sufficient number of equals in it to prevent decision by sheer authority.[44] For "proof" is the set of procedures which are expected to compel assent in a given community, just as "logic" is a set of

[43] Childe, *op. cit.,* pp. 82–122.
[44] Crowther, *op. cit.,* pp. 49–50.

rules for the combination of statements that are to be held valid in a particular logical system. The rules of logic may be those of Aristotle, or those of Mr. Bertrand Russell, or those observed in the arguments of Central African Negroes by British anthropologists;[45] the rules of proof may include the competitive piling up of oaths by numbers of freeborn "oath helpers," as in early medieval German law, or magical procedures, such as the ordeal.

"Reason," "logic," and "proofs" are products of social organization, but they are only one of the elements needed for the rise of science. To be sure, any explicit scheme of general concepts, any accepted set of rules for recombining symbols will permit potentially *some* demonstrations, proof, and criticism, suggest new questions and predict new discoveries. Whether and to what extent these technical possibilities will be utilized, and whether they will be utilized for the development of science may depend on other factors.

From Reason to Science: Steps and Conditions

Another element essential for science is interest in the prediction and control of actual events *in nature*. The behavior of men and animals can be predicted and controlled at least to some extent by signalling to them through signs or sounds, by luring them with food or whatever else they desire, and by threatening them with pain or whatever else they fear. *Magic* is the application of these methods to inanimate nature. But mixed in with magic, practical control of nature was achieved, in agriculture, metallurgy, and all the other crafts, through unanalyzed trial and error, or unanalyzed insight. If magical spells were learned by heart, these practical techniques were transmitted through concrete example and unanalyzed imitation. "Transmission of such lore is largely imitative and therefore conservative. The process need not be described in abstract terms. All the apprentice need do is to imitate as closely as

[45]George and Monica Wilson, *Social Change*, Cambridge University Press, Cambridge, England, 1945, pp. 53-56.

"Primarily, logic is the avoidance of contradiction between people, and hence of conceptual contradiction. . . . Logic . . . is maintained by social pressure. Accepted definitions and qualifications are imposed on those who flout them by the weight of intellectual authority; the group or its representative impose them on the individual, those of higher status on those of lower. . . . The pressure . . . consists sometimes of scientific facts and connections, sometimes of dogmatic opinions, which are generally accepted in the society or group concerned . . ." *Ibid.*, p. 56.

possible every operation of the master. In so doing he has no opportunity of introducing a variation which might be beneficial."[46]

The dynamic activity which we call science arose when effectiveness in predicting and controlling events in nature became a major factor in developing and selecting the particular systems of proof and logic, the particular rules for the recombination of symbols, in actual use in a society. Every scientific system is rational, but not every rational system is scientific, though it may be a proper object of sciences studying such systems. A decisive step toward science is in the acceptance of the reliable forecasting and control of repeatable physical events as a major criterion for the selection of any system of reasoning. In short, if reason is the recombination of symbols according to explicit rules, with the step by step marking of a retraceable trail, then science is such reason controlled by the need for its applicability to the successful prediction and control of physical events.

Here, perhaps, we can see the root of the power of mathematics to describe the world in which we live—a power which the historian Charles Singer has called a "mystery."[47] Perhaps mathematics has this power because of all possible symbolic patterns and rules of recombination those were developed and selected which fitted the world in which its students operated. Symbols of integers were selected to fit the stable discontinuities marking off each finger or pebble from all others; Euclidean geometry and Euclidean space corresponded to the actual operations and measurements with which those and many later ages were concerned; independence of the results of matching or adding operations from the sequence in which they were carried out occurs in sufficiently many real situations, from which mathematics were derived or to which they could be applied later. We may note here, by way of contrast, the insistence on strict and unique sequence in magic spells, and the long persistence of such magic in the lore of agriculture, metallurgy, and chemistry, which involve operations and processes too complex for easy mathematization, with results often dependent on the sequence in which steps are taken.

Science implies the application of the social technique of reason to physical nature. It implies conflict, sooner or later, in field after field, with the alternative social techniques of magic and imitation. And for

[46]Childe, *op. cit.*, pp. 71, 126.
[47]Singer, *op. cit.*, p. 19.

its success, it requires the aid of two further concepts rooted in society: the notions of "fact" and "law."

A *"fact"* is an event or experience which can be regularly repeated, directly or in its traces, by different observers; or more strictly speaking, which can be regularly and closely paralleled by similar events on repetition of the relevant aspects of its attending situation. A "fact" involves, therefore, only a certain kind of event, excluding those which are untraceable or unrepeatable in any particular historical technology. Its reception involves a certain kind of observers, for it excludes those who cannot transmit comparable information to each other, or who cannot store and transmit in their own memory or records comparable information from one time to the next.[48] The efficient dealing with "facts" involves, therefore, a certain kind of society and culture: one in which memories, new experiences, and testimony from different persons are all accepted as relevant, not for blind belief, but as relevant for comparison and criticism, and that again implies a society with some measure of individualism and equality within a sizable and influential group of its members.

Law: From City to Cosmos

A sizable number of individuals or groups of approximately equal power, in frequent touch with each other, as in trade, may develop just these notions of equality or "equal justice" in their dealings with each other. Retaliation and blood feuds among evenly matched parties will be inconclusive, and the experience of trade may suggest the cancelling out of injuries, as through the payment of *"wergeld"* among Germanic tribes or of *"diké"* among Homer's Greeks. Rough notions of such equality at the emergence from barbarism may then develop in the stable market relations of the city state into settled law—law both as an operating social institution and law as a generalized tool of thought applicable to nature.[49] It is this application of the market's concept of exchange and the city state's concept of law and justice to nature which

---

[48]To be sure, a regularly repeatable event, rejected from symbolic transmission through the channels of a particular culture, may still have traces or consequences which will function as facts regularly repeated in the lives of the people of that culture which denies it. Those who fail to recognize wars or epidemics may still die of them.

[49]Jaeger, *op. cit.,* pp. 103–111, 151–161; Childe, *op. cit.,* pp. 208–209; G. H. Sabine, *A History of Political Theory,* Henry Holt & Company, New York, 1937, 1947, pp. 25–27.

is at the bottom of the Ionian philosophers' image of the universe as an ordered and understandable cosmos,[50] and of their principle of *cause* which "was originally the same as the idea of Retribution, and was transferred from legal to physical terminology."[51] The concept of law here is that of a general rule of exchange, impersonal and indefeasible, predicting accurately, completely, and without exceptions, the consequences of all actions or events to which it applies. This idea of law in the universe reappears in Parmenides's assertion of the compulsive character of logical thought, and, developed in a different direction, it is reapplied to the guidance of society in the "wisdom" (*sophia*) of Xenophanes and the *logos* of Heraclitus—the conscious rational insight into the law and structure of the cosmos, which teaches men to act "while awake" instead of "while asleep"; with which they can strengthen themselves "as a city strengthens itself with law"; and by which man can live as a cosmic being, voluntarily learning and obeying the cosmic laws.[52]

The Tragedy of Greek Science

The sweep of these philosophical generalizations should not hide from us the penetrating power of the science that could result from the combination of reason and law with the accurate observation and attempted prediction and control of physical events.

Greek science developed its insights, its accurate concepts, its amazingly suggestive theories of evolution (Anaximander), the quantitative nature of the universe (Anaxines, Pythagoras), elements (Empedocles), and atoms (Democritus), not by mere speculation. Between 600 and 500 B.C., the great century of Ionian science, we find recorded such inventions or innovations as the potter's wheel, bellows, the anchor with two arms (all these ascribed to Anacharsis, fl. 592 B.C., the Scythian prince who came to Athens, friend of Solon); the soldering of iron (Glaucus of Chios, c. 580 B.C.); the art of moving and placing huge

---

[50] ". . . the word originally signifies the *right order* in a state or other community." Jaeger, *op. cit.*, p. 110. "The Greek name . . . *cosmos* is derived from a root that in the earlier Greek of Homer is applied to the marshalling of clans for war and the settlement of tribes on the land." Childe, *op. cit.*, p. 208.

[51] Jaeger, *op. cit.*, p. 161.

[52] *Ibid.*, pp. 172–174, 179–182. Jaeger's discussion should remain a landmark in the history of ideas.

columns (Chersiphron of Cnossus and his son Metagenes, c. 550 B.C.); the level, square rule, lathe, key, the polishing of the natural surfaces of precious stones, and, introduced from Egypt, the casting of bronze (all these ascribed to Theodorus of Samos, fl. at Ephesus c. 532 B.C.); and the building of water conduits including a tunnel 1,000 meters long (Eupalinus of Megara, at Samos, before 522 B.C.). There is no other century in Greek history with so many major inventions or innovations and so many inventors, actual or alleged, honored by the recording of their names. Nor is there in Greek history any other century in which so many of the recorded innovations have direct application to the manufacturing or working of physical objects.[53]

Similarly, close observation of events in nature is found at that stage. We find the early Greek scientists concerned with the loadstone (Thales), sundials and maps (Anaximander), fossils (Xenophanes); acoustics and the quantitative relation between length of string and height of pitch (Pythagoras). We find them recorded as making experiments, dissecting animals, dissecting the brain, studying meteoric stone (Anaxagoras); proving experimentally the corporeality of air, discovering the labyrinth of the ear, studying respiration and the flux and reflux of the blood (Empedocles); deriving the atomic theory from the observation of the evaporation of water, the diffusion of scent, the gradual wearing away of plowshares, stone steps, and stones under eaves (Leucippus and Democritus);[54] and the sustained scientific approach and practice of the Hippocratic school of medicine.[55]

The Greeks were perhaps uniquely placed for the making of their twofold contribution of broad intellectual synthesis and deep penetration. Their trade and colonies made them the economic and intellectual focus for the goods and knowledge of the whole Mediterranean and even much of Persia, Babylon, and Egypt. Their geography and social structure encouraged the degree of equality needed for proof and generalized thought. Their use of alphabetic letters even for vowels freed reading and writing from dependence on the context, and allowed each new combination of letters to stand by itself; their use of standardized small coins prepared the way for thinking of numbers and atoms. The social

---

[53] Sarton, *op. cit.*, pp. 75–76, and chronological surveys, pp. 61–388.
[54] The observations are listed in Lucretius, *De Rerum Natura*.
[55] Sarton, *loc. cit.*; B. Farrington, *Science and Politics in the Ancient World*, Oxford University Press, New York, 1940, pp. 57–67.

structure of their city states where law came to override personal loyalties, and where often the measured quantity of an individual's wealth determined the quality of his voting rights, as in the Solonic system of Athens after 594 B.C.—all these encouraged the development of the most powerful methods of abstract reasoning.

None of these conditions had grown automatically. Greek science was not a mere byproduct of location and climate. Indirectly and directly, it was the result of the finding of real answers to real problems by the Greeks. The social innovation of the city state based on contract rather than kinship, the economic innovation of abandoning self-sufficient wheat growing for cash crop olive oil production for export in manufactured pottery in the "Solonian economic revolution," and the political changes in the franchise that followed it—all these involved new social inventions, new patterns of behavior, new creative responses to the challenge of physically and historically given conditions. Men made their own history when they responded to existing conditions by the creation of Greek institutions and Greek science.[56]

It is at a later stage that Greek science turns from quantity to quality, from ideas as tools to predict the course of changing reality to ideas as unmoving and unchallenged patterns beyond space and time, from nature, first to the city state, and, finally, to the consolation of the individual—it is then, with the important exception of abstract mathematics, that the flow of significant new ideas dwindles, that experiments disappear, that dissection falls into disuse, that magic superstition reoccupies the fields attempted by science, that even men like Archimedes and Hero apply their science to the construction mainly of war machines and toys. Historians have called the period after 300 B.C. "the failure of nerve,"[57] or, in a broader framework, the "disintegration" of Hellenic civilization.[58]

This failure cannot be blamed on Christianity. It was patent a century before Jesus. Ancient and modern writers have blamed a variety of causes: the economic system of slavery (Crowther, Childe), the deliberate encouragement of superstition by oligarchic governments (Polybius, Farrington), the divorce between scientific thought and technological

---

[56] Cf. Toynbee, *op. cit.*, II, pp. 37–42, 97–98; III, pp. 273, 336–339; IV, pp. 201–202.
[57] Singer, *op. cit.*, pp. 56–93; followed by "The Failure of Inspiration" (50 B.C.–400 A.D.) and "The Failure of Knowledge" (400–1000); *ibid.*, pp. 94–128.
[58] Toynbee, *op. cit.*, VI, pp. 287–291; and elsewhere.

practice (Childe), or the general political, moral, and spiritual breakdown of classical civilization (St. Augustine, A. J. Toynbee).

Perhaps the different aspects of the record stressed by these writers may help us to derive two things about science from the experience of its breakdown in antiquity: first, the peculiar vulnerability of science to the injury of the critical elements on which it depends for life; and second, the fundamental contribution made by Christianity to the ultimate resurrection of science on a far wider and more powerful basis.

What Science Needs to Live

It seems that science depends on a continuing three way flow and reflow of information: technical, between men and physical operations; social, between men and men; and intellectual, between a man's unanalyzed experiences and his ensemble of secondary symbols derived from them for conscious analysis and recombination, and between his own knowledge and the accumulated knowledge of men before him. Each of these three depends on a set of channels of communication of some kind; and it appears that the breakdown or loss of any one of these three classes of communication can destroy the growth of science.

The history of the civilizations of antiquity suggests the occurrence of subtle breakdowns in these channels of social communication well before the visible breakdowns of social cohesion or authority.

How does a once flourishing civilization lose its centuries old power to unite men from many regions despite any "innate" or "irreducible" differences in their social outlook, ambition, and purpose? When and how—perhaps without any further increase in area or numbers—do previously manageable differences become truly "irreducible"?[59]

In search for an answer, A. J. Toynbee has investigated in some detail the recorded cases of such internal breakdowns in many civilizations of the past.[60] He describes the typical pattern of breakdown as a "loss of creativity" on the part of the civilization's "creative minority"—that is, their failure to find a successful response to the current major "challenge" or problem before the community. This failure to create is then

[59]Of course, there are differences of outlook within any flourishing civilization. Unity is not uniformity. But these differences are not mutually incompatible to a critical degree. When and why their incompatibilities become fatal, is precisely our question.

[60]*Ibid.*, IV, esp. pp. 5–6, 119–133, 232–244.

followed, according to this view, by the minority's failure to charm or awe the majority of the members of their civilization into continuing to imitate their leaders. These leaders then attempt to replace the broken down process of mimesis by an appeal to force. The former creative minority now becomes a merely "dominant" minority. Their former followers refuse to imitate them. There ensues a schism in the body social. An "internal proletariat" secedes at the center of the civilization, while an "external proletariat" secedes in its outlying regions; and gradually the whole civilization breaks down in a rhythmical sequence of "routs" and "rallies"—renewed but unsuccessful attempts to respond adequately to the challenge which was not answered in the first instance—until the pattern ends in "rigor mortis" or in dissolution.[61]

If we accept Mr. Toynbee's examples, it could perhaps now be shown that the original breakdowns of accomplishment are due to a preceding breakdown of communication, either between the members of that society ("minority" and "majority" in Toynbee's terms), or between the leading group of that society and the external situation surrounding them.

This stress on communication is ours rather than Toynbee's, but Toynbee's examples seem to bear it out. In the instances he cites, the minority either overstressed their earlier "withdrawal" from the rest of the community, omit to return into full social intercourse with it, and become an esoteric, closed circle, at the price of impotence to move or lead the mass of their contemporaries in their own civilization;[62] or the minority "infect themselves with the hypnotism which they have deliberately induced in their followers";[63] now "rest on their oars," or they, after having responded successfully to some earlier challenge, refuse to meet the next challenge, and rather idolize some ephemeral aspect of their own past; or they fall victim to the intoxication of some earlier victory purchased at the price of "excessive," that is, structure-distorting and habit-forming, effort.[64]

Whatever one's reservation about particular conclusions, or particular selections of evidence, in Professor Toynbee's vast work,[65] the observa-

[61] *Ibid.*, I–VI, *passim.*
[62] *Ibid.*, IV, pp. 122, 232–233.
[63] *Ibid.*, p. 129.
[64] *Ibid.*, pp. 232–581.
[65] Cf. *e.g.*, the criticism by P. Geyl, "Toynbee's System of Civilizations," *Journal of the History of Ideas*, IX, 1948, pp. 93–125. Even stronger objections could be raised against

tions recorded by him are too massive and too relevant to be ignored in any subsequent treatment of the history of thought. They point to patterns noticed by other observers—as in Thorstein Veblen's notion of the "penalty of taking the lead"—and relevant to our question: What are the particular kinds of communication which must continue to function if knowledge is to grow?

Perhaps the first set of channels is that which might involve the communication of *novelty,* of new experiences or discoveries of facts, of new combinations between things or men or symbols, even in the mind of a single individual. From the discovery of the previously unknown to the making of the previously non-existing, from the putting together of "two and two" to the making of new recombinations and their comparison with reality, these channels are closed by the fear of new behavior which may lead to fear of new thoughts, or fear of acting on them.

The second set of channels are those which permit the *sharing of knowledge* between those persons who have it and others who want to acquire or increase it. This kind of communication is choked off if knowledge becomes a secret or a monopoly of a chosen few.

The third set of communications might involve the *sharing of experiences* between different human beings: It withers away if other human beings are rejected as witnesses; their testimony cut off as untrustworthy; their fate ignored as insignificant and their feelings as not comparable with those of the members of the group which excludes them.

The fourth set of communications might be that *between men and nature:* It breaks down if "sense impressions," the results of physical interaction with nature, are rejected as illusory or irrelevant; if observations are not made, or not remembered or transmitted; if nature is viewed as unintelligible or not worth understanding; or if observations of nature remain on the spectator level, but if that actual experience of nature is cut off which comes from *making* things, or making them happen, from the active and deliberate interaction with nature which we call work.

The history of each breakdown of ancient science reveals the gradual

---

some of the basic concepts which Professor Toynbee seems to have accepted, such as the simple one way relationship between individuals and their society, which is defined merely as "the coincidence of their individual fields of action." Toynbee, *op. cit.,* III, p. 230, *et seq.*

earlier breakdown of one or more of these essential kinds of communication.

We may discern the growing hostility to new behavior and new ideas in the story of the petrification of science in Egypt and the other irrigation civilizations as these civilizations complete their great irrigation works, increase their population more nearly up to the limits of the new food supply, and find henceforth their essential task no longer innovation or improvement but sheer maintenance of the physical facilities and populations dependent on them, brought into being by their previous expansion.[66]

We may find there, too, the growth of secrecy, the monopolization of organized knowledge by bureaucratic castes, and even the deliberate indoctrination of the people with irrationality and superstition. The retraceable trail of rational knowledge is not only barred to most men by social prohibitions, but deliberately obscured, or made untraceable, for those outside a small minority.

The refusal to share knowledge is accompanied in some of these civilizations by the refusal to share experience: the experience of the *fellah,* the slave, the serf, the "untouchable," are largely excluded from the effective intake of information of the thinkers of the society in which they live.

And lastly, since so many of the laboring members of society are held in low esteem, this low esteem comes to include much of the particular aspects of physical nature with which they are dealing in their work. Indeed, not only are their observations rejected and the very things ignored which they might have occasion to observe or to control; finally, the very idea is rejected of deliberately controlling physical objects through sustained painstaking operations or experiments. It smacks too much of work which is held as contemptible as the men who perform it.

It is striking to note how these breakdowns in the four main channels of communications come to a climax in time well before the actual breakdown of the growth of Hellenic science and ultimately of Hellenic civilization.

The wide introduction of plantation slavery after 480 B.C.; the peak

[66] On "irrigation bureaucracies" generally, cf. Max Weber, *Wirtschaft und Gesellschaft,* p. 542; K. A. Wittfogel, *Geschichte der Buergerlichen Gesellschaft,* Wien, 1924, pp. 116-118; Alfred Weber, *Kulturgeschichte als Kultursoziologie,* Leiden, 1935, pp. 35-45.

in the exploitation of slaves in the silver mines of Laurion during the same century; the reversal of Athenian policy from Solon's ready grants of citizenship for artisans to Pericles's restriction of Athenian citizenship —resembling more modern "grandfather laws"—to those both of whose parents were Athenians;[67] the growing importance of foreign tributes and public bounties for the welfare of the poorer citizens; the growing contempt for the artisan (as *e.g.,* for the tinker in Plato's *Republic;* and later even for the sculptor in Polybius's dream of *"Techne"* and *"Paidea"*) —all these testify to the drying up of the channels between thought and work, between symbols and reality, between idea and experiment.

The estrangement from work is paralleled by growing hostility to new thought, which is not only shown in the banishment of Anaxagoras and the death of Socrates, but in the proposal of Socrates's pupil Plato to outlaw all further innovations in his *Republic,* including all innovations in the style of poetry or music. The conflict is dramatized in Aristophanes's attacks on science and scientists, and from a different point of view, in Aeschylus's *Prometheus Bound.* If Plato had still claimed the right, at least for philosophers in his own image, to "follow the argument wherever it might lead," we find by the second century B.C. the historian Polybius praising "the foundation of Roman greatness . . . superstition. This element has been introduced in every aspect of their private and public life, with every artifice to awe the imagination. . . . It has been done to impress the masses . . . (which) are unstable, full of lawless desires . . . to hold them in check by fears of the unseen and other shams of the same sort." And Polybius agrees that it would be "folly and heedlessness . . . to dispel such illusions."[68]

Perhaps the most significant breakdown is the breakdown of empathy, the breakdown of fundamental human relations. There is a terrible contrast between the audience of the time of Euripides, which still expects to be moved to terror and pity by tragedies played by actors in a theater, and the spectators of a Roman circus shouting for the pitiless killing of real gladiators in the arena. Between the two scenes lay a long history of merciless differentiation between human beings. There has been Plato's comment in the *Republic* on the cruel and murderous warfare among Greeks, to the effect that such things should not be done by

---

[67]W. L. Langer, editor, *An Encyclopedia of World History,* Houghton Mifflin Company, Boston, 1940, pp. 51, 56.
[68]Polybius, *Histories,* VI, 56; cited in Farrington, *op. cit.,* p. 167.

Greeks to Greeks, but rather by all Greeks together to the non-Greek "barbarians."[69] There had been the same philosopher's proposals in the *Laws,* to tighten and harden the existing Athenian law of slavery and to abolish judicial punishment for a slave who had killed a free man, but rather to have the state hand over the slave to the family of his victim for such revenge as they might see fit.[70]

There had been Plato's proposal of the famous "royal lie" to stabilize the social order: to convince the members of the various social classes in his Republic that they were descended not from human beings but from the soil of their city, and so forever different from other people; and separately descended in each class from a different metal in that native soil, and so forever different—with few and rare exceptions—from all other classes in their own community.[71] What had been boldly proposed by Plato as a stabilizing myth—a decisive inborn qualitative difference between human beings—was calmly set down by Aristotle as a fact: the division of mankind between natural born free men and natural born slaves.[72]

The emotional barrier between slave and freeman, and between Greek and barbarian, became generalized into the divisions between the dominant minority of the Greco-Roman civilization and the underlying "proletariat." This broad mass of the disinherited comprised not only most of the slaves, but included also Greeks and Roman citizens uprooted or expropriated by wars, civil wars, or economic changes, and the mass of the populations of the Roman provinces, ground down by usury and taxation. The fear and contempt of the rulers and the smouldering hatred of the ruled kept breaking through in a series of uprisings, massacres, and mass atrocities—beginning with those recorded by Thucydides—until by the first century B.C. the abyss between different groups of people became illustrated in broad daylight by the six thousand crosses erected by Lucinius Crassus along the Via Appia, "with a captured follower of the insurgent gladiator Spartacus nailed alive on each."[73]

[69]*Republic,* par. 471, Modern Library, Inc., New York, n.d., p. 200.
[70]Glenn R. Morrow, *Plato's Law of Slavery in Its Relation to Greek Law,* University of Illinois Press, Urbana, 1939, pp. 120–133.
[71]*Republic,* III, par. 414–415, pp. 124–125.
[72]"Aristotle admits . . . that this is often not true in fact, but at all events it is the theory upon which slavery is justified. For this reason the slave is the master's living tool, to be kindly, but still used for the master's good." Sabine, *op. cit.,* pp. 93–94.
[73]Toynbee, *op. cit.,* V, p. 36; cf. other instances, *ibid.,* pp. 36–38, 58–72; L. M. Hartman, *Weltgeschichte,* Gotha, Perthes, 1921, I, p. 3: L. M. Hartmaltz and J. Kromayer, *Roemische Geschichte,* p. 128.

No choking off of channels between human beings is likely to be complete. There were humane individuals as administrators and emperors; and physicians like Galen continued to practice dissection and experiment.[74] But all these were minor modifications, brief resting places, on the road of decline. If knowledge was ever to rise again at a rate worthy of its earlier growth, a more radical change would be needed to open again the sources of its life.

Christianity and the Resurrection of Science

One decisive step toward that change was the rise of Christianity. Any revival of the growth of knowledge and science must have been remote from the preoccupations of the early Christians—and yet there is some reason to suggest that the profound reorientation of human motives in the course of the rise of their faith opened the fundamental channels of communication so much more deeply and widely as to lay the foundations for later centuries of unparalleled intellectual and technological growth.

Christianity implied a new attitude of man to man, a radical acceptance of empathy, a willingness to accept full communication of the fate and experience of other persons, however poor or low, and a feeling: "Here but for the grace of God go I." This feeling is expressed in Jesus's saying: "What you have done to the least of these, you have done to me"; in Paul's conviction that, in the things that truly matter, there is "neither Jew nor Gentile, neither bond nor free," and that men must come to view themselves as "members of one another."

Beyond the language of faith, these are statements of essential aspects of communication. Men are viewed as potential *substitutes* for each other in their external fate, their external interactions with their environment, their experiences of nature and society—to such a degree that "but for the grace of God" the fate of another might be mine. This accepted possibility of substitution implies that the behavior and experiences of other men are relevant for me as potential test cases of my own.

This view embraces operations. A tentative modern definition of the relationship of *complementarity*—that is, of the relationship between broadcasting and receiving radio sets tuned to each other, or between a key and all the locks which it fits—might be that it consists essentially in

---

[74]Sarton, *op. cit.*, p. 301; but "in Galen's time . . . the knowledge of anatomy had . . . declined." Singer, *op. cit.*, p. 90.

the possibility of performing an operation in one set of facilities which is effective in the other, while preserving a significant number of its characteristics in both sets. These characteristics of the operation, or chain of events, may be described in statistical terms as a pattern of "yeses" and "noes," and may then be called "information."[75] Is not this relationship stated in the words: "What you have done to the least of these, that you have done to me"? By restoring and deepening the community of human experience and communication, Christianity restored and deepened one of the essential foundations, not only for common belief or common superstition but also for every future community of science.

It should be clear that Christianity cannot claim any exclusive monopoly in that contribution. The vision of the Hebrew prophets who took the side of the poor "sold for a pair of shoes," the pity of Buddha, and the trend of some currents of Hellenistic thought, all implied some awareness of men's relationship as potential substitutes and test cases for each other. What seems to me to have been new in Christianity was the consistency with which this insight was carried toward the conclusions of seeing all human beings as "members of one another," and of recognizing love to one's neighbor (regardless of that neighbor's religion) as the visible test of love to God.

Less directly, and less dramatically, early Christianity laid the foundations of a later restoration of a fuller communication between men and nature. The doctrine of creation and of the fatherhood of God, already found in Judaism, favors the notion of a friendly universe. It implies that the universe is such that men can live in it—that it is not fundamentally hostile to either life or understanding, and indeed that understanding may reveal a friendly wisdom behind it all. There is a minority tradition in Christian thought which denies this and sees the created world as radically irrational or radically evil. To be sure, such a view may seek this understanding by quite non-scientific or irrational methods, through vision, intuition, or some form of revelation. It may even for a time reject the study of most of the physical aspects of nature, and insist on the sequence of historical and religious events as the only kind of rational information that matters. But it retains the assumption of meaning, that is, of underlying recognizable order in the world, and Christianity, like much of Judaism before it, saw this order in time as an order of non-cyclical history, moving from a beginning toward a recog-

---

[75]Cf. Wiener, *op. cit.*, pp. 75–82.

nizable goal. It should be noted that this fundamental intellectual framework of Christian thought is far more favorable to our modern ideas of science, of evolution, and of history, than the hopeless cyclical world view of eternally recurrent patterns in so much of pagan thought.[76]

More important still than the Christians' theoretical ideas of nature was their practical attitude to work, to manual labor, that is, to the main practical channel through which most men deal with nature in their daily lives. The living examples of the carpenter Jesus and the fisherman Peter were reinforced by the parables of good shepherds and of laborers in vineyards, and underlined in Paul's insistence that every man laboring faithfully at his calling was praising the Lord with the work of his hands.

These views of labor and one's neighbors had long lived implications. According to Max Weber, Paul's "shattering of the ritual barriers against commensalism . . . meant the origin of Christian 'freedom' . . . which cut across nations and status groups," and "was . . . the hour of conception for the Occidental 'citizenry.' This was the case even though its birth occurred more than a thousand years later in the revolutionary *conjurationes* of the medieval cities. For . . . without the Lord's Supper in common . . . no oath bound fraternity and no medieval urban citizenry would have been possible."[77]

Let us recall again at this point that Christianity was only one of the major elements in the laying of the foundations of modern Western civilization. Just as Christianity arose out of a new combination of the great traditions of Judaism and of Hellenism, and became different from either of its parents, so it could perhaps be said that Western civilization arose in the Middle Ages in Western Europe out of the union of the Christian faith and Hellenic civilization with the social and cultural traditions of the communities of barbarian peoples who came to settle and govern these regions after the fall of the Roman Empire.

This was not simply a combination of Christian ideas and barbarian blood. Both were present in the Byzantine Empire which extended a Christian state religion over many barbarian immigrants. But in Western Europe these immigrants—Franks, Visigoths, Langobards, and others—came not in scattered families but as compact conquering peoples, bring-

---

[76]Cf. Collingwood, *op. cit.*, pp. 46–52; E. Rosenstock-Huessy, *The Christian Future*, Charles Scribner's Sons, New York, 1946, pp. 61–91.
[77]*Essays in Sociology*, tr. by H. H. Gerth and C. W. Mills, Oxford University Press, New York, 1946, pp. 403–404.

ing with them large parts of their cultural preferences and social institutions—preferences and institutions which centered in the fact that these peoples still largely consisted of free men and that they had a greater possibility for communication between each other, between men and women, and between men and physical nature, than had been characteristic of the slaves and slave holders of ancient Rome. The legal position of an unfree Frankish peasant of the tenth century might resemble that of a fourth century Roman colonist, just as the jointed armor of a fourth century Roman cavalryman (a *clibanarius* or "hardware boy," as he was popularly called) resembled externally the armor of an early medieval knight. What separated these men of the tenth century from their counterparts in the fourth was the difference in the culture of which they were a part, due to a decisive difference in their history: a decisively different past permitted to each of these two generations a decisively different future.

One large step toward the working out of these potentialities is perhaps marked after 400 A.D. by St. Augustine's conception of the "City of God" as an unbreakable and indestructible community and organization of Christians, independent from the fortunes and misfortunes of the "City of Robbers," the worldly governments—a notion which implied the casting off of the lifeboat of the organized church from the sinking "Titanic," the Roman Empire, which was perishing before Augustine's eyes.

Another major step toward the working out of these underlying trends occurred about a century later in the actual turning to labor as an organized concern of a Christian community, in the movement of the Benedictine monks after 500 A.D. In the place of the hermits' search for personal salvation in solitude, the Benedictine monks built a disciplined community dedicated not only to prayer but to sustained work and service of their fellow men. Pledged by St. Benedict's rule to seven hours of daily labor in the fields (in addition to four daily hours of prayer), and owning no property except that owned in common by their monasteries, these Benedictines came to serve as a kind of collective "shock troops" of their faith, carrying both Christianity and a measure of Roman agricultural, industrial, and intellectual skills to peoples and regions which the Roman armies had failed to conquer. The next four centuries are marked by their accomplishment of an unprecedented task of religious conversion, technological and intellectual dissemination, and elementary administrative organization in Western Europe, Switzerland, Austria, and Western Germany.

Out of the union of these three elements, Judeo-Christian thought, barbaric traditions of a measure of rough equality and freedom, and the remnants of Roman science, technology, and commerce, there became possible a new type of merchant and artisan, and the rise of a new type of town. And with it there came from about 800 A.D. onward the first stirrings of a new wave of inventions and innovations in economics and technology: the wide introduction of the heavy plow, the spread of the three field system, the invention of the horse collar—forerunners of an ever widening stream of technical inventions and innovations during the High Middle Ages after the year 1000.

It is in the course of this long range process of social change that we find the decisive reorientation of Western Christianity which has separated it from the Church of Byzantium and put an enduring mark on Western civilization to this day. The task of the Benedictine monks for four centuries had been one of cultural diffusion. To bring Christianity and civilization to the heathen, monks and clerics had made whatever alliances seemed expedient with the heavy handed tribal chieftains, lords, kings, and war band leaders of the age. Now that the church had transmitted much of its culture and information to the newly converted peoples, it seemed to be left in little more than a subordinate position under the effective power of the Carolingian nobility. Lords who gave land for a church claimed and obtained the right to *Eigenkirchen,* that is, to churches where they appointed incumbents for the priesthood. And the orders a local baron gave to the chaplain on his lands were echoed by the orders which, during the generations after Charlemagne, the emperors of Germany gave to the Popes of Rome. To have revolted against this subordination of the institutions of the spirit under a rule of worldly violence, was the meaning and the merit of the reform movement of Cluny, which initiated what Eugene Rosenstock-Huessy has called the first European revolution.[78]

The Christian Revolution of the Middle Ages

Among the monks, this revolution was characterized by a shift away from labor in the fields to a stress on will power, discipline, and or-

[78]*Die Europaeischen Revolutionen,* Jena, Diederichs, 1931, *passim; Out of Revolution; Autobiography of Western Man,* pp. 485-561.

ganization. In the calendar it was dramatized by the shift from the celebration of All Saints' Day to All Souls' Day, with its unmistakable implication of the vanity and powerlessness of all earthly things and the ultimate weakness of all earthly political powers. Among the saints it was marked by the deliberate elevation of the Apostle Paul, the wielder of the sword, to equal if not superior rank with the Apostle Peter, the keeper of the keys; at least four pointed references to the Apostle Paul figure prominently in the charter of Cluny from the year 910 A.D.

In time the implications of the new movement became evident. The defiance of imperial power was set to music in the hymn *"Veni, Creator Spiritus,"* the new movement's fighting hymn of the spirit which "listeth where it will." The movement acquired a political battle cry in the concept of the sin of simony, that is, the sin of yielding spiritual service or position in consideration of worldly inducements or worldly pressure—that is to say, the proclamation as a damnable sin of that which had been current practice in the days of the Carolingians and their successors. The clerical revolution acquired a political program in the *dictatus papae* of Pope Gregory VII. It fought its battles against the German emperor in the struggle about investitures, and it won a shattering victory over the German Empire with the beheading of the last German emperor of the house of Hohenstaufen, Konradin, on a public square in Naples in 1268. In the process of this revolution, the church found allies in the new elements of European society: the towns, as in the League of Lombard cities; the guilds, an alliance made visible in stone in the cathedral building movement; and the knights, both free men and ministerials—an alliance confirmed in the Crusades, and sealed in the emergence of European chivalry.[79]

In their implications, it was perhaps these three hundred years of social and spiritual transformation which made Western civilization into the dynamic thing it has remained until this day. The transformation involved a new attitude toward labor in the guilds, with the major emphasis put on the dignity and the imagination of the skilled working man himself. It involved a new method of teaching, local and interregional, through the institutions of apprenticeship, the journeyman's journey, the masterpiece, the title of master. This craftsman's method of teaching finds its parallel in the pattern of training from page boy

---

[79]Cf. Rosenstock-Huessy, *loc. cit.;* Sabine, *op. cit.,* pp. 227–237.

to knight, and in the organization of the university, the guild of craftsmen of words whose apprentices are students, whose journeymen are Bachelors of Art, and whose masters are called Doctors and have the right to teach everywhere in Christendom.[80] And it is in these centuries that the social inventions and innovations of the self-governing town, the self-governing guild, and the crusading knights, are paralleled by the technological inventions and innovations of the crossbow, the orrery, the gothic arch, and the flying buttress, improved types of millwheels and vastly greater use of water power—to be followed by the stream of innovations which has not ceased until our day.[81]

It is obvious that the foregoing account has been sketchy in the extreme. It has been an attempt to condense into one section of this paper an outline of some of the problems which occur in the history of thought which one might study during a half year. The second term might then deal with the more detailed examination of medieval religious, scientific, and social thought, and of the break up from within which finally overtook so many of these ideas and institutions in their medieval form. This break up, and the gain and loss involved in the replacement of the old by new ideas, might then be traced through the ages of William of Ockham, Niccolo Machiavelli, Galileo, Newton, perhaps up to the crucial work of Lavoisier on the eve of the French Revolution. The third term might then deal with the century that was characterized by the consequences of the eighteenth century revolutions, from Robespierre to Bismarck, or from Lavoisier to Planck, and the fourth term might then be devoted to scientific, intellectual, and moral problems of the past two generations, the age of worldwide wars and unrest from the 1890's until the present.

Above all it should be remembered that the purpose of such a course

---

[80]Cf. A. Dempf, *Das Mittelalterliche Menschenbild, Proceedings of the Tenth International Congress of Philosophy*, Amsterdam, 1948, 1, p. 27.

[81]Some interesting control data on the historical and technological significance of early and medieval Christianity might be gained from a comparison between the growth of technology in Japan and in any leading country of Western Europe, say between 800 and 1800 A.D. According to K. A. Wittfogel, prenineteenth century Japan had the main economic and technological factors for the rise of industry: it had towns, merchants, capital, and a feudalism which made displaced peasants or their children available for labor (*op. cit.*, p. 119). If investigation should confirm these similarities in social structure, and yet reveal significant differences in the actual flow of innovations, the importance of such historical factors as time sequence and kinds of communication, ideas, and value systems, might be strikingly borne out.

would be not antiquarian but practical. It would study the history of problem solving, in order to equip us for the new chapter that we now must add to it. In each period studied, the task would be to recognize and investigate some of its major social, technological, intellectual, or moral problems in their historical setting, together with a study of the symbolic models and practical operations used in the search for their solution. The problems would be chosen for their relevance to our own problems today; and the conceptual schemes and models would be studied with an eye to their relative efficiency, capacity for improvement, and fruitfulness in terms of new concepts and new operations.[g] To tackle this job well, however, it may prove necessary in many instances to do more background research on the fundamental concepts, analogs, and models in social and scientific thought than has been done so far.

2. Research on the Role of Models in the Natural and Social Sciences

(The section which follows is pertinent to this inquiry. It discusses some fundamental research problems, in the working out of some of the philosophical and ethical foundations of the program proposed in this paper, and some possible advances which may result from their solution.

[g] Comment by Henry Margenau:

The problem to which Professor Deutsch directs attention, if I understand it correctly, is one of the most important of our time; the need for solving it is so great that all methods for its solution should be examined with care. The problem is how to make the theories of society and of history able to predict, or how to make them scientific.

The author's analysis of former crises in the unity of knowledge has elements of remarkable power and significance. One wished he had continued this kind of discussion to its end and drawn from it whatever information is relevant to the problems of our day. Instead he chose to follow a more fashionable road to scientific respectability.

Under the label of an operational approach he imposes upon history, upon the functioning of the human mind and of society, the external trappings of communications engineering. The term "operational" denotes either a philosophic attitude or a special scientific method. Operational philosophy is a version of empiricism which has been successful in correlating the less fundamental sciences. It slights basic theory in favor of experimental procedures. When it denotes scientific method the operational approach acknowledges its limitations and presumes a parallel approach of a theoretical kind on a more basic plane. I have not been able to reach a conclusion as to whether Professor Deutsch wants the whole of the history of thought viewed in the sense of operational philosophy or whether he wishes to examine it in a partial way from the vantage point of operational procedures. I fear that he would favor the former alternative.

Higher Education and the Unity of Knowledge

Readers interested in a more general survey may prefer to go on directly to the next section.)

Men have tended to order their thoughts in terms of pictorial models since the beginnings of organized thought. The model itself was usually drawn from something in their immediate experience, available from their technology, and acceptable to their society and culture. Once adopted, it served, more or less efficiently, to order and correlate the experiences which men had, and the habits they had learned, and perhaps to suggest a selection of new guesses and behavior patterns for new or unfamiliar situations.

Thus men used the image of their own society (where men influence one another's behavior by talking to each other) as a model for physical nature which was pictured as a society of animated objects which could be magically influenced by talking to them through the right kind of incantations, that is, through the language socially accepted in that imaginary society of things. The inefficiency of this sort of model is considerable, since it permits very little analysis and only very poor predictions.

Later models were drawn by men from the work of their hands, that is, from processes and things which they themselves could bring into existence, put together or take to pieces, and which they therefore could analyze and elaborate more adequately in their parts and interrelations.

There is the simple model of the artisan who makes things with his hands, particularly the potter who shapes clay. Once men have ceased to think of trees as of a society of animated beings to be talked to, they may think of them as a collection of green pots made by some invisible potter. After having assumed that things have minds and either existed forever or were born and died like men, it is now assumed, on the second model, that things have neither will nor mind but are so many inert products made by the invisible craftsman. Here again, however, the model permits very little correlation between experience with one kind of thing and experience with another. Nor does it permit much analysis or prediction of the invisible craftsman's past behavior or future intentions.

More complex models become available when men have learned to produce more complex contrivances and when the fruits of their labor can be combined and piled up into houses, towns, and pyramids, which dwarf the size and the life span of the individual beholding them. The impersonal plan or law of the city may then come to serve as a model for an assumed impersonal plan or law of nature, and the structure of this impersonal law or architecture appears to remain effective regardless of the subsequent activities of any invisible architect or lawgiver who might have originated it. These new models permit a clear and more specific correlation of experience. They imply rigid and often immovable arrangements in space, which lend themselves readily to pictorial representation. In this manner the Egyptian pyramid, with its rigorous order of a very few stones at its apex and the many stones bearing all the burden at the bottom, has served as a "social pyramid," a model for that conception of human society from which the Jews walked out under Moses. More broadly the pyramid has served as a model for the conception of a "hierarchy," because a hierarchy, whether of priests, army officers, or ideas, values, and purposes, such as in Aristotelian philosophy, turns out to be an Egyptian pyramid writ large, with its stones replaced by officers, or words, or human beings. A significant characteristic of the pyramid model is its static character. The pyramids were deliberately built to be unchanging. They were a prototype of that "graven image" in which a dynamic religion might fear a grave of life.

Two other simple models involve at least some movement, and therefore some implication of time. The first of these is the wheel. In its simple rotary motion, elevating and casting down each part of its circumference in regular succession, it has been conceived of as a model of human affairs and human history, whether "wheel of fortune," "wheel of fate," or Fortune standing on a ball—in each case suggesting instability of the parts with stability of overall performance; and it was projected to the skies in the spheres, cycles, and epicycles of Ptolemaic astronomy.

The other of these models is the balance, the pair of scales which yields the concept of stable equilibrium, with its implication that the adverse reaction must be the greater, the more the true position of balance has been destroyed. The notion of *diké,* of "nothing too much," of the golden mean, and the statue holding the scales of justice in front of many Western lawcourts, all testify to the suggestive power of that model. Both wheel and balance imply movement but only movement which either continues permanently or else eventually returns to the original position. "The more it changes, the more it stays the same."

Other simple technological operations began to yield models which implied the notions of process, progress, and history in the simplest, most elementary form. Perhaps the two outstanding models here are the model of the thread taken from spinning, whether as the thread of fate, or the thread of an argument, or the thread of human life. A web woven from these threads is then an obvious extension of this model, implying now, however, the notion of interaction. The German word for reality, *Wirklichkeit,* is related to the word denoting such a textile operation. Goethe has embodied this picture in the Earth Spirit in *Faust:* "*So steh' ich am sausenden Webstuhl der Zeit und wirke der Gottheit lebendiges Kleid.*"

The very continuity of thread and skein and warp and woof make these textile models unsuitable for analysis. It is only with the development of far more complex operations, toward the end of the Middle Ages, that we find mechanical models of greater complexity, slightly less inadequate for describing the world around us. Mechanisms can be taken apart and reassembled. This is crucial for the new models. The development of the making and understanding of mechanical pumps to a fair level of efficiency made it finally possible for Harvey to write his scientific classic, *De Motu Cordis,* using the analogy of valves and pumps for the first adequate description of the circulation of the blood.[82]

The Classical Model of Mechanism

The development of clockwork, under progress ever since the thirteenth century, finally yields the classical model of a "mechanism" which is then applied to a description of the stars in the system of Newton; to the system of government in the writings of Hobbes, and in the "checks and balances" of Locke, Montesquieu, and the founding fathers of the American Constitution; and to the human body by such writers as La Mettrie, author of the book, *Man A Machine,* in the eighteenth century. It is extended to God as the "first mechanic" by Tom Paine; and to joy in Schiller's lyric, "Ode to Joy," as the "watchspring of the universe."

The transfer of the idea of mechanism, from the experience of pumps and clockworks to a general description of reality, was encouraged in the days of Newton by the success of gravitational astronomy where the movements of the planets, isolated from each other by vast distances

[82]Pledge, *op. cit.,* p. 29.

of space, proved peculiarly suited to mechanical interpretations; though it has appeared since that they seem to be peculiarly unrepresentative of most of the events in nature.[83]

The classical concept or model of mechanism implied the notion of a whole which was completely equal to the sum of its parts; which could be run in reverse; and which would behave in exactly identical fashion no matter how often those parts were disassembled and put together again, and irrespective of the sequence in which the disassembling or reassembling would take place. It implied consequently the notion that the parts were never significantly modified by each other, nor by their own past, and that each part once placed into its appropriate position, with its appropriate momentum, would stay exactly there and continue to fulfil its completely and uniquely determined function.

These few remarks already show that the classical notion of mechanism is a strictly metaphysical concept. No thing completely fulfilling these conditions has ever been on land or sea, nor even, as our cosmologists have told us, among the stars. The more complicated a modern mechanical device becomes in practice, the more important becomes the interdependence and mutual interaction of its parts through wear and friction, and the interdependence of all those parts with their environment, as to temperature, moisture, magnetic and electrical influences, etc. The more exacting we make the standards for the performance of a real "mechanism," the less "mechanical" in the classical sense does it become. Even an automobile engine must be "broken in," and a highly accurate timing device depends so much on its environment that it must be assembled in strictly air conditioned workrooms by workers with dry fingertips.

The Classical Concept of Organism

Conspicuous breakdowns of the concept of mechanism became most obvious in the fields of the social sciences and biology. Attacks on the inadequacy of mechanical thinking form a major part of the political writings of Edmund Burke, and the emphasis on wholeness, interrelatedness, growth and evolution, proclaimed in literature and education by Rousseau, and in politics by Burke, was then powerfully reinforced in the nineteenth century through the growth of the biological

[83]Cf. Wiener, *op. cit.*, pp. 40–56.

sciences, resulting in the wide popularity of the concept of "organism" in its classical nineteenth century form, as the proper model for reality.

According to this classical view, an "organism" is unanalyzable, at least in part. It cannot be taken apart and put together again without damage. As Wordsworth put it, "We murder to dissect." The parts of a classical organism, in so far as they can be identified at all, not only retain the functions which they have been assigned but in fact cannot be put to any other functions (except within narrow limits of "dedifferention" which were often ignored), without destroying the organism. The classical organism's behavior is irreversible. It has a significant past and a history—two things which the classical mechanism lacks—but it is only half historical because it was believed to follow its own peculiar "organic law" which governs its birth, maturity, and death and cannot be analyzed in terms of clearly identifiable "mechanical" causes.

Attempts have been frequent to apply this classical concept of organism to biology and to human society. On the whole they have been unsuccessful. While "organismic" models might sometimes help to balance the onesidedness of a "mechanical" approach, biologists have failed to derive significant predictions or experiments from the supposed "life force" of nineteenth century "vitalists," and the inadequacies of organismic theories of society or history have been even more conspicuous.

Both mechanistic and organismic models were based substantially on experiences and operations known before 1850. Since then, the experience of almost a century of scientific and technological progress has so far not been utilized for any significant new model for the study of organization, and in particular of human society and human thought.

Perhaps it is now becoming possible to develop such a new model in the field of scientific theory, since such new models during the past fifty years have actually been developed in the world of physical fact. The developments in this connection have been the developments of communications engineering. Telegraphs, telephones, and switchboards have often been compared with the nerves of an organism, but this comparison has usually remained a figure of speech. But by continuing to *make* things which fulfil the functions of communication and organization, we cannot help in the long run but gain significant opportunities for a clearer understanding of those functions themselves. Given a development of peace and progress in the next few decades, we ought to gain an unprecedented chance to find out vastly more about the processes of communication, organization, and learning, since we have in fact been engaged in making an ever larger number of physical facilities which actually do these things.[h]

If we should rate this chance less highly we may yet not be willing to neglect it. At a time when we all still know so little of communication, organization, and learning in the working of the human mind and the behavior of societies, we may welcome any help toward organizing our scanty data and clarifying our elusive concepts for the investigations still so urgently needed.

Self-modifying Networks as Generalized Models of Organization in Machines, Minds, and Societies

Modern studies of communications engineering suggest that the behavior of human organizations, peoples, and societies has important relations in common with manmade communications networks, such as servomechanisms, switchboards, and calculating machines, as well as with the behavior of the human nervous system and the human mind.[84] It now seems possible to analyze and describe the *common patterns*

[h]Comment by Herman Finer:
   What arguments does Dr. Deutsch bring forward for the coherence of the whole of society; what for its articulation? This is the standing problem of education: the nature of obligations, the nature of rights. I defy the power of any natural science analogy, even the most modern, to give us guidance on this.

Dr. Deutsch's reply:
   Dr. Finer is right in stressing the importance of understanding the nature of social coherence and of social obligations. I believe that they can be understood best as aspects of communication. It is communication and the fitness for it—that is, complementarity—which make societies cohere. It is by operations of communication that coherence is tested, and it is the maintenance or increase of communication (and the conditions for it) which is the fundamental social obligation. These matters are discussed in the historical example of the contribution of early Christianity to the rise of Western Civilization, and in more general terms in the section on "Societies." (The moral aspect of communication is also stressed in Karl Jaspers's recent book, *Der Philosophische Glaube*.)

[84]*E.g.*, A Rosenblueth, N. Wiener, and J. Bigelow, "Behavior, Purpose and Teleology," *Philosophy of Science*, X, 1, January, 1943, pp. 18–24; W. S. McCulloch and W. Pitts, "A Logical Calculus of the Ideas Immanent in Nervous Activity," *Bulletin of Mathematical Biophyres*, V, 1943, pp. 115–133; F. S. C. Northrop, "The Neurological and Behavioristic Basis of the Ordering of Society by Means of Ideas," *Science*, 107, N. 2782, April 23, 1948.

of behavior of self-modifying communications networks in general terms, apart from the question whether their messages are transmitted and their functions carried out by circuits of electric current in an electronic device, by chemical and neural processes inside a living body, or by spoken, written, or other communications between individuals in an organization, group, nation, or society.

There are several advantages in using electric networks, nerve systems, and societies as analogs for each other, provided we remember that analogy implies similarity *only in certain relations* between the constituent elements of each system.[85] We gain the aid of new and perhaps more efficient models for our thinking about minds and societies. These new models offer suggestive analogies for such relationships as "purpose," "learning," "free will," "consciousness," and "social cohesion"—that is, precisely for those relationships which have often been considered crucial in social science but were found incapable of effective representation by earlier models.[i] Until now, these relationships

[i]Comment by Herman Finer:

Generally, I cannot see the point of substituting a new analogy from the natural sciences to make easier or more comprehensible social science. Dr. Deutsch has shown that all the old ones, *e.g.,* the Newtonian system and "checks and balances," were fallacious, even if suggestive, that they omitted something of decisive significance in their suggestion that the human mind worked in such a wise. Why, then, attempt once again the analogy? Why not admit at once that there is something unique in the mind which no mechanical or nonhuman natural things can represent or explain? Why not teach the human mind directly, as a thing *sui generis*? I suppose the answer must be that it is not acknowledged, or not admitted fully enough, that the human mind is a distinct, unmatchable phenomenon. *If* this is so, no amount of teaching by Dr. Deutsch's syllabus will help mankind. Omit mind and destroy education.

Dr. Deutsch's reply:

If the mind cannot be represented by anything "non-human," as Dr. Finer says, how could it be represented by symbols? Symbols are in themselves "non-human": they are dots, dashes, lines, colors, letters, sounds. Yet they can represent things of the mind. How else could we speak or write about it? Indeed, if any particular mind consists of dynamic interrelationships of symbols—Shakespeare's "stuff dreams are made of"—in appropriate physical facilities or channels, why could not that which consists of symbols be described by symbols, too?

The history of thought is full of attempts to apply principles of order, organization, and even mathematics to the mind—from Socrates and Plato to Leibnitz and the moderns. It cannot prove or disprove the validity or usefulness of further attempts at such interpretation. What seems new about the present attempts in this direction is their larger scale and more powerful equipment.

[85]Cf. Polya, *op. cit.,* pp. 37–46.

could at most be treated qualitatively, by recognition or description. The new models suggest observations and experiments to seek data for their treatment in quantitative terms.

A modern radar tracking and computing device can "sense" an object in the air, interacting with its beam; it can "interpret" it as an airplane (and may be subject to error in this "perception"); it can apply records of past experience, which are stored within its network, and with the aid of these data from "memory" it can predict the probable location of the plane several seconds ahead in the future (being again potentially subject to error in its "recollections" as well as in its "guess," and to "disappointment," if its calculation of probability was correct, but if the airplane should take a less probable course); it can turn a battery of anti-aircraft guns on the calculated spot and shoot down the airplane; and it can then "perceive," predict, and shoot down the next. If it should spot more than one airplane at the same time, it must become "infirm of purpose," or else decide ("make up its mind") which one to shoot down first.

This is contemporary engineering practice. It would be out of place to describe here other existing devices, such as thermostats, automatic airplane pilots, or electronic calculators. Suffice it to say that manmade machines actually operating or designable today have devices which function as "sense organs," furnish "interpretations" of stimuli, perform acts of recognition, have "memory," "learn" from experience, carry out motor actions, are subject to conflicts and jamming, make decisions between conflicting alternatives, and follow operating rules of preference or "value" in distributing their "attention," giving preferred treatment to some messages over others, and making other decisions, or even conceivably overriding previous operating rules in the light of newly "learned" and "remembered" information. Parallels for this behavior in the fields of psychology, neurophysiology, and cultural anthropology are striking.

None of these devices approach the overall complexity of the human mind. While some of them excel it in specific fields (such as the mechanical or electronic calculators), they are not likely to approach its general range for a long time to come. But, as simplified models, they can aid our understanding of more complex mental and social processes, much as sixteenth century pumps were still far simpler than the human heart, but had become elaborate enough to aid Harvey in his understanding of the circulation of the blood.[j]

The Feedback Concept

With the aid of these models, we may recognize a basic pattern which minds, societies, and self-modifying communications networks have in common. Engineers have called this pattern the "feedback." "In a broad sense (feedback) may denote that some of the output energy of an apparatus or machine is returned as input . . . (If) the behavior of an object is controlled by the margin of error at which the object stands at a given time with reference to a relatively specific goal . . . (the) feedback is . . . negative, that is, the signals from the goal are used to restrict outputs which would otherwise go beyond the goal. It is this . . . meaning of the term feedback that is used here."[86] "By output is meant any change produced in the surroundings by the object. By input, conversely, is meant any event external to the object that modifies this object in any manner."[87]

In other words, by feedback is meant a communications network which produces action in response to an input of information and *includes the results of its own action in the new information by which it*

[j]Comment by Herman Finer:
There are several advantages in using "electric networks," etc., for analogical education: yes: there is one supreme one—it leaves out the human. It is not in "complexity" that the human mind differs from the machines—it is the origin of living *purpose*.

Dr. Deutsch's reply:
I agree with Dr. Finer on the importance of *purpose* in the human mind. A major portion of my paper deals with the importance of analyzing and understanding the nature of purpose with the help of our new goal seeking machines, just as the generation of Harvey came to understand the *living* circulation of the blood by comparing it to a circulation system of *non-living* valves and pumps.

[86]Rosenblueth-Wiener-Bigelow, *op. cit.*, p. 19. A more refined definition of feedback would put "output *information*" in place of "output *energy*," in accordance with the distinction between "communications engineering" and "power engineering." Cf. Wiener, *op. cit.*, p. 50.

[87]Rosenblueth-Wiener-Bigelow, *op. cit.*, p. 18. There is also another kind of feedback, different from the negative feedback discussed in the text: "The feedback is . . . positive (if) the fraction of the output which re-enters the object has the same sign as the original input signal. Positive feedback adds to the input signals, it does not correct them . . ." *Ibid.*, p. 19, see also Wiener, *op. cit.*, pp. 113–136. Only self-correcting, *i.e.*, negative, feedback is discussed in the present paper.

modifies its subsequent behavior. A simple feedback network contains arrangements to react to an outside event—*e.g.*, a target—in a specified manner—*e.g.*, by directing guns at it—until a specified state of affairs has been brought about—*e.g.*, the guns cover the target perfectly; or the automatic push button tuning adjustment on a radio has been accurately set on the wavelength approached. If the action of the network has fallen short of reaching fully the sought adjustment, it is continued; if it has overshot the mark, it is reversed. Both continuation and reversals may take place in proportion to the extent to which the goal has not yet been reached. If the feedback is well designed, the result will be a series of diminishing mistakes—a dwindling series of under- and-over-corrections converging on the goal. If the functioning of the feedback or servomechanism is not adequate to its task (if it is inadequately "dampened"), the mistakes may become greater; the network may be "hunting" over a cyclical or widening range of tentative and "incorrect" responses, ending in a breakdown of the mechanism. These failures of feedback networks have specific parallels in the pathology of the human nervous system ("purpose tremor") and perhaps even, in a looser sense, in the behavior of animals, men, and whole communities.[88]

Learning and Purpose

Already the simple feedback network shows the basic characteristics of the "learning process" as described by John Dollard. According to Dollard—who is speaking of animals and men—"there must be (1) drive, (2) cue, (3) response, and (4) reward." In a manmade feedback network, "drive" might be represented by "internal tension," or better, mechanical, chemical, or electric "disequilibrium"; input and output would function as "cue" and "response"; and the "reward" could be defined analogously for both organisms and manmade nets as a "reduction in intensity" (or extent) of the initial "drive" or internal disequilibrium.[89]

[88] Wiener, *loc. cit.*
[89] Cf. John Dollard, "The Acquisition of New Social Habits," in Linton, *op. cit.*, p. 442; with further references. "Drives . . . are 'reward,' that is . . . they are reduced in intensity . . ." A. Irving Hallowell, "Sociopsychological Aspects of Acculturation," in Linton, *op. cit.*, p. 183; cf. in the same volume, Kluckhohn and Kelly, "The Concept of Culture," pp. 84–86.

A simple feedback mechanism implies already a measure of "purpose" or "goal" which does not only exist within the mind of a human observer, but has relative objective reality within the context of a particular feedback net, once that net has physically come into existence. A "goal" has been defined as "a final condition in which the behaving object reaches a definite correlation in time or in space with another object or event."[90]

This definition of a goal, or purpose, may need further development. There is usually at least one such external goal, *i.e.,* a relation of the net as a whole to some external object, which is associated with one state of relatively least internal disequilibrium within the net. Very often, however, a very nearly equivalent reduction in internal disequilibrium can be reached through an internal rearrangement of the relations between some of the constituent parts of the net, which would then provide a more or less effective substitute for the actual reaching of the goal relation in the world external to the net. There are many cases of such surrogate goals or *ersatz* satisfactions, as a shortcircuit in an electronic calculator, intoxication in certain insects, drug addiction or suicide in a man, or outbursts against scapegoat members in a "tense" community. They suggest the need for a distinction between internal readjustments sought through pathways which include as an essential part the reaching of a goal relationship with some part of the outside world.

This brings us to a more complex kind of learning. Simple learning is goal seeking feedback, as in a homing torpedo. It consists in adjusting responses, so as to reach a goal situation of a type which is given once for all by certain internal arrangements of the net; these arrangements remain fixed throughout its life. A more complex type of learning is the self-modifying or *goal changing* feedback. It includes feedback readjustments also of those internal arrangements which implied its original goal, so that the net will change its goal, or set itself new goals which it will now have to reach if its internal disequilibrium is to be lessened. Goal changing feedback contrasts, therefore, with Aristotelian teleology, in which each thing was supposed to be characterized by its unchanging *telos,* but it has parallels in Darwinian evolution. The per-

---

[90]Rosenblueth-Wiener-Bigelow, *op. cit.,* p. 18. "By behavior is meant any change of an entity with respect to its surroundings . . . Accordingly, any modification of an object, detectable externally, may be denoted as behavior." *Ibid.*

formance of a human goal seeker who strives for new goals on reaching each old one has been immortalized in Goethe's *Faust:*

> *Im Weiterschreiten find't er Qual und Glueck,*
> *Er, unbefriedigt jeden Augenblick.*[91]

We can now restate our earlier distinction as one between two kinds of goal changing by internal rearrangement. Internal rearrangements which are still relevant to goal seeking in the outside world we may call "learning." Internal rearrangements which reduce the net's goal seeking effectiveness belong to the pathology of learning. Their eventual results are self-frustration and self-destruction. Pathological learning resembles what some moralists call "sin."

Perhaps the distinction could be carried further by thinking of several orders of purposes.

A first order purpose in a feedback net would be an internal state in which internal disequilibrium would be less than in any alternative state within the range of operations of the net. This first order purpose would correspond to the concepts of "adjustment" and "reward" in studies of the learning process. Self-destructive purposes or rewards would be included in this class.

By a second order purpose would be meant that internal and external state of the net which would seem to offer to the net the largest probability, or predictive value derived from past experience, for the net's continued ability to seek first order purposes. This would imply self-preservation as a second order purpose of the net, overriding first order purposes. It would require a far more complex net.

A third order purpose might then mean a state of high probability for the continuation of the process of search for first and second order purposes by a "group" of nets beyond the "lifetime" of an individual net. This would include such purposes as the "preservation of the group" or "preservation of the species." Third order purposes require several complex nets in interaction. Such interaction between several nets, sufficiently similar to make their experiences relevant test cases for one another, sufficiently different to permit division of labor, and sufficiently complex and readjustable to permit reliable communication between

---

[91] Analytical understanding of a process need not diminish its sublimity, that is, its emotional impact on us in our experience of recognition. *Faust* becomes no more trivial by our knowledge of goal changing feedbacks than a sunrise becomes trivial by our knowledge of the laws of refraction.

them—in short, such a "society" is in turn essential for the higher levels of the learning process which could lead beyond third order purposes.

Among fourth order purposes we might include states offering high probabilities for the preservation of processes of purpose seeking, even beyond the preservation of any particular group or species of nets. Such purposes as the preservation or growth of "life," "thought," "learning," "order in the universe," and all the other purposes envisaged in science, philosophy, or religion, could be included here.[92]

Complex Networks: Messages and Symbols

Several simple feedback mechanisms can be combined in a feedback network of a higher order. The derivation of abbreviated symbols from the interactions of the network's "sensory structures" with the outside world can be made more elaborate and more precise. These symbols can be stored in, and "recalled" from, more elaborate "memory facilities" (modern electronic calculators may have several such "memories"). They can be recombined according to previously specified rules to produce new results, that is, new combinations of symbols which may or may not correspond to outside events past, present, or possible, depending on the efficiency of the network, the accuracy, relevance, and relative completeness of the symbols, and the relative "realism" or applicability of the specific "logic" or rules of recombination applied to them by the network.

Complex feedback networks, like their constituent simpler circuits, deal with "messages" and "symbols." For purposes of definition, a "network" is a system of physical objects interacting with each other in such a manner that a change in the state of some elements is followed by a determinate pattern of changes in other related elements, in such a manner that the changes remain more or less localized and independent of other changes in the system from other sources. A "state description" is a specification of which of its possible states each element of the

[92] The four orders overlap; their boundaries blur; and there seems no limit to the number of orders of purposes we may set up as aids to our thinking. Yet it may be worthwhile to order purposes in some such fashion, and to retain, as far as possible, the model of the feedback net which permits us to compare these purposes to some degree with physical arrangements and operations. The purpose of this procedure would not be to reduce intellectual and spiritual purposes to the level of neurophysiology or mechanics. Rather it would be to show that consistent elaboration of the simpler processes can elevate their results to higher levels.

network is in. A "message" is any change in the state description of a network or part of it.[93] Similar definitions have been suggested by Norbert Wiener: A "message" is a reproducible pattern of changes regularly followed by determinate processes depending on that pattern. A "channel" is a physical system within which a pattern of change can be transmitted so that the properties of that pattern (or message) are more or less isolated from other changes in the system.[94] Any message may be interpreted as a set of alternatives or decisions.[95]

The point is that a message is not a physical object in the sense of everyday language. It is a pattern of physical changes of physical objects. It has physical reality: it can be measured and subjected to repetitive treatment. Only by physical processes can it be preserved, received, transmitted, destroyed, or operated on, in any way whatever. Yet it can be transferred in succession or duplication from one set of physical objects to another. It can be in several places at once. Unlike "matter" and "energy," "information"—that is, the patterns that can be abstracted from messages—is not subject to their laws of conservation. It can be created and annihilated. It differs greatly from those aspects of reality stressed so heavily by the mechanical "materialism" of the nineteenth century. And it permits us to deal with the hitherto supposedly "intangible" aspects of pattern, *Gestalt*, configuration, order, novelty, as physical realities accessible "in principle" to analytical, quantitative, and operational treatment, as against the intuitive approach of metaphysics and "idealistic" philosophy from Plato to the present.[96]

In complex feedback nets, any message may be treated by the network as a symbol, or symbols may be derived from it. By a "symbol" is meant

---

[93]Communication from Walter Pitts, Massachusetts Institute of Technology, April 8, 1949.

[94]Communication, Massachusetts Institute of Technology, April 11, 1949; cf. *netics,* pp. 74–82; C. E. Shannon, "A Mathematical Theory of Communication, System Technical Journal,* July, 1948, pp. 380–382.

[95]This applies, as do the preceding definitions, to continuous, as well as to discontinuous physical processes. Information in television, for instance, is transmitted as a set of alternatives between bright and dark image points, or between points of discriminably different levels of brightness. These decisions can be represented mathematically on the binary scale. Such representation is also possible for any kind of continuous signal, since in practice it always is transmitted against a background of noise. Any variations in the signal which can actually be picked up can be represented very closely by a sequence of binary choices. Wiener, communication, April 11, 1949; Shannon, *loc. cit.*

[96]"It is indeed possible to conceive all order in terms of message." Wiener, Massachusetts Institute of Technology, March 4, 1948.

any message within such a network which has acquired a relatively stable association with another event outside the net, or with any other message within it.[97] As a symbol, a message within the network functions as what Charles Morris has called a "sign vehicle." It is treated by the net as associated with ("interpreted as referring to") an outside event or group of events (or with another inside message), which Morris calls its "designatum," and it may result in some specific behavior by the net, which Morris calls its "operand," and which students of the learning process might perhaps associate with their concepts of "cue" and "response."[98]

Switchboards and Values

The movements of messages through complex feedback networks may involve the problem of "value," or the "switchboard problem," that is, the problem of choice between different possibilities of routing different incoming messages through different channels or "associative trails"[99] within the network. If a relatively large number of alternative channels is available for a small number of messages, the functioning of the network may be impeded by indecision; if many messages have to compete for few channels, it may be impeded by "jamming." The efficient functioning of any complex switchboard requires, therefore, some relatively stable operating rules, explicit or implied in the arrangement of the channels, that is to say, rules deciding the relative preferences and priorities in the reception, screening, and routing of all signals entering the network from outside or originating within it.

Simple examples of such rules are the priority given fire alarms in many telephone systems, or the rules determining the channels through which transcontinental telephone calls are routed at different loads of traffic—including even the "hunting" of an automatic switchboard for a free circuit when the routing channels are fully loaded. They illustrate the general need of any complex network to decide in some way on how to distribute its "attention" and its priorities in expediting competing

---

[97] What is labelled in this latter case is not, in an electric net, a voltage pulse, but the state in which particular parts of the net are at a particular time. Such internal labeling of states of parts of the net itself is used in the automatic recall of stored information in electronic calculators.
[98] Morris, *loc. cit.*; Dollard, Hallowell, *loc. cit.*
[99] Vannevar Bush, *op. cit.*

messages and how to choose between its large number of different possibilities for combination, association, and recombination for each message.

What operating rules accomplish in switchboards and calculating machines, is accomplished to some extent by "emotional preferences" in the nervous systems of animals and men, and by cultural or institutional preferences, obstacles, and "values" in groups and societies. Nowhere have investigators found any mind of that type which John Locke supposed "to be, as we say, white paper." Everywhere they have found structure and relative function.

In much of the communications machinery currently used, the operating rules are rigid in relation to the content of the information dealt with by the network. However, there seems no reason why these operating rules themselves should not be made subject to some feedback process. Just as human directors of a telephone company today may react to a traffic count by changing some of their network's operating rules, we might imagine an automatic telephone exchange carrying out its own traffic counts and analyses, and modifying accordingly its operating rules and even the physical structure of some of its channels, such as adding or dropping additional microwave beams—which fulfil the function of telephone cables—in the light of the traffic or financial data "experienced" by the network.[100]

What seems a possibility in the case of manmade machinery seems to be a fact in living nerve systems, minds, and societies. The establishment and abolition of "conditioned reflexes" long studied in animals and men, and the results of individual and group learning, often include changes in such "operating rules" determining the organisms' treatment of subsequent items of information reaching it.

Any network whose operating rules, that is, preference structures, can be modified by feedback processes, is subject to internal conflict between its established working preferences and the impact of new information. The simpler, relatively, the network, the more readily internal conflicts can be resolved by automatically assigning a clear preponderance to one or another of two competing "channels" or "reflexes" at any particular

---

[100] An automatic telephone exchange capable of opening new channels in response to its own traffic counts was reported under construction by the Phillips Company at Eyndthoven, Holland. *Science News Letter*, Washington, D. C., April 10, 1948, p. 233. A telephone exchange which would install such a channel control itself would represent one more extension of the same principle.

moment, swinging from one trend of behavior to another with a minimum of delay. The more complex, relatively, the switchboards and network involved, the richer the possibilities of choice, the more prolonged may be the periods of indecision or internal conflict. Since the net acquires its preferences through a process of history, its "values" need not be all consistent with each other. They may form circular configurations of preference, which later may trap some of the impulses of the net in circular pathways of frustration. Since the human nervous network is complex, it remains subject to the possibilities of conflicts, indecision, jamming, and circular frustration. Whatever pattern or preferences or operating rules may govern its behavior at any particular time can only reduce this affliction, but cannot abolish it.

But since the network of the human mind behaves with some degree of plasticity, it can change many of its operating rules under the impact of experience. That is to say, that with the aid of experience the network of the human mind can change its own structure of preference, rejections, and associations. And what seems true of the general plasticity of the individual human mind in its evolution during the life of the individual, seems even more the case of the plasticity of the channels which make up human cultures and social institutions and those particular individual habit patterns which go with them, at least in some proportion to the ability of those cultures to survive and to spread.

So far, we have described two kinds of feedback "goal seeking," the feedback of new external data into a net whose operating channels remain unchanged; and "learning," the feedback of external data for the changing of these operating channels themselves. A third important type of possible feedback would be the feedback of internal data, analogous to the problem of what usually is called "consciousness."

Consciousness

"Consciousness" may be defined, for the purposes of this discussion, as a collection of internal feedbacks of secondary messages. "Secondary messages" are messages about changes in the state of parts of the system, that is, about primary messages. "Primary messages" are those which move through the system in consequence of its interaction with the outside world; or any secondary message or combination of messages may in turn serve as a primary message, in that a further secondary message may be attached to any combination of primary messages, or to other secondary messages, or their combinations, up to any level of regress.

In all these cases, secondary messages function as symbols or internal labels for changes of state within the net itself, and are fed back into it as additional information, influencing, together with all other feedback data, the net's subsequent behavior. "Consciousness" does not consist in these labels, but in the processes by which they are derived from the net and fed back into it.

Such feedback messages about some of the net's internal states occur in simple form in electronic calculators where they serve important functions in recall. They may occur, in extremely complex patterns, in the human nervous system, where they would be extremely hard to isolate for study. But they also occur, and can be studied with relative ease, in the division of labor of large human teams which process information and fulfil collectively certain functions of thought, such as industrial research laboratories or political or military intelligence organizations.

In cases of this last group we can observe how guide cards and index tabs are added to the information moving through, or stored within, filing systems, libraries, card catalogues, or the document control centers of intelligence organizations such as the State Department or the wartime Office of Strategic Services; and how these secondary symbols influence the further treatment of the information. The heads, policy boards, or project committees of such organizations cannot deal with all the vast information in the original documents. They are dealing mostly with titles, description sheets, summaries, project requests, routing slips, and other secondary symbols, while a great deal of the material continues to be processed "below the level of consciousness" of the guiding and policy making parts of the organization. Only those feedback circuits and decisions which are "picked up" through the attachment and feedback of secondary symbols, become directly "conscious" for the organization.

To be sure, selective function of any network is by no means limited to this "conscious" zone of secondary symbols. On the contrary, what reaches that zone for separately labeled and recorded processing, depends in turn on what has been selected or rejected, associated or dissociated, routed or blocked, recorded or misfiled or erased, within the rest of the system. What seems true of the screening function of the reporter on the beat and the desk analyst in the intelligence organization, seems similarly true of the "non-conscious" remembering and forgetting, the "aversions" and "hunches" of the individual human mind, as well as of many of the "unverbalized" conventions and assumptions, preferences and taboos of human societies and cultures.[101]

The powers of the "non-conscious," internally unlabeled circuits and processes within a network, can be positive as well as negative. An experience may be built up into a perception and recorded in memory, two and two may be put together, new associations, and indeed significant discoveries and insights, may be put together "non-consciously" without intervention of secondary symbols, until secondary symbols are attached to the new combination and suddenly the image of the new synthesis breaks through into the realm of consciousness, seemingly all ready and armored like Pallas Athene springing forth from the head of Zeus in the Greek legend.[102]

Yet it is by means of these secondary symbols that we may be conscious of some or all of our relevant steps in a calculation, or of some or all of our steps in a sequence of behavior. Since these secondary symbols are fed back into the net, the message of which the net has become "conscious" may appear in that net with greater frequency than its unlabeled alternatives, and remain more readily available for preferred treatment: be it preferred association, recording, transmission, blocking, or suppression, under the current operating rules of the system.

If secondary symbols become attached to parts or connections in the net, which embody these operating rules, these rules themselves become "conscious" for the net, and, by being fed back into it, become statistically reinforced for more effective application, or else for easier modification, if possible modification of the rules themselves is included in the net. The effects of such internal labeling may be thought of as to some extent comparable to the effect of dramatic symbols or publicity devices being attached to particular ideas, practices, or laws in a society, lifting

---

[101] "By 'culture' we mean those historically created selective processes which channel men's reactions both to internal and to external stimuli." Kluckhohn and Kelly, *op. cit.,* p. 84.

[102] For a general description of this experience of "sudden insight" and its unreliability, see Russell, *History of Western Philosophy,* pp. 123–124.

them from their previous obscure existence into the crossfire of public attention within that community.[103]

The ensemble of secondary symbols may easily misrepresent the net's actual content. Some primary symbols may be "overrepresented" by ample feedback, while others may not be made "conscious" at all. Consciousness, therefore, may be false consciousness; much as the actual personality of a man may be quite different from what he thinks it is. Similarly, by attaching suitable symbols and feedbacks to suitably chosen aspects of their behavior, groups or nations can be given highly misleading ideas of their own character.

How does the feedback notion of consciousness compare with other approaches? In the behaviorist school of psychology, we are told, "consciousness and conscious processes are excluded as not subject to scientific investigation, or . . . reinterpreted as cover language responses."[104] In social science writings, consciousness is often stressed, and ascribed to groups, but usually this is done without definition or description in any but intuitive terms.[105] Two recent writers describe individual consciousness as follows:

> (The) integrative (regnant) processes in the brain . . . according to the findings and speculations of neurophysiologists . . . are capable of self-awareness (as if they had a mirror in which to see themselves). During the passage of one event many, but not all, of the regnant processes have the property of consciousness, at the moment of their occurrence or soon afterwards if recalled by retrospection. Thus the stream of consciousness is nothing more than the subjective (inner) awareness of some of the momentary forces operating at the regnant level of integration in the brain field.[106]

This is a suggestive description in the language of everyday life in which processes behave like small individuals who "reign," "see them-

---

[103] The importance of consciousness in the growth of nationalism is stressed, without defining consciousness itself, in Hans Kohn, *The Idea of Nationalism,* The Macmillan Company, New York, 1944, pp. 6–16.

[104] Gardner Murphy, *Personality,* Harper & Brothers, New York, 1947, p. 981. "Consciousness" and "awareness" are referred to in the text, but do not appear in the elaborate glossary and subject index.

[105] Kohn, *op. cit.;* H. D. Lasswell, *The Analysis of Political Behavior,* Oxford University Press, New York, 1947, p. 143; Royal Institute of International Affairs, *Nationalism,* Oxford University Press, London, 1939, pp. 22, 108, 115, 116, 240, 284; etc.

[106] Clyde Kluckhohn and Henry A. Murray, *Personality in Nature, Society, and Culture,* Alfred A. Knopf, New York, 1948, p. 9.

selves as if they had a mirror," and "have the property of consciousness" which "is nothing more than . . . subjective (inner) awareness." But how helpful is it as a concept from which we might derive new observations and experiments?

If consciousness is a feedback process, then it requires material facilities, and is carried on at some material cost in terms of facilities and time. Some of the facilities tied up, and some of the delay imposed on primary processes, should be capable of measurement. Furthermore, feedback processes have structures, circuits, channels, switching relationships, incompatibilities, and discontinuities, which might be susceptible of mapping. If we cannot isolate the physical facilities involved, we might devise functional tests for possible patterns, limits, and discontinuities in the performance of the process of consciousness. If these tests should yield a map of discontinuities in performance, we might derive a basis for further inferences about the structure of the underlying facilities and processes themselves.

Similar considerations might apply to the processes of "consciousness" in nations, classes, or other social groups. If there are such processes, how are they organized and patterned? What are the manpower, facilities, symbols, learning processes, and teamwork relations by which they are carried on? If consciousness resembles a feedback, does it also resemble its peculiar kinds of instability? A small change in a feedback circuit can bring about a large change in its overall performance. Are there analogies for this in social life?

The feedback model of consciousness is more than a verbal explanation. It is a concept. For it suggests many questions which sooner or later should be answered, one way or another, by observation and experiment.

Will

Consciousness seems related to "will"—or to that sense of conation or of making autonomous decisions which we mean when asserting that "our will is free." This notion of will includes not only decisions with internal labels attached to the very moment of action, or to several steps within an action; it includes also mere decisions to start an action now or on a later signal, with the actual parts of the action following automatically without any "conscious" labels attached to them.[107] "Will"

[107]*E.g.*, in the pressing of a key on a signal in N. Ach's experiment, where "at the very

in all these cases may be tentatively defined in any sufficiently complex net, nervous system, or social group as the set of internal labels attached to various stages of certain channels within the net, which are represented by these labels as relatively unchanging, so that "we merely trip the purpose and the reaction follows automatically," or at least we expect it so to follow.[108]

In other words, *will* may be called the *set of internally labeled decisions and anticipated results, proposed by the application of data from the system's past, and by the blocking of incompatible impulses or data from the system's present or future.* Since the net cannot foretell with certainty either the outcome of the subsequent trains of its own internal messages and switching orders, or the outcome of its own efforts to inhibit information incompatible with the "willed" result, it knows only what it "will do," not what it "shall do." It may "know its mind," but it cannot know with certainty whether or when it will change it.[109]

A fundamental problem of "will" in any self-steering network seems to be that of carrying forward and translating into action data from the net's past, up to the instant that the "will" is formed (the determination becomes "set," or the decision "hardens"), while endeavoring to screen out all subsequent information which might tend to modify the "willed" decision. Will, in short, could be called the internally labeled effort to maintain preference for predecision messages over postdecision ones. The "moment of decision" might then be seen at that threshold where the cumulative outcome of a combination of past information begins to inhibit effectively the transmission of contradictory data.

This general problem of "will" seems to apply, at least to some extent, to manmade devices whose operations can be accurately specified. Automatic pilots or steering mechanisms exclude or compensate subsequent "experiences," such as gusts of storm, which might deflect them from their course. Modern guided missiles, homing torpedoes, proximity fuses, and similar weapons, involved in their design problems of this

---

instant of action no consciousness of will need appear," but "such a consciousness was nonetheless present as a 'determining tendency' prior to the action and governing it." Mueller-Freienfels, *op. cit.*, pp. 109 f., cf. also pp. 41, 69, 236.

[108]Rosenblueth-Wiener-Bigelow, *op. cit.*, p. 19; cf. also Warren S. McCulloch, "Finality and Form in Nervous Activity," Fifteenth James Arthur Lecture, American Museum of Natural History, New York, May 2, 1946, p. 4 (multigraphed).

[109]McCulloch, *loc. cit.*

kind. Electronic wave filters screen out "noise" from the "desired" messages.

Isolating the pattern of "will" in feedback machines may help us to recognize it in men and communities. Men may shut out the experiences of pain or fear or doubt or pity which might deflect them from their "fell purpose." Cultures or states, ever since the days of the Spartans, may put informal social or religious taboos or explicit legal prohibitions in the way of all messages which might change their previously determined patterns of behavior. Modern nations, governments, or political parties may strive in war or peace to perpetuate their policies by blocking all incompatible experiences from the life of their community by all the methods of legislation, indoctrination, pressure, censorship, police, or propaganda, of which they may dispose. It is in that sense, perhaps, of a pattern of relatively consolidated preferences and inhibitions, derived from the past experiences of a social group and consciously labeled for at least a relevant portion of its members, and applied to the guiding and restricting of the subsequent experiences of that group, that the concept of "will" can be applied meaningfully to the behavior of political movements, peoples, and social organizations.[110]

In what sense is this "will" free?

First of all, this will is relatively free from the pressures of the outside world at any one moment, since it represents the stored outcome of the net's past now being fed back into the making of present decisions. Without effective feedback of its past, the net's behavior would be determined largely by outside pressures. It would not steer, but drift, in both its external and internal arrangements.

If autonomous goal seeking or goal changing is treated as a value—if "to be in hell is to drift, to be in heaven is to steer," in the words of G. B. Shaw—then a corresponding value attaches to this material precondition of autonomy, the continued possession of an effective past. Here is the foundation of the value of *integrity*, that is, a structure of internal feedback controls and connections, undisrupted by excessive inputs from outside. Integrity can be destroyed by excessive rates of input, either by internal disruption of the net, or by such a speed-up of the learning rate that the net's past becomes negligible in predicting its future behavior. It seems, then, that we learn in the long run by not

[110] On the importance of "will" in nationalism and nationality, see again Kohn, *loc. cit.*

learning too much at any one moment, and that the net that learns too much becomes a thing. This case differs in kind from that of a net which finds its effectors temporarily ineffective due to outside forces, but retains its internal structure, much as a ship may be tossed by a storm but retain intact its steering mechanism, or a prisoner still may "call his soul his own."

Men, or whole communities, may treat destruction of their "integrity" as equivalent to physical destruction. Faced with the need for rapid readjustment, they may find themselves now with past habits shaped by a pathological learning process which has deprived them of the capacity to adjust freely to new realities, and see no further choice but internal loss of integrity or external destruction. There are at least three types of pathological learning—through drifting, through *rigor mortis*, through internal breakdown—and there is a fourth, relative type: through failure to learn freely[111] and yet rapidly enough to keep up with a given rate of change in the environment.

So long as it has autonomy, the net wills what it is. It wills the behavior patterns (the "personality") which it has acquired in the past, and which it is changing and remaking with each decision in the present. Thanks to what it has learned in the past, it is not wholly subject to the present. Thanks to what it still can learn, it is not wholly subject to the past. Its internal rearrangements in response to each new challenge are made by the interplay between its present and its past. In this interplay we might see one kind of "inner freedom."

In its external actions, the net does what it can do. Its outward behavior will be the result of the interplay between the orders transmitted to its effectors, and the feedback data about their results among the pressures of the outside world. In this type of interplay we may see a kind of external freedom for the net to continue its efforts to reach its goal.

Freedom in a feedback network could go further. A chess playing machine could be constructed which would rapidly compute all admissible moves on both sides for two or three moves ahead, and choose the ones most profitable for its side according to a schedule of values derived from the rules of the game. It would play mediocre chess.[112] It could be improved by giving it a suitable memory and additional

---

[111] That is, retaining at each step a significant part of its preceding past.
[112] Wiener, *Cybernetics*, pp. 193–194.

circuits, so that it could learn to modify its play on the basis of experience. The quality of its playing would then depend largely on that of its experience. It could be spoiled by poor teachers or stupid opponents. If all its past opponents were mediocre, the machine might never learn to play brilliantly. It would remain imprisoned by the limitations of its past. But it could be aided to play better, by building into it a device to break or override sometimes the patterns learned from its past, and to give it a chance for initiative and creativity.

This function of autonomous internal habit breaking could be fulfilled by building into the machine a circuit breaker controlled by some "internal receptor," such as the flipping of a coin, that is, by some element of the network, whose state would be "not altogether determined by the previous states of other parts of the net."[113] Such a device could be connected in such a way as to break up from time to time established connections or patterns of response, and to permit new combinations within the net to be formed, recorded internally in memory, and carried through into external action.

The results might resemble those of a "spontaneous impulse." Like all "spontaneity," they would be subject to limitations. All they could do would be to replace an old or highly probable configuration by a new or less probable one, *provided that the elements for the new configuration were already present in the net at the critical moment*—even though they might have got there only through the input in the immediately preceding instant.[114] The range of possible new combinations would therefore also depend, among other factors, on the range of possible new input information from the outside world, and on the effectiveness of the inner "habit breaker" in breaking up blocks against its integration with other data in the net. Apart from facilitating this in-

---

[113]*Receptors* are elements of a network whose state may be influenced from outside, *i.e.*, which is not altogether determined by the previous states of other elements." Communication from Pitts, Massachusetts Institute of Technology, April 6, 1948. "Outside the network" need not refer to physical location. Any element influenced by any process other than those in the other elements of the network—for instance, an inner element varying randomly—counts as a receptor under this definition. It is this last type of arrangement that I have called "internal receptor" in the text. It would differ from ordinary "external" receptors in that it might be largely independent from most other processes acting on the other receptors of the net.

[114]There are two kinds of new information for a network. The first is outside information not previously present in the net. The second is an internal recombination of symbols not previously *recognized*, that is, not previously matched in this configuration by a new secondary symbol or symbols.

flow of new information, "spontaneity" could only bring out a wider range of the potentialities already contained within the net.

This type of feedback network might provide an analog for the problem of "Free Will." Such an analog might be found in a machine combining a determinate store of memories with a randomly varying inner receptor in the circuits governing recall and recombination. The random effects of the inner receptor (or "sudden impulse") are then limited by the statistical weight of the alternatives available from the stored past of the machine (its "personality"). Such a machine might act "freely," with initiative, but "in character."

The analogy suggests that "moral responsibility" is conferred by the determinate, cumulatively learned element in the combination. Each of us is responsible for what he is now, for the personality he himself has acquired by his past actions.

But no single act—and hence none of the past ones—was wholly determinate. Each act could have been different by the small but finite probability of the random internal "circuit breaker" producing a different outcome. Nor are we wholly prisoners of any one decision or any one experience. Ordinarily, it takes many repetitions so to stock a mind with memories and habits that at long last all roads lead to the same city, whether it be taken, in religious language, as the City of Destruction, or the City of Salvation.

This view seems to clash with the traditional one. Tradition sees responsibility for the "wholly" free act, as a limiting case, and no responsibility for the act wholly determined from within a person's past. The view explored here would take the opposite view of these limiting cases. It sees in the actual moment of decision only a *dénouement* in which we reveal to ourselves and to others what we already have become—or perhaps better, what we have become thus far. This view has parallels to that of St. Augustine, and more recently perhaps of Karl Jaspers and other existentialists, but it does not involve outside predestination. For each step on the road to "heaven" or to "hell," to harmonious autonomy or to disintegration, was marked by a free decision. Each was an act of free interplay between the randomness of the internal "pattern breaker" and the determinacy of the character, the memories, and habits accumulated up to that step. The determinate part of our behavior is the stored result of our past free decisions.[115]

[115] This view of moral responsibility would exclude those determinate elements of

Freedom and Coherence in Societies

We have glanced at a few suggestive analogies between mechanical or electrical feedback nets, nerve systems, and societies. Let us conclude this brief survey of learning nets with a glance at some of the major differences among them.[116]

A "machine" has been defined as an "apparatus for applying mechanical power, having several *parts each with definite function"*; and an organism as a "body with *connected interdependent parts* sharing common life"; and an "organ" as a "part of animal or vegetable body *adapted for special vital functions."*[117] Both machines and organisms are here characterized by a high degree of permanence in the functions assigned to each part, be it a cog in the wheel or an organ grown permanently in its place in the body. Learning nets may conform to these limitations, if they are of mechanical or organic construction, but their functions as learning nets may point beyond these limits, to the different characteristics of societies.

Already modern calculating machines involve a balance between subassemblies permanently constructed for specific purposes, and transitory subassemblies put together from general elements to serve temporary needs. Multipliers in electronic calculators, *e.g.*, are usually permanent subassemblies, but more highly specialized operations, such as use of one or several algebras, would ordinarily be performed by general equipment temporarily brought into a suitable sequence or configuration of activities.[118]

Perhaps it could be said that this *possibility of relatively free transfer and recombination,* not only of the symbols treated, but *of the very physical elements of a learning net* for the performance of new operations, is the critical property which makes a given learning net into a *society*.

A learning net functions as a society, in this view, *to the extent* that

---

behavior which are not freely learned through intake of information, but are the results of heredity, mutilation, organic disease, or functional mental illness after it has disrupted significantly the processes of learning or decision making.

[116] Another discussion of such differences, stressing considerations other than the ones in this paper, will be found in Rosenblueth-Wiener-Bigelow, *op. cit.*, pp. 22–23.

[117] *Concise Oxford Dictionary,* Clarendon Press, Oxford, 1934, pp. 688, 804; my italics.

[118] Communication from Norbert Wiener, Massachusetts Institute of Technology, June, 1948. See also *Cybernetics,* pp. 155, 160.

its constituent physical parts are capable of regrouping themselves into new patterns of activity in response to changes in the net's surroundings, or in response to the internally accumulating results of their own or the net's past.

The twin tests by which we can tell a society from an organism or a machine, on this showing, would be the freedom of its parts to regroup themselves; and the nature of the regroupings which must imply new coherent patterns of activity—in contrast to the mere wearing of a machine or the aging of an organism, which are marked by relatively few degrees of freedom and by the gradual disappearance of coherent patterns of activity. The distinction between learning nets which are machines or organisms, and learning nets which are societies, appears here as a matter of degree which turns into a difference in kind, that is, in overall behavior.[119]

The difference between organisms and societies rests, then, in the degree of freedom of their parts, and the degree of effectiveness of their recombinations to new coherent patterns of activity.

This in turn may rest on specific properties of their members: their *capacity for readjustment to new configurations, with renewed complementarity and sustained or renewed communication.*

The degree of complementarity between the members of a society may determine its capacity for sustained coherence, while their degree of freedom—and their range of readjustments available without loss of complementarity—may determine the society's capacity for sustained

[119] In some calculating machines, and perhaps in the cells of the human brain, there is some degree of reassignment of general elements to specific tasks or temporary sub-assemblies serving as "task forces." In some societies, such as that of the Eciton army ants, there seems to be such a high degree of permanency of specialized function for each ant or class of ants, and so few degrees of freedom for an individual's choice of path that the entire column of ants may trap itself in a circular "suicide mill" where the path of each ant becomes determined by "the vector of the individual ant's centrifugal impulse to resume the march and the centripetal force of trophallaxis (food-exchange) which binds it to its group," so that the ants continue circling until most of them are dead. T. C. Schneirla and Gerard Piel, "The Army Ant," *Scientific American,* June, 1948, p. 22. The authors believe that communication among ants "resembles the action of a row of dominoes more than it does the communication of information from man to man. The difference in the two kinds of 'communication' requires two entirely different conceptual schemes . . . " *Ibid.* The concepts suggested in Norbert Wiener's *Cybernetics* and in the other literature on learning nets, cited elsewhere in this paper, could perhaps be applied to both kinds of communication. The action of rows of falling blocks or dominoes has been used by McCulloch to demonstrate more general principles of communication relevant for the understanding of more complex nets. McCulloch, *loc. cit., passim.*

Higher Education and the Unity of Knowledge

growth. If the essence of growth, according to Toynbee, is increase in self-determination, then this concept of growth should prove applicable to societies and other complex learning nets. The more complex and readjustable the constituent parts of a society become, the greater the coherence and freedom of each of its subassemblies, the greater should be the society's possibilities of itself achieving greater coherence and freedom in the course of its history. Learning nets and societies do not grow best by simplifying or rigidly subordinating their parts or members, but rather with the complexity and freedom of these members, so long as they succeed in maintaining or increasing mutual communication.[k]

Perhaps these few remarks will indicate the potential aid which our thinking might derive from these new advances in the fields of engineering and organization, and from the gradual emergence of a generalized model of a "learning net."[1] The chances for a successful

[k]Comment by Herman Finer:
The trouble with the world today is emphatically *not* the refusal of communication: it is a clash of different views of the teaching of history and different ambitions and different *telos*, accompanied by great mobility of ideas and much communication. But the element of TIME enters in: we cannot expect all men to spend all their life on a quest: to expect it is to be disappointed. If they were re-educated to the effect that all their life should be a quest of somebody else's insight that education would fail, for their nature would not tolerate it: there are other goods that they want.

Dr. Deutsch's reply:
Dr. Finer is right again when he reminds us that "the trouble with the world today is . . . clash of different . . . ambitions and different *telos,* accompanied by . . . much communication." The point is, perhaps, that "much communication" of a highly selected kind is no substitute for enough communication of the sort that matters—which is communication of relevant data about the external and internal consequences of our aims and actions.

[l]Comment by Philipp Frank:
The basic idea of this paper seems very sound. However, it seems to me that the conception of "mechanism" should be defined in a more general way. The author distinguishes between the model of a "clockwork," which turned out not to be sufficient in biology and sociology and the model of "feedback mechanism" which seems to be a good model for these fields. From the viewpoint of theoretical physics there is no real distinction between a clockwork and a feedback mechanism. Both operate according to the laws of Newtonian mechanics and are classical electrodynamics. The clockwork is just a simple case of mechanism, the feedback mechanism a more complex one. If one had told La Mettrie of feedback mechanisms he would have hailed it as a brilliant elaboration of his program to regard the human organism as a machine. There is nowhere in La Mettrie and contemporary materialists the idea that a "mechanism" has to be of the simple character of a clockwork and that the parts of a mechanism cannot be rearranged by the operation of the mechanism.

The breakdown of the mechanism as a model in the twentieth century is due to the

development of such new models are perhaps increased by the parallel development of a growing division of the labor of fact finding and thinking in human organizations, as exemplified in the division and reorganization of intellectual labor in industrial research and in social research and intelligence organizations.[120] In the light of such a generalized model of a learning net, it should now become possible to carry forward a systematic comparison of key concepts in the natural and social sciences in terms of operations.[m]

---

impossibility of constructing a mechanism for the phenomena within the atom, for instance, a mechanism for the conversion of mass into energy as it happens in the atom bomb. If one says that for a certain phenomenon there is no mechanical model one can only mean that this phenomenon cannot be derived from the laws of Newtonian mechanics and classical electrodynamics, and that one needs the new physical theories like relativity and quantum theory.

The discussion of the feedback mechanisms shows clearly that the phenomena of biology and sociology can be described approximately by using mechanical models in the old Newtonian sense and that they are not affected by what one calls the breakdown of "mechanism" in the twentieth century.

[120] For a major treatment of the principles of communication and organization: cf. Wiener, *loc. cit.*

[m] Comment by C. P. Haskins:
I believe that this is in many ways the most remarkable paper that has ever been presented to the Conference that I have read. In its grasp of the processes of history, and in its really remarkable integration of anthropological and historical backgrounds with modern concepts in sociology, and especially in psychology, it is, to my mind, unique. It is the only good exposition that I have read in a historical framework of the exceedingly important work which Wiener and his associates have been carrying forward for a number of years at the Massachusetts Institute of Technology in the field of mechanical analogs of brain activity. The whole concept of the "feedback" mechanism in relation to processes of thinking, and, especially, of initiation of new trains of thought and action will, I am very sure, have important and profound consequences in our understanding of historic and social processes—as they have already had important repercussions in the realm of physiology in such work as that of J. Z. Young.

Comment by Henry Margenau:
Without prejudice to the success or failure of the communications approach to the problems of psychology and sociology, one wonders a bit after reading this persuasive account whether its author is pointing to anything more significant than *analogies* between social and natural science. To put the matter most unflatteringly, the historian has discovered the outline of a horse in the clouds. He sees clearly its head, its ears, legs and feet, and therefore forthwith proceeds to apply mammalian anatomy to the clouds. I suggest that the theory of communications engineering, while applicable to many problems at present, is very far from accounting for consciousness.

This criticism, however, is far too harsh. It does injustice to the unique worthwhileness of the author's endeavor.

3. Research on Key Concepts

If concepts can be used as tools for organizing our experience and solving our problems, why do universities not help us to get a kit of them? If every self-respecting safe cracker aims to acquire a set of tools adequate to the problems he expects to encounter, why could we not aid our students to equip themselves with a set of "heuristic devices," that is, with ways of asking questions and organizing answers, so as to recognize and solve problems with the greatest effectiveness?

When we speak of a set of tools, we imply that the tools themselves should be matched or related to each other in some fashion. Actually the tools must be matched in two ways: like a set of burglar's keys, for each lock which they may encounter there should be among them at least one key that may be used to work on it; but all of them together without exception must fit the hand of the man who is going to use them, so that he himself can transfer his efforts from one tool to the other.

It is regrettable that many of the concepts of science today fall far short of these standards of the burglar's craft. General concepts, as used in every day language, will fit almost every man's hand, but they are so blunt and ill defined that they lack precision and incisiveness for dealing with many more complex problems. Specialized tools, defined with great accuracy by craftsmen working on one particular set of problems, such as mathematicians or biologists, are usually so highly specialized that they do not fit the hand of anyone outside the field. And so the "generally educated" person finds himself confronted with concepts which are frequently either so general as to be useless or so specialized as to be unusable.

What could be done here might be something which has already been started in a very small and very modest research project at the Massachusetts Institute of Technology, the attempt to put together, side by side, in the most precise operational terms that can be found, descrip-

---

Dr. Deutsch's reply:

The original draft of the discussion of minds, thinking machines, and societies was justly criticized by Professor Margenau for a number of unclear or vulnerable formulations. It has now been reformulated in part and amplified.

[In view of Dr. Deutsch's reformulations, several of Dr. Margenau's original technical criticisms, for which Dr. Deutsch has expressed appreciation, have been omitted.]

tions and definitions of key concepts which are used in a number of different sciences. The concept of group, for instance, can be defined with precision by mathematicians. We can specify the operations by which a mathematician identifies a group, and we can note on the same card not only the operational procedures but perhaps also the fields of unsuccessful application of this concept defined by these operations. We may then, next to it, put down a card on which a chemist tells us just what the concept of group means in chemistry and by what operations it is identified, and we may note the field in which these operations have been applied successfully, and possibly the instances where they have proven inapplicable. We may go on to the concept of group as used by the biologist, and then to the anthropologist, and to the student of economics and political science, and having specified in each case the operations by which the concepts are identified by each group, we may possibly know whether there is an analogy between these different operations. As a result, we might possibly arrive at a more precise understanding of the group concept in general and at a more accurate statement of the specific changes which have to be made when the group concept is transferred from one of these fields to the other; and we may secondly gain a set of five or eight concepts of group and of operations for identifying groups which may be helpful or at least suggestive to anyone who finds himself dealing with a new group problem not obviously covered by any one of the standard approaches in the established fields.

The same technique could be applied to concepts which are often left undefined because they seem so familiar to us that we usually do not bother to specify the operations of measurement which they involve. Perhaps it may be sufficient here to outline a few series of concepts which might benefit from such comparison and operational analysis:

1. Sign
   Symbol
   Language
   Thought
   Mind

2. Sense Organ
   Sensation
   Recognition
   Perception

Comprehension
   Quantity
   Quality
   Reason

3. Thing
   Identity
   Concept
   Pattern
   Universals
   Gestalt

4. Uniqueness
   Cause
   Necessity
   Probability
   Prediction

5. Reflex
   Association
   Habit

6. Secondary symbol
   Consciousness
   Will

7. Compatibility
   Preference
   Paradox
   Value

8. Reason
   Abstraction
   Intuition
   Knowledge

9. Memory
   Learning
   Integrity
   Conversion
   The sublime (in art, philosophy, religion)

It is clear that none of these concepts will be explained or defined exhaustively. But there is reason to believe that for each of them either something new and worthwhile about them can be found by this approach, or else at least that known and familiar descriptions of the processes which these concepts imply may now be learned faster, and more easily connected with, or transferred to, different but relevant concepts and operations in other fields."[n][121]

4. Some Specialized Courses and a Tentative Curriculum

On the exact nature of the specialized technical courses, men other than I will be competent to speak. Generally it can only be suggested that we consider the possibility of a college curriculum which gives fundamental courses in mathematics (including two terms of elementary calculus) and biology (perhaps including one term of *systematics* and anatomy and one term of genetics and embryology) in the freshman year, in addition to history of thought and one elective subject in the humanities and the social sciences. In the second year, it would contain a term of mathematics and a term of mathematical logic and a term of physics, including dynamics above the high school level. The third subject would again be the history of thought comprising the period from 1790 to the present. The fourth subject might again be elective in the social sciences or humanities. The selection of the history of industrialization in this year might be desirable for social science majors. The third year might contain a year's work in electricity and communications, including in the first term possibly such subjects as the theory of electric currents, elementary electromagnetism, harmonic oscillation, and circuits. The second term of this course might introduce the student to harmonic analysis, to the concept and treatment of the

---

[n]Comment by Philipp Frank:

The importance of this very good and helpful suggestion of Dr. Deutsch becomes evident from this paper itself. A great part of the argument is based upon tracing the meaning of the term "mechanism" through the fields of physics, engineering, biology, and sociology. This kind of study seems to me very valuable for the goal of integration of the knowledge of the student. One point has, however, to be carefully watched. This study is of great use only if the definition of terms is based upon a definite theory of meaning. Otherwise one would only achieve a collection of historical facts about usage of words. But this study would be of immense educational value, if one would try to give every word what the semanticists call an "extensional definition," which is about the same thing that is called a "pragmatic definition."

[121]Similar collections of significant operational meanings could be sought for certain basic terms of ethics or religion, such as "justice," "mercy," "responsibility," etc.

message, of filters, and of information, followed by an introduction to elementary feedback mechanisms or circuits, switchboards, and storage and recall of information. All other courses in the third year should be elective and so should be all four courses in the senior year. Among these electives, courses on statistical techniques, and a senior course in philosophy might be recommended.

Such a program, possibly suitable for a future social science major, would require the student to spend one third of his time on science and two thirds on the humanities. The natural science major might only be required to take the same prescribed courses, but would be free to use all his electives in the sciences, provided only that he selects at least one social science during each year. Modifications from these very general patterns could of course be developed in practice.

The essential point of the entire scheme rests in the nature of the seven required courses. Two of them, represented by the two years of the history of thought, cut across the natural and social sciences, since they supply information relevant to the understanding of both. The five courses in mathematics, mathematical logic, physics, biology, electricity, and communication, are courses in the sciences, but in sciences specifically selected for their importance in unifying and understanding the fundamentals of the entire range of modern knowledge, of scientific thinking, and of the principles of experimentation.

Perhaps the most practical way of introducing such a program might be to make it available on an optional basis to a few students at an institution large enough to have the equipment and faculty for such a program. It could then be modified in the light of these experiences, but might in the meantime train a number of special workers, perhaps for a degree of Bachelor of General Science and Coordination, or General Science and Social Development, similar to the degrees in general science and engineering or in engineering and economics which are now being offered at the Massachusetts Institute of Technology.

VII. *Some Possible Results of This Curriculum*

What could such a type of training accomplish? Perhaps in the most general terms it could aid students to achieve a larger measure of understanding of processes and of the nature of change and growth.

It might aid them to achieve a better understanding of the nature of values and a greater openness to the values of other peoples and other cultures without weakening their understanding and attachment to their own. It might help students to acquire a rational appreciation of reason, and at the same time not only of the function but of the nature of tradition and intuition, and perhaps, to some degree, of mysticism and religion: it might help them to keep their minds open to the insights and values which have been attained and which may be attained again through any and all of these approaches without forcing them at the same time to despair of the powers of reason.[o]

In a more concrete framework, such an education could teach specific skills in the organization of thoughts and knowledge. It might teach men to think more accurately in terms of compatibilities. It might supply a general educational background for such varied later specialized careers as logistics, traffic engineering, town planning, and administration in business or public life. It might help men to overcome the isolation of their own specialized fields, and to facilitate the transfer of their experiences and skills from one situation to another.

Most important, perhaps, it might aid them to understand more clearly the problems involved in the transfer of values and institutions

---

[o]Comment by David Bidney:

Since we have been informed that a knowledge of ultimate values lies beyond the sphere of science and pertains to the realm of religion and philosophy, it is difficult to see how a comprehensive course in the history of science, or research on the role of models in the natural and social sciences, together with an analysis of "key concepts," will produce the above result.

The issue must be squarely faced: either philosophy and religion in conjunction with the natural and social sciences have something of their own to contribute toward a common understanding and appreciation of human values or else we are limited to the discrete facts of science and to a common faith in scientific methodology. Dr. Deutsch, it would appear, has not shown how it is possible to pass from scientific methodology to an appreciation of normative cultural values. As Dr. Robert Ulich puts it in Chapter I, "On the Rise and Decline of Higher Education": "In other words, unification of parts can never come from the parts themselves, but only from a principle that unites them, and this, in turn, is not only a principle in the sense of a method, but it is a mode of thinking which ultimately springs from the power of a conviction. In all great periods of higher learning there worked, explicitly or silently, an integrating philosophy behind the various scholarly activities." If, however, as Dr. Deutsch appears to suggest, the university is not to attempt the task of a philosophical interpretation of our contemporary culture because of its inability to "enforce agreement" upon ultimate values, then the "unity of knowledge" which he seeks will be an empty and formal unity conducive neither to individual peace of mind nor sociocultural harmony.

[For further comment on the above paragraphs of Dr. Deutsch's chapter, see Chapter VIII by Alain L. Locke, who quotes and discusses Dr. Deutsch's remarks.]

over time, and through a period of change. Starting out with an analysis of their own historical situation and an appreciation of the substantial reasons behind it, they may at the same time learn to weigh the probabilities of further change. They may come to assess more concretely the alternatives for themselves and their communities in terms of risks and sacrifices, of time and effort, of institutions, habits, and values. They can perhaps be aided, to that extent, with more usable information to preserve and renovate our industrial civilization with the integrity of its spiritual heritage: a free community whose members are their brothers' keepers, but call their souls their own.[p]

[p]Comment by Louis J. A. Mercier:

This paper seems to me the most original and up to the minute contribution to the Conference. As an historian, Professor Deutsch shows enough objectivity to give their due to the Middle Ages, and he even brings out, along with Toynbee, the economic contribution of the medieval monasteries. His uniqueness seems to come from the fact that, an historian, he works in a scientific institution in touch with the latest mechanical developments of scientific methods. This rare combination of historical and scientific knowledge at once gives him a wider humanistic view than that of the average scientist, and a keener desire to draft plans of research more exactly than usual with the humanist or the philosophical naturalist.

Still, he remains confronted with our fundamental dilemma, as Dr. David Bidney has clearly brought out in his comments on the paper. The problem is, as Professor Deutsch puts it: "to know which loyalties by their very nature can be agreed upon."

I agree with the concern for the perfecting of our methods of determining the universal moral values according to which all sociocultural modes of life should be judged, and which all ages should make an effort to approximate. The physical sciences can throw no light on this. Social studies—they are but pseudo-scientific, though they may perhaps be made less so by such perfecting of methods as Dr. Deutsch indicates—can throw some light on man's behavior. But ultimately we shall have to resort to metaphysics, because only metaphysics can enable us to distinguish by reason what is the universal nature of man out of which flow universal duties, rights, and values. Therein only can be found by reason that integrating principle of which Dr. Ulich stressed the need.

Comment by Herman Finer:

Generally I think the paper is too worshipful of natural science. When a student has about four years of university life, one third of his time on science is far too much, except for those whose vocation is to be a natural scientist, and even that I question. I am interested in the making of citizens of the world: three months out of forty-eight is quite enough for techniques: forty-five will still be too little for them to have learned something from the millennia about human nature. To give more to science is to go back to Comte's first age of man: to be ruled by the Fetish. I have been appalled by students having to spend a year tickling a frog's feet with electrodes in the unexamined conviction handed to them that they were thereby learning something about *man*, and yet being nonplussed by simple problems about two thousand years in the record of Frenchmen or Germans. The paper gives us no clue how to know our duty, but does offer some clue as to the valid procedures by which we might seek to know it.

CHAPTER V

The Unity of Knowledge

By SCOTT BUCHANAN
Director, Liberal Arts, Inc.

> Ah love! could you and I with Him conspire
> To grasp this Sorry Scheme of Things entire
> Would not we shatter it to bits—and then
> Re-mould it to the Heart's Desire!

NINE YEARS ago Mortimer J. Adler read a paper from the platform of the first session of this Conference, entitled *God and the Professors*. It was an attempt to point out the conditions, scientific, philosophic, and religious, which would make the aim of the Conference possible. It said in effect that tracing the relations between the diverse universes of discourse presupposed the unity of knowledge, and that these together demanded a common faith in the attainability of truth. But the paper was written in terms of dogmatic theology, and it broke rather than supported the available rhetorical forms of communication. I shall never forget the atmosphere of tension in which the paper was read, and the chaotic outburst of passion that it released. Cassandra had spoken again, and could be neither believed nor understood.

I am hoping that the four lines above, written by a great mathematician with pathos and irony, will provide a happier atmosphere for a restatement of Mr. Adler's thesis. The theme is today, nine years later, ubiquitous and unavoidable, the need for the unification of human knowledge. Theology has gone underground and become a conspiracy inside each universe of discourse; knowledge has not only been shattered to bits, it is being ground to dust by whatever gods there be; hearts' desires live in the labyrinth and the catacomb. Nevertheless, as on previous similar occasions, the despair in this process is generating a faith in the necessity and therefore the possibility of remolding the sorry scheme.

World government, like communism a hundred years ago, has become a specter. It is invoked and feared everywhere. The wisest thing that has been said about it comes from A. J. Toynbee: it is coming sooner than we think. Nations and classes are being ground down to fit it. No one yet knows whether it will be just and wise or whether it will be tyrannical and violent. That is why we fear it, and that is the decision we have to make. The difference between the possible outcomes is the measure of the knowledge and wisdom we can bring to bear upon the process of accepting it. The effective applications of knowledge will not be merely increments of empirical and speculative science, not merely humanitarian improvisation, not merely the invention and codification of laws. The intelligent functions of government must be founded in penetrative knowledge of nature, technology, and man. One of its conditions would seem to be the discovery of a new unified basis of all our knowledge.

The system of our technology and its reflection in the great associations of men make economic planning practically unavoidable. It is obvious that a little planning is a dangerous thing, that so-called private planning is inadequate, and that state planning has not yet found its matrix of justice and freedom. Here again the difference between freedom and slavery seems to depend upon the degree to which intelligence can penetrate the automatisms of the factory and marketplace. We do not believe that at present we have the grasp of things that would enable us to face the inevitable task.

Modern science has been and is a going concern; it throws off radiations, powerful and suggestive of human good, but so far only fragmentary and destructive of the foundations of use and want upon which our common life moves. The mechanical, the chemical, the electrical, the energetic, the organic, the psychic, these are all slivers split off some central rational root, upon which reason works only to split and distinguish further. Applied science is almost by definition and common consent bastard and unassimilated science. Atomic energy is only the latest and some would say the final demonstration of unassimilable science, the final refutation of the Scholastic maxim, distinguish in order to unite. The earlier hostile gap between mechanism and teleology was only the first narrow crack in Pandora's box of intellectual troubles. The trouble at bottom is not ethical and moral fixation, as the human engineer thinks; it is epistemic, a matter of knowledge. Science, a new kind of knowledge has been born a twin with a new kind of ignorance, and there is no Socratic midwife to provide knowledge of what we do not know. We are even suspicious that the new knowledge is a new disguise for systematic sophistic ignorance. The general public meetings of the Associations for The Advancement of Science may impregnate the body politic with a new monstrous ideology, a technocracy and a revolution of managerial violence. A new atomic explosion may burn the world up before a new virus has denuded it of life. These are the phantom fears that spread from laboratories of industrial and governmental research. The legal unification of science in the name of the control of atomic energy may well bring off the revolution that will prevent any genuine unification of knowledge in our time.

The ferment in democratic education that has worked from the kindergarten up through the grammar and high schools to the colleges and universities in the past two generations, has been trying to keep up with the multiplication of knowledges and the new varieties of experience. In a pseudo-clinical concern with individual pathology it is treating each individual mind as if it were a broken universe of discourse, and it has turned to a therapeutic occupation with the fine arts to pacify the symptoms, while it throws every variety of nostrum into the witch's pot known as general education. The liberal education which was once the common medium in which the individual accepted and revolutionized his tradition has now become for the first time in its long history the genteel specialization for the new irresponsibles, the scholar and the fine artist. Education is no longer the torch of truth, the inciter to curiosity, the nurse of useful learning. It pounds and kneads the whole man while his intellect sleeps.

The cause of this degradation of education is not malice, perversity, and laziness, but rather the failure of a desperate attempt to find out what ought to be taught, or to find the authority which might enable the teacher to teach. As we do not know the ignorance that goes with science, we do not know what we ought to learn in education. We have not been able to discern the pattern in our knowledges that would make them one knowledge.

In all these samples of our common life government, industry, science, and education, it is clear that there are despair and signs of desperation, there is whoring after strange gods, but these are, like high fever, healthy signs of constitutional vitality. If there were no despair in a sick world, there would be no faith. It is fairly clear where the trouble lies. We have been living for several centuries, particularly the past one, under a code of individual liberty. The strides of progress that we have taken in government, in industry, in science, and in education have been daring and bold steps in the division of labor. Individual initiative and effort have been the terms in which freedom has been understood. This meaning of freedom has spread to the whole world and has had profound effects, but perhaps the deepest effects in our own minds; we have divided the labor of our own minds. But disintegrative as this may be, it has also been dynamic and productive. We have changed the world and brought about a situation in which collective effort and common thinking have become absolutely essential to our continued common life. This is what makes communism the most moving and vital political idea in the world today; it also makes its inversion and failure in Russian practice today a horrifying spectacle. The application of the collective idea in economics and politics is undergoing its crucial experiment, and the crisis has frightened us who view it at a distance. And yet it is perfectly clear that the situation we have created in the world and for ourselves demands agreement and cooperation among ourselves; our problems can no longer be solved by independent thought and action. We must find some kind of collective intellectual freedom.

It may be true that our contribution to the historical process has been made through the basic pattern of individual civil liberties as we have understood and applied them throughout our common life, and that we ought not to expect and to accept the solution of the consequent problems from elsewhere. It seems that that is what we shall have to do, if we do not discover and teach ourselves new common intellectual habits. Russia has discovered and is using a plan of collaboration in industry and business that once looked like the logical consequences of our own principles of liberty, but she has combined this plan with patterns in government and education that horrify us with their barbarism. We have a sharper sense of our own pattern because of this development; it could excite us to the further exploration of this pattern. We once conspired with God to grasp and shatter a sorry scheme of things, and we rebuilt it to the heart's desire. We might now try to rebuild our structure of civil liberties nearer to our collective heart's desire.

I have a suggestion that I would like to make for the permanent organization of this Conference, but before I make the suggestion, I would like to make some observations on three great historic models which it distantly imitates.

The Unity of Knowledge

The first one is the work of Plato and Aristotle which was done in rather full awareness of the breakdown of Greek civilization at the end of the Peloponnesian War. In separate but providentially connected ways these men undertook the criticism and unification of human knowledge. The two minds, one searching, explorative, and critical, the other inventive and constructive, brought about an extraordinary single and exhaustive view of a very rich and manifold world. One can regret the haunting doctrinaire influence that their achievements have had on the rest of our tradition, but it would be hard now to justify such regrets by formulating any alternative intellectual reflections of truth that would have provided even a fraction of the light and guidance that they have contributed to Western human life. They were able to do this by the organization of institutions of learning, the Academy and the Lyceum, in which the burden of teaching and research gave substance and vitality to their speculations. It is also notable that they and their institutions were concerned with and impregnated by a political purpose. They were institutions that watched over the political fates, first to the Greek peoples, and then finally over vast areas of the globe through the Alexandrian and Roman Empires. Alexander and certain Roman emperors even imagined themselves to be philosopher-kings.

Another historic model is to be found in the intellectual labors of Scholastics in the medieval universities. They were so successful in their drive toward unity that they have falsified history; the Middle Ages are for us, among other things, a time of great synthesis, although we know with a little second thought, that this was a time of physical violence, of misery and spiritual darkness, and of irrepressible intellectual conflict. In spite of this the angelic and subtle doctors, working in a medium of ecclesiastical and monastic institutions, pushed their minds through the warring doctrines to points of vision from which order could be seen in the world. There were many such views, as the readers of more than one *Summa* know, but they knew better than modern pluralists how diverse unities can be, and how important sincereness of view can be in human wisdom.[a] Here again, it is important to note that the intellectual work was done in an institutional framework, and that it had a watchful concern with politics, the deeply subtle politics of the church.

---

[a] [Cf. the discussion of medieval and Renaissance education in Chapter I by Robert Ulich, Chapter VII by Charles W. Hendel, Chapter IX by Howard Mumford Jones, and Chapter XII by Louis J. A. Mercier.]

146   *Goals for American Education*

The third instance of recognition of the need of unity in knowledge and action to achieve it is the abortive, but nonetheless influential, attempt of the French Encyclopedists. The eighteenth century fell into the project almost by mistake. The occasion was a publisher's attempt to get Chamber's *Cyclopedia* translated into French. He found Diderot to do the job. Diderot in turn persuaded some of his friends to help him revise as well as translate the work. Church and state protested the revisions and the publishers suppressed portions that they thought would irritate the authorities; they did this without letting Diderot know. Diderot was harassed by enemies and deserted by friends, and the project suffered delay and fragmentation. But its effect is now attested by the fact that most of the new material is taken for granted by us, and we hardly can reconstruct the world which it replaced. Its drive again had been the unification of knowledge and its locus of discourse was politics to which all other concerns were related, although it lacked institutional support.[b]

These examples help to clarify the suggestion I want to make to this Conference. It is that we grasp the sorry scheme of things as our assignment in this time of troubles, that we recognize that its entirety includes the shattered things of science, philosophy, and religion, and that we undertake to remold it in terms of politics, taking as our matrix the American way of intellectual life as it is formulated in the Bill of Rights

---

[b]Comment by Louis W. Norris:

Dr. Buchanan's historical illustrations are not convincing. Politics for Plato was a live concern, to be sure. But he always conceived political plans, as indeed all others, derivative from the realm of ideas. Plato was first of all a metaphysician, and all phases of his philosophy stem from his scheme of eternal forms. He would think of the unity in knowledge as resting in this realm of concepts by which all politics is to be judged.

Aristotle did of course hold that man is a "political animal," but for him, too, the "forms" of things were the points of reference. Politics is subject to ethics, for Aristotle, and human actions are good when they express most adequately the forms of human nature. Here again, politics is subject to criticism by rational principles. Also, Aristotle held that the political scheme any given people should follow varies according to their ability, experience, and location. Hence he did not believe there was any one political plan which could unify people's knowledge. If there is no timeless truth, there is no use trying to unify knowledge.

Aquinas was interested in the good society, but his first concern was in showing that the revelation was rational. His scheme was oriented toward metaphysics and theology. Politics was but a minor part of his larger frame of thought. It is dubious, at least to me, whether the *Encyclopedia* of Diderot had enough influence to be of much help in launching the plan Dr. Buchanan favors.

Plato, Aristotle, and Aquinas would rather suggest to me that unity of knowledge should be sought through "first," rather than political principles.

and the other political, scientific, philosophic, and religious documents that helped and are helping to formulate it.[c]

Albert Einstein has recently been quoted as saying that the only way today to think about human destiny is in political terms. I do not know what reasons he would give for this statement, but we can all guess what they are and we can add reasons from our own experience. Judging from the points I have stressed in the historic models, we could be right if we said that no one has ever been able to think about human destiny without political terms. At any rate it appears now to be true that political terms are almost the only ones left available to us for our pressing task.

Theology is the queen of the sciences, it was once held, and I believe truly. It was the science that submitted its findings to the highest standard of truth that men knew, and it persuaded men by reason out of their own hearts. But this is no longer available, partly because the theologians do not accept the assignment, and partly because men are not being persuaded in terms of the highest truth they know. Similarly, the philosopher no longer presides over the intellectual affairs of a university, although a few philosophers may try to be kings of Boards of Trustees. Philosophy is a department in a university, only lending its name in the degree of Doctor of Philosophy to the achievements of all parts of the university in research. Medicine and science do play the role of bringing learning to bear upon human affairs; they are coming to realize that their proper focus is the whole human being from the cradle to the grave; but the fragmentary nature of their theoretical achievements, and their uncertain grasp of the political framework within which they must work make them subject to the designs of quacks and ideologists. In fact the task of unifying knowledge, pressing and inevitable as it is, is passing from the irresponsible scholar and professional to the private enterprise of the self-appointed tyrants and demagogues who are devotees of the

[c]Comment by Alexander Meiklejohn:

This proposal seems to me fundamentally wise. Both by practical experience in teaching and by reflection upon it, I am convinced that this is the road which leads most surely and directly toward the construction of an intelligent plan of education. If we Americans would enter upon a sober and passionate study of the provisions and deeper implications of our Constitution, we would be finding our way toward insight into the forms of life which are worth living and, hence, worth teaching. Such self-critical insight would have value, not only for ourselves, but also for the total human community of which we are a part.

black mass and the black arts. Ideology has become the only focus of human knowledge.[d]

When the god no longer inhabits the temple, the folk find him in the theater. When the intellect no longer lives in the school, the university, or the professional guild, the common man and the intellectual look for each other in the marketplace and the forum. There are signs that the common man has begun his search, but there are pitifully few signs that the intellectual is joining the assembly. It is time that we looked to our common humanity and rediscovered our political animality.

Starting where each of us is we ought to begin a study of the Declaration of Independence, the Constitution, the Federalist Papers, and move on as fast as we can into a thorough study of the decisions of the Supreme Court, where some of the finest American writing and thinking about our common problems has been done. At the same time we should join in the efforts of our respective political parties where the sickness of our political life is most acute. We should meet regularly to report and discuss our findings, and to follow the issues wherever they lead. I would not doubt that these discussions would fall within the limits of Science, Philosophy, and Religion in relation to the Democratic Way of Life, and I hope they would lead to the acceptance of the responsibilities they imply. One of these practical implications might be undertaken immedi-

[d]Comment by John D. Wild:

I am glad that Dr. Buchanan employs the word "ideology" for that vital and essential mode of awareness by which every group to some degree apprehends itself and its unifying purpose. But his statement that "Ideology has become the only focus of human knowledge," seems to be attended by some regret, which I cannot share. If, as I am convinced, there is no such thing as a "group-substance" or "group-soul," then the ultimate source of group unity, indeed of group existence in a human sense, must be found in the sharing of a single common purpose which is to some degree understood. Sound social life is dependent upon the formulation and maintenance of an adequate ideology capable of calling forth the integral devotion of all its members. When its ideology loses its clarity and appeal, the human group disintegrates. Hence it seems to me that, as against the acute individualism which at first exercised such a dominant influence on modern thought, the recent concern for ideology is a most healthy and hopeful symptom, which should be supported without any overt or latent qualms.

It seems worth pointing out that this recent concern has so far been guided by philosophic conceptions emanating from Hegelian idealism. Both communism and national socialism have arisen from this source. The practical implications of classical and medieval realistic thought have never been thoroughly considered and developed—at least at the *natural* level. I throw this out merely as a suggestion concerning an unexplored direction which might be of peculiar interest to the sort of practical investigation which Dr. Buchanan has outlined.

ately, the extension of our incomplete system of universal education to the entire adult population.

The proposal I am making to this Conference does not envisage a group of researchers who will catalogue and index the products of our learned societies; it does not suggest the building of ivory towers for the private cultivation of the contemplative virtues; I am not even thinking of a board of jurists to codify world law. Each of these might be a useful enterprise if there were a receptacle to recognize and accept the resulting formulations. I am thinking rather of an institution like the European Academies, which are well named after the Platonic Academy, to which reports could be made and from which judgments could issue on the state of the intellectual arts, and their operations in our common life. It should be assumed that the common medium of discourse is political and the style of discussion should be deliberative, that is, directed to practical conclusions. This should not be understood to eliminate abstract thought and dialectic with speculative dimensions, or to avoid any universe of discourse, but rather to begin and end in the consideration of ends and means. I believe political thought is the rational receptacle we must construct, or reconstruct, if our common life is to fulfil a common good. It would be the function of this Conference to rediscover and to set in motion the institutional processes by which our common life may again reach a common good.[e]

This suggestion is giving up or postponing much that is desired when

[e]Comment by Louis W. Norris:
The dangers of totalitarianism in Dr. Buchanan's plan do not seem to be sufficiently identified. Recent experience of German, Italian, and Russian leaders in tooling their scholarly pursuits to mesh with their political beliefs, should be dire warning that this way lies disaster for democracy and the search for truth which Dr. Buchanan's academy envisages. The real hazard lies in the ease with which such scholarly pursuits come to support the existing political system, thus stifling the independent criticism and creative experiment that keeps political life healthy. As soon as any society confines itself to coordination of its functions on merely practical levels, these functions lose their orientation. Dr. Buchanan asserts that abstract speculation is not to be eliminated, but his stress upon the practical outcome of knowledge suggests that he will not expect much from such generalizations. A framework of criticism for these practical concerns must be established if knowledge is to serve its day.

Because the trend of the time is away from metaphysics and theology, it does not follow that unification of knowledge on purely practical levels is the chief task before us. Leaders of science, philosophy, and religion should provide a platform of knowledge that constitutes a valid unification first, rather than working from public tastes primarily. Getting the public to recognize such unity after it is established, is a secondary and not insoluble problem.

we speak of unifying knowledge. It is not a new thing to discover that truth, or the mind of God, as it was once called, is beyond human reach, and that men's minds are a little lower than the angels', but I think we are even farther than this would indicate from our heart's desire. We cannot hope to do now what we can in time train ourselves to do, that is, to measure our knowledge and our ignorance against a wisdom that is humanly attainable. There is abundant evidence at present that we do not even want metaphysics or theology as the focus of our view of the world; there is considerable evidence that we do want such a focus in our politics.

I suppose I am thinking in the back of my mind about what Plato did in a time of troubles similar to our own. Through the highly dramatic intellectual personality of Socrates and with his own soaring faith in the human intellect he first wrote a series of dialogues that held the mirror up to Greek human nature. The process in these dialogues was then institutionalized in the Academy, where it went on for a thousand years. The *Republic* was the charter of the Academy. With this institution as background and medium he continued the work with comrades, some of whom became philosopher-kings and guided the ancient world through stormy times. Plato himself continued to write increasingly speculative dialogues, but he ended where he began in political considerations, and he never forgot the political theme, least of all when he took time off to try practical politics in Syracuse. The range of these written works is tremendous. The dialogues contain a complete survey of the

---

Comment by John D. Wild:

Dr. Buchanan suggests that the discussions of this Conference in the future be given a more distinct and conscious *political* focus. He supports this suggestion by arguments which strike me as very sound and cogent. I should like to supplement them by a few further considerations which seem to me quite relevant.

Dr. Buchanan makes it clear that he does not mean "to eliminate abstract thought and dialectic with speculative dimensions." I should suggest an even stronger statement. Any responsible consideration of the ultimate end of political action must involve the raising of the most profound theoretical issues concerning the nature of man and the world which he inhabits. The building of a social order requires at least the *tacit* acceptance of a metaphysical point of view, though theoretical speculation may be carried on without any reference to its practical implications. This is why the most sweeping philosophic syntheses have been achieved under practical rather than under theoretical auspices in the past. Hence Dr. Buchanan's suggestion is to be taken in no sense as a restriction, but rather as a clarification and intensification of the integrative aims of this Conference.

The Unity of Knowledge

human arts as practised in the Greek cities and an ordering of them under the master art of government. They contain the highest speculation, including the model for all later metaphysics and theology in the *Parmenides*. In between these extremes there are places indicated for the sciences, morals, and institutions as the objects of human knowledge and love. Plato did not accomplish the unification of knowledge, but his life and work have made the necessity of it seem possible ever since.[f]

---

[f] Comment by Alexander Meiklejohn:

Dr. Buchanan's prescription for an ailing education seems to me sound in principle and promising in practice. It is obvious, however, that when an idea has been so incompletely formulated, the proper response is not one of acceptance or rejection. We must try to discover what the idea means. To that end I offer some comments and queries about the puzzling principle of "the unifying of knowledge" upon which Dr. Buchanan rests his case.

First, the project of making "many knowledges into one knowledge"—if it be interpreted as a merely intellectual achievement—seems to me in danger of substituting a means to an end for the end itself. The goal toward which education should strive is practical rather than cognitive. It is a mode of human behavior which, though it includes right thinking, is far wider and deeper than right thinking. This fact is, I think, implied in Dr. Buchanan's suggestion that the focus of our study of education should be political. Politics is action and the planning of action. It is the art of forming the life of a community and, hence, of the individuals who constitute the community. It deals with opinions only as they give direction to decisions. If, then, we study politics, our goal is a Plan of Action. We are not, in the last resort, seeking for knowledge, unified or ununified. We are searching for a Faith which can command our allegiance, a Cause which can bring us all together into active, intelligent, and friendly cooperation. Nothing short of that universal practical commitment can be the goal of teaching.

Next, then, we inquire, "Has humanity a Faith, a Single Purpose, in relation to which all our intellectual activities may be given relevance to one another, may, thereby, become the proper materials of teaching?" The answer is, I think, a sure, though not very clear, affirmative. Blindly or clearly, Humanity has a Faith. We human beings have a Common Cause to which we all alike owe allegiance, with respect to which, therefore, we are morally obliged to be, as far as possible, intelligent. That Cause is the forming and maintaining of a World Community, in which every person, every group, every race, shall have its rightful place. In the name of the Brotherhood of Man, we demand that all men shall be free, that all men shall be equal, that peace shall be established, that justice shall be done.

Finally, Dr. Buchanan has told us that the replanning and redirecting of education is a desperately difficult task. That statement cannot be doubted. Hence one must deplore what seems to be the irresponsible expression of an opinion which dangerously threatens the foundations of our undertaking. The opinion in question was recently attributed to Arnold Toynbee, when he was quoted as saying, "We must have Unity. But it is quite possible that in making One World our *primary* hope, we may fail by aiming too low. For the Brotherhood of Man is, I am convinced, an utterly impossible ideal, unless men are bound together by belief in a Transcendent God." That opinion seems to me to have the same intellectual and emotional status as the corresponding opinion which contradicts it in the words, "Religion is the opium of the people." And, apart from some superficial validities, the two dicta are equally ill founded. As we human beings work together toward the making of One World, some of us find grounds for believing that our efforts have Divine support. Others can find no such grounds. But the essential fact is that, whether we believe in God or not, the Common Cause is there as a human aspiration which demands our loyalty, our intelligence, our action. We have a Common Human Faith.

CHAPTER VI

The Contemporary Devaluation of Intelligence

By JOHN COURTNEY MURRAY, S.J.
Professor of Theology, Woodstock College

THE PHENOMENON of contemporary life with which I attempt to deal is so Protean in its manifestations, so subtle, so pervasive, that its full exploration would be a lengthy business. I am not even sure that I name it aptly. One could give it other names: the decay of metaphysics, the despair of reason, the loss of the full object of thought, the narrowing of man's mental vision, the disappearance of the "Transcendental" into the "Unknown," the embrace of purposelessness, the triumph of the Irrational, or perhaps most generally, man's absence from himself. However one may name the phenomenon, its frightening reality is beyond question. Consider these testimonies to it, selected at random, without pretense of completeness.

At the conclusion of his book, *Political Thought from Spencer to Today,* Ernest Barker years ago spoke of "a certain trend of anti-intellectualism which is one of the features of the age." He detects the trend in certain currents of political thought that incline to depreciate the element of rationality that had traditionally been supposed to animate the structures and processes of political life. Increasingly, he says, men seek the origins of the State in irrational forces, and look to these same forces for the achievement of the purposes of the State. This same flight to the irrational, then noted in the field of political theory, was even more strikingly the dynamism of the political movements that convulsed the world after Barker wrote. The great political myths of our century, the pseudo-religious creeds of Fascism, Nazism, and Communism, are, for all their differences, characterized by the same exultant dethronement of intelligence as the ultimate dynamic and norm of social life, and the enthronement of a subrational element of human nature (blood or race) or of some material determinant of human life (class, the economic order). The whole power of these movements lies in their demand for the unconditional surrender of individual reason and conscience unto absorption in irrational mass-feelings and unto blind, irrational obedience to a power beyond reason or reason's juridical incarnation which is law. I do not have to elaborate this subject.

In the field of jurisprudence, too, our phenomenon appears. In the school of sociological jurisprudence it appears in the substitution for the concept of "rights" of the concepts of "interests," whose characteristic is that they possess no absolute value and are determined and measured by no fixed rational norm. "Justice" is a balancing, more or less mechanical, of "interests" into a more or less stable equilibrium of forces. And natural rights, as Dean Pound has said, "mean simply interests that we think ought to be secured," because of their recognition at the moment as social values. An even more profound denial of rationality in law is made by the school of legal realism, in which the so-called "is element" in law is pushed to the exclusion of the "ought element"; that is, law ceases to be reason (what *ought* to be) and becomes simply the factual will of the legislator (what *is*), that is, law because it is a threat of the application of state force. In this theory "rights" become, in Karl N. Llewellyn's phrase, "factual terms, nothing more"; they evidence simply the existence of a particular pattern of social behavior; they are therefore, Llewellyn says, "statements of the result likely in a given case." Without going farther into the subject, let me say, in the words of a distinguished law teacher, that we are witnessing today in the field of jurisprudence a "contest between the force and validity of principles, precedents, reason, free will, and impartial justice" and "the impact of emotion, irrationalism, bias, environment, and juristic skepticism in the legal order."

In the field of religion the contemporary discount of reason and intelligence is perhaps most obvious in Barthian neo-orthodoxy, with its tendency to a radical separation of the domains of reason and religious faith, to the denial of the possibility of a natural theology and of a natural law and morality, and to the complete exclusion of reason from any instrumental function in regard of faith, just as human effort is excluded from any instrumental function in regard of the "coming of the Kingdom." From another point of view, and in another form, intelligence is seen at a discount in what today remains of Liberal Protestantism on the Schleiermacher model, in which "religion" becomes simply "religiosity," the *Sinn und Geschmack fuer das Unendliche,* that issues from the region of sentiment wherein man chances to have experience of his dependence —an experience, however, that possesses no intellectual content, and connotes no rational knowledge of God, Who is for reason, on Kantian grounds, forever unknowable.

There are other instances of man's loss of grip upon his own intellect and its potentialities. Professor John U. Nef, for instance, pointed to one when he spoke of "the loss of the common cultural inheritance in the intellectual sense, which existed among the learned and cultured down to the nineteenth century";[a] this loss of grip upon the mind's historic achievements argues, I think, some more profound loss of grip of the mind upon itself. Furthermore, we have all noted that particularly insidious attack upon the rational that emanates from the more undisciplined theorists and practitioners of the "depth psychologies"—those, I mean, who deny the dualism in human nature, and in the single quest for unconscious motivations rising from subrational depths in man deny, too, or diminish to a vanishing point, the determinate influence of the choices of rational freedom. All of us, moreover, are aware of the devaluation of intelligence evident in Marxism—in its atheistic postulate, in its determinist interpretation of history as ruled by the "objective" factors of material environment, in its concept of the spiritual life of man as secondary to, and derivative from, the sheerly materially conditioning factors of human life, in its reduction of intelligence to the degrading position of a mere tool for the manipulation of economic processes, and in the denial to intelligence of freedom to pursue any quests other than that of furthering the dialectic movement toward the Marxist social ideal.

However, not unduly to prolong this paper, let me cite just one more expression of the modern abdication of intellect—the recent article by Professor W. T. Stace, "Man Against Darkness" (*Atlantic Monthly,* September, 1948). Its central thesis is the statement of what purports to be a fact: "Belief in the ultimate irrationality of everything is the quintessence of what is called the modern mind." It is science, says Professor Stace, that has ushered in this belief, not by reason of anything it has proved or disproved, but simply by reason of its domination of men's minds, in consequence of which there has grown up in the minds of men "a new imaginative picture of the world," as "purposeless, senseless, meaningless." Moreover, from this scientific view of reality men have

[a] [Cf. Chapter XI by John U. Nef.]

drawn the consequence: "If the scheme of things is purposeless and meaningless, then the life of man is purposeless and meaningless, too. Everything is futile, all effort is in the end worthless." The further consequences are relativism in morals and determinism in human action in general. This is the modern situation, says Professor Stace. It is to be accepted as simply "there"; and man's duty is to face honestly the question it puts to him: "Can he grasp the real world as it actually is, stark and bleak, without its romantic or religious halo, and still retain his ideals, striving for great ends and noble achievements?"

I do not know whether Professor Stace is practising a bit of Socratic midwifery or stating his own convictions. At all events, I have not seen a better statement of how the "noble mind is here o'erthrown." The abdication of intelligence is threefold. There is first the abdication involved in acceptance of irrationality as ultimate in all nature, whether material or human. There is secondly the abdication involved in accepting the ultimate irrationality of all things by a "belief" that is itself known to be irrational; for Professor Stace seems to know that it is quite irrational for science to assert, and for us on its word to believe, that the world of nature and of man is an irrational world. Science can ask of man and of the world only limited questions; it cannot therefore give to the problem of man and the world a complete answer. For its limited purposes it can disregard the problems of finality in nature and of the destiny of man; but because science disregards the questions, is it rational to suppose that they are not meaningful questions or that no answer to them is possible? Finally, there is the last abdication—this time a fortunate one. It is the abdication that Dostoievsky's Kirilov refused to make and therefore killed himself. If human life is without sense, direction, meaning, purpose, it is because there is no God; and if there be no God, as Kirilov saw, then the intelligent thing is suicide. The absolute atheist must know himself to be the ultimate, divine, since there is no other ultimate, no other divinity. And if he is divine, he is absolutely independent, *a se;* and if he is such, he must have an act wherein to express this independence. And there is no other such act than the subordination of his own existence to his sovereign freedom: "I shall kill myself," said Kirilov, "to prove my independence and my terrible new freedom." Professor Stace's modern man refuses this last conclusion from his premises; it is his final irrationality. (I call it a fortunate one, because the sober fact remains—however recalcitrant the Humes and Huxleys, the Sartres and Staces may choose to be about it—that it is not necessary for a man to believe in hell in order to go there.)

I cite Professor Stace primarily in testimony to the reality of the phenomenon which I began to describe; if it be not a despair of reason, a devaluation of the power of intelligence, irrationally to accept an irrational "belief in the ultimate irrationality of everything," concepts have lost all meaning. Secondly, I want his testimony to the fact that "science" is somehow at the root of this appalling situation. If this be the fact, close scrutiny must be bent on the thing called "science" by those who have at heart the cause of intelligence as well as of religion.

It would, of course, be untrue to suppose that atheism or ethical relativism or determinism was somehow an intrinsic exigence of the scientific spirit; and it would be naive to imagine that science is singly to blame for the fact, noted by Professor Stace, that man today so largely finds "his life hollow at the center." The secularist assumption that is now so widespread is not ordinarily, if ever, reached by man as the term of a scientific induction, much less of a metaphysical journey; it is usually a starting point adopted in obedience to the pressures of a climate of opinion. And certainly there are no resources in scientific method to validate the extraordinary illation that is the crucial point of Professor Stace's analysis of the modern temper—the illation from the purposelessness of the world of nature (as supposedly established by science) to the parallel purposelessness of the life of man. The monistic view of reality that underlies such an illation is a philosophical position, and all the empirical data that scientific method may accumulate must always fall short of its proof or disproof. Finally, the form of militant, "scientific" atheism that looms today as the successor, far more dangerous than they, of yesterday's critical or agnostic atheism, does not owe its basic inspiration to science. It springs, as Maritain and others have pointed out, from an obscure, passionate, subrational resentment against God, to Whom man refuses forgiveness for the fact of evil in the world; it springs, too, from a resentment against Christianity, whose followers have faltered so badly in the war they should have waged against injustice and the frustration of human freedom.

This said, one must still agree with Professor Stace that science has in fact, though not of necessity, had much to do with the creation of the "darkness," the "stark and bleak" world, with which modern man feels himself confronted. If one accepts, say, as phenomenologically correct,

Comte's division of the ages of the world into the theological, the metaphysical, and the positive, one must realize that each age has had its special temptation. The temptation of the theological age, in an era of highly simple, agrarian culture, was to superstition—an irrational worship of the unknown in nature, and an ignorant identification of it with the divine. The temptation of the metaphysical age, as it ran out in the eighteenth century era of surging social revolution, was to rationalism—an irrational worship of reason as capable of destroying forever the concept of the unknown, the mysterious, the divine. The proper temptation of our positive, scientific age, in an era of industrial, urban, mass civilization, has been to skepticism—a disinclination to worship anything at all, a disposition to stand before the unknown neither in awe nor in anger but in total disinterest.

This skepticism doubtless is the result of sheer materialism—the immersion of the human spirit in matter unto the "loss" of itself and its power to perceive the realities of the spiritual world. But it is also in part the obverse of that illusion of total knowledge that science has tended to create. So knowing has man become, that in strange, paradoxical fashion he has managed to lose contact with the fundamental thing in him that knows—his own spiritual, intelligent soul. He has learned so much about the realities that he can measure and transform into mathematical equations, that he has lost sight of the world whose higher realities measure him. And he has so deepened his knowledge of the nature that he has in common with the animal, that he has tragically cut himself off from contact with that "high point of the soul" wherein he is most himself, a human person. He has come to suffer an hypertrophy of one part of his reason—the part that guides his hand and the tools it fashions, the part that deals with the fugitive realities of matter, space, and time. And in consequence of an old, mysterious law that somehow dictates that the discovery of new values should at least for a time bring about the depreciation of older ones, man has strangely come loose from the part of himself whereby he inhabits the invisible kingdom of the spirit, that escapes the contingencies of matter, space, and time.

"Western man," says Gabriel Marcel, the Christian existentialist, "behaves officially more and more as if what I have called the higher soul were a survival, a useless relic of a fossilized species." For this higher soul science has no use. It cannot be the object of science because it is its subject; and it cannot be the tool of science because its proper search is for the essence of things, their "form," and their finality; and for essences and finalities science has no concern. Therefore this higher soul has been left to atrophy, and the result has been the mutilation of man, a life "hollow at the center," a loss of ultimate purpose, a despairing involvement in the purposelessness of a material world upon which man was destined to stamp his own purposes. Originally, under the intoxication of the "Cartesian dream," man took the sword of science to slay with it his material enemies and make himself "master and owner of the forces of nature"; actually, it seems that with it he has simply slit his own intellectual throat, and now he must either offer himself in meaningless enslavement to the ultimate irrationality of everything, or else stand helpless, head in hands, waiting for some repetition of the miracle of St. Denis of Paris, that will enable him to walk, headless, to some possibly human goal.

In saying all this, I am not for one moment decrying science or any of its works. By all means let it be Prometheus, to light fires on the earth; the God of Abraham, the Father of our Lord Jesus Christ, does not begrudge man fire or other creations of His human genius. On the contrary, He, the Creator and Lord of Creation, has made man in His own image, that man may be himself a creator and a lord of creation. I believe, with Paul Claudel, that "Nature must hear in the depths of her being the orders we bring her in the name of God"; and I know that it is by the techniques of science that those orders are issued, commanding that nature be harnessed to the purposes of man and made to serve his dignity. All that is understood. What troubles me, as it troubles Professor Stace, is that on his account (which experiences of my own have verified) science has not proved to be Prometheus, bringing light and warmth to the life of man. Its legacy has been darkness, the death of the spirit in that which is highest in it, and a stark, bleak world in which man wanders with futile steps to a destiny that is nothingness. Professor Stace has the intelligence to dismiss the complacency of the Russells and the Deweys with the remark: "It is not likely that science, which is basically the cause of our spiritual troubles, is likely also to produce the cure for them." I agree, with the reservation that science is not basically the cause of our spiritual troubles, and therefore all the more cannot be the cure for them.

This whole situation, thus inadequately described, is highly significant for the problem of the goals of education. Initially, I suppose, it raises the question of the suppositions of education. Is one antecedently to consent to such a domination of the human mind by science as will result in a concept of the material world as purposeless and in a concept of man as so continuous with matter that his life is likewise purposeless? Is one to agree that the sole "truth" accessible to man is the "truth" of the quantitative relations between entities (whose nature and finality remain unknowable), that is the quest of science? Is there no other rational technique for reaching reality than scientific method?[b] Must one deny that there is a power inherent in intelligence to perceive metaphysical truth and falsity, moral value and unvalue, by an intellectual intuition that may indeed lack the hard clarity of insight into a mathematical equation but that possesses nonetheless an absolute certainty? According to one's answers to these questions, one will have a set of assumptions on which to predicate the educational process. And since the questions are so widely propounded, it will at least be well to be clear about the answers before one enters a classroom.

In regard of the goals of education, the problem about reduces itself to this: are we to educate men to live in darkness, or to find the light? Professor Stace takes the former alternative. His position seems to be that "honesty" demands that man relinquish "the Great Illusion," God as existent, and as the end of man, and as actively willing the subordination of the forces and processes of nature to both the temporal and the transcendent end of man. Professor Stace further maintains that it is possible for "very highly educated" men "to live moral lives without religious convictions," as it is possible for the cultured intelligence to provide "a genuine secular basis for morals to replace the religious basis which has disappeared." On this new basis human ideals are possible of conception and even of achievement. The ultimate goal of education therefore will be to coax men out of their childish illusions, turn them aside from being "sham civilized beings" (*i.e.,* men who live out of a sense of religious sanction for human and moral obligations), and form them into "genuinely civilized beings," who will live "decent lives" in a sense beyond the dreams of Pelagius. Be good, Pelagius said, because goodness is possible to the inherent resources of human intelligence and will. Be decent, say his successors, even in spite of the fact that the scientific intelligence assures you of what Pelagius denied, that a decent life is ultimately as futile and meaningless as an indecent one; for both end in ashes.

[b] [Cf. Chapter VIII by Alain L. Locke, for a proposed revision of scientific method to enable it to deal with areas where it has formerly been inapplicable.]

This may be an extreme statement of the matter; but I think one should be grateful to Doctor Stace for having given such an extreme statement. It clarifies the issues that are often obscured in less forthright presentations. In one or other form and in varying degrees of dilution the same philosophy of life (and therefore of education) is very widely held today. Professor Stace's prime merit lies in his exposition of the frank dogmatism of the view. He makes it clear that we have here to do not with a reasoned view, but with an "imaginative picture" of the world of man, that has been precipitated out of a climate of opinion and got itself unthinkingly accepted. In other words, he has called attention, perhaps unwittingly, to what is really "the Great Illusion" of our times —the illusion that the life of man is purposeless, or, if it have a purpose, that that purpose is consummated in time, and has no transcendent reference. Having no more use for illusions than Professor Stace, I suggest that a cardinal task of education is to turn all the forces of the critical intelligence (understanding intelligence in its full scope, and including all the forms of intellectual critique) upon that Great Illusion, than which no more hollow one has ever clouded and crippled the spirit of man.

The scrutiny of this illusion must also lead to the analysis of the climate of opinion which generated it; there is a task of intellectual history here to be done. Professor Stace speaks of science having operated "the greatest revolution in human history"; well, we have had enough of experience to know that revolutions always destroy too much, and never, until counter-revolution sets in, achieve a just balance of values. I suggest then that it is time for the counter-revolution. By a curious inversion modern philosophy, as influenced by modern science, has become as false as was medieval science, as influenced by medieval philosophy. E. I. Watkin has said: "It is hardly an exaggeration to say that the medieval Catholic and the modern secularist keep a different eye open on the world. Where one sees, the other is blind; where one is blind, the other sees." The difference, I should add, is that the medieval eye, in that era of world history, had not yet been opened; but the modern eye has deliberately shut itself. The need today is that both eyes be opened, each to gaze clearly and unafraid at all there is to see, each knowing at once the scope and the limits of its field of vision—the scientific eye seeing the totality of observable or conceivable relationships between the quantities of matter or energy that fall under its scrutiny; and the eye of reflective intelligence, aware of all that science sees, seeing in turn, to what depth it may, into the natures of things, their ends, their order, their character of "vestige" or "image" of the Supreme Reality, God, the origin and ground of truth.

It is the fashion to ridicule the metaphysicians of Galileo's day because they insisted on solving the problem of the movement of the heavenly bodies by pondering on abstractions in their chambers, and would not go out under the sky to look through Galileo's telescope. Far more ridiculous today are the scientists (fortunately relatively few, but highly vocal) who insist on solving the problem of man's purpose in life by bending over benches in a laboratory, and refuse to retire into the chambers of their own souls, there to open themselves, under abnegation of the narrowness of view that is legitimate for a scientist but not for a man, to that flash of awareness of what it *is* to be a *man* that must by a primal law of humanity force itself with all the power of primitive, inescapable truth upon the intelligence that humbly, courageously unveils its native eyes.

This fact—what a man *is*—is not one fully to be explored by scientific method, which necessarily pauses on the periphery of things; but it is for all that a fact that needs to be explored, and there are methods of reaching it. They are the methods of philosophical reflection, brought to bear on the full data of experience, and purified for its work both by the moral discipline that strengthens the spirit to accept the consequences of what it sees, and by the intellectual asceticism that prepares the spirit to see all there is to be seen. Here perhaps is something of a goal for education; I should call it the cultivation of a genuine intellectualism. It is a broader, higher, more human thing than a myopic scientism or an equally myopic rationalism; and it is certainly a more respectable thing than a compromising attempt to rescue "values" by appeal to sentiment in support of a sagging intelligence.

I should not, of course, maintain that this true intellectualism is education's highest goal, any more than it is a total solution to the problem of human life. I should make only the more modest assertion that apart from this intellectualism, as a habit of mind, one will not and cannot even see what the problem of life is. In that sense at least it is a goal of education; for surely, if it be too much to ask that education should solve the problem of life, it is not too much to ask that it help one to see what the problem is.

CHAPTER VII

Education and Politics: The Problem of Responsibility

By CHARLES W. HENDEL

Professor of Moral Philosophy and Metaphysics, Yale University

I

"This nation hath extreme need . . . —of a better education . . ."
Milton, *Letter on Education*, 1644.

FOR VARIOUS REASONS there is an increasing concern about education in our country. As we now look back on the past war we are more than ever appalled at what happened to the minds of civilized nations like ourselves that induced them to conduct war in ways inhuman beyond belief. A few in our own country fell to thinking of our enemies as inherently evil and beyond the pale of humanity but such notions, born of a mood of hate, have yielded to the more intelligent judgment that the fault was really in the education of those people. Further reflection has made us wonder whether such opinions in our own ranks about other nations is not evidence of that deepseated fault in our own minds which we call national or racial prejudice. We cannot help asking, then, if we ourselves have a firm enough foundation in morality.

There is an increasing social conscience, too, about every sort of discrimination. This is a matter of the fundamental ethics of our democracy. So deep and strong have the convictions become in this regard that immediate action is now demanded on behalf of the rights of man in American democracy. The first thought has been that this equality of right can be secured and enforced by law. But serious objection is often made that such recourse to the power of the State means imposing a standard of moral behavior which ought to develop naturally in the hearts of men. When those who argue thus do sincerely believe in equal rights, they offer education as their solution. And the more they stress the value of education as a cure for social prejudice the greater becomes our obligation to extend its benefits to all persons without exception.[1]

This public feeling about prejudice and discrimination results in a view of education as essentially an instrument of social policy, a means for achieving a finer sort of democracy than we have heretofore known.

A further purpose occupies those whose vision extends to the larger community beyond the nation. Considerable discouragement has come over us since the first days of hope at the signing of the charter and the launching of the United Nations. The differences between those pledged to democratic methods and others who follow authoritarian methods have so far proved too great to permit of any common procedure to which all parties will faithfully adhere so that some common law will govern the conduct of all alike in international relations. Of course, when the United Nations was started, it was understood that any such institution cannot work without an actual universal allegiance which in turn must depend upon all the peoples' understanding and appreciation of the cause of peace. Hence UNESCO was set up within the organization to help bring about a universal education in world-community. But this agency itself has shared in the initial weakness of the United Nations. People generally have little conviction about it. Moreover, it is something very new in history for the people of a State to learn to be more than patriotic. Now those in our own country who see the imperative need of an education for the international community place their immediate hopes in what we ourselves can do to develop the understanding and the attitude necessary for world peace.

In the past the morality we have here been considering has been nurtured by religion, which sustained the belief in the spiritual worth of the individual person and taught the duty of man to his fellow and to the universal fellowship of man. The ideal of equal personal rights sprang, in part certainly, from the religious conception of man and life.

---

[1]This is the spirit of the Report of the President's Commission on Higher Education, presented December 11, 1947, and published as *Higher Education for American Democracy*, Harper and Brothers, New York, 1948. See especially the individual reports therein entitled: I, "Establishing the Goals"; and II, "Equalizing and Expanding Individual Opportunity."

[For further discussion of the report of the President's Commission, see Chapter I by Robert Ulich (including comment by Rowland W. Dunham), Louis J. A. Mercier's comment on Chapter II by Lyman Bryson, Chapter IV by Karl W. Deutsch, Chapter XIII by Mordecai M. Kaplan, Chapter XVII by Ordway Tead.]

Education and Politics: The Problem of Responsibility

Those who value religion solely for its support of these moral, social, and political aspirations of men join today with others who call for a secular education in a truly "common faith," which means, to them, faith in democracy, and they urge it with a religious fervor. They believe education should serve as the handmaid to our democratic faith.

But more than faith is now being demanded—nothing less than unqualified loyalty to American democracy. The insecurity and fear which beset us, along with the other nations of the civilized world, have produced a spiritual malaise and inner conflict. While we seek constructively to promote trade, recovery, and better understanding, at least in Europe, we are busy preparing for a possible conflict which could rend and destroy much of what remains as civilization. It is hard to live with such opposite purposes in mind, with efforts for peace and warfare at the same time. There appears to be no way of changing the policy of those who hold to communism. Our proper role seems to be to stand firm against any assault on the independence of the other peaceful nations. Yet there is always the fear that despite the clear showing of our position, some reckless step might be taken which will precipitate war. We may hope to keep cool and to see that our own foreign policy shall not be either provocative or misleading. But such self-restraint is very difficult, for the emotions clamor for action: "We must do something." And now one outlet has been found through which the full charge of the present emotional tension is being vented. There is the enemy within, the communist and the near-communist, and the alleged or suspected communist. The apprehension of danger so close at hand has absorbed into itself the fears and frustrations over the *external* situation. Here, at least, men think, is something for us to do: to stamp out obvious treason and to oust from all places of office or influence anyone whose activities are believed to be subversive of American democracy and to require of everyone an outright, unquestioning, all-American faith. The first recourse has been to try to secure this loyalty by act of law. But by tradition, and especially through their experience of prohibition, Americans know that laws cannot control opinion and belief. So there must be another sort of recourse—education—which will receive the mandate to instil loyalty in all the youth of the land.

Everything focuses on a moral education. We want to see men treat each other as equals, that is, as persons who have equal rights to life, liberty, and the pursuit of happiness. Keenly conscious of the extent to which this democratic principle is violated, we look to education as the cure for the habits of prejudice on grounds that have nothing to do with the inherent worth of other persons or with their real usefulness in society. We need to understand the actual interdependence of men in any community, large or small. The same mutual dependence and respect for common rights is necessary for a peaceful world.

Yet our thoughts are not wholly on peace but on war, too, and this seriously affects our conception of the purposes of education. We see embattled democracy in conflict with aggressive communism and we marshal our resources and our weapons. Education is expected to contribute to our strength by producing a firm, unshakable democratic faith and a loyalty to America.

In 1945, before the war was over, some American soldiers spoke their minds on American education. They were men fresh from combat service after several years of duty in the United States Army. They were very thoughtful observers of the war in which they had taken an important part. They were also concerned about the peace they hoped for ahead. At the moment they were enjoying a few weeks of study, away from their units, at the Shrivenham American Army University in England. They took a very serious view of the future. In a discussion of some problem of philosophy, these men turned aside from the immediate subject and volunteered some remarks about their own education. Among their remarks was the following: "We have not been taught principles and so we have not been responsible in combat and in the other things we did afterwards. . . . The worst thing about war is the loss of personal responsibility."[2]

These were prophetic words. They revealed a deep, philosophic insight into essentials. For most of the faults and positive evils in society today, which education is now being called upon to set right are due to moral failure or inadequacy in man. There is something wrong in the attitude of man to man and of men toward the State, the community, and the wider society of the world. There is a defect in the prevailing ideas about conduct. Somehow, in the complex circumstances of life, the caring about what happens to others is lost in the shuffle. The phrase used by those soldiers, "personal responsibility," has since then come into constant use today. We hear many comments about the absence of

[2] Quoted from *Civilization and Religion*, by Charles W. Hendel, Yale University Press, New Haven, 1948, pp. 4, 23.

Education and Politics: The Problem of Responsibility

good workmanship or honest service—it is, people say, due to lack of responsibility. It is the same fault we see when individuals, social groups, nations, violate or disregard their own solemn agreements with others or their recognized moral obligations. We are concerned about evidences of irresponsibility of that sort in any quarter, in the citizen or in the workshop or in the officers of our government.

The idea of responsibility contains the essence of morality. There is the idea of duty in it, namely, that which one person owes to others, and at the same time it means that the mature individual has the right to make his own decision as to what his duty is. This reveals that responsibility is linked in our thought with the idea of man's personal freedom.

II. *Lessons from Experience*

"All other men take pains to get previous knowledge of the profession to which they belong." Erasmus: *The Education of a Christian Prince.*

The peoples of modern Europe have had for centuries to live through wars as catastrophic and threatening to the values of human life as the two wars have been in our time. They had to rebuild a peaceful order again and again. They were concerned, likewise, about loyalty, faith, the preservation of a civilized way of life, and peace. We may profit by their previous experience.

At the beginning of what we recognize as the modern, European civilization,[a] when men of learning were inspired by the discoveries they were making in the arts and the knowledge of ancient culture and civilizations, Erasmus, one of that enthusiastic company of humanists, published his *Education of a Christian Prince* (1516). Europe was about to be engaged in a religious conflict which would divide the peoples of civilization into two warring camps. A native of Holland, he thought and wrote as a good European and a tolerant Christian. Fearing a breakdown of the whole social order of Christendom, he worked all his life for peace. His aim was to introduce more of a spirit of broad and rational humanity into public affairs. He tried his influence personally with the various princes and with the Pope, in the hope of averting the wars that

[a] [Cf. the discussion of medieval and Renaissance education in Chapter I by Robert Ulich, Chapter V by Scott Buchanan, Chapter IX by Howard Mumford Jones, Chapter XII by Louis J. A. Mercier.]

actually ensued in spite of such efforts. His book was intended to be salutary instruction for everyone who exercised political authority, all princes of Church or of State, all supposed to be truly Christian princes.

Actually another kind of counsel to princes quite opposite to that of the humane Erasmus then held the field. Many were the voices heard in Europe repeating the maxim of Machiavelli's *Prince*—the prudent ruler must learn to be "half beast, half man." It was cunningly insinuated that the Machiavellian politics was only necessary of course for the sheer survival of the nation itself and that the national end justified the immoral means. But this politics in practice was in exact accordance with the pattern of Thrasymachus in the *Republic* of Plato, where everything ministers to the interest of the princely power, really regardless of the private interests of the subjects. Perhaps toward the ruled the ruler could afford to be "half man"; and thus win them to identify his whole policy with their own good; but toward the foreign people and princes certainly the ruler should be the "half beast." Erasmus himself could be as "realistic," too, with respect to the actual course of events resulting from such politics.

> "Now . . . every Englishman hates a Frenchman, and every Frenchman hates the Englishman, for no other reason than that he is English. The Scot, only because he is a Scot, hates the Briton; the Italian hates the German, the Suabian, the Swiss, and so on for the rest, region hates region and city city. Why," Erasmus appealed, "are we divided by these stupid names, rather than bound together by the common name of Christ?"[3]

But it would not suffice merely to invoke the name of Christ. All parties called upon Him even as they went to do battle. It was His Gospel that they failed to appreciate. They had too little conscience about it, once the traditional moral authority of the Church was thrown off. So it had to be through the minds of men, Erasmus thought, that the pacification of Europe would have to take place. There was indeed some relevant "previous knowledge" about man and his life in society that needed to be recalled or learned anew by the men of that day. They had to regain the classical and Christian wisdom concerning human values.

---

[3] Erasmus, *Institutio Principis Christiani*, translated by Percy Ellwood Corbett, the Grotius Society Publications, No. 1, 1921, reprinted by the Peace Book Company, *Peace Classics*, 1, London, 1939. I have modernized some of the proper names in the passage quoted.

Education and Politics: The Problem of Responsibility

One particular lesson was needed, one that had been taught of old by Socrates and Plato among the Greeks, as well as by the inspired prophets and saints of the ancient Scriptures: wherever political power resides, there must also be a moral responsibility, for otherwise the sovereignty of man will not work for the common good but always for evil. This was what men should learn for themselves by fresh study of the Greek and Roman sources and those of the Christian doctrine. And the scholarship of the time was providing more accurate versions of the old books, and interpretations and translations, so that the saving message for humanity and peace could be known more widely. This was an essential goal of sixteenth century humanistic education.

The Education of Men of Affairs

We are not concerned, in this retrospect of the past, with universities or schools of learning but with a few typical leaders of thought who contributed to the education of the modern age. Education in this broad sense is not an affair of the young exclusively; learning was sought for by grown men, as they lived and moved in the world of affairs. It was in their work that they had their individual power to do good or evil. The "moral philosophy" of the new learning was addressed to them.

In this aspect Hugo Grotius can be taken as another example of the humanistic "profession." He, too, happened to come from Holland, like Erasmus. He was likewise greatly concerned about war. The particular war that troubled Europe was that of the Austrian Succession and it was in reality a struggle for title to the Empire. The imperial authority, however, was fast becoming weaker as the military power of those independent sovereigns of the different nation-states of Europe grew stronger. Grotius's aim at this juncture seems to have been to preserve the Christian European civilization against a total disintegration. The policy would be to make the new princely power of the independent States a *de jure* sovereignty, and therefore, a responsible authority, instead of leaving the power perfectly free and unlimited, or rather, limited solely by the measure of military success of the prince and by his ability afterwards to administer the territory gained by force of conquest. This policy had an internal as well as an external application. The right to govern a people, according to this theory, comes only from a contract which invests the power in the sovereign for the sake of the benefits of law, order, and peace which he can vouchsafe to the people. The sovereign thus has his obligations to the people and they have their natural rights. Further, there are laws ascertainable by reason which should govern the conduct of all nations and sovereigns alike—these laws are "of perpetual obligation" and must be observed in war even as in peace. Thus alone can civilization be preserved through a period of armed conflict between nations. These natural laws or laws of the nations are nothing less than the universal conditions for any enduring human society whatsoever. They are absolute principles of right and under them men are entitled to their natural rights which ought to be respected by their governments that possess only the particular right to govern. These were the teachings of the book, *The Rights of War and Peace* (1625). Not content with publishing this work, Grotius added a complementary treatise on the Christian religion in which, without reliance upon any doctrine of special revelation, he established common tenets of the Christian creed, in the belief and hope that if others were persuaded by such rational thinking about the common faith, the wounds in Christendom might be healed. Enlightened piety would surely help bring about a disposition in sovereigns to compose their national and religious disputes. It would strengthen their moral obligation to abide by the universal principles of right which were demonstrated in the other book on politics.

The teaching of Grotius was another version for his time of the basic moral philosophy of civilization which Erasmus had recalled a century earlier: where power resides, there must be an obligation to both man and God. And Grotius the humanist hoped, too, that sovereigns could be convinced by reason, which so clearly showed the necessity of those universal laws of right which were the laws of nature and God. While his *Rights of War and Peace* was dedicated to Louis XIII of France, Grotius sought actually to reach a wider circle of men than Erasmus who addressed himself chiefly to the princes themselves, for the leaven of modern learning had been doing its work and men of parts were to be found everywhere who could read and receive the instruction of such books. These scholars might some time become the counsellors of the kings who had to know about the political order and its true economy. There were merchant princes in that world, the entrepreneurs who understood something of the conditions of peace necessary for thriving commerce. For this growingly powerful class of men who in fact shared with monarchs in the exercise of the great increasing power of the new modern State, Grotius's work constituted a higher education of the duties of men of affairs.

Nothing has been said of the moral education of the people. That was not yet a matter of great concern. The "common man" talked of in our time was not yet a problem in those circumstances. The peasant or laborer, "the small man," needed no new instruction—his duties were still taught him by his religion and by his very occupational status in the social order. His work in society called for certain virtues and his station itself prescribed what he should do on all occasions. Besides his powers to do good or evil were limited. But it was where such limitation was not the case, where political power claimed to know no higher law beyond the will of the sovereign, it was there that the humanistic thinkers who were so concerned for the future of civilization focused their efforts and attention—those who have such superior power or advantage must learn to act as persons responsible both to man and to God.

The Education for a New Commonwealth

Grotius hoped that the effect of his doctrine concerning sovereignty and law would be to avert internal civil wars, as well as wars between the nations. That depended somewhat, however, on what the sovereigns actually believed about their power. They might solemnly avow their responsibility to God but roundly reject any accountability to man, especially if that were thought of as the lawful consequence of a contract between people and king. If the king held that his power came solely by divine right, nothing could be allowed to stand between the king's own conscience and his God. The people had no right to question their prince before any tribunal; he was judged only in Heaven. They were wrong to imagine, too, that they should have any part in the making of the laws by which they were governed.

Such was the high doctrine of the Stuart kings of England. But the tradition of English liberty was strong and Parliament was an instrument through which the people's rights could be asserted. Thus within two decades after Grotius's book came out England witnessed a civil war. It was a revolution that cast out the claim to absolute sovereignty. The king himself became a prisoner of the army. But this event was no old story being repeated of a military overthrow managed by rival princes or captains. The victory was that of a new model army, an army drawn from and representing the English people. Political power was now in new hands—indeed, for a time it was not certain where authority was really lodged, in the Parliament or in the army. However that might be, the State was to be a new Commonwealth, a community in which the people should count in the sense not only that their good was the object of their government, but also that they must be governed by their own laws. It was "a noble and puissant nation rousing herself," in Milton's eloquent words.

How would the power be used? The Revolution enlisted vigorous minds and pens in the cause. They found many problems of statesmanship: how was the commonwealth to be constituted and how were the people to be represented in their government so that they could secure their rights and liberties? Among them was John Milton, poet, puritan, and humanist. He recounted years later, in his *Second Defense of the English People* (1654), that he paid a visit to Grotius, "whose acquaintance I anxiously desired," then in France serving as Ambassador from Sweden, who "gave me letters to the English merchants on my route (to Italy) that they might show me any civilities in their power."[4] Milton's visit to Grotius is interesting evidence of the esteem in which that author of the *Laws of War and Peace* was held by the generation who were fighting the doctrine of the "divine right" of kings with the philosophy of "natural right" derived from the laws of nature and God. But Milton went on to tell that after a few months living in Italy he was about to go across to Sicily and Greece when the "melancholy intelligence I received of the civil commotion in England made me alter my purpose; for I thought it base to be traveling for amusement abroad, while my fellow-citizens were fighting for liberty at home."[5] At first, he said, he hoped merely to look on, trusting in "the wise conduct of Providence" and "the courage of the people." But he perceived that "a way was opening for the establishment of real liberty . . . that the principles of religion, which were the first objects of our case, would exert a salutary influence on the manners and constitution of the republic . . . and I perceived that if I ever wished to be of use, I ought at least not to

---

[4] Quoted from *Areopagitica and Other Tracts,* edited by C. E. Vaughan, Temple Classics, J. M. Dent and Sons, Ltd., London, 1907, p. 94. (The translation from Latin is by Robert Fellowes.)

[5] *Ibid.,* p. 95.

be wanting to my country, to the church, and to so many of my fellow-Christians, in a crisis of so much danger. I therefore determined to relinquish the other pursuits in which I was engaged, and to transfer the whole force of my talents and my industry to this one important object."

Thus Milton embarked on his work for the new commonwealth. His attention was focused on the "principles" which would "exert a salutary influence" on the morals and politics of the new republic. It was especially in this connection, Milton explained, that he had "discussed the principles of education . . . than which nothing can be more necessary to principle the minds of men in virtue, the only genuine source of political and individual liberty, the only true safeguard of states, the bulwark of their prosperity and renown."[6]

That short treatise on education took the form of a letter to Samuel Hartlib, a German Pole residing in England, another humanist full of ideas about reform. In his letter Milton divulged to this colleague his own ideas on the reforming of education which should help "both to the enlargement of truth and honest living with much more peace," . . . "for this nation hath extreme need" of "a better education in extent and comprehension far more large and yet of time far shorter, and of attainment far more certain than hath been yet in practice."[7] Milton's discourse, though "short" and "summary," was nevertheless the outcome, he declared, of a laborious "search of religious and civil knowledge."[8]

"The end, then, of learning is, to repair the ruins of our first parents by regaining to know God aright, and out of that knowledge to love him, to imitate him, to be like him, as we may the nearest." Here is the needed religious knowledge.

And, further, "seeing every nation affords not experience and tradition enough for all kinds of learning, therefore we are chiefly taught the languages of those people who have at any time been most industrious after wisdom; so that language is but the instrument conveying to us things useful to be known." That passage is reminiscent of St. Paul's: "the Greeks search after wisdom" (I Cor. I, 22).

It seems as if such education was only backward looking. Back to the pure teaching of religion and to the wisdom of ancient Greece and

[6] *Ibid.*, pp. 99–100.
[7] *Ibid.*, p. 73.
[8] *Ibid.*, p. 74.

Rome. But Milton went on to show the meaning of his declaration that words are but "instruments," for he attacked the absorption with Latin and Greek languages as such. He was "progressive" enough in his own time. He had gone traveling to learn from the "experience and tradition" of modern peoples in science and politics, as well as in literature. He visited Galileo in Italy and the men of letters and, as we have seen, Grotius, the modern writer on war and peace. He was alive to the needs of contemporary England and Europe and it is in reference to the situation at that time that we should interpret the following statement about the proper end of education: "I call, therefore, a complete and generous education, that which befits a man to perform justly, skilfully, and magnanimously, all the offices, both private and public, of peace and war."

The term "offices" is reminiscent of Cicero the moralist with his *De officiis*. Milton was speaking about the duties and responsibilities of a man in peace and war. But why in war? Is there a different morality in war from that in peace? One who conferred with a Grotius could only believe that there is one moral order whose laws are of "perpetual obligation," binding at all times. Such a belief alone would be in the Platonic tradition that essential virtue is really one and undivided. But if this be the meaning, why mention war at all? It is not so strange if we recall the kind of performance Milton wanted to see in men at such a time, "justly, skilfully, magnanimously." For a war is precisely the situation in which the virtue of a people is tested.

A test case was at hand at the very time of writing. The Parliament of the English people on gaining the upper hand in the struggle with the king, entertained a proposal to continue the objectionable royal practice of censorship and control of printing. It is natural, and perhaps almost unavoidable, for the victors in a revolution to try to safeguard the cause as well as their own new won power, by not letting the disorder in the State progress farther in the name of liberty, and thus they will use the very coercion they rebelled against. In the present case the Parliament would be using its power to stifle liberty of thought. These were "the liberties and freedom" the English people were fighting for, and it ill behooved their government and their representatives in it to act so inconsistently with the principle of their revolution. The liberty of speech and writing, though it might make difficult the keeping of order, was to them an essential good. So Milton spoke out in his *Areopagitica* which was published the same year (1644) as his *Letter on Education*.

Education and Politics: The Problem of Responsibility

And Milton himself, when telling the story later in his *Second Defense of the English People,* connected this work on political and religious liberty with that short treatise on education. Both were works of education. The *Areopagitica* was virtually a book of instruction for Christian parliamentarians in the same way that Erasmus's book had been instruction for a Christian prince. In this period of history, as in the earlier time, the actual holders of political power needed an education in moral principle and responsibility.

The Education of a Revolutionary Army

Three years after Milton's public advice to Parliament on liberty of thought and discussion, the men of the army were engaged in numerous debates over the fundamental problems of government in their new civil and religious order. They had formed a Council of the Army to which in English fashion the various regiments sent representatives. An Agreement of the People had been drawn up, a proposed basis for peace. They desired a voice in the "settlement of the kingdom" and particularly in what was to be done about the royal prerogative, the authority of Parliament, and parliamentary representation. On the last question issues developed over the property qualification for suffrage. But the debates as a whole revolved around the liberties and rights of a nation of free men.

There is a verbatim record of their meetings at Putney in 1647 and at Whitehall in 1648. In these papers are heard again the fresh and extemporaneous speeches of men who were deeply concerned for the future of their nation. They discussed fundamental political issues, on which they found themselves divided, with earnestness and a remarkable sense of responsibility which has since been regarded as a characteristic mark of the Puritan.

They had struggled together for their liberties. Everyone who had served in that revolutionary army had a life of his own to lead, the poorest as well as the richest, and many of them had been impoverished precisely because they had risked all their estates for the cause, and they demanded equality of moral right to representation in the government along with those who owned property. Thus they argued about political right and privilege, authority and liberty. Some employed the abstract, philosophical terms of natural law and right, calling on Grotius to be witness, as it were, for their case, but most of them used the language and the imagery of a higher witness, the Scripture and word of God, for these men of that army were versed in their Bible. The old events told in the Holy Writ were living occurrences to them and were relived again in their own time. They believed in the idea of a covenant with God. They envisaged themselves as a nation living and obliged to act under the scrutiny of God and His supreme law. Throughout their discussion they spoke as men of deep spiritual conviction. Often very plain men or small holders of no consequence would deliver their views courageously and frankly in the presence of their superiors in authority, and with confidence, too, quoting their authority of Scripture. And when some became too hot and belligerent in argument, the others would remind them of their duty of Christian charity and patience with each other and their submission to the will of God. They acknowledged a spiritual law of righteousness common to them as well as the law of their traditional English liberties. Though they frequently reached an impasse in debate they came out of it time and time again, humbling themselves before their Supreme Judge, and in a chastised spirit seeking to reach agreement. They formed a genuine community with common principles and convictions. They practiced self-discipline among themselves. They were men responsible to each other and to God. It was a good augury of things to come in the commonwealth which they were here seeking to inaugurate.

Yet their virtue was not complete or fine enough. The power of the English nation was really lodged in that army. Their power came not from their having arms but from their being representative of the whole nation. Yet Parliament was strictly the sole and legal representative of the people. Hence there was continual friction in the relations between the two powers, Parliament and the army. In dealing with Parliament they did not show the forbearance they had learned in their own debates on politics. Parliament was like an external body. They were not thinking in the same terms and they were not together in purpose. Their arguments were often like the dealings of alien powers. They could not get together in their plans for the kingdom or commonwealth. The conservative interests of commerce, finance, property, and privilege, centralized in the City of London, where Parliament met, stood opposed to the broad claims for liberty and equality. The army became impatient at the

Education and Politics: The Problem of Responsibility 177

delays and alleged stalling. And it enjoyed considerable popular support and knew that it could enforce its will by arms. It was actually proposed, then, that without further parley they should march on London and force the decisions they believed right for the settlement.

Then Cromwell and his lieutenant Ireton were obliged to argue mightily against the motion and dissuade them from such violent action, as being quite irresponsible: their original rebellion as an army against the royal command had been lawful enough because it had been authorized by their own Parliament, which, according to their own ancient laws and precedents, possessed some share in the government, because the laws were made there, but if they now marched against Parliament itself and made that body bend to their will, they would take away the only remaining vestige of lawful government in the commonwealth. Of course they had the power to act, but they ought not to use it in that way. Their force could never make whatever they would do right and they would only perpetuate disorder. There must be an order of common law in their liberty, by which all parties should be bound. Thus this revolutionary army received its necessary instruction in responsibility.

Cromwell himself transgressed later in his own subsequent dealings with Parliament. The inauguration of the new English commonwealth came with the drastic act of beheading the king of England. The story is a commentary on Milton's earlier words, "Our nation hath extreme need of a better education," more complete and generous, to the end of obtaining magnanimous and responsible conduct in all the duties of life.

It is a familiar story, how the impetus of that Puritan revolution and its political, moral, and religious convictions traveled across the Atlantic to the new world. Men sought to establish in a New England the free commonwealth which had failed of establishment in the Old England. They solemnly made their covenant with each other and God. They intended that their community should be reared always under the law of their relation with God. Churches raised their spires in every village and town. Their town meetings were to be those of free holders and responsible citizens. The political form of their society was to be of the type in which such free men or their representatives in assembly would have a voice and power in all matters concerning the general welfare. Those colonial commonwealths ultimately united to form our American federal republic.

III. Moral Education and Education in Freedom

Before turning at once to the problem of responsibility as it exists now in American civilization, we should look once more at those three scenes of the past. The moral so far has been this—an education for personal responsibility is necessary to the progress, and even the survival, of civilization. Yet this is not the whole of the lesson. We have not noted all that actually happened on those previous occasions. What we have finally to take into our reckoning is the manner in which those men performed their part in carrying on the moral tradition. The spirit of their *example* is even more important and instructive than the contents of the tradition itself. We learn more from the men themselves, in short, than from their books, records, doctrines, all their works.

Erasmus, Grotius, and Milton were alive to critical problems of their time and were vigorously seeking to use the wisdom of the past to help in charting the present course of life. They believed in the saving *power of mind*. They worked intelligently and resolutely for a proper education of man in decent, civilized, humane living. The ideas which they learned from ancient culture and from their own religious tradition were appreciated as directly relevant to their own circumstances. They found them to be useful and consequently held that there were real principles by means of which human relationships and conduct ought always to be governed.

Such principles were nothing less than the natural law of human existence. Any attempt to override that supreme law is foolish because it disregards nature and attempts to order human affairs in ways that must necessarily fail and bring ruin upon the whole society. This was the typical folly of rulers and all who have sovereignty or any power that claims to have no limits. Such proud men need the knowledge of that law above men. And such knowledge of moral principle surely must put the man himself into virtue, so that he will act with regard to the true good of himself and others. Socrates had long ago proposed the question: Does not knowledge of itself constitute virtue? But these early teachers of the modern world were already so convinced of its truth in their examination of the life of their own day, that they spent no time in further questioning. Their own purpose was quite clear: it was to provide for a moral education through the mind of the individual man.

Consider the effect of their own education, in these three particular examples. Far more than the meaning of Latin, Greek, and Hebrew words and letters passed into their experience. They did not copy; they used, they created, they acted. They made modern literature. They transmitted an inspiring vision of the vocation of man. No one could read the literature of antiquity without encountering that original figure of Socrates at almost every turn. It was a daring Socrates, too, who had proposed the boldest and most paradoxical ideas. The one proposal that he himself pretended to find most shocking was reported by Plato, that there could really be no safety nor good for man in any State unless philosophers were the kings, or, what is more possible in practice, unless men who had the knowledge of true principle would at least be associated with kings. Each of these moderns had been caught by that vision of the philosopher which made them emulate him. Erasmus went to see the Pope and princes offering counsel and instruction; Grotius found a post as an active diplomat where he might apply what he had written about those laws that are perpetually obligatory on all nations; and Milton returned from an excursion for the private good of his own development in Italy to take active part in the founding of the new republic and he rendered his statesman's service, not by repeating antique general formulas, but by an active intervention in a political and religious issue concerning liberty of the press and freedom of discussion. These leaders in their time learned from the example of ancient wise men how to do their own original work in the world.

The Education of the Free Mind

Milton attacked a problem that was, indeed, critical for the whole future of education. The possibility that men of learning ever could be kings or even kings' counsellors was quite as remote in the large sovereign State as in the city state that Socrates had lived in. They could not reach the mighty directly but they still made very good use of a new modern resource at their disposal—the printing press and books. They had to begin by teaching a few who could learn the ancient languages. In time, the commentaries upon the old books and translations would spread the learning more widely. The Bible in particular was early made accessible in the vernacular languages of the different nations. So if those holding authority were not immediately affected by the vital knowledge themselves, there was an increasing body of people who had what Milton alluded to, "the desire to learn." Though sovereigns could not or would not learn the law of nature and their own duty to follow and abide by it, some of their subjects, at any rate, came to understand these things very well and wrote freely about the responsibilities of their rulers to themselves, the people, as well as to God. In this respect, the new education accomplished its practical purpose, by rearing such a class of people in a common understanding of principles. For the people who were so instructed were disposed to act on their knowledge and to insist upon observance of the principles by their rulers. Thus the English revolution was a forerunner of a century and more of political struggle in Europe which was to establish what we call the modern liberal order. In this aspect the new education became something of political and social consequence in the modern world. When Milton pleaded so eloquently, then, for the liberty of printing, he was doing work which was just as effective, though it would take longer time, as if he had actually been the Socratic philosopher standing beside a king and counseling him in his duties.

What is important here is not simply the knowledge itself nor any doctrines that such men taught, for those things form but the body, as it were, of learning. The true learning is not merely repetition, whether of phrase, line, figure, or style, but reacting with the same dynamic spirit as first created the works.

The vision of Socrates and philosophy can be a spark to touch off a kindred flame in him who studies the philosophy, for he himself becomes the philosopher addressing himself to the conditions of his own time. So it is with all the arts and with science. The best part of education is the calling forth of the "virtue" of a man, which means his individual power to do great and fine things.

At first sight those who engaged in learning seem to have been wholly occupied with mere tradition, that is, with something already done in the past which they transmit from one generation to another as a currency passes from hand to hand. But this is not the true art of the educator. In the examples here observed, there was a *revival* of mind and spirit. The creative elan of life must pass on with and through the tradition. The mind of him who learns catches, from the silent words on the page or from the life sketched on the canvas, or in the structure that is reared into the heavens, the art itself of thinking, or making music, or painting, or building. The tradition is the medium that starts one on the way—then must come the *initiative* of the liberated mind which will leave a record, too, of works and deeds of enduring value for the man of that time and for the future.

Milton himself explained that the recourse to ancient languages and letters had been necessary at first because the modern nations had not yet acquired "experience and tradition" in all forms of learning. The time was coming when they would have their own traditions. They would gain experience in the arts and sciences and be able to create for themselves. Modern man could learn from the knowledge of modern man. When Milton feared the imposition of Parliament's censorship, it was not because the official censors would be likely to discontinue the publishing of the ancient books of learning but because they would frown on modern novelties, on the publication of the discoveries of the present era, the new astronomy, as well as the new theology. The consequence of the revival of learning had been that men learning to write first in the ancient language soon took to writing their own language with fresh inspiration and knowledge of what language can do. It was the same with Renaissance art—from understanding ancient works they went on to create their own in their own individual styles. It was even the case in religion itself, which though it was anchored, as doctrine, to the Scripture, for those who broke away from the church, was a matter, too, of individual experience—and discovery. The demand for religious liberty among the Puritans was also a claim to the right "to continue seeking" for themselves and to have their own discovery of God in their lives. Then, too, a whole nation demonstrated, in the English civil war, that they were minded to have self-government and a new order, and they were then gaining their own experience in the political art. One can see the dangers of a censorship in this situation where there were such new trends toward freedom in politics and religion.

In the van of this advance of the mind was physical science. When Milton wanted to dramatize the meaning of censorship by the state in the *Areopagitica,* he told an episode of his early sojourn in Italy. "I found and visited the famous Galileo, grown old a prisoner to the Inquisition, for thinking in astronomy otherwise than the Franciscan and Dominican licensers thought." And he told further how people there came to him to tell of the blight of unfreedom that was upon them, and how they looked with hope to England as a place where men could be free and work at their discoveries about nature or man and society and God.

Liberty in science, "Christian liberty," political liberty, liberty of the mind in all provinces of experience and knowledge—this was the coming philosophy of the modern tradition. Milton struck it off in his phrase "philosophic freedom."

IV. *Our Own Case*

Now the power once attributed to princes belongs to all the people. A *democratic* responsibility is needed—a sense of duty, an allegiance to moral principle, and the recognition of a universal law which stands above the will of the people.

Is it really the case, some may ask, that the people now have supreme power? Of course they are the acknowledged source of all authority. The laws of government usually contain an appropriate reference to their good and are submitted, as it were, for their general approval or disapproval. The policies of the governments which they elect are given every appearance of being dictated by their will and purpose. In this respect certainly, their sovereign majesty is recognized, and this is true even in dictatorships whose powerful leaders have gone through the motions of free elections as if deriving their authority from the people. They have presented themselves as "the people's choice." We can object that this is only a pretense and no evidence whatsoever of democracy. But in our own case, too, political machinery is not of itself genuine democracy. More is needed than such formalities of government. The substance of democracy must be found beyond such appearances. Yet even the semblance of it is arresting—that in civilized countries today all who wield political power must pay their tribute to the opinion of the nation. Power does depend upon what the people at large are willing to have done in their name. This confirms Montesquieu's discovery two centuries ago when "English liberty" was an object of general admiration and an ideal for all Europe. After examining the various regimes of government, past and present, Montesquieu showed that all were in actual practice limited by long-established customs and beliefs and that even the most despotic rulers had not really possessed the absolute power to which they pretended, because they could not ignore such "fundamental law" of their nation. This was law in an ultimate sense, something beyond any rulings which governments may make and alter at their will. So today the false deference of dictators to the people is a necessity of *their* government. There is an ultimate law founded on the nature of things in society which constitutes a limiting principle on all political power.

The form of democracy we know was begun by a people who had grown up together and who had long been governed together—they were already, as Milton said, "a nation." By struggle and strenuous common effort and with considerable self-discipline and even self-sacrifice they won their right to freedom and to a share in the exercise of the political power which sprang from their being one community. They believed in individual enterprise and the right to property. But they were a people, too, whose lives were governed by an inward pattern of moral duties and convictions. In their practical dealings with each other they lived under a common law. Their plan of government included the idea that throughout the whole of their lives the regulation thereof should be by laws truly common and founded upon their own consent. Their unity was assured and was not their prime concern, much less a dominating passion, as it came to be with other peoples. They were already established as a free and independent sovereign state. The people simply wanted their liberty, in the form of self-government.

Other nations of Europe had suffered long under a decadent empire which could at last no longer hold together nor rule them well. They had been nations for centuries before they became merely parts of an agglomerate body politic. They had memories of that past. The idea of liberty that flashed through nineteenth century Europe awakened them to consciousness of their own worth and the spiritual values of their national cultures. To them "liberty" meant the gaining of their national independence and with it the power to be sovereign nations, too, as the others were. In compensation for their long and humiliating subjection to a rule now felt to have been alien they saw a "destiny" ahead for them, when they in turn would rule. These nations tended to act as slaves do who have not known what it means to be free, and who, when liberated, want only to reverse the roles of master and slave. So the spirit of modern nationalism is often proud, envious, ruthless, and restrained by no scruples or respect for sister nations.

Nationalism has been deliberately cultivated, too, in politics. It spells power for those who can indoctrinate the people with the belief that the individual's life is identical with that of the nation and state. This makes for an immense allegiance—the minds, hearts, interests, and aspirations are all enlisted. Yet the individual does not feel himself a non-entity. For nationalistic politics adroitly makes use of the democratic idea that the individual is free to have his own property and to pursue private gain.

The present complexion of affairs in the world is something like this: a tradition of political liberty and self-government combined with a tradition of economic individualism and nationalism. These have been historical companions. The upshot today is a condition in each civilized society where the people are organized in democratic form and, thanks to their private enterprise and their belief both in their nation and in democracy, they make available national power greater in sheer effectiveness than anything ever known.

We live now in a world of tremendously large national organizations possessing a vast mobilized energy. In international politics the moves are made on a world scale through the concentration of power in national governments which decide the fate of millions who have actually little, if anything, to say about the matter. The expenditures of governments, whether for armaments or for the economic and social recovery of Europe and Asia, are grandiose sums. Yet they represent ultimately only what willing hands and the labor of many will produce. Such resources of power have become available to political use because the people believe in their nation and state and consent to the operations of their governments, and because, too, they identify their own life with the existence and welfare of the collective body to which they belong. The upshot is a massive national power in a number of separate states.

Consider now the great nations of the earth, how they act, the character they display in their relations with each other. They stand arrayed as almost solid masses of people—fearful and in hostile opposition to each other. The *nationalistic* organization of life is their dominating feature. Any question about the security of the state stops all argument about right and overrides any objections to measures. There is no law of life above national security and national interest. Thus international law cannot have any meaning or effectiveness, and the power of these great masses of people in the nations is largely focused on preparation for war.

The dangerous power of the organized collective is the most challenging political and moral problem of our time. And it is a national problem as well as an international one. The modern state itself contains precisely the same fault within its own social organization, though, of course, it is in lesser degree. It is a common practice of groups of people within our own state, for instance, to organize for collective action to gain their own particular ends, and again and again they will press their claims regardless of the consequences to the whole community. Some seek to keep secure their special privileges against the claims of others for justice. Those who challenge such vested interests and who organize to assert their power of union may at first aim only at their own minimal claims of their just rights, but they, too, proceed to go as far as they can toward securing for themselves a position of permanent advantage which will safeguard them against future reverses. These aggressive groups tend to recognize no limit to the use of their power except a superior opposing force. On occasion, the government, spurred by an alarmed and angry public opinion, forces a settlement upon the parties. Everywhere, however, there is witnessed the attempt to use pressure, coercion, and sheer unprincipled force. The practice prevails throughout the economic world of industry, commerce, finance and labor, and it even pervades other institutions, secular and religious.

Such militant activity of collective bodies is nothing but a form of group warfare, restrained only by the stern demands of the whole country that the struggles between their groups shall not endanger the state. But even when this discipline is applied, it is often for reasons merely of national security rather than for justice. Many serious injustices remain because "security reasons" are the chief grounds for state action. The *nationalistic* theme thus runs through all our politics. The internal and the external politics are of an identical character which we call, unflatteringly, "power politics."

The scene today is vaster and more complex than any we have surveyed in the previous parts of this study. Our wars are total, engaging everyone and everything in a battle of powers. Our internal struggles tend to take on a similar character. Organizations compete with organizations. The sense of inclusive community in which all can live together at peace is hard to keep alive in these circumstances. Universal principles of conduct, binding upon all alike, do not seem to have much reality or commanding authority. "One's right extends as far as his power," is the maxim on which men and groups and nations now appear to act.

The ancient Greek philosophers had seen in the democracy of their time simply a rule of numbers *without ethical purpose,* that is, without caring for the good of the community and for the others in it, without seeking to render justice, without acknowledging any higher law than simply their edict or will. The "many" will tend to go wrong as well as one man or a few.

These are not antiquated criteria for the judgment of a social and political order. We, too, are troubled today by this same unethical character in the workings of our own democracy. That is why we hear on every hand that call for more social responsibility in everyone, for this is the term we use, in lieu of the one the ancient peoples used, namely, "justice."

But a distinctively modern criticism has developed, too, characteristic of ourselves because we consider the individual foremost rather than the state. Thus we are critical of nationalism today because under its dominant influence men cannot think of each other as men, as plain human beings, as persons having any intrinsic worth in their own right but *only* as nationals. They are reckoned as so many hands or bearers of arms. The value of human life itself is almost nothing in such reckoning. Whatever esteem there is for man confines itself to one's fellow nationals.

What is the effect on the human personality of the operations of all these large scale collective organizations in our modern society? Philosophers ask the question because they value above all else the personal and spiritual development of man. The following passage from A. A. Bowman is a fine example of such ethical criticism.

> The tendency to conduct human affairs more and more upon the basis of class organization is one of the striking phenomena of our modern civilization, and reflects man's profound distrust of his neighbors, and the failure of the social systems based on man's regard for man. The tragedy of human existence in these later days is nowhere more marked than in the desperate efforts that are being made to improve the conditions of human life by ceasing to treat human beings as persons, and by trying to fashion their lives on patterns derived from a study, not of the individual, but of the mass. Not that such methods are illegitimate or inexpedient. They are in fact profoundly necessary. The social structure demands the handling of men in groups, and calls for an elaborate technique. But in so far as the maintenance of existing structures and the more or less forcible creation of new combinations become the all absorbing business of life, in so far as the individual is lost outside the limits of

his technical habits, there is a corresponding loss of those supreme meanings that have their seat in personality. Of all the forms of wanton self-destruction there is none more pathetic than that in which the human individual demands that in the vital relationships of life—the relationships which imply reciprocity and mutual understanding—he be treated not as an individual, but as a member of some organization.

The full significance of this cult of organization is apt to be lost upon those who are most competent to deal with its detail . . . Even its critics have usually advocated an increased application of the very methods from which the evil springs. What they fail to see is that as society integrates itself more and more upon a basis of political and economic organization, the general effect upon individual character is not always that of an integrating power. On the contrary, increased organization may retard the process of integration in the individual . . . The forms of activity called for, the interests appealed to, bear unequally upon the funded resources of the soul; and this means the consolidation of character around one set of impulses, to the neglect and atrophy of others no less vital. The acquisitive instinct and the instinct of pugnacity in particular are kept in a constant state of overstimulation . . . The results . . . appear in those deep and unbridgable fissures that divide the human race into rival and potentially hostile societies . . . In the associations of employers and in labor groups, we see what human life becomes when organized by the instinct of acquisition. In every instance the issue is the same; in every instance men are found endeavoring to secure the fullest outlet for their acquisitive propensities by restricting an identical instinct in others. The same thing is true of political organization . . . [It] is to be expected of a well organized society that it will find means of binding the citizen to it without depersonalizing him, and that, by relieving him of much mechanizing drudgery, it will set him free to find the larger life that makes for a completed personality.[9]

"Social responsibility" is apparently the great need of our nation today. The people must act with responsibility themselves, and require it of all those who are authorized by their consent or by their tolerance to act for them. And we imagine such a community, regardful of each individual and pursuing the welfare and continuing existence of the whole, as reaching beyond the present national state so that it comprises all the people who co-exist with us in "one world." Yet to speak of social

---

[9] A. A. Bowman, *Studies in the Philosophy of Religion* (edited posthumously by Norman Kemp Smith), The Macmillan Company, London, 1938, II, Chapter XVIII, "Christianity and the Completed Concept of Religion," pp. 130–134.

responsibility is not enough. For it is what the individual person is in himself that matters and not only how he acts in his relationships with others. His responsibility must issue from himself as an individual who will treat others as free and equal persons. Our "better education" must have this personal responsibility as its goal and purpose.

V. *Our Special Problems in Education*

All the people need to be "principled"—to use the words of Milton—not simply those who have "the desire to learn." The conditions of education are now vastly different from those of the earlier time. Classical literature and philosophy, the treasure house of "Greek wisdom," is no longer so important in most men's eyes. Nor are the examples of sanctity and righteousness in the Bible nearly so influential in the lives of men. The reason Milton gave in 1644 for an education through the classics, that "all nations," had not yet "experience and tradition enough for all kinds of learning," is hardly valid today, since the moderns have now their own experience, their own traditions, and above all, their science. They seem to feel, unfortunately, that it is quite unnecessary to seek for truth as well as beauty in those works of the past. Yet those books had much of priceless value and appeal. There was power of vision in them, eloquence, music of language, and the whole expression of man when he is fully aroused and his reason, imagination, and senses are all united in a creative achievement. Men who were wrestling with the universal problems of human life had put into their books all their mind and soul in the conviction that their "knowledge" would yield "virtue."

But there is a perennial problem about moral education. Even if we had the old discipline still, we should have that deeper question remaining, which has faced everyone who thought seriously about the improvement of man through education: "*Can* virtue be taught?" If even Socrates wondered about it, in connection with his circle of disciples and friends, can we who depend so much on books and on school teaching expect an easy answer in our time?

The Role of Family Life

Even in the days when the wisdom of books seemed to count for so much more than in the present, the chief role was played by the family. The significance of early life in the home for the formation of character is well known. From birth youngsters grow up experiencing some affection and care, however ill advised it may be at times or mixed with impatience. They may become accustomed to the ministrations of their elders and take them for granted. They may resent it, too, when they want to choose their own sweet way. But they come to cherish their family later, as they go about in the world, where they meet with so much less consideration. Before that retrospective appreciation arrives, however, a certain natural discipline will have taken place in their own attitude and in their actual conduct. Through their common daily experience of the same situations the needs, strivings, successes and failures, joys and sorrows of one and all are reflected in the consciousness of every one of them. They can see right at hand the consequences of any of their actions on their family group. They learn to be careful and to have a care for each other. They place a value on the considerate attitude and judge themselves, as well as others, by reference to it. Here moral judgment is formed, and here, too, the first real sense of personal responsibility comes alive, and finds its demonstration in conduct. Naturally enough, the family or home has always been referred to as a model for the other social relationships that obtain in the larger world beyond. Plato sought to realize in the whole state this sort of real justice, felt in the bones of all and not simply conceived in philosophers' heads. And religion, too, has used the images of parental love and sacrifice and of the filial response to inspire men to achieve that desperately needed spiritual fellowship in the wider world.

Beyond the right education in the family, however, what can be done for man as a moral being? Or if the family fails, what later corrective is possible? Indeed, it would seem from the experience of mankind that the education of the home, even at its best, is never sufficient in and by itself. There has to be a subsequent education, concurrent with the active life beyond it. As a man moves into the world about him he must learn there, in the particular circumstances in which he finds himself, the moral principles that should guide his conduct in those conditions. It is not possible to store up merit at home and then go abroad all armed for life's "snares." But if the case of the home is taken as a good example of what is possible, we may infer in general that man learns best how to be responsible and moral precisely in those relationships which can be *personal,* as in his occupation and work with others, in any other association or enterprise where whatever one person does is plainly seen in its bearings on the lives of others. In such situations a social conscience can form. But there does not seem to be any *wholesale* way of making men moral beings—only this slow growth into a membership in this or that community and development of a spirit of mutual regard and service to one another.

The Educative Society

But what chiefly educates the generality of the people at any time are the obvious, prevailing ways and practices of the society in which they happen to live. These "teach" more than professed teachers ever can. They are influences which are constant and almost ever present. They pull men along with the force of custom. This was something the Greeks knew very well. When Socrates was on trial, charged with being the source of the corruption of the youth of Athens by his teaching alone, he crossquestioned one of his accusers and made him admit that it was really "the whole city" which educated in such matters, whereupon Socrates invited the jury of fellow Athenians to consider what little he alone could do compared with the moral influences in the general tenor of life of their community. The fault in the youth was some fault in them all—and it was that very fault, he pleaded, which he himself had been attacking in all his questioning to which people had objected. His charge against them all was that they did not have any "care about the soul" of man but only about wealth, power, honor, or some other less important matters, in the pursuit of which men were constantly guilty of doing injustice to each other.

What, then, about our own present case? We are living in a society which is powerfully "educative," with all the democratic facilities for communication which makes the whole society affect every member and with a force never perhaps witnessed before in history. The "many" are in a position to be affected, not only by what goes on around them but by what is going on everywhere in the world.[10] Consider their natural inference, for example, from what they can observe about the practices of nations. The conduct of states in their international relations

[10]See the problem posed by Sir Fred Clarke, in *Freedom in the Educative Society*, University of London Press, London, 1948.

teaches that "national interest" is the sole principle of political action at any time.

The code of the world contains other articles of practice which teach similar *de facto* ethical lessons to the people. The primary object of the vast economic activity in a modern society is the supplying of our material needs and wants. All people are eager for material goods—the market is wide and unlimited. So, too, are the desires of man. The same enterprises which can succeed in producing goods for the mass of the people and improving their material standard of living are able "to do more business" by creating new desires. It is very profitable to search the desires of man's heart, but not, as the Almighty does, according to the Scripture, in order to chasten him. The aim is rather to solicit desire and satisfy it, and then again to stimulate it. The tendency is to keep man demanding things which others will have to supply for him. The individual is made increasingly dependent, not only on material goods themselves but also on the purveyors of them from whom he derives his very ideas of what is good. Having so many things to choose from, he now has little chance to weigh, and discriminate for himself—his values are determined for him. All business, too, is "big"; the rewards for enterprise great; the social emoluments of wealth make for prestige —which induces people to believe that the good of life is summed up in the possession of wealth and external goods. All this affects man's belief about himself and leads him to think that he is solely motivated by a materialistic self-interest.

There is nothing in this *ethos* of our economy and our politics to hold men together. Their particular interest on any occasion may or may not be what others should expect or find reasonable. It may happen to coincide with that of others one moment, but be quite opposite at another. Any *common* interest is then purely an accident and ephemeral. Any so-called common purpose has no real quality of *purpose,* unless it contains a guiding principle which eliminates individual vagary or wilfulness. And if we can *only* be motivated by self-interest, then we can never have any obligation nor any lasting confidence in each other. And without some *faith* in each other it is impossible to give up a personal advantage for the sake of the general good of the whole community. Real sacrifice *is* required. But no shadow of that can exist in such a world of sheer self-interest.

The Necessity of the Free Mind

The picture is one of man against Moloch—what chances has man of saving himself? That phrase, "saving himself," is quite appropriate in this connection, for we tend to assume, in our plans of education, a role which does not allow for any self-reliance in the individual. We act like a father who would make every provision possible for the life long security of his children, an attempt as foolish as it is vain, for they will be more secure through what they make of themselves. So here, as we study the strong tendencies in our economic and political order to deny man his individuality, we should trust more the individual's own powers of resistance and independence. The brave *Ethic* of Spinoza has a lesson here: the true strength to resist evil influences is within, in the thinking of the mind itself. It is through winning a "freedom of the mind" that one has "strength," a dauntless strength, too, that cannot be overcome by external powers of the world. The goal of education, according to this philosophy, should be exactly the same as that of democratic politics: to provide for freedom of the mind in everyone, so that the individual can determine his own life and escape the "human bondage" of a confusion due to the pressures of the society and civilization in which he finds himself.

Problems about Freedom of Mind in our Time

The modern philosophers began with such a trust in individual reason. Spinoza and Kant recognized this power of the free mind in themselves and they valued it above everything else. Hence they honored modern science, too, for it is the signal achievement of the free intellect. Science is the very model for us of straight, rational thinking. This we depend upon greatly today for any education of man in freedom.

But the liberty of the mind may be taken away before we have even realized that it is in danger. When a mind has been previously subjected to "evil communications," it is hardly able to take the straight way and follow reason.

Even in the "age of reason" it was recognized that a preparation is necessary for "the state of maturity" when a man is truly free in virtue of his reason. John Locke told of the responsibility of the parent for the child, and particularly the duty to see to "the necessities of his life, the health of his body, and the information of his mind," and in regard to the last of these he further remarked "to turn him loose to an unrestrained liberty before he has reason to guide him is not allowing him the privilege of his nature to be free but to thrust him out amongst brutes."[11] Care is required, then, about what youth are exposed to. Later J. J. Rousseau, more than ever concerned about the liberty of man, was even more emphatic about guarding the early experience and the sensibilities and imagination of youth against the distorting arts, prejudices, and practices of the world.

In Plato's philosophy education has a more positive function. The arts and handiwork of man express man as he now is and as he dreams and aspires to be. They reveal man to himself. But they are not merely private revelations; they are put forth for public enjoyment. There are public readings, performances, spectacles. There is music in the air. One cannot escape the impress of these things. There is no sheltering of man behind the walls of a house—the arts pervade the whole of life, from the child's earliest experience to the very last years. Consequently the arts truly form the man of any society. And if we are ever concerned with effecting any improvement in human life we should look first to these primings of the spirit in imagination and feeling. Only a nature that is well balanced and harmonious in its upbringing and in its own self-expression can attain to genuine maturity and a complete life in a good society.

It follows from this philosophy of education that the values of human life are actually learned first in the form of *appreciation*. A distorted "education," if we may call it by the name of education, of the sensibilities, emotions, and imagination imparts unbalanced tendencies before the mind is free enough to exercise any individual discretion and choice. Only through the genuinely "fine" arts can there be a suitable cultivation of esthetic and moral judgment.[b]

In our day such education in the traditional arts is of course continued in school and university and available to the few who are able to pursue their studies at this higher level. But in our "educative society" the "mass communications" have the first innings—the press, the cinema, the

[b] [Cf. the discussion of education of the emotions and imagination through art in Chapter XIX by Rowland W. Dunham.]

[11] John Locke, *The Second Treatise on Civil Government,* Chapter VI, "Of Paternal Power," sections 59, 61, 63.

radio are ubiquitous. The popular and cheap magazines are out on stands by the thousands; the radio is heard any time in every home and place of gathering; the moving pictures have habitués from infancy to old age. Everyone is exposed. There is no escaping the outpouring of words, advertisements, solicitations. Today these new agencies of communication are servants of business and they have a vast field for commercial exploitation. They amuse, excite desires, and in some instances direct the very interests and the living habits of millions of people—and chiefly for gain. So far as this pecuniary purpose directs these tremendously potent influences, their effect as education is largely negative in value. The amount of poor stuff turned out and spread abroad, far and wide, tends to produce an unrefined taste as well as ethos which are not calculated to aid in forming a sound, balanced character nor in developing a mind that is strong and individual enough to be free.

We are not considering the large question of policy regarding the responsibilities of such agencies which have so great a power in the shaping of the destinies of the nation. They are public in their operation and should, like anything else of that category, come under the supreme law of civilized society that they shall be conducted with paramount regard for the public welfare. We are reckoning here only with this one aspect of the matter, that these agencies are for the most part at present actually working against the right kind of education.

The Arts and Freedom

In this respect a saving policy is being adopted. The "fine arts" are really so much finer than these "communications" which are so much more in evidence that, given the chance, men and women do prefer them. True drama has a lasting appeal and means more than melodrama. Poetry still expresses intimate thought or experience which does not suffer from a cheapening effect of publicity. The very dissociation from all utility is a characteristic of the arts. And it makes them a genuine recreation. They are more enjoyable in their own integrity, too, than in any version which is made of them to serve industry and commerce or the propaganda purposes of governments. They are expressive of the creative freedom of man, and this is something man has loved from the earliest times, even prehistoric. The works that have weathered the test of time exemplify and establish within the mind of the beholder

Education and Politics: The Problem of Responsibility

really authentic standards of truth, beauty, and good. They summon the mind to effort, too, since the appreciation of art is no mere case of passive relaxation of mind as amusement. And the effort is not only that to know but also that *to make art* for oneself. The genuinely fine arts inspire men actively to create with their own hands.

It is the practical recognition of the importance of this active expression through art that vitalizes education today. Such activity is of immense consequence, too, for the freedom of man, for when the individual has an opportunity to learn the best of art, and above all, to do creative work in any of its forms, he is the better able to judge values for himself and reject, with "a mind of his own," whatever seems spurious, cheap, and meretricious. He will also have the courage to demand both for himself and for his community that which expresses the best of which mankind is capable in imagination, feeling, and thought. The hope of coming through our present morass in the exploitation of mass audiences or spectators lies in giving all the people a taste of creatively doing something for their own enjoyment instead of merely buying it from others.[12]

Just as man has obtained good government only in so far as he takes the trouble to govern himself, so he will establish genuine values of human life through winning them for himself. This is the way to freedom.

Freedom and Science

Let us return now to science, to consider its part in education for freedom. Science has been of great sustaining power to the moral life of man, for it supports the conviction that there is an "order of nature" and existence into which man must fit himself, if he is to live in right relations with other beings in the world. This is the aspect of "pure science" that men attain when they have searched profoundly into its meaning.

But science wears another aspect, in the general opinion about its role in life. Primitively man's interest in nature was that of gaining in the sheer power to survive. Magic began with that purpose. Science has succeeded remarkably well in that role by means of discovery after

---

[12] See Herbert Read's various writings, particularly, *Education through Art* and *Education for Peace*, Charles Scribner's Sons, New York, 1949.

discovery that can be put to technical and manufacturing use. Now questions arise about the meaning of science for our time.

Those who know science best have seen far beyond that primary utilitarian aim and they have transformed a technique of magic into an art of knowledge which is far more than a technique to satisfy the desires for material goods. But are people generally, who are acquainted with the wonderful *uses* of science, transformed in understanding, too, as are those scholars and scientists whose disinterested search for truth has yielded so great and valuable a body of knowledge? What sort of benefit is science to them and their thinking, and above all to their freedom as persons endowed with minds?

The mantle of utilitarian purpose is spread like a dust over everything in our civilization. What is most obvious to men about science nowadays is its power to wrest useful secrets from nature. The talk is always spiritually proud about man's "conquest over nature," a phrase which is inadvertently carried over from military exploits, though we profess generally to abhor the very idea of conquest. But that sort of language betrays a tendency of which we are repeatedly being warned today. We have consented to a reckless exploitation of the land and its resources which has been accompanied by an utter disregard for the welfare of the community and future generations. This mentality of exploitation is a dangerous one. It is not so far a cry from the acceptance of the idea of plundering a planet to that of exploiting even man himself and using him as material for explosives as Nazis did or, if not going to such an extreme, still making him serve as a means to some end. The worth of human life may easily be forgotten. And wherever any man is not being treated as an end in himself, he is in danger of losing the freedom that is essential to his humanity.

Pure science can liberalize and sublimate the primitive quest for power over nature and convert it into a search for truth and an enterprise, too, that satisfies the mind in a way which no profits or material benefits can do. Education in genuine scientific thinking can also help the arts restore to us an appreciative interest in nature. For science discloses not only nature's order but also her variety and inexhaustible riches for the spirit of man. There is a direct moral value in the right application of science to man's needs, for just as action and reaction are equal in its simple law of motion, so man in his relation to nature must give in order to receive. And this elementary lesson in justice may be supplemented with a further one, for what is received is really more than one deserves and so is kindled a thankfulness as well as a reverence that are religious in character. These dispositions in the spirit of man increase his sense of being responsible to something beyond himself.

Religion

Almost inadvertently we have passed in thought from Nature to God. It is hard to separate them. The example of that is in philosophy, in the thought of Spinoza who simply left us with the alternative, call it "God or Nature." The life of the thinking and free man is most complete in "the intellectual love of God." Therein man eventually attains his full freedom of mind. When the later philosopher Kant analyzed man's experience of duty, the absolute respect for the moral law, he saw that it practically implied a belief in God and in the everlasting significance or immortality of a person whose life is moral. And the freedom of man stood first among these "postulates of morality," as Kant called them. This was the only way that he could make sense of man's dignity as a person.

What the philosophers here recognized, in the terminology of their respective systems of thought about man, nature, and God, is what would be called religion in our ordinary language. There is some essential connection between religion and the moral life—how much or how essential is a subject of continuing argument. More arguable, too, is what particular religion is to be regarded as necessary. But there seems, in any case, to be actually no choice between a religion and no religion. Men need and they search for something that is ultimately significant beyond their transitory experience. These religious proclivities of men tend to find some outlet or other and an object of allegiance. Such tendencies toward a "faith" are forces of great power for social action, and in our time large masses of people have been thus religiously exploited for the political purposes of nationalism. The result has been, in those cases, a degradation of man and destruction of freedom and of other personal values. Such worship of the state or nation or whatever it be called is still with us in contemporary life. And exactly as the individual moral judgment and taste are constantly obscured by the prevailing ethos of our politics and commerce, so the native springs of religion are muddied by these religions "of the world" which are but servants of political and social power instead of being the chief instruments of discipline for those who have such power.

An education in religion is then another need of our nation. It poses a problem of immense difficulty. We have a common religious tradition. But today we are acutely conscious of our differences and that we are "worlds apart." As long as men intend to be free, it is not possible to have them of one faith with such perfection of unanimity in their belief that they will not differ on vital points. Modern men may temporarily be forced, or led without their knowledge, into one fold; but so far as they are men with free minds they will have their own individual convictions and will group themselves with others who believe much the same way. It is not by one uniform authoritative doctrine, therefore, that they will acquire a common religious spirit so that they will live at peace and with due regard for their fellow men. There is for the Christian the Bible, and for some of them, the interpretation of a church. But the religious literature and the instructions alike depend, for their purchase on the mind, upon some experience of the individual himself which opens up to him the meaning of the things that have been mysterious in what was read or told him. In this respect all religion has essentially an individual character. This accounts perhaps for the many different kinds of testimony which become part of the religious heritage and which cannot be summarized merely in a few articles of a creed. So the problem of a religious education, especially in our society, is very great—how can anything be set down as requisite without offense to genuine religious conviction in some quarter or other. Many today even resent the traditional and institutional religion. They would rule it out of education as detrimental to straight-going morality and open democratic politics.

It appears, however, that there will always be something or other that is actually a man's religion. If so, an education which is to accomplish its purposes—and in the present discussion these are two, moral responsibility and freedom of the mind—must consider the *relevance* of religion.

This question is too large and profound to be followed through in further argument. There is one story in the annals of philosophy, however, which seems to come close to showing what is chiefly essential for us in the circumstances of our time. Just a few minutes before Socrates was on trial for his life, accused of irreligion in his teaching, he questioned a youth named *Euthyphro,* who had that mixture of very primitive notions and high ethical ideals which so often characterizes so-called civilized people, who yet lack sound sense as well as the simplest sort of piety. Socrates in his conversation with that youth spoke of reverence as the true mark of the religious man's life. It is reverence for the Divine and reverence for those like one's parents to whom one owes love and honor. That is something in man which needs to be cultivated, extended, and enlightened. The first expression of piety is in the home where morals, too, are first learned. But the spirit of reverence for man and for God knows no such confinement to the home or to any particular group of worshippers or even to one's own nation. It shows, too, in man's attitude to nature as well as to man. The artist knows this reverent care, and the scientist, without saying so, proclaims it in his strict observance of fact, and the plain man knows it in his parenthood and family life and sometimes even in his workmanship. In a democratic society such reverence is needed in all the relationships and activities of people, in their work and in their politics, in whatever they are busy about in the world.

All through this discussion we see two essentials of education which should have "priority" but not, of course, to the exclusion of other ends. Moral responsibility and freedom must be our foremost concern. To focus on anything less than these two is to endanger the foundations of our civilization and our human values.[13] Education for democracy, if we must use so limited a conception of our purpose, can be oppressive and destructive of democracy if it looks only to the solidarity of the nation but not to the other goal of liberty and freedom of the mind. We may have erred from the way in thinking only of freedom without social responsibility, but we do not redeem ourselves by going to the other extreme of forcing men to believe what they do not understand.

---

[13] See Carl L. Becker, *Freedom and Responsibility in the American Way of Life,* Alfred A. Knopf, New York, 1945.

CHAPTER VIII

The Need for a New Organon in Education

By ALAIN L. LOCKE
Professor of Philosophy, Howard University

For nearly two decades, scholars and educators have been intensively engaged, though too often on divided fronts, in what now appears a quest for a common objective—the discovery of integrating elements for knowledge and the search for focalizing approaches in education. Though not altogether fruitless on either side, these explorations have been unduly confusing and not overwhelmingly successful because of the lack of coordination between the philosophical and the educational activity and effort. The prospects of ultimate solution and success at present are immeasurably improved, however, through the comparatively recent realization of the common cause character of their problem and interests on the part of philosophers and educators. Both groups, accordingly, find themselves in a more strategic and hopeful position. There is agreed coordination, it seems to me, on three points; and pending tactical cooperation. The points of agreement are: first, that contemporary learning suffers from a serious and immobilizing lack of any vital and effective integration, both as a body of knowledge and as a taught curriculum (excepting, of course, the pragmatic vocational clusters in the various professional fields); second, that this "ineffectiveness" is not so much an internal fault as it is an external dislocation in the relationship of knowledge to the problems of the social culture; and third, that unless some revitalizing integration is soon attained, not only the social impotence of our knowledge must be conceded in spite of its technological effectiveness, but a breakdown of the culture itself may be anticipated.

These pragmatic pressures of a culture crisis, when added to the normal concerns for the systematization of knowledge and to our special contemporary need for "unified knowledge" after decades of an unprecedented expansion of the scientifically known, result cumulatively in a problem of great weight and urgency. To the natural desire on the part of educators not to evade their traditional social responsibility is added an anxiety not to forfeit their customary intellectual leadership. Although felt only vaguely in the earlier stages—that period of educational reform when "orientation courses" were proposed as the problem's "solution"—these concerns have now deepened to reach the present widespread preoccupation with the problem in terms of "general education" and the "core-curriculum." I have no desire to deprecate any of these promising and in many cases galvanizing reorganizations of the college curriculum, or to prejudge their coordinating potentialities, especially since so many are yet in the experimental stage. Particularly not to be thus minimized should be those programs which, in contradistinction to the "Great Books" plan, aim at broadening directly the student's present day perspectives of social vision and at connecting student thinking realistically with major practical interests of contemporary life, be they personal or social, local or global. Common to all such educational directives is the laudable attempt to link academic learning with the practical issues of living, and thus develop critical acumen and trained aptitudes for responsible intelligent action.

My ground of general criticism (and generalized criticism has its admitted limitations and risks) rests not on the contention that such general education plans lack merit and usefulness, but that, to use Matthew Arnold's phrase, "one thing more is also necessary." Accordingly, these suggestions of a much needed supplementation are brought forward in the conviction that mere curriculum extension or revision is insufficient, and that a more fundamental methodological change both in ways of teaching and in ways of thinking is necessary, if we are to achieve the objectives of reorientation and integration so obviously required and so ardently sought.

Any educational reconstruction adapted to a culture crisis as acute and deepseated as ours should be expected to be radical enough to call for more than mere realignment of subject-matter content or just new emphases in focus and perspective. Comparable culture transitions in the past have been characterized by a new methodology as well as a "new learning"; each age or stage of scholarship seems to have developed a new way, as well as a new scope, of thinking. In illustration, one need only cite the priority of the inductive logic which the scientific

Renaissance instated, and its eventual methodological revolution of the laboratory method itself. However, to be even more specific, one might mention such later methodological departures as the genetic-functional approach which initiated evolutionary theory and scientific naturalism, the historico-comparative and statistical methodologies which combined to produce our modern social science, or quantum mechanics and mathematical relativity which evoked our contemporary atomic science. A new phase of scholarship and learning, so far as historical precedent shows, presupposes a new organon.

It seems somehow curious, then, that in this whole educational consideration of the present culture shift, whereas proposals of curriculum revision have been legion, suggestions of new methodology have been so few. And of these few, only the proposals of the semanticists and the "logical positivists" have been at all thoroughgoing and systematic. On one point, certainly, one can tangentially agree with the logical positivists to the extent that their project of "unified knowledge" calls for a more precise and more relevant logic than the verbalist and formalistic one, which, even when it is renounced as a formal logic, still dominates us so tyrannically through its deep embodiment in our language terms and the modes of thinking they have conditioned. But from there on, those of us interested primarily in a pedagogically useful organon, will, I take it, not pin our hopes on a "new logic" which, instead of yielding a clarifying and critical instrument, remains up to the present more recondite and abstract than the old logic it plans to supersede.

One can also find oneself in passing agreement with one of the prime objectives of the "Chicago Plan"—its insistence on the need for sharpening the instruments of critical thinking as an educational prolegomenon. But here again, as with its companion school of thought, the approach is too aridly formalistic.[a] As practical integrations of knowledge neither new "encyclopedic unity," nor the disciplinary unity of formal training in the abstract virtues of clear thinking, seems immediately promising. So, if for no other reason than its practical orientation toward the contemporary world and its problems, the curriculum reorganizations proposed by the "general education" plans seem to offer the wisest

[a] [For further discussion of the "Chicago Plan," see Chapter II by Lyman Bryson, Chapter III by T. V. Smith, Chapter IX by Howard Mumford Jones, Chapter XI by John U. Nef, Chapter XIII by Mordecai M. Kaplan, Chapter XV by George N. Shuster, Chapter XVI by Earl J. McGrath, Chapter XVII by Ordway Tead, and George B. de Huszar's comment in Appendix III.]

preference in the present field of choice. Even without a corrective methodology aimed expressly at implementing integration, they have considerable educational promise.

But it is by no means an excluded possibility to envisage a methodological approach superimposed on the new type curriculum, which would be calculated to assure the development of new ways of thinking *about* its newly reorganized content. It is such supplementation that this paper suggests. For without some specific correctives for traditional ways of thinking, it would by no means be certain that the wider horizons and broader content correlations of the general education program would really broaden the student's thinking, actually integrate it sufficiently to ensure a process understanding of the facts reviewed, and develop in him the capacity for evaluative criticism. We are making the assumption, of course, that global thinking, and what has been called "process understanding," and the capacity for evaluative criticism are compositely the prime objectives of the several general education schemes.

As a matter of fact, none of these objectives is assured except as the student's way of thinking is made the focus of pedagogic attention and ability for interpretation and capacity for critical evaluation explicitly placed above information and analytic skills. Can we be sure that content coordination and broadening the curriculum in time and space perspective will, of themselves, produce these results? Let us suppose, for example, that we have extended the study of history or of man and his cultures from the conventional Western hemispheric scope to a global range and setting, have we automatically exorcised parochial thinking and corrected traditional culture bias? As I see it, not necessarily. It surely is a patent fallacy to assume that a change in the *scope* of thinking will change the *way* of thinking. To convert parochial thinking into global thinking, involves meeting head on their issues of conflict, realistically accounting for their differences by tracing the history of their development, and out of a process-logic of this development, bravely to take a normative stand. If on the other hand, we keep scholarship's traditional neutrality as to values in the name of impartial objectivity, if we proceed with the old academic balancings of *pros* and *cons,* no matter how wide the scope of the curriculum, we are likely to have as an end-product a student, more widely informed, but with the same old mind-sets, perhaps more substantially entrenched in the conceit of knowing more. In that event, we have augmented rather than resolved the problems which, as intellectual defaults and dilemmas, constitute so large a part of the current "culture crisis."

If modernized contemporary education is to deal with attitudes, it must perforce grapple realistically with values and value judgments; if it is to build constructive mind-sets, or even fashion efficient critical ones, it must somehow restore the normative element in education. On more elementary educational levels, under the pressure of critical social issues and their behavior problems, a considerable vanguard of progressive teaching, particularly in the areas of "social" and "intercultural" education, has already crossed this educational Rubicon. Only in retrospect will it be realized what a departure this initiates from the standard educational traditions of descriptive objectivity, and *laissez-faire* neutrality with its "hands off" policy on controversial issues. The new programs openly involve a normative responsibility for attitude formation and even for remedial attitude reconstruction. In the latter, we go beyond the reconditioning of the pupil's thinking to situational recasting, in some cases, of his behavior patterns. Yet because this new "doctrine" has for its base objective findings in anthropology, social psychology, mental hygiene, and scientific child study, there is an authoritative consensus back of these newer educational procedures that few would care to challenge. Certainly no one would think of putting them in the same category, let us say, with religious teaching or political indoctrination.

But it is not easy to discover analogous procedures on the level of higher education, where independent thinking and self-forming opinion are conceded objectives. No matter how urgent the educational need for developing critical discrimination or inducing constructive attitudes, I take it we would not seriously consider reinstating, even in a modified modern guise, the old doctrinal didacticism which, at such pains and effort, education shed several generations ago. So our problem resolves itself into the very difficult and crucial one of finding a way to treat materials on this level with critical and normative regard for values, but without becoming didactic or dogmatic.

These difficult specifications set up criteria for a basic new methodology, as suited to meeting these new demands for our contemporary problems and interests as the empirical method, with laboratory science as its embodiment, was suited to the characteristic problems and interests of the first scientific age. Ironically, it was just the latter's fixation on fact to the exclusion of value, which led—by its neutral objectivity and consequent incapacity to consider values and their goals—to the present day bankruptcy of the objective scientific method in certain important areas of contemporary concern. It is for just these areas and their problems that intellectually and educationally a new organon is a pressing need. Adequate thinking on social issues needs above all to be critically evaluative rather than stop short at descriptive neutrality. So far as possible we must learn to handle values as objectively as we are able to handle facts, but in the social science fields we stand in further need of some way of correlating significantly and realistically their factual *and* their value aspects.

Objectively critical and normative judgments have been the despair of the social sciences (and for that matter, too, of the humanities in problems of comparative criticism), ever since scholarship subscribed to its modern scientific basis. However urgent our normative social interests or educational needs may become, we cannot secede from that alliance. So the only practical alternative is to discover a way of projecting into the study of social fact a normative dimension objective enough to be scientifically commensurable.

Though difficult, such a development is methodologically feasible. It could stem from a broadly comparative and critical study of values so devised as to make clear the vital correlations between such values and their historical and cultural backgrounds. By so regarding civilizations and cultures as objective institutionalizations of their associated values, beliefs, and ideologies, a realistic basis can be developed not only for a scientific comparison of cultures but for an objective critique of the values and ideologies themselves. Study and training in such analyses and interpretations should develop in students a capacity for thinking objectively but critically about situations and problems involving social and cultural values.

Considerable ground has already been broken for such an approach in recent studies undertaking realistic historical analyses of the ideological framework of various periods of civilization and systematic value comparisons between varying types of culture. The well known work of Arnold J. Toynbee, F. S. C. Northrop,[1] Charles Morris, Margaret Mead, Geoffrey Gorer and others in this field, attempts this extension

---

[1] With limiting reservations in the cases of Toynbee and Northrop because of the remnants in their thinking of the abstract dialectical principles of interpretation.

of the study of culture and history into the history and development of ideas and ideologies and the formation of various value orientations in social cultures. They are pioneering, in their several ways, in the techniques of objective and comparative social value analysis. "Area studies," also, from another angle of emphasis on the study of all aspects of a given society or culture as organically correlated, have similar, if not so clearly developed potentialities. These new approaches, emphasizing "civilization-type," "overall culture pattern," "paths of life" and "culture orientations," as determined by historical value emphases and predilections, all seem to reflect a common trend toward bridging the gap between the "factual" and the value aspects of the social sciences by using values objectively as key concepts for historical interpretation.

The methodological basis of such studies must be carefully distinguished from the earlier nonrealistic philosophies of history with their superimposed dialectics. These newer attempts, on the contrary, with no preconceived dialectics of history, try to make history reveal its own process logic, by following on a comparative historical basis the operational connection between an age and its beliefs, a culture and its system of values, a society and its ideological rationale. Here in this sort of integrated study of history may lie the implementation of a new scholarship that will not only afford us an objective panoramic outlook on history, but will also develop critical criteria for analyzing, comparing, and evaluating the varieties of human culture, and for explaining their cultural differences. The advantages from the point of view of a more objective understanding of society, culture, and history are rather immediately apparent; the normative implications, of equal if not greater importance, will be presently considered.

In this connection it is interesting to note, that with very few exceptions, the general education curricula center around the history of civilization. This seems a general recognition of the prime importance today of a fuller and more comprehending knowledge of man. This generally conceded goal of an "integrated" education is, of course, the old humanist ideal and objective of the best possible human and self-understanding. But it recurs in our age in a radically new context, and as something only realizable in an essentially scientific way. Instead of being based as before on the universal, common character of man, abstractly and rationalistically conceived, it rests on the concrete study of man in all his infinite variety. If it is to yield any effective integration, that must be derived from an objective appraisal and understanding of the particularities of difference, both cultural and ideological. These it must trace to the differentiating factors of time, place, and circumstance, largely on the framework laid down by recent cultural anthropology. The modern version of the "proper study of mankind is man" is, therefore a comprehensive, comparative study of mankind with realistic regard for difference, instead of a rationalistic study with a zeal for commonalities and conformity. We face, accordingly, a type of scientific humanism, with an essentially critical and relativistic basis. Its normative potential can issue only from the more objective understanding of difference and the laying down of a scientific rather than a sentimental kind of tolerance and understanding. If we are not to renounce the scientific approach, the hopes for integrated understanding must be grounded not on any doctrinaire normativism of agreement but upon this relativistic normativism of the realistic understanding of difference. And the question there has always been—how integrating can that be?

Although proposing a scientific type of core-curriculum, Professor Deutsch[b] in his paper for the current Conference, faces this same question, and from a somewhat similar methodological approach envisages a sound and constructive normativism derived, however, from relativistic premises. Answering his own query, "What could such a type of training accomplish," he remarks: "Perhaps in the most general terms it could aid students to achieve a larger measure of understanding of processes and of the nature of change and growth. It might aid them to achieve a better understanding of the nature of values and a greater openness to the values of other peoples and other cultures without weakening their understanding and attachment to their own. It might help students to acquire a rational appreciation of reason, and at the same time not only of the function but of the nature of tradition and intuition and perhaps, to some degree, of mysticism and religion; it might help them to keep their minds open to the insights and values which have been attained and which may be attained again through any and all of these approaches without forcing them at the same time to despair of the powers of reason."

A more rigorous and systematic program of value analysis and comparison would not leave such admittedly desirable results to chance or indirection. These broadening intellectual emancipations should be

[b][See Chapter IV by Karl W. Deutsch.]

considered direct normative objectives of the process of education. The historical-comparative approach could then warrantably be maintained as the only proper (in the sense of the only scientific) way of understanding values, including particularly those of one's own culture and way of life. It would be regarded as educationally mandatory to view values relativistically in time perspective, so as to comprehend value change and development, and likewise, to see them in comparative perspective, so as to understand and appreciate value diversity. Thus there could be derived from critical relativism a corrective discipline aimed at the undermining of dogma-forming attitudes in thinking and the elimination of the partisan hundred percentist mentality at its very psychological roots. Instead of correcting here and there in palliative fashion specifically objectionable manifestations and superficial symptoms of an intellectually reinforced irrationality, we should then be attacking it at its generic source. For all absolutistic thinking, however idealist, has totalitarian potential; the characteristic end-product of the abstract intellectual tradition is dogma.[c]

We have come to a partial realization of this in our modern study of public opinion and in propaganda analysis. We have grappled with the problem at a deeper level in semantics, by searching out the mechanisms of dogmatic thinking and exposing the fallacies of symbol identification and the like. But until we have based the training of the student mind on a thoroughly grounded educational corrective for dogmatic thinking and its traditional rationalizations, we will not have effectively established scientific critical thinking in general, and objective thinking about values in particular.

The normative consequences of such a critical relativism can be realized only when it is carried through to a consistent and coordinated methodology. It then reveals not only how extensive are its normative implications, even though based on essentially non-normative scientific procedures, but how radically reformative its effect can be. One can survey these in general outline by making an inventory with their limiting and in many cases, corrective criteria. Carried through as a consistent methodological approach, *Critical Relativism* would

    1. implement an objective interpretation of values by referring them

[c] [For further discussion of the problems of ethical absolutism and relativism, see Chapter X by Donald C. Stone (including comments by Quincy Wright and Clem C. Linnenberg, Jr.) and Chapter XIV by Theodore Brameld (including comments by B. Othanel Smith, John D. Wild, and Louis J. A. Mercier).]

realistically to their social and cultural backgrounds,
2. interpret values concretely as functional adaptations to these backgrounds, and thus make clear their historical and functional relativity. An objective criterion of functional sufficiency and insufficiency would thereby be set up as a pragmatic test of value adequacy or inadequacy,
3. claim or impute no validity for values beyond this relativistic framework, and so counteract value dogmatism based on regarding them as universals good and true for all times and all places,
4. confine its consideration of ideology to the prime function and real status of being the adjunct rationalization of values and value interests,
5. trace value development and change as a dynamic process instead of in terms of unrealistic analytic categories, and so eliminating the traditional illusions produced by generalized value terms—*viz.,* static values and fixed value concepts and "ideals,"
6. reinforce current semantic criticism of academic value controversy by stressing this realistic value dynamics as a substitute for traditional value analytics, with its unrealistic symbols and overgeneralized concepts.

It should be made clear that this approach does not necessarily involve substantive agreement on specific value interpretations, but merely methodological agreement to keep value analysis and discussion on a plane of realism and the maximum attainable degree of scientific objectivity. It could even be a conceded educational device to maintain neutrality and permit constructive educational consideration of value issues so controversial as to be irreconcilable otherwise, especially with public educational institutions.

Critical thinking, however, could make no greater headway in a single line of uncompromising advance than, with such a strategic methodology as tactic, to invade the innermost citadel of dogmatic thinking, the realm of values. Nor could it provide a more vital integrating element in a modernly oriented general education than by carrying the scientific approach into content areas hitherto closed to objective scientific treatment. Conversely, it would be a real supplementation to scientific method itself, which has its admitted limitations, to be stretched by the necessity of handling value materials to the inclusion of new techniques of critical appraisal and formative attitude-conditioning. The gains would thus be mutual, to value analysis on the one hand, and to scientific method, on the other.[d]

Such methodological procedure could not be expected to settle many of these controversial value issues, especially their theoretical aspects, in concrete answers or demonstrable conclusions. But there would at least be an end to the inconclusive neutrality which education has been forced to exercise on many vital matters. It should be an educational boon to be able to handle them realistically and systematically off the plane of dogmatic solutions.

But while it is possible, and even strategic, to sidestep opposition with specific dogma not directly refutable by scientific proof, it is also nearly impossible to generate and implement critical thinking without challenging dogmatic thinking in general. As previously pointed out, it is necessary to attack the psychological roots of dogmatism. No restricted, formalistic discipline seems to me calculated to accomplish this in the present day college curriculum; neither the new scientific logic, nor the newer semantic logic, not to mention a rejuvenated traditional logic. We should remember that in the days when the traditional logic was effective and vitally alive, it was a real organon of learning, developed in application to the content of almost every other subject in the curriculum. Accordingly any reform in methodological approach which can carry its techniques, discipline, and influence into a large area of curriculum content has, it would seem, a favorable chance of being effective in the training and orientation of student thinking. A realistic critique of values, aspects of which run importantly throughout the whole range of the social science and humanistic subjects of the curriculum, has a definite advantage and wide prospect of influence, once adopted and set to work. It can become a new organon of critical thinking as well as a new apparatus of integration in the present educational situation, which is one of extreme, almost emergency need, with respect to both critical thinking and integration. Beside internal integration within the areas of the subjects with important value aspects and problems, there is a further overall curriculum integration in the extension of the scientific method to cover so much more intellectual territory. After all its success in the natural science segment, and for that matter,

---

[d] [Cf. Chapter VI by John Courtney Murray, S.J., for a criticism of the limits of scientific method with the proposal that there are other rational techniques available for dealing with questions of value and metaphysics.]

wherever facts are in question, has already established potential dominance of the scientific method and approach throughout the scope of modern scholarship. The conquest of the field of values would be almost the concluding triumph.

CHAPTER IX

Education and One World

By HOWARD MUMFORD JONES
Professor of English, Harvard University

MODERN AMERICAN COLLEGES and universities descend from the Middle Ages. This can be shown by a number of familiar examples. The very concept of a college of liberal arts, a college in which neither painter nor poet nor pianist feels quite at home, is a concept originating in the medieval division of learning into seven arts—grammar, logic, rhetoric, arithmetic, geometry, music, and astronomy—only one of which has much to do with art as we understand the term. This college presumably has a dean, that is, a *decanus,* which is medieval Latin for the supervisor of ten monks in a monastery; and its students enroll in lecture courses because the medieval doctor of philosophy or master of arts read aloud from a manuscript in order that students might write down his dictation in their notebooks. We still continue the process. If the student is successful, he becomes a bachelor of arts, whether he is married or not, because the medieval student was called a *baccalaureus,* a word that originally seems to have referred to a farm; and we admit him at commencement to the first degree in the arts with all its rights and privileges, meaning that he can avoid being hanged at the order of a secular court, a privilege students, I imagine, still enthusiastically endorse. And when conferring this remarkable degree upon the young American, we professors dress in black nightgowns with brightly colored hoods (mostly rented from a costume company), because in the Middle Ages these hoods were useful protection against bad weather. Thus quaintly garbed, we walk in procession, swaying gently, two by two, like monks in a monastery, to affirm our descent from the medieval University of Paris.

The tremendous inheritance I hint at is, however, something more than the survival of obsolete customs. It is a weighty intellectual inheritance as well. It goes back at least to the year 1000, when teachers of law laid the foundations of the University of Bologna. As we study this vast intellectual history, we can divide it into three great stages, medieval, Renaissance, and industrial. The central idea of university education in the medieval university was knowledge of God. The central idea in Renaissance education was knowledge of the world and of man. The central and necessary idea of the industrial order of today is knowledge of society. No one of these excludes the others, since the medieval theory of God also included a theory of society, and in the industrial order we need to know more than we do about the nature of man and of the universe, but for our purposes my distinction is roughly true. I want now to glance briefly at each of these three phases of university education.[a]

A striking fact about medieval education is that it was put together by and for men without women, without families, without individual economic necessities and without any personal responsibility for the welfare of society as we understand the phrase today. By and large, medieval education was largely a monkish invention, one in which theology was always central because, by definition, the right knowledge of God was worth infinitely more to the soul than any other conceivable kind of knowledge. Since the monkish community was wholly male; and since, in the Middle Ages, women were not only an inferior sex, but also a temptation to holy men, the curriculum established for bachelors of arts blandly ignored one half the human race. The effects of this monkish attitude toward learning are still found in America, not only in the general prejudice against employing women professors, but also in the passive copying by women's colleges of a curriculum originally intended for men only, without inquiring whether this was either the only, or the best, way to prove that women have brains. Moreover, since the man in the monastery was without family responsibility, this curriculum did nothing to prepare those who studied it for family life; and to this hour our colleges, whether coeducational or otherwise, in most cases, elaborately pretend that young people are never going to face this serious and intimate responsibility. Finally, since the religious communities of the Middle Ages were characteristically supported by

---

[a] [Cf. the discussion of medieval and Renaissance education in Chapter I by Robert Ulich, Chapter V by Scott Buchanan, Chapter VII by Charles W. Hendel, and Chapter XII by Louis J. A. Mercier.]

contributions from the faithful or by taxes, the individual teacher, though he might collect fees for his lectures, was under no obligation to prepare anybody to get a job in a fiercely competitive society; to this day the more ancient, respectable, and economically useless departments in American colleges, such as Latin, Greek, and philosophy, characteristically will not admit the obvious fact that colleges prepare students for jobs. For older and more conservative members of our faculties a liberal education is still a mysterious something that takes place in a timeless and spaceless world of pure intelligence, without boom or bust, without rising prices or falling incomes, without salaries or taxes, sex or family, illness or retirement, political parties or global warfare.

I have said the medieval curriculum was built around the knowledge of God, or theology. By an ironic turn of events this is the one element of medieval education which, except in the Catholic colleges, has not come down to us. In publicly supported institutions, our separation of church and state forbids the support of theologians by tax money; and in privately endowed Protestant institutions the school of divinity is overshadowed by other schools, and the knowledge of God now customary among students is what can be picked up in a fifteen minute chapel service, once required but now voluntary. In other words, our colleges keep parts of their medieval inheritance that are sometimes a real hindrance to educating young people, but abandon the central living idea of the medieval university.

Let me turn to learning in the Renaissance. Scholars have refined or explained away the famous phrase that the Renaissance marked a rediscovery of the world and of man, meaning in the one case actual observation of natural phenomena and in the other the study of human nature outside of theology. I shall, however, cling to this form of words because it is sufficiently exact for my purposes. In the Renaissance, human nature was freshly examined in the light of Greek and Latin literature and of conduct at the courts of Western Europe, until a new ideal of man replaced the theological concept of man the sinner. This ideal is the ideal of the European gentleman. Along with this reexamination of human nature went the study of physical nature. The theory of this reexamination of human nature was formulated by Francis Bacon, its practice was brilliantly exemplified by Galileo. Consequently the concept of experimental science was felt to be beneath the dignity of universities, so that into British and American colleges, the laboratory scientist entered rather late, often in the guise of a Christian philosopher explaining the wonders of God's universe to the young. Meanwhile, however, the cult of the gentleman overspread the Western world.

A thousand books, from Castiglione to Cardinal Newman, celebrated the virtues of the gentleman. The concept is, of course, aristocratic. It assumes that a small fraction of the human race can be severed from the great mass of men who toil, and that these separated men, through birth, endowment, or training, can be entrusted with the conduct of the state. Freedom from the necessity of earning one's living by any vulgar trade or occupation is essential to the concept, since, by definition, manual labor was supposed to degrade, retail trade was mean, and any form of crude toil involved servile education. The training of the gentleman was made synonymous with liberal education; or rather, a liberal education was made synonymous with the training of gentlemen. It assumed either that he did not have to earn his living or that he earned it only by something remote and delicate like wholesale brewing or collecting rents. As a member of the leisure class the gentleman was under obligation to study philosophy, literature, and science (though only in an elegant way); and if, in addition, he took up book collecting, the patronage of painters, or the support of musicians, these became honorable parts of culture. To become a certified public accountant or a railway engineer, to run a garage acceptably or to set up a retail grocery store for personal profit, to become a professional football player, a mortician, a register of deeds, or a saloon keeper, no matter how honest one might be—occupations like these were beneath the dignity of the gentleman, who could deal with politics or business or trade or banking only in the grand manner and without soiling his hands with actual coin.

These sentiments may seem mildly shocking. I am being deliberately severe because one of the great problems of our society—I had almost said the overwhelming problem of our society—is that everybody wants a white collar job.[b] Now a white collar job is not necessarily a good job or an interesting job or a secure job. But it has prestige. This prestige is the latest phase of the cult of the gentleman. It springs from the curious assumption that it is liberalizing to know Greek but not liberalizing to

[b][Cf. Chapter II by Lyman Bryson (including comments by George N. Shuster and Louis J. A. Mercier).]

repair a carburetor, that writing a paper about imaginary people in a novel is cultural but writing about actual people for a paper is merely vocational, that working with books connotes wisdom and working with tools connotes ignorance. These seem to me rather astonishing assumptions.

So long as Western society was organized into ranks and classes the cult of the gentleman furnished acceptable leaders. Emerson, in his *English Traits,* found the English gentleman, member of Parliament and justice of the peace, an excellent specimen of humanity. But today the whole basis of leadership in our society has shifted, whereas the assumptions of the college have not shifted, or have not shifted sufficiently to give us the kind of leadership we need. Because, decade after decade, our colleges have turned out amateurs who have been shielded for four years from the necessity of facing real choices in industrial society, Dean Donham, late of the Harvard Business School, I think rightly, charges that the colleges talk about training for leadership and do almost nothing to furnish it in any real sense. They do not attempt to ascertain what kinds of leaders are needed in the industrial order, how you train them, or what manner of persons with what sort of qualifications are to be trained.[c]

The cult of the gentleman has had another unexpected result, upon which I can touch only briefly. The greatest need of labor in this country is for broad-gauge leadership, which can result only from the right education of the right people. The interest of labor in labor education is real, is great, and is increasing. But I think even the most sympathetic observer must say that the notion of labor education common in the movement is doctrinaire; and I suggest that this is one of the prices we pay for the cult of the gentleman. For, though our colleges are theoretically open to all and are increasingly representative of all parts of American society, it is still an historic truth that the cult of the gentleman has been associated with the interests of the employers, its

[c] Comment by Herman Finer:

It is a serious question whether you can train for *leadership.* Leadership lies rather in character than in intellectual furniture. A good many men sat in the same classes with Franklin Delano Roosevelt but he was the only one with the unique unteachable qualities. The attempt has been made for many decades to find leaders in public administration. Where are the best results? In Britain, where Macaulay and his colleagues and successors deliberately rejected the specific job of producing leaders and applied themselves to producing *minds,* or rather of discovering them, and then inducting them into the fellowship of learned and public spirited men?

assumptions have been sometimes violently, though often innocently, anti-labor; and labor in this country has not enjoyed the same quality of leadership that has apparently been developed in Great Britain. It is only in the past decade, in fact, that the colleges have really faced this problem, and they are still too often condescending in their attitude to labor.[d]

But it is now time to turn to that other human being descending to us from the Renaissance, the laboratory scientist. In order to be appointed to a college faculty in the eighteenth century (and even later), the scientist, as I said, had for a long time to pretend that he, too, was a theologian. His chair was called the chair of natural philosophy, a phrase common to Scholastic thought, and he spent his classroom hours teaching the wonders of God's handiwork as revealed by the telescope and microscope. Outside of the university, meanwhile, he was becoming what he has since everywhere become—he was turning into a specialist in zoology or physics or engineering or non-Euclidean geometry, until about the middle of the past century, the universities began to capitulate and admitted him not because he was a philosopher, but because he was a specialist.

Almost immediately the concept of specialism swept the colleges and universities off their feet. Not only did the research worker conquer natural philosophy, but by infection and imitation he also conquered the arts. History ceased to be literary and became a research problem, as the monograph took the place of the narrative. Philology, or the scientific study of language, replaced *belles-lettres* in literature. Teachers of ethics sought by statistical inquiry to establish what is right and wrong.

[d]Comment by Herman Finer:

I cannot accept the suggestion that the poverty of labor education in the United States of America is due to the cult of the gentleman in the colleges. The reason labor education is as it is, is because the labor leaders are still in the throes of what may be called the "combat" stage in their fights with the employers. I speak as a friend of labor, and I think that the wants of the rank and file are too crudely materialistic to allow of an education in a "sense of State." It is hardly fair to compare American labor leaders with those in Britain, for firstly, the British labor movement began at the turn of the eighteenth into the nineteenth century, a long time ago, since which time both workers and employers have taken measure of the other side. Secondly, the British movement was born in a society where a sense of social obligation was already widely diffused. Thirdly, many British labor leaders came directly out of the noncomformist and the established Churches—they were born of and raised in Christian ethics. Indeed, they became "gentlemen"! It will be appreciated, therefore, that it was not formal education that alone produced the British labor leaders, nor principally: they were formed by their social environment of which education was but a part.

Education and One World

Philosophy gave birth to psychology, which soon adopted a laboratory technique. Specialists in education multiplied. Schools of engineering increased from six to one hundred and fifty in half a century. Technological institutes multiplied. We have not merely developed them in engineering and business, but we have also developed an institute for religious and social studies, an English institute, an institute for current world affairs, and eventually an institute so advanced, dizzy, and rarified that it is known simply as The Institute of Advanced Studies, Princeton, New Jersey.

The triumph of the specialists, notably after 1876 when The Johns Hopkins University opened its doors with an avowed program of pursuing graduate study for its own sake—that is, of creating and continuing specialisms, was a double triumph, immediate, spectacular, dazzling. One part of this triumph was his conquest of higher education. The specialist took over the graduate school, which is now completely in his control. He created a rich variety of schools and colleges for his specialisms—in medicine, in dentistry, in public health, in business, in library science, in journalism, in engineering, in agriculture, in public administration. He invented or caused to be invented a variety of non-academic specialist institutions unsullied by the necessity of teaching and wholly dedicated to research, such as the General Electric Laboratories in Schenectady, the Brookings Institution in Washington, and the School of Classical Studies in Rome.[e] He created the university press, so that his findings might be reported to his colleagues at the expense of somebody else. He is now demanding support from the federal government in a bill to subsidize research and research workers at an expense of hundreds of millions of dollars a year. And, of course, he invaded the undergraduate college, so successfully that the last two

---

[e]Comment by Herman Finer:

I do not think that the significance of institutes like Brookings is properly brought out in the slightly ironic account of their establishment. The three institutes mentioned are, by the way, not on a par, and do not fulfil the same social function. I put this question: in a democratic country, where law is made by public opinion, but where public opinion is itself simply the clumsy result of the collision of the self-created opinion of many little publics, what organs are necessary to attempt to clarify the facts and issues free from egoism which obscures some of the issues all or some of the time, and which is the very life of each egocentric group? This service is necessary to modern tumultuous and segmented society: something of objectivity and a higher view of distant and long-range consequences needs to be made evident to the struggling groups, partially blinded by self-interest.

years of its four year course were henceforth devoted to specialism rather than to leadership. It is with difficulty that some part of the first two years, or the awkward age, has been reserved for general education. He even reaches down into the high schools through such instruments as Science Talent Search, and appears in the intervals of symphony concerts to publicize the results of his labors. In the Middle Ages this same period would presumably have been reserved to proclaim a knowledge of God.

All this was possible because in Western society generally, but particularly in the United States, the other side of his triumph, beginning in the eighteenth century, was also spectacular, dazzling, and critical. This was his creation and conquest of industry. Pure science led to applied science; applied science fed its problems to pure science; and the application of the scientific method in industrial society to the production, advertising, and distribution of goods, from the earliest known engineering concept through the invention of the interchangeable part down to the singing commercial recorded on a disk and heard simultaneously in twenty million places—this has revolutionized the whole structure of our society, all Western values, our human relation to the earth, the connection between population and warfare—indeed, everything from babies' diapers to the atom bomb. So critical has been this revolution that thoughtful men came to see that, unless the social process of the industrial order were itself understood, mankind might be broken on machines of its own contriving. Accordingly, as the industrial revolution developed, the third great component was added to the burden of higher education—the concept of the social sciences.

It was not until the mercantile revolution of the eighteenth century was well under way that Adam Smith published his *Wealth of Nations,* from which we conventionally date modern economic theory; it was not until the industrial order was established that Comte in France and Spencer in England founded modern sociology; it was not until industrial imperialism threw the men of the West into violent contact with so-called backward nations that anthropology reached its present importance; and it was not until the maladjustments of Western society grew more and more disturbing and less and less soluble in religious terms that psychiatry and social psychology became therapeutic instruments in the modern state. Today it can almost be said that courses in social relations, social psychology, and anthropology seem to many of our young people their chief hope for understanding the anarchy of the contemporary world—an anarchy created by our former unbounded faith that the industrial society, made and manned by specialists, requires no guidance from us. The development of departments of social science in universities has been as rapid, as startling, and as significant as was the development of the research scientist in the nineteenth century; and in college after college you will find today that a significant proportion of undergraduates—sometimes more than half the school—is concentrating in one or more of the social sciences and related fields. Indeed, the study of literature, of the fine arts, of philosophy is not seldom undertaken in terms of the social revelation they can give; and there are even those who, in place of explaining the social order by theological truth, prefer to explain philosophic and scientific systems as products of particular phases of social development. Particularly in the United States the wide acceptance of the theories of William James and of John Dewey, with their strong sociological overtones, our national distrust of metaphysics, our comfortable belief that *ad hoc* solutions will get us through, have given us that bent toward the social gospel that foreigners remark. "Service" as a motto is a unique American word, but it is a motto with social overtones.

But here, too, the specialist has been triumphant. Seeking to understand society, the student confronted not merely a department of economics, but a specialist in economic history, one in money and banking, a third in the theory of the business cycle, and a fourth in economic statistics. If he turned to the sociologists, he had to choose among courses in the social and psychological foundations of behavior, culture change, the sociology of the family, social pathology, opinion and communication, and introduction to quantitative methods. If he tried public administration, he faced an expert in constitutional law, a second in commodity controls, a third in the legislative process, and a fourth in fiscal policy. Man and society disappear from his vision as men and specialties crowd them out. And because each of these expensively trained professors is enthusiastic for his topic and sure that the student requires the discipline of his particular specialty, the general understanding of society as a whole by average men is not greatly advanced.

This situation is worsened by our educational accounting system, which I may call the savings bank deposit theory. All conceivable knowledge, we believe, can be cut up into units, each exactly like another, and each of these courses, with a few exceptions, is worth precisely as much at the bank as any other of them. When your savings bank book shows that you have accumulated sixteen or thirty-two of them, you can graduate, but not before. If you have thirty-one units you cannot graduate, and if you have thirty-three, you throw one away. The principle of the interchangeable part was never more strikingly illustrated than by the accumulation of thirty-two credits for a B.A. degree.

The doctrine of the interchangeable part is in turn the product of the departmental system, and this in turn is the product of the supreme importance of the specialist. The student is supposed to thread his way among courses and departments, like Christian going among the lions in *Pilgrim's Progress,* or if I may change my figure, like an aboriginal hunter. The young man develops considerable skill in stalking game easy to kill; but if we suppose he seriously wants to understand the world in which he lives, our collegiate customs often make it difficult for him to do so. Let me illustrate my meaning.

I will begin with my own department—the department of English. It is supposed to arouse in the student an enthusiasm for books. If, however, my undergraduate wants to find out about books written in some other language, he will have to bow himself out of the English department and knock at the door of another department—let us say, Romance languages. If in the department of Romance languages, he becomes interested in the French novel and curious as to what led Balzac and Flaubert and Zola to write as they did about French workingmen, Parisian shopkeepers, and provincial wives, the department of Romance languages says to him: "Your curiosity is laudable, but we are not permitted to satisfy it in any thorough way. Go across the campus to the history department; if they are not too crowded, you can perhaps enroll in a course in the history of Europe in the nineteenth century and learn about the political and social conditions of Zola's time." If the student, now enrolled in the history course, casually discovers that the philosophy we call positivism had much to do with what Frenchmen thought; or if he is told that Saint-Simon and Louis Blanc formulated theories of society and the state; or if he discovers that serious differences of opinion about the nature of truth eventually came to influence French national policy about the church and education; the history department will in turn have to extrude him and advise him to take a relevant course in philosophy, if he can find one. I say "if he can find one," because literary instruction and much history tend to be organized on nationalistic lines, whereas instruction in philosophy and science is not organized on nationalistic lines but assumes that God has scattered genius through the human race without regard to racial origins—except as we assume that genius is a monopoly of Europeans and Americans.

I shall not send my undergraduate further—for example, to fine arts or anthropology—for the reason that it is clear how curiously we play the departmental game. Of course, I have assumed an extreme case, but you will observe that any synthesis of ideas about France the young man may arrive at, he will have to achieve privately and by himself. And this places a burden on him no adult would bear. Moreover, the information he has now acquired about France and French ways comes to him haphazardly and in contradictory forms. For example, his knowledge of French philosophers came to him, not because they were French but because they were philosophers, whereas his information about language came to him, not because it was language but because it was French. In studying French literature he received good instruction, let us say, in the poetry of the seventeenth century, when France was an absolute monarchy and the court had a monopoly on culture, but not even Frenchmen would argue that this was much help in understanding the present problems of the French empire. And my point is that, because we have to live in a world exhibiting the most terrible clash of cultures that history has ever known, we cannot much longer, if we are to survive in it, trust to this casual method of studying the cultures that are in conflict. What I am saying is that when you have specialized instruction, you are going to have compartmentalized information—and it is asking too much of the American high school graduate, when he goes to college, to make privately a synthesis his teachers refuse to make for him professionally.

At this point upholders of a more conservative tradition have something to say. They rightly look upon themselves as guardians of a great intellectual tradition that is constantly under attack—a tradition which begins with the Greeks and the ancient Hebrews and comes down to us. In this tradition thinkers like Plato and Thomas Aquinas and Descartes, poets like Sophocles and Shakespeare and Goethe, elements of thought like pure mathematics and formal logic and literary composition—all these have something to tell us, something, indeed, so powerful and useful, they argue, as to create almost automatically in the right student that insight, that judgment, that breadth which will yield understanding of life, right decisions in social issues, and support for the right social order. To deny that existing college curricula have produced many admirable alumni would be absurd. To say that in the simpler situations of the past—for example, the society which gave us our Constitution—leadership of this sort proved wise and good is true. But our situation is complicated; and the radical defect of this theory of education is that it assumes that understanding society is so simple and plain a problem, any student can make a useful transfer of practical inferences from a study of *Julius Caesar,* Plato's *Republic,* and John Locke, to practical problems of municipal elections, after he has left college. I fear this seldom happens in this direct way. The theory lays on the ordinary student an even greater burden of synthesis than does my supposititious case about France; and in fact, of course, college after college has tried to institute some integrative principle, some mode of bringing these remote traditional matters into useful relationship with the fearful problems of our time.[f]

In a book called *Education and World Tragedy* published a little over a year ago I tentatively proposed another approach to the problem.[g] I shall have to refer my reader to that volume for a more detailed discussion of my idea; and I freely admit that a thousand practical details of administration and teaching would have to be changed if my proposals were accepted by the customary college. But it is sometimes useful to be speculative; and to avoid improvement because present systems of bookkeeping are not geared to change, is no argument against alteration. In these parlous times it seems to me not only proper but necessary for anybody with an idea making, as he hopes, for peace, to come forward with it and to defend it if he can.

I proposed there a six-point program as an ideal for our college education. The six points enumerated in my book are these: 1) Professional or vocational training for all; 2) the study of the theory of science and of the application of scientific discoveries to our technology; 3) the study of personal relationships in modern society; 4) the assumptions

---

[f] [Cf. Comment by George B. de Huszar, in Appendix III, dealing with Dr. Jones's discussion of the use of "great books."]

[g] [Cf. Comment by I. L. Kandel in Appendix III, on this book and on Dr. Jones's chapter.]

and workings of representative government, particularly in the United States and in the British Commonwealth of Nations; 5) the study of Russia; 6) the study of the Orient.[h]

Reflection will show that these six objects of study fall into two main divisions: 1) Studies intended to illuminate Western industrial society, particularly in the United States; and 2) studies intended to make it clear that we are living in one world, and not merely in the world of Western man.[i]

[h]Comment by Paul L. Essert:
I believe there is one other area of study which should be added to the six: the consistent, continuous participation of the student throughout his liberal arts studies in democratic processes in situations which test his practical application of his theoretical studies of these cultures.

Comment by Louis W. Norris:
No one should doubt the value of Professor Jones's educational program. Many would want, as I do, however, to see a seventh proposition added which makes place for studies in philosophy or metaphysics, and perhaps an eighth one to cover the history of civilization. Chancellor Hutchins's belief that "educating a man to live in any particular time or place . . . is . . . foreign to a true conception of education," is at least a pole of thought that should stand in continuous tension with Professor Jones's view of contemporaneity in education.

Comment by Swami Nikhilananda:
It is a matter for surprise that Professor Jones has omitted the study of religion and the humanities from his six point program, though he acknowledges the tremendous influence of the medieval and Renaissance cultures upon modern Western education. If religious study is excluded from the healthy atmosphere of the universities and is left to private initiative, the entire phenomenon of religion will be encrusted with more and more superstition. Two great wars in one generation have demonstrated the inadequacy of a purely mechanistic interpretation of life and the universe. Ethics, economics, and esthetics, divorced from genuine spiritual experience, degenerate into selfishness, greed, and lustfulness.

It is contended, perhaps with truth, that a basic antagonism exists between Christianity and the physical sciences. Their methods are different. Hence religion is regarded as incompatible with the scientific method that dominates the education in the universities today. It is equally true, however, that there are many professors who are eager to effect a *rapprochement* between religion and science without abandoning the unique features of each. In the cultural tradition of India one does not find an incompatibility of secular and spiritual knowledge. Known as the "lower" and the "higher" knowledge, both were studied with zeal. Both were considered necessary for the realization of truth. The science of the soul, the science of matter, and the science of Ultimate Reality were integrated by the ancient Hindus, revealing a true picture of "One World."
[i]Comment by Clem C. Linnenberg, Jr.:
This program reflects far more of a "world view of man" than is to be found in those programs which try to attain such a view but are limited in focus to Western culture, whether in the neo-medievalist manner or otherwise. To ignore important areas and cultures merely because one dislikes them or because they are different from one's own,

If there were time, I should like to demonstrate why I think the liberal college makes a mistake in theoretically ignoring the truth that its graduates are going to have to seek jobs in a highly competitive social scheme. I can argue the point here no further than to say it is my belief that the college ought normally to admit no one to its classes until he has given some reasonable assurance that he proposes to pursue a course of professional or vocational training. It is wonderful how, when the individual establishes such a goal, his education comes into focus, and how, by postponing the necessity for such a decision, we permit freshmen and sophomores to wander aimlessly through vague courses until as juniors they begin what seems to them their real education.[j] I shall

---

is to invite disaster, as Professor Jones has lucidly shown. The only change I would make in Professor Jones's program of education would be to add an explicit treatment of the problems and possibilities of world federation and the alternatives to it as conceived by diversely but thoroughly informed people—pacifism without federation; a *pax Romana* (this is at least two different alternatives, depending upon which country gets to be Rome); and so on.

Comment by Herman Finer:

What is clear about our living "in one world"? We live in one world geographically, and only that. It is not suggested, is it, that the world is morally one? Is it intended by Professor Jones to say that we ought to be morally one? How much in common ethically must the various societies of the world possess to be just to each other, and peaceful in their search for the standards of justice? This problem might be the starting point of an inquiry into the nature of education.

[j]Comment by Clem C. Linnenberg, Jr.:

Professor Jones presents the case for requiring every liberal arts student to decide upon a vocational goal before he is admitted to college. The idea is rather persuasive; but the choice of a vocation is vastly facilitated by exposure, even on a humble level, to the opportunity of close observation of a few occupations. This will ordinarily mean some work experience. Such a thing lies outside of the designing of a college curriculum; but it must in some way be arranged if Professor Jones's tough but useful rule be adopted. In the case of youths who have the stuff to fit them for a more intellectual sort of work than that engaged in by their adult relatives, it is especially true that to make the decision demanded by Professor Jones at home is to make it in a vacuum.

While a vocational slant can benefit liberal education, it is also true that liberal education can make a person more effective in his job, if the job is of a professional sort. Every field of professional knowledge is constantly absorbing facts and ideas from beyond its borders. Once these are properly authenticated as relevant to the particular profession, even its dullest member may possibly recognize their existence. An equally fruitful process, but one which involves much more individual initiative, is to expose the student to a field of knowledge which is not yet formally recognized as a part of his professional training but which has a general relationship to it—and then let him discover for himself the impact of the allied field upon his own. An economist who is trained in anthropology is likely to be much more alert in economic analysis than is an economist who, in his training, devoted to economics the amount of time which the first man spent on the two fields combined. It is difficult to think there is one obvious answer

likewise not argue for the desirability of general instruction, not merely in science and the assumptions of science, but also in what happens to society when you turn the specialist loose to invent whatever he pleases. I have said elsewhere that it seems to me insufficient to praise research for its own sake, since the tremendous (and sometimes tragic) results of research for its own sake, when these results take the form of widespread technological change in modern society, are as basic to an understanding of the modern world as is any part of science. As for instruction in the actual workings of democratic government, this is so patent a need, it is surprising to me that college students can be graduated without instruction in the subject, as they too frequently are. By instruction in this area, I do not refer to a mere paper knowledge of the Constitution, but to what I may call the actual sociology of the representative process. And, finally, it would take a very long time indeed for me to expound what I think is needed in the way of re-establishing faith in personal relationships in the world today.[k]

and only one answer to a given economic question when you know that there are cultures which never have conceived the question.

[k]Comment by John D. Wild:

This is a most delightful and refreshing paper, but I emerge from it with a feeling that Mr. Jones really means something rather different from what he says.

In a very vivid and forceful manner he describes how our colleges and universities have preserved the trappings, paraphernalia, and structure of the medieval schools, almost everything in fact but the central, living idea, and how they have embalmed the language, philology, and machinery of classicism without its vital spirit of critical reflection. All this would seem to point very clearly to the need not of more courses, fields, and machinery, but of a new vital spirit emanating from a sound, intelligible point of view, or what Mr. Jones calls a "central living idea." But in the constructive part of his paper he gives us nothing of this, but only a list of courses, fields, and subjects to be dealt with. Frankly this is a great disappointment.

I simply cannot agree with his preference for more vocational training, nor do I see how this fits in with his keen awareness of the dangers of narrow specialism. The recent collapse of German culture has given us first hand evidence of the ease with which masses of highly trained vocational specialists may be misled to disaster by childish forms of propaganda to which any half-educated person should have been completely impervious. For the reasons given by Mr. Jones himself, I believe that the professional, vocational element of our college training should be weakened rather than strengthened. We are not going to be saved from the crises now confronting us by technical engineers or laboratory specialists.

[Cf. the discussion of the place of vocational preparation in the goals of education in Chapter II by Lyman Bryson (including comment by George N. Shuster), Chapter III by T. V. Smith, Chapter XV by Dr. Shuster, Chapter XVI by Earl J. McGrath (including comment by Louis J. A. Mercier), Chapter XVIII by Harold Taylor (including comments by Mason W. Gross and Dr. Mercier), and comment by George B. de Huszar in Appendix III.]

Recognizing that these are vast and perplexing problems, I wish to devote my remaining space briefly to two points: the study of the Orient and the study of Russia. I spoke earlier of the medieval inheritance of our universities, and it may surprise you if I now say that, in some sense, it is to that medieval inheritance these two points return. What was essentially right in medieval education was that it was directed toward a world view of man. The medieval curriculum bounded the known earth; it afforded a clear and sufficient theory of human life before the rise of nationalism and before the existence of peoples other than those of Western Europe and the Near East was generally known. The great virtue of that point of view was unity. But to return, as some people at the University of Chicago want to do, to that inheritance with a view to regaining unity without recognizing the complete change in the complexion of the world seems to me, at any rate, a romantic impossibility.[1] We can no longer interpret life solely in terms of Europe. And the error of those who, wishing to avoid the excessive specialism of our college education, want to restore general education, is that they have instituted courses in Western thought and culture, contemporary civilization, or the like, which underline or overemphasize the supposed superiority of the Western world to all other cultures on the earth whatsoever. Western culture has very great value, but I doubt that it has the value of monopoly. When so much of the globe is in open or covert revolt against the fruits of Europeanism, to reorganize general education around a merely Western idea, seems to me unfortunate and parochial. If ever there was a time when we should teach and learn what values, hopes, and ambitions are cherished in the vast areas of Russia, the rest of Asia, Africa, South America, and the islands of the sea, now is the time humbly and patiently to begin. I fear that the academic mind has not everywhere adjusted itself to the meaning of the atomic age. In the interests of peace, and even of survival, I believe that liberal education in this country must recognize the primacy of this problem.[m] In fact, I believe this so thoroughly that I am prepared to face with equa-

---

[1] [For further discussion of the "Chicago Plan," see Chapter II by Lyman Bryson, Chapter III by T. V. Smith, Chapter VIII by Alain L. Locke, Chapter XI by John U. Nef, Chapter XIII by Mordecai M. Kaplan, Chapter XV by George N. Shuster, Chapter XVI by Earl J. McGrath, Chapter XVII by Ordway Tead, and George B. de Huszar's comment in Appendix III.]

[m] [Cf. Comment by Harry J. Carman, in Appendix III, dealing with Dr. Jones's discussion of Western provincialism.]

nimity the enormous charge that to ignore the ancient languages, not to make a place for Shakespeare, or to call into question the value of our present courses in poetry, history, or the arts, means that I have merely a Philistine notion of education.[n]

However, if my program represents a real return to the unity of man, it represents also a real revival of the Greek spirit of curiosity about the contemporary world.[o] The Greeks were not, so to speak, scholars of Latin and Greek. They were not a cloistered race. Their culture, in its great period, was unburdened by libraries, erudition, and scholarship comparable to our own. They were a people, as St. Paul said, eager after each new thing, acute, lively, cosmopolitan. Socrates did not talk

[n]Comment by Swami Akhilananda:
It seems to a sympathetic and objective observer that American higher educational institutions have almost ignored the cultures of the Orient. The result has been disastrous. Today, when the Orient is fully awakened to its ancient heritage and national aspirations, Americans, however powerful and wealthy they may be, cannot afford to continue unjustifiable attitudes and behavior patterns in interracial and interpersonal relationships without disastrous results. It should be realized by the authorities of higher educational institutions that they should assure, especially for their young scholars, a clear understanding of the ideals and functionings of such great cultures as India and China, and they should also be prepared to receive the contributions of these civilizations. A civilization begins to deteriorate when it becomes self-sufficient and closes its mind to the contributions of other cultures.

Comment by Swami Nikhilananda:
Up till now America has excluded, to all intents and purposes, the study of Indian culture. American professors of history, philosophy, religion, and sociology know next to nothing about those subjects as related to India. The Indian civilization is very old. That it is producing great men like Gandhi, Tagore, and Raman, not to speak of mystics like Ramakrishna and Vivekananda, proves its vitality. It is recognized by all that the region of southeast Asia is fast acquiring importance in the political, economic, and cultural fields. The realization of the ideal of "One World" and also of American leadership in world affairs requires that American youths should be familiar with the ancient civilization of India. Through the study of Oriental culture in a sympathetic spirit the West will broaden its religious outlook, discover the intimate relationship between the world of matter and the world of spirit, and help to usher in a world renaissance before whose scope and depth the European Renaissance, resulting from the contact with Hellenic culture, will appear small indeed.

[o]Comment by Clem C. Linnenberg, Jr.:
Professor Jones's "real return to the unity of man" and his "real revival of the Greek spirit of curiosity about the contemporary world" would assuredly be, as he hopes, a force for peace. It would contribute to peace directly, by promoting understanding, and indirectly by immeasurably helping to bring about world federation. Without world federation, including at least the United States and the Soviet Union at the outset and all countries eventually, there is no hope of long lasting peace, no matter how faithfully individuals may strive to understand each other.

for posterity but like a radio commentator; Plato wrote no conscious masterpieces, but like Churchill, Gandhi, Truman, Henry Wallace, whom you will, struggled with the local political problem, just as Thucydides wrote, not a classic, but a commentary something like Walter Lippmann. When we bind our colleges into attitudes of reverence for the Greeks, we are never less Hellenic; we far more resemble the old Manchu empire with its emphasis on keeping behind a Chinese wall than we resemble the free and open life of Hellas. I venture to suggest that Demosthenes would be far more interested in the program I have outlined than he would be in attending a class in Greek 5 every Tuesday, Thursday, and Saturday at nine.

My program is a difficult one. It implies that books and ideas have meaning in the cultural context which produced them, not as moral absolutes in college courses; it implies that we can replace the departmental separatism of the specialist by an integrated approach in studying an area, a language, and a culture, in terms of coherence and unity; it implies that, before catastrophe arrives, we can overcome our woeful lack of teachers competent to deal with cultures other than European ones. Particularly in the Oriental field enormous linguistic barriers exist, though I cannot admit that these barriers are greater for Westerners to overcome than those which Orientals surmount in learning about Europe and the United States. It implies more deeply still a kind of shock and reversal of our customary modes of thought—those modes of thought which the Oriental finds so condescending and blind. And, finally, it implies that a knowledge of Russia and of communism is a central fact in liberal education today.[p]

The fury of hysteria, prejudice, religious fanaticism, and political chicanery which has fallen upon the Russian question is incredible, is tragic, is disastrous, is insane. Newspapers drove one Russian institute out of Cornell University to Columbia; and the attitude of the attorney general, of the Committee on Un-American Activities, and

[p]Comment by Swami Akhilananda:
  It is indeed important that scholars should study carefully the background, philosophical interpretation, and actual working out of the teachings of Karl Marx, Lenin, and Stalin, in order to understand the hopes and aspirations of the Russian people. One may not find one's self in total sympathy with communistic activity, yet one must have clear knowledge of that important revolutionary movement, in order properly to face the present critical situation and handle it in a successful and peaceful manner. If the democratic countries really want peace they should adopt peaceful means, and this is possible only when there is real and deep understanding of the conflicting cultures.

of other branches of the government toward any society—for example, the Friends of Soviet Russia—trying to work for understanding between the two cultures is, indeed, discouraging. I can only quote from Mr. Salisbury's review of *Russia and the Russians* by Edward Crankshaw as it appeared in the conservative *New York Times Book Review* for February 15, 1948. Said Mr. Salisbury of this author:

". . . we have only two choices with Russia. We must understand her or we must destroy her. If we destroy her there is every reason to suppose that, along with Russia, we will destroy ourselves." (There is an even more horrible prospect, which he suggests without too much emphasis, that Russia might destroy us.) Mr. Crankshaw does not regard this as a mere exercise in logic or philosophy. He believes that the question of Russia and the West is here and now. "We have to ask what happens *now*," is the idea with which Mr. Crankshaw closes his book. "Russia is a force, potentially the greatest force in the world . . . We are left with the task of discovering how these people are to fit into the modern world. They exist, a nation of overwhelming and exuberantly increasing numbers. Russia, in a word, is one more fact of life, and a decisive one. Thus, the only answer, as it seems to me, is that our whole conception of society, of the way in which human beings live together, will have to be remodelled to allow for this new and unprecedented fact."

Mr. Salisbury and Mr. Crankshaw have between them said with force and eloquence what I am trying to say; namely, that a wider understanding of the forces at work in world society must be secured at whatever cost. This problem is now the central and tragic problem of American education. I do not say that the American liberal college is obsolete; but I do say that much of our thinking about liberal education in its relation to the world of today is obsolescent, and it is to a statement of a program of educational betterment that I have directed this paper.[q]

[q]Comment by John D. Wild:
 I gather that Mr. Jones is worried about our capacity really to understand Russia, and to set up a cooperative world community. So am I. But I am unable to follow him in the assumption that these crucially important aims will be achieved merely by setting up more machinery, professors, and secretaries, more fields and areas called "the study of Russia" and the "study of the Orient." *How* are these things to be studied; from what sort of integrating point of view? Is he proposing an amalgam of Western, Chinese, and Russian culture? If so, what would this be like? Or is he proposing a sort of cultural

relativism in which everyone seeks to divest himself so far as possible from all the culture he has?

I do not believe that Mr. Jones is advocating either of these alternatives. I gather that he is interested in correcting the economic and social injustices that distort our present civilization, that he wishes to see the vast power which modern technology has put into our hands used intelligently for the common good. All this is in line with the best philosophical and religious thought of our Western tradition, when properly understood. I gather further that he feels we should be humble about the rather rudimentary civilization we now possess at this early stage, precious as it is, and that we should be open to suggestion from alien sources. This also is thoroughly in line with what is best in our own tradition. If this is what Mr. Jones means, then what we need most of all is to recapture the basic insights and principles (religious as well as philosophical) upon which our Western culture was founded, and then to apply them to the critical problems of our time.

Comment by Ruth Strang:

The paper of Howard Mumford Jones is a convincing and exciting blueprint for higher education, but in order to build higher education according to this pattern, we must face two major difficulties: (1) the difficulty of finding teachers who have broad cultural background, integrity, mental alertness, and a constructive orientation to the modern world, (2) the difficulty of obtaining accurate, complete understanding of the values, philosophies, and secret plans of the leaders in Russia and the Eastern nations, and of preventing persuasive persons from indoctrinating impressionable young students with one-sided points of view. The Russian Primer, written soon after the Russian Revolution, proposed a realistic, constructive plan for developing the vast Russian natural resources for the welfare of the people. In contrast, a recent translation of a Russian textbook out-Hitlers Hitler in its aggressive attitude toward other nations. It is no easy task to get and weigh the facts and translate facts into truth. Perhaps a national fact-finding group, with high integrity, could furnish teachers with carefully evaluated information. If these difficulties could be overcome, and if all of these aspects of education were developed in the light of the guiding star of spiritual and moral values, Professor Jones's plan would have a good chance of contributing to the salvation of the world. [Cf. Professor Strang's further comment in Appendix III.]

Comment by I. L. Kandel:

Howard Mumford Jones is sound in his criticism of the aridity of college teaching but in criticizing the specialist's approach he is in danger of denying the value of the subjects properly taught. The paper is stimulating but, strong in its criticisms, it is weak in failing to offer some constructive suggestions. Is the issue that faces the world or the United States today due to a lack of knowledge and understanding of Russia and the Orient, or the cult of the Western tradition of culture, or is it the gradual disappearance of an emphasis in education on the development of moral standards?

Comment by Louis J. A. Mercier:

No fault can be found with Professor Jones's call to a widening of our horizons to take in Oriental thought. He might also have mentioned that there would be great value in studying the Arabic civilization which parallels the development of the Christian, since its knowledge seems to be necessary to understand not only the philosophical but the literary development in the West. Nor is there anything to be startled at in his call to study Russian thought. There is much more to Russian thought than communism. In fact, communism, out of Marx and ultimately Hegel, is not Russian at all. The real Russian thought which goes back to Oriental thought is deeply religious and even very interestingly mystical. It will no doubt blossom again when the Russian people will have a chance to rid itself of its forced importation of monistic Western thought. Though its mysticism may need the correction of Western intellectualism, we could greatly profit from the study of Oriental thought in general. It is certainly significant that such a humanistically trained educator as Professor Jones disregards the importance of Jewish and Christian thought, though they are essential even for a half-intelligent understanding of modern history and of our problems. It is a first indication of the one-sidedness of our academic circles.

Comment by Louis W. Norris:

Professor Jones has entered a strong and just plea for the relevance of education to its times. But there is grave danger here that the timeliness of education should obscure its timelessness. Socrates and Plato, as Professor Jones says (and even more truly Aristotle), "struggled with the local political problem." But the very reason they were able to make such helpful comments about social, ethical, and political questions was, that they were even more concerned to find out the "forms" of things that were timeless. Without the "definitions" of Socrates, the "ideas" of Plato, and the "forms" of Aristotle, their "radio commentating" would have been shallow jibberish forgotten as soon as ninety-nine per cent of present commentary. A frantic concern to understand Russia or the Orient will lead us nowhere, unless the student brings to these problems skill in analysis, order in valuing, knowledge of history, and such social experience as gives him a basis for judging what he finds out about Russia and the Orient.

CHAPTER X

The Function of the University in a Free Society

By DONALD C. STONE

Director of Administration, Economic Cooperation Administration

THE EUROPEAN RECOVERY PROGRAM, one of the boldest and most imaginative efforts in human history to preserve a civilization, requires professional and technical skill of great variety and resourcefulness. The universities of the United States and of Western Europe have produced during the past quarter century a large number of economists, scientists, and technicians of many kinds without whom it would be impossible to carry the program forward. While there are many gaps in the supply of such skills, particularly in Europe where university education came almost to a standstill during the war, it is not this lack which is most crucial to recovery. Neither will the mere supplying of several billion dollars worth of commodities and credits bring about the increased production of foods and industrial products which is so essential.

Rather, the main question is whether the participating countries and the United States of America will pull together in promoting those common measures which are essential to economic well being. Imperative as material aid may be, increased production and economic well being will be achieved only if the peoples of these countries and of the United States have the right motivation and the will to do the job. If labor and management will resolve their animosities, if political factions will bury their petty jealousies, if the different national and racial groups will forget their prejudices, an environment can be established within which efforts toward recovery will flourish.

Economic recovery could be attained in a remarkably short time if this environment possessed more positive qualities. Absence of acute frictions and disruptive influences is not enough. Such an environment or culture could be created if enough people possessed a dynamic spirit, devotion to ideals, humility, a faith which gives meaning and coherence to life, and were willing to place the principles underlying this faith above all other values.

The need for more persons in all walks of life to provide this type of leadership is essential at this hour, for worldwide battlelines have been drawn between those, on the one hand, who believe in the sacredness of human personality, in freedom of mankind to realize the highest potentialities God has destined for it, and in love as the basis for all human relationships, and those, on the other hand, who exalt the materialistic state and employ whatever means they find advantageous, no matter how treacherous, and corrupting, to achieve manmade purposes. We find many of the latter group attracted to communism, which follows the thesis that any means—no matter how vicious—are justified by the end. The main characteristic of man's plight in the world today is not the East-West conflict as such, but the struggle between democracy and dictatorship, freedom and enslavement, and righteousness and evil, wherever these issues flourish. The conflict is worldwide and arises within the United States and other democracies as well as between nations.

Just being "against" dictatorship, injustice, and other social ills is unfortunately not enough. "You can't lick something with nothing." If the course of democracy and freedom is to survive, something more dynamic and appealing to the minds and hearts of men must motivate those who subscribe to this way of life than "pleasant fortune" or material well being as the crown of human existence. Too many people have good intentions, but are ineffectual. European recovery and, for that matter, economic well being in the United States will depend on the uniting of people for higher values. Only in this way can there be born the new spirit so urgently needed. The economics can be worked out readily if sustained by a healthy moral and spiritual environment.

But in these days the university does not talk much about such things. They are matters just a bit below its dignity to consider, except in a rather detached philosophical light. The aim seems to be to stifle emotion in youth and make them "fishy eyed," so that they will not be susceptible to propaganda. Whereas what is needed above all else is to arouse constructive emotion—indeed a passion for doing battle until the men behind the iron curtain are free, until injustice, prejudice, corruption, hate, and greed are supplanted at home and abroad.

It is within this elementary context that I discuss the function of the university. In the early days of the university its main contribution was to preserve the scholarship of the past, to find the key to the good life, and to explore those requisites for human behavior which would improve the condition of society.

Later it was found that science could contribute to man's existence, and a whole new world of activity arose in which scientific research and the teaching of the professions became the dominant feature of the university. As ethics and philosophical studies became crowded out and as we began to place our main reliance in science for bringing "the Kingdom of God on Earth," the university began to take for granted the desirability of an environment of freedom and democracy and to give little thought to the necessity of developing young men and women who would make its achievement their primary life purpose.

One of the most disheartening efforts is to inventory the number of scientists, artists, and members of the professions who directly or indirectly apply their talents in enterprises which corrupt youth as well as adults. Neat salaries are garnered by the artist, the chemist, and the social psychologist, as they demonstrate conclusively to one hundred million Americans that since more physicians smoke Fumettes than any other brand, they cannot share in the more abundant life unless they do likewise. Even an egg beater cannot be sold today without the aid of an alluring female form to attract man's furtive eye. However, the educated man is broadminded, so he yields readily to the era of beneficent Fumettes and more lustful egg beaters.

Not only do we focus attention in the university upon what a diploma will mean in getting ahead and in being successful—as the marketplace judges success, but also the attention given to the more fundamental aspect of society and the plight of man is largely one of analysis. We analyze and diagnose, we observe and comment, we take opinion polls and editorialize. The universities produce graduates who can talk glibly about social ills and moral disintegration, but they produce few people with the passion and ability to do anything about them. The competition among university graduates for achievement on the moral and spiritual front is not very great.

Obviously, university graduates must earn a living and provide for the necessities of life. Too many of us like to make our way by turning a deal rather than by hard labor in which we produce "food, clothing, and shelter." Vocational proficiency is essential. But man lives in society. Thus he has need also for moral and spiritual development which gives cosmic significance to his life and sustains him as he works out his relationships with others.

Modern science has given us undreamed of powers for the harnessing of nature. Through the social sciences, psychology, and biology we have learned much about human behavior and culture. But man's ability to harness himself to moral ends and maintain satisfactory relations with his fellow beings has failed woefully in keeping up with the powers which technology has placed in his hands.

In the university today the student learns very little about the moral nature of the universe. Few graduates have any real appreciation that there are certain inherent laws stamped into the fabric of life which govern human behavior. Except in a vague way it is little understood that if mankind is to secure peace and security and to establish an environment in which he can realize his best potentialities, he must conform to these requisites. This is difficult to comprehend, because the failure to observe these moral imperatives, either deliberately or through ignorance, is inevitably paid for in suffering—collective suffering as the result of entire countries following an immoral ideology; individual suffering because we try to run against the grain of life and it crosses us up.[a]

We can understand these moral imperatives through intellectual processes and through the study of social experience. We come into full

[a] Comment by Quincy Wright:
  It seems to me that education to fit people into one shrinking world in which change accelerates and conflict becomes more destructive must have a large element of tentativeness and relativity in the values it teaches. Instead of uniting and fighting for higher values, should we not reflect, and compare and apply wisdom to see whether apparent conflicts cannot be synthesized or error eliminated by reason and diplomacy? Mr. Stone's battling for the good is stirring, but may not some of our good be superseded by a better in our changing and inventive world? I appreciate the evidence that argument is of little avail against such dogmatic religions as that professed in Moscow. But let us not hasten a war which may not be necessary, by abandoning the tentativeness and experimentation and flexibility which is the essence of democracy.
  The argument on the one hand for commitment to action to preserve threatened values, and on the other hand for reflection to consider the possibility of synthesis and reconciliation of apparent opposites, are both strong and both arguments must be kept constantly in mind. Civilization may lag if the will to preserve our values becomes "sicklied o'er by the pale cast of thought," and also if discussion and reason and the possibility of error are forgotten in crusading for values which seem obvious, adequate, and acceptable, to all but the wicked or perverse. The problem cannot be solved by knowledge or logic, but only by wisdom and balance.
  [Cf. Chapter VIII by Alain L. Locke.]

realization of them when we drink at the fountain of the great prophets and humble our spirits before the Son of Man. But only when we tap divine resources do we find the faith and power to transform society.

The world abounds in examples of men and women who through a new found apprehension of God have harnessed a perverse human nature to great ends, have been changed from self-centered, lustful, or ineffective persons to generous, loving, and dynamic characters. Yet the university, which should be in the vanguard of analyzing such cases and building its teaching on the basis of scientific observation, lets these amazing phenomena pass by almost unnoticed. I have often wondered if the explanation of this is fear on the part of the psychologists and other social scientists that they would be forced to commit themselves to the way of life which their findings demonstrated to be valid.

Heretofore in human history pockets of free people survived for long periods in a world where most people were enslaved. Gradually the more appealing conception of life of the free people would win new converts. Such societies struggling to maintain democratic values would often be destroyed by conquest, making it necessary for the process to begin all over again.

With extraordinary development of weapons of mass destruction and techniques of corruption, is there not now a question whether civilization can be perpetuated so long as pockets of totalitarianism exist? These weapons in the hands of a small minority can quickly and decisively bring a peace loving majority within or without a country to its destruction. Either we must convert these threatening pockets to the democratic conception of life and reduce the cells which are alien to the principles of a free society to such small dimensions that threats they may make to peace can be readily controlled, or we might as well surrender now hope that the disruptive forces which inevitably break out in a police state will somehow in future generations give mankind a better start. The time is not long.

At the 1945 meeting of the Conference on Science, Philosophy and Religion, there was a consensus that no common culture existed throughout the world which provided an adequate basis for the maintenance of peace and security. By culture was meant the scale or system of ideas by which people live throughout the world. Culture was viewed as the sum total of our convictions as to the relative value of ideas and ideals, those which are to be esteemed and those which are not.

Consequently, the aim of the university must be not merely to further knowledge, to teach professions, and to carry on scientific research, but withal to help instil in all students the ethical and spiritual ideals which we must share in common if the world's culture is to provide a suitable environment for democracy and a free world society. Otherwise, the end product of education tends to be the training of individuals to make their profession an end in itself and to get ahead by accumulating material goods for purely self-centered purposes. The professions call for only small, specialized groups. Democracy and freedom concern everyone, and we are all equally responsible.

Yet we tend increasingly to leave this field of ethical and spiritual ideals to some special faculty and group of students. Such an attitude, of course, is comforting because it relieves us of responsibility. Politics are readily shunned as something sordid. The church in Germany, and only to a lesser extent elsewhere, could view the morality of politics as something apart from its concern. "Good people" could remain relatively indifferent to the horrors of the concentration camp.

Specifically, all graduates must sustain and contribute to these higher freedoms through new moral infusion. No generation can advance by living off of another generation's morality.

It is for these reasons I propose that the *first* obligation of the university is to prepare all students to help create and actively sustain a free society everywhere. Any narrower approach to education will not only lead to the collapse of what freedoms we have but also to frustration and bitterness on the part of the individual, because he lacks not only a synthesis of knowledge, but also a synthesis of life without which there can be no realization of his higher potentialities. Individual action in both private and public endeavors will falter unless the individuals initiating such action embody zeal, wisdom, and moral purpose. Just as security cannot exist among nations when they rely upon military power rather than upon establishment of a suitable moral climate and culture, so, too, individual security comes only in the development of a satisfying philosophy of life and the application of moral and spiritual principles to daily living.

I have come to the conclusion, based upon my own experience as well as upon the record of human efforts to find "the good life," that the only scale of values—the only culture—which provides a key for coping with the spreading pockets of totalitarianism within the United States and without is that reflected in Christianity.[b] In Christ we find carried to highest fulfilment the moral values and spiritual potentiality of human life which the world has been seeking through the ages. Only when the leaders who are emerging from our universities zealously apply Christian principles to all problems—ranging from individual behavior on the one hand to the execution of the European Recovery Program on the other—will we establish a solid basis for personal self-realization and a "one world" free society. The university must recognize that the two go hand in hand.

Nota bene:

The addition of a required course or the conduct of an "inspirational" chapel series will not solve the problem.

[b]Comment by Clem C. Linnenberg, Jr.:
The mass conversion which Mr. Stone envisages raises some deeply perplexing questions. In rejecting non-Christian contributions to the good life, what would he have done about Mr. Justice Brandeis, than whom there has never been a more devoted friend of democracy? Or Mr. Justice Cardozo, whose gentle, compassionate nature evoked a vision of Christ considerably more readily than does the bellicose Christianity of Mr. Stone? Or Mr. Justice Holmes, that profoundly skeptical old gentleman whose healthy influence on the national life, however one might characterize it, was hardly Christian? In Mr. Stone's grand crusade for democracy, would he have rejected Gandhi as an ally? Is Nehru's India to be brought to heel for its religious heresy?

And when the universities are instilling Mr. Stone's faith into their students, when young people are relearning a sectarian self-righteousness against which the most decent elements throughout the world have struggled for centuries, at what point is this process of narrowing the choice of satisfactory "cultures" to stop? When that remarkably diverse aggregation of faiths which includes the Unitarians, the Southern Baptists, Jehovah's Witnesses, and the Church of Rome, has at last made itself dominant, is the process of selecting the one satisfactory creed to stop there? There is an abyss between the doctrine of Mr. Stone and Professor Kaplan's view that all "civilizations, religions, economic systems, and social ways of . . . mankind" are ". . . the source of its miseries as well as of its hopes and aspirations."

[Cf. Chapter XIII by Mordecai M. Kaplan.]

CHAPTER XI

The Goal of American Education

By JOHN U. NEF

Chairman, Committee on Social Thought, The University of Chicago

※

IN A UNIVERSITY of the Far West the chairman of the board of trustees remarked recently to two visiting professors that their task is to change the thinking of the American people. Making harmless visitors feel pleased with themselves is one of the most innocent and agreeable weapons in the still well-stocked arsenal of Far Western hospitality. The visiting professors would have made a mistake if they had taken the chairman's remark seriously as a compliment to them. They would have made an even greater mistake if they had been misled, by the social occasion on which the compliment was paid, into supposing that the actual assignment was devoid of serious content. The chairman was convinced that the thinking of the American people needs to be changed.

During the past twenty years Americans have begun to lose the confidence they once had that the courses they have been following in business, in the professions, in amusements, and in education are the right courses. During the past ten years, the once pervasive optimism in this country has changed to an almost equally pervasive pessimism concerning the future of the world in general and the United States in particular. If a class of graduating students had been asked before the outbreak of the Second World War whether man's lot is happier now than it was in eighteenth century Europe, more than ninety-eight out of a hundred would have given an affirmative answer with complete assurance. Now it is by no means uncommon to find nearly half the pupils in such a class assuming that men were at least as happy in the eighteenth century.

The growing doubts which Americans feel over the validity of the lives they lead have had little effect on their conduct, or on such thought as lies behind it. While pessimists are replacing optimists, the new breed is one of fatalistic pessimists. Apart from the sentimentalists, who talk as if the millennium could be achieved simply by speaking in favor of it, and the communists, who talk as if the millennium could be achieved simply by giving absolute authority to a leader pledged to dispossess and shoot the rich, the very great majority of Americans, including most of the sentimentalists and the communists, never think of altering their conventional conduct in the specialized work and the specialized recreation which engage them. They do what is expected no matter how uneasy they become lest the consequence of everyone's doing what is expected of him may be the destruction of all. This combination of worry with indifference reaches an extreme in the numerous persons who say in one breath that another world war will destroy civilization and that such a war is inevitable. The prospect of collective suicide has lost something of its absurdity in societies where individual suicide has become so prevalent and where the means of destruction seem to promise, most fallaciously, that collective suicide will be easy and comparatively painless.

If the world is dividing politically into two camps, is this not to a considerable degree a result of the intellectual and spiritual poverty that have accompanied the material triumphs which the novel use of power and machinery during the past hundred years made possible? If mankind has open to it only two mutually exclusive ways of meeting the great recurring problem of happiness in the material world, then its intellectual resources must have become small indeed. The result of serious thought and reflection, combined with humanity and love, might be conceivably a single faith, but it would hardly be two so-called "ways of life" here below, each bent on crushing the other.

A single formula for existence in an eternity beyond human experience is not rationally indefensible. Almost anything is possible in that eternity. As Pascal remarked, it is no more irrational to assume that eternity exists than to assume it does not. If it exists then we may rationally suppose eternal life to be very different from the temporal life we know, to be beyond the realm of controversy, competition and strife to which on earth human beings are condemned by their nature.

Since controversy, competition, and strife are an inevitable part of temporal existence, the problem of the wise is to divert them into constructive channels, and to prevent them as far as possible from producing violence. History and philosophy alike show that the conditions of human happiness on earth are many rather than one, and that diversity of experience in temporal joys and sorrows and in daily work is itself an important condition of happiness. The precise ways of living that enable men and women to fulfil their human potentialities are as fleeting as life itself. The vision of perfection combined with the universality of many imperfections would be the only basis for any enduring unity among human beings everywhere. Black or white, fascism or communism, Panslavism or Americanism, capitalism or socialism, as the alternatives in the temporal affairs of men and women, are the result less of wrong thinking than of no thinking. They are the result, not of faith, love, and charity, but of spiritual nihilism and hatred. The task of education is not so much to change the thinking of the American people as to help them and other peoples throughout the world to *think*, and to recognize that thought and action, thought and history, are not independent but interdependent. Fatalism and intolerance are near twins. They can prevail only to the extent that men and women lose their belief, their hope in the specifically human powers of rational thought, imagination, love, and charity, the powers with which according to the Christian faith God has endowed human beings through minds and souls that are independent of time, space, and matter.

The goal of education is to help in building up a world which provides rich alternatives to fatalism and intolerance, alternatives capable of claiming the allegiance now given only to extreme, irrational positions which set group against group, nation against nation, with a violence that our most famous eighteenth century ancestors assumed to be impossible among civilized peoples. For many decades the higher learning has given in the main a bad example. It has focused the attention of scholars and teachers upon the special and the particular, at the very period in Western history when specialization and particularism in economic and political, and even in artistic life have been carried to extremes unknown in earlier civilized societies. One effect has been to deprive the most gifted minds of even the normal hope of influencing men and women for the better. The subject matter which the ordinary scholar commands is usually so small and unimportant for history as to be inconsequential. The audience he can reach with the fruits of his special studies is so tiny as to seem even more inconsequential than the subject matter. That is why the need is now so great, if we are to serve the goal of education, to relate the special studies we pursue to the whole of man's nature and to those common aspirations, to the common strength and the common weaknesses, which are to be found in human beings everywhere—in Asia and Africa as well as in Europe, in South America and the islands of the oceans as well as in the United States, in dark and yellow skinned as well as white skinned men and women. At a time when all parts, all races, all creeds of the world have been brought into economic, social, and military interdependence as never before in history, what happens to the whole (so neglected by men's minds in recent times) is bound to have immense effects on the parts, on the special groups and nations whose interests their members so jealously guard.

If we are to work toward the goal we have defined for education, sharp comprehensive changes in the intellectual and moral outlook of men and women everywhere are required, nowhere more perhaps, unless it be in Russia, than in America. Modern democracy and communism may be poles apart concerning the nature of freedom and the nature of justice. They are at one in conceiving of both freedom and justice and other human values predominantly in terms of material goods. They are at one in assuming that if men only wring all they can from the natural resources of the earth, if they only go on working to increase the volume of output and to decrease the death rate from disease, the future welfare of mankind will be assured, provided their way of seeking these objectives triumphs over all other ways. What both fail to recognize is that the pursuit of these objectives is full of dangers for human happiness. War, overpopulation, the exhaustion of resources, can deprive men of the possibility of pursuing these objectives at the very time when they have deprived themselves by habit of their faculties for seeking other equally human objectives, beauty, truth, and morality foremost among them.

If education in the United States at this critical stage in civilized history is to set an example, is to be of service to human nature in its variety and richness, education should cease to serve the material at the expense of the spiritual, the special at the expense of the general. It should cease to serve the interests of the nation at the expense of world community, upon the creation of which the welfare of every nation, our own not least, has come to depend.

The Goal of American Education

I

The movement in American education led during the past fifteen years or so by Chancellor Hutchins of the University of Chicago has had from the beginning such objects in view. In a symposium devoted to the goals of American education, it is desirable therefore to take stock of what this movement has tried to accomplish, what it should try to accomplish, how its objectives are related to peace and good will among men and to the prevalence of an orderly, disciplined, yet varied and intelligent life, in which claims of the spirit are given a dignified place neither inferior to nor in conflict with those of the body.[a]

The new educational movement which centers at Chicago aims to make Americans more adult in their thinking, more complete in their view of human existence. From colonial times the people in America have had to meet difficult practical problems if they were to take advantage (in the interest of a high material standard of living) of the rich natural resources provided by a sparsely settled and for the most part uncivilized continent. The solution of one practical problem usually created many new ones. Business enterprise, whatever its faults and whatever its corruption, has met these multiplying problems with extraordinary energy and with remarkable success. By concentrating on the practical material problems of special individuals, of special regions, special subjects—by treating these practical material problems, which specialization helped to solve in a great continent at peace, as the only problems worthy of the serious and undivided attention of our most gifted young men, we have starved a part of our nature. We have largely lost the faculty of recognizing and revealing the permanent in the particular, and thus of giving actual content to abstract propositions, even of giving meaning to the words which we use all the more freely for their lack of substance and for the abundance of paper and other materials needed for verbal communication. We have diverted our energy, our generosity, our kindliness, our love, and such charity as has been vouchsafed us, into the service of the very particular, individual, and selfish interests and causes which divide. In these ways Americans have

[a] [For further discussion of the "Chicago Plan," see Chapter II by Lyman Bryson, Chapter III by T. V. Smith, Chapter VIII by Alain L. Locke, Chapter IX by Howard Mumford Jones, Chapter XIII by Mordecai M. Kaplan, Chapter XV by George N. Shuster, Chapter XVI by Earl J. McGrath, Chapter XVII by Ordway Tead, and George B. de Huszar's comment in Appendix III.]

largely deprived themselves of those human faculties, the power of thought and of contemplation which are man's chief resource when he is left to himself, and which paradoxically provide him with the more enduring means of human intercommunication for which mechanical efficiency and speed in transmitting messages are no substitute. It is this starvation of an enriching side of human nature that has made us so afraid of being left alone, that has prodded us to occupy every minute of our days and evenings with activities.

The program of the Chicago school starts with the conviction that college work should have serious meaning, that it should fill the lives of students, and that it should prepare them to assume responsibilities at an earlier age. With these objectives, Chancellor Hutchins introduced certain clearly conceived reforms. Some merely cleared the ground for intellectual work. Manifold are the extra-curricular activities which deprive college students of opportunities to taste the more enduring delights of the life of the mind and spirit, but the central one is intercollegiate football. By abolishing it at the University of Chicago in 1939, Dr. Hutchins attacked the vice of college triviality in its citadel.

Some months ago as an eminent colleague of mine, who has a great reputation in sociology, was coming out of the University Club, he met a football hero of some thirty years ago. The two had not seen each other since college days, when my colleague had been an inconspicuous member of the class and had confined his athletic activities to amateur skating and occasional games of tennis. In the intervening decades the other man had disappeared from the limelight which had played upon him in the football era at the University of Chicago, when he had made the third All-American team. But my colleague had a good memory and so was able to call his old classmate by his nickname of "Red."

Red was still living in his adolescence. He learned with astonishment that my colleague was employed at the University of Chicago. This knowledge enabled him to launch into an enthusiastic account of a broadcast he had listened to the night before. It had featured "old man" Stagg, the original University of Chicago coach and athletic director, now in his upper eighties.

After the account my colleague gave me of his meeting with Red, we could not help reflecting that a meeting thirty years hence between two classmates now in the college at Chicago could not have as its staple this particular triviality.

It may be desirable for many colleges to retain some restrained kinds of intercollegiate athletic competition. But if the leading universities of the country should follow Chicago's example in eliminating semi-professional football, this would help promising young persons to acquire a taste for serious thought and contemplation at an age when it is still easy to form good habits.[b]

In 1942, three years after the abolition of football at the University of Chicago, a reduction was made in the age at which college work can be completed. This was accomplished by opening the doors to students two years earlier than is the custom in other reputable educational institutes in the United States, and by granting the terminal bachelor's degree two years sooner. Students with first rate records are now admitted to the college after they have completed their second year of high school. After accomplishing work which is estimated to require on the average four years, they are eligible for the bachelor's degree. Other students who complete four years of high school are given the opportunity of graduating from college after following a course of study estimated to require two years. The new college is designed to graduate men and women at twenty instead of at twenty-two.

Graduate and professional training is now much more prolonged than it was a century or even a generation ago. Surgeons, for example, have frequently to study and serve for at least eight years after graduation from college before they can set up as full fledged practitioners. All over the world the young men of this and of the preceding generation have had long periods lifted out of their productive lives by the obligation to join the armed forces of their countries. Under these cir-

---

[b]Comment by George B. de Huszar:

Professor Nef fails to point out that other things than football have been eliminated at Chicago. Mr. Hutchins has stated that "We have excluded body-building and character-building. We have excluded the social graces." Mr. Hutchins also maintains that the university "should relax its desire to train students in the moral virtues," and objects to the fact that "Universities have developed the idea in parents, or parents have forced it upon universities, that the institution is in some way responsible for the moral, social, physical welfare of the students." (It should be pointed out that many of the distinguished scholars at Chicago do not agree with such notions and policies.) Thus it is maintained that since athletics, personality, character, and social graces have been eliminated and teen-agers have been given books, intellectual life flourishes. It is assumed that by rejecting ordinary and simple standards on which any civilized community is based, one will become an intellectual —a pose which can be attained by carrying books around, chattering about them, and conceiving oneself a privileged and superior being. However, true intellectuals do not talk *about* but are genuinely interested *in* thought and insight and are concretely concerned with quality and taste.

cumstances the persons who should be potentially the most gifted are hardly in a position to assume major responsibilities until they have reached a greater age than the one at which Keats, Schubert, Alexander the Great, or even Mozart, had completed their life work. If the drifts of the past half century continue, we might keep our best equipped men and women at some kind of school or in some kind of apprenticeship until they reach the age of retirement, which oddly enough has been frequently lowered. The reduction of the college graduation age represents an effort to halt processes which threaten to turn us into a nation of persons who enter their second childhood as soon as they have completed their childhood!

The administrative changes of the Chicago school so far mentioned are constructive only in the sense that, without them, construction would be more difficult. They help prepare the ground for building. We shall not lead men and women to be more adult and responsible simply by taking away some of their toys and by substituting for a system which divides education into three major units of 8-4-4 years, another which divides it into units of 8-2-4 or, if, as is our hope, the high schools reach into the elementary schools for their youngest pupils, 6-4-4. We must try to educate our citizens from their tenderest years in ways which will make them more adult at twenty than they now are at twenty-two, which will enable them to acquire disciplined habits of work before they enter graduate or professional schools, rather than waiting, as is now the case, until afterwards.

No doubt the achievement of this objective depends upon the early training received by children in homes and schools before they enter college. But it is up to the universities through their leadership, through their graduate schools and their adult education programs, as well as through their colleges, to indicate to fathers and mothers and to elementary school teachers what the best kinds of early training are, and to show what are the objectives of human existence that should arouse the enthusiasm and love of the very young. The reforms of the Chicago school all aim at such leadership.

The positive side of the college program consists, first, in setting up, in place of the system of electives, popularized at the end of the nineteenth century on the initiative of the late President Eliot of Harvard, a series of general courses in the natural and biological sciences, the humanities, and the social sciences. The generation now in middle life was graduated, some few with a knowledge of Greek or Latin, some with a knowledge of economics or political science, some others with a knowledge of history or sociology, others with a knowledge of one or two modern languages or of English literature and composition, others still with a knowledge of chemistry or physics, biology or mathematics, etc. The new program aims to provide all college students with one body of knowledge. In connection with it has been introduced a series of courses aiming to make sense of the whole. The most ambitious of these is entitled "Observation, Integration, and Interpretation." This course attempts to provide the students with the philosophical principles underlying intellectual, moral, and esthetic judgments.

The decisive questions are, of course, how good this curriculum is, how well it is taught, and how effectively the students master it. We are still in an experimental stage. Considerable differences have existed from the beginning between the curriculum developed at the University of Chicago and that in Annapolis at St. John's College, which has been until recently under the direction of two of Hutchins's early colleagues —Stringfellow Barr, the historian, and Scott Buchanan, the mathematician and scientist. At St. John's the student is trained in science with four years of active laboratory work. He is expected to learn four foreign languages.

At both St. John's and Chicago emphasis has been laid upon the reading of books of enduring value. It is here that the change in conditions produced by the reforms of the Chicago school is most marked. Twenty years ago, before the movement of reform began, it was with the utmost difficulty that I managed to get my associates at Swarthmore College to let me introduce in a course in economics such books as *The Wealth of Nations, The Spirit of the Laws,* and *The Social Contract.* I was finally permitted to use them as "collateral reading," which is reading of a kind nobody has time to do. The main business of the course was to master Raymond Bye's *Principles of Economics.* Getting-bye became the only concern of the student.

If a cultured visitor to the University of Chicago were now unwittingly to collide on a slippery winter's day with a college student burdened with an armful of books, he would see the familiar names of, say, Herodotus, Aristotle, Shakespeare, Homer, Dante, or Kant. Eighteen years or so ago a cultured visitor who had a similar collision would not have been able to recognize the author of a single one of the books lying scattered in the snow. If the collision had the slightest charm for him it was only that of the body with which he collided.

At the end of the new four year college, men and women are ready to start on a career or to enter a professional school or university. They have had an experience fundamentally different from the generations that preceded them—the generations that fought in the two world wars.[c]

II

The strategy of the Chicago school does not end with the colleges. Its objectives extend to the education of adults, the reform of schools of law and theology, even to the foundation alongside the old university graduate schools of a small university of a new kind.

The adult education program aims to reach as large a number of citizens as possible. It grew out of experience gained by Chancellor Hutchins and Professor Mortimer J. Adler, the American philosopher,

[c]Comment by George B. de Huszar:
I have read Professor Nef's paper with a great deal of interest, particularly because it deals with Mr. Hutchins's educational experiment, a subject on which I have been writing a book entitled, *Education for Chaos*. It is my thesis that the educational experiment under discussion is a failure basically for intellectual reasons. An immature and improperly conceived philosophy, when applied, is bound to create chaos. Plato has pointed out in the *Republic* that an improper conception of philosophy will bring upon it the charge so often made against it, that it undermines morality and unsettles the mind. According to Plato the study of "dialectic" should come at a proper age, and steadiness of character should be combined with speculative activity. At Chicago, intellectual training comes before the teen-age student has a chance to develop morally and emotionally. And without the chest, the seat of sentiment, the cerebral man surrenders to the visceral man. [Cf. Dr. de Huszar's comment in Appendix III.]

Comment by Louis J. A. Mercier:
This able exposition of Chancellor Hutchins's school of thought calls for little comment as I have already recognized the value of Hutchins's recovery of metaphysics. By all means, let all those capable of understanding them read "the great books"; but an exhaustive study of the St. John's list leaves me in doubt whether that list really includes all the books necessary to grasp thoroughly the opposition between the two fundamental alternatives of thought: monism which gives us a pantheistic or atheistic total evolutionism, and dualism which gives us theism, a philosophy of the abiding above and in the changing, and the possibility of accepting Christianity. Even if they do, the question remains whether their reading will issue in dilettantes, skeptics, or believers in the saving alternative.

It may be, however, that the American university can do no more than to give its students an honest survey of the fundamental alternatives of thought, of their ramifications, and of the history of their consequences. If it did, it would do a great deal more than it is doing now. The mere thought that it might do so is enough to make us realize how little it is really doing now, save in the physical sciences.

in a kind of seminar which they offered jointly for many years for groups of some twenty to thirty college students. The seminar was devoted to the discussion of various great books of the Western world, selected to instruct participants in the common moral and intellectual tradition which we derive from our European forebears. Eight years ago the experiment was tried of setting up a series of some six seminars of this kind, and of opening them to the public upon payment of a fee. A particular great book or part of it was assigned as a basis for the discussion at each meeting. The discussion aimed to bring out ideas of enduring value derived from the book and to illustrate them with the help of experiences with which members of the classes were familiar.

During the past seven years these seminars have multiplied in Chicago and have extended to many other cities. They are now under the direction of a corporation of the University of Chicago, called "The Great Books Foundation." Some forty thousand or more people are taking part in the classes this year [1948] as compared with some seven thousand last year. It is hoped that the number will increase in geometrical progression from year to year until it reaches into the millions. In anticipation, the *Encyclopaedia Britannica,* now affiliated with the University of Chicago with Dr. Hutchins as chairman of its Board, hopes eventually to print a set of the "Great Books," as these have been selected by a committee presided over by Dr. Hutchins.

American law schools have become increasingly pragmatic in their training during the past fifty years. The "case method," which like the elective system originated at Harvard, forsook ethical principles almost altogether as a part of the program of instruction. In the early years of the century a student at the Harvard Law School remarked in Professor Beale's class: "I shouldn't think that the law on this point should be as it is." To which Beale answered, "We are not teaching what the law ought to be but what it is." So the students have been schooled in the precedents set by the judges in series of litigations and trials until, when they graduate, they can estimate how, in the light of past experience, a particular case will probably go and advise their clients accordingly. These methods are deeply intrenched, and no radical departure has yet been made from them even at Chicago. But courses in the fundamental principles of jurisprudence and ethics have been introduced. It is intended that the validity of decisions in particular cases shall be considered in the light of principles instead of being taken for granted.

It is hoped that eventually this new training in principles may be adopted more extensively at Chicago and then by many law schools, that it may inculcate a sense of the moral good as such among lawyers and judges throughout the country and also among politicians many of whom have been practicing lawyers or judges before they enter politics.

Studies for the ministry at the University of Chicago were formerly divided between a number of independent theological schools, each with its own curriculum. These separate faculties have now been federated. As neither the Roman nor the Episcopalian communion (nor for that matter the Lutheran) is represented in the study of theology at the University of Chicago, the federation falls somewhat short of Christian completeness! It is nevertheless symbolical of a will toward unification which inspired it. There is always in the dim indistinct background the possibility that Hamlet might appear in the play.

Some of us have more generous and comprehensive hopes for Christianity. We hope that there will be a great resurgence and extension of the Christian faith, based, like the first extensions during the early centuries of our era, not upon force and fear but upon belief and trust. A universal, worldwide Christian society obviously could not be brought into being by pedagogy, even if teachers and scholars generally were believers in the divinity of Christ, which most of them are not. In all matters of education and creative thought, work of the mind loses its force when there is a straining for results which do not emerge as an inevitable consequence of free inquiry, of artistic and intellectual integrity. But for those who believe and who belong to universities, the problem of reconciling all the dogmas and all the learning of the past four centuries of Western scholarship with the Truth of Christian revelation is bound to arise in any work that has a trace of cosmic significance. Such persons should not be intimidated either by the prevalent unbelief or by the doctrinaire nature of most of the religion now expounded by the churches. They should face the problem of reconciling theology, philosophy, and science, the problem which has concerned this Conference from its inception.[d]

[d]Comment by John D. Wild:
   I sympathize with Mr. Nef's hope for "a great resurgence and extension of the Christian faith," but this suggests to me a further problem. It is certainly a scandal that students in our colleges and universities are now cut off from any instruction in religious thought and life which have played such a predominant role in the formation and history of our culture. But how can religious instruction (aside from a mere account of the historical

Thus envisaged, the hopes which we put in the Christian faith are not in conflict with the desires Mr. Hutchins shares with his friends to make an impression upon thought, even upon art, and through thought and art upon the life of our time. The reforms discussed hitherto are all of a pedagogical nature. They aim to revive the common Western moral and intellectual inheritance which existed among the learned and cultured down to the nineteenth century.[e] They aim to extend that inheritance to the majority of the population. But beyond these pedagogical reforms plans exist to provide a center (perhaps eventually several centers) for creative thinking and writing aiming at the unification of knowledge in the light of wisdom. An *Institut de Sagesse,* Jacques Maritain has called it. A beginning has been made by the Committee on Social Thought at the University of Chicago.

Modern knowledge presents difficulties which seem almost insuperable to the scholar or thinker who is seeking to unify and who is searching for universals. The enormous quantity of information, of ideas, and of theories, divided among the almost innumerable compartments into which knowledge has been split, confuses such a scholar and leaves him with a sense of impotence. The possibility of surmounting these difficulties rests, it may be suggested, in combining an instructed view of man and the universe, such as can be derived from the great intellectual and cultural traditions to which we are heirs, with the creative handling of one or more special subjects. The Committee on Social Thought aims to make possible such an approach to knowledge by a small faculty and

---

"facts" which is not necessarily religious, and is usually definitely anti-religious) be given in a present day college without being "doctrinaire"? Mr. Nef is aware of this difficulty, and I gather that he thinks it can be met. But he does not outline the mode of solution in any detail.

[e]Comment by John D. Wild:

I think that Mr. Nef is right in pointing to a ubiquitous trend of materialistic thought and a resulting subordination of education and indeed all human activity to the values of "success" as the chief disruptive factor in our contemporary civilization. The task of counteracting this tendency, usually masking itself in a disguise of supposedly "scientific" doctrine is now the major problem confronting American education. But I am not quite clear as to the strategy which Mr. Nef is recommending.

Mr. Nef speaks of "the common Western moral and intellectual inheritance which existed among the learned and cultured down to the nineteenth century." But this "inheritance" contains a vast number of disparate elements many of which are essentially opposed. Unless they are studied critically from some integrating point of view, they are apt to elicit merely an attitude of skeptical indifference which is the normal result of a survey course in the so-called history of philosophy. What is this integrating point of view? How for example, is Kant made to lie peacefully by the side of Aristotle?

a limited number of carefully selected graduate students. The purpose of the Committee is to discover interrelations which will help to relate the fragments into which knowledge has been split, especially during the past hundred years, and eventually to facilitate a unified vision such as existed in the limited area of Western Europe in the eighteenth century.

This Committee has recently issued a volume—*The Works of the Mind,* with contributions by Hutchins and a number of other distinguished men—which, it is hoped, may contribute to an understanding of the common purposes that are embodied in true works of scholarship, thought, art, and creative administration, and of the contributions which all such works—aiming as they do to reveal the universal in the particular—might make to a growing sense of world community. D. J. Boorstin's *The Lost World of Thomas Jefferson* and G. O. von Simson's *Sacred Fortress* are two works of synthesis by members of the Committee which have just appeared. The first reveals the common theological starting point from which all members of the Jeffersonian circle approached most diverse subjects. The second brings out the interdependence of religion, art, and politics in the great ecclesiastical monuments of sixth century Ravenna. Other books on the stocks are concerned with uniting knowledge which has been artificially separated by the growing specialization of learning during the past century.

In providing for the graduate students, the pervasive systems of memory tests and course credits have been abandoned. The students demonstrate their knowledge by written essays, by lectures, by the passing of general examinations which emphasize reason rather than memory, and by the composition of works of the mind. Graduate students are accepted as junior colleagues into what is intended to be a community of scholars aiming at the unification of knowledge.

In his *Higher Learning in America,* published in 1936, Mr. Hutchins remarked that American academies for graduate study, with their scores of separate and almost hermetically sealed departments, resemble encyclopedias rather than universities. The only unifying principle is supplied by the letters of the alphabet. He suggested that the natural sciences, the humanities, and the social sciences should all become more philosophical in their objectives.

It is the intention of those who formed the Committee on Social Thought to make them so. Original thought is the necessary lifeblood of a true university. It is only when researches are undertaken not for their own sake but for the higher purposes of humanity everywhere and always that they can command the allegiance, the imaginative insight, and the force necessary for the creation of lasting works of the mind. Graduate students of the Committee are introduced, through supervised reading and tutorial instruction, to the problems of the unification of knowledge by a study called "Fundamentals." An attempt is made to arouse their interest in basic issues of theological, philosophical, and historical knowledge. Each individual is encouraged to reconcile the contradictions that appear in these subjects.

The object is to help him with the work of synthesis. During the past centuries the general effect of the increase in empirical studies in the natural sciences, the social sciences, and the humanities has been to divide. Philosophical principles and imaginative insight are the generating forces that can reveal what it is important to bring together and how the unification can take place. As the reason for the existence of the Committee on Social Thought is to enable its faculty and students to contribute, as individuals, however humbly, to syntheses of knowledge, the training in "Fundamentals" is intended to be an integral part of the creative writing that each is invited to undertake. To be valid any partial synthesis of modern knowledge must rest, it is felt, on theological, metaphysical, and historical foundations.

The Committee aims to provide the conditions under which ideas may form and grow in gifted minds, helped by contact with older, more mature, thinkers in a number of different scholarly disciplines and even with men of letters and other artists. The instruction which the Committee aims to give is training in thinking combined with serious sustained research, begun as soon as possible in the student's graduate career. This research is not concerned with the indiscriminate collection of bits of knowledge or with the achievement of immediate practical results of a material kind. It is concerned rather with the examination and the testing of data in the light of an evolving philosophical, esthetic, or moral purpose—evolving because the continued exploration of interesting data helps the purpose itself to take on the tangibility and meaning without which no work can have substance or durability.

If such work of unification is to flourish at Chicago and elsewhere, it is indispensable that it should be carried on in a small and intimate way, independently of the means of mass communication—the radio, the cheap newspapers, and magazines—which have done so much to mechanize what should be natural, to stereotype what should be creative, to cheapen what should be valuable and even sacred. As Henry Adams wrote, "Any large body of students stifles the student. No one can instruct more than half a dozen students at once." What is true for the instruction of students is equally true of creative relations and great conversations among colleagues.

III

Is there a conflict between the two different sides of the program of the Chicago school—the education of the very many and the cultivation of creative thought among the very few? If knowledge could in fact be effectively unified, then the resulting work of unification should have a message for all. The fracturing of knowledge has much to do with the destruction of a general audience. This splitting of our cultural inheritance has made a present of the very large audience to the purveyors of sport, cheap entertainment, and sensationally presented news. The creative thinker or writer receives his ideas in trust for a large audience. The potential reader of the "great books" might conceivably provide this audience. One of the evils of the modern world is the enormous size of its enterprises. The evils of size are especially pronounced in the American universities of which there are hundreds, some with tens of thousands of students. In such enormous entities stereotyped and mechanized rules impede creative thought and discussion. Yet with a world of two billion people, made largely interdependent by modern technology, civilization cannot escape large units. The hope for the creative mind seems to lie in the establishment within those oceans of people of small islands devoted to creative thought, to letters, and to art, that is, to work which could have great meaning for many. What these groups need is independence, freedom, and security to work, and recognition for work which deserves recognition. The prizes which now go to cinema "stars," radio commentators, and some writers of best sellers are not for members of these groups. They must not be for sale.

The program of the Chicago school is still in an embryonic stage. Whether it lives up to its promise depends largely upon the persons who are entrusted to carry it out. How widespread and deep an impression it will make, the years alone can decide. This program is only one of many means of working toward the goal of building a Christian world community based on charity, love, and justice, rather than on force and murder or on confusion and individualism run wild. What universities can do is only a small part of what education can do—because the years before children are ready for college are in many ways of far greater importance than those at college in forming habits. University education, even college education, is not for everyone. We suffer today from too much education almost as much as from bad education. The goal of education ought to be the goal of human endeavor. Only by ceasing to be pedagogical in the narrow sense, only by appealing to the latent desires of men everywhere for a world in which mechanical efficiency is subordinated to wisdom, force both to charity and justice, and freedom to responsibility, can education contribute to the eternal happiness which all men and women have the right to seek.[f]

[f]Comment by Paul L. Essert:
This paper is an excellent statement of what the University of Chicago is trying to do to synthesize our specializations of knowledge, with their disastrous effect, into broad generalizations of wisdom. I believe that Dr. Nef's program presents a great need of our social life and a significant goal of education, but that the means adopted for attaining this goal will create further fragmentation and specialization. Nowhere does the paper point out the need for education to help the people think through the meaning of their own experiences, to take the daily distressing and specialized experiences and to get new meanings and new goods from them.
In brief, it seems to me that the illustration of the thesis, namely the Chicago plan, entirely overlooks the insistence of the paper upon the interdependency of thought and action.

Comment by Ruth Strang:
In order to change the intellectual and moral outlook of the American people in every way, Professor Nef has one main solution: Teach them how to think. Although he says that thought and action "are not independent but interdependent," his proposed system of education does not bridge the gap between learning to think and acting for the common good. Our doubts about the efficacy of this program center upon the following questions:
1. Does an education which emphasizes ideas almost exclusively equip students with the techniques and skills needed to implement ideas? Many such skills are practiced and learned in the extra-class activities in which students nominate and elect leaders, work together for the welfare of the group, engage in service activities, acquire skills and interests for the creative use of leisure—music, drama, art, handwork, sports.
2. Is there not a possible danger of swinging too far in the ideological direction, to the neglect of the physical aspects of life? Should not the practical arts of everyday life be developed as they have been in the *folkschule* of the Scandinavian countries? Has not thought itself developed in close association with the work of one's hands?
3. Is it a sound idea that "small islands devoted to creative thought" will leaven the masses? Are not large numbers of persons capable of creative thought within the range

of their own experience? There is some evidence from a new type of intelligence test featuring thinking and problem solving instead of verbal tasks, that children in high and low socio-economic groups do not differ greatly.

4. What evidence do we have that thinking leads to desirable action? Have there been follow-up studies which show that students educated according to the Chicago plan function better than other young people as workers, as citizens, and as members of families? Does this kind of education help them to start where they are and to contribute to the making of a better world?

Comment by Harold Taylor:

Mr. Nef states that the goal of education is to help in building up a world which provides rich alternatives to fatalism and intolerance. He then drops the matter of goals quickly, and moves on to a description of the means by which Mr. Hutchins has been trying to reform the University of Chicago for some years. The goal of these reforms is not stated, although by implication it would seem to be to make everything in higher education a little tidier and get it over a little faster, to justify Christian theology as ultimate explanation, and to order knowledge to that end on a set of basic rational principles. It is tempting to discuss the instruments of the Chicago program, the value of the practical reforms involved, the naive rationalism of the implicit philosophy, the passion for order which it indicates, and the urgent request which it seems to make to each student to nestle in the safety of the genteel tradition. But I content myself with pointing out the only two explicit instances cited by Mr. Nef of the values inherent in the program. First, that thirty years from now no University of Chicago graduate will discuss Mr. Stagg or football with any other graduate. I am not sure that this is an advantage. The conversation which I foresee in its place seems pretty dull, and would probably start with, "Do you feel that the natural sciences are now sufficiently integrated with rational theology?" It is also possible that there would be nothing to talk about at all, since if the Chicago program is successful, the conversation of each graduate would consist of a series of commentaries on Mr. Hutchins, Mr. Adler, and St. Thomas. I cannot help liking Mr. Nef's *Red,* who was so successful in the field of his choice, was still interested in it, and was loyal to Alonzo Stagg and the old regime.

The other instance is equally illuminating. If any of us were to collide with a student from the University of Chicago, says Mr. Nef, we would find that we had knocked down a little walking library of the Great Books from Herodotus to Kant, and that we had spread the ground with approved materials of the higher learning. Eighteen years ago, according to Mr. Nef, this would not have happened. The student, I imagine at that time, would have been wearing a raccoon coat, with pockets jammed with hip-flasks, *College Humor,* Hemingway, André Breton, Gide, football tickets, and the *Police Gazette.* Mr. Nef's example had the effect upon me of producing nostalgia for those earlier times when we had Sandburg, Dewey, John Reed, Dos Passos, Farrell, and a simpler world. If the new Chicago student is reading and carrying books whose titles and authors we would all recognize, that is a sign of change, if not progress. But for my part, I am looking for a system of education and society which will give us another Sandburg, even a Whitman, or perhaps an A. N. Whitehead.

CHAPTER XII

What Should Be the Goals of Education Above the Secondary School Level?

By LOUIS J. A. MERCIER

Professor of Comparative Philosophy and Literature, Georgetown University

THE DISCUSSION of the goals of education above the secondary school level is inextricably bound with that of those below.

The scope of secondary education was clear in the classical program developed at the University of Paris in the early sixteenth century, borrowed from it by Ignatius of Loyola, experimented with and tested out in the Jesuit colleges, and finally summed up as to curriculum and methods in the *Ratio Studiorum* of 1599.

Secondary education remained strictly classical and primarily formative, very specially in France, till the end of the nineteenth century. The fact remained that it had been devised at the beginning of the sixteenth century to meet the challenge of the Renaissance and of the emergence of a society in which the aristocracy was to dominate and the bourgeoisie to rise through sharing the new culture. It was therefore inevitable that three centuries later, after the aristocracy had been displaced by the bourgeoisie, and the masses in turn aspired to equal rights, and especially after the new challenge of the industrial revolution and its call for personnel, that the education devised to make cultured gentlemen should be considered inadequate. Not only the new social demands, but the new possibility of education for a larger number due to the growth of national income, could not but raise the issue of a more elastic system of secondary education which would allow an introduction to the new techniques, and, moreover, of the building up of a system of higher education necessary to pass on the rapidly accumulating achievements in the physical and social sciences, and of training for their further development.

The question then was: how much attention was it possible to give to these new demands within the college, the formative education unit, and what other units needed to be created or developed further to take care of them. Thus it is seen that our question: "What should be the goals of education above the secondary school level?" depends first on what should now be the goals of secondary education.

In Europe, and in the South American countries, and Canada, which continued to follow the lead of Europe, the problem remained comparatively simple. First, the college or lycée was retained as the secondary, formative, adolescent education unit, with graduation as Bachelor of Arts or Sciences before the twentieth year; and the university was developed as an entirely separate plant to which the college graduate went for graduate work in a chosen specialty. Secondly, within the college, the problem of the reorganization of secondary education was solved by the introduction of alternative programs. In fact, when the Jesuit colleges had been reopened at the beginning of the nineteenth century, a new program of studies had already been elaborated in the *Ratio Studiorum* of 1832. The native language was taught as a separate study throughout the course along with the retained Latin and Greek, and some place was made for history, mathematics, and gradually for chemistry and physics. The same held for the secular colleges. But by the end of the century this was far from enough. As the social and industrial revolution continued, the facilitated intercourse and commercial relations called notably for the teaching of modern languages, nor could it be ignored that the rapid growth of the secondary school population introduced a greater amount of individual differences as opposed to the comparatively small socially screened constituency of the seventeenth and eighteenth century colleges. In France, at the very beginning of the nineteenth century, a solution was found by offering four alternative programs: Latin-Greek, Latin-science, Latin-modern languages, modern languages-science. The consequences have often been criticized. It meant that Greek was largely abandoned and Latin less generally studied, with the consequence, it was said, that general culture and even accuracy in writing French deteriorated. It was also claimed that with the effort to introduce also large doses of history and some philosophy, all the programs were overloaded.

These, however, were questions of details. The goals of secondary and higher education remained clearly differentiated. That of secondary education continued to be formation, the acquiring of tools with consequent habits of analysis and expression, and an introduction to the main fields of knowledge. The goals of higher education were consequently the pursuit of specialties in the graduate schools of law and medicine, and in the faculties of letters, history, and geography, the physical sciences, philosophy, etc., in the universities. As there was no electivism within the alternate college programs; and as candidates for the higher humanities would certainly have taken at least the Latin course; and those electing science, if not Latin, the modern languages; all had a cultural background, linguistic tools, and at least a common well organized formation.

In the United States the picture has been wholly different. It is true that the colonial colleges were classical, close to the European pattern, and also had a socially screened constituency. But after the education of the masses became recognized as a state responsibility, an eight year elementary public school developed to be followed by a four year high school. The college was thus pushed up as a sequel to the high school, at first still for the few, but gradually, and especially since 1900, for an ever greater number, especially through the development of state universities.

This meant graduation from the elementary school at about thirteen years of age, from the high school after seventeen, and from the college after twenty-one, with consequent blurring of secondary education as such. Since the classical college graduated its students at about eighteen, the high school became its parallel. Was then the high school to replace the college as the organ of formative adolescent education? But the classical college began its work at least two years earlier. What then, too, of the post high school college? Was it to be also a secondary education institution? As formative education was hardly completed in the high school, it might well be, and yet evidently it should be more, since it kept its students well past their twentieth year. Was the college then after its first two years, still at the secondary school level, to introduce, in its last two years, studies at what was in Europe the university level, with implied specialization, requiring special methods and a special staff?

All these questions remained to plague us because with the elementary school reaching into the secondary education age, the high school far into the European classical college age, and the college at least two years into the European university age, the whole American educational system was completely scrambled.[a]

That is why when we ask, what should be the goals of education above the secondary school level, we must first determine where the secondary school level begins and ends, since it is in so far as we have not done so that all our educational discussions have remained hopelessly muddled, and too often our students could say with President Hutchins: "I went through high school in order to go to college, and through two years of college without knowing why."

This saying recalls that the high school, at least for those who plan to go to college, has tended to be not an autonomous institution with its own goal, but a coaching school for college entrance examinations. On the other hand, the general course for such students as did not envisage college has been a battleground for curriculum makers. What should the goal of the general course be, general or cultural education? If general, should Latin be retained, should modern languages, or should they not all be replaced by social studies? In fact, should not even the college preparatory course be stripped of language study, and the colleges asked to modify their entrance conditions?

At the college level, the debate has waxed no less fiercely. The state universities in particular have been accused of having completely sabotaged liberal and general education by offering and giving equal standing to all types of utilitarian studies throughout their four years. But furthermore it was not clear just where education of the secondary school type should stop in college and the university type begin.

It is significant, however, that out of this turmoil a tendency has emerged to unscramble our educational units by relabeling them. At least, the last two years of the elementary school have been distinguished as the junior high school, the first two years of the college as the junior college, and the last two as the senior college.

[a]Comment by John LaFarge, S.J.:
Anyone who has wrestled with the problem of trying to explain the American curriculum to the European mind will appreciate Dr. Mercier's clearcut analysis of the differences between their system and ours. It is easy—and laudable—to talk of exchange scholarships, but much time and effort will be lost if those who are exchanged, whether they come from Europe to the United States or *vice versa,* have no exact idea of what channel they are sailing in the educational sea. Clarification of goals, particular as well as general, is one of the most obvious preliminaries to any real international cultural understanding.

This is most interesting because if you take the junior high school, the high school, and the junior college, you get back the equivalent of the European–Canadian–South American college, or traditional institution for secondary, formative, adolescent education, in other words, an educational combination for students from about twelve to twenty years of age.

As soon as you do this, you may begin to discuss the goals of education in the same terms as in the European tradition: The combination junior high-high school-junior college is the domain of secondary as opposed to primary and higher education. Its natural goal is formation and general information. The senior college, on the contrary, belongs to the university, its legitimate goal is some specialization.

In fact this is not far from the present practice which developed after the reaction against unorganized electives. At least to some degree the colleges, again in the wake of Harvard, passed after 1910 from a system of free electivism to one of concentration and distribution. Their last two years, being given over to this concentration, offered courses open to both graduates and undergraduates at the university level, taught by professors in the graduate school.

From this it may be seen that the first two years of the present college, distinguishable as the junior college, really belong to secondary, formative education, while the last two years belong to higher or university education. For instance, at Harvard for the past thirty-five years, a typical freshman program consisted of English A, a fourth year of modern language, History 1, and one or two of the distribution subjects, necessarily of an introductory nature: a science, mathematics or philosophy, government, etc.; while the sophomore year, although the concentration was then chosen, still consisted of introductory courses, though more according to the specialty; a second modern language, a science, a survey course in literature, etc.

In the light of all this, it would seem that the question: "What should be the goals of education above the secondary school level?" should be restated as follows: "What should be the goals of higher education, understanding that it starts with the senior college, and follows upon a secondary education to be given in the junior high school, high school, and the junior college?"

However, as the work possible in the senior college will depend on the equipment obtained in the secondary education units, and as education should be a continuous process of concentric development, what secondary education should be may more profitably be taken up after recalling the progress made in recent years in elementary education.

There is value in considering that education is, as the etymology of the word may indicate, a drawing out, a development of existing powers and, as these powers are to be exercised on some objects, that it also implies the development of information about the self and other beings, about their natures, their consequent essential relations as means and ends, and about the history and expression of those relations.

We should therefore be ready to grant that elementary education demands first the education of the senses and of the power of generalizing upon sense data through organized observation of nature; and that the use of tools for recording such observation and induction, arithmetic, writing, reading, should be taught after the need of such records has been shown through experience.

The next group of experiences to be gained may well be such as give the consciousness of the needs of man for survival and for bettering his condition, the production of food, clothing, shelter, security, recreation. This may lead at once to two types of activities: personal experience in such production, a study of historical record of such production, and personal expression of personal production and of reflection upon the history of the production of others.

Nature study and the comparative study of nomadic shepherd life, agricultural life, of the crafts, of dwellings, of growing trade and industry, of town development, of the growing complexity of social and political relations, eventually of all the arts, and of the dependence of all human occupations on geography, and hence on geology, mineralogy, meteorology, and further still on chemistry and physics, are thus the natural subjects, at least in their elements, for elementary education. As the early progressives have shown, and in particular in this country Francis W. Parker between 1880 and 1900, all these subjects in their most elementary and general aspects which so naturally grow out of one another, can form a correlation, a compenetration of knowledge, through the grasp of life as a dynamic whole, which will beget interest in the child because he naturally seeks to know more about the various concrete aspects of the world he lives in. This natural, concrete approach to education is generally linked with the naturalistic movement in the wake of Rousseau, and has since been associated with purely materialistic doctrines, but it is really good Aristotelianism, since the fundamental principle of the epistemology of Aristotle is the induction of the universal out of particulars, which means to start with experience and to generalize from experience.

Elementary education can thus be made a fascinatingly happy period in the child's life, one, too, in which the practice of various games may prepare to make skilful use of the body in sports, as well as in physical work. Nor need or should secondary education remain short of the study of values. Physical values such as those of food, shelter, etc., will become readily obvious; but many occasions may also be found to bring out moral values: the need of justice for stable social relations and the maintenance of peace, the need of knowledge, prudence, courage, for personal success and happiness. Finally, as any study of history brings out, the constant effort of man to understand his origin and the possibility of his immortality reveals his spontaneous belief in supernatural beings, and of some duties to them. Hence, the question of religion cannot be kept out of education, even at the elementary level, without falsifying the record.

What then may secondary education be after an elementary education so understood?

In general, it cannot be said that the progressive approach through motivation through correlation of studies, based on the developing natural interests of students, has been so successfully worked out for the high school as it has been for the elementary school.

There are many reasons for this. The most basic is the educational tradition. How limited and one-sided is that tradition is not yet sufficiently appreciated.

It is well known that elementary education, even in the more advanced countries, had a haphazard organization until it was recognized as a state responsibility in the nineteenth century, but only the richer states could develop it adequately on a national scale, hence the continued high percentage of illiteracy in so many countries. Even where organized, elementary education generally remained the uncorrelated initiation to a few tools, "the three R's," and to a few facts, mostly of geography and of national history.

It is less generally realized how the educational tradition of secondary education developed.

In the Middle Ages it was necessarily for the few, who for the most part would become ecclesiastical leaders, or else secular leaders through the study of law and the practice of administration. The Middle Ages, as a consequence, developed a high quality of higher education, in law, philosophy, and theology.

But it was only at the beginning of the sixteenth century that, at the challenge of the Renaissance and because of the growth of cities and the consequent development of a middle class, secondary education was widely organized specially for laymen. As we have already recalled, the Jesuit colleges were the greatest influence for its propagation throughout Europe.

Because Latin had been used as a living language by the universities throughout the Middle Ages, medieval Latin had become laden with colloquialisms and technical terms. The Renaissance challenge was to recover classical Latin and to learn again to write with Ciceronian elegance. To do so, the method developed by Quintilian for the education of Roman youths, and abundantly discussed in his *Institutes of Oratory*, was used. It can therefore be said that Quintilian became the professor of education of the post-Renaissance era as the Jesuits elaborated and systematized his teachings.

Hence the curious consequence. Secondary education in the sixteenth and seventeenth centuries began as soon as pupils could read and write and had for its aim the speaking and the writing, in both prose and verse, of Latin, and even of Greek. This became the more readily the central aim as learned vernacular literatures did not yet exist and the physical sciences were in their infancy. The by-product was an acquaintance with the carefully expurgated greater classical writings and, as a complement, some study of mathematics and Aristotelian philosophy; but what the student was applauded for in solemn ceremonies of prize distribution were his Latin orations and poems, not to speak of the acting of Latin plays often written by his teachers. The central tradition of secondary education is, then, the teaching of Latin, and in a minor way of Greek, as living languages, which means as powers or skills.

Nor should it be forgotten that the results of such teaching produced startling results. Jesuit students so trained achieved the first masterpieces in their own tongue. In France, Balzac passed from the practice of Ciceronian Latin to organic French prose; Corneille from the study of Seneca and Stoic thought to pithy antithetical expression of man's faith in his will power; while Bossuet expressed the deepest philosophical and religious insight in oratorical masterpieces, and St. Francis de Sales the most confident piety with a humanistic sense of the duties of the state of life. Molière, less true to his masters in following a Christian philosophy of life, at least lifted comedy above the coarseness in which it had wallowed, and made it a realistic study of the foibles of men.

All these surpassing achievements might well be quoted in support of the thesis that thorough analysis and assimilation of the classical authors, of their keen discrimination and exactness of expression in the study of human behavior, make for what Newman called "the force, the steadiness, the comprehensiveness, and the versatility of intellect, the command over our own powers, the instinctive just estimate of things," or as he sums it up, "the culture of intellect." The fact that these great neo-classical French writers showed such a many-sided originality would also prove that to start in imitation of the greatest is a way of achieving greatness in turn, though this supposes the attitude of the French neo-classics themselves, as expressed by La Fontaine: imitation should not be slavish and should serve, as it were, rather as a priming to one's own originality.

Nevertheless, it was inevitable that in the early nineteenth century, the need of training in the new standardized vernacular languages, the development of the vernacular literatures, and the accumulating scientific data should call for a displacement of the classical languages as central subjects, the more so as they were no longer the vehicle of discussion for the learned.

What happened? Here we may note one of the most farreaching facts in the subsequent development of secondary education. The classical languages were displaced as spoken languages, but they were retained for the content of their literatures and for the study of their grammar. The study of the literature became a translation exercise, and the study of the grammar the learning of abstract rules to be applied in written exercises. It was then argued that there was much disciplinary value, much mental training in these processes, and this remained a chief argument for the retention of the classics. But this meant that the study of the classics became primarily a knowledge-subject instead of a skill-subject in that the grammar-translation method replaced an oral and written self-expression method. One consequence was that when the modern languages won admittance to the curriculum of secondary education, they borrowed this grammar-translation method, so that while the classics were taught as living languages in modern times, the modern foreign languages have largely been taught as dead languages.

The tradition of secondary education has then at its core the study of the ancient languages and literatures, partly because other subjects were little developed when it began, and it has come down to us essentially distorted. Partly, at least, a utilitarian subject in the sixteenth and seventeenth centuries, it has become with us a cultural and disciplinary subject as a preparation for higher education. In planning for the best possible reorganization of secondary education, it may well then be that we should restudy just where and how Latin and Greek are to be utilized.

Before discussing this reorganization, however, we must recall that in our democratic society with education open to all, we must first take into consideration the need of the differentiation of the school population. Since at least one third of the elementary school constituency may have intelligence quotients below eighty, we need high schools for special purposes. Students with I.Q.s between eighty and a hundred can hardly do well in primarily academic programs. Other students, though capable of making successful efforts in languages and the humanities, still may prefer more technical and practical subjects. It may therefore be estimated that for some sixty per cent, high school courses should be devised to prepare directly for trades and occupations, with the amount of cultural subjects to be introduced in such programs, and the special methods to be used to motivate them, remaining an interesting problem. Evidently such groups of courses should be considered as giving a terminative rather than a secondary education.

What we have to deal with therefore in planning a secondary education which would include the first two years of college, as part of an organic system of development, to be continued in the senior college and the graduate school, is at the most some forty per cent of the adolescents of a generation and more likely twenty-five to thirty per cent.

One way to attack the subject is to note that all possible courses offered in the high school, the college, or the university have to do with either the development of skills or the imparting of knowledge. Much of our confusion in education is due to our failure to distinguish between power or skill which functions unconsciously, and requires the formation of habits, and knowledge which can be acquired only by prolonged consideration in consciousness, and which may be retained without issuing into habits. Thus a child may have acquired the skill to express himself in his native language without being conscious of its structure, and, on the other hand, one may study the grammar of a language and develop no skill in using it.

It is essential therefore in the discussion of programs to distinguish between primarily skill-subjects and primarily knowledge-subjects. Evidently the languages are primarily skill-subjects, and so are the fine arts and music. The literatures, history, geography, government, economics, philosophy, theology, the physical sciences, and mathematics, are primarily knowledge-subjects. Many of the latter subjects, however, require or lead to manipulative skills, in fact all experimental sciences, at least for their improvement, and likewise, all knowledge-subjects which may be put into practice, such as law, medicine, surgery, engineering, government, teaching. One great problem in the organization of education is therefore to determine the distribution of subjects that are primarily skill-subjects and of those that are primarily knowledge-subjects, and the relative time and place to be assigned to the development of knowledge and to the development of skill in the study of such subjects as call more or less for both.

Taking up, then, the organization of a secondary education program for our selected group in terms of knowledge-subjects and skill-subjects, we must further keep in mind that the basic principle for an organic system of development is motivation. Witness the pathos in President Hutchins's saying: "I went through high school in order to go to college, and through two years of college without knowing why."

The problem of motivating the subjects of elementary education has been solved, as we saw, thanks to the progressive schools. In the high school motivation is still generally neglected. One reason is that in the elementary school there is a class teacher in charge of most subjects. The teacher may then more readily understand that she must teach in terms of the child and not of the subjects, that the development of the child is the goal and the subjects the means. In the high school, on the contrary, there are as many teachers as there are subjects, and it is hard for each to realize this, especially as each is a specialist.

The classical college of the sixteenth and seventeenth centuries, as we saw, solved the problem for its times. It was truly progressive. It made the organic development of the child its goal. Latin, Greek, the incidental handling of the vernacular, were taught by the same teacher. The humanistic course was a unit. What was to be done with the student was to develop in him the habits necessary for expressing himself in Latin and in Greek, and history, geography, mythology, were taught in commentaries to explain the texts the assimilation of which was to lead to self-expression. Through the reading of the basic classics and such commentaries upon them, the humanistic content of the Greco-Latin tradition was transmitted, an introduction to the dualistic humanism of the Aristotelian tradition was given, and the Christian tradition held up as a pattern of life. So far as it went, the original secondary education college was most progressive even in the modern sense.[b]

What we need is to learn to do as well as it did. Our trouble is that there are now so many more skills to be taught to the student, and so much more knowledge to which we must introduce him. The consequence has been an electivism which has steeped down from the college. The high school student may or may not have Latin or modern foreign languages. He may have Spanish but not French, United States history and modern history but no ancient history or *vice versa*. He will surely have courses in English, one language other than his own, some history, some mathematics, one science. Until very recently Harvard required three years of Latin for admission to the B.A. Now three years of mathematics may be substituted. But, in general, these studies remain dissociated in the student's mind as separate college entrance requirements; and often within the subjects, the units studied are never visualized in their proper relation to the whole. How many students have had some Caesar, Virgil, and Cicero, without getting the perspective of Latin literature or of its relation to Greek, or of the relation of both to history! How many have studied French or German only to read inconsequential texts selected for the degree of their difficulty! How many have studied algebra without knowing why they should!

And yet, it should not be difficult to motivate the secondary education program, and to make it organically concentric. We need only to

---

[b] [Cf. the discussion of medieval and Renaissance education in Chapter I by Robert Ulich, Chapter V by Scott Buchanan, Chapter VII by Charles W. Hendel, Chapter IX by Howard Mumford Jones.]

keep in mind that to do this we must recognize that the distinct human power is the power of generalizing from the comparison of individual data.

Granting that the elementary school child may best do this at first on the basis of personal concrete experiences, it would stunt his growth to limit his possibilities of further generalization to personal experiences. The record of the race is there for him to study: the political and economic history of the world, the history of religion, ethics, philosophy, science, and all the literatures. Moreover, the adolescent becomes capable of being motivated by more distant ends than the child. As he gradually becomes conscious of the importance of other peoples in the history of the world, of their written achievements, of his necessary or possible relations with them, the study of their languages and literatures may become an interest as spontaneous as was the child's interest in nature. The more detailed study of history thus becomes vitally motivated, increasing in turn his interest in the achievements of his own race. Finally the adolescent's growing experience with nature and the products of industry can easily be made to awaken his interest in the sciences.

It should therefore be easy for the junior high school and high school teacher to motivate the study of the ancient and modern languages, of general history and government, and of the elements of economics, with plentiful references to geography and allied sciences, especially geology. This in turn may motivate a special systematic though still elementary study of physics and of chemistry with references to mineralogy, while biology, physiology, hygiene, can even more easily be shown to be direct human concerns.

The division of subjects into skill-subjects and knowledge-subjects which we have discussed should enable us to see more readily how this can be done.

First, then, we have as skill-subjects, the languages and mathematics, with mathematics leading us directly to the discussion of the sciences.

Mathematics is well ensconced in the high school program. There remains only to take every precaution to motivate it by showing that it furnishes a skill necessary in the physical sciences. This may be done by giving the student such experiences as require the use of mathematics, thus satisfying the principle: motivate through the experience of a need. A further valuable approach to this is through the history of the experiences of the race which have led to the first scientific and mathematical discoveries. This approach has been well explored at St. John's, Annapolis (cf. catalogues) at the college level, and could be used in the high school. Such higher tools as analytical geometry and calculus could go into the junior college, but trigonometry might well be integrated with geometry as it has so many practical applications.

As for high school science, it can be motivated in terms of human needs: the need of physiological information, of hygiene, of geology, mineralogy, etc., as essential to the understanding of geography, of chemistry and physics in terms of their application in the home and environment, of the appliances which use the principles of kinetics, light, heat, electricity. How mathematics is used even in the most elementary statements of physical laws and the devising of machines should be emphasized.

The general motivation and goal should be to awaken the student fully to the fact that all material progress has been due to the development of the physical sciences and mathematics, and that they are the key to his understanding of the physical world around him. The science teacher might also point out that the development of industry based on the sciences is necessary for the production of sufficient wealth for the raising of the masses above a mere subsistence and low standard of living, for the development of schools, and even for the support of churches. Some reference might be made to the submerged populations, perhaps two-thirds of the earth's population in tropical and Asiatic lands, because of a lack of industrial development. This would in turn motivate the study of history, geography, and economics. Such a science course, which might be a two year course, might be more general in the first year and devote a semester each to chemistry and physics. It should develop a permanent interest in at least popularized scientific literature and awaken the particular interests of those having special aptitudes for such studies. There should of course be laboratory and shop work in the school and it should be encouraged as extracurricular at home through school exhibitions of completed projects. Nature study begun in the elementary school could also be continued by clubs of specially interested groups. The outside reading of biographies of scientists, of popular histories of science, of work, of popularization of recent discoveries, could be encouraged both in the science course and in English courses. Further cooperation between the English and science departments could include an encouragement to write for the English class compositions on scientific experiences and knowledge acquired.

The high school course in science and mathematics could thus insure that even those who would later specialize in the humanities would retain scientific interests.

Science and mathematics being thus taken care of, let us now see about the humanities, and the languages as skill-subjects.[c]

Here we are challenged by the needs of our day, as the educators of the sixteenth century were by those of theirs. And immediately, we may see that we are forced to consider a displacement of the classical languages on the very principle which installed them at the center of the secondary curriculum.

Latin, and even Greek, were necessary oral skills on the morrow of the Renaissance. They are no longer so. Why should they remain central subjects? Because their study is a good mental discipline? No doubt it is. But even granting that Latin and Greek, because more compact and synthetic languages, offer superior exercise in discrimination, and that such discrimination, induction, and deduction have disciplinary value because any exercise of such fundamental operations develops the habit of such operations, it cannot be said that the study of modern languages does not offer many such opportunities.

Especially should we realize that the classics were not studied, in the sixteenth and seventeenth centuries, for their disciplinary value but as practical skills, really as utilitarian subjects, and that, therefore, as such, their place today belongs to the modern languages.

[c]Comment by Paul L. Essert:
From here on Dr. Mercier seems to overlook the central fact of all cultures, the search for truth that would bring man out of the mire of poverty, disease, fear, and despair, and recall the university to the French–Canadian–South American positions of classical isolationism. My major disappointment in the paper is that it does not recognize the important relationship of the humanities and the sciences in both the secondary and higher levels. The exciting beginning which tends to recognize that a unifying philosophy might be evolved out of our world absorbing problems of the industrial production and distribution of goods should, in the light of modern needs, have been expanded throughout the program. The heart of the unifying principle is in the languages, from which broad knowledges are to be evolved; and as the student enters the university he is prepared for his specializations by having a basic working knowledge of the ideas of men expressed in their literature, particularly of the Western culture. While it is true that Dr. Mercier gives a parallel time value throughout secondary education to mathematics and science with the humanities, I did not seem to find that they came together in any close relationship. In brief, there is a close interrelationship between ideas and machines which the proposals do not seem entirely to recognize.

Let us then be ready to recognize that the place of the classical languages in the present day curriculum may well be readjusted in view of the new demands, so that we may have the necessary time to study the modern as the ancient were studied: as practical skills pushed so far that the students could use them in written and oral composition or self-expression.

If such astonishing results were attained in the classical college in the use of Latin and Greek, it was not only because of the excellent method of assimilation but because they were begun at an early age. So with us a modern language should be begun in the junior high school, and continued through at least three years of the high school. Such practice, on the basis of oral methods in Massachusetts schools has, in the present writer's experience, sent students to college who had good habits for self-expression in French, and who could carry on college work much as French born students. Even better results have been attained in the schools of Cleveland under the direction of Dr. E. de Sauzé who controls completely the method of training teachers, and the selection of pupils on the basis of at least one hundred I.Q.

It is then entirely possible to give our students adequate skill in a modern language such as the seventeenth century teacher gave his Latin pupils. It is also highly advisable that a second modern language be started in the high school, at least to the extent of giving habits of good pronunciation, reading habits, and some practice in oral and written synopsis work.

Does this mean that the classical languages should be eliminated from the secondary education of those who are to go to college? On the contrary. Their displacement should mean only this: that their inclusion is to be considered in terms of the type of skill which belongs to them in our day. We no longer need to use them for expression, but we do need to be able to understand texts written in them, if we are not to lose the tradition of the origin, and of some of the finest expression of Western thought. Latin should still be studied three years in the high school by all those who are likely to specialize in the humanities as an indispensable tool of introduction to the ancient world. Those who are likely to specialize in science should at least have a year of initiation to its easier texts and structure.

Although the Latin course may still be three years, Latin teachers should study whether the method of teaching Latin should not be completely renovated by dropping the grammar-translation method which represents a decadence as opposed to the very efficient sixteenth to seventeenth century method, the aim of which was assimilation of texts leading to their imitation.[d]

Deciphering the text with the help of dictionaries was not then held to be a virtue. On the contrary, the teacher first elucidated and discussed the text with the students in a prelection. He saw to it that they understood it before leaving the classroom by comments, the giving of the necessary erudition, and translation when necessary. The effort thus saved could be put on the assimilation of the elements of the text, and frequently by memorization of part of the text.

The same could be done today by preparing texts on the model of the Hachette-Paris series as follows:

> *Arma, virumque cano, Trojae qui primus ab oris*
> *Italiam, fato profugus. Lavinaque venit*
> *Littora: multum ille et terris jactatus et alto*
> *Vi Superum.*

(On opposite page or on back page:)

Cano arma, virumque	I sing the arms and the hero
qui profugus fato,	who a fugitive from fate
venit primus	came the first
ab oris Trojae	from the shores of Troy
Italiam	to Italy
littoraque Lavina	and the Lavinian shore:
ille jactatus multum	he much thrown about
et terris et alto	on lands and the high seas
vi superum.	by the power of the gods.

Students should then be instructed to read the original text till the meaning is spontaneously evident. This would provide the necessary eye training for the development of reading power which we now know to be necessary, and would insure far better results than now ob-

---

[d]Comment by John LaFarge, S.J.:

All those who, like myself, have pondered over the place of Latin in the scheme of modern liberal education will appreciate Professor Mercier's contribution to this particular discussion. As a humanist, trained in the full stream of the humanist tradition, Dr. Mercier is concerned with preserving the humanistic values of Latin, and does so by separating this, its true function, from the much less essential function of providing a useful type of intellectual gymnastics.

tained. Original composition could even be practiced on the basis of the texts, and gradually straight texts only could be used.

With such a control of tools: a fair capacity to use French, German, or Spanish, skill in reading another of those languages, and a fair reading knowledge of Latin—a student could go into college well equipped for work in the humanities, science, social studies, and foreign relations; and moreover know how to study other languages, as he would catch the need of them in the junior college which should provide additional courses at least in Italian, Portuguese, and Greek, designed to give the student correct habits of pronunciation, a knowledge of essential structures, and some practice in reading and synopsis. The development of correct pronunciation habits should be stressed in all cases, because, with a good pronunciation, a student can practice by himself profitably.

The skill-subjects and physical sciences thus disposed of, we may now turn to the humanities, that is, to all studies pertaining to man.

The student needs to have the whole perspective at least of the history of the West, ancient and modern. He should also be given, before the time comes for him in the senior college for specialization, an idea of the whole perspective of the development of Western literature and art, and of the main schools of thought.

How should these humanistic subjects be grouped, and how can their teaching be organized to reach these goals and be most effectively motivated?

It would seem that the centralizing subject for motivation in the humanities is literature.

The following scheme shows how naturally the other humanistic subjects may be grouped around it in the high school:

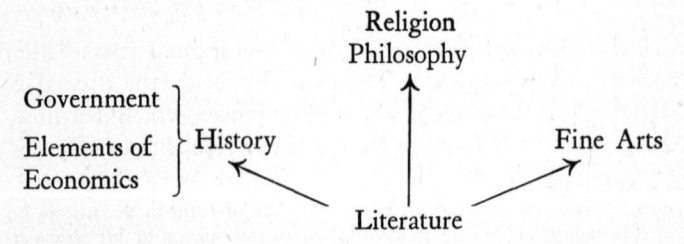

```
           Religion
          Philosophy
              ↑
Government  ⎫
Elements of ⎬ History         Fine Arts
Economics   ⎭       ↖       ↗
                    Literature
```

The following table[e] shows a possible time-distribution:

[e]Comment by John D. Wild:
  As I regard Professor Mercier's lucid presentation, one question arises in my mind, concerning the secondary level. Is this scheme not too narrowly concentrated on our own

What Should Be the Goals of Education?

	First Modern Language	Latin	English and English Literature	American History and Government	Math.
9th Gr.	First Modern Language	Latin	English and English Literature	American History and Government	Math.
10th Gr.	"	Latin	"	"	"
11th Gr.	"	Latin	"	Modern History	Math. or Science
12th Gr.	Second Modern Language	Ancient History and Culture	Eng. Lit. and Essay Writing	"	Science

The writing of English and the study of English literature is made the central subject.

The tool-subjects, the foreign modern languages, mathematics, and science are on the wings. The organization of their teaching has been discussed.

The spirit in which the humanistic subjects can be correlated with the study of English literature, so that the whole program will be concentric and motivated, may be briefly indicated.

The teaching of English composition should not be dissociated from content, nor should the history of literature be taught without constant references to history and geography.

Therefore throughout the first three years of the English course, devoted to the reading of masterpieces, the teacher will sketch the development of English literature and do so in connection with history. An elementary textbook should be available. The early history of England gives occasion to take up briefly the history of Western civilization, its Mediterranean-Greco-Latin-Hebraic-Christian-Roman origin, its spread through France to England and Germany, the northern tribal inroads, their final latinization. Modernized extracts from the early and

---

Western culture, and even here on the British and American phases of this culture? In the light of the growing interdependence of the parts of the world, is it not necessary to give the child a somewhat broader perspective on other civilizations, and the nature and history of civilization itself? I fail to see why two years should be devoted to American History and Government. One year I believe should suffice, the other being devoted to some different culture. Our present educational system is too self-centered and nationalistic. To a mitigated degree I feel that this is still true of Professor Mercier's revision.

Anglo-Norman literatures should be available. Medieval England and the age of Chaucer require reference to further French history, the Elizabethan age to Spain and Italy, while, from the seventeenth century on, English social progress may be shown to be revealed in the literature, and to parallel the same evolution, particularly in France.

During the fourth year both the social and literary history should be amplified and systematized, and should furnish the subject matter for English composition.

The study of Latin may most easily be motivated through this general comparative approach. Caesar's Gallic war becomes significant as the means through which Mediterranean civilization was implanted on the bridge of France; the *Aeneid* as the annals of the Roman people, and an occasion to refer the students back to the *Iliad* which they should read in translation, and to the basic importance of Greek literature; Horace as the master of neo-classicism both in France and in England. In this connection, Latin teachers might well study the question of reading less Caesar and Virgil in the text, though they should be finished in translations, and of having textbooks which would give a running brief introduction to the development of the whole Latin literature, illustrated by extracts from all the principal authors on the model of Marcel Braunschvig's textbook of French literature, *Notre Littérature étudiée dans les textes*. The breaking up of Latin texts for the more rapid development of reading power has already been discussed. Such a textbook could have such texts. The goal should be to give the student the perspective of the whole of Latin literature instead of sending him out of a three year Latin course knowing only three or four authors without much idea of where they fit in.

The fourth year should complete this work. Devoted to a more special course on Ancient History and Culture, some Latin texts could still be used, but a summing up and amplified study of Latin literature could be made through the many textbooks available, and some idea of Greek history, culture, and authors, through translated extracts, should be given. In short, the student must get the chance to secure a good view of the Mediterranean inheritance. Something should also be said of the spread of Greek culture after Alexander, and of the Arabic civilization in Africa. Needless to say, references to the fine arts and illustrations from the masterpieces should parallel the literary studies throughout.

But not only may Latin be motivated through English history and literature, but so may the modern languages, especially French.

English literature is written in terms of the French throughout the Norman period which brings us into the Renaissance at least in Italy. Italian needs to be referred to for the three centuries of this renaissance of letters. Spanish may also be referred to, as it was the Spain of the golden age that had to be defeated by England. German is the language of the Protestant Revolt and is indispensable for the understanding of the romantic revolt against neo-classicism, and German thought since Kant we must recognize as dominating the nineteenth century even though that influence may seem to us fatal. Moreover, in spite of this, German scholarship cannot be ignored, so that German is indispensable for the reading of authorities in many fields.

In the high school, there is no doubt that French literature, so closely allied with English, reinforces the study of English masterpieces, and can best be motivated by their study. Though languages are to be studied as tools, language work must remain based on reading and that reading can readily be made to give a glimpse of their literatures. With French, in particular, it is easy to give the students an idea of the fundamental literary schools in all languages, the realistic, the romantic, and the classical.

Understanding thus that the four year English course is the basis for the correlation of the parallel courses in Latin and the modern languages, it is easy to see how the history courses may be motivated as reinforcements. American history, to be studied in the first two years, is easily linked up with European history up to the War of 1812. It also furnishes an occasion to discuss government and the elements of economics in connection with the development of the West and the Civil War. After that, it becomes interestingly linked again with European history, both through the study of immigration and the development of democracy; and, finally, with the fight for democracy and the rights of the human person in the World Wars. Nor is it difficult to see how the development of the fine arts throughout history can be referred to constantly as following the development of the literatures and throwing light throughout on the progress in the ornamentation of life.

There remains the question of religion and philosophy. They constantly come up in the study of literature. In the French college which leads directly to the university, and yet which, as we saw, graduates its students with a B.A. or B.S. at about the same age as the American high school, there is a year's work in systematic philosophy. It is also understood that the students are free to practice their religion, in fact, in principle, chaplains are attached to every college. In this country, a systematic study of philosophy had perhaps better be left to the college, but the teachers of literature and of history may certainly, and in fact should, make references to the philosophy and attitude toward religion of the various authors they treat.[f] In what spirit this should be done, will be discussed in connection with college work.

Along some such lines, it would seem that we can solve the problem of making the high school course as motivated and concentric as that of the elementary school has been made by the "progressives." Incidentally the program just outlined corresponds to the Latin-modern language course in the French colleges which certainly succeed in giving a coordinated general education, and is, for most students, the sole preparation for university work.

Life reflected in history, literature, philosophy, religion, is an organic, dynamic whole. To treat any subject apart from the whole is to kill it. Language, too, is a dynamism, hence the need of teaching its mechanisms through living wholes, significant texts illustrating the mechanisms but of interest to the student. Finally, the student himself is a combination of powers which must be organically developed, skill-subjects to yield habits, and knowledge-subjects to yield understanding through

[f] Comment by Louis W. Norris:

There is no reason to think that maturation of American high school students should be delayed longer than their European contemporaries. Experience in talks and discussions of simple philosophic principles with selected high school seniors indicates to me that American high schools are missing an important opportunity to hasten the maturity of their graduates. The wasted time of high school seniors is notorious. They are capable of more comprehensive and basic learning of principles than is generally supposed.

Basic principles of psychology, logic, and ethics, could be presented with profit. The fact that such a small percentage (between five and ten per cent) of high school graduates go to college means that the vast majority of American youth never gets any systematic understanding of the mind or training in the ordering of its processes. Self-understanding and direction are supposed to sprout mysteriously like Topsy, or else, to be imported into the student's life by sophisticated "counsellors."

If it be objected that these subjects are too difficult, the answer is that logic is no more difficult than mathematics, and high schools have not balked at mathematics on this ground yet. Ethics and psychology are no more difficult than history or literature. Every teacher inevitably makes moral judgments of leaders in history, or characters in literature, and it is impossible to keep students from doing so. Students are expected to observe the psychological and ethical workings of others. Why can they not learn something of the principles on which they themselves act and on which they should act?

comparison of experiences personal and recorded.

The classical college represented such a concentric education in terms of its time: human experience as recorded in the books made available by the discovery of printing and the scholarship of the Renaissance of letters. But since then, we have had the development of the physical sciences. Education was challenged not to be so much in terms of books. "Progressivism" has seen to it that in the elementary school at least it should be made more concrete. In the domain of secondary education vast materials have also been added since the Renaissance to history, literature, and social studies in general. The need of speaking elegant Latin has been wholly replaced by the need of control over new tools, the modern languages, and more experience with the sciences. The organizing of a wider concentric development in the high school is therefore essential as a preparation to reach the goals of higher education. It remains our most difficult educational problem.

This problem cannot be solved unless all teachers concerned understand fully the goals to be reached and work at perfecting the integration of the curriculum and the methods to be used. This has been extensively done by progressive elementary teachers at their level. It must be done by high school teachers under the direction of their principal. For this reason, there should be in high schools, as there are in progressive elementary schools, frequent faculty meetings for the candid and earnest discussion of all such problems.

With a secondary education so organized in the high school, its continuation in the junior college should be simplified.

Care should be taken to complete the equipment of the student with the tools and with the introduction to subjects which he should have to round out his general education before becoming completely absorbed by a specialty in the senior college.

The junior college is therefore the place to continue the study of the second modern language begun in the high school. A third language might well be begun, as it will never be so easily learned; Greek, Spanish, Italian, Hebrew, Russian, Arabic, Chinese, or Japanese, through the method already discussed. Even the mere power of controlling the original text of a translation is valuable. For instance, there is a great difference between a student of philosophy who knows no Greek and can only use translations, and one who knows enough Greek to compare the text of Plato or Aristotle with a translation.

The junior college should also take up, at least in the second year, the initiation to philosophy which the high school could not begin; while, in the first year, a course in psychology and educational psychology would obviously be most valuable and no doubt improve his learning methods.

This would still leave the possibility of two year courses in the social studies and two in mathematics-science:

First Yr. =Freshman	Second Modern Language	Psychology, especially "Educational"	Social Studies	Math. and Science	English if necessary
Second Yr. = Sophomore	Third Language	Introduction to Philosophy	"	"	

It has been recognized that the student should be oriented toward concentration or specialization in the second year of the junior college, otherwise called sophomore year. It has also been felt at Harvard after over thirty years of experience that the concentration of six to eight full courses with a four course distribution did not sufficiently protect the possibility of continuing general education in college, while the distribution courses came to be considered as artificial chores instead of the guarantee of a more general education. This has led at Harvard to the proposition of introducing six courses in general education of which three would be taken during the first two years of college, that is, in the junior college. The St. John's experiment has even more drastically organized the reading of "the great books" as a remedy.

Such a development of secondary education including the junior college as discussed here, would evidently ease the problem of general culture.

A junior college course for a student who had elected to specialize in Romance or in English literature might be as follows:

Second Modern Language	Psychology	History or Economics	Math. Science or Hist. Science	English composition if necessary
Second or Third Language	Introduction to Philosophy	Survey of French Literature	Survey of English Literature	

A junior college course for a student who had elected to specialize in science might still include a modern language and educational psychology and philosophy, a survey course in literature or history, and surely a course in the history of science. But some of these courses would parallel some of the general education courses or be replaced by them, and there could still be three courses in science.

What we have tried to do is to apply the principle which should govern the organization of secondary education including the junior college: equip the student with the necessary tools and initiate him to all the main fields of knowledge so that he may have a general cultural background.

With the senior college we really reach the university level, as shown by the fact that courses taken those two years are open to both graduate and undergraduate and are taught by the professors who teach in the graduate school. The time has come for specialization; still the specialization should not be so exclusive as to shut off completely general education. The principle which should govern the goals of higher education may then be the following: pursue a specialized training, but in such a way as to continue to see its relation to other fields of human knowledge.

For instance, if the specialty is Romance languages and literatures, the courses in the literatures should contain some parallel readings in the history, political but especially social, of the countries concerned, the necessary references to other literatures and to the general history of ideas. If this cannot be done in the subject courses, it should be done in special courses. A Romance student should not ignore English literature at the college level, nor should an English literature student ignore French and Italian literatures. He may also need to deepen his knowledge of the basic philosophical systems. The approach to the study of any literature should be historical, economic, philosophical, comparative. If the specialty is science, the student should carry several cultural courses, and especially study the ethical and economic aspects of the uses of science.

To reach the goal of specialization against a cultural background at the college level, or more precisely at the university level, since the senior college belongs to the university, much can no doubt be borrowed from the idea of the systematic reading of "the great books" sponsored at St. John's, either by checking the inclusion of these books in the cultural courses, by having special reading courses which senior college students might follow, or by some tutorials as at Harvard. The great value of tutoring is that it can be done in terms of the student rather than of the subject, the tutor finding easily by questioning what the student lacks and directing him to the necessary readings. Tutoring may also help the student to pursue an interest which he has developed. The courses in general education inaugurated at Harvard will also bear watching from this point of view.

No attempt need be or can be made here to go further into the details of the organization of the concentrations in the senior college. This is a matter of departmental organization. However another principle needs to be introduced as to the goal and spirit of all general courses:

General courses should be so organized as to present religious and philosophical questions and the philosophy of history in terms of the general and objectively presented perspective of all the basic alternatives of thought.

As long as courses were elective, students could omit all courses taught from what was to them an objectionable point of view, but if general courses are obligatory, students may be forced to take courses against their own philosophy of life if they are taught from some other point of view. As Norman Foerster has pointed out in his *The American State University,* too often there is liberty of thought in American universities only along naturalistic lines. The positions of Judaism and Christianity are dismissed *a priori* and their records distorted. Moreover, to be intellectually respectable, colleges and universities should label their courses properly. For instance, a course in the history of Christianity taught by a modernist should not be labeled "History of Christianity," but "The modernist interpretation of Christianity"; a course in the philosophy of history taught by an atheist should be called "The Atheistic Philosophy of History." Courses may respectably have general labels only when they objectively present all the historical alternatives of thought on the given subject. All general courses which all students are obliged to take should be taught from this objective point of view.[g]

[g]Comment by John D. Wild:
One of the major defects of our education, especially in its higher branches, is its lack of philosophical and religious integration. Professor Mercier, aware of this lack, suggests general courses in which the major opposed philosophical integrations are presented in a wholly detached and "objective manner." But such courses, as he himself points out,

The question of the goals of higher education also calls for a discussion of the low estate to which the Ph.D. degree has fallen, and of the original weaknesses in the organization of that degree.

First of all, the designation is misleading, just as was that of the B.S. which was given to students who had no Latin though they might have a little science. This has been changed at Harvard by giving the B.A. to all students, but this is a loss and a blow at the humanities. As to the Ph.D., obviously it is not a doctorate in philosophy. It should be broken up into Doctor in Letters, Doctor in Science, Doctor in Philosophy, etc., as is done in French and Canadian universities.

In any case, the doctorate should be a badge of broad culture, of intimate acquaintance with an area of knowledge, and a certification of the proved capacity for research at least in one part of that area.

What often happens in the United States is that B.A.'s with a very limited cultural background are asked to do extensive elementary work on the outskirts of their area, in philology, for instance, in the case of language and literature students, and to write a thesis which is often only secretarial work, such as isolating and tracing an item in a body of readings. While doing so, they neglect further readings in the general field so that the comprehensive Ph.D. examination is often inferior to those in undergraduate courses. Yet they are granted the degree because it has become a teaching certificate and the jury is loath to shut them out of teaching positions after three years of study.

Here again, there has been a mix up in educational goals. An effort should be made, as Irving Babbitt in his *Literature and the American College* and Norman Foerster in the work already cited have pointed out, to distinguish, as is done in France, between what is represented by the *"licence,"* the *"agrégation,"* and the *"doctorat."*

The *"licence"* is a certification for instructorships, the *"agrégation"* for professorships in the higher classes of secondary education, or assistant professorships in universities, and the *"doctorat"* for election to chairs in universities.

What we need is therefore a Master's degree requiring at least two

---

quoting Foerster, are usually veiled forms of materialism or naturalism. If they are really objective, they are dull and lifeless, and elicit only a final skepticism and indifference in the student. Pending the time when more cultural agreement can be reached, I think that the other course of allowing the student an option between alternative courses in each of which the instructor openly defends an important point of view, is far preferable.

years of study with wider reading in the field and allied subjects, as well as some study of the parts of the field or allied subjects not opened up in undergraduate work (*e.g.,* further philosophy in connection with literature), and which could profitably include one course in education. A Master's thesis should be required as evidence not so much of original research as of the capacity to organize and present available knowledge. This plan could be perfected to represent the *"licence"* and *"agrégation."*

The holder of this M.A. could then either devote two years exclusively to the writing of a thesis of genuine importance; or begin to teach in the college, and, as is done in France, devote at least five years to the writing of a thesis that would really constitute a contribution to existing knowledge.[h]

Before concluding, more should be said about the problem of the objective attitude toward philosophical and religious questions which should permeate teaching at every level.

Because man has the power of reasoning, he was brought to inquire what kind of being he was, as opposed to other kinds: to try to determine his own nature, and also to wonder as to his origin, the possibility of his immortality, and his consequent ultimate end. The study of these and allied questions through reason, man called philosophy. It included natural theology or religion: surmises about the existence and nature of a Supreme Being. It also came to consider what should be the relations of man to other beings, and we had natural ethics. In general, this is the Greco-Roman philosophical tradition.

Men also came to believe that there had been revelations from the Supreme Being as to man's origin and destiny, and explanations of his present fallen state. So the Western world had the Hebraic tradition.

Other men came to believe that the Supreme Being had taken on man's humanity in the person of Jesus Christ, the promised Messiah of the Hebrew tradition, that humanity had thus been relinked to God so that man was again able to have a supernatural life through grace, made possible again by the redemption, which restored to him the possibility of the vision of God for eternity. Those who believed in the redemption, considered to be confirmed especially by the indubitable resurrection of

[h][Cf. the discussion of this subject in Chapter XVI by Earl J. McGrath and Dr. Mercier's comment thereto.]

Christ after His death on the Cross, constituted the Church of Christ which His apostles were commissioned to preach to all the nations, and whose means of grace they were to dispense according to the powers bequeathed to them by Christ. So we have the tradition of the Catholic Church, generally called Roman because the successor of Peter, designated by Christ as Head of His Church, came to live and center the administration of the Church in the capital of the Roman empire.

For geographical, political, and a special doctrinal reason, a large portion of the Church broke away in the tenth and eleventh centuries and became known generally as the Greek Orthodox Church.

In the sixteenth century, for many varied reasons, political, economic, as well as doctrinal, there was a wide exodus from the allegiance to Rome, mostly in northern Europe, known as the Protestant Revolt or Reformation. This was much more drastic than the Greek schism, because it repudiated the priesthood, as dispenser of the sacraments as means of grace, and as authoritative expounder of the Creed, and left to the individual the private interpretation of the Bible, encouraging him also to believe in personal revelations from God. In spite of the attempt of the first Protestant groups to formulate creeds, this led to the foundation of a great number of separate churches.

The consequent quarrels between the churches as to the nature and the means of grace, and as to their legitimacy, divided peoples, led to numerous wars, and finally, in the course of the eighteenth century, to the repudiation by many of the whole Christian point of view. A return was made practically to the Deism of Aristotle, though the idea of a personal God and of the after life as one of reward and punishment was retained from the Christian tradition.

Toward the end of the eighteenth century, a much greater break was made with the whole past of Western thought, in fact the first totally radical revolution since the days of Aristotle. Fichte, Schelling, and Hegel definitely broke with Deism which was still dualistic and inaugurated the reign of a monism which merged God, man, and nature in one current of becoming. This was given a materialistic interpretation, especially after Darwin. The upshot was our present naturalism which considers that "the time has passed for Deism and Theism." This doctrine makes traditional Christianity and Judaism impossible, commits the Protestant churches to modernism, and is necessarily opposed to the doctrine of the inalienable rights of man based on a God-given nature, and to an ethics based on abiding relations between men, and between men and God.

All these doctrines divide us today. They are reflected in the literatures. From each is derived a distinct philosophy of history and criteria for criticism. All texts are therefore more or less directly written from one or another of these alternatives of thought. Moreover, all books treating of literature and history, especially those written for secondary schools, are apt to be nationalistically partisan.

How to guarantee the student the objective perspective of history to which he is entitled is therefore one of the most difficult goals to be attained by secondary and higher education.

The solution would seem to be in an effort on the part of all teachers to reach an objective attitude toward the study of all the above alternatives of thought, and to point out from which alternative the authors of all books studied have written, when they have not been strictly objective.

This presupposes that all the alternatives of thought have been outlined to all students.

Schools, colleges, and universities have begun to recognize this, and also the right of their students to seek, from representatives of the alternative which appeals most to them, enlightenment as to the arguments, historical and logical, in its support.

This has led, especially at the college and university level, to the encouragement of church foundations on or near the campus for that purpose. Less has been done at the high school and elementary school level, though the organization of religious classes on released time was a move in that direction.

In any case, we need here another principle: the college and university should take an objective stand as to the alternatives of thought, and should encourage the student to seek further information upon them from their representatives. If courses are offered from the point of view of any one of the alternatives, they should be so labeled.

Adherents of some of the alternatives of thought who consider that they imply a way of life, and that the school as such should practice that life, will of course insist upon their right to have schools of their own. They should, however, acquaint their students objectively with the other alternatives.

In Canada, and some other countries, such schools are also supported at least partly by the state, on the principle that every citizen has the right to the philosophical and religious education which he desires, and that schools that provide it have a right to public funds if they also provide adequate education in the secular subjects.

This pluralistic approach is evidently more liberal than our own which runs the danger of totalitarianism, in so far as it would enforce within the state schools a supposed neutrality which is often, as Norman Foerster has pointed out, a state indoctrination in naturalism.[1]

[1] Comment by Louis W. Norris:
From many points of view the last two paragraphs of this paper are the most important. Professor Mercier rightly points out that American democracy in fact indoctrinates its students in naturalism by prohibiting state support of schools which teach that religion and morality are elemental in the whole educational process, and by prohibiting religious instruction in public schools. By default of such instruction in religious and moral values the state tacitly teaches that these are unimportant.

This point made by a Catholic educator is the more interesting because it is shared by an outstanding Protestant leader, namely, Umphrey Lee, President of Southern Methodist University, in his book, *Render Unto the People* (The Abingdon Press, New York, 1947). Lee shows, too, that a popular majority can inflict its outlook upon minorities to their harm, and it may provide such thoughtless educational philosophy as to deteriorate the moral fiber of even the majority. In this way, the moral outcome of democracy may be subject to as serious criticism as that of totalitarian governments. The point of advantage accruing to democracy lies, of course, in the fact that the will of the majority can change, with the resulting change in the outlook educationally, which is exacted within the state. In America, therefore, the chief problem *does* lie in the question of how to fertilize the majority so that it will insist that the valuational core of education gets a hearing commensurate with so-called "secular" subjects.

If all independent schools which provide such philosophical and religious education as "every citizen has a right to," were given state support, the problem then arises of how differing religious outlooks could retain their standing. Inevitably there would be competition by religious groups to put such political leaders in office as would favor their own outlook, even as is now done in our supposedly "free" democracy. The Cincinnati public schools case is in point. This would be the end of religious freedom in America.

Could Professor Mercier suggest how the undoubted need for education with a philosophical or valuational rootage could be provided, without the jockeying for ascendency which state aid to "religious" schools would generate?

[For further discussion of this chapter see comment by I. L. Kandel, in Appendix III.]

CHAPTER XIII

The Need for Normative Unity in Higher Education

By MORDECAI M. KAPLAN
Professor of the Philosophies of Religion, The Jewish Theological Seminary of America

I

IN THE RACE between catastrophe and education, education is fated to play the role of the tortoise, although catastrophe is far from acting like the hare in the fable. Catastrophe is anything but dilatory, and leaves nothing to chance in its eagerness to gain its ends. Fortunately, there are some who still keep their heads on their shoulders, and refuse to escape their responsibility for the future by joining the chorus of "After us the deluge."

It is undoubtedly true, as a distinguished educator maintains, that "if war is a gigantic error, education alone will not cure it." To prove his point, he adds that education "might as well promise to find every man the right wife." Nevertheless, even if we do not expect education to help every man find the right wife, it ought to help a man know the difference between the right and the wrong kind of wife. And by the same token, even if education alone cannot cure us of the error of war, it ought to help us discover what would cure us of that error. If education cannot prevent us in the least from bungling in matters like marriage or war, what is it good for? We are talking about education and not about vocational training.

It is well that some of the outstanding educators and leading educational institutions are taking time off to reexamine the goals of education and to reorganize the curricula of the schools, in the light of what they regard as indispensable to the mental and moral growth of the coming generations. Of particular significance is the informative and illuminating Report of the Federal Commission on "Higher Education for American Democracy." That commission was appointed by the President who charged its members with "the task of examining the functions of higher education in our democracy and the means by which they can best be performed." These and similar efforts cannot by themselves stem the advancing tide of disaster. Nevertheless, we must not abandon them. Perchance by some miracle they might, in conjunction with other salutary forces that are latent in human life, help to avert the impending doom.

As long as there is any hope of a future, we must do all in our power to forestall the miseries to which it is bound to be heir, by reason of the mistakes we keep on repeating in our educational endeavors from generation to generation. The attempts to reconsider our educational aims should not be permitted to remain sporadic. All of us should be made to realize that no matter what is in store for us, we are sure to be better prepared to meet it, if our young people, particularly those who will receive a higher education, will be adequately equipped in body, mind, and spirit. Moreover, it devolves upon groups like the Conference on Science, Philosophy and Religion and similar bodies to examine the educational studies that have recently been made and to weigh their conclusions. It can hardly be claimed that those studies are so definitive that all we need is to implement the practical suggestions they offer. The main symptoms of what ails present day education are generally known by this time, but it cannot be said that the diagnosticians have really gone to the root of the trouble. Remedies based on the present stage of educational investigation are not likely to bring about anything more than superficial improvement.

Among the most noted efforts at reconstructing our higher educational system are, first, the one at The University of Chicago, which is of several years standing; second, the Harvard Report on *General Education in a Free Society* issued in 1945; and third, the *Report of the President's Commission on Higher Education* issued in 1947. They constitute three distinct types of approach to the problem of higher education. If institutional religion is to be left out of account as a means of synthesizing the educational process, then those three types of approach are virtually exhaustive of what can be tried, from the standpoint of the one purpose they all aim to achieve: that of having the higher educa-

The Need for Normative Unity in Higher Education 295

tion function at least as a partial means of integrating the character and personality of the student.

The Harvard Commission found the heart of the problem of higher education to be the irrelevance of the cultural subject matter to the vocational subject matter, and the irrelevance of both to the building of a free society. The solution the Commission suggests is mainly of a curricular and administrative character. They offer no definite proposal as to the nature of the intellectual unity to be aimed at. They stress the importance of achieving some common frame of reference for the sciences and the humanities. For a likely source of such a frame of reference they point to the procedures followed at Chicago University with its emphasis on the reading of the great books and at Columbia University with its civilizational survey courses. As far as the relevance of higher education to a free society is concerned, that is identified with the question of reconciling the element of experiment and change with the element of tradition and permanence. Nothing specific, however, is said concerning the nature of the changes, the areas in which they have to be effected, or what constitutes permanence.

The sponsors of the Chicago plan—and that goes for St. John's College which has served them as a kind of educational laboratory—are more critical of the present condition of higher education.[a] They find that education to be fragmentary, disjointed, and incapable of getting the students to see life steadily and whole. Students are not given, as in the past, some religion to infuse their disparate studies with common purposes and attitudes. Nor are they provided with a common background of ideas and values on which to base their own thinking and evaluations. As they undergo training for their respective vocations they move into totally different universes of thought, and before long they are hardly on speaking terms about anything of general human interest, other than the weather, sports, and the most recent movies. If they happen to carry on a serious conversation, the words they use carry for each of them entirely different auras of meaning. The remedy lies, according to the Chicago plan, in having students of all departments

[a][For further discussion of the "Chicago Plan," see Chapter II by Lyman Bryson, Chapter III by T. V. Smith, Chapter VIII by Alain L. Locke, Chapter IX by Howard Mumford Jones, Chapter XI by John U. Nef, Chapter XV by George N. Shuster, Chapter XVI by Earl J. McGrath, Chapter XVII by Ordway Tead, and George B. de Huszar's comment in Appendix III.]

engage in guided reading of a number of the world's classics which present the basic ideas and values of Western civilization. That, however, might only give the students intellectual unity, but not normative unity. It is, therefore, important to aim deliberately at achieving in the students a common attitude toward life and all its problems. That calls for interpreting the great classics in the light of some tested metaphysics or philosophy, a requirement which, in the opinion of the sponsors of that school, is best met by what is designated as Neo-Thomism.

Both the Chicago and the Harvard plan suffer from a narrowness of horizon, which is a source of practical danger in our day. The reading and survey courses to which they both attach so much importance are certain to habituate the students in the assumption that civilization is synonymous with Western civilization. That assumption is analogous to the one which prevailed in the past with regard to religion, when it was considered synonymous only with Christian religion. The Oriental world does not seem to exist, educationally and culturally, for the educational leaders of either the Chicago or Harvard sponsors of educational reform. It should be the business of educational reform to combat the cultivation of blind spots for any aspect of human life the world over. All mankind is at present embroiled in tension and strife. There is no phase of its life which does not scream at one time or another from the daily headlines or does not barge into every home that has a radio set. We, therefore, cannot afford to ignore the existence of civilizations, religions, economic systems, and social ways of any part of mankind. They are all the source of mankind's miseries as well as of its hopes and aspirations. Who knows but that we might have averted the Pearl Harbor attack had we known something about the development of Shintoism during the half century before World War II? That no modern outlook can afford to ignore the Oriental civilizations is cogently argued in Northrop's *The Meeting of East and West*.

Due probably to freedom from association with any particular college or university in which suggestions have to be immediately translated into a program, the report of the President's Commission could afford to be incomparably broader in outlook and more comprehensive in vision than any university commission.[b] It defines the goals in terms

[b] [For further discussion of the report of the President's Commission, see Chapter I by Robert Ulich (including comment by Rowland W. Dunham), Louis J. A. Mercier's comment on Chapter II by Lyman Bryson, Chapter IV by Karl W. Deutsch, Chapter VII by Charles W. Hendel, and Chapter XVII by Ordway Tead.]

The Need for Normative Unity in Higher Education

of "Education for a Better Nation and a Better World" which it specifies in the following three propositions: 1) Education for a fuller realization of democracy in every phase of living; 2) Education directly and explicitly for international understanding and cooperation; and 3) Education for the application of creative imagination and trained intelligence to the solution of social problems and to the administration of public affairs. Here the problem is viewed not merely as one of intellectual integration or of relevance of the humanities to the sciences, but fundamentally as one of normative unity, of relevance to a particular type of conduct and attitude in all human relations. The particular type of conduct the Commission is concerned with goes by the name of democracy. Its members conceive democracy so broadly that they deem it essential in the home and in the shop as well as in international dealings of a global character.

The Report of the President's Commission (henceforth referred to as the Federal Report) does not content itself with large generalizations. It breaks them up into eleven specific objectives which are so eminently desirable as to render their very statement edifying and stimulating. Detailed provision is indicated for methods and means that have to be employed in order to translate those objectives into reality. The relationship between general and vocational education is not only taken cognizance of, but the way to exploit it is clearly set forth. The importance of counseling and of realizing the strategic significance of graduate schools in the whole endeavor of educational reform is dealt with in realistic fashion.

II

When we compare the three foregoing programs, we note the following: The Chicago program recognizes the importance of *normative* unity. In the past such unity could be achieved with comparative ease, for everybody had to subscribe to the dominant religion. Since that is no longer feasible under democratic conditions, the Chicago program advocates the next best, namely, the cultivation of some recognized metaphysics or philosophy. Such cultivation is expected to lead ultimately to normative unity. If, however, we are to regard a recent publication by a member of that school of thought as typical of the kind of normative unity the Chicago program would lead to, we cannot but foresee a sharp and dangerous cleavage in American life between those who have faith in democracy and those who oppose it and all its works. *Ideas Have Consequences,* by Richard M. Weaver, a member of the Chicago University Faculty, is an anti-democratic tract. It condemns democracy as materialistic and vulgar. That kind of contempt for whatever progress has been made to emancipate Western man from medieval obscurantism and from all notions of class distinction, brings into sharp relief the contrast between the normative unity aimed at by the Chicago plan and that aimed at by the President's Commission on Higher Education.

In the Harvard program normative unity does not figure at all. The impression it conveys is that even to aim at that kind of unity is beyond the scope of an institution of learning. The limit of a university's ambition should be intellectual unity. Under present conditions, even that unity is recognized as lacking between the humanities and the sciences, or between the so-called liberal or general education and vocational education. In the Federal Report, the achievement of normative unity is the all pervading purpose to which all else is to be subordinated. That normative unity is based on the acceptance of "democracy in every phase of living." *"In the future as in the past,"* we are told, *"American higher education will embody the principle of diversity in unity: each institution, State or other agency will continue to make its own contribution in its own way. But educational leaders should try to agree on certain common objectives that can serve as a stimulus and guide to individual decision and action."*

A striking fact which is common to the three plans in question is the tacit assumption that there is no place for religion in higher education. That cannot be said of either the Princeton or the Yale plan. The probable reason for making that assumption is that institutional religions continue to regard one another as rivals. It is therefore impossible to have any one of them serve as a basis for either intellectual or normative unity. An institutional religion might help its own adherents, but it would at the same time widen the gulf between them and the adherents of the other religions. If that is the reason—and it is difficult to conceive any other—nothing is gained by failing to state it frankly. It is surely unnatural to by-pass religion as though it did not exist, or to pretend that it is the concern only of the church and the home. With all the emphasis that is being placed upon the importance of integrating every phase of human life into some intellectual and spiritual unity, such a division of labor is quite absurd. That is certainly a matter which this Conference, which accords parity to religion with both science and philosophy, cannot afford to ignore.

In the entire Federal Report the very word, religion, is not mentioned even once. The Harvard report makes passive reference to it, and drops it as though it were a hot coal. The Chicago plan deplores its enforced absence from the curriculum and proposes a substitute for it, or rather tacitly proposes that, instead of having education consummate the evolution suggested by Comte, namely, from theology to metaphysics and from metaphysics to science, education stop at metaphysics. In the Chicago program there is at least a definite recognition that the passing of traditional religion leaves a vacuum which has to be filled. But if we are seriously concerned with the need of reconstructing our educational goals because of the passing of traditional religion, we ought not merely be informed of that passing and have some substitute arbitrarily imposed upon us without our being consulted either about the fact of the passing of religion or the eligibility of the substitute.

The truth is that, though the Federal Report makes no mention of religion, it implies, in the very place it assigns to democracy as the dominant principle in all of its objectives, an unmistakable awareness of the vacuum created by the passing of traditional religion as the basis of normative unity and of the need for looking to democracy to function in that capacity.[c] What the Chicago plan expects of Neo-Thomist metaphysics, the Federal Report expects of democracy. We must realize, however, that though the educators ignore institutional religion, it still plays an important part in the lives of at least sixty per cent of the American people, and therefore has to be reckoned with in any educational reform that counts upon being generally adopted. Whether that is pos-

---

[c]Comment by Herman Finer:
    There is here an acknowledgment of the replacement of traditional religions by democracy, as "the basis of normative unity." This is true and most important. The question that should next be asked is, is this not inevitable in states of enormous area, where self-government is craved for, and where multitudes of convictions must be peaceably reconciled? And is it not desirable? If the answer were in the affirmative, as it is for me, then Professor Kaplan would have to proceed to put democracy as a faith over religious faiths. Why not? To discover through the democratic process the substantial content of the General Will would be the substance of education. The General Will, created by democratic procedures and institutions and self-restraints, like those proposed by Mill and Bentham, would now be God.

sible without trespassing on the principle of separation of church and state is the heart of the very problem of education as well as of democracy. The main reason we are at present far from any likelihood of a solution is not that the problem is inherently insoluble, but that we have been playing possum with the problem so long that we do not seem to know how to face it frankly. It is my purpose in what follows more to bring the problem out into the open than to suggest a possible way of meeting it, though some such way will be intimated.

III

The issue between the Chicago plan and the Federal Report turns upon the question whether the normative unity to be aimed at shall be of the authoritarian or of the democratic type.[d] We cannot discuss the merits of either proposal of educational reform without realizing the significance of the basic assumptions implied in authoritarianism and democracy. The literature on the political assumptions underlying authoritarianism and democracy is mountain high. That literature has to do with the question: Where is the ultimate seat of sovereignty or authority? Authoritarianism has always affirmed that the sovereignty or authority comes from above. Throughout premodern times God alone was universally regarded as the seat of authority. The verse, "Thine, O Lord, is the greatness and the power and the glory" (I Chron. 29:11), was not taken to be merely an expression of fervent adoration. It was interpreted as a doctrine concerning the ultimate source of authority. It still is the openly professed doctrine of the Roman Catholic Church. Archbishop Lucey of San Antonio, in a letter to Dr. Everett R. Clinchy, excerpts of which appear in the April 26, 1948, issue of *Christianity and Crisis,* stated as follows: "There is no power but from God. Civil authority and ecclesiastical power have the same source and therefore, by the will of God Himself, church and state must be allies in procuring the temporal and eternal welfare of citizens. . . . God's power which He gives to the civil authority should in logic and theory be used to assist God's power given to the ecclesiastical authority." On that assumption, the only ones authorized to exercise authority, to formu-

---

[d]Comment by Gerald B. Phelan:

The word "authoritarian" is not antonymous to "democratic." "Authoritarian" means simply advocating the principle of obedience to authority, not the abdicating of all freedom and of all rights in the face of an arbitrary or dictatorial despot.

late and execute the law, are those who are recognized as having been directly commissioned by God, or by those whom, in the last instance, God directly commissioned. That is the conception of authority in the historical religions of Judaism, Christianity, and Mohammedanism.[e]

In each of those religions, in their pristine form, only supernatural revelation can be the ultimate validation of laws governing every phase of human life and the ultimate sanction of those who administer those laws and exercise authority over their fellow men whether as priest, prophet, or king. When those three religions encountered the stream of philosophic thought emanating from Greece, they extended the range of those laws which might be regarded as deriving their authority from God and of those authorized to exercise power over their fellow men. The laws which were mediated by reason and were recognized as natural law, also came to be viewed as divine and binding as the revealed or "positive" laws. That entitled the theologian who was expert in the use of reason, as well as in the knowledge of revealed law, to be the authoritative guide in human life. That led to the recognition of Theology as the "Queen of the Sciences." Such has been the attitude toward "natural law" on the part of the historical religions ever since they attained the zenith of clarity in self-definition.

In the light of the foregoing brief survey of authoritarianism as a way of life, the purpose of the Chicago plan is to have higher learning in our day retrieve that aspect of normative unity enjoyed by higher learning in the past when it was dominated by Queen Theology. Since it is not possible, for very evident reasons, to have the revelational element of that theology brought into play in the modern academic set-up, it should be possible to introduce at least the metaphysical or rational element. That element, however, must be left intact as deriving its validity entirely from above, from those angelic doctors of reason, whose rationality is of such extraordinary lucidity and is so endowed with intuitive insight as to be only little less than supernatural revelation.

That approach possesses an uncontestable advantage which democracy lacks. Being authoritarian, and falling back upon traditional ways of thought, which are of long standing, it cannot be accused by the ad-

[e]Comment by Gerald B. Phelan:
  These two sentences give a false picture of Christianity. I claim to be a Christian and I recognize the right of the President of the United States to exercise authority although he has never been *directly* commissioned by God but elected to office by the votes of the people.

herents of institutional religions of either competing with or undermining their respective religions. On the contrary, they have good reason to feel that they have in that approach a strong ally. While they depend upon the college or university to provide the rational background of traditional religion, they can look to their own religions to provide *revelational* content. The matter stands altogether differently with the democratic approach.

Democracy, for good or for ill, is based upon an assumption which is the very antithesis of that underlying authoritarianism. The antithesis does not consist, as those who have always sought to malign democracy have tried to maintain, in negating authority or sovereignty altogether, but in affirming with deep conviction that all authority or sovereignty has its seat in the will of the people who can, and for the most part do, delegate but never abdicate it.[f] What that has meant politically constitutes the story of the political revolutions which have put an end to feudalism and rendered monarchy where it still exists entirely impotent. But *political* application of the democratic principle of authority or sovereignty is only the beginning of the revolution which that principle is bound to effect in the economic, social, and cultural areas of civilization. It is these other areas that are first beginning to feel the effects of the democratic revolution.

The fact that the problem of goals of higher education is being raised at this time signifies that democracy, with its unique conception of authority and sovereignty, finds it necessary to have that conception permeate the entire educational system. The present attempt follows upon the heels of the movement, which began during the first decade of this century, to democratize education. What is known as progressive education consisted in the main of rendering education student centered instead of subject centered. To progressive education in those years,

---

[f] Comment by Gerald B. Phelan:

There are so many good things in Dr. Kaplan's paper, so many keen insights and wise counsels, that I regret to have to differ with some of its basic principles. The conception of democracy upon which it rests is to me quite unacceptable. A democracy for which "all authority or sovereignty has its seat in the will of the people" constitutes a system or mode of life basically capricious and any "authority" based upon such a conception will ultimately rest on power—the power of those who are astute enough to influence, and eventually control, the will, not of the *people,* but of the *majority*. An educational policy arising from such a condition of affairs is bound to be completely state controlled. And, I fear that Dr. Kaplan, in defending such a view is unwittingly laying the foundation for the building up of those hideous manifestations of totalitarianism which he is so eager to destroy.

subject material represented not only the accumulated knowledge, but also the authority, of the past. To be interested mainly in having the student master subject matter was really to make him slave to it and rob him of the freedom and the normal development of his own personality. The mistake which those educators made was in assuming that the student can be permitted to experiment with whatever potentialities of self-development he possesses, including those of self-government.[g] That was as absurd as it would have been to assume that a child should not be taught any language in particular, on the assumption that he would of his own accord come to speak in the vernacular of his environment.

At the present time the motivation to democratize education comes from the recognition that, so long as the theory and practice of democracy are confined to the political area of civilization, it has not the ghost of a chance against authoritarianism, especially in its latest manifestations as fascism and communism. The place to begin the democratization of education is with the goals of higher education. Those who receive such an education are likely to be leaders in all walks of life. They themselves will actually exercise authority in one form or another. It is therefore important that before they go out into the world, they be thoroughly imbued with democracy as a norm of human life in all its aspects. This is unquestionably the spirit in which the sponsors and those who worked on the Federal Report conceived their task. Thus we are told that "the first goal of education is the fuller realization of democracy in every phase of life." The meaning of democracy is described there as "residing in the human values and ethical ideas on which democratic living is based." The main objective of democratic education is defined as being "the full, rounded and continuing development of

[g] Comment by Ruth Strang:
  Dr. Kaplan throughout this paper offers a splendid theoretical construct, but seems to reject the most important means of putting this concept to work in higher education— namely, the resources within the individual himself. The statement to which this note is appended is in complete opposition to the client centered approach to individual development advocated by Frederick Allen, Carl Rogers, Jessie Taft, and many others in the field of psychotherapy and social work. Dr. Kaplan's paper is curiously institution centered. Programs seem to be superimposed from above. Little reference is made to the student, whose needs, abilities, attitudes, present ways of thinking and feeling are ignored. Yet it is here that education must start—with the resources within the individual to be educated. In the effort to extricate higher education from pseudo forms of progressive education, Dr. Kaplan has failed to recognize and build on resources within the student for his full development as a social being.

the person." All of which leads to the conclusion that "it is the responsibility of higher education to devise programs and methods which will make clear the ethical values and the concept of human relations upon which our political system rests."

IV

In the peaceful contest which is being waged between democracy and authoritarianism, and which, we hope, will remain peaceful as long as that contest lasts, authoritarianism possesses a further advantage over democracy, in addition to the one of support from the adherents of the institutional religions. I refer to the advantage of having a well knit and consistent ideology of human destiny, or of what constitutes the fulfilment of human life. That is the concept of salvation which, in authoritarianism, is backed up by a long and rich tradition. In contrast, democracy having busied itself, since its inception, with politics, has not had the chance to formulate an ideology of human destiny or of salvation. The possession of a long tradition for any such ideology is, consequently, out of the question. Those, therefore, who are interested in seeing that in the contest between democracy and authoritarianism the two be evenly matched, to say nothing of those who definitely want democracy to win, cannot afford to have it continue in its present condition. *Democracy without a philosophy of salvation is a headless torso.* The time is more than ripe for that lack to be made good. Otherwise all possibility of having democracy function as the basis for normative unity in higher education is precluded.

The traditional conception of salvation, which is organically related to the authoritarian approach underlying the Chicago plan, definitely looks upon human destiny as incapable of being fulfilled in the natural order as we know it. Salvation, though conditioned by what man makes of this worldly life, is by no means achievable in this world. The consummation of human life is regarded as belonging to the same order of existence as all that makes man distinctively human such as his knowledge of God, or his deference to law and authority. As these are part of a world order that is "wholly other," so does the consummation of human existence belong to that world. In other words, salvation is, to the traditionally minded, inherently other worldly. It is hardly necessary to dwell upon the fascination which this view of human destiny and salvation is likely to have for us nowadays. With every item in the daily newspapers proclaiming man's failure to make this world habitable, and announcing the doom awaiting us as we are speeding toward the precipice ahead of us, unless by some miracle we turn the corner, to use Robert A. Hutchins's analogy, little other comfort is left to us, except to hug this hope of the possible bliss that awaits us in the beyond.

Nevertheless, there will always be some, and may their tribe increase, who refuse to be reconciled to an interpretation of human destiny that, in the last analysis, *justifies,* even if it does not necessarily advocate, inaction and passive waiting upon miracle. There still are people who do not despair of the possibility of making this world safe for man, and with safety there can come salvation. But they must not content themselves with "unexamined" effort, with effort that is not related to a philosophy of salvation. They should prove Mark Van Doren wrong, who, unfortunately, is at present so altogether right, when he says that "educators today are breathlessly confessing that the past generation of students was not taught to believe enough things. There is little evidence, however, of a search into the metaphysics or even the psychology of belief; and there is less evidence of an anxiety in educators to believe something themselves."[1]

Even, therefore, at the risk of being tentative and groping in our search, *those of us who have the cause of democracy at heart should take our courage into our hands and set out to explore the possibilities of formulating a philosophy of salvation that can speak the language of democracy.* Such a philosophy is indispensable, if a report like the one of the President's Commission on Higher Education is to have anything like the authority and prestige which authoritarian education still possesses with large numbers of people and with the most influential among them.[h]

[1] *Liberal Education,* Henry Holt and Company, New York, 1943, p. 5.

[h] Comment by Herman Finer:
Is not democracy itself a philosophy of salvation? Is it not all the better for not having any one God, unless it be the sacredness of the principle of majority rule, and the principles of human nature and the universe upon which this is based? If unity is sought by a gospel of salvation which depends on any one of the Gods of the different churches, will not the unity of the fellowship that can come spontaneously in freedom (imperfect as it may be) be lost in the ardor of a dominant gospel? Is not what is wanted a gospel, that, up to a point, all doctrines of salvation shall be free and equal in their quest for acceptance by humanity; and is not the only system of government which offers this (even if imperfectly) better than any other system, however ardent and brilliant it may appear to be?

V

Before we undertake to formulate a democratic philosophy of salvation which is to be a means of educational unity, we must be satisfied in our own minds that it is desirable to use education for such a purpose. We all know how easily education can be misused as a means of indoctrinating young people with all kinds of false notions. It is not enough to say that indoctrination, like all forces and instrumentalities, is inherently neutral and capable of being put to beneficent or evil uses, and that we must merely be sure that what we are indoctrinating is compatible with the ideal of democracy. Unfortunately, the human mind is so susceptible to self-delusion and so capable of making the worse appear the better cause that it can smuggle in, under the concept of democracy, the worst kind of tyranny. Nevertheless, we cannot go to the extreme of avoiding all references to universal norms and standards in our conduct and our human relations. The very lack of ethical and spiritual norms and standards of a universal character, to replace those which have become obsolete, is responsible for much of the present amoralism, nihilism, and cynicism.

Norms and standards that are universal in their reference and application must form an integral part of all education, higher as well as elementary. Indoctrination is therefore inevitable. But if the norms are to be in keeping with the spirit of democracy, then even the *method* of indoctrination must likewise be democratic. That is the antithesis of the dogmatic or doctrinaire method. Democratic indoctrination is not the inculcation of fixed or inviolately sacred tenets. It is a process of teaching in which the learner is aware that he is given the choice between alternatives in ideas, beliefs, and values. It is possible for indoctrination to communicate affirmations without ruling out the experimental and hypothetical attitude. It can cultivate in the student that open-mindedness which enables him to discipline himself into living by truths, though he knows them to be subject to the limitations of the human mind, and by standards and norms which he can freely choose,

---

I answer, Yes, to my own questions: my system of education begins with the analysis of democracy, in all its main principles and major detail. It is my principle of emphasis, my criterion in the examination of past stages of human symbiosis and the struggle between systems. Professor Kaplan recognizes the supreme importance of following out the consequences of democratic principles in education: and it would be interesting to read his full analysis and the educational conclusions he would draw.

even though he should be prepared to change them when circumstances render them obsolete. This attitude of approximation and tentativeness is democracy as applied to ideas, events, and experiences. This is neither anarchy nor uncontrolled *laissez-faire*. It treats normative unity as a desideratum, the search for which would constitute an endless self-correcting inquiry, rather than as an attainment.

Some time ago the American Philosophical Association conducted an inquiry to find out what educators and people interested in higher education expected of the study of philosophy. The results of that inquiry are summarized in the first chapter of the book entitled *Philosophy in American Education*. According to Professor Brand Blanshard, the author of that chapter, four kinds of demands have been voiced by those who were interrogated: 1) the demand for integration, 2) the demand for community of mind, 3) the demand for a reinterpretation of democracy, and 4) the demand for a "philosophy of life."

From what we know of the relation of the history of philosophy to the history of education, it is not too much to say that there is a definite correlation between what people view as the function of education in general and what they expect of the formal study of philosophy. This correlation is strikingly illustrated in the three programs of educational reform which we have been examining. It is apparent that the Harvard program reflects the expectation that philosophy serve as a means of counteracting the fragmentation of knowledge. That fragmentation results from the tendency of young people to begin to specialize in their studies long before they are sufficiently grounded in general knowledge. Particularly, the gap between the sciences and the humanities is one that is viewed in that report as in special need of being bridged. On the other hand, the Chicago program corresponds to the demand that philosophy be a means to achieving a community of mind, or the acceptance of common standards of thought and action. That program looks particularly to the study of the great books to bring about enough of a community of mind to make it possible for people of different intellectual interests and vocations to have their minds meet and exchange ideas instead of being completely walled off from each other. Finally, the educational approach of the Federal Report corresponds to the demand that philosophy lead to a better understanding of the meaning of democracy as a way of life. What this essay attempts to set forth concerning the goals of higher education corresponds with belief that the study of philosophy should give one "a philosophy of life." Accordingly, higher education should not only serve all the three functions mentioned above, but also help the student achieve a world outlook that is so integrated and that has so direct a bearing on one's conduct that it is tantamount to a philosophy of salvation.

Mark Van Doren puts his finger upon the weakest spot in our educational efforts, when he tells us that nobody who has been subjected to a college education comes away with a "reasonably deep and clear feeling," of having been anywhere near the center of things from which the various elements of culture radiate, elements like art, science, and religion. No student is made to realize their bearings upon one another. Where else can being at the center of things mean than being at that point where we come to know what it is to be human, in the deepest and most comprehensive sense of that term? In other words, there really can be no mental, moral, or spiritual integration, which is what we are aiming at in this inquiry, without some idea of human destiny or self-fulfilment. Let not the fact that this idea has been the main concern of institutional religions, and that for many of us those religions have failed to do justice to this idea, prejudice us against exploring it. For without an idea of human destiny or salvation, we are merely trying to make ropes out of sand or laying foundations on quicksand.

VI

The elemental fact on which it is possible to build a philosophy of salvation is that of self-preservation, which is characteristic of all living beings. That is generally identified as the will to live. Self-preservation, or the will to live, need not be conceived as a conscious purpose of living beings, whether human or sub-human. It is merely a generalization of the infinite variety of their outward behavior, with its accompanying inner experiences. There is, however, a qualitative difference between the way the will to live functions in the human being from the way it functions in the sub-human being. In the human being the will to live is accompanied by powers of memory, imagination, and abstraction which make him aware of numerous alternatives of thought and action. His mind is forever engaged in the play of choices and preferences. This constitutes, or results in, the trait of self-awareness which, reduced to its lowest terms, means identifying oneself mentally with alternative states of mind or forms of behavior.

The first consequence of these distinctive capacities in the human being is that he cannot have enough of life. The more alive he is, the wider the horizon of the potentialities he envisages. By climbing higher, he sees more clearly that which had limited his view before he climbed. At the same time the new vistas bring into his ken more objects that excite his powers. Climbing higher is here a metaphor for that all inclusive trait which is the human differentia, that of transforming environment and self. Thus in man the will to live becomes the will to maximum life, or the will to salvation.

By virtue of man's extraordinary mental powers, his will to live possesses the capacity of changing his environment to a degree which not even the most clever among the animals ever approaches. Bees and beavers and all species of birds and fish perform what for animals are remarkable feats in changing environment for purposes of shelter, breeding, and storing up food, but their capacity is limited to a routinized procedure. Once that is interfered with, they are helpless. Man's capacity to transform environment is not only incomparably more complex, and includes not only the subordination of other living beings; it includes his own personality. Man not only refuses to accept the environment as he finds it and insists on rendering it more habitable: he also refuses to accept himself as he happens to be; he always strives to make of himself more than what he is. Unlike the unmodifiable hungers and drives of the sub-human, man's hungers and drives are subject to indefinite change and development, not in their original nature but in their outward manifestations and forms of satisfactions. His ability to distinguish between means and ends, primary and secondary, essential and unessential, allows room for modification in the very manner of satisfying his primal hungers. As his habits and wishes, his ideas and goals undergo change, he devises new instruments for satisfying them. In that way the process of transformation was so slow in the methods of peaceful life or of warfare as hardly to be perceptible. During the past thousand years, however, the process of transformation of self (*i.e.,* changes in ideas, habits, wishes, and goals) and of physical environment have been gaining in speed. This is particularly true of Western civilization. By now enough changes take place in the lifetime of

Western man to render both him and environment at the end of it almost unrecognizably different from what they were at the beginning. *The very need of reconsidering and modifying the goals of higher education is an index of the changes that have taken place in the ideas, habits, wishes, and goals of the American person.*

As a result, however, of the rapidity with which the environment is transformed in response to some of the more elemental wants of man, in contrast with the slowness with which the higher wants of man respond to the new responsibilities and the increased opportunities inherent in the expanded environment, we get what is known as "cultural lag," with its accompanying maladjustments, crises, and catastrophes. That state of affairs has become more menacing with each generation. At the present time the cultural lag or inner maladjustment is manifest in the feeling of insecurity, forlornness, and loss of a sense of purpose or meaning to life. This accounts for the present uncertainty with regard to the meaning of salvation and the hopelessness of attaining it.

Ever since the Renaissance, the idea of salvation as interpreted by traditional religion has begun to disintegrate. The Enlightenment which flourished in the eighteenth century marks the beginning of an attempt to achieve an idea of mundane salvation to fill the vacuum which that disintegration creates. But the Enlightenment was diverted from its goal by the violence of economic revolutions and international wars. The changes which have come about in human relations and ways of life have been so convulsive as to preclude all orderly evolution. That accounts for man's failure to bring the human self with its ideas, habits, wishes, and goals abreast of the new environment which has come into being as a result of the extraordinary technological development in recent years.

That the task, however, of formulating a working conception of salvation can no longer be postponed, is implied in the restiveness manifest in institutions of higher learning. The need they express of revising their goals is not merely a need for some educational technique that would render their activities more efficient. But unfortunately *the various studies of the problem of higher education are inhibited from acknowledging the full significance of what they themselves are attempting, namely, to articulate a mundane conception of salvation which shall function in men's minds with the same authority and effectiveness in transforming men's lives as did the traditional conception of salvation during the centuries before the Renaissance.*[1] *Unless that fact is clearly recognized and reckoned with in the determination of the new goals for higher education, the results are bound to be disappointing.*

VII

When Chesterton asked: "What's wrong with human life?" the answer he gave was: "We don't know what's right." Though we are as yet unable to be entirely specific as to what is right, we know at least the direction in which we should go to find specific answers. We know, to begin with, that the main thing that is wrong with human life is the imbalance caused by the failure to use our capacity to transform our ideas, habits, wishes, goals, and values in correspondence with the extent and speed of the transformation effected in our environment. If we want to achieve the necessary balance we should treat the area of life both inner and outer which we are in a position to influence or transform, in the same way as the sculptor, in the analogy employed by Aristotle, treats the statue which he makes.

Aristotle employs that analogy to point out that we cannot understand reality or any part of it, unless we reckon with each of the four factors, causes, or as he terms them, *archai* (principles) which go into the making of a statue, *viz.,* the material, the efficient, the formal, and the final. Without necessarily assenting to this conception of what constitutes knowledge of reality as a whole, or any part of it, it is a fact that we cannot produce any work of art or artisanship, if we ignore any of the above mentioned four factors. *If we want to know how education can help the young in the shaping of their lives, we have to view human life itself as an art.* Gregory Nazianzen spoke better than he knew when he said that "to educate man is the art of arts." That implies

[1]Comment by Herman Finer:
  Did the medieval doctrine of salvation in fact bind men together? It is said to have done so; but they seem to have fought each other badly. The doctrine of salvation then taught was synonymous with the darkest ignorance of the masses. This raises the relationship between a faith in salvation and the corpus of knowledge available to the masses today through schools and the mass media of communication. A single doctrine might have succeeded when men knew no alternatives: is it feasible today? I think not. And democracy itself is also open to continuous challenge—there is no harm in that. I should like to know exactly which centuries, or decades, or even years, exhibited a union of mankind much better than in our own time, except when men were coerced.

reckoning with human life as an art process, in which each of the four factors named above has to be translated into knowledge, values, and habits. Though habits may not come within the purview of higher education, ideas and values certainly do.

The raw material which is to be shaped into human life is none other than life itself, which is a form of energy. It differs from inanimate energy. We may denote that difference by calling it will. In so far as we think of it apart from any of its specific manifestations we term it as the will to live. But we also have reason to differentiate the will to live as manifest in the human being from the will to live in other living beings. As pointed out above, that difference consists in choosing among alternatives the one that promises more life and ever more life. Hence, when we generalize that fact, we may say that the human will to live differs from other forms of that will, in that it strives to achieve life abundant. The fact that in traditional religion life abundant is synonymous with salvation need not restrict the concept of salvation to what traditional religion has identified it with. We may, therefore, describe the human will to live as the will to salvation.

As the raw material of human life, the will to salvation constitutes the material factor. It is the datum with which we operate. Whatever a human being begins life with is not a matter of choice. The choice among alternatives operates only within the scope of the other three factors. Unlike the artist who can choose the particular medium he wants to work with, the human being has to work with the will to salvation as represented by his body with its psychic potentialities and the environment, both physical and social, into which he is born. The process of education consists in accepting that datum and helping the youth bring out all the good that it is capable of. What that good is we can best determine by exploring each of the three factors which, in their combined working with the material factor, produce the living result —a human being.

Each one of the factors in the shaping of human life operates through the medium of recognizable wants or hungers. Each of those wants or hungers, however, is only one phase of any manifestation of man's will to live. In its entirety such a manifestation, which is designated as "an interest," consists of three elements or aspects: conation, emotion, and cognition, represented respectively by the drive, the want, and the value or good. Throughout the rest of the discussion, whenever we have occasion to refer to values or goods, we shall understand by that term the *cognitive* aspects of all human interests. A value or good is any conceivable object, person, event, process, or relationship, from the standpoint of its capacity to satisfy any particular interest and, therefore, as a means to life abundant or salvation in general. A "disvalue," or evil, is any one of these things, in so far as it is capable of frustrating any particular interest, or salvation in general.

Each of the three factors in the art of living may be conceived as a distinct dimension of human life. Each such dimension is organically related to the two others, and the three are, therefore, interdependent. Nevertheless, each dimension is sufficiently distinct to be regarded as qualitatively different from the other two. One of the most prevalent fallacies known as "reductionism" which is particularly characteristic of scholars and thinkers to a far greater degree than of the unlearned, would be averted, had this qualitative difference between each of the three dimensions of human life been carefully noted. Reductionism is the tendency of the human mind to reduce the various aspects of any phenomenon to the one aspect which happens to interest us most.

The entire history of human thought and endeavor in the art of living is a history either of egregious failure to recognize any such distinctions in the vast maze of human strivings, or of stupid blundering in identifying the true nature of human interests. It would be presumptuous for any man to claim that he has hit upon a principle of classification that is infallible, or even that he can always apply his own principle correctly and consistently. In suggesting the Aristotelian principle of the four *archai* as a kind of Ariadne's thread in the labyrinthine maze of human life, we do so in hope that it will call forth similar attempts on the part of others, and that out of all those attempts, one that approximates reality most closely will be evolved.

VIII

The efficient factor in the art of living may be designated as the *dimension of power*. The interests in which the human will to live manifests itself in this dimension are physical, mental, and social. So urgent is their satisfaction that in comparison with the interests in the other dimensions of human life they may be characterized as vital. These interests, though of infinite variety, may be classified into categories like the following which are not necessarily exhaustive: *health, security, work, companionship, mating, play, recreation, and new experience.*

None of these interests can be satisfied without effort to overcome the resistances to their attainment. The exercise of such effort is the exertion of power. The more difficult it is to secure the goods or values to satisfy those interests the greater the power we must possess. Hence, the fundamental problem in securing the vital goods or satisfying the vital interests is the problem of augmenting power. This is where physical strength, endurance, and mental ability come into play. Knowledge is power, that is, the more we know about objects, persons, etc., the greater the chances of our attaining the goods or values necessary to satisfy our vital interests. Intelligence and imagination are mental traits which, making use of knowledge, enable us to bring about all kinds of theoretic and practical combinations and permutations whereby we can gain control of the requisite goods or values.

The resistances to the attainment of the vital goods or values are of two kinds, impersonal and personal. The impersonal resistances call for the acquisition of impersonal power, *i.e.,* power which does not implicate interpersonal relations; it calls for ability to exercise control over things. The main problems of human life, however, arise from personal resistances, due to the fact that the supply of goods for the satisfaction of the vital interests is seldom such as to be enough for all who want those goods. Every person, therefore, is animated by the fear of being deprived by his neighbor of what he regards as indispensable to his own welfare. That sets up in him resistance against the efforts of his neighbor. Thus arises the struggle for power, not over things but over other persons.

The problem of personal power is further complicated by the fact that it is impossible for any individual to rely entirely upon himself and his limited resources for the attainment of what is indispensable. In his dependence upon others, he must submit himself to them for guidance and help. Those who have the power to impose their will upon their fellows are all too often tempted to abuse that power. Before long, human beings are confronted by the situation which is universal, that of exploiter and exploited. This situation develops within each group, and in the relations of groups to one another. When clans, tribes, or peoples engage in war as a result of invasion or aggression, entire populations are reduced to slavery or serfdom. Thus arise all the injustices and inequities that have ever marred human society, whether savage, barbarous, or civilized.

Within the limits of the smaller groups, particularly those of the face to face type, it is inevitable for those engaged in the struggle for power over others to become aware sooner or later that such struggle cannot be permitted to go on indefinitely without internecine consequences. That awareness is supplemented by such other expressions of the will to live as the need for companionship, work, play, none of which can be realized without bringing under control one's will to power. Those needs are accompanied by a form of sympathy which, without being intended, sometimes breaks through the wall of otherness that isolates us from our fellows. We then come to understand that the only way to live is to live together, and that we have to work out some *modus vivendi*. When that takes place an altogether new dimension of goods or values emerges: the dimension of wisdom.

IX

The sense in which the concept, "wisdom," is used in this discussion is in keeping with the one it has in the great classics of religion and philosophy. In the Bible, and particularly in what is known as "Wisdom Literature," the term wisdom denotes virtue and truth. The struggle for personal power in every society is, as we have seen, more or less mitigated by the values identified with the interests of wisdom. Sincerity, good faith, justice, mercy, and love emerge from the process of satisfying our vital interests, and are as much an expression of man's will to live as are the vital interests, or the interests of power. However, in so far as they are brought into the focus of consciousness, and come to be recognized as possessing intrinsic worth apart from their being necessary to survival, the values of wisdom become distinctively human traits, and come to figure in the differentia which marks off the will to salvation from the mere will to live, which man has in common with the subhuman.

An entirely different account of the emergence of what is called "the ethical mechanism" is given by Julian Huxley.[2] His is not a sociological but an individual psychological approach. The baby, according to him,

---

[2] "The New Evolution," in *Our Emergent Civilization*, Ruth Nanda Ansken, editor, Harper & Brothers, New York, 1947.

during its second and third year, experiences the beginnings of inner conflict. The mother who represents the external world to the baby has a twofold meaning for it. She is the child's chief object of love and fountainhead of satisfaction, security, and peace. But she is also "authority . . . arbitrarily thwarting some of the impulses along whose paths its new life quests outward." Torn between anger and hate on the one hand, and love on the other, the conflict is finally resolved, when the love gets the upper hand, but it is loaded with a sense of guilt. Thus is built up a new mental structure which comes to function as an "ethical mechanism." That mechanism gains in complexity with the growth of experience. The concept of "ethical mechanism" is Julian Huxley's way of saying that the ethical evolution of the human being is not merely a form of biological evolution but represents a different dimension. This corresponds with the principal point which I am trying to make that, however viewed, whether sociologically or psychologically, the sense of right and wrong, or the power of wisdom, is a qualitative human differentia.

An aspect of the sincerity which is basic to all the categories of wisdom is the love of truth, not only in action but in and for itself, as a matter of cognition or knowledge. That aspect of sincerity is the one that philosophy has always emphasized in its glorification of reason. Fundamentally, reason is an expression of that something in the human mind which demands complete objectivity and reality and which rebels against illusion and all forms of unreality. The very tendency to misuse reason as a means of self-delusion and of deluding others, proves how deeply rooted in human nature is the need for reason. The very tendency to "rationalize" implies how easily reason may be appealed to. Even those who are intolerant of the views or tastes of others seem to have a sense of guilt, which they try to throw off by means of all kinds of sophistries. Had they not inwardly felt frustrated as a result of their intolerance they would not work so hard to justify it.

Henry Lanz, the author of *In Quest of Morals*, suggests a fantastic way of proving that, despite the apparently limited role of reason and of the demand for objectivity in human life, we cannot afford to disregard them. He supposes that by a kind of Mephistophelian bargain you are offered a life in which all your heart's desires meet with fulfilment, but on one condition, namely, "that it will all happen in a dream," without your being aware that it is a dream. It is either that or continuing your own humdrum existence. Which would you choose? "The mere fact," says the author, "that you would hesitate shows what a hold the want of reality has on you and how destructive of satisfaction the least suspicion of illusion." James Farley in his recent book, *Jim Farley's Story,* tells of his having received ten honorary degrees and adds, "While these are flattering to my vanity, I would trade them all for an earned B.A." This ethical want inherent in human nature takes the form of the quest for objective truth. One who is obsessed by that quest is a philosopher, a lover of wisdom. Socrates assumed that the most important truth in search of which the philosopher should engage is not that which concerns man's environment but man himself, particularly truth in action, or the ethical life.

Without involving ourselves in the epistemological problem of the difference between the objective and the subjective, between reality and illusion, it will suffice to point out that the essence of wisdom or of reason both in thought and in action consists in an inner consistency or lawfulness. Wisdom is the antithesis of arbitrariness. That is perhaps what those who stress the absolute character of the moral law really want to emphasize. Inner consistency in being and acting makes possible dependability, without which it is impossible to plan for or direct the future. Whatever makes the future possible makes for life. So intimate is the relation between the categories of wisdom and the traits of consistency and lawfulness which are the bases of dependability, that Richard C. Cabot, in *The Meaning of Right and Wrong,* assumes that it is possible to build the entire ethical system on the dependability which is created by agreement or *"declaration of intention arrived at, in view of an understanding of facts by the various tendencies within one person, or by two or more persons."*

Not only truth and justice are based on law, but also love and mercy. Love cannot be the antithesis of law as such, of law that expresses the inherent nature of some reality; love itself is a law of human nature, in so far as no human being can be sufficient unto himself. Those whose souls are filled with hate for the stranger, would go insane, if they were not to love at least those who are akin to them in body or spirit. But apart from being a law of human nature, love must abide by its own law, else it degenerate into mushy and undependable sentimentality.

X

The factor of purpose, or the final cause, in the shaping of man's destiny has to be something that gives unity to the manifold of interests in the process of living, both in the dimension of power and in the dimension of wisdom. There is bound to be more than one unity in this third dimension. The unity of the self, or one's inner life, which we identify as personality, cannot suffice to mobilize the various interests in the process of living. While those interests have their roots in one's own personality, they cannot exist without the social and the physical environment. These are as essential to personality as earth, water, and sunshine are essential to the tree. The social environment provides the indispensable cooperation, and the physical environment provides the physical conditions and means of satisfaction. These three unities are related to one another in a kind of concentric fashion. In this relationship, one's personality, the society with which one identifies oneself, and the world viewed as cosmos or ordered reality in which one can feel at home, are the three foci in one that give unity of purpose to human life; these give to human life destiny or destination.

Personality, as such a focus, is not to be identified with the psychic or organic unity that constitutes an empirical fact. It is rather that unity which is spoken of as soul, and that carries with it certain religious implications. In institutional religions, the assumption of personal immortality is one such implication. *In the type of democratic religion, which is emerging, the concept of personality, or soul, carries with it the principle of intrinsic worth or dignity that is inviolable, and of rights and duties that are inalienable. Among these rights and duties is the right to be different and the duty to be oneself or true to oneself, one's real self which, paradoxically enough, is one's ideal self.* For that reason we may well characterize personality, which is the unity of the individual human being, as transcendent. This is probably what Pascal meant when he said: "We must love a being who is in us and is not ourselves." As transcendent, personality is not a static entity, nor a completed process, so long as one is alive. It becomes more of a unifying factor in our experiences with every success that it achieves. In that capacity, it grows in significance as one of the three purpose categories of human life.

Likewise, *Society,* which is the second category in this third dimension of man's will to salvation is not the empirical group of human beings that constitutes the social world of the individual. It is rather the community of the past, present, and future generations of one's clan, city, tribe, nation, or church, which those who compose it envisage in their most zestful moments and apotheosize as transcendent. It is a chosen people or City of God. It is the main bearer of all those ways and customs and laws which form part, or the whole of wisdom. That society forms the second focus around which are centered all of man's outgoing efforts that make of him a social being, and break down the walls of his self-centeredness. That unity is assumed to possess the traits of immortality and high worth to a far greater degree than the unity identified as soul or personality. Its immortality is almost an empirically verifiable fact, in so far as with the passing of one generation there is another to take up the life of the society. That in itself is sufficient to endow the society with far greater worth than the individual.

But even the society is not entirely self-sustaining. It needs the physical world, the earth, sea, and sky, the sun, moon, and stars to constitute for it a unity, as the source of its own life and the life which it mediates to the individuals that compose it. As a focus of attention in the pursuit of our various interests, *the world* is a unity which gives meaning and direction to our will to life abundant, to say nothing of its actually enabling us to achieve it. *The world, regarded as a cosmos or as salvation conditioned, may be viewed as the creation or the revelation of God. No matter how many the kinds of gods human beings actually worship, they cannot help intuitively sensing in all of them one common function, that of rendering the environment conducive to the fulfilment of man's needs and destiny.*

The effect of these three unities in mobilizing all human interests around the purpose of salvation, or the achievement of human destiny, is to call forth in the human being the courage and perseverance without which he would not be able to get very far in his effort to make the most of his life. The incidence of failure and frustration is so frequent that man is ever in need of drawing upon these unities to provide him with the necessary morale, which is usually conceived as persistence in the pursuit of a purpose and tenacity in the face of adversity. But even in the day to day performance of one's routine tasks there is room for morale in the form of efficient and upright service. Consequently, *in addition to the dimensions of power and wisdom, we have the di-*

mension of morale with its value categories of personality, society, and cosmos, as aiding man to fulfil his destiny to give purpose to his life, incentive to be and do his best, and courage to bear the worst that may befall him. It is this aspect of education Rousseau must have had in mind when he said: "Those of us who can best endure the good and evil in life are the best educated."

The dimension of morale is the specific concern of the religion of a people or of a church. To that end, each religion orients its adherents in a world outlook in which the significance of its three unities, personality, group, and salvation conditioned world is emphasized by various means, such as rituals, legends, histories. Certain persons, objects, places, events which happen to have figured as sources of strength, victory, sustenance, or guidance are singled out for homage, worship, or glorification. These objects of homage constitute the *sancta* or the elements of holiness in the civilization which is their context. They help to focus attention on the three main unities, and render them sources of morale in the struggle against all manner of difficulties, dangers, and frustrations. *The function of a religion as such is not to make men good but to keep them strong.* As far as *making* them strong, most men, especially those who are scientifically minded rely upon the vitality values.

It is at this point that institutional religions have the opportunity to make their contribution to democracy. It is also at this point that democracy must recognize its need of whatever institutional religions the students bring with them from their home background. Democracy is virtually still in its infancy. Its very conception has hitherto been limited to political and national experience. The struggle for it hitherto could not possibly have evolved those values of personality, society, and cosmos which we all need for persistence in being and doing our best, and the fortitude necessary to bear the worst. Since we can do as little without morale as we can without morals, we must necessarily fall back upon the religions which all of us have brought with us. Those religions have a rich accumulation of tradition which, interpreted in the light of human nature and destiny, can easily be shown to abound in permanent values of heart, mind, and spirit.

On the other hand, if those religions which we have brought with us want to serve in that capacity, they will have to renounce their respective claims to the exclusive possession of the key to salvation. They will have

The Need for Normative Unity in Higher Education

to concede that for each people, church, or denomination, its own religion is the one best calculated to contribute toward the salvation of its adherents.[j] But even that purpose it should not expect to accomplish without the cooperation of all elements in the life of the nation whose common interest is the furtherance of democracy in "every phase of human life." It is needless to say that this entire discussion is meaningless from the standpoint of the Roman Catholic Church whose fundamental philosophy is "that there is one true church, and the power of God in the civil arm should be used prudently to assist the power of God in the ecclesiastical arm."[3]

The author of the foregoing makes no secret of the fact that in a predominantly Catholic state minority religions would be tolerated only because "proscription of a substantial minority would cause civil and religious disputes, dissensions and conflicts." Such doctrine is the antipode of democracy.

XI

The plausibility of this soterical[4] classification of the various interests of human life is confirmed every time a thinker has occasion to summarize the various phases of human life or education. Thus Aristotle's three main attributes of temperance, justice, and fortitude are

---

[j]Comment by John LaFarge, S.J.:

Dr. Kaplan seems to say that *all* gods are helpful, or conceived as helpful to human society. But is this true? Are all gods outside of the living God of Abraham, Isaac, and Jacob necessarily helpful? I find very little social helpfulness in Thor and Wotan, or even in Zeus and Hermes, not to speak of countless other polytheistic or pantheistic divinities. They may be magnificent and inspiring, but how many of them have love?

Dr. Kaplan's reply:

The question whether all gods are helpful is answered by Father LaFarge himself, when he says that "they may be magnificent or inspiring." To be magnificent or inspiring is certainly to be helpful in furthering a nation's or a despot's ambition which may end in their destruction. The God of Abraham, Isaac, and Jacob is helpful to men and nations that strive for salvation which transcends ambition by including *all* the categories of wisdom and holiness.

[3]From the letter of Archbishop Lucey of San Antonio mentioned above.

[4]Soterical—pertaining to salvation as a synonym for the maximum life or to soterics as the study of salvation.

Cf. "Toward a Philosophy of Cultural Integration," *Approaches to Group Understanding*, Lyman Bryson, Louis Finkelstein, R. M. MacIver, editors, Conference on Science, Philosophy and Religion in their Relation to the Democratic Way of Life, Inc., New York, 1947, pp. 589–600.

evidently the virtues respectively of power, wisdom, and morale. Or when Milton says: "I call therefore a complete generous education that which fits a man to perform justly, skilfully, and magnanimously all the offices, both private and public, of peace and war," he anticipated some such design for living as the one here suggested. We perform *justly* in the dimension of wisdom, *skilfully* in that of power, and *magnanimously* in that of morale.

A detailed analysis of the content of human life, and likewise of educational subject matter, based on the life pattern of the four factors suggested by Aristotle would require the gift of a Thomas Aquinas for encyclopedic organization of human knowledge. For the purposes of this discussion, it will suffice to answer a few questions that naturally come to mind in connection with this life pattern. Wherein, for example, does this life pattern enable us to see the relation between the sciences and the humanities?

The sciences are of two kinds: pure and applied. The purpose of pure science is to arrive at a knowledge of reality, and to dispel all error which is the result of imagination impelled by fears and desires, or of mistaken notions. Such knowledge is wisdom. It is also a form of power, but not power over things, and least of all over human beings. It is moral power which we identify as purity or nobility of character and a good in itself, without being a means to aught else. On the other hand, applied science is power over things or conditions of life, the ability to control and manipulate them for all those interests which belong to the dimension of power or the vitalities. We would avoid considerable confusion, if we confined the use of the term, "reason," to the categories in the dimension of wisdom, including *pure* science, and the term, "intelligence," to the categories in the dimension of power, and therefore to *applied* science.

Whether as part of wisdom, or of power over things and conditions of life, science aims on the whole to see objects, events, relations, and processes in their respective contexts, to distinguish the permanent from the changing, to identify the quality and quantity of things, their similitude and dissimilitude, the relationships of cause and effect, to recognize the one in the many. The same approach is implied in the human sciences, whether in their pure or applied form.

It is only in recent times that the dangerous possibilities inherent in the applied human sciences have come to be realized. The use to which

The Need for Normative Unity in Higher Education

they can be put in the struggle for power over other human beings is unlimited. There is nothing in the human sciences themselves, any more than in the physical sciences, that can serve as a criterion of the uses to which they are to be put. Just as the physicist and the chemist have, in their capacity as scientists, nothing to say about the right or wrong of the making of atomic bombs, so the psychologist and the sociologist, as scientists, have no rule to go by concerning the ethical character of propaganda.

It is at this point that the place of the humanities in education is vividly experienced as indispensable to human life. *It should be the function of history and literature to inculcate those values in the dimensions of wisdom and morale without which no amount of applied science can make a human being really human. It should be the function of education, particularly of higher education as distinct from technical training, so to integrate the scientific studies with the humanistic that, with every application of science which confers any kind of control, the student would at once become aware of its implications in terms of the categories of wisdom and morale.* How that is to be accomplished is a matter of pedagogic technique. We may nevertheless suggest that one sure way of *failing* to accomplish it is to present this entire approach merely as the function of a special department, as is done with philosophy or English. Indeed just as the student fails to get the most out of those studies, because they are usually confined to their own departments, so would he fail to work out the necessary syntheses between the sciences and humanities, unless something of the humanities forms part of the courses in the sciences and *vice versa*. That integration is of particular urgency and most capable of achievement between the *human* sciences and the humanities.

XII

It is evident that the soterical design for living calls for a different classification of human values from that which is the heritage of Hellenic civilization. The division of human values into the true, the good, and the beautiful is largely responsible for much of the confusion in the aims of education. *Western civilization which is a synthesis of Hellenic and Judeo-Christian values could not, without considerable distortion, fit into a frame of values which is purely Hellenic.* The organization of educational content into trivium and quadrivium may well have fitted the classic pattern, but really never corresponded to the educational needs of the post Roman world. In the modern world it is a complete misfit. All the homiletic reinterpretation given to it by Mark Van Doren in his *Liberal Education* fails to be convincing. The basic difficulty with the trivium and quadrivium is that the classic division of human values upon which that program is based is totally inadequate.

The Hellenic classification of human values is inherently not balanced and, in relation to the actualities of life, either leaves out the area of religion or forces upon it a wrong evaluation. If good, for example, denotes the ethical good, there is no reason why "the true" should not be a "good." Moreover, to put the good and the true side by side with the beautiful, as though they were coordinate, is ridiculous. Since, according to Matthew Arnold, conduct is three-fourths of life, it ill becomes the beautiful, which shares the remaining fourth with truth, to claim that it is coordinate with the good.

In all this, where does religion come in? To say that it is synonymous with the good is not altogether true. Religion itself may be good or bad. As such, therefore, religion must belong to some fourth category which is overlooked in the classic formula. That is, indeed, the category of the holy. I doubt whether in any of the recent treatises dealing with the problem of higher education, the word, "holy," occurs even once. It has become a Sunday word, and the assumption is that higher education is intended mainly for the other days of the week. This is on the face of it quite absurd. The concept, "holiness," has a great history behind it. It is like a flowing river always and never the same. The fact that its meaning cannot be the same as what it had for the ancients should no more be a reason for ignoring it than there would be for ignoring the concepts of truth, goodness, and beauty on account of the ever changing content with which they are associated. It is easy to understand what has happened to the concept, "holy," if we examine it in the light of the soterical analysis. It is a concept which has functioned mainly in the two dimensions of power and morale. In the dimension of power, it denoted a quality which is related to the magical control of whatever is of *vital* value to the human being. As for the dimension of morale, "holy" is really the historic term for whatever inspires morale. Everything that gives us courage, fortitude, endurance, and a sense of life's worthwhileness has always been treated with reverence and always will be, because it is holy.[k]

As for the category of the beautiful, we believe that the soterical analysis can assign to it a far more appropriate place in the design for living and education than the Hellenic classification. Beautiful is the sensuous experience, actual or imagined, of whatever contributes effervescence and zest to the fulfilment of any of the needs of human life. Beautiful objects in nature and art are sources of such sensuous experience. Poetry is the source of imagined sensuous experience of that kind. What stimulates zest and effervescence is a matter for the science of esthetics. Just as physical beauty in one of the opposite sex activates the sex glands, and a beautifully set table whets the appetite, so a beautiful landscape activates the feeling of the cosmic, and beautiful music may activate the feeling of any or all of the three unities in the dimension of morale. Beauty is rarely associated with truth or goodness. Yet we have heard of some who derive esthetic pleasure from geometric forms and formulas. And not a few have attempted to interpret ethics as a phase of the "Dance of Life." The part played by the fine arts—architecture, music, pantomime, drama, and dance in rendering religion exciting and fascinating is well known. The fine arts actually rouse in those who can appreciate them the zest for living. Without beauty, human life becomes stale, flat, and boring. A life which is devoid of all beauty is, at its best, like champagne that has become vapid.

There is no doubt, therefore, that *we would be able to plan more intelligently and more rationally life as a whole and the educational process in particular, if we replaced the traditional classification of the true, the good, and the beautiful with the soterical classification of the vital, the wise, and the holy.*

XIII

It should not at all be difficult from the standpoint of the soterical design for living to orient ourselves anew with regard to the inalienable

---

[k]Comment by John D. Wild:

Mr. Kaplan seems to identify religion with whatever inspires morale. This strikes me as a far too anthropocentric line of thought. Is it not the essence of the religious claim that it puts us in communion with something higher and more important than we ourselves and our human desires? In so far as this really happens it cannot fail to have an *incidental* moral effect. But those who embrace religion for the sake of the good it can do them are apt to emerge with something which is neither very religious nor very good.

rights and duties of the individual as conceived by democracy. The rights to life, liberty, and the pursuit of happiness would thus receive their validation from what may be described as a philosophy of mundane salvation. There can be no question that democracy teaches a different conception of the ultimate authority which validates the ethical values of human life from that taught by institutional religion.

According to institutional religion, the source of authority or validation is exclusively of a supernatural character. That is right which God wills, whether through the medium of revelation, or through that of reason. Even the reverse assumption—that whatever is right God wills—does not get us very far, since the rightness of what is right has to be validated by supernatural revelation. According to democracy, on the other hand, the source of authority or validation is immanent in the very nature of man in that part of his nature which we identify as personality. But personality itself is, as we have seen, not reducible to scientific categories. It is indeed, a transcendent element in man, a manifestation of the Power in the cosmos that makes for man's salvation, or God. Accordingly, that is right which is deliberately intended to help man achieve his salvation.[1]

The negation of supernaturalism, by no means, necessarily implies the negation of the transcendental significance of human life. The difference between, on the one hand, viewing man as self-sufficient and thus devoid of all transcendence, and, on the other, viewing him as the terminus of a transcendent process, is like the difference between a geometrical point and a pen point. The point of a pen derives its distinctive character from that which is beyond it. *Man, viewed transcendentally, is man in the context of the cosmos, as the stage with its properties so*

---

[1] Comment by Thurston N. Davis, S.J.:
  Dr. Kaplan sees clearly the necessity of our keeping pace in our social and educational thinking with the vast changes taking place in the contemporary world. No one could quarrel with him in these matters. But with Dr. Kaplan's conception of a new religion of Democracy there is more reason to disagree. If his concern is for a religion without authority, then we might profitably discuss the whole metaphysic which underlies the historical fact of divine revelation. If, however, his new religion is meant to be merely a "soterical design for living," "a philosophy of mundane salvation," then it might be useful to debate the question as to whether such an amalgam of sentiments—though it might be very "democratic"—would be "religious" in any recognizable sense. On this whole matter of a religion of democracy we might well be guided by the historical lessons which the French Revolution has to teach us. It is interesting to observe how rapidly this one important past experiment in a religion of democracy was changed into a reign of terror and tyranny.

The Need for Normative Unity in Higher Education

set as to enable him to play the role of a being with an insatiable hunger for maximum life.[m]

The fact that the values of democracy are generally presented as though they had no transcendental implications, and independently of their relation to salvation and to the God concept, is misleading. That fact is taken to imply that democracy and religion are mutually heterogeneous. Such is not at all the case. As a rule, the reason for omitting the concepts of salvation and of God from discussions of democracy is that for most people those concepts are limited to the other worldly interpretation given them by institutional religion. But once we realize not only the possibility, but also the need, of giving them a mundane interpretation, as when we deal with basic problems of life and especially of education, we should not feel inhibited in making use of those concepts. *We must educate ourselves in the process of defrosting the traditional usage of the great terms of the religious tradition of mankind. That process might carry us very far in the better understanding of the great books, to say nothing of the better ability in understanding one another.*[n]

[m]Comment by John D. Wild:
Mr. Kaplan's discussion of the transcendent leaves me rather confused. On the one hand he seems to deny anything transcending man in the cosmos, admitting only "a transcendent element in man, a manifestation of the Power in the cosmos that makes for man's salvation, or God." Yet he has previously stated that "the world, regarded as a cosmos or as salvation conditioned may be viewed as the creation or the revelation of God." *This* view is either true or false. If false, it has no place in higher education and must be discarded as a delusion. But Mr. Kaplan does not apparently wish to discard it. If true, then there is a cosmic power higher than man, for man did not bring himself into existence, nor did he condition the cosmos to any plan of salvation. Does Mr. Kaplan really believe in such a power or not? I am not clear on this. If so, I can see how he may find a place for religion in his scheme. If not, I think that he should frankly dispense with it.

Dr. Kaplan's reply:
Professor Wild quotes two statements which *presumably* set forth my conception of God, and which seem to contradict each other. The fact, however, is that the first statement refers to personality in man and not to God. I cannot find any statement in my paper which is open to ambiguity with regard to God's transcendence. The fact that I assume also God's immanence is certainly no reason for inferring that I question God's transcendence.

[n]Comment by B. Othanel Smith:
The search for a theory of salvation which will be compatible with democracy is much needed. But Professor Kaplan's proposal troubles me at three points. First, any theory of salvation which fails to build and to sustain personal morale in the face of death will be short of satisfactory. How is this problem to be handled by a mundane theory of salvation? The second point has to do with the cosmic view underwriting morale. Here Professor Kaplan falls back upon the historic religions which all of us have borrowed from prior cultural periods. How the cosmic views of these religions can be accepted as the bases of

If, however, we persist in keeping the traditional usage of those great terms in its frozen state, we shall be inhibited from carrying our endeavors at educational reform to their consummation. To give a typical illustration of how we unnecessarily inhibit ourselves by refraining from a rational reinterpretation of the great terms of religion: "The fundamental concept of democracy," we read in the Federal Report, "is a belief in the inherent worth of the individual, in the dignity and value of human life." This statement, as it stands, is empirically unverifiable. There is no valid logic by which we can derive this idea from any demonstrable experience. This assumption like many another in democracy is not only inescapable, but also derives its significance or validation from a source beyond itself. The question of other worldliness apart, democracy manifests emotionally and practically all the traits we associate with religion. Why then should democracy discard the advantage of the emotional and practical momentum accumulated by the institutional religions?°

---

morale without accepting also their theories of salvation, is certainly not clear. This would seem to be a case of trying to eat your cake and have it, too. The third point derives from the obvious fact that cosmic views are today arising not from traditional religions but from the "religion of science." More and more theoretical physics is appropriating the territory once claimed by metaphysics and religion. Today it is hardly possible for a person to be a first class metaphysician without a thorough going discipline in theoretical physics.

It may well be that whatever theory of salvation is finally evolved will be one compatible with the world view of modern science even down to its criterion of truth. How are the humanities and scientific studies to be integrated? History and literature which are to be used to inculcate values in the dimensions of wisdom and morale are filled with all sorts of contradictory views and normative rules and judgments. How we are to know which of these views, rules, and judgments are to be accepted, is by no means clear from Professor Kaplan's paper. Are there to be two criteria of truth: one for the sciences and another for the humanities? If so, how are these disciplines to be integrated?

°Comment by I. L. Kandel:

Somehow the implication that the way of democracy is the way to God, sounds like the attempt to combine religion and politics in the Nazi statement that the "way of Hitler is the way to God." Instead of inventing or applying new terminologies it would have been well if one with authority could have discussed the importance of including in a college curriculum the development of sane understanding of the place of religion as a part of American culture, leaving to the denominations the formal and specific training.

Dr. Kaplan's reply:

To object to the implication that "the way of democracy is the way to God" on the ground that "it sounds like the Nazi statement, 'the way of Hitler is the way to God,'" is to find fault with the sound, not with the sense of what is implied. Nor is the attempt to combine religion (not church) with politics as absurd as it seems to Dr. Kandel. After all, not even the prophets of the Judeo-Christian tradition, could prevent the Nazis' perversion of their teaching which dealt for the most part with the problem of combining religion with politics.

One of the crucial problems of mundane salvation is how to keep human nature functioning simultaneously in the three dimensions of power, wisdom, and morale in such a way as not to throw them out of kilter. The very capacity of the human mind, which enables man to abstract mentally one or more phases from a situation or event, overreaches itself. That capacity is carried to a point which leads the human being to react to life not with the whole of his nature, but only with that part which happens to be disturbed or maladjusted. Most of the time, of course, it is the part which responds to the vital hungers. Least often, it is the part which responds to the demands for wisdom. But whichever part it is, it is generally treated, particularly when under tension, as if it were the whole of human nature. The rest of human nature is then usually ignored or slighted. Hence, *education, whose main function it should be to enable the human being to live as full a life as possible, should have as its chief objective so to train all human capacities in their mutual relationship as to produce not a fractional man but a whole man.* It should counteract all tendencies to upset the mutually organic character of the three dimensions in the art of living. It should aim at such development of each of them that their equilibrium would be maintained through the normal and adequate activity of each.[p]

The function of education to maintain the balance in the development of human nature is not only one of desperate urgency by reason of the present condition of man. It is also one which man's past aberrations point to as indispensable to man's salvation. The history of the many civilizations that at one time played a great role in the world is a history of their overextending themselves in the struggle for power, without due regard to the demands of wisdom and morale. The heritage which Western civilization has taken over from Hebraism and Hellenism consists for the most part of its emphasis on wisdom as indispensable to the wholesome fulfilment of the needs of power and morale. Hebraism stressed the category of goodness and truth in action, and Hellenism stressed the category of truth in thought. The prophets reminded Israel time and again that social injustice, power politics, and magical religion destroy the morale of a nation. The philosophers sought to impress upon their contemporaries that disregard of the realities and that any "unexamined life" led to the disintegration of personality, the mainstay of one's morale. But thus far that Hebreo-Hellenic heritage has not been trans-

[p][Cf. Comment by I. L. Kandel in Appendix III, and Dr. Kaplan's reply.]

lated into the art of living nor into the policy of nations. In the meantime the undreamed of developments of technology with their thousandfold augmentation of man's power have tended to render man more oblivious than ever to the indispensability of wisdom. Only by reinterpreting democracy so as to have it apply, as the Federal Report suggests, "to every phase of living," and only by reinterpreting the great terms of the institutional religions so that they may fully articulate the redemptive qualities of democracy, will we know what has to be done educationally to replace the striving for power with the striving for salvation.[q]

[q]Comment by David Bidney:
Regardless of the considerable merits of Dr. Kaplan's particular philosophy of life and education, it may be questioned whether a fuller realization of democracy "in every phase of living" requires the acceptance of any one particular philosophy of life such as his. The God of the various traditional religions, it seems, is not democratic enough and He is to be superseded by a Democrat immanent in the heart of man. The point at issue is whether democracy in religion requires some one philosophy of life such as Dr. Kaplan's, or whether it implies rather a diversity of philosophies which share certain common objectives. The experience of this Conference during the past eight years has been that any attempt to provide some one particular philosophy of life and culture as the sole justification for the democratic way of life will prove unacceptable.

Is democracy to be conceived as a sociocultural method of resolving the problems of human society, or does it entail a common philosophy of salvation as well? Dr. Kaplan appears to assume that the latter alternative is the only acceptable one, thereby setting up a new monistic ideology in the supposed interest of the democratic way of life. Is it possible to adhere to the democratic persuasion without a common philosophy of salvation, of the type suggested in his paper? Must one deny a faith in extramundane salvation in order to agree upon common objectives for the democratic attainment of a maximum of happiness for man on earth? Personally, I see no reason why one should feel compelled to choose *between* these alternatives as if it were a question of *either or*.

In any event, we must be clear on one issue: whether democracy is to be considered as a new religious faith supplanting in large measure the traditional religions, or whether democracy as applied to every phase of living is a liberal attitude of mind compatible with the variety of traditional religions and metaphysical systems. Are we to have a new *religion of democracy*, or are we to have *democracy in religion*, regardless of the claims of its adherents, so long as it is compatible with humane, democratic objectives?

Dr. Kaplan's reply:
I am thankful to Dr. Bidney for putting bluntly the question to me whether "democracy is to be conceived as a sociocultural method of resolving the problems of human society, or does it entail a common philosophy of salvation as well." That gives me a chance to state that, in my opinion, there is a third alternative to which I subscribe, *viz.*, democracy should be conceived as a sociocultural method. As such, *it presupposes not a common philosophy but a common method of achieving salvation.*

In other words, the soterical approach developed in the paper does not presume to be *a philosophy* or an ideology of salvation, but a *method* whereby it is possible for people of diverse cultural background and belief to achieve their salvation, or to make the most of

XIV

It is entirely beyond the scope of this paper to discuss the many areas in which democracy would have to be interpreted in the light of the soterical design for the art of living. It will suffice to mention two or three problems that come to mind as linked up with the application of democracy to education.

That application demands, in the first place, regard for the principle of equality. What equality means has been clearly set forth in a document which emanates from the Chicago school of thought. The document is designated as a "Preliminary Draft for Global Federation." There is hardly any direct connection between that document and the thought pattern of the Chicago school, except in an occasional phrase or two which does not affect the substance of the argument. None of the assumptions and provisions of the Constitution is made to depend upon the acceptance of any particular metaphysics. They are all based upon the principle of equality which, though not mentioned by name, is implied in the following: "It shall be the right of everyone everywhere to claim and maintain for himself and his fellowmen release from the bondage of poverty and from the servitude and exploitation of labor, with rewards and security according to merit and needs; freedom of

---

their own lives without hindering their neighbors from making the most of theirs as they conceive it. The soterical approach to the problem of salvation is analogous to the rational approach to the problems of the physical world. The rational approach being based upon reason, which is common to all normally minded human beings, is the best method of achieving the greatest amount of knowledge of the physical world and of control over its forces. That does not preclude difference of opinion and interpretation. Similarly the soterical approach is *a hypothetical method,* which can justify itself only by the success in actually integrating human life in the individual and the group and giving it purpose and direction.

As for Dr. Bidney's question: "Must one deny a faith in extramundane salvation in order to agree upon common objectives for the attainment of a maximum of happiness of man on earth?" I would certainly say: No. I agree fully with his own reply.

The only alternative I do set up is either the authoritative approach which confers authority upon those who validate it on the basis of a revealed code or apostolic succession, or the democratic approach which confers authority upon those who are elected or appointed by the people on grounds which are validated by some such method as indicated in the soterical pattern of human values. The latter calls for much more than "democracy in religion." We have been having "democracy in religion" ever since the establishment of the Constitution. From that arrangement there has accrued most advantage to political democracy, less to economic democracy and least, if any at all, to religion and to social democracy. If we wish to see advantage accrue also to religion and social democracy (or genuine equality), we need, "a religion of democracy."

peaceful assembly ... protection of individuals and groups against subjugation and tyrannical rule, racial and national, doctrinal or cultural ... and any such other freedoms and franchises as are inherent in man's inalienable claims to life, liberty and the dignity of the human person. These rights are accompanied by the duties of everyone everywhere ... to serve with word and deed, and with productive labor according to his ability, the physical and spiritual advancement of the living and of those to come, as the common cause of all generations of men; to do unto others as he would like them to do unto him; to abstain from violence."

The soterical design for living merely fills out the outline of what the freedom of "everyone everywhere" is for, or that wherein all human beings in the world regardless of creed, color, race, or nationality are equal. That means, in the first place, that "everyone everywhere" is fully entitled to every available opportunity to achieve mundane salvation, by realizing the optimum of which he is capable in the values of power, wisdom, and holiness. That is a far cry from the vulgarized conception of democratic education which is based on the assumption that its main function is to train the common man to make a living as a hand worker or brain worker, and that education for the art of living is not a concern of the state but is to be left to the home and the church. Secondly, the principle of equality in higher education places upon the state the responsibility for enabling all young people, regardless of economic status or home background, to continue their all around mental, moral, and spiritual growth as far as their abilities can carry them. In the words of the Federal Report, "Free and universal access to education, in terms of the interest, ability and need of the student must be a major goal in American education." "This means," the Report adds, "that we shall aim at making higher education equally available to all young people."

Another important corollary which derives from education for democracy, in the light of the soterical design for living, bears on the problem of leadership. This is where the *political* aspect of democracy is principally involved. It is impossible for human needs to be fulfilled without human society, and it is impossible for society to exist without the few to exercise authority and the many to submit to it. From a consistently authoritarian point of view, the many should have nothing to do with determining who is to exercise authority, nor with what qualifies anyone for authority. Both of these matters should be determined by those who derive their authority from a source that transcends the rights of the many.

From a democratic point of view, however, the determination of who should govern and what qualifies one for government is itself the prerogative of the many. They are the seat of authority which they usually decide to delegate to their chosen representatives. Moreover, it is the many who are entitled to use their discretion as to what constitutes fitness to act as their representatives or to be leaders. This places a heavy responsibility upon the individual as citizen. *The success of democracy depends entirely upon the ability of the people to choose the right kind of representatives or leaders.* We need everywhere in politics, in industry and finance, in law and medicine, in journalism, in church and social work, and above all, in education, men and women of intelligence, uprightness and spiritual courage, whether they be leaders or followers. *One of the main functions, therefore, of all education, and especially of higher education, should be to qualify the student to recognize among candidates for leadership those who will strengthen and improve democracy.*

Indeed, there is good warrant for viewing democracy as the culmination of a long historical process in which human beings have been experimenting with all kinds of leadership to help it achieve their destiny. The three dimensional analysis of man's will to salvation enables us to identify the various experiments with leadership. The shaman or medicine man and the warrior who were the first leaders to appear on the human scene, functioned in the dimension of the vital needs to achieve power necessary, in the one case, for obtaining food and health, and in the other, for overcoming enemies. The priest who evolved out of the shaman or medicine man came to function as the medium of the agencies that are the sources of morale. The age old struggle between warrior and priest has continued down to our own day in the rivalry between state and church. In time there arose a new type of leader, namely, lawgivers, prophets, and philosophers; the lawgivers as spokesmen for the right, the prophets and philosophers as critics of the *status quo,* in the name of the right and of the truth. These leaders articulated the categories of wisdom.

The reason democracy has not realized the hopes of its founders is that it has not as yet discovered the kind of leadership that can adequately meet men's needs. In contrast with the types of leadership which governed society in the past and which represented the values either of power or of morale, the leadership which was to function in the spirit of democracy was to represent the values of wisdom. This accounts for the advent of the lawyer instead of the soldier or priest as the political leader. As a lawyer he incarnates the spirit of the law which is assumed to be the embodiment of justice. Actually, however, he has generally served merely as a front for powerful industrial and financial interests whose will he articulates in the form of law. Thanks to the economic crisis from which democratic society suffers in times of peace and to the dangers to which it is exposed in times of war, some ingenious technicians recently advised us to scrap democracy and to adopt technocracy. That meant putting technical experts instead of civilians into the seat of authority. Instead, however, of the soldier being leader, it would now be the technical expert. That would have been a reversion to the dimension of power and the vitalities as the locus of leadership. Fortunately, it did not take long for people to discover the absurdity of that proposal. Technocracy was a short lived dream.

Incidentally, if a serious attempt is ever made to democratize higher education, it would have to begin with the selection of trustees for the universities who are representative of various interests and callings. Just as political leadership has, for the most part, passed out of the hands of those who represent merely the values of morale, or of religion, in the conventional sense of the term, so has education leadership. A recent study[5] points out that the practice of having clergymen constitute a large percentage of university boards of trustees is a thing of the past. Their place has been taken by business and professional leaders, by manufacturers, bankers, and lawyers. The author proposes that, in addition to increasing the proportion of women, those who represent the interests of agriculture and labor, and also faculty members and students, should serve as trustees.

So far there has been little attention paid to this entire problem of leadership. That fact is prejudicial to the interests of democracy. The strength which fascism was able to develop for a time, and which communism still possesses, is due to a keen awareness that the question of leadership is crucial in the set up of society. If democracy is to be strong enough to meet these two rivals not merely in the contest of war,

[5] H. P. Beck, *Men Who Control Our Universities,* Kings Crown Press, New York, 1948.

The Need for Normative Unity in Higher Education

but what is far more important, in their respective claims upon the human heart, then together with a philosophy of salvation democracy should develop a philosophy of leadership.

Without attempting to outline a democratic philosophy of leadership, it will suffice to set down as a general principle the following: *No one kind of leadership can possibly meet the needs of society in accordance with the principles of democracy.* A way will have to be found whereby each of the three groups of interests of human life will have its own spokesmen. That would necessitate the formation of three bodies in which the right to legislate would be vested. The possibility of our adopting that type of representation in our national government is, indeed, remote. Nevertheless, it may not be long before it will come to be seriously considered. That the very idea of having government conducted by three different types of leadership, very much along the lines of a three dimensional system of values, should have spontaneously occurred to the Chicago group is extremely significant. It indicates a certain correspondence between that idea and the real needs of modern society. The three Special Bodies which, according to the proposed constitution of the Federal Republic of the World, are to be set up within the first three years of the World Government, are the following: a) "A House of Nationalities and States, with the representatives from each, for the safeguarding of local institutions and autonomies and the protection of minorities; b) a Syndical or functional Senate, for the representation of syndicates and unions or occupational associations and any other corporate interests of transnational significance . . . ; c) an Institute of Science, Education and Culture." The House, the Senate, and the Institute correspond, respectively, to the interests of morale, of power, and of wisdom.

Before this kind of governmental set up ever comes into being, it is important that the citizen be fully aware of the nature of the authority he entrusts to those who are to speak in his name politically, economically, or morally. *Only by having clear discernment of each type of authority, of their relation to one another, and of the responsibilities which each type should be competent to discharge, will the citizen of a democratic nation be in a position to exercise properly the rights and duties of citizenship.*

A third corollary which derives from the democratic philosophy of salvation is the following: *The democratic philosophy of authority, as vested in the living members of society, is compatible only with a world in which international war would be outlawed, and nations would submit to a world government.* With the Damocles sword of war ever hanging over our heads, we cannot even afford to live up to the Atlantic Charter with its Four Freedoms. We have to suppress freedom of expression. We have to stimulate fear instead of promote freedom from it. We have to divert attention from the problem of freedom from want. And we have to impress the freedom of worship into the service of national patriotism. Hence, by the same token, that we strive toward "a fuller realization of democracy," we must strive toward international understanding and cooperation, both of which goals are emphatically set forth and defined in the Federal Report.[r]

This means that instead of the nation being the largest societal unit to which the individual is to look for the values that are to give him the morale for living, the whole of mankind will henceforth have to be that societal unit. If we will not at least begin to dream of world citizenship, we shall be ridden by the nightmare of world destruction. "Modern man," adds significantly the Federal Report, "needs to sense the sweep

[r]Comment by Herman Finer:
 I cannot agree that democracy is incompatible with a world which suffers international war, if we are talking in relative terms. If there is such a thing as an absolutely perfect, immaculate system of democratic government, then maybe war would be its constant assailant. But a large part of the world can be very democratic indeed, while war is still part of its life, so long, of course, as it has the power and resources and the will to defend itself. It is possible even that it might be all the more democratic if it is obliged to defend itself. Do not seek perfection; or if so, only in speculation, at any rate.

Comment by Clem C. Linnenberg, Jr.:
 I wholeheartedly share Professor Kaplan's opposition to authoritarianism and his attachment to democracy, freedom, and equality. I fully agree with him as to the urgent need for world government. But world federalists are disposed to assume that a world constitution must either have no bill of rights at all, or have a bill of rights which would operate against *all* levels of government. Professor Kaplan apparently assumes a world bill of rights which would operate against all levels of government and which would guarantee to the individual everywhere both liberty and economic security, now emphasized respectively in Western and Soviet declarations of faith. To attempt to achieve a bill of rights immediately which would operate not only against the world government but also against national and local governments is, I believe, to erect a needless barrier to the reasonably early attainment of world federation.
 Americans can help to protect what freedom they now possess by working for world federation even if—in order to attain federation—they refrain at least temporarily from trying to make over all the rest of the world in the libertarian design which they themselves would like to exhibit and which, in some degree, they do possess. Any country which felt safe from war would be less inclined to demand conformism.

of world history in order to see his own civilization in the context of other world cultures." This should suggest the urgent need for some philosophy of salvation which might serve as a bridge among the various cultures of the world. Elsewhere[6] I have sought to indicate how, with the proper interpretation of the values in each of the dimensions of the soterical design for life, that design might serve as a kind of evaluational Esperanto. By means of it the various studies in the college curriculum might well contribute to that international-mindedness without which all political machinery to establish peace is futile.

In sum, the present plight of mankind may be interpreted as due chiefly to men's moral and spiritual unpreparedness to cope with the power released by the recent technological developments. Whether or not it is too late for education to catch up with those developments and to render them safe for the world, we dare not give way to despair. We must reeducate ourselves as well as the nations which are mainly responsible for having accelerated the present crisis. In the process of reeducation priority should be given to higher education. The present tendency of colleges, universities, and the Federal Government to reexamine the entire process of higher education should not be limited to education and academicians. It should take hold of our entire population.

The fundamental educational issue at the present time is: With what shall we refill the vacuum created by the removal of the authority of institutional religion from the political life of the nation? The Chicago plan proposes the adoption of Neo-Thomism as an intellectual creed. The Federal Report proposes a farreaching application of the principle of democracy. This Conference is known as a "Conference on Science, Philosophy and Religion in Their Relation to the Democratic Way of Life." It seems, therefore, appropriate that this Conference should align itself with the Federal Report. It should point the way whereby science, philosophy, and religion may provide a philosophy that would serve as sanction and authority for the democratic way of life. That philosophy would have to be a philosophy of mundane salvation.

With the wide diversity of ideas concerning what constitutes mundane salvation, the task of formulating a philosophy of it might at first seem hopeless. Nevertheless, with an approach that sounds plausible, that takes into account all that men strive for, and that provides helpful criteria for practical guidance in education, a philosophy of salvation

---

[6]"Toward a Philosophy of Cultural Integration," *loc. cit.*

may meet with general acceptance. These qualities seem to the writer to be possessed by the soterical design for the art of living outlined in this paper. In any event, without some such philosophy of salvation all our attempts to reconstruct our higher educational system are bound to end up in mere tinkering or wishful thinking.[8]

[8]Comment by Paul L. Essert:

Dr. Kaplan's contribution to a clarification of objectives in higher education is stimulating and heartening because (1) it clarifies strengths and weaknesses in current philosophies and schools of thought objectively and fairly; (2) it is a convincing challenge to education that it has either stopped short of coming to grips with religion in education or dodged it entirely; (3) it makes a splendid presentation and defense of the soterical classification but does not defend it as a final or absolute; (4) it makes a significant contribution to our concept of democracy in its religious aspect.

Comment by John LaFarge, S.J.:

Professor Kaplan's paper is undoubtedly a basic contribution to this entire discussion, since it sets out in such thorough, lucid, and objective form the various major solutions to the problems of higher education which have been proposed in the United States in recent years. I wish I could share Dr. Kaplan's optimism, however, as to the ability of man to settle his problems by a merely mundane scheme of salvation. Dr. Kaplan himself recognizes, with his usual clarity and frankness the danger that the concept of democracy may be used as an instrument of political tyranny. But if this is so in the merely political order is not the danger all the greater when the concept of democracy is elevated to the transcendental order of human ultimates? It is my fear that the attempt to enthrone democracy, as a symbol (if I am correct) of a mundane salvation, in the very seat of God Himself, will lead to the very opposite of that which Dr. Kaplan so earnestly desires, the securing of human freedom and the establishment of human rights: that democracy may find itself betrayed in the house of its best friends; and universal doubt can be the instrument of tyrants quite as much as absolutism. I realize, however, that I am probably overstating Dr. Kaplan's idea; for I feel that much of what he says is motivated by a deep sense of moral revolt against the wickedness that a gospel of hate and spiritual nihilism has produced in the world. If by mundane salvation he means a scheme of salvation that takes into account the realities of history and the fullness of all that the world reveals of God and all that man himself can learn about the world, a salvation which *includes the world,* but *does not exclude the world's Creator* and ultimate meaning and man's ultimate justification, then the phrase should not present such difficulty.

Dr. Kaplan's reply:

Father LaFarge's last sentence states exactly what I do mean. He overshoots, however, the mark when he thinks he might ascribe to me "the attempt to enthrone democracy as a symbol of a mundane salvation in the very seat of God Himself." It is true that I would like to see genuine democracy enthroned, not in the seat of God, but in a seat of authority that might render it worthy to mediate God's will. Does that mean enthroning democracy in the seat of the Church? Not necessarily by any means. There is no reason why we cannot have more than one authority mediate God's will, provided they appeal to a common frame of reference. In the paper I wrote for the 1945 Conference on Science, Philosophy and Religion, I indicate in what way the frame of reference I describe in this year's paper might well serve as a bridge between tradition and reason or as a *modus vivendi* between democracy and institutional religions ("Toward a Philosophy of Cultural Integration," *op. cit.*).

I do not wish, however, any of the foregoing to be interpreted as a retreat from the position I take with regard to the incompatibility of authoritarianism, in theory as well as in practice, with the theory, if not always the practice, of democracy. I do not, as Father LaFarge recognizes, minimize the danger of democracy's degenerating into bureaucracy or mobocracy. But what prize worth having is ever gained without risk? The greater the prize, the greater the risk. What greater risk than entrusting man with the freedom to choose between good and evil? Yet that seems to be the method of the Creator.

Comment by Louis J. A. Mercier:

Professor Kaplan does make an avowal of Theism, at least in his reply to Father LaFarge. As he puts his whole emphasis on the salvific power of democracy, his paper belongs with Dr. Taylor's [Cf. Chapter XVIII], but as a Theist, Professor Kaplan seems to me much better placed than I thought Dr. Taylor to be, in equating our "mundane salvation" with "the democratic way of life." A democratic majority will not necessarily vote according to moral values. It might vote against the Ten Commandments, but a Theistic democrat would not. As a Theist, he recognizes above the mundane sovereign, whether king, dictator, oligarchy, or majority, the sovereignty of God's natural law.

Theistic democracy can truly give us a doctrine of "mundane salvation" and since this "mundane salvation" includes the respect of inalienable rights, the inalienable right of worshipping God according to one's conscience would open the way to an extramundane salvation, and leave the liberty of studying what it might be, and of accepting whatever means to reach it that may be at our disposal.

If Theistic democracy is objectively true, and can be proved to be such, even if metaphysics have to be utilized to do so, then there is no reason why the university should not recognize it, and stand behind the principles of the American Declaration of Independence, as principles objectively capable of giving us our long sought universal unifying principle.

I am more confirmed than ever, after reading all the papers of the Conference, that it is on this Theism that we must make our stand, so much so that I find a practical program for us in the Interfaith Pattern for Peace issued in 1943 by high representatives of the Catholic, Protestant, and Jewish churches. Its first article boldly states their common faith in Theism: "The organization of a just peace depends upon the practical recognition of the fact that not only individuals, but nations, states, and international society are subject to the sovereignty of God, and to the moral law which comes from God."

Out of that first article, and the implied dignity of the human person, the Interfaith Peace Pattern deduces a full social and international program. I believe that to that program could easily be added a more specific educational program. In fact, it already contains many of the goals mentioned in the various papers.

If the university cannot help in carrying it out, then I am afraid the university will be of little use except to develop the physical sciences which may at any time, as we fail to solve the moral problem, usher in our nemesis.

CHAPTER XIV

Prolegomena to a Future Centered Education

By THEODORE BRAMELD

*Professor of Educational Philosophy, School of Education,
New York University*

IN CONTRADISTINCTION from those, and they are legion, who like to dismiss a certain type of thought from serious consideration by labeling it "utopian," my thesis is that the single most profound need of our day is to revivify and magnetize the utopian spirit. The monotonous regularity with which the "practical minded"—who too often, upon scrutiny, turn out to be the pedestrian, visionless, compromising, or cynical—attach invidious adjectives like "starry eyed" to anyone so presumptuous as to project imagination-stretching goals for society and education alike, is actually a commentary on their own failure either to perceive the character of our present culture or to grasp the central responsibility of philosophy to it.

By the character of our present culture, I mean particularly its condition of chronic and acute crisis, the manifestations of which have now reached so explosive a point that we are being warned even by our hypercautious brethren, the physical scientists, that civilization itself is in danger of literal annihilation.

By the central responsibility of philosophy, I mean not only that it should contribute importantly to the diagnosis of our crisis culture, but more especially that it should delineate as clearly and audaciously as possible the alternatives to annihilation.[a]

[a]Comment by Harry B. Friedgood:

Although Dr. Brameld believes this course of action to be the province and central responsibility of philosophy, I doubt that anything short of the collective and integrated opinion of social and medical scientists, who have studied the broad field of human relations, will be adequate to the task at hand. Politicians and statesmen negotiate their differences at all levels of the social structure through a variety of sociopolitical mechanisms that are interrelated through a common denominator, *viz.*, they deal on an empirical basis

Of these alternatives, the single one deserving of exhaustive consideration would aim to assure mankind that, amidst the grim and fearful dangers which threaten us, our own future is simultaneously if ironically abundant with unprecedented promise: with as yet unfulfilled, certainly unguaranteed, but entirely realizable ends. The crystallization of ends appropriate to a revolutionary period of history—ends sufficiently powerful at once to neutralize the false lure of defeatism or escapism, and to generate by their own compulsions the strategies required to win them —here is the utopian spirit which should permeate philosophy in general and educational philosophy in particular. No other obligation begins to compare with this in urgency or importance.

It is an obligation, however, of such immense breadth and depth that adequate accomplishment would touch upon virtually every issue and belief of modern life. I shall select but six of a considerably larger group of premises relevant to the needed outlook. These may be called: (a) history as future; (b) man, the goal seeking animal; (c) social consensus in future building; (d) the "group mind" as end and means; (e) blueprints for a reconstructed culture; and (f) the role of the cultural myth.

Each of these deserves far more elaborate treatment, of course, than is possible in barely an outline. Each, indeed, should be judged as an invitation to all educational theorists who agree upon the imperative of the central task. Each likewise requires an almost infinite range of experimental application. In these prolegomena I cannot enter the area of practice. But let the conviction at least be recorded that the significance of each premise for learning, for curriculum designing, for teaching, for administration, for the relation of school and community, for patterns of control, for every level from nursery school to university, is so farreaching as to amount virtually to an educational revolution.

I

Although the first premise, a conception of history as future, must be treated even more briefly than the five which follow, it is nonetheless

---

with the *end-result* of a worldwide disintegrating culture. But what about the fundamental factors responsible for the desperate plight of twentieth century civilization? Before one can recommend and undertake specific therapy for the diseased state of our body politic, we must have a clear concept not only of the nature and course of the malady, but also of its primary causes.

indispensable, in order to provide a meaningful sense of reality to the goals we are capable of winning. To think otherwise—to assume, for example, that the real is confined wholly to what has *already* occurred or is *now* occurring—is at the outset to deny any ontological foundation for our legitimate hopes; it is to stunt our creative and visionary energies. In this respect there is, I think, a subtler significance in traditional teleologies than some contemporary students of the philosophy of history readily appreciate; for, though they are right in repudiating any doctrine of metaphysical purpose, they are wrong when they reject also the groping intent of teleologies to locate some kind of natural expectancy or potentiality in historic development.

Actually, almost any modern ontology of time itself supports our premise of history as future. We need only recall the philosophic truism that time as duration is a flow extending in *both* directions from the present instant, and that men therefore live in the future by the simple fact that they live in time. The present is indeed much more difficult to grasp than the other two dimensions: we all appreciate that, as we focus upon any passing moment, it immediately slips from our grasp into the past and is replaced by another moment which, an instant earlier, belonged to the future. We can, of course, expand our conception of the present to include a long succession of moments, and this is how we usually behave in everyday life. When we do so, however, we in fact already reach both into the past and into the future—that is, we include moments in our continuum which extend in both directions from the present instant.

Here, then, is an excellent reason for holding that, not only the past, but the future also is real for purposes of practical experience. We constantly embrace it even when we assume we are concerned chiefly with the present. In one sense, indeed, it is more genuine than the latter, for like the past it is of sufficient duration to provide a degree of coherence which no fleeting present instant can ever provide.

But if the future is real in any case, our business is to make sure that it is given at least as adequate and scrutinizing attention as are the other two dimensions of time. We should by no means reject the importance of those other dimensions; but we should say that while they determine the future in important part, so the latter determines them also in important part. In this sense utopianism itself has a basis in ontology.

While this principle is true for every historic period, there is, however, special need in our own culture of devoting meticulous attention to the reality of history as future—a need engendered first of all by the critical junction through which we are passing, and beyond which lies a choice of avenues leading to contraction or expansion of freedom, to destruction or peace. This is not to say that by analyzing future trends it is possible to answer in advance the question of whither we are inevitably bound; we do not presume that the groove of the future is already mysteriously cut. But to know what the future *should* be like is essential to what it *could* be like; and if we then implement our choices with power and strategy, we can determine what it *will* be like.[b]

As a great future looking philosopher of the nineteenth century said: "That which is ahead is just as much a condition of what is present as that which is past. What should be and must be is the ground of that which is." Thus spake Frederick Nietzsche. To him, as it should be to us, history as future is the history of men making real their hopes and purposes.

II

The second premise is, in a sense, the first premise restated as a philosophy of psychology rather than as philosophy of history. It therefore involves aspects of both epistemology and axiology in the respect that psychology always deals sooner or later, and sometimes despite itself, with aspects of both knowledge and value.

Thus the belief that man is a goal seeking animal has long been believed by both philosophy *and* psychology. Indeed no single view could better be selected to illustrate how implicit philosophic beliefs hover amidst the coldly impartial atmosphere of laboratories.

Yet to an extraordinary extent, recent psychologists have failed both

[b]Comment by Quincy Wright:
I am worried by the confidence displayed in such a sentence. Perhaps, if a large enough number of people agree on what the future should be like, this "determination" can be made peacefully. But experience shows that individuals and groups tend to differ greatly in their vision of the future and the more distant is that future, the more different are their visions. Overconfidence in the will to create and to achieve, produces conflict, war, and mutual frustration. The remedy is to be found in an objective view of the universe, firmly grounded in facts of the past. I am afraid that abstract conceptions of the future, of the goal seeking characteristics of man, and of the social consensus, are likely to prove unsafe guides unless planted on the firm ground of concrete situations with which the student and the group are confronted.

to clarify their own language or to test their own assertions. Some psychologists have shied away from the problem of goal seeking for fear they will become enmeshed in speculation. Others, especially of mechanist predilections, have fairly well begged the question by identifying goal seeking with the "pleasure principle"; or they have given a great deal of attention to "drives" which are so bound up with the process of stimulus-response that these become little more than synonyms in a different context.

Psychologists closer to the functionalist school have paid more careful attention to goal seeking because of their concern for the organism developing in space and time. The principle central to their position is the interactive relation of goals (preferably defined as aims) and means. They insist therefore that while, in one perspective, an "end-in-view" conditions and refines the functions needed to arrive at its consummation, in another perspective these functions constantly remake and hence determine the nature of the outcome itself.

More technically, the stimulus is constituted by the response quite as much as the reverse, and both are inseparable relations of total organic action.

Now the practical effect of this theory is a concern with the dynamics of growing—with the continuity of adjustments and readjustments. It recognizes, to be sure, ends as well as means, both "consummatory" and "instrumental" experiences. At no time, however, does it allow either —and above all, the former—to crystallize or absolutize in such a way as to become a criterion of the other. Passages in the writings of the philosophers of progressive education which seem to stress ends or goals or outcomes more than the *seeking* of those ends or goals or outcomes, must always be judged in the larger context of their full meaning. And when they are so judged we are invariably brought back again to the key focus of interest—not to the product, but to the process or *method* which we call intelligence. Progressivism offers a psychology perfectly in accord with the philosophy needed by a *present* centered culture; for the human being, too, is above all concerned with the ongoing present of continuous means-ends-means-ends-means. . . .

I should like to raise at least two criticisms of this doctrine—the one practical, the other more theoretical. The first follows from the assumption that we now face a major crisis in history which forces us to consider the alternatives before us with a thoroughness which was earlier much less compelling. The endless method of problem solving experience, granting its psychological validity up to a point, is even dangerous at such a moment as this: despite its activism, the method has the paradoxical effect of complacency—of resting content with temporary and *present* actions rather than giving utmost concern also to the outlines and forms of the culture which we have yet to build for the *future*. In short, *it is now imperative that we know as clearly as we can where we want to go,* not only because it provides contrast with where we do not; but also because, so long as we do not know, we shall be unprepared to get there: our means will bog down along with our ends.

Or, to relate this first question to our discussion of "history as future," is not the need to broaden the present time continuum to embrace a much wider segment of its future dimension? A stable culture can be satisfied with a fairly narrow continuum; a culture such as ours cannot. The goals needed for a period of crisis are more farreaching, both more extensive and expansive.[c] Granting for the moment that the means-ends process is thus far in accord with psychological experience, its range then must be greatly expanded and both its ends and means fashioned more solidly if it is to be effective for today and tomorrow.

The other question raises the more difficult issue of whether the nature of goal seeking can itself be deepened further. More precisely, what do we mean by *goals,* and what do we mean by *seeking* them?

Now the theory advocated here is strongly influenced up to a point by the behaviorist principle that men are complex bundles of tendencies rather than walking department stores of instincts or faculties. Therefore it, too, would look dubiously upon any fixed compulsions of human nature—goals which man at all times endeavors to achieve because they are the inevitable ends of his very destiny.

Also, the present theory hesitates to divide "primary" and "secondary" drives or desires. To say, for example, that man inherits the primary desire for food or sex, but acquires the desire for music or companion-

---

[c]Comment by Quincy Wright:

I wholly disagree with this proposition. The very essence of a period of crisis is that individuals and groups differ radically as to their goals. Precisely in such circumstances, agreement can be reached only upon procedures and upon very immediate practical ends. An effort today, for example, of either the United States or the Soviet Union to formulate, plan, and execute their long range goals would only lead to World War III and the probable extermination of civilization. Long range planning, especially in periods of crisis, is a formula for oppression.

ship, is at best a convenient division which, in the course of history, has become less and less empirically meaningful. The fact is that, in actual cultures, so-called secondary desires may become far more potent than so-called primary: many a primitive society testifies to the power of taboos which, though clearly the creation of culture, take precedence over the seemingly most urgent needs of life. For these reasons, I do not propose to distinguish between "needs" and "wants," as has often been tried: the term, "wants," embraces all types of goal seeking interests.[d]

To say, however, that human nature is an almost limitless array of diverse impulses is not the same as to say that we should therefore largely disregard attempts to delineate and specify what the most important of them may be for a given period in the history of culture. The easiest corollary of flexibility and complexity is, of course, that any systematic organization or classification is so artificial and oversimplified that we may as well not attempt it. But such a statement is precisely the issue which disturbs: it too much parallels the argument that since means continually modify ends therefore it is both impractical and illogical to determine the precise nature of those ends.

On the contrary, to specify the goals of our culture and accordingly the ends of human nature is to perform an imperative task. The terms which are used by various authorities to characterize these goals and ends are, to be sure, various. Sometimes "interests" if sufficiently specified may be adequate; sometimes "drives." In any case, with the aid of

[d] Comment by B. Othanel Smith:

Some students of education, among whom I would number Professor Brameld, have attempted to ground the goals of education in the universal needs of man—needs so basic that they appear in all peoples of all cultures. If this were possible, statements of educational goals could be judged in terms of whether or not their materialization would contribute to the fulfilment of these needs. Goals could then be validated, in part at least, by facts that cut across all cultural systems and ideological outlooks. Ideologies could be validated in terms of the extent to which they make possible the fulfilment of basic human needs.

Professor Brameld subscribes to the view that goals must be judged by reference to human needs. But he refuses to distinguish between basic and derived needs and thus commits us to a thoroughgoing social relativism in which it is difficult, if not impossible, to say that one set of goals is better than another. Social anthropologists and psychologists usually distinguish between needs which are given in the original nature of man and his environment, and those which are derived from these basic needs operating in a particular cultural system. Since derived needs are culturally induced, they cannot be used as bases of judging educational goals without accepting a naive relativism. If we incorporate these needs in our judgments we are only judging a culture by itself. Then it is only to be expected that individuals of different orientations will look upon derived needs in entirely different ways.

anthropology, social psychology, and other sciences, as well as philosophy, evidence is now accumulating toward a workable formulation. Fourier was on the right track when he sought to classify the basic appetites of the "senses" and of the "soul" and to harmonize them into an all controlling impulse which is both egoistic and social. Marx and Engels are proving to be correct in their own lifelong contention that the sheer "necessities of life"—food, shelter, clothing, health—are potent goals. Freud is right in his emphasis upon the need for love—sexual, yes—but also familial, and even love of much larger groups such as humanity. Thomas is right in his designation of man's four "wishes": (a) for new experiences; (b) for security; (c) for response (most reminiscent of Freud); and (d) for recognition. Lynd is likely to be right in his analysis of human "cravings" as including not only those above but such still more subtle ones as a "natural tempo and rhythm," or a "sense of fairly immediate meaning."

If we ask next what we mean more exactly by "seeking" goals like these, the answer is that, consciously or not, scientifically or not, cooperatively or not, most people in our culture so passionately desire to achieve them that their lives are devoted to that effort even when they fail to realize that they are. Frustration and tension, in the present context, are effects of denial of such goals—sometimes self-imposed by ascetics or others who think they can destroy desires by suppressing them; oftener imposed by social institutions which thwart or warp man's natural propensities. But the seeking still goes on; and whether by magic, supplication, force, by conscious and systematic effort, or simply by the sheer immediacy of organic hunger, men everywhere exert their energies so that such goals may finally be realized.

From this viewpoint, then, the means-ends process is something more than growing, something more than the analyzed description of an ongoing dynamic which everlastingly goes on because such is the way of experience. At least in our modern era men struggle to realize *certain purposes*—purposes which need not, moreover, remain forever ambiguous and undefined, but which can and must become specified as powerful and definite objectives. Fused together, they are capable of generating the intense white light of guidance and action toward a new society. Seeking becomes seeking *for*. Growing becomes growing *toward*. It is precisely here that the utopian thinkers in philosophy grasped a psychological insight of profound significance.

What now is the import of this all too briefly discussed principle for knowledge and values?

First, if we are agreed on the conception of man as goal seeker, we have in our hands a powerful instrument by which to determine, on the one hand, how and why men *learn,* and, on the other hand, what knowledge and values are ultimately for—indeed, to determine whether what passes often for knowledge and values can be so classified properly at all.

Second, it is possible to *know* both the chief goals of our culture and how we ought to seek them. This is not to say that we know them fully now; nor, let me repeat, that they are everlastingly inherent in *all* men or *all* cultures at *all* times. What is important is that we can determine that they are relatively universal to the men and the culture of *our* time, and accordingly that they can become dependable, in the sense of *known,* criteria by which to reorganize the culture with the aim of realizing them to the maximum.

Third, goal seeking is indispensable to knowledge and values because clearly it is essential to those future political, economic, educational, and other institutions which themselves depend on knowledge and values. Such institutions are far from mere ephemeral creations of speculative minds: to be sure, they are thoroughly utopian, but for our time they are also thoroughly practical in that they can and should rest upon all possible available evidence about man's resources and capacities. In short, those ends or goals which are most central psychologically are synthesized with institutional patterns which are most tangible and systematic sociologically. And both are finally accepted or rejected by the test of whether they are able to sustain the rigid scrutiny of public examination and social acceptability.

The importance of goal seeking for a reconstructed theory of education may be underscored, finally, by recalling the concept of prehension. The term has been coined by Whitehead, we recall, to suggest a type of experience which experimental intelligence has insufficiently analyzed —perhaps because the experience falls too much outside its favorite canons of explanation. Stated as succinctly as possible, prehension means the *unity,* organic wholeness, of any event in nature. It is a unity which precedes *apprehension,* or the analyzed awareness of an event by which we recognize or perceive its component parts. Time, for example, is prehended before it is apprehended: it is, as we have already said, a duration or continuum first of all; only secondarily do we become cognizant of the fact that it can be divided into distinct units or instants which succeed one another like ticks of a clock. Yet its prehended meaning not only is just as real, if not more real, to us than its apprehended meaning; it is the indispensable basis of the latter.

The future oriented purposes of the needed philosophy, however, give a special turn to prehension which one scarcely detects in a thinker of such strong realist interests as Whitehead himself. Thus we are now prepared to go further in our discussion of the nature of goal seeking by observing how the important goals of man are themselves prehended. Is it not evident that apparently even the simplest needs of man—food, for example—are motivated by basic hungers which have their own persistent patterns of rhythm, their own organic unity, even their own duration or continuum which flows toward consummation? Is not sexual desire similarly unified? And if we prehend such needs as these —they are there in our natures as unified events long before and long after we examine and explain them—would not the same fact be certain of still more subtle patterns of desire, such as recognition or adventure?

This does not mean, of course, that reflective, scientific analysis is not also—and perhaps equally—important. But now we are prepared to assert that knowledge and values have not one, but at least two, interdependent aspects: first, the prehended unities which are everywhere around us—in time, in the contours of the earth, or, what is most *à propos* for us, in the urges of man—and, second, the apprehensions of intelligence with which we then perceive and analyze prehensions themselves.

Furthermore, this concept serves the important role not only of grasping single unities—time or hunger, for example—but of binding each with other unities. Nature, says Whitehead, is an *organic* process, "necessarily transitional from prehension to prehension." Hunger is not hunger for food alone; as we both prehend it and later analyze it, we find it commingled with a strange continuum of hungers the totality of which is man striving to achieve his goals—the organism as a living whole.

The role of prehension as an integrating force may also be extended beyond the individual, for if it pervades nature everywhere, then it pervades that social nature which is culture. It affords some expectation that the goal seeking of one man, which is increasingly grasped as an organic pattern of goals, is in turn the expression of a goal seeking culture likewise prehended as an organic pattern.

Thus we may have reason to expect that variety among purposes becomes gradually governed by unifying purpose—not, to be sure, a Purpose ordained by some spiritual Being, but one which becomes clear to men and to the culture as their partial unities coalesce in a prehended whole.

III

The third premise emerges from, or at any rate is necessitated by, the two we have already considered. By social consensus as a principle of future centered educational theory, I mean that the truths and values of those experiences most vital to the social life of our culture are determined not merely by the needful satisfactions they produce, but also by the extent they are *agreed upon* by the largest possible number of the group concerned. Involved in this preliminary definition are several general aspects which should be weighed together before we are ready to decide for or against its soundness.

It is unnecessary, for example, to argue that here is to be found *the* criterion of knowledge or value or both. Certainly the experimental method is useful in many situations. Moreover, as enthusiasts of that method may or may not wish to insist, the theory of social consensus may already be more or less implicit in their own formulation. The only contention here is that the principle needs to be much more heavily emphasized and clearly explicated; and that, for *purposes of goal seeking and future building,* it is of singular importance.

Social consensus is a way of submitting the evidence about goals which are sought as fundamental to an open court of recognition and appraisal. For example, while such wants as food, sex, or recognition are ultimately evident only immediately or directly to people who experience them, they can be brought into the sphere of communication where each individual and group may testify before others that they actually do so experience them. The importance of the seemingly obvious need of testifying about evidence is that it at once takes the prehensions, idlike desires, and goals of men and groups out of their inner sanctuaries: instead of being any longer purely private, inscrutable, and hence subjective, the aim is as far as possible to make them now public, expressible, and in this sense objective.

As the step which follows, social consensus proper now becomes merely the expressed consent on, say, your part, that the testimony I have offered seems to make sense in so far as it articulates an experience which you recognize equally with mine. Of course there is nothing strange about this method: all science, even physical science, presupposes the ability to communicate and to agree about the evidence appropriate to a given field. What we need now to be especially interested in, however, is the kind of agreement obtained by the many who constitute a *group* (or, still more, agreement between the many groups who constitute a culture) about the interests which are here defined as goal seeking interests. Once delineated, the *process* for all groups is similar, and the *product* which is reached—a consensus that here is a truth or a value or both which we can now proceed to utilize for the social purposes and practices with which we are concerned—is also similar.

This rather superficial outline of the premise under examination is rich with implications which are by no means so superficial. Let us consider several.

For one thing, it implies that however far we may proceed with the aid of scientific evidence, however cautious we are in both self-examination and communication, there is always a point at which we must simply stop and either agree or disagree upon testimony we have offered as to the nature of the goals we seek.

This moment of commitment or noncommitment could of course follow a period of prolonged consideration. As we testify, we may experiment with various ways of couching our experience. With the psychoanalyists, we may become increasingly sensitive to the ease with which we deceive ourselves about the desires we are trying to express. With the semanticists, we may become aware of how readily we distort our testimony even when we have no wish to do so. With the clinical psychologists, we may even utilize the reports of experimentation upon animals or other overt approaches to behavior in order to increase our grasp upon what we report as our own experience.

At last, however, we reach a point where our own goal seeking interests defy any such aid: they are too prehensive, too unrational, too immediate, too qualitative, in their basic character. Like awareness of time or hunger for food, they are grasped as direct awarenesses—awarenesses which analyses and apprehensions deepen in content or sharpen in refinement, but which both precede and succeed those analyses and apprehensions.

Another large implication from the outline of this principle is that no individual or group should, if uncoerced, consent to the testimony of another individual or group unless or until convinced as far as possible that such testimony is in accord with his or its own awareness of the experience being communicated.

Theoretically, of course, it would be possible to cease before the step of consent is ever gained. Thus the solipsist could insist that there is no actual way of guaranteeing that my experience is identical with yours; and so he would simply refuse to agree that there is any proved similarity between our experiences. In the same way, the pure anarchist in political philosophy could deny that there is any sound principle of social order other than the be-all and end-all of the individual himself.

We have just seen, moreover, something of the difficulty of guaranteeing similarity between two experiences—of how, after all possible cautions have been taken, you and I must fall back upon the sheer awareness of those experiences as such. And it is precisely because of the constant possibility of inadequacy—of incorrect testimony or self-deception, for example—that no individual and no group should agree with another quickly or impulsively. It is often their business to serve rather as critic and corrector of those who have agreed.

Finally, it is important to ask to what extent social consensus is a practical device. How can it be defended, if at all, against the criticism that it is too theoretical and much too ideal for the confused, already violent issues which beset our culture?

Now it is only too clear that, as any cursory review of history shows, the principle of social consensus has seldom if ever functioned perfectly. Neither individuals nor groups often unite through the process of testimony and agreement exclusively. Economic classes, racial groups, religious sects, and nations, alike consist of people who find themselves usually united rather because they have been born or coerced into such groups. Also, the goals which govern their activity are by no means always enunciated clearly: in primitive groups, for example, motivating purposes are likely to be mingled with powerful customs from which it is difficult even for an anthropologist to separate one from the other.

Occasionally, a purpose even when fairly clear to the members of a group may in a sense seem as negative as it is positive—that is, as in the case of some Negro groups, or associations concerned to establish a world order, their ultimate objective may be to supplant isolation of race or sovereignty of nation by a wider, more inclusive unity which would eliminate their own reasons for existing. Again the ends of an individual or group which are openly enunciated may upon careful scrutiny prove to be shockingly different from, or at least mingled confusingly with, those ends which in reality dominate that individual or group. Moreover, a social consensus achieved by one group is still in some fashion and at the same moment usually in conflict with that of another group—a fact abundantly proved by the frequency of hostilities, suspicions, even battles, precipitated between races, classes, and states. Indeed, even when one agrees with another's testimony *privately,* still an individual or group may yet refuse to do so *publicly* because of some supposed self-interest gained by so refusing. A final important inference from these limitations is that social consensus turns out to be too often the consensus of a *part* of some group—a part which, small or large, is yet able to dominate the rest because it controls the instruments of power, or perhaps also because the rest are at the time simply too indifferent or ignorant to care.

A future centered theory of education, in reply to these observations, would begin by agreeing with their seriousness. At the same time, it defends the principle with the same vehemence that it admits and even emphasizes obstacles. I shall sketch here six points in that defense.

1. Despite its clumsy and partial operation, consensus does actually operate in social experience. Even primitive human beings do proceed to live together, and they do reach group decisions upon the more or less enunciated belief that they are understanding one another's interests. In some respects, the process historically is more common than we have perhaps seemed to imply—in fact, too common in the sense that consensus is often arrived at hastily or uncritically.

Moreover, the circle of group consensus sometimes widens to embrace a much larger number of individuals and groups than at other times. In this process an earlier consensus may be superseded by a later one which, judged by agreement about the goals we seek, is clearly more expressive of and therefore closer to the truth about them. Politically, we see the process of social consensus enormously strengthened by popular government. Economically, we see it strengthened by the conscious self-assertiveness of such class unities as the trade union or the business association. Technologically, through communication and transportation, we see how even the most remote groups of the earth have gradually been brought into closer and closer proximity with all other groups.

2. The practicality of social consensus is enhanced further by increasing knowledge from such social sciences as anthropology that goals are not, in any case, purely or even chiefly individual, but above all *shared* goals. In actual practice, we do not first testify about our own desires and then seek to convince others; we first learn about those desires from relations with others and then afterward gradually recognize them in ourselves.

That the typical ends in which we become most interested, far from being isolated or private, are thoroughly mutual, is clearly illustrated by love, security, appreciation, and a dozen others which depend for their very existence and meaning upon participation with others. Hence the process of achieving agreement through testifying is enormously aided, and the reliability of its product enhanced, by the indubitable fact that it rests upon this common denominator of culture: the *sociality* of most if not all the goals that both individuals and groups struggle to attain.

3. This historic and scientific evidence is still further bolstered by such recent deliberate experimentation as collective bargaining and intergroup relations. Economic groups, however acute their deeper conflicts may remain, sometimes learn how to resolve their most immediate differences through conciliatory means like labor management committees. Religious denominations have made beginnings in bringing together Protestants, Catholics, and Jews upon a common ground. Even nations, more conscious than ever before of the dangers of destruction, have been at least trying to devise new machinery of testimony and agreement which might succeed in resolving disputes through international consensus.

Most of these efforts are, to be sure, fragmentary and crude. Yet they still point to the fact that, to a degree never before reached, there is worldwide concern over the need of agreement in almost every sphere of contemporary culture.

4. These very differences, moreover, may serve to refine social consensus as a working principle. While, for example, an ideological picture of a culture is often used to divide groups from one another, or to con-

fuse people about their interests so that they can neither honestly testify nor clearly agree, on occasion it also performs other roles. During the youth and virile maturity of a culture an ideology may even interpret purposes with considerable accuracy, and as it is forced on the defensive by thinkers of reformist or revolutionary (that is to say, utopian) tendencies it may seek to express its own consensus with renewed thoroughness.

Even more significant is the practical role of the utopian thinker. As the critic of ideologies he points out facts and meanings which have been overlooked if not perhaps deliberately rationalized or hidden by those ideologies. Utopian thinkers of the Renaissance like Bacon were powerful contributors both to truths about the inadequacies of the culture they attacked and the culture they envisaged. More recently, Marx and Engels have played the same double role. In our own day, the utopian mentality may often be more willing to deal with facts, to expose false beliefs, to rationalize less often, than could usually be expected from ideologists. Indeed, while utopians also are too often incorrect, they may turn out to be so much more frequently correct, both in revealing the failures of the cultural configurations they oppose and in widening consensus for the configuration they support, that strenuous effort is often exerted to still or at least muffle their voices.

5. Social consensus is defended still further on the ground that it is itself a dynamic and, in some ways, experimental principle. Accordingly, it is never in any case to be judged by its unqualified success or failure, but by how well it operates in the long run as it is more and more widely exercised. Furthermore, there is no pretense that the truths and values it creates are wholly applicable to every culture at every time.

Such a precaution has already been implied. Goals, for example, are relative to our delineation of human nature—social and individual—at a given period: the means with which men seek their satisfaction likewise vary with the nature of those goals. Again, we have seen how the facility with which an individual or group learns to testify is, at its best, always subject to improvement both because of increased scientific knowledge and because of the immediacy and directness of its own goal seeking experiences—a contingency which in turn leaves open the never ceasing need for criticism of testimony and agreements previously made. It follows, too, that the most universally agreed upon formulations of cultural objectives are in the course of time subject to modification and supplementation.

6. In the last analysis, however, the principle is important not so much because it thus somewhat resembles the hypothetical, tentative, and methodological characteristics already supported by the experimentalist philosophy, but *in spite of* such resemblances. What is needed above all is a principle guaranteeing positiveness, direction, and clearcut commitment—qualities without which social strategies are themselves now likely to become totally ineffective and perhaps helpless. This principle is sought, however, by a procedure which aims to avoid such pitfalls as dogmatism and passivity of mind both of which, among other frailties, permeate powerful philosophies inimical both to orthodox experimentalism and to the position here developed.

This defense of social consensus might end, accordingly, on a question which is largely rhetorical. If, in our search for knowledge and values by which we can be guided in our age of crisis, we do not wish, on the one hand, to be saved by some intellectual elite, by some supernatural or metaphysical authority, or by belief in the preordained fixity of mechanized laws; yet if, on the other hand, we can no longer effectively function merely with an ongoing problem solving method which in any case imperfectly analyzes the goal seeking interests of individuals and especially of groups—if, we say, we want neither of these, then the alternative of necessity is inescapable. Translated into cultural programs and objectives, *truth seeking and value seeking through social consensus is the attempt of an entire culture to rediscover and then to reconstruct itself*—a culture which, left unreconstructed, suffers chronically from disintegrating pressures.[e]

[e] Comment by John D. Wild:
    I believe that Mr. Brameld is quite correct in defending the theses that the future is in some sense real, and that man is a "goal seeking animal." I believe that he is also correct in calling our attention to the major importance of achieving social agreement with respect to "blueprints for a reconstructed culture" and the means of realizing them by means of "cultural myth" as well as rational persuasion [See Parts V, VI of Dr. Brameld's chapter, below]. But it seems to me that he has failed to do justice to the crucial role in all this which is played by rational cognition of the universal, as over against sensory experience of the particular, which we share with the other animals.
    Our concrete sensory experiences, and the images or imagination can never be exactly transmitted from one mind to another. At best, my image is only similar to yours. They cannot be identically *the same!* Hence, communication at the sensory and imaginative level is always vague, inexact, and uncertain. It is only in so far as we can abstract some

IV

The "group mind" as end and means, the fourth premise selected for attention, is anticipated by the principle of social consensus in the sense that the "mind" with which this viewpoint is most concerned is that of the group—how the group thinks, and what it does with its thinking in behalf of the ends which stimulate its efforts and organize institutional patterns commensurate with those ends. In the sense of a mysterious entity existing in and of itself with characteristics totally distinct from individual minds, the concept of the group mind has no meaning. But in another sense which we shall now discuss it is of very real significance. I outline that meaning first as end, and then as means.

The group mind as end implies that a number of individuals or groups—only a few, perhaps, or again millions—have united for a purpose, and that further they have more or less clearly defined this purpose in the form of goals which they endeavor to realize. Obviously such a group mind is a normative standard as well as descriptive fact. As I have taken some pains to observe, social consensus as its central char-

---

phase of such an experience or image in the form of a universal concept, that we arrive at something which can be transmitted to another mind without any alteration. Hence the very life of a human group depends upon the cultivation of rational discipline in its members. Unless they are capable of clear, *i.e.*, abstract reflection, they cannot *exactly* communicate their ideas and purposes. Without such communication there can be no common understanding of a common end, and the group will begin to disintegrate.

I therefore suggest the disciplines of abstract reflection to Mr. Brameld, as the most potent instruments for the attainment of "social consensus," or should we say, "social understanding." I should suggest that in spite of all the individual differences between individual men and groups, our human reason is capable of abstracting an essential aspect that is always and everywhere the same—call it human nature or what you will. One cannot clearly apprehend this universal nature without at the same time apprehending to some degree of clarity, that universal pattern of cultural activity which is required by this nature, always and everywhere for its perfection or completion. It seems to me that it is such a *universal* pattern of action which Mr. Brameld is seeking to clarify and express. Such an abstract pattern is of course compatible with all sorts of variations in the particular acts and circumstances of this or that group. But it is not compatible with such an unmitigated cultural relativism as Mr. Brameld sometimes seems to suggest.

Comment by B. Othanel Smith:

I am confident that Professor Brameld's approach to the problem of determining educational goals is more promising than a historical one. The most serious problem arises when sincere men of equal devotion to fact and to the best methods of thought and communication reach diverse conclusions. Each of us encounters just such irreconcilable differences of opinion. When we do, we usually go away convinced that the other fellow is prejudiced, that he cannot think straight, that he will not face the facts. And the other fellow retires

acterizing feature always operates at best imperfectly in actual cultural experience. Yet it is also evident that historically groups do collect evidence, carry on communication, and effect agreements; they do act on their decisions; and sometimes they even improve in the range and reliability of their consensuses. Here then *is* the group mind already functioning.

What has not been examined sufficiently thus far is the influence of the dominant ideology of socioeconomic arrangements and relations in developing the typical group mind of our century. As Mannheim has shown, this ideology tends to shape the thinking and actions of groups in ways which precipitate a whole variety of beliefs and habits, stubborn ethnocentricisms, tensions, and at times overt conflicts—realities which must be recognized frankly for what they are and included in any complete delineation of the group mind itself. Without such inclusion, moreover, we can neither clearly interpret the meaning and role of ideology as a consensus aiming to preserve a particular socioeconomic order, nor of utopia as a consensus aiming to reconstruct that order.

While such additional and crucial influences still do not produce a group mind different *in kind* from the individual mind, the *degree* of difference is often of farreaching significance. True, individuals, too, may be and usually are basically affected by any socioeconomic configuration with its accompanying ideology. But they may at least on occasion isolate themselves in their experimental laboratories, or in the privacy of psychoanalytic clinics. They may then analyze as dispassionately as possible the forces at work within and upon them, and thus attain a certain number of reflective judgments with commendable success. Groups are much less able, however, to achieve such isolation: Negro

---

with the same convictions not about himself, but about us. There was a time when such differences were chiefly between individuals and minor social groups. But now such cleavages divide the people of the nation and of the world and somehow they must be resolved.

In order to resolve these differences by peaceful methods it will be necessary to avoid the doctrine of extreme social relativity which Professor Brameld apparently accepts. The notion of consensus as a criterion of worth involves the further idea that the consensus rests upon the actual or imagined social consequences of proposed goals. The consequences in turn are judged by various social groups in terms of their perspectives. And so we come back to our differences in our search for agreements. In raising this question I am not assuming that the social consequences of educational goals are irrelevant to the determination of the worth of such goals. The question is whether or not goals can be judged solely on this basis without committing us to a crude form of social relativity.

and Jewish groups have repeatedly tried and failed; economic groups like trade unions depend for their existence upon participation in, not separation from, economic struggle; and nations cannot isolate themselves from our "one world" even if they would.

Testimony and agreement by the group mind about the goals it seeks are influenced, then, not merely by rational considerations, not merely by such considerations as prehensive interests and unities, but also by the configurations of a socioeconomic order which groups defend or attack, or about which they are simply very much confused.

And yet the chief inference to be drawn is not that the group mind must merely *submit* to such configurations—certainly not to our own. Rather only by clear recognition of their enormous influence shall we be equipped, on the one hand, to diagnose the chief conflicts of our own culture and, on the other hand, to build a new and more encompassing consensus—a utopian consensus in which the group mind, while still hardly universal, can be much more comprehensive in its agreement about fundamental goals, and the means to reach those goals, than history has ever yet achieved.

Mention of means leads us to the other aspect of group mind in which we are now interested. If ends are, especially for our culture, the goal seeking interests of men as these are agreed upon by social consensus and then encompassed in adequate institutional arrangements, means are the strategies by which group minds attain their ends.

Means, in other words, are equally based upon social consensus and all that this implies. Here again, therefore, a great problem of our time is one of reaching the *widest possible consensus about means*—of building a broadly organized strategy by which those who agree upon the goals of a new order may concertedly, aggressively, *act*.

This problem is complicated by the ticklish issue of just *when* and *where* action should take place. The present theory argues that we should lose no time in agreeing about our ends, for history has already reached a grim junction of opposing choices. This still leaves uncertain, however, that *moment* of commitment which, to be more than verbal, is a moment of action as well. To reach it prematurely is always dangerous: it may produce arbitrary, impulsive, or weak strategies which in turn may only boomerang by generating more hostility or stronger counter strategy than prevailed before. Yet to reach active commitment tardily is just as dangerous: the utopian group mind can be, as it sometimes has been, fairly well destroyed by other groups whose own ends and means have earlier crystallized.

No automatic formula is available by which both of these twin dangers can be surely averted. The general principle that concerted effort to reach a fresh consensus about ends will in turn assist enormously in reaching commitment and action about means is, nonetheless, of such paramount importance that it can scarcely be overemphasized. The group mind as end and means becomes at once a mind which knows both what it wants and how to gain satisfaction of its wants.

V

The fifth premise, which I have designated by the phrase, "blueprints for a reconstructed culture," is projected here chiefly to illustrate the consequences which flow from accepting the premises that (1) history is future as well as past and present, that (2) man is a goal seeking animal, and that (3) social consensus is the central principle through which (4) the group mind acts both as to its goals and as to the means by which its goals are won.

By "blueprints" I mean the specific while flexible outlines of political, economic, scientific, esthetic, educational, and other major institutions and practices which should be formulated as guides to the culture of the future. In political terms they are crystallized policies bolstered beneath by values and projected above toward detailed legislative implementation. It may be helpful, first, to dispel certain misconceptions about blueprints: and, second, to formulate several to typify their meaning.

Besides their need for flexibility, blueprints should never be regarded as ends utterly divorced from means. The psychology of goal seeking which bolsters this philosophy is, we remember, one of both *goals* and *seeking*—a psychology applicable not only today while advocates of a future centered theory are acting as the critical minority, but equally tomorrow when and if their institutional proposals are tested on a grand scale by the culture itself. The temporal ontology always presupposed by this theory should in itself be sufficient reason, however, to dismiss any notion that blueprints could be completely fixed or static; or that they should lack provision for the *modus operandi* by which institutions are actively to realize human ends.

And yet after these precautions, the very term *blueprint* should imply a radically different orientation from various other influential philosophies of our day. It implies deliberate, systematic, organized construction of future cultural objectives. It implies not merely the everlasting process of *planning* alone, but also *plans*—concrete, definite plans. It implies that, despite the impossibility of proving logically or scientifically in advance of the future that our plans will inevitably be tried fairly or will work successfully, we are nonetheless now obliged to obtain the widest possible consensus about them in the present. It implies that we already possess vast, almost unused reservoirs of scientific knowledge about the kind of culture we could and should have—physical, biological, psychological, social knowledge to be vitalized and organized in order to determine whether it is true and good. It implies esthetic creativity—that cultural blueprints can become prehensive designs of creative, imaginative vision and beauty. It implies choice and thus commitment—taking sides with one kind of order as against another, more specifically with the kind of order which will integrate cultural arrangements in behalf of an expansion of freedom for the masses of common people. It implies the full spirit and content of a *utopian* approach to the crisis of our time. Finally, it implies maximum, although never exact, correlation between general values and specific plans—the objective throughout being to assure that only the richest possible satisfaction of goal seeking interests for the largest number of individuals and groups is a sufficient test of that correlation.

Permit me, then, to sketch the kind of blueprints for the culture of the future which these remarks challenge us to specify:

1. *An economy of abundance,* to: (a) satisfy the maximum wants of the consumer rather than to win profits for the producer; (b) assure full employment for all citizens, in accordance with their abilities and interests, and under working conditions determined through their own organizations; (c) guarantee minimum income for all families sufficient to meet expertly determined standards of adequate nourishment, shelter, dress, medical care, education, recreation; (d) utilize all natural resources and all enterprises of monopolistic tendency in the interests and under the control of the majority of the people.

2. A *service state,* responsible for: (a) unifying and collectivizing major industrial and agricultural enterprises of the economy of abundance; (b) integrating and supervising transportation and communica-

tion systems, utilities, health, and other public services; (c) maintaining a balance of strong federal authority and direction with a maximum of local or regional administration and participation; (d) providing legislative, executive, and judicial representation in direct coordination with the chief occupations and purposes of those represented.

3. A *scientific society,* committed to: (a) subsidizing pure and applied scientific research as a chief need and interest of the service state; (b) making technological, medical, and all other scientific discoveries available to and basically controlled in the interests of the economy of abundance; (c) assuring complete experimental freedom to the scientist, but also assuming his direct concern for and responsibility to the public welfare; (d) utilizing large numbers of men and women trained in the social sciences for democratic leadership and governmental service.

4. A *cultural design,* to: (a) allow esthetic participation in remaking the culture by as many creative individuals and groups as possible; (b) express organic, functional unity and direction in the planning and reconstruction of homes, cities, agricultural regions, recreation centers; (c) encourage artistic talent and reward creative achievement as a public responsibility but also encourage the same complete freedom of expression assumed for the scientist; (d) offer free facilities and works of fine and applied arts (music, drama, movies, painting, architecture, decoration, etc.) to all citizens as a public privilege.[f]

5. An *educational system:* (a) supported chiefly by federal taxation, supplemented by local resources, and controlled by the service state;[g]

[f] Comment by Rowland W. Dunham:
The matter of encouragement and reward "to creative achievement as a public responsibility" would call for careful discrimination and adequate administration. In music, for example, the spurious creations by dilettantes may easily be mistaken for genuine art products. This is a decision that can only be made by a trained expert of unquestioned integrity. The musical profession has long been reluctant to approve governmental sponsorship. "Free facilities and works of fine and applied arts" may also have certain questionable connotations. It has been notable that musical composers who have not made great economic sacrifices in securing their training have rarely been writers of masterpieces.

[g] Comment by John D. Wild:
If I am right in urging the profound practical importance of theoretical research and contemplation, I think that it should be more definitely recognized in the cultural blueprint which Mr. Brameld outlines. Thus under 5a there might be a heading reading as follows: Purely theoretical research in the fields of science, philosophy, and theology, together with those logical disciplines which are required for their maintenance and further advance. Such disciplines must be widely supported and respected, or education will be deprived of sound guiding principles, and as a result the whole culture will run the risk of falling into chaos and confusion.

(b) offering completely free universal education from the nursery school through the university and adult levels; (c) gearing curricula, teaching, guidance, and administration to the purposes of the economy of abundance, service state, scientific society, and esthetic order; (d) bringing newspapers, radio chains, and other instruments of public enlightenment into direct cooperation with education and under similar controls.[h]

6. A *humane order,* which: (a) regards sexual expression as a positive value of great power and great beauty; (b) protects and encourages family life (which however may conceivably require reorganization of traditional forms) in order to achieve maximum fulfilment as a medium of devotion and belongingness, but also as a way of sharing interests both within and between families; (c) provides complete security and rich companionship to citizens of old age and to the helpless; (d) guarantees full participation in all phases of cultural life by members of all minority groups.

7. A *world democracy,* dedicated to: (a) agreement among the great

[h]Comment by E. V. Sayers:

The changes in the social patterns which Professor Brameld advocates may or may not be desirable, but the proposal to use the schools to obtain the specified changes has no ground to stand on in America. The measure advocated is appropriate to a social and political order such as at present is unacceptable to the American people. I am for any experiment along lines which promise to make our schools more democratic, but I cannot subscribe to a policy which is aimed at making them even less expressive of the common will of the people than they now are. The blueprints offered us specify the features of the social heaven Professor Brameld would usher in by means of school education. This use of the schools would be strictly a propagandizing and indoctrinating of young people with his program of social reconstruction. I see no way around this conclusion, so long as specific social patterns are set up as educational objectives. If American teachers adopted goals of the sort advocated by Professor Brameld (assuming the possibility), American education would become identical in its "utopian" aspect with the education appropriate to Marxist and Fascist regimes. Democratic education (distinctive education for democracy) cannot be employed to bring in a blueprinted heaven.

Nevertheless, Professor Brameld does want American teachers to have clear and compelling goals. That idea will stand repeating. But these goals cannot be utopian and intelligent at the same time, any more than can the goals of science, or technology. To do for us what we need them to do, they must conform both to foreseen consequences and to present resources. If the "utopian thinker" could study the discipline of mind and disposition needed by people, in order to engage maturely and effectively in the process of democratic social reconstruction, and if he could, furthermore, study the teaching techniques required for this discipline, he might come to see 1) that children and young people can engage in such social reconstruction as the community and their own maturity permit and 2) that the work of the teacher through the whole program is properly focused upon the disciplining of character for cooperative practical judgment. For such goals, in contrast with those proposed by the "utopian thinker" we have general consent, if not an imperative consensus.

and small nations that national sovereignty must now be subordinated to enforceable international authority; (b) inclusion of the exploited peoples of colonial territories within the widening social consensus of peoples committed to the new order; (c) maximum educational, scientific, esthetic, and economic intercourse between nations (including immigration); (d) application internationally of all principles enunciated in the six blueprints above.[1]

VI

Now it is at once clear that these outlines lack the color, the flesh and blood, even quite the audacity that they must possess if they are to serve the crucial role for which they are intended. Or, to put it differently, they lack the quality which a sixth and final premise aims to supply—namely, that kind of quality intrinsic to the cultural "myth."

The term, "myth," is always a hazardous one to praise. It is commonly identified with superstitions and doctrinaire dogmas of the past, or fanatical sectarian faith and uncritical tradition worship. In recent decades it has been given renewed and deliberate use in the perversions of fascist propaganda: the "myth" of the Italian nation, for example, or the "myth" of a racial elite. Accordingly, we should expect a good deal of skepticism toward the concept, and properly so, from philosophies which pride themselves on their rational and scientific approaches to life.

Yet we should also be over hasty in concluding that the myth has always been, or necessarily need be, solely an iniquitous device to distort reality, conceal truth, or pervert values. The history of the great myths of civilization reveals that they are something like huge panoramic canvases which attempt to blend together and ennoble by the use of colors and designs and symbols the most comprehensive, most profound meanings and purposes which men can unfathom from a given culture. In this sense, all great philosophies are themselves in certain ways myths:

---

[1] Comment by Gerald B. Phelan:

Mr. Brameld's utopianism is nothing but a determined and hardheaded effort to settle in one's mind the ideals toward which one should strive and the principles which should govern one's efforts to realize them. But I do not seem to want to go where Mr. Brameld thinks we ought to. There is something frightening about those "blueprints." They conjure up memories of Hitlerian educational regimentation or visions of the "democratic" system of Stalin. A democracy for which religion is a "myth" [See Part VI, below] can never be anything but either an anarchy or a despotism. Blueprint number five for an educational system, has all the earmarks of a totalitarian plan of indoctrination under rigid state control.

Platonism may be interpreted as an intellectual poetic portrait of Athenian culture, Thomism of medieval culture. Even experimentalism, despite the loud protests we may expect to hear from certain of its advocates, is in some ironic ways the rather too dispassionate myth of the scientific technological culture through which we have been speeding.

The point, then, is that there may be "good" as well "bad" myths, depending upon the values which they symbolize. And there may be "true" as well as "false" myths, depending upon the extent to which they serve more to unveil or to disguise the common character of the periods in which they are influential.

The significance of myths is exemplified further by a religion like Christianity. That this giant force in Western civilization has its own strong mythical qualities would be denied today by no one except, perhaps, the most rabid fundamentalist. Not only is the story of its founding perhaps the most powerful symbolic poem of all time. The significance of its doctrines for both past and present cultures—its belief, for example, in "eternal salvation"—is vibrant with a profound sense of human destiny, and so defiant of literal translation that only a Michelangelo can portray the Christian myth so that all may understand.

That Christianity has frequently served as co-partner of ideologies is, however, also an historic fact. It served thus in the Middle Ages. It serves thus today when the Church collaborates with fascism; or when American ministers and captains of industry join hands to celebrate business competition as a fine example of Christian virtue.

Yet, while the ideological use of religion is a chief reason why the whole concept of myth is so often legitimately frowned upon both by present minded and future looking intellectuals, the fact is also true that Christianity has its own potent utopian propensities. The encompassing value of maximum goal satisfaction, for example, is anticipated if not sufficiently delineated in its emphasis upon the dignity of personality and the brotherhood of man. Indeed, among certain contemporary Christian leaders one even hears the contention that the one hope for religion's own salvation is to throw its energies and ideals into the struggle for a rehabilitated, socialized, goal satisfying culture.

The theory I am proposing does not, of course, advocate merely a utopianizing of the Christian myth. What it is most interested in here is "radiation"—in how to energize its blueprints with that spirit of commitment and enthusiasm which, it contends, progressivism on the one hand lacks, and theories like neo-Thomism on the other hand futilely seek to engender by reincarnating too largely obsolete and, for our culture, often dangerous beliefs. The myth it seeks is a social therapeutic: to lessen the tensions and resolve the bewilderments from which too many of us suffer, but also to substitute for these a constructive aim in which we may join, for which we may fight, knowing we are once more on the side of righteousness.[j]

As a matter of fact, the role of the myth in this kind of context has been too carefully considered to be impatiently dismissed at once as inevitably playing into the hands of fascists and other barbarians. Its subject matter is, of course, already provided by practical blueprints themselves—materials which are voluminous, substantial, and to an extraordinary sense scientifically respectable. Its form and order are provided by the several arts working upon this subject matter to create prehensive unities—to harmonize our personal and institutional activities into marvelously organic, balanced, dynamic, social designs. Its motivation and direction derive from and are sustained by goal seeking interests of individuals and groups who find prehended, as well as apprehended, mean-

---

[j]Comment by Louis J. A. Mercier:

Is not Dr. Brameld in danger of falling into unrestricted totalitarianism, as it would seem, the humanitarian naturalist must inevitably do?

The argument would run as follows: Yes, all animals are goal seeking. What characterizes man is that he can initiate goals. A common goal seeking unites, it creates a group: an orchestra, a team, a tribe, a people. But what goal seeking can unite all men, create humanity? Only an end above all times and places: God. If there is no being above time and space whose will, the natural law, may be a universal end, for all times and places, there can be no humanity, only groups with local conflicting goals. Yes, blueprints are needed but they must be according to that law.

Now, the humanitarian naturalist, as a humanitarian seeks the material good of man, but as a naturalist he does not believe in a personal God, nor can he believe in a personal man, or in a universal justice; he has merged God and man in nature. Well, nature begets conflicting drives, desires, interests. To put an end to these conflicts, even within his group, constituted by local goal seeking, man will necessarily have to call upon the state; to put an end to intergroup conflicts, he will have to devise a superstate. If above the state, and the superstate, there is a universal justice, a natural law which the state has to respect on the basis of a consequent Bill of Rights for man, well and good. We do need the state. But the naturalist does not believe in such a universal law, because he does not believe in God. Therefore the will of the state will have to be the law for him, even if it runs counter to the universal nature of man. Minorities can have no appeal. There is no one to appeal to, and no eternal law such that even Antigone could appeal to against Creon. There can be no Bill of Rights. Only a God given common nature of man can safeguard inalienable rights. We have to choose at least the Theism of Thomas Jefferson, or we shall get the totalitarianism of Hitler and Stalin, and a much clearer religion than the sentimental myth of humanitarianism is needed to safeguard our Theism.

ings in the very fact that they are participating together in both utilizing the subject matter and forming the patterns of a new culture of which they are fellow members. Only as you and I, in short, are included in a great social consensus committed to goal seeking and goal reaching shall we, too, be sharing in the making of a myth which becomes, at the same time by its fulfilment, ever more real.[k]

Various thinkers have sought in various terms to express this elusive but indispensable need for the mythical element in utopian thought. Sorel tried with exciting but abortive effects to transform the aims of Marxism into a myth. More recently, Randolph Bourne has coined the term, "impossiblism," to challenge the cautious, pedestrian provisionalism of the experimentalists, and to suggest the urgent need for uncautious, daring devotion to value creation. Even a thinker usually thought of as a pragmatist, Edward Scribner Ames, has defended the "practical absolute" as that kind of social and axiological decision which should at some point follow rational deliberation, and toward which one may have all the constructive attitudes which one associates with the most authentic spirit of religion. The more than usually courageous social scientist, Robert S. Lynd, speaks of "outrageous hypotheses" which often turn out to be exceedingly close to phases of the blueprints outlined above.

Many democratic artists likewise defend the utopian myth in their individual idioms. Babette Deutsch: "The poet who speaks out of deepest instincts of man will be heard. The poet who creates a myth beyond the power of man to realize is gagged at the peril of the group that binds him. He is the true revolutionary: he builds a new world."[1] Waldo

[k] Comment by Quincy Wright:
  I have no doubt that groups, especially large groups, require a mystical faith in symbols and objectives to hold them together, but the very strength of such symbols and myths lies in their vagueness and ambiguity. Efforts to convert them into concrete plans lead either to civil or to intergroup war.
  I have no objection to the building of utopias and the elaboration of myths so long as they remain in the realm of fantasy and imagination. The child, however, should be taught the difference between irresponsible relaxation in fairyland and responsible action in the world of men. He should be taught to distinguish "the impossible," "the possible," "the probable," and "the actual." He should realize that the distinctions between them may be measured by the ticking of a clock, but that in the affairs of men nothing is more important than time. He should not let his fantasies as to what is desirable and perhaps possible in a thousand years interfere with his appreciation of what exists today and what is probable within the next year.

[1] *This Modern Poetry*, W. W. Norton Company, Inc., New York, 1935.

Prolegomena to a Future Centered Education

Frank: "In a world where a chaos of forces is breaking down the life of man before our eyes, the chief conditioning art—although all arts have their place—must be one to synthesize our complex pasts and present, and to direct them. This is the art of words, by which man captures the worlds and selves that have borne him, and renders them alive with his own vision."[2] Harry Slochower (speaking about Thomas Mann's great story of the Biblical figure, Joseph): "The myth would render homage to man's ancestral and traditional roots. It is a work of piety and loyalty to essential forms in an age of unrest and bewildering change . . . However, Mann's work is not a mere retelling of the primitive legend. It is not pure regression and literal recurrence. His myth is garbed in all the complex forms of modern insights . . . the myth is still *to be fulfilled,* and that depends on our work in the present and future."[3][1]

All this is merely to put in different ways what Professor William P. Montague suggests in speaking of philosophy's own richest role as that of vision. Or, to quote the greatest of all utopian prognosticators of the coming scientific age, "By far the greatest obstacle to the progress of science and the undertaking of new tasks . . . is found in this, that men despair and think things impossible." These words of Francis Bacon

[2]*In the American Jungle 1925–1936,* Farrar & Rinehart, Inc., New York, 1937.
[3]*No Voice is Wholly Lost. Writers and Thinkers in War and Peace,* Creative Age Press, New York, 1945, p. 338.

[1]Comment by Harry Slochower:
Mr. Brameld's introduction of the myth category contains the idea of man as a symbolic (meaning and goal seeking) being and the principle that the future determines the present. It is rooted in the notion that culture is a composite folk product, expressive of man's communal status and interest. One thing which bothers me is Mr. Brameld's tendency to identify myth and utopia. At the close of his paper where he discusses the role of the cultural myth, he uses "utopia" in its traditional meaning as the "no-where" realm of the "impossible." But in this sense, myth is opposed to utopia. The vision and imagination of the myth are completely related to living practical activity. Myth deals with the actual world of real problems and difficulties which preclude "utopian" or perfectionist achievement. We find this in its role among primitive societies and in its symbolic function of unifying and organizing cultural forms. To be sure, as Ernst Bloch has shown, the historical Utopias (More, Campanella, etc.) are themselves conditioned by their respective historic settings. But their final vision is that of "the impossible." Myth, rather than utopia, points to the eternal man, to the universal potentialities of thought, feeling, and will by which man labors toward completeness and a unified world. It seems to me that myth is a more accurate designation of Mr. Brameld's actual alternative to non-substantive ideologies. He clinches his thesis by urging the myth as an important means for countering our present crises of divisions.

might well become the clarion call of any theory which would seek to demonstrate with Bourne again four centuries later that the impossible is, after all, possible.[m]

[m] Comment by I. L. Kandel:

Dr. Brameld's paper is a restatement of the proposal that education should be devoted to the reconstruction of society. Those who do not agree with him are put out of bounds as "pedestrian, visionless, compromising, or cynical," because they are practical minded, have no feeling for the utopian spirit, and regard those who have vision as starry eyed. The difficulty for those who, like myself, regard such proposals as naive is that the proponents never give a blueprint. Dr. Brameld's paper is an interesting exercise but when one asks how what would "amount virtually to an educational revolution" is to be put into practice, he is informed that, "In this (*sic*) prolegomenon I cannot enter the area of practice." It would be interesting to find out what formal education had to do with social advances in such countries as Australia, Great Britain, New Zealand, and Sweden.

Comment by E. V. Sayers:

Has not serious utopian thinking typically assumed, with Professor Brameld, that man's first task was to project a heaven that *should* be and, holding fixedly to this as if he *knew* it should be, to let this heaven represent for him what it actually *could* be and thus determine for him what he should do? This is the kind of thinking earnest people frequently do when they find the present too much for them.

Concern with present events, sensitiveness to movements and participation in their direction in the light of evolved values and knowledge—this is what we need. No longer need we employ the myth either of a far off event to which we all move nor of a heaven compounded of our frustrated wishes. The controls that a modern world offers have originated in observation of present moving events, and they can function for us only in the management of present moving events. Such futures as we need to bring into our work with present events are the possible futures (consequences, conclusions) of those same present events. To be real futures, they must be the futures of actual present affairs. And to get hold in imagination of these futures (predictive knowledge) as means in the management of present affairs, is to employ intelligence.

A most serious question arises regarding what happens to the present values of people when utopias actually take hold of the energies of people. I think it is not out of place to say that the thing most repulsive to Americans about our modern example of utopia centered societies is their inhumane and unrealistic disregard of the present. On the road to their goals they ride roughshod over the present values of their own people, to say nothing of the values of others. I am sorry if I may seem to Professor Brameld to employ innuendo in thus coupling his theory with the world's most notorious instances of policy based on utopian thinking. But criticism seems to require this association.

In a last comment, I would say that the past does not, in its accumulated wisdom, afford us the answers to our problems, but it does afford us disciplines which, if used to the full as we face our problems, even though they may not get us into Professor Brameld's particular heaven, can, nevertheless, provide us with the best earthly assurance of a safe escape from any number of hells.

Comment by Ronald B. Levy:

Although Professor Brameld has pointed out that we are at a critical junction in our history, it is necessary to explicate the dynamic nature of our crisis situation. Ours is a culture in which instability is on the increase. In such a cultural matrix where are men to find their source of security?

Instead of gaining security through *ownership* or possession of things, we must learn how to gain security through effective functioning in the society—in the successful solution of social problems. Professor Brameld does emphasize this point in his blueprints for the future. Virtually all of them are designed in terms of active processes which are to be learned and made possible for everyone to participate in. Nevertheless the great body of his prolegomena seems to me to emphasize the achieving of *specific goals* or ends which may all too soon *end* the process by which they were achieved. Instead of asking to what *place* do we want to go, we might rather ask in what *direction* do we want to go. Our "goal" then contains a direction. Goods will be attained in the process—specific goals will be achieved—but these are not ends in themselves. They are signposts on the path by means of which our direction may be checked and maintained.

When we see our purpose as the mastery of a directed process rather than the achievement of a finite goal, then social consensus becomes a matter of striving for a greater feeling of belongingness in our community—a greater and more nearly unlimited emotional involvement in our group—rather than the amassing of a greater total *number* of members, or a larger count of votes, as Professor Brameld seems to suggest. Community or consensus becomes a *quality* of group life, not its *quantity* or geographical extension.

The security gaining method for our culture, then, is clearly indicated to be the practice of effective social and group processes, so that this quality of community life will permeate the individual members and thus give them reinforcement and security in their social functioning. It is when one feels that he belongs to a group or community that he functions in a socially secure fashion. When this feeling is one approaching total involvement, then the community will also spread and become quantitatively larger as well. Therefore, it is in the processes of group discussion, deliberation, and decision that society is democratically centered.

Basic to this type of group process is the final point on which I intend to comment. It is in the area of conflict and its solution that the method of group process becomes important. Shall social processes be directed at sharpening conflict for the purpose of the elimination or exclusion of one party to it, or shall social processes be directed toward undercutting the conflict situation—restructuring the stimulus field—so that those factors which appeared to be conflicting are seen to be at least potentially compatible? It is in maximum inclusion—maximum participation and involvement in social problems—that security is born and bred for the individual community members. It is therefore my suggestion that the most effective method for attaining Professor Brameld's blueprint of our future culture is through a social process whose direction is toward the maximum inclusion and participation of all social groups in this directive process itself. This process gains its depth and breadth of inclusiveness through infusing community members with a deep and total sense of belonging and being emotionally involved in their community activities. It is my belief that education directed in this fashion can be an ever evolving social process focused in the future, and giving with the help of utopian visionaries reinforcement and security to individuals through their effective participation in an inclusive well functioning society.

[Cf. Chapter III by T. V. Smith, for a discussion stressing the need of thinking in terms of practical goals rather than "utopian" or "impossible" ideals.]

CHAPTER XV

The Administration of a Municipal College

By GEORGE N. SHUSTER
President, Hunter College of the City of New York

I HAVE SOMETIMES permitted myself to believe that colleagues in the fraternity of college presidents might profitably read two great treatises on education—*Don Quixote* and the dramas of Euripides—which are not alluded to as frequently as seems desirable. In the one there is to be found a terse and searching discussion of what happens to the public mind when values are ignored and integrity is dissipated; and in the other a man of notable wisdom and experience weighs the limitations of the intelligence and the perils that attend what are known as intuitions or urges. But the mere use of the term, "great book," makes many a lip quiver. While it is true that Matthew Arnold counseled seeking out "the best that has been known and thought in the world," our contemporaries often appear to feel that to call anything "best" is to commit an act of metaphysical obscurantism. To legislate that two times two are four would, one surmises, be deemed undemocratic effrontery; and if so unpardonable an offense were perpetrated, the matter would no doubt eventually be referred to the Supreme Court, which body might well opine that two and two are seven, with Mr. Justice Reed demurring, and Mr. Justice Frankfurter delivering a classic and quite competently documented defense of the traditional view.

The mixture of opinions now served up is, in short, so very like a traffic jam that it has become almost impossible for any number of people to proceed in any direction together. The other day I was invited to comment on an article, accepted for publication by one of the more popular magazines, which called for the condoning of murder when the victims could not be proved to have been socially useful beings. The author, it appeared, believed that a great many people would serve humanity most effectively by assenting in advance to their somewhat untidy demises. I remonstrated rather feebly that there existed no evidence to prove that the writer of the piece was not hoist by his own petard, and suggested that it was quite unfair to propose so beguiling a temptation as this sort of homicide to one so weak as I. The incident is related here because it strengthened an impulse to live anew with Euripides in my pocket and *Don Quixote* on my desk. The educational ideal which is here taken for granted is, as a result, fairly simple and uncomplicated.

I hold it to be the first business of a college to be a friendly, literate, and sometimes amusing place, in which a relatively few things are taken very seriously, indeed. They do not include the integration of the curriculum, or even the elimination of vocational courses in favor of a vigorous emphasis on abstract thought. I shall enumerate them. First, a person who is not deeply interested in teaching and more than willing to work hard at it ought not to take money for being employed by a college, however important his research may be. Second, the college, if it is to be any good, must provide the instructor with some little place on the campus which he can call his own, and in which he can confer with students—in short it must equip Mark Hopkins with a log. Third, some provision must be made for listening to what the students themselves think of the proceedings. And fourth, the young people who come should be expected to work as hard as other young people do who are not in college. An institution which lives by these principles will, I think, win the allegiance of its students, and its alumni will see to it that it has support. I do not consider it my professional obligation to save souls, or even to make an atomic age say to itself each morning that it is the atomic age.

As I see it, my business as an administrator is to try to create a college such as I have described. The situation prevailing at a municipal college is of course in some respects different, and an attempt will be made in what follows to outline the problems and to set forth some of the efforts being made to solve them. It is abundantly clear, of course, that effort is not success. It is often just an experiment, or perhaps an act of trusting to luck in the absence of recipes which can be guaranteed to produce results.

A municipal college may be defined as one financed out of the City treasury, administered by a Board of Higher Education, and subject to the provisions of the Education Law of the State. This means that the administrator must work inside a sort of triple enclosure, the presence of which he is often made aware of by a bump to his bones. Cities are no doubt much alike, but I can speak at first hand only of New York. This has been very generous to higher education, though its budgetary procedures are by no means as elastic as are those of many states. That is at once an advantage and a handicap. One can be reasonably sure of avoiding drastic curtailments, but one must also realize early that one's native eloquence, however remarkable, will not loosen the purse strings to any memorable extent. In my time I have found the City administration notably honest and unbiased. Indicating that this is true has done no harm. Woe betide the man who is in debt for political favors! But let us extend our regrets also to him who is not generously aware of the virtues of those who are in political life.

A Board of Higher Education—or a similar Board under whatever name—differs from a Board of Trustees serving a private college in that its members are seldom selected from among the graduates of the institution. They are appointed to represent important component groups of the population, and for this reason will normally be public spirited citizens who are sincerely interested in education. They are therefore without any special sentimental attachment to a given college, but they are likely to manifest a deep concern for fair play, honesty of administration, and faculty welfare, while strongly opposing any kind of intolerance or quackery. Sometimes a member of the Board may ride his own hobbies, or put all his eggs into one basket. But on the whole I believe that the great majority of municipal college presidents will say that their cities have appointed year after year ladies and gentlemen who continue to be regarded affectionately as ladies and gentlemen; who support the presidents of their choosing loyally and intelligently; and whose awareness of community feeling has been proved a dependable barometer. It costs heavily in time and money to be a member of a Board, and if anything goes wrong one is in the doghouse. Nevertheless I cherish the feeling that nearly all Board members I have known considered the sacrifice worthwhile. The administrator must learn to work with such men and women and to respect their opinions even when they diverge sharply from his own. In view of the fact that the powers of publicly appointed Boards are likely to be very broad, and that in the final analysis responsibility is coupled with power, it seems to me quite surprising that so few major decisions prove to be utterly wrong.

State Education Laws differ, and so I shall use that of New York as an illustration. It is a many faceted and important document. It confers tenure and salary upon teachers, so that on the one hand these teachers are likely to be frozen into their posts very early, while on the other hand movements to improve the economic status of the faculty proceed quite independently of the administration of the College and are supported with such pressure as the staff itself can muster. The Law also limits freedom of instruction, particularly in the sense that anything smacking of religious exhortation is taboo. Personally I consider this ban an anachronism. It is of course undesirable that students belonging to different churches or creeds be subjected unilaterally to teaching which incorporates the dogmas of any one church or creed. But just why one should be so squeamish about the presentation of religious views to students who desire to see such views expounded remains a mystery. And of course the outcome is that opinions detrimental to any religious point of view must likewise be exercised.

So much for the framework. Perhaps the sorest trial which a college administrator thus constrained is likely to encounter at the outset is the realization that the alma mater he fosters is looked upon as a poor relation. So sacred to the American are ivy and private property that an institution which charges very little, if anything at all, which admits children regardless of the status of their ancestors, and which probably does not list among its alumni many Presidents of the United States, is often considered the habitat of unfortunate beings who, but for the absentmindedness of the taxpayer, would be scouring pans for the rest of their lives. Therefore the administrator husbands every ounce of prestige as carefully as Mr. Lilienthal does atomic energy. His big task is to convince his own students and faculty that they can look the world in the face with confidence. Unless he is perennially careful the morale of his institution will bog down like a Buick on a Ukrainian dirt road. He must, with a kind of virtuous unscrupulousness, take advantage of every bit of glitter he can amass; and yet he must at the same time remain intellectually honest and, indeed, just the least bit cynical.

He profits from the fact that his student material is the best in the world. The great majority of the youngsters who come to his college have a price tag on their chests. It would be far more advantageous economically for their families if after leaving high school they got some sort of a job—if they addressed envelopes or wrapped parcels in a department store. But a deep respect and hunger for learning persists, together with the hope that eventually the scion of hard working parents may strut the stage in a better role. Students, therefore, have all the faults of American youth save one. They seldom feel that Dad will bail them out even if their four years at college are what my contemporaries defined as a complete "flop." They may write atrocious English. They may never have heard of Emily Post. But they are not vagabonds on their way to and from the Social Register. They need to be cajoled a little, and to be prodded more than a little. They are the salt of the earth which has to find out what salt is. And we fail miserably whenever they do not find out.

You must remember that such students will not often be taught by the most glamorous of American teachers. Sometimes indeed—and I regret to say this—they are addressed by instructors who entertain a profound contempt for their charges, and compensate for their nostalgic evocations of Oxford by looking about them with aversion. But it is pleasant to note that while a municipal college may not number among its employees many of the most highly touted, it does assemble some of the most devoted of professors. These are men and women who have plumbed at first hand the meaning of scholarship but who remain nonetheless the patient guides and friends of youth; who have trained their hearts to draw no line of demarcation between student and student for any extraneous reason; and who, if they themselves have risen from among the less widely acclaimed sections of the population have, while surrendering no cherished principle of religious belief or national heritage, put on a garment one can only refer to as charity because it is more luminous than humanism, is indeed the product of faith in the meaningfulness of the origin and destiny of man.

To build a community of the best of such students and their teachers, against the background of numerous and diverse urban homes (for the municipal college student does not live on the campus) is no doubt the basic, continuing problem. There are so many young people that one cannot hope to know any great number of them. But one can recall that nothing is so sacred to college students as are traditions, and proceed to create things that will be remembered—say, a Christmas assembly and luncheon, with community singing; a place in which to browse among books, or to argue incessantly; a bench on which sitting is forbidden, and therefore especially attractive. One can make an effort to help young people through a program of guidance that makes sense because it deals on a personal basis with each individual girl or boy.

Above all one must put no credence in either of two favorite myths. One must not believe that merely taking a program in the liberal arts will equip a youngster who has no arrows in her bow for hitting the bull's-eye which is a livelihood. I could illustrate in a thousand ways the quite pathetic helplessness of graduates who despite the reading they have done in Thucydides and Homer have not the foggiest notion about what action to take in order to fit in somewhere. An aspect of the liberal arts myth which invites special criticism is that which has to do with what one may term inculcated highmindedness. This is something quite different from honesty, loyalty, humility, or any other of the traditional virtues. It is a state of being so chockfull of good advice to the world that one has literally moved out of the world. One could be a United States Senator, no doubt, or possibly even a Vice President. But that one should be destined to toil as a clerk in the office of the Peterkin Thermos Bottle Company, or to change diapers, or to market cigars, is first of all incredible and secondly utterly disillusioning. I may add that we who are along in years too often forget that the average young person has to be pushed first out of home and then out of college. At home, mother is a factotum, supplying everything from cereal to television. And at college the dean is currently a sort of expanded incubator, which can hatch every problematical egg. But whereas the fledgling bird need only learn how to fly and how to grub for a worm, the young human being must make a difficult social and psychological adjustment to living—so difficult, indeed, that the market for books which purport to explain how it is to be done is always a staggeringly profitable one.

The municipal college cannot afford to be unrealistic about such matters. I have unshamefacedly urged all language and literature majors to take courses in typewriting and stenography, and I have just as persistently cajoled feminine students into finding out what a baby looks like, what has to be done to help it grow up, and what a strange sort of creature its father is likely to be. Yes, I am persuaded that the issues here alluded to are so important that until they have been dealt with any further extension of college facilities might well be relatively catastrophic. I concede that perhaps society ought to reimburse everyone who can sing an aria from *Martha;* but if the singers have to take up a collection from amongst themselves, because the performers outnumber the audience, something has gone wrong, and it is not the capitalist system. I believe in the values of education as ardently as does anyone else. But it seems to me inconceivable that a college exists in order to help young people fail in everything else than their classes.

Now for the second myth. Can we really teach students either professions or vocations? The answer is, of course, no. A man qualifies for such a calling as medicine or law by taking advantage of what a school can offer him, of what he finds out afterward, and of what he has in himself. A good physician is a man of knowledge, character, insight, and magnanimity. And the really bad doctor is not the quack who "cures" arthritis with herb tea, but the impostor who sells patients his wholly worthless degree. Accordingly there is little need to point out that what an undergraduate college can do to help train students to be writers or concert pianists, advertising salesmen or teachers, is relatively insignificant. But it is equally apparent that it can do something. One can, for example, foster a bent toward journalism by providing some sort of work experience that resembles journalistic activity. Harm is done only when more is attempted than can be essayed realistically—when, for instance, the teaching of educational psychology in segments as numerous as are the products of Heinz is looked upon as a satisfactory preparation for classroom instruction.[a]

In short I do not believe in the "pure" college, the sole business of which is to feed its infants an extract of world culture. The value of the Hutchins "great books" idea seems to me to lie not in the choice of the books (though it is a pretty good one) but rather in the proposed method of studying them.[b] This method is a revamping of what the French call *explication des textes,* which in turn is part of the age old teaching of rhetoric, designed to train orators, lawyers, statesmen, and teachers. One has only to note that Mr. Winston Churchill's words have played so sig-

---

[a] [Cf. the discussion of the place of vocational preparation in the goals of education in Chapter II by Lyman Bryson (including comment by Dr. Shuster), Chapter III by T. V. Smith, Chapter IX by Howard Mumford Jones, Chapter XVI by Earl J. McGrath (including comment by Louis J. A. Mercier), Chapter XVIII by Harold Taylor (including comments by Mason W. Gross and Dr. Mercier), and comment by George B. de Huszar in Appendix III.]

[b] [For further discussion of the "great books" and the "Chicago Plan," see Chapter II by Lyman Bryson, Chapter III by T. V. Smith, Chapter VIII by Alain L. Locke, Chapter IX by Howard Mumford Jones, Chapter XI by John U. Nef, Chapter XIII by Mordecai M. Kaplan, Chapter XVI by Earl J. McGrath, Chapter XVII by Ordway Tead, and George B. de Huszar's comment in Appendix III.]

nificant a part in modern history because like Cicero's they were hammered on the anvil of a great intellectual and art tradition, in order to see that by bringing to life again, though perhaps with a larger number of cabalistic signs than was wholly necessary, the teaching of rhetoric, in the true sense, Mr. Hutchins has rendered a very important service to our democracy. This democracy must assume that each citizen is in some modest way a statesman. It is not "culture" that Mr. Hutchins is trying to sell (whether he knows it or not) but the art of becoming a cultivated and communicative man.

But I do not see why the cult of the *disputatio* and the *colloquium* should be hermetically sealed off from contact with vocational or work experiences such as I have described.[c] In my lifetime, which included formative years spent in a gymnasium of the Swiss type, I think I have learned that some strenuous thinking about what one is going to do as well as about what one is going to be, is a vital part of growing up. And so our own college pattern of instruction includes always some room for what, for lack of a better term I have called "vocational inlays," and which may be described as modest essays in the art of preparing for life. At any rate, our record seems to indicate that such inlays give the student confidence and a sense of direction. Our difficulty is not one of finding that vocational considerations occupy too much of our time. It is rather that we cannot soon enough give our students some insight into the ultimate unifying purpose of their collegiate life.

Here, of course, we, too, are brought face to face with the enigma which everybody is discussing and with which, alas, a college administrator can do nothing as an administrator but only as a sort of philosopher or even poet—which even if he were able he could seldom find time to be. The root of the problem is obviously this: the college, like the university, exists to husband, distribute, and even to increase knowledge; but the deepest insight into the meaning and the drift of life comes not from knowledge but from belief. By belief I do not mean credulity but a

[c]Comment by Louis J. A. Mercier:
President Shuster would praise the Hutchins program not for "giving an extract of world culture," but for teaching "the art of becoming a cultivated and communicative man," and for him this need not be "sealed off from contact with vocational and work experiences." It would have been helpful if he had given us more details on how it can be sealed in. However, we might note once for all that education was always utilitarian. Sixteenth to seventeenth century classical colleges taught Latin as a living language for would be leaders in the professions and government. In those days college graduates had to understand what was written on their diplomas.

willing personal venture, exacting and even at times heart rending, amidst the eternal landmarks of holiness, awe, universally valid law, tragedy, and comedy. Just as the college cannot produce genius or great poetry, so also is it unable to inculcate sanctity or wisdom. Knowledge will remain forever the centrifugal activity of the mind face to face with reality. It is the quest for the parts of which the Whole is compounded; and each part is in turn so infinitely complex that in its microcosm one rediscovers the endless depth that the world everywhere manifests.

Therefore when I personally talk of these things I try to say that the experience of knowing, of accumulating knowledge, is valuable because of the dexterity, accuracy, and perspective which it can bring to one's performance of the quite relative tasks one is to assume in an always necessarily relative human world. Knowledge, in other words, is functional. It will help a doctor to diagnose and properly deal with pneumonia, and it will assist the psychologist in warding off some potentially dangerous psychosis. The proper teaching of rhetoric would revitalize what are called the Humanities.[d] But one cannot alter the fact that man's existence, like the existence of the cosmos, is a profound mystery, the confrontation of which by each human being is his personal religious experience. Perhaps art and literature and philosophy can bring one to this

[d]Comment by John D. Wild:
  I have learned a great deal from this winsome and penetrating discussion of the problems confronting a college administrator at the present time. With respect to its major themes I find myself in hearty agreement. One small question, however, emerges from Mr. Shuster's remarks on "the great books idea." I think he is quite right in pointing out the sense in which this represents "a revamping of what the French call *explication des textes*," and a partial revival of what was once called the discipline of rhetoric. Mr. Shuster seems satisfied with the purely formal aspects of this discipline, "the art of becoming a cultivated and communicative man." But does this art not require some sound and systematic *content* for its completion? Can we teach the art of becoming cultivated without also teaching cultural principles at the same time? Can we teach a man to communicate well without also teaching him some truth to communicate? As Plato points out in the *Phaedrus,* the art of rhetoric is apt to degenerate into a purposeless manipulation of psychic responses, unless it is governed by dialectic and philosophy. We must not become so impressed by the medieval *trivium* as to forget the *quadrivium* with which it was so intimately intertwined.
  I should very much like to know what Mr. Shuster would say along this line. When he says that "the proper teaching of rhetoric would revitalize what are called the Humanities," I cannot believe that he means rhetoric *alone*.

Dr. Shuster's reply:
  Professor Wild's comment would, under ordinary circumstances, tempt me to write still another paper but matters being what they are in this hectic world, I shall content myself with a word or two. The art of *explication des textes* depends, of course, upon the skill and honesty with which the texts are selected but in my humble opinion far more upon the in-

point. Beyond that each single soul is on its own. I believe it would be well to express openly and humbly such a sense of the limitations of education. Knowledge cannot be integrated. It may within limits be more rationally organized, and possibly it may also be quite tentatively synthesized into what is called "general knowledge." But should we really succeed even if we added the Encyclopedia to the Hundred Best Books? Integration in the ultimate, final sense is something quite different. It is silence.[e]

So then I go back to where we were before. A good college is a place where a young generation associates with older generations in order to learn how to be useful and cultivated participants in the business of life. This living together should be as good spirited, stimulating, industrious, and courteous as possible, because in the end a civilization is worth saving only if it is these things. One has the right to go home smiling at the foibles of one's colleagues and oneself. But one is forever stigmatized by pettiness and pride. The good teacher, in a word, is a good friend. He can utter the truth that hurts, but only because he realizes also that it can heal.

If I may at the end formulate a few opinions about some of the special problems of the municipal college, I shall single out two from among so many that the mere enumeration of them would be confusing. First, this college is an integral part of the community it serves. Like the public school, it is more than a school—is, in fact, a sort of "center" to which the neighborhood and it may be the city as a whole look for a variety of serv-

---

tegrity and talent of the *explicator*. From what I have seen of Professor Wild's own comment on Plato, I am sure that at Harvard a great book has been associated with an excellent teacher. On the other hand, I am perhaps heretical enough to assume that regardless of all the virtues of Greek philosophy, that philosophy would be more than useless in the hands of a bungler.

In short, I believe that Mr. Hutchins should constantly revise his list of great books in accordance with experience as to the effectiveness with which they are presented by the available interpreters. My point is that the pattern cannot be envisaged without reference to the human environment to which it is inevitably appended.

[e]Comment by Louis J. A. Mercier:

The greatest value of President Shuster's paper is perhaps his recognition that the problem of ideally combining vocational knowledge with culture that would issue in character is largely insoluble by the college: "The college cannot produce genius or great poetry, sanctity or wisdom." "Man's existence like that of the cosmos is a profound mystery, the confrontation of which by each human being is his personal religious experience." "Beyond art, literature, and philosophy, each single soul remains on its own."

It is indeed invaluable to have these statements, because after all our discussion of man in social terms, we shall have to ask whether we did not forget his personal intangibility.

ices. Second, a municipal institution, being non-residential, cannot provide opportunity for the experience of living in common under direction which is among the noblest duties performed by a good campus college, and which is rooted in the age old monastic practice of idealistic intellectuals, of whatever creed or persuasion. This experience is one for which our age, formed by individualism, ardently yearns, as witness on the one level such movements as the French *Resistance* and even, when they are young and fervent, Communist cells, or, on the other hand, such evocations of a pattern of living as that of Hermann Hesse in *Das Glasperlenspiel,* which won for its author the Nobel Prize.

Viewed as a community center, the municipal college offers a broad program of what, for lack of a better term, is called "adult education." There are formal cultural and vocational courses; supervised activities which are properly recreational in character; and such more ambitious enterprises as the Hunter College Concert Series. And, in addition, room and facilities are made available to a great variety of educational and cultural groups, sometimes famous as is the Boston Symphony Orchestra and sometimes young and experimental. The fostering of such associations and the selection of those which most merit what is always looked upon as approval by the college is an important administrative function. I think that these various kinds of community education are bound to prove more and more significant. There is still a good deal of feeling around in the dark here, and more than a little charlatanism. But I am convinced that the answer to America's educational problem does not lie in the multiplication of colleges at which still other tens of thousands will spend four years. It is to be found rather in a decision so to reorganize secondary education that young people will be channeled into the working and culturally advancing community in accordance with their aptitudes and abilities, and then to create a virile and creative "adult education" movement to which a portion of leisure time can be devoted. This is, however, a complex and difficult topic, which cannot be elaborated here. It is apparent, however, that the college administrator cannot run away from it—and that he cannot persist in the leisurely belief that four years of life on the campus will be significant at all unless they are rich in meaning for the whole lives of the individuals affected. Let us also note that while it is most certainly true that no qualified young person should be denied the benefits of higher education because of inability to pay for those benefits, it is also true that Ph.D. degrees cost more than they ever before have and that, in purely economic terms, they are worth less than they have ever been worth. But the participation of the whole community in the making of its common culture is above all price.

Viewed as a "city pavement" institution, the municipal college assuredly needs supplementing with some place in the country, supported in part by the students themselves, at which they can participate for limited periods of time in a community building experience. Out of such experience altruism will grow, and altruism is the indispensable concomitant of leadership. I hope that my own college will in the not too far distant future have such facilities available, and I am sure that the use we can make of them could be rewarding beyond all claims that I could now make. There would then be ready for realization a pattern of education in which life in the home environment would conjoin with initiation into the academic community, in order to humanize the fruits of study.

I have said these are problems among many. To state them even briefly is to make evident once more that the job of a college administrator is one which no human being in his right mind would willingly assume. One takes on such assignments when one is momentarily drunk with a vision of what might be accomplished if one were somebody else and the world a more malleable affair than it unfortunately is, and muses then during subsequent hours of relative sobriety upon one's limitations, errors, and inability to surmount circumstances. One sees clearly then that if one were Augustine, one would still have a tiff with one's colleague, Jerome, and that if one were Plato, the Republic would get itself on paper well enough but not off it again. But one is not Augustine or Plato but only a rather dowdy duffer of a little more than middle age, wondering where the next eruption is likely to take place. And perhaps that is as it should be. One must have a stout heart, a tough skin, a sense of humor, and somewhere in the background like an icon in a crypt a core of unflinching and indestructible honor. One can then safely permit oneself to marvel daily at the glory and the beauty of youth, without minding too much the portent of the dire fate which will some day be meted out to it also—the fate of starting all over again for its successors the process to which it itself is subjected.

CHAPTER XVI

The Goals of Higher Education[1]

By EARL J. McGRATH

Dean of the College of Liberal Arts, State University of Iowa

UNIVERSITIES HAVE four primary functions: (1) training the members of the professions and other vocations which require formal education beyond the high school; (2) performing informal educational services in the community at large; (3) encouraging research and preparing scholars to extend the frontiers of knowledge; (4) and educating youth to perform intelligently and responsibly all the activities of life in a democracy.[a]

On the efficient performance of the first of these functions, the material prosperity of a commonwealth and the physical well being of its citizens largely depend. Competence in the professions has increased as their members have had the advantages of formal education. The gains made during the past century in the diagnosis, treatment, and prevention of disease, for example, have resulted largely from the institutionalization of medical education and research. Comparable social benefits have come with the transfer of the education of other occupational groups, such as engineers, social workers, and librarians, from practitioners to institutions of higher education.

Public recognition of the value of this type of education is amply shown by the increase in the number and variety of professional schools. To the early courses of study in medicine, law, and theology, have been added dentistry, pharmacy, engineering, agriculture, education, business administration, and others, and these instructional units are

---

[a] [For discussion of this classification of functions, with regard to Dr. McGrath's paper and others, see comment by Quincy Wright in Appendix III.]

[1] Though this paper at the request of the officers of the Conference on Science, Philosophy, and Religion deals primarily with higher education in state universities, almost all the statements apply with equal force to private universities.

constantly being subdivided into more specialized branches. The demand for new types of specialized education beyond the high school will increase as vocations undergo greater differentiation. Hence, universities, especially state universities, established as they are to meet all the varied educational needs of society, may be expected to increase the number and to expand the offerings of their professional divisions. In achieving this objective—training the future members of the occupational groups requiring advanced education—the American university has been signally successful.[b]

The second function, performing informal educational services, is assuming increasing importance, especially in publicly controlled universities. These activities include extension classes for adults, casual lectures for civic organizations, occasional investigations for industry, farming, and governmental agencies, and professional counsel to public and private bodies. Schools of agriculture and engineering have developed these informal services most fully, but other divisions increasingly extend their work into the everyday life of the state. Schools of journalism, for example, operate institutes and short courses for newspaper personnel. Departments of psychology make surveys of public opinion on matters of interest to the state at large or to various economic and social groups. Schools of social work, library science, commerce, public administration, and law, often render similar services of teaching or research which draw the universities and the communities which

[b]Comment by Louis J. A. Mercier:

Dean McGrath does us a real service in stressing the benefits that have come from vocational training. The humanistic reaction against it has too often minimized them, since they have given the United States their power, their high standards of material life, and even the opportunity for a greater number to have a chance at cultural education. The question is then not to disparage vocational training in an age where competence is the only badge of superiority. The question is how much humanistic and religious training do we need alongside of vocational training, and how are the three to be secured?

If a professional man, even learned and skilled in his profession, knows little or nothing of the complete humanistic and religious tradition of the West, and even of the East, he is a barbarian. He may be an aseptic barbarian and better gadgeted for comfortable living, but he cannot lead an intellectual life, because without an introduction to the thought inheritance of the race, he can begin thinking only at zero, and is at the mercy of the pressure groups of his time and place.

[Cf. the discussion of the place of vocational preparation in the goals of education in Chapter II by Lyman Bryson (including comment by George N. Shuster), Chapter III by T. V. Smith, Chapter IX by Howard Mumford Jones, Chapter XV by Dr. Shuster, Chapter XVIII by Harold Taylor (including comments by Mason W. Gross and Dr. Mercier), and comment by George B. de Huszar in Appendix III.]

support them into closer and mutually beneficial relationships. Traditionally, especially in the aristocratic European universities, these services were not provided. Now, however, they are a vital and growing element in the American educational system, and in our democratic way of life.

Universities have been less successful in reaching the two other goals of higher education. Hence it is with these that this discussion is primarily concerned.

The third objective, encouraging research and educating scholars, fails of full realization because it is confused with the first, training the members of the professions. Universities carry on activities in the graduate schools which properly belong in the professional divisions. Before the confusion of ends in graduate and professional education is examined, however, the research activities of universities deserve review.

In state institutions, especially those with agricultural and engineering units, research has often been concerned with matters close to the economic and social life of the commonwealth. The improvement in methods for processing oil, the development of economically superior breeds of animals, and the experimental production of grain which flourishes in regions with little rainfall, are examples of research which has benefited the supporting community and the entire nation. Its value is incalculable. These investigative activities of universities have raised the American standard of living, increased the comforts of life, and so improved the material well being of our people that we are in this respect the envy of other nations.

Nor have these publicly supported institutions, concerned as they rightly are with investigations closely related to the lives of the people, neglected pure research—studies of no apparent immediate practical utility. In their laboratories, libraries, and studios nuclear research has been done, the boundless oceans of astronomical space explored, novels written, and symphonies composed. Their faculties include world renowned students of Milton and Chaucer. There is little evidence that truth and beauty have been less zealously pursued in these public institutions than in private universities because of a preoccupation with practical things or a niggardly public support of fundamental research.

Investigative activities, both theoretical and applied, must, however, be intensified and more largely supported if the state universities are to make their maximum contribution to the life of the time and to the continued improvement of the lot of humanity. Especially in the social sciences and the humanities is imaginative inquiry needed if men are to come to grips with the political, social, and moral problems which now beset them. Contemporary misunderstanding and conflict can be relieved by the steady application of the investigative techniques of the scholar to human problems. In the realm of art the activities of scholars and producers of beauty must be increased in order that our people may gain a keener awareness of the meaning of life through artistic appreciation and expression. Research in all the fields of learning, and especially in the seldom explored no-man's-land between the various disciplines, must be vigorously carried forward. If the activities of scholars should cease, society would become static, disease flourish, the mind of civilized man atrophy, and biological forms with a more enterprising spirit take over the earth.

Universities have the responsibility of encouraging research and providing the necessary laboratory, library, and other facilities needed by men of learning in the practice of their craft. But they must do more than this! They must also provide a place where the skills, attitudes, and habits of scholarship can be acquired. Universities must stir the spirit of inquiry, inspire a devotion to the life of the mind, pass on the sacred traditions of learning, in short, breed succeeding generations of scholars. To be a university it is not enough that an institution offer advanced instruction. Many corporations like Westinghouse and General Electric conduct classes in the most advanced branches of physics, mathematics, and engineering. But they are not universities! Nor does the maintenance of a research program, no matter how large, comprehensive, or costly, give an institution the right to call itself a university. Without teaching such an agency is no more than an institute.

A university is a place, therefore, where research and teaching are done, but where special responsibility is assumed for the preparation of those who will continue the traditions and the work of scholarship after the present generation of teachers and investigators has passed. In the absence of a company of teaching scholars there can be no real university. Where such a fraternity dwells there a university will exist, even though, as in the case of the Chinese institutions during the war, the normal physical characteristics—buildings, books, and laboratories —are missing.

Are the universities of America producing scholars? Swelling graduate enrollments, the multiplication of doctor's degrees, the increase in learned societies, the growth of scholarly literature, all suggest an affirmative answer. Two common measures of success, at least, size and numbers, indicate a flourishing program of graduate education. But a second question must be asked before the first can be definitively answered. To what extent does the present graduate program actually nourish the most imaginative and vital minds—minds that may be expected to engage in a productive life of scholarship after the compulsions of formal schooling are removed? It must be admitted that some creative minds have flowered in the graduate schools.

Nevertheless, the most reliable available evidence of intellectual fecundity and the capacity for scholarship—the published results of research—suggest that graduate schools are less successful in cultivating habits of creative thought and scholarly production than might be desired. A group of distinguished mathematicians, for example, after examining the publications of holders of the Ph.D. in mathematics, concluded that "it is no apparent overstatement to assert that, under present conditions, at least eighty per cent of those receiving the doctorate in mathematics will publish no useful research beyond their doctoral theses."[2] A study of historians revealed a similar barrenness.[3] These figures for two of the older disciplines surely raise some doubt concerning the efficacy of graduate study in stimulating the creative faculties and in cultivating the capacity for original research. Confirmatory evidence regarding the failure of the graduate schools to stimulate imaginative thought may be found among scientists who, viewing the scientific enterprise at work during the war years, made the observation that American scientists had been less imaginative in conceiving and doing fundamental research than their European colleagues. These facts arouse speculation as to whether graduate education in its present American form attracts and nurtures superior minds, whether the atmosphere of graduate schools is congenial to independent thinking and productive scholarship.

It is now time to return to the thesis that the third objective of university education, the encouragement of research and the preparation of scholars to extend the frontiers of knowledge, is not adequately

[2] The Commission on the Training and Utilization of Advanced Students of Mathematics (E. J. Moulton, chairman), "Report on the Training of Teachers of Mathematics," *American Mathematical Monthly*, XLII, 5, May, 1935.

[3] Marcus W. Jernegan, "The Productivity of Doctors of Philosophy in History," *American Historical Review*, XXXIII, October, 1927, pp. 1-22.

achieved because it has been confused with another responsibility of these institutions, the training of the members of the various professions and other occupations requiring education beyond the high school. Graduate faculties are attempting to perform two dissimilar functions, without apparently recognizing their difference. The primary responsibility of the graduate school is to produce creative minds capable of the most original investigative work. It should not dissipate its energies, as has increasingly become the custom, in the training of professional practitioners. It should educate scholars and research workers, not librarians, ophthalmologists, social workers, and college teachers. It should select and cultivate generative minds capable of sustained scholarly endeavor. The training of men and women for practice in the various professions, on the other hand, should be the responsibility of the professional schools.

The present confusion of graduate with professional education weakens both. Those who seek to become theorists and scholarly investigators are handicapped by being subjected to the academic routines in the training of a practitioner. Those, on the other hand, who wish to learn the practice of a profession such as social work, nursing, or college teaching, needlessly spend their time and energy in learning the techniques of scholarly investigation, in satisfying foreign language requirements, and in preparing a thesis often of questionable quality as an original piece of investigative work. To correct the present shortcomings in both graduate and professional education their functions need to be differentiated, and a specific educational program designed for each.[c]

For the education of the few who have extraordinary gifts for creative intellectual activity, a new type of institution, or at least a new type of administrative unit is required. This division need not be large, nor involve elaborate administrative machinery and faculty relationships. Indeed, regulations, time schedules, course credits, academic bookkeeping, and all the other obstructive features of higher education should be completely abandoned. Those who seemed to possess the habits of mind and character essential to a life of scholarship should be admitted to

[c]Comment by Louis J. A. Mercier:
   Dean McGrath calls to our attention the fact that the Ph.D. system has not produced many permanently producing scholars. His proposal for a distinction between the preparation of college teachers and that of professional researchers, supports the contention in my own paper that we should distinguish a Ph.D. in teaching from a Ph.D. in research, along the lines of the French *agrégation* and *doctorat*. [Cf. Chapter XII by Louis J. A. Mercier.]

this institution, which might be called an *Institute of Higher Studies,* placed under the supervision and guidance of an accomplished scholar, permitted to attend lectures, work in the library or laboratory, or travel, as in each case seemed best. They should be left completely free to pursue their chief intellectual interests, find a challenging problem the solution of which would be their own responsibility, and at the end of three, four, or five years, demonstrate their competence for creative scholarship by exhibiting the product of their work and by passing an examination set by their peers.

Spoon feeding devitalizes the present graduate program. The first prerequisite of continuous scholarly production is the capacity to identify potentially profitable areas of study and to devise appropriate techniques for their investigation. Yet inquiry among sponsors of graduate students concerning the number who actually discover their own problem and devise suitable methods of investigation, reveals that at best fifteen or twenty per cent of graduate students actually display these simple evidences of intellectual originality. More commonly, a sponsoring professor identifies a problem, an area of study (usually adjacent to his own plot of research), and suggests a "sure fire" technique for its successful solution. The student is thus deprived of that sense of exhilaration which comes from genuine intellectual prospecting, that psychological reward which drives the real adventurer ever forward to unexplored regions. Instead of prospecting on his own, the student becomes a mere academic laborer who enters the shaft of the already discovered mine with the provided pick and shovel, and follows the routine of digging out the facts. That this procedure produces only a small percentage of creative minds is not surprising. Those who are to become real intellectual leaders require a more stimulating experience.

Students who wish, on the other hand, to take postgraduate work in medicine, law, library science, social work, engineering, and accounting, and those who wish to pursue advanced studies in the arts and sciences for the purpose of becoming college teachers, should be educated differently. Other divisions of the university should offer advanced instruction preparatory to the practice of a specialty in one of the professions. In medicine, for example, students commonly pursue a graduate program with the aim not of continuing a life of research but rather of entering specialized practice as an internist, ophthalmologist, or otolaryngologist. Likewise in schools of social work they study to become psychiatric social workers, probation officers, or public welfare administrators. It is unfortunate that these students have been expected to make original contributions to knowledge in the sense of doing fundamental research or led to believe that they have done so. Only confusion has eventuated from the practice of putting the development of a new technique in medical treatment, or the collection of a body of data on a particular social problem, in the same category with basic research. The fact of the matter is that a large percentage of these so-called contributions to knowledge are nothing of the sort in any honest sense. They are routine compilations of data on pedestrian subjects according to mechanical procedures. That is all they need be for the purpose they serve, and there can be no objection to awarding a graduate degree to one who goes through this process. The evil lies in confusing it with imaginative research, to the detriment of both.

The failure to recognize the essential differences between the work of the scholar and research worker, and the activities of practitioners, and of the consequent need for different educational programs for each, has had particularly unfortunate consequences in the case of college teachers. On the assumption that research and teaching are similar activities, the graduate program has been built around the work of the scholarly investigator, and the future college teacher has learned little of the art and science of his calling. The research worker, concerned with the minute analysis of an ever narrower area of reality, requires a knowledge of research techniques and skill in their use. The prospective teacher, on the other hand, though he should have an imaginative and vital mind and the capacity for critical analysis, must master wide ranges of subject matter, learn the habit of philosophic synthesis, and acquire certain pedagogical skills and professional attitudes.[d] It is not essential that the teacher spend much time in research activities (as earlier described) either as a graduate student or in his later life. If he has the special aptitude to do research, has an interest in it, and can find time for it without slighting his teaching, well and good. But

[d] Comment by Norman Foerster:
 Logically, such a stand seems unassailable. If you want investigators, produce them; if you want teachers, produce them. Yet I raise the question whether we can afford to be so literal. The practical facts themselves are averse: most of the good minds looking forward to a life of investigation are also looking forward, with varying degrees of interest, to a life of teaching. Admittedly, to combine the two objectives has some awkward consequences; but to separate them might well have still more awkward consequences.

for teaching, it is enough that he become acquainted with the sources of knowledge, acquire the habit of familiarizing himself with new knowledge, and cultivate the faculty of reflective synthesis. The vast majority of college teachers cannot hope to produce new knowledge. They have not done so in the past as the record so clearly shows. They should not be driven to try to do so in the future. But the graduate program is not based on a realistic view of these facts.

The future teacher may be handicapped by the very features of the graduate program which develop the research specialist, and *vice versa*. The education of investigators is one thing. The education of teachers is another. The prospective teacher should learn the art of teaching, the research worker the art of investigating. The failure to recognize that the two arts are not the same accounts for much mediocrity among those who attempt to practice them without possessing the necessary skills. Though they have elements in common each is sufficiently different to require special training. And students should decide at the earliest possible time in their graduate work which objective they are pursuing. Some who intend to become investigators will later decide that they wish to become teachers. If so, the period of their graduate study will have to be extended. If the research worker later decides to become a teacher he will have to learn the skills of his newly chosen profession. In no other profession would this requirement be considered unjust. If a Ph.D. in physiology chooses to become a physician, he must learn the art of the practice of medicine by studying clinical subjects. It is generally recognized that though they possess knowledge in common, a physiologist is not a physician. College education will be palpably improved when it is also generally recognized that a philosopher is not a pedagogue, nor a taxonomist, a teacher.[e]

[e]Comment by Norman Foerster:

The analysis does not appear to be a happy one. I cannot speak for the sciences, but when applied to the humanities the proposal opens up a melancholy prospect. Research in the humanities has long suffered too much from the kind of training suggested. What it needs today is a wide awareness, a critical sense of values, a genuine pertinence, and other qualities that enter equally into enlightened research and sound teaching. It is time for us to escape from the narrow positivistic and atomistic concept of research in the humanities, which flourished in Europe and America in the nineteenth century. Europe rejected it after the First World War; it lingers with us after the Second. Clearly, the first thing needed today is a reform of our education of investigating scholars. Once this has been achieved, we shall be gratified to find that scholars proposing to enter college teaching will be vastly better prepared for teaching, as well as for scholarship, and then the temptation to sunder the two functions and invite new problems and discontents will be removed.

Society urgently needs thousands of broadly educated, devoted, skillful college teachers to prepare the youth of the nation to cope with the urgent and complex problems of our time. These teachers can best be educated in institutions established for this specific purpose and attended by students dedicated to a life of teaching, just as medical schools are established to train doctors and are attended by those who aspire to membership in this profession. College teachers should be prepared by a graduate faculty charged with this particular responsibility and devoted to this task of such determinative significance in the life of our nation and of our time.[f]

This responsibility of universities to improve the education of college teachers is directly related to a fourth major goal, the education of youth to perform intelligently and responsibly all the activities of life in a democratic society. For the first two centuries of American higher education this was its almost exclusive function, but during the past hundred years liberal education has been gradually reduced to the position of handmaiden to the graduate and professional schools. Here again there is a confusion of ends. The liberal arts colleges once educated youth for the general activities of civic and personal life—and this was their sole function, all the tales about the training of ministers in early Harvard to the contrary, notwithstanding. Many colleges continue to declare such purposes in high sounding language and doubtless believe they are in a measure realizing the ends of liberal education, but these institutions devote their energies primarily to giving instruction which constitutes the first step in graduate or professional education. If a student gets a liberal education it is his own responsibility.

German university scholarship having become the dominant force in American higher education, the center of gravity even in the liberal arts colleges has shifted from the student to knowledge, from the education of the layman for the responsibilities of life, to the education of

---

However, these are minor objections to what I regard as the most statesmanlike utterance (whether address, article, or book) by an American leader in education in many a long year. It is even somewhat embarrassing for me to comment on Dean McGrath's paper, because I agree with it so heartily.

Of the four sections of the paper the most valuable, in my opinion, is the last and longest, dealing with the need of education for intelligent, responsible living in a democratic society. But I could not discuss it without virtually repeating what the author has said.

[f] [For discussion of this separation of functions in contrast with the views of Robert Ulich (Chapter I), see comment by Quincy Wright in Appendix III.]

the expert for the specialized activities of the library and the laboratory. Faculties have become preoccupied with research and the writing of learned treatises. Teaching young people how to live has become a matter of secondary importance. Except in a few universities such as Chicago and Columbia, the view of the liberal arts as the unifying and central element in higher education has disappeared. Universities are now aggregations of specialized teaching faculties, and liberal arts colleges assemblages of departments with little organic connection. The consequence of this separatism is a company of ostensibly educated men possessing no common knowledge, tastes, skills, attitudes, or compelling convictions.

Under the influence of this philosophy institutions of higher education have glorified vocationalism. Hence our people have become highly competent physicians, engineers, and social workers, but they have not gained in wisdom. As Ortega y Gasset has put it:

> Compared with the medieval university, the contemporary university has developed the mere seed of professional instruction into an enormous activity; it has added the function of research; and it has abandoned almost entirely the teaching or transmission of culture. It is evident that the change has been pernicious. Europe today is taking its sinister consequences. The convulsive situation in Europe at the present moment is due to the fact that the average Englishman, the average Frenchman, the average German are *uncultured:* they are ignorant of the essential system of ideas concerning the world and man, which belong to our time. This average person is the new barbarian, a laggard behind the contemporary civilization, archaic and primitive in contrast with his problems, which are grimly, relentlessly modern. This new barbarian is above all the professional man, more learned than ever before, but at the same time more uncultured—the engineer, the physician, the lawyer, the scientist.

If higher education is to educate the leaders of the nation and prepare citizens generally for the trying responsibilities of life in the modern world, liberal studies must again become the essential component in post high school education. The work of the colleges of liberal arts must be transformed from a preparation for advanced specialized study or professional education, into a preparation for life in a world that demands ever increasing knowledge and wisdom. This reorientation will be difficult to accomplish, for at present the professional schools and the graduate divisions with their emphasis on vocationalism, specialism, and utilitarianism, dominate higher education. Their philosophy has gradually been accepted in the colleges themselves. An embarrassing fact must be faced with candor and honesty before any real reform can occur. That fact is that *the academic profession itself is largely responsible for the present emphasis on specialized education and for the sickly condition of the liberal arts.* Education to equip this generation with the broad knowledge and the intellectual habits they will need more than any other men in history, if they are to survive and achieve the good life—this kind of higher education—many of our people want. And more would want it if its values were made clear to them by those who are supposed to be the stewards of the liberal traditions of Western European culture.

Many Americans, even those with little formal schooling, believe that their sons and daughters should be educated to understand this complex world and their place in it. They recognize that however well their own formal education may have prepared them to earn a living, it cultivated neither the understanding to cope intelligently and decisively with the pressing problems of the day, nor steadiness of view to see meaning in an age of swiftly changing values. There is abundant evidence that both adults and college students, when not misguided by vested academic interests with respect to the relative values of specialized, vocational instruction and the study of the great works of the Western intellectual tradition, will eagerly choose the latter. The naive mind uninfluenced by the proponents of specialized learning finds in the liberal disciplines a rich experience with the continuing problems of mankind, an experience which all human beings appreciate, for they know that these problems are their problems, that they will be the problems of their children, and of their children's children.

Educators who assert that the common run of men are interested only in subjects related to their occupation or the current practical problems of life, are usually expressing their own wishes and interests, for whenever students are given an opportunity, and are encouraged, to study the subjects which challenge the mind, elevate the spirit, and nurture wisdom, they seize it. Those who question this statement should observe the adult education program of the University of Chicago in which thousands of men and women in all walks of life, all levels of society, all types of vocation, and all varieties of faith, continue year after year to attend classes in which the great texts of literature, science, and philosophy are analyzed and discussed. To some of these men and women the earning of a better living is an urgent matter. Yet they choose to spend their evenings not in studying accounting, engineering, or drafting, but *The Apology, The Republic,* and *The Decline and Fall of the Roman Empire.* Likewise the students in the college at Chicago and at Columbia, where a real education in the liberal arts and sciences is available, are not resentful because they are required for the better part of four years to study the same works.[g] They are vitally interested in their studies, they participate eagerly in class discussions, and they carry these discussions forward in the corridors, the dormitories, and the eating halls. But neither these adults nor these students, are subject to the pressures and the baleful influence of the specialist. Hence they do not "know enough" to be uninterested in the subjects that will help them most to understand their fellow men and the world in which they live.

No, the average American, if unadvised by the members of the profession, will not embrace the specialistic philosophy of the schoolmen. Men and women outside the universities are asking that higher education minister to the intellectual and spiritual needs of all men, not the peculiar needs of the physician, the accountant, the lawyer, the nurse, or the radio operator, but the needs which these and all other human beings have in common.

Let one, whose voice is now sadly stilled, speak on this subject. In 1943, Wendell Willkie, observing the nation engaged in the most inhuman war in history, said,

> I think it can be stated as almost an historical truism that the greatest civilizations of history have been the best educated civilizations. And when I speak of education in this sense I do not have in mind what so many today claim as education, namely, special training to do particular jobs. Clearly, in a technological age like ours, a great deal of training is necessary. Some of us must learn how to be mechanics, some how to be architects, or chemists. Some will have a special aptitude for medicine. And a great many will have—or think they have—a mysterious talent which induces them to undertake the practice of law.

[g] [For further discussion of the "Chicago Plan," see Chapter II by Lyman Bryson, Chapter III by T. V. Smith, Chapter VIII by Alain L. Locke, Chapter IX by Howard Mumford Jones, Chapter XI by John U. Nef, Chapter XIII by Mordecai M. Kaplan, Chapter XV by George N. Shuster, Chapter XVII by Ordway Tead, and George B. de Huszar's comment in Appendix III.]

But none of these specialties constitute true education. They are training for skills by which men live. I am thinking, rather, of what we call the liberal arts. I am speaking of education for its own sake; to know for the sheer joy of understanding; to speculate, to analyze, to compare, and to imagine.

. . . you are told that they are of little help to a man in earning his living or in making a contribution to his fellow men. The thing to do, you are told, is to get trained; learn an occupation; make yourself proficient in some trade or profession. Of course this advice is sound, so far as it goes. But the inference, and sometimes the outright declaration that frequently follows it, strikes at the very roots of our society. The liberal arts, we are told, are luxuries. At best you should fit them into your leisure time. They are mere decorations upon the sterner pattern of life which must be lived in action and by the application of skills. When such arguments gain acceptance that is the end of us as a civilized nation.[4]

It is claimed that the taxpayer will not support liberal education because he considers it a luxury. If this be so, educators are to blame. They have not been the proponents of liberal studies. How many legislative halls have resounded with pleas for liberal education? Is it strange that funds are easily obtained for a new pig barn at the college of agriculture, or a new cyclotron at the university? These projects have their advocates. But when have university officers requested a hundred thousand dollars for the improvement of instruction in political science the better to prepare the young for the responsibilities of citizenship in a troubled world? It yet remains to be shown that legislatures have more interest in pigs than in children, more interest in horticulture than human culture.

The public has relied upon educators to maintain a balanced program of instruction to prepare the young not only to earn a living, but to live intelligently in all the various phases of life. But the universities, and increasingly in recent decades the colleges, as well, have been interested primarily in the former. At least they have been more successful in preparing the members of the professional and managerial classes for their occupational responsibilities than for civic and social leadership. The

---

[4] Wendell Willkie, "The Importance of Liberal Education Policies," address at Duke University, January 14, 1943, broadcast over the Mutual Broadcasting Company network. Published in *Vital Speeches*, IX, February 15, 1943.

latter they cannot do until liberal studies again become the cornerstone of all higher education.

This proposal that the liberal subjects be restored to a central place in the university does not require that all youth who seek post high school education be herded together on one campus in an enormous liberal arts college. It is doubtful indeed whether the chief values of humane learning can be realized amid the current hurly-burly of university life. The turbulence and confusion of the campus is hardly more conducive to reflective thought and calm judgment than the excitement of the ball park. It is time to reduce the size of these institutions to manageable proportions by establishing new units in state educational systems, removed from the main campus and devoted principally to undergraduate education. Large private universities might accomplish a similar reduction in the size of liberal arts divisions by encouraging young people to attend the small private colleges which would be able to provide a better liberal education if they devoted their energies and their limited resources solely to this purpose and stopped the practice of trying to match the professional instruction of larger and more adequately endowed institutions.

The advantages in such a plan of decentralization are numerous, the disadvantages negligible. In many states it could be put into effect quickly by transforming some existing junior colleges into four year institutions, or by taking under public auspices four year colleges now struggling for existence under the handicap of too few students or inadequate resources. In some instances entirely new institutions would have to be built, but the cost to the state would be more than justified by the added educational opportunities thus made available to its youth. This proposal to decentralize education is consonant with a recommendation of the President's Commission on Higher Education which found that opportunity for higher education varied with the region in which a young person lived. To make college education more generally available to American youth it recommended the founding of additional institutions in educationally underprivileged areas.[h]

[h][For further discussion of the report of the President's Commission, cf. Chapter I by Robert Ulich (including comment by Rowland W. Dunham), Louis J. A. Mercier's comment on Chapter II by Lyman Bryson, Chapter VII by Charles W. Hendel, and Chapter XIII by Mordecai M. Kaplan.]

The greatest advantages of a system of separate four year liberal arts colleges, however, would be pedagogical in character. There is no exact scientific formula for determining the optimal size of a class or an institution. Universities, however, which crowd twenty or thirty thousand students together on a single campus have probably reached a size which actually interferes with educational efficiency. In any case a college of one or two thousand students with a curriculum limited to essential subjects would be better able to maintain classes of manageable size, sound teaching procedures, and stimulating faculty student relationships than the larger universities. Such a college might nourish the qualities of mind and spirit that have been the justifiable pride of those private liberal arts colleges which have not tried to imitate the larger institutions by becoming all things to all men. A system of state colleges properly located with relation to distribution of population and the sites of existing institutions, would increase the opportunity for, and improve the quality of, higher education. In these institutions superior education in the liberal arts could be provided at relatively small expense.

In the future, liberal arts education will probably flourish best if it is entirely removed from the university community. It will then be free from many of the influences which now stifle and stultify it. But this will be a slow process. For the present it can at best be hoped that an increasing number of students will attend these separate liberal arts colleges. Traditions and vested interests within the universities and pressure groups of alumni and townspeople outside will no doubt prevent the complete removal of liberal arts colleges from large university campuses for some years. If, however, they remain a part of the university community the liberal arts colleges must become identifiable corporate entities with their own purposes and their own integrity. The liberal arts college cannot remain what it is at present, a collection of loosely related, semi-autonomous departments primarily concerned with the teaching of preprofessional and prospective graduate students. It must have a mission of its own, a purpose as vital as that which now animates the life of the other divisions of the university. As long as the faculties of the college of liberal arts give their first loyalty and principal interest to the graduate and professional schools, the college will continue to have inferior teaching, a weak *esprit de corps,* confused purposes, and students who do not understand the value of liberal education and hence do not believe in it.

In order to have a being of its own, the liberal arts college should have a plant, a faculty, and a budget of its own. There is no more justification for erecting special classrooms, dormitories, and laboratories for medical students, or law courts, and libraries for law students, than for providing suitable accommodations for liberal arts students. These colleges, now so enormous in state institutions ought to be divided into units of a few hundred students, a corporate body very much like the college in the English universities, with living quarters, eating halls, library facilities, classrooms, and a common hall for public discussions and other group activities. If only the small number of courses needed for a genuine liberal education were offered the majority of classes could be held in such houses. The wasteful multiplication of courses in the advanced branches of the various disciplines which now constitutes such a heavy and unnecessary expense, and at the same time a vitiation of true liberal education, could be avoided.

The program and the educational policy of such a college should be determined by a group of liberally educated faculty members, who no longer pressed by the need to do research (though some could and would do so) might devote their efforts and their imagination to the education of youth for responsible and informed citizenship in a society of free men. For the present they would have to gain a liberal education after leaving the graduate schools, as these institutions often not only do not provide, but actually forbid, it. As members of a liberal arts faculty, freed from the extraneous pressures of research, writing, and specialized teaching, such a faculty could instruct students in the basic liberal disciplines and cultivate those intellectual habits of analysis, reflection, criticism, and synthesis which have always characterized men of learning and of culture. In time statesmen and leaders in all walks of life might be so educated as to direct the energies of their countrymen into humanly useful enterprises. Eventually a citizenry possessing common ideals, a common knowledge, and a common social purpose, might evolve.

The education of citizens for a responsible life in a free society—this is the first responsibility of a system of higher education. If higher education does this it will eventually give intellectual direction and spiritual force to American life. If higher education does less, it will have broken faith with the great intellectual and moral traditions of Western culture and in time it will go down with this culture.[1]

These, then, are the objectives of higher education in the United States. Two of these purposes have been substantially realized in the development of the schools which train the members of the professions and the managerial occupations, and in the teaching and research activities which meet the day by day needs of the supporting constituency. Two other objectives, the encouragement of research and the training of scholars, and the education of youth to perform intelligently and responsibly all the activities of life in a democratic society, have not been sufficiently realized. What is required at this juncture in American life is a studious reconsideration of these two latter objectives of university education and a critical analysis of the policies and practices which make their attainment impossible.

Any genuine improvement, however, must await a general recognition of the fact that we have been successful in the areas of higher instruction which deal with the application of knowledge to the practical problems of life, the building of bridges, the improvement of sanitation, the nurture of crops, the preservation of food, the development of television, and the creation of enormous industrial organizations. We have been less successful in the building of philosophic systems, the improvement of morals, the nurture of spiritual resources, the preservation of

---

[1] Comment by B. Othanel Smith:
Most of what Dean McGrath asserts about the restructuring of universities claims my favorable reaction. We cannot properly educate either for the professions or research so long as these two functions are under the same administrative head. When Dean McGrath turns to liberal education, however, his views seem to be developed less from a careful social diagnosis of our times than from traditional class notions of education. The liberal arts, as they are conceived of historically, may develop the kind of persons Dean McGrath wishes no more than the colleges of liberal arts and sciences are now developing them. It may be that we shall have to develop a new conception of liberal education for our times if democratic men are to be built. I see no reason to suppose that those who now claim discipline in the great books, or in the liberal arts, are any more understanding and considerate of their fellow men than those who claim no such discipline. The students who have completed the so-called better liberal arts programs show no more of the characteristics of democratic men than students who have gone through colleges of agriculture and other vocational schools. To say the least, it would be wiser to ask for the evidence before we accept some of the notions of a liberal education now being paraded by various individuals. If a liberal education is to do anything more than change the way individuals talk, it will be necessary to redefine such an education in terms of modern psychological and sociological knowledge of human nature and human behavior.

peace, the development of character, and the creation of great masterpieces of art and literature. Perhaps this is what should have been expected in an infant culture engaged in the enervating task of conquering a great continent, a culture in which the rewards of life went to those whose wits provided relief from the crudities, the hardships, and the frustrations of a life close to nature. But America has physically come of age. With the collapse of European culture and the devitalization of the universities which sustained it, the cultural center of gravity has shifted to the United States. The universities of this nation now have the responsibility to promote and encourage the fundamental type of investigation which has distinguished their sister institutions in Europe, while at the same time educating our people not only for the trying responsibilities within our own land, but also for citizenship in a troubled and restless world. Such education must create a broader understanding, a greater poise, a more serene spirit, a more balanced judgment, and a more comprehensive wisdom than institutions of higher education have hitherto produced. The recent war demonstrated that the universities have tremendous capacity for adapting their programs to the needs of a national emergency. In a very real sense a larger emergency now exists in which the values for which universities through the ages have stood and fought are in jeopardy at home and abroad. All Americans may confidently expect these institutions so to change their purposes and their ways as to prepare our people to meet this emergency with courage and with wisdom.[j]

[j] Comment by Harry B. Friedgood:

Many of us, who are concerned with the problems of medical education, would not hesitate to apply Dean McGrath's constructive criticisms of higher education in the university at large directly to the context and methodology of the medical curriculum—in consequence of which I am inclined to question his remark that "the American university has been signally successful" in training physicians. It is true that we have graduated relatively large numbers of doctors who are as qualified to practice medicine as any in the world; but to express satisfaction with their understanding of the social implications of medicine is another matter. With the ever increasing recognition that medicine is essentially a social science, this is a serious indictment of the university training offered to candidates for the M.D. degree.

The conventional approach to the study of medicine has been made by what may be termed the departmentalized or compartmentalized method, inasmuch as each course of the four year schedule is taught in separate departments without adequate reference to continuity with, or relation to, the other subjects. Although efforts are being made in many schools to depart from this orthodox practice, the medical curriculum still persists largely in its original form. The departmentalization which characterizes the latter resembles the organizational structure of grade schools, secondary schools, colleges, graduate institutions and other professional schools. This pattern of pedagogy has perpetuated a fundamental archaic defect since it reflects the scholastic philosophy of antecedent generations based upon the concept that knowledge, *per se,* is the ultimate purpose of education. This viewpoint fails to give proper emphasis to another primary objective of education, namely the application of knowledge to an understanding of man and of his relations to the dynamic social and natural forces of the world in which he lives. The widespread recognition of this more comprehensive approach to the meaning of education demands the correlation of allied fields of knowledge. The failure to achieve adequately this correlation, particularly in the medical sciences, is a matter of historical record.

There is also a lack of correlation between the basic natural and medical sciences and the social sciences, which are taught in the graduate and undergraduate divisions of the rest of the university. It has become increasingly clear of late that the social sciences (psychology, sociology, anthropology, history, political science, etc.) have a direct bearing on the modern practice of medicine. The ever increasing realization that social factors play a basically important role in the etiology of disease dovetails with a dynamic view of the total personality structure.

I would also underscore the importance of what Dean McGrath has said about the vast difference between the training of scholarly investigators and the preparation of individuals for a professional career. In principle, I find myself completely in accord with his view on this matter; but from a practical viewpoint one is tempted to amend his suggestion that "these two functions of the university need to be differentiated, and an educational program designed specifically for each." There is the risk that his proposal will be interpreted too literally, and that the source of inspiration which stems from contact with scholarly investigators, and which should touch upon the life of each medical student, will be denied to those who need it most; for without the research point of view, the pursuit of medical practice loses its main dynamic component.

CHAPTER XVII

The Role of Objectives in Higher Education

By ORDWAY TEAD
Chairman, Board of Higher Education, City of New York

THE BIBLICAL STATEMENT that of the making of books there is no end can be paraphrased to a similar truth that of the making of college objectives there is no end.

And my theme will be suggested by invoking another familiar saying that there is many a slip 'twixt the cup and the lip. In other words, it is one thing to state desirable objectives; it is something else again to be sure that they are given effect. And the major problem with which I am here concerned is as to the ways and means of translating statements of college objectives into the actual performance of suitable educational activities.

Formulations of college objectives add up today to an embarrassment of riches—an observation not intended in any way to belittle their importance. It has to be recognized, however, that such formulations are easy to make; they are usually cast in noble, beguiling, and general phrases; their very nobility and generality are deceptive because of the human tendency to assume that handsome is as handsome says. Also, the diversity of objectives to be examined readily becomes confusing to those who read them, even before the operating problem of implementing them may arise.

Presented as we are, therefore, with this seeming embarrassment of riches as to what colleges are trying to do, it seems worthwhile to explore the role of objectives in terms which place less stress upon what they say than on what they do operationally in making college education more effective.

I propose, therefore, to consider the following facets of the problem:

Why do we have objectives?

What are examples of typical expressions of these from differing points of view?

How have they come to be formulated?

Under what conditions do they actually have any relation to changes in the method and content of instruction?

Do we know from experience how it is that formulations of objective, aim, or purpose, do in fact get translated into instructional changes of a significant character?

Also, do we have any adequate ways of evaluating the worth of new or different objectives?

In other words, is the whole question of what goes on educationally a matter which can be tested in order to determine whether outcomes in the minds and behavior of students are better or worse as objectives are studied, shaped, and altered?

My reason for posing these questions is that a mere scrutinizing of the abundance of such formulations as have been made in recent years may supply less evidence of educational advance in and of itself, than of the wishfulness and the verbal felicity of those who may have the boldness to proffer such new aims.

I do not question that statements of educational objectives can serve a useful purpose. Whether they do or not depends on a variety of factors which I propose to consider. But, generally speaking, when, as, and if, such statements can come to have some close relation to educational behavior, they can clearly serve as something of a compass, something of a bill of rights, something of a charter of authority as to the obligations, powers, and techniques controlling those who conduct the education.

Indeed, it is important to recognize that objectives can have value at several different levels of operation. They might have some guiding value in relation to a national educational policy which for good or ill our country does not yet possess. They clearly can have an institutional value in that each college would wisely enunciate what its specific purposes are. Beyond that there is the objective of an individual department or division of instruction. There is the objective of a specific full year or half year course in a particular subject; and there should be the objective of each specific class hour.

It is on the whole with institutional, long range objectives that I am here primarily concerned.

The Value in Diversity of Statements of Objectives

The question may well be initially faced as to the desirability of the wide variety of statements of college objectives. The time has certainly not yet come when we can safely say that the present multiplicity is undesirable. Rather our awareness of the importance of such statements is relatively so new found that we stand to profit by as much diversity here as is consistent with broad ends which any substantial number of people, educators and others, stand ready to defend. They can thus be a stimulus to exploratory thinking even before they reach the stage of shaping any particular curriculum.

In our American tradition, moreover, there is undoubted value in varied approaches to the stating and realizing of objectives. And to characterize some of the different types of formulations should be helpful to fuller understanding. Indeed, the present danger is not in diversity but in too great fixity or too great inflexibility of aims that may be held to by those in any particular institutions over too long a time without periodic reexamination and appraisal.

Several kinds of possible justifiable diversity of objectives may be initially noted as having potential value—or at least excuse for being. Perhaps the largest two way division today is that to be found as between colleges conducted under public support and those privately controlled. There is the further division between solely undergraduate colleges, usually smaller in size and in smaller communities, and those which are affiliates of a great university.

There is, finally, the distinction between objectives to be observed in the so-called church related colleges and in those which have no explicit religious affiliation.

It is impossible within the scope of this discussion to spell out all the possible differences in general objectives as they might arise under these different institutional settings. That certain differences can be justified here is obvious almost by definition. But beyond this obvious point, I see no intrinsic reason why the basic approach to and content of objectives of these several different kinds of college have necessarily to be profoundly different. The possible theoretical difference between colleges supported by religious bodies and those not so supported is no doubt an exception to this statement, although operationally the differences are often less pronounced.

This similarity seems true despite the fact that the quality of educational *experience* in a small college in a country community may clearly result for the student in something quite different from his total experience in the college of a Columbia or Harvard University, even though on paper the objectives may read similarly.

A deeper reason for diversity is that a genuine confusion or at least lack of agreement among competent students as to what is desired and how it is desired to achieve it, are facts of our educational scene. The disparity stems from profound philosophical and theological causes. And to attempt at this time to discourage exploration both as to ends and as to means would be like trying to order a moratorium on scientific discovery. Rather we shall all be the gainers by the contributions of diverse, and indeed of contradictory, formulations.

Kinds of Objectives

Summarily viewed, we find a number of broad categories of objectives. The first type of difference is that between *general* statements of independent thinkers designed for wide public enlightenment and formulations made *ad hoc* to clarify policy for a single institution. One could, for example, cull much of a general nature from such a volume as Dr. Robert Ulich's *Three Thousand Years of Educational Wisdom*.[1] And the illumination and inspiration of such good historic utterances can be great. As of our own day, Alfred North Whitehead and John Dewey come at once to mind as generalizers of objectives which have without doubt had large influence.

Another division *sui generis* is that between objectives which have either a philosophical or *a priori* theological basis and those more inductively derived. Such induction may grow out of psychological, educational (methodologically viewed), or nationalistic premises.

The broad division between the intellectualistic, the "character" and the total personality approach, is another way of characterizing certain features of familiar differentiation. Indeed, so much to the fore is the controversy about these alternatives that it is worthwhile to let Chan-

[1] Harvard University Press, Cambridge, 1947.

cellor Robert M. Hutchins of the University of Chicago[a] set forth his intellectualistic position as follows:

> One purpose of education is to draw out the elements of our common human nature. These elements are the same in any time or place. The notion of educating a man to live in any particular time or place, to adjust him to any particular environment, is therefore foreign to a true conception of education.
>
> Education implies teaching. Teaching implies knowledge. Knowledge is truth. The truth is everywhere the same. Hence education should be everywhere the same. I do not overlook the possibilities of differences in organization, in administration, in local habits and customs. These are details. I suggest that the heart of any course of study designed for the whole people will be, if education is rightly understood, the same at any time, in any place, under any political, social or economic conditions. Even the administrative details are likely to be similar because all societies have generic similarity.
>
> If education is rightly understood, it will be understood as the cultivation of the intellect. The cultivation of the intellect is the same good for all men in all societies. It is, moreover, the good for which all other goods are only means. Material prosperity, peace and civil order, justice and the moral virtues are means to the cultivation of the intellect.[2]

As brilliant an exponent as any of the *character* objective is the Vice Chancellor of the University of Oxford, Sir Richard Livingston. In his volume, *Some Tasks for Education*,[3] he says:

> It is not surprising that human character has not improved, for we have never taken its improvement seriously in hand. We have spent time and careful thought on physical health; but what have we done comparable for the health of the character? Our system of spiritual or ethical medicine (if I may so phrase it) is in much the same position as medicine itself in the eighteenth century; good in patches, but wholly inadequate and generally unprogressive, and needing, if any real advance is to be made, hard thought, exact study, and methodical treatment.

---

[a] [For further discussion of the "Chicago Plan," see Chapter II by Lyman Bryson, Chapter III by T. V. Smith, Chapter VIII by Alain L. Locke, Chapter IX by Howard Mumford Jones, Chapter XI by John U. Nef, Chapter XIII by Mordecai M. Kaplan, Chapter XV by George N. Shuster, Chapter XVI by Earl J. McGrath, and George B. de Huszar's comment in Appendix III.]

[2] *The Higher Learning in America*, Yale University Press, New Haven, 1936, pp. 66–67.
[3] Oxford University Press, London, 1946, p. 33.

And in his lecture, "Plato and Modern Education,"[4] he pronounces as follows:

> Finally—and most important—everyone needs a philosophy of life, a sense of values by which to judge and use the gifts of material civilization. The perfectly educated man would have a standard, a perception of values, in every province—physical, aesthetic, intellectual, moral; in his profession or occupation; in personal, national and international life. He would know the first rate in all of them and run no risk of being deceived by the inferior. Further, as far as this is possible, he would have a hierarchy of values, so that lesser did not dominate greater goods. No age needs a sense of the first rate more than our own. We are individualists; without standards to control it, individualism is apt to reveal itself as eccentricity and to end in chaos. We are free; without standards freedom only gives greater latitude of error. Our possessions and opportunities multiply; without standards we have no idea of their relative value, no principle of choice among them, except the whim of the moment. No doubt the perfectly educated man does not exist and never will exist. But the quality of a civilization depends on the number of people in it who approximate to this standard, and we should at least set such an ideal before us.

Another kind of classification is possible in terms of an emphasis in aims upon the passing on of a total cultural heritage and equipment for dealing with a presumably known set of social facts and forces as contrasted with an emphasis upon education as directed toward social reorganization or the reconstruction of society. Advocates of the latter position have a strong exponent, for example, in the writings among others of George S. Counts of Teachers College, Columbia University.

In current curriculum building, we see the influence of aims which may be characterized in these three ways—the offering of a common body of needed content to enable the student to function in our times, of which Columbia College of Columbia University stands as the most impressive witness; the "student centered" approach which builds on individual student interests and capabilities of which Sarah Lawrence is an outstanding exemplar;[b] and the "functional" approach of building around life interests and activities such as citizenship, parenthood, vocation, etc., of which Stephens College is the proud devotee.

[b] [Cf. Chapter XVIII by President Harold Taylor of Sarah Lawrence College.]

[4] The Macmillan Company, New York, 1944, p. 25.

The Role of Objectives in Higher Education 411

Each of these types proceeds from objectives more or less clearly formulated and definitely controlling educational policy and practice.

I mention without elaboration the further possibility of which Soviet Russia supplies us with an impressive illustration, namely, of objectives shaped by ends of national philosophy and policy, in which the ends of the "state" are paramount.

Samples of Objectives

Coming now to a brief view of representative, individual statements in the current scene, the following by Professor Howard Mumford Jones is interesting for its concreteness:

> I suggest then, that American colleges ought to consider some such program as this:
> 1. Professional or vocational training for all.
> 2. The study of the theory of science and of the application of scientific discoveries to our technology.
> 3. The assumptions and workings of representative government, particularly in the United States and in the British Commonwealth of Nations.
> 4. The study of Russia.
> 5. The study of the Orient.
> 6. The study of personal relationships in modern society.[5]

In the light of Professor Jones's formulation, it is interesting to note the emphasis in the following paragraph from Professor F. S. C. Northrop's *The Meeting of East and West:*[6]

> The task of the contemporary world falls into four major parts: (1) the relating of the East and the West; (2) the similar merging of the Latin and Anglo-Saxon cultures; (3) the mutual reinforcement of democratic and communistic values; and (4) the reconciliation of the true and valuable portions of the Western medieval and modern worlds. Running through all these special tasks is the more general one, made imperative with the advent of the atomic bomb, of harmonizing the sciences and the humanities.

[5] *Education and World Tragedy,* Harvard University Press, Cambridge, 1946, p. 91. [Cf. Chapter IX in this volume, by Howard Mumford Jones.]
[6] The Macmillan Company, New York, 1946, p. 436.

The emphasis in the statements both of Professor Jones and Professor Northrop gains added importance in the light of an interesting and forthright *critical* statement about American educational aims expressed by a South American scholar:

> But the feeling that we are without roots, or, what is still more serious, that our roots tie us to a world different from that which surrounds us, is a common ailment in both Americas. Hence, in the case of the United States, education has been conceived as a huge laboratory for the absorption into the North American nationality of people from all parts of the world, having the most varied and unmatched cultural, linguistic, ethnic and religious backgrounds. . . .
>
> Contrary to what is generally said, the yield of the great melting pot of the United States has not been left to chance. Whether they wanted to or not, the successive waves of immigrants who arrived at the shores of North America had to fit themselves to the mold of the civilization established by the first English colonists on the Atlantic Coast. A code was thus evolved which has permitted one hundred and fifty million people, whose affinity is not based on any of the postulates which contributed to the formation of the old nations of Europe, to fit together, in the environment of moral and psychological monotony which characterizes the United States.
>
> By refusing to assimilate the non-European ethnic groups—Negroes, Indians and Asiatics—the United States, though it has achieved organic unity of the nation for the moment, has only put off for the future a problem bristling with difficulties.[7]

One of the most widely heralded recent statements of objectives of higher education is that to be found in the Report of the President's Commission on Higher Education.[c] Because of the official character of this utterance and because it draws upon a widely accepted contemporary view of educational purposes, it is worthy of reproduction here:

1. To develop for the regulation of one's personal and civic life a code of behavior based on ethical principles consistent with democratic ideas.

---

[c] [For further discussion of the report of the President's Commission, see Chapter I by Robert Ulich (including comment by Rowland W. Dunham), Louis J. A. Mercier's comment on Chapter II by Lyman Bryson, Chapter IV by Karl W. Deutsch, Chapter VII by Charles W. Hendel, Chapter XIII by Mordecai M. Kaplan.]

[7] Juan Oropesa, "Contrasting Philosophies of Education North and South," *Points of View*, 10, Pan American Union, Washington, D.C., September, 1947.

The Role of Objectives in Higher Education 413

2. To participate actively as an informed and responsible citizen in solving the social, economic, and political problems of one's community, State and Nation.
3. To recognize the interdependence of the different peoples of the world and one's personal responsibility for fostering international understanding and peace.
4. To understand the common phenomena in one's physical environment, to apply habits of scientific thought to both personal and civic problems, and to appreciate the implications of scientific discoveries for human welfare.
5. To understand the ideas of others and to express one's own effectively.
6. To attain a satisfactory emotional and social adjustment.
7. To maintain and improve one's own health and to cooperate actively and intelligently in solving community health problems.
8. To understand and enjoy literature, art, music and other cultural activities as expressions of personal and social experience, and to participate to some extent in some form of creative activity.
9. To acquire the knowledge and attitudes basic to a satisfying family life.
10. To choose a socially useful and personally satisfying vocation that will permit one to use to the full his particular interests and abilities.
11. To acquire and use the skills and habits involved in critical and constructive thinking.[8]

Further evidence of a growing consensus of outlook upon objectives is indicated by the following from the excellent volume, *Higher Education in the South*:[9]

> The cooperative studies on which this report is based are in general agreement that the aims of collegiate instruction are:
> 1. To enable the student to acquire a relatively large amount of information and skill (physical and mental) and to further such attainment by developing habits of sustained intellectual effort in the mastery of subject-matter and skill;
> 2. To develop clearness and accuracy of thought and expression;
> 3. To develop intellectual independence and initiative together with the ability to form sound judgments;
> 4. To establish fundamental interests which result in continuous intellectual curiosity and activity and in respect for the intellectual way of life;

---

[8] *Higher Education for American Democracy*, A Report of the President's Commission on Higher Education, Harper & Brothers, New York, 1948, I, Chapter III, pp. 50–57.
[9] The University of North Carolina Press, Chapel Hill, 1947, p. 71.

5. To inculcate a sense of social responsibility based upon a sound conception of human values;
6. To develop aesthetic, moral, and spiritual standards and values, thereby permanently elevating and enriching life.

Coming now to formulations which have been derived close to the scene of action in the individual institution, I shall content myself with three representative offerings. The first is from the widely known *General Education in a Free Society*, a report of a Harvard Faculty Committee on which policy changes have been based.[10]

> Education looks both to the nature of knowledge and to the good of man in society. It is to the latter aspect that we shall now turn our attention—more particularly to the traits and characteristics of mind fostered by education.
>
> By characteristics we mean aims so important as to prescribe how general education should be carried out and which abilities should be sought above all others in every part of it. These abilities, in our opinion, are: *to think effectively, to communicate thought, to make relevant judgments, to discriminate among values.* They are not in practice separable and are not to be developed in isolation. Nor can they be even analyzed in separation. Each is an indispensable coexistent function of a sanely growing mind.

Amherst College has published (January, 1945) its *Report of the Faculty Committee on Long Range Policy*, and here again, we have a document which has been put directly into use in shaping the reorganized curriculum of the postwar period.

In this report we find the following:[11]

> If a liberal education is to be comprehensive, it should be organized in such a way as to unify the most fundamental cultural interests of the society in which we live. The curriculum, we believe, should be organized around three basic foci of interest: the mathematical, physical and biological sciences, history and the social sciences, and literature and the fine arts. The organization and exposition of subjects should be in terms of these great divisions rather than in terms of a number of diverse departments and a multitude of separate courses. Every student should be required to do at least as much work in each of these three divisions of the curriculum as will give him the sense that he has a community of knowledge and interests with all of his fellow students.

[10] Harvard University Printing Office, Cambridge, 1945, pp. 64–65.
[11] Pp. 25–26.

Nothing is more in contradiction with the purpose of a liberal education than a curriculum composed of large numbers of discrete and uncoordinated courses all treated as though they were of equal importance. This kind of laissez-faire program is a confession of intellectual bankruptcy. That a faculty should not prescribe certain courses as an essential part of a liberal education is as if a physician should refuse to prescribe specifically for his patient on the ground that all the available remedies would undoubtedly have *some* effect. It is the elective system more than any other thing that has led to the disconnected way of treating subjects which has done so much to destroy the vitality of our modern curriculum. If students are taught fragments, they cannot learn to think in terms of wholes. This means that the curriculum should be strictly limited in character. There should be far fewer courses than there are now in the program of the average college. To limit the number of courses is not to say that a knowledge of excluded subjects is undesirable. Everything, obviously, is worth knowing in some relation or for some purpose. But some things are in general better worth knowing because they have more relations and fulfil larger purposes than do others.

And one final exhibit is offered because of the concrete no less than comprehensive nature of the objectives defined. The following comes from the Pennsylvania College for Women:

> The areas of knowledge in which every intelligent person should acquire understanding fall conveniently into five.
>
> 1. A study of man as a human organism.
> 2. A study of the universe he inhabits.
> 3. A study of his social relationships.
> 4. A study of his esthetic achievements.
> 5. A study of his attempt to organize his experience.
>
> The faculty at Pennsylvania College for Women regards knowledge as a means, not an end. The end is wisdom, a deep understanding of life and an effective means of adjustment to it. Wisdom in action, therefore, requires more than acquaintance with fact; it involves the acquisition of certain basic abilities, and attitudes.
>
> The abilities which a student is expected to acquire are:
>
> 1. The ability to express oneself clearly in speech and writing.
> 2. The ability to demonstrate critical insight and imagination.
> 3. The ability to seek out sources of information adequate to the task involved.
> 4. The ability to remember selectively and precisely.

5. The ability to observe with care and discrimination.
6. The ability to concentrate on a given problem until an adequate conclusion is reached.
7. The ability to make unbiased, objective judgments, based upon knowledge.
8. The ability to synthesize and correlate.
9. The ability to express oneself creatively.
10. The ability to demonstrate taste in perception.[d]
11. The ability to apportion one's time wisely and to use it productively.
12. The ability to live and to cooperate with others.

The socially contrived attitudes which the student is expected to express in his living are:

1. Perseverance in the pursuit of knowledge and understanding.
2. Integrity in thought and action.
3. Courage to take the initiative.
4. Critical appraisal of one's abilities and achievements.
5. Understanding of and appreciation for other races and cultures.
6. Eagerness to develop spiritual insight.[12]

Methods of Formulation of Objectives

I have already intimated that general philosophical or educational utterances have undoubtedly had a stimulative value upon the thinking of individual educators. But the problem of the hour is as to how single institutions fertilize their thinking for a revamping of ends and means. Typically, we find the procedures employed to be the selection of a faculty committee, instigated usually by the president or dean of the college. Such committees have in some instances been handpicked by appointment from above and in others been elected by the appropriate faculty body. And their mandates and their resources may vary con-

[d]Comment by Rowland W. Dunham:
Dr. Tead's study of objectives, as formulated by individual educators and groups, causes a certain disappointment to me, as a professional musician, due to the neglect of an area that seems vital indeed to educating any person. This area is, of course, the emotions and imagination along with the matter of discrimination. In this statement by the faculty at Pennsylvania College for Women items 2 and 10 might well be quite as applicable to men as to women. The lack of taste and imagination in all sorts of application are two of the general characteristics of college people which irritate me most. With these qualifications lacking I cannot accept even the most brilliant Phi Beta Kappas as actually cultured people.

[12]"Educating for Tomorrow," *Bulletin of Pennsylvania College for Women,* XLII, September, 1946, pp. 7–8.

siderably. Perhaps the most important features of the outstanding and influential efforts here are: first, strong encouragement and support from the administrative head; second, the according of sufficient time away from teaching to allow the committee or at least its chairman to do the necessary thinking, studying, interviewing, and traveling; and third, some broad initial agreement among the leaders of this effort as to the general line of policy to be followed. Here as in other types of inquiry, it is clearly necessary to have premises, and to establish the validity of the premises is one of the proper intentions of the study.

In practical terms, one of the most urgent problems is to assure that the committee is rigorously taking an attitude of concern for the *over all* educational processes of the college and is not being unduly influenced in its thinking or decisions by the special interests of the several teachers preoccupied to protect the interests of individual departments, subjects, or favorite courses. It has not proved easy in certain institutions for faculties to rise above preconceptions and presuppositions of their own particular subject matter fields. And the generalization is warranted that the value of these faculty reports has therefore varied considerably from college to college. Indeed, there have been cases where faculties have reaffirmed existing objectives and methods despite strong minority reports to the contrary. To secure the collaboration of faculty members on a basis of disinterested educational inquiry rather than on the level of special pleading for particular subjects, is *the* condition prerequisite to progress here.

It is this consideration which lends special interest to further inquiry into the methods of helping faculties in their deliberations to transcend departmental interests and be concerned for total educational effectiveness as defined by a fresh and contemporary view of objectives for the particular institution.[e]

[e]Comment by Louis W. Norris:
There is much value, by way of cross-fertilization, in the great variety of aims found in American education by Dr. Tead. Nevertheless the common charge made by fascists and communists alike, that democracy in general and American democracy in particular, has no clearly defined policy on anything (and also their readiness to take advantage of this indecision), suggests that we would do well to struggle manfully for a unity of aims. The Report of the President's Commission on Higher Education might well serve as a starting point. All American schools are parts of American democracy, and presumably their graduates expect to take their place in such a system.

This does not mean that the *first* aim of education is political, nor that all schools must agree on all their aims. It does mean, however, that democracy with all its plurality of aims

Goals for American Education

How Objectives and Curriculum Alterations Are Wisely Forwarded

Several conclusions emerge from first hand knowledge of the way in which some colleges have moved forward in a productive way. One conclusion is that to start with an effort to get agreement in general terms about first principles in what are essentially philosophical generalizations, is to go at it the hard way.

A second conclusion which in principle would presumably have general acceptance, is that if people are to be asked to agree about new programs, they had better, so far as is humanly possible, be parties to the deliberations in which the programs are being formulated. This is a counsel of common sense, of democratic procedure, and of psychological wisdom. The experience of agreeing upon a course of action is at its best the result of a shared experience of discussion and reflection as to what changes are desirable. Human nature is such that if it is not to act on the basis of command, it has to act on the basis of prior desire and conviction of those involved that the proposed action is wise and good for them. And this means something more than taking a finished statement of objectives and program into a faculty meeting and asking for their acceptance.

Another general conclusion is that the process of application is desirably approached cooperatively, experimentally, and with a determination to continue in cooperative search to be sure that sound answers are in the making.

The wise chairman of one such faculty committee on the study of objectives writes me as follows:

> If I had begun the meetings of our committee by asking for agreement on principles at the outset, that is, if I had said let us define our ends

---

and free play of initiative, must have some common ends shared by its citizens if it is to retain its privileges.

An important explanation for the ascendency of fascists, and the present establishment of communism, has been the philosophy of history which lay, and lies, at the bottom of their educational programs. They each have had a sense of *destiny,* a belief that the time for certain ideals and ends had come. Such a conception is strikingly absent in American education now, though it did pervade the outlook of our Puritan ancestors. I suggest that the philosophy of history might well become a common denominator for the aims of American education. Every educator has some, expressed or unexpressed, assumptions on this theme in any case. Their articulation and criticism could stabilize American education and serve American democracy.

before we decide on our means, the committee would soon have broken into several warring groups and nothing of any importance so far as education at this college is concerned, would ever have come out of it.

The only way we can proceed in a democratic society to achieve more community is to start with whatever community of interest happens to exist and to try and find and put into effect ways of utilizing that community of interest more effectively. . . .

At the very end, after we had agreed unanimously on our practical program, I sat down and wrote what I thought in general as to the objectives which our program implied. At that point the committee found no objection to this general formulation.

This letter may seem to belie what has been suggested above about the operative importance of a faculty agreeing upon a statement of objectives. But a more penetrating analysis of what can wisely happen reveals that there have undoubtedly to be in the minds of the leaders of such a committee some fairly clear ideas as to new directions which it is desired to take. The point is not that reorganization problems are to be discussed in a philosophic vacuum, but that the emphasis in deliberation is placed upon admittedly desirable changes as to which there is some initial common sympathy because there are common agreements that improvements are necessary. Indeed, the writer of the above letter in subsequent correspondence reaffirms this very point as follows:

Only the subtle means of personal relationships will, I think, accomplish what is wanted. Given a group of people, say a president or dean and some leading faculty members, who have achieved a *prior* agreement on a program and whose ideals are at stake and whose personal prestige is involved, you have a situation where effective leadership is almost bound to occur. In a situation of that sort certain people have to assume responsibility for the *execution* of a plan. The problem, as I see it, is how to establish that sort of situation.

Obviously, no committee can be sufficiently representative to take account of *all* faculty points of view at every moment. It becomes essential strategy, therefore, to do a good deal of conference work with departments and individuals who can naturally offer much invaluable assistance in giving detailed substance to ideas which the committee is entertaining in more general terms. In other words, the committee deliberations will be most effective if they represent a constant interweaving back and forth of committee meetings and personalized discussions with department members throughout the college.

My whole emphasis here is that statements of objectives are operationally no more valuable than their acceptance in good faith for application by those who have to do the applying. And the assumption is, of course, that usually a modern educational program may entail embarking upon methods which depart from the experience and habits of many faculty members. Efforts to carry on courses in general science supply, for example, a good instance of a kind of program problem which is often met with resistance by science teachers who have been schooled in a different tradition. And the practical steps toward alteration in science instruction for general students requires on the part of the science teachers the desire, the understanding, the experimental disposition, and the willingness to spend ample time in conference—all of which are the prior conditions of an altered program.

The same situation prevails to a greater or less degree in the changing of curricular procedures in all subject areas.

The faculty of Columbia College in their valuable study after twenty-five years of struggling with "general" courses, supplies a documentation of the conclusions I have set forth about how objectives are translated into effective action. As Dean Harry J. Carman reminds us in his Preface to that study,[13] "I feel it a pleasant duty to recall that the Columbia College curriculum here anatomized is not the work solely of one mind or one committee or even one Faculty now in charge; it has been a collaborative enterprise which for a generation has drawn on the thought and energies of many men."

Dean Carman has usefully supplemented this preface in a personal letter which discusses the whole problem of the acceptance of new objectives from the point of view of the Columbia experience. He says:

> In the first place, one of the greatest tasks of all is to get a faculty to the point where its members are not only willing but anxious to take stock of its objectives with a view to ascertaining whether or not it can do a better educational job. Many faculty members are slaves to a routine way of doing things and, for reasons which we both know, oppose change. This opposition can be overcome—not entirely I grant you—by the right kind of leadership. If the president or the dean of the college knows how to select key men and to win these men to his point of view,

[13] *A College Program in Action*, Columbia University Press, New York, 1946.

namely, to take inventory of present college objectives with a view to their improvement, he has won half the battle, for these key men can be used to convert other members of the faculty. In this connection, it is the part of wisdom, it seems to me, to build up a tradition or habit in your faculty of taking inventory from time to time of both objectives and methods.

When such inventory is taken and it seems advisable to introduce a new course or courses either departmental or divisional, the greatest care should be exercised in staffing. Only those should be selected who believe in and have enthusiasm for the course and its objective. Objectives can easily be defeated and courses designed for the realization of such objectives ruined.

Second, unless the actual formulation of the objectives is participated in by those who will give them effect there is loss. Take the Contemporary Civilization course at Columbia for example. This course both in its inception and revision was built by those members of the staff who gave instruction in it. Furthermore, your thought that there be conferences with representative or key faculty members while the committee is at work on the course's formulation is very much to the point. This can be done by conferences with individuals or by means of staff smokers which because of their informality encourage discussion.

To emphasize what I have said in support of your suggestions let me briefly outline the Columbia machinery. The Dean is supposed to be more than a mere administrator. He should be (and hopes he is) an educational leader and spokesman for his staff. He is continuously taking stock of objectives and methods. Out of his head come what seem to him to be constructive proposals. Not all such proposals come from him however. Many come from alert faculty members. These proposals go to the Committee on Instruction composed of six elected faculty members with the Dean and Associate Dean, *ex officio*. (The Dean is the Chairman.) Here they are discussed and worthwhile items if approved by the Committee are mimeographed and circulated to all members of the staff for their information. Then the staff is invited to a smoker where the proposal or proposals are further discussed. They then go back to the Committee where they are either adopted or rejected. If adopted they are then reported to the Faculty for official action. This machinery is in itself a means of educating the staff.

Third, it is sound procedure always to work closely with the department or departments involved. Otherwise instead of cooperation there is likely to be opposition. Always create an atmosphere to the effect that the affected department or departments are bringing about the change.

Fourth, that the experience of other institutions be utilized there can be no question. No institution should *slavishly* follow the experience of another institution. Rather it should attempt to know as accurately as possible what the educational objectives of other institutions are and how these objectives are being realized. If any part of another institution's program can be utilized all well and good. In the last analysis, however, any institution must cut its own cloth to fit its educational garment.

Mutual criticism among all those involved in working out of the applications is very important. Weekly staff seminars at which the work for the coming week is discussed and the method of instruction emphasized are very useful. Chicago uses this technique very successfully and it has long been employed by Columbia College in both its Humanities and Contemporary Civilization courses. For many years prior to World War II the Contemporary Civilization staff spent a week together at camp where it combined recreation with serious proposals for the improvement of the course in content and instruction.

Student criticism is also valuable. Each year every section of the Contemporary Civilization course elects a student representative. This representative confers with his fellow students in the section and with representatives of the other sections. At the end of each semester the staff plays host at a dinner to all the student representatives where all aspects of the course are discussed and suggestions made for its improvement. The revisions which have been made in the course—and they are many—have resulted in large measure from these student suggestions.

The last point is that applications be kept fluid in method and the actual teachers keep on conferring is most essential. If this situation does not prevail the course tends to regress and the staff to become stale. Frequent—indeed almost continuous—inventory is the method which we have found to be the most successful. Nothing is more fatal to an educational institution than the prevalence of an atmosphere that things are perfect and that change is unnecessary.

In short, effective application of new educational proposals requires the active and willing involvement of the teachers affected. It requires this from the very outset; it requires this continuously. And all concerned must be prepared to take the enormous amount of time needed for self-criticism, for mutual criticism, for experimental efforts which may have to be abandoned, and for an eagerness to profit by similar experience wherever it can be found in other institutions which have faced the same problems. More than that, programs have to be kept fluid. Methods of measuring results should be considered and appraisals of results should be rigorously prosecuted. There is, in short, no easy and rapid road to the transferring of objectives from a report into classroom conduct. And any meritorious proposals deserve a trial of at least three or four college generations in order to have any comparative basis for judging the wisdom or success of the program.[f]

Also, a detail of no minor importance is that faculty members who remain unconvinced or who are patently ill equipped or intransigent about joining in any new program, have in some way to be coped with, so that the program is not being subtly obstructed by the carping criticism of the disaffected. Some institutions can afford to build their labors around such teachers and leave them to their own traditional labors. Others have successfully given leaves of absence for a year's study to help equip men for new assignments. And others have found, out of the experiences of the past war, that certain teachers can be more versatile than they had themselves realized. But to provide some way to prevent the teachers who will not or cannot implement new objectives from sabotaging the program, is *essential*.

Evaluative Procedures

Final emphasis should now be given to the problem of evaluation and appraisal to which I have alluded. There is the problem of the evaluation of the soundness of any specific formulation of objectives for a given institution. There is next the added problem of how well these objectives are being translated into action. And, finally, the vital and all too often ignored question as to how beneficial the results of application are in terms of the quality of life subsequently experienced by the students who have been educated under a specific plan. On all three counts, we are still in the elementary stages of knowledge as to ways and means.

With regard to the soundness of any particular formulation of objectives, it is not here my purpose to occupy the role of critic. This paper

---

[f]Comment by Louis W. Norris:

Dr. Tead makes a valuable suggestion in stressing the educational value *to the faculty* of periodic and corporate study of a school's own objectives. School bulletins usually carry statements of purpose but they are rarely embedded in the muscle tissue of its teachers. These objectives should change to some degree but even if a school's objectives do not change, it is helpful for a faculty to restate them in new phrases occasionally, in order that each professor may have an articulate end continuously in view as he goes about his work.

is not designed to be a comparative appraisal of individual statements of objectives or of the philosophies behind them. I am rather pressing the point that we need more study to help us determine how good any given statement is and how we know it is good. And obviously such judgments and such study depend upon the ultimate social philosophies of those conducting the inquiry.

It does, however, seem logical that at least the educational objectives of single institutions should bear a demonstrably close relation to the purposes and aspirations of the nation within which the institution functions. Yet even here we find that within the frame of a democratic nation like our own, there is room for considerable difference of view as to the statement of democratic objectives and accompanying methods as they may seem valid in different institutions.[g]

That it may eventually be possible to make some further statement of *criteria* of good aims is hopefully true; but that this has been satisfactorily undertaken in any sources with which I am familiar is not yet the case.[14]

How Effective is the Application?

The effectiveness with which fresh objectives are given concrete expression in any particular institution is a relatively simple problem. Theoretically, it calls for some grasp of both ends and means on the part of trustees, administrators, and teachers. In actuality, however, the

[g]Comment by B. Othanel Smith:

Mr. Tead has raised the sixty-four dollar question, namely, how can we ascertain "the soundness of any specific formulation of objectives for a given institution"? He apparently assumes that objectives can be sound for one institution and not for another. But I hardly see how this can be the case unless the institution is to be divorced from the society which sustains it. Mr. Tead recognizes this difficulty and concludes "that at least the educational objectives of single institutions should bear a demonstrably close relation to the purposes and aspirations of the nation within which the institution functions." But why this is the case, or what consideration led him to that conclusion, is not revealed to us. It would seem that in our interdependent world the objectives of education must be grounded in something that transcends national aspirations and purposes. There is no question more pressing or more in need of thorough exploration than the question of how to validate the objectives of education.

[Cf. Chapter I by Robert Ulich and Dr. Smith's comments on Chapter XIV by Theodore Brameld.]

[14]An interesting attempt in this direction has been made by Dr. Frederick Rogers in a pamphlet published January 10, 1945, in California, entitled, "A Rational Approach to Aims in Education."

faculty and its leaders, especially those who have had a formative influence in any program of curricular reorganization, will be best equipped to appraise the relation of specific action to aspiration. And this emphatically requires that there be those who constantly maintain a critical and comprehensive view of the over all operation of the program, and who are at pains to keep sufficiently in touch with all its parts as they together impinge on student personality. Also, occasionally to bring in for consultation some friendly critic sympathetic with the newly applied objectives has sometimes proved to be beneficial.

To some undetermined extent, also, it is true that the students themselves should be able to voice some significant opinion about the satisfactions, intellectual and otherwise, which the revised program is bringing for them. Student judgments have proved on numerous campuses to have been exceedingly perceptive on such issues. But much depends upon the way in which their opinion is sought, the mood of responsibility in which they voice their judgments, and the comparative experience they can draw upon in making judgments.

In general, however, it seems true that a combination of faculty and student judgments to the effect that a program is proceeding satisfactorily can be a reasonably sound index of a program's success in so far as that is to be measured by its fulfilment of accepted objectives.

It is when we reach the third question that we are left with no landmarks, no objective measures, no devices of appraisal, subjective or objective, which have thus far stood the test of time. It is true that there have been various studies of the results of college education in terms of income earned, relative numbers in Who's Who, leisure time habits and similar tests. But such studies do not really address themselves to the heart of the problem. For what we would like to know is, how and to what degree different academic programs really do comparatively give beneficial shape and guidance to the unfolding of body, mind, and spirit. And sooner or later, it is to be earnestly hoped that studies can be undertaken over a twenty or thirty year period and with some objectivity of measuring methods, which may supply more clues on this score than exist at present. For the painful truth is that the estimations of educational success attained under different programs remain still largely in the realm of opinion. This is not to say that we are completely without guides or criteria. And it would seem that with a growing body of knowledge about the nature of society and about the nature of man in society, we will be able to come closer and closer to a body of educational practice which will have increasing efficacy under defined premises of defensible aims.[h]

Conclusion

As the work of faculty study of educational programs goes forward in increasing volume in the next few years under all the pressures for the improved social competence of college graduates, it will be important to realize that the role of objectives is, if I may say so, both absolute and relative.

It is absolute in the sense that we may gradually hope to attain a wider sense of agreement as to the philosophical presuppositions which underlie our thinking about program. And it is relative in the sense that, as the above discussion has shown, college teachers may be expected to reach an agreement more readily upon matters of program than upon the formalized statements of objectives which may derive from such programs. And in the present state of our knowledge, widely differing kinds of program can undoubtedly serve good ends and yield good satisfactions, especially since the ends and satisfactions are at present so relatively viewed both by college teachers and by society in general.

The central theme of this discussion, therefore, has been the vital need for a sharing in an open minded and experimental way by *all* the teachers involved, in the thinking and planning as well as the operating of revised programs.

It is, finally, to be hoped that as the work of reorganizing the graduate

[h]Comment by Paul L. Essert:
I am particularly impressed with the comments regarding evaluation of our objectives. Not only is it true in higher education that we spend a great deal of time, energy, effort, and money in clarifying objectives without adequate appraisal of the effectiveness on the behavior of the student, but this is true all the way down the line in elementary and secondary education as well. Certainly we need a great deal of research and systematic thinking about all of this.

Comment by Louis J. A. Mercier:
We have here a special caution. It is all very well for an institution to state or restate objectives, but what precautions must be taken to insure their being earnestly pursued, and how can the results of the new programs be evaluated?
The particularly sobering thought which Dr. Tead leaves with us is how difficult it will be to evaluate results produced by changes in objectives. Who shall distinguish, and when, and on what basis what effects changed programs have had on the students? Apparently no one else thought of raising that important question.

instruction of prospective college teachers goes on, there will be included in that instruction some genuine experience of thinking about higher educational aims and correlative procedures as a whole, rather than merely intensive study of discrete bodies of knowledge. If wise objectives are to be newly shaped and instructional processes are to be appropriately revamped, this depends in the last analysis on a point of view and an intellectual equipment on the part of a new generation of teachers, which will help them to espouse flexible educational experiments more eagerly than has usually been true in the past.

The role of objectives is, in short, vital. But equally important is the role of those leaders who struggle to translate them into actuality by virtue of a democratic process of shared deliberation. And that cooperative thinking has to be designed to earn consent for improved aims and methods calculated to make improved objectives work.[1]

[1]Comment by Swami Akhilananda:
We would like to offer our humble suggestions to Dr. Tead in connection with the application of the objectives of educational institutions. The study of human nature reveals to us that one may have intellectual comprehension of the supreme goal of life, namely, the manifestation of perfection; yet if the individuals who are in charge of institutions are not thoroughly established in those ideals then they cannot disseminate the spirit to their students. On the other hand, students should also be inspired by those ideals, for then alone will there be a harmonious working relationship between the faculty and student body.

One should also consider the patronizing agencies of the educational institutions. The controlling agents may be governments, industrial groups, and so on. But if they do not have the greatest good of mankind in view and if they have the wrong objective in life, however rationalized they may be in the name of freedom, social justice, etc., they will certainly force the administration to carry out their own aims by making the faculty and students subservient to their aspirations and goals.

So the highest ideal of the greatest good for man and society cannot be carried out by higher education unless the institutions are in charge of thoroughly integrated personalities who are well established in moral and spiritual ideals and free from the control of interested individuals and groups. It may seem that we are suggesting utopian ideas regarding the controlling agencies. However, there have been many historical facts to prove to us that time and again the world produces strong personalities who can carry out the highest ideal in their own lives and who can inspire others to do the same. So it is the duty of the educators to remember that their life is one of nobility and sacrifice for the common good of mankind.

CHAPTER XVIII

Education as Experiment

By HAROLD TAYLOR
President, Sarah Lawrence College

AMERICAN EDUCATION has lost touch with many of the realities of contemporary life. The world has moved past it, leaving its theories dated, its philosophy discursive, and its energies dissipated in managing practical problems which have only incidental relations with education itself. The result is that American education is overorganized, while the American student continues to be undereducated.

Reality in contemporary life is not academic, abstract, or genteel. It consists of people, in and out of trouble, in varying degrees of social tension. What is real is that prices rise, civil wars are fought, politicians are jailed, governments are overthrown, workers riot, music and poetry are written, new lives are formed. It is true and real that the moral values by which Western civilization has lived its past are shattered in Europe, that the economic and political unity designed to support those values is broken, and new values, with new social systems to support them, are coming into existence. The reality in which we live is one where old societies are breaking up and new societies are developing, where India, China, Japan, and the whole of Europe show us man in social crisis and active revolution, with only America and Russia in comparative stability. Even that degree of stability and power is relative, and in a large degree illusory, since it is also true that man himself is in a critical stage in his own transition from an old world into a new, where each is vulnerable and each is tormented by contemporary necessities. This crisis, in which men are either brutally certain of their powers and convictions, or frighteningly uncertain of their feelings and beliefs, is at the center of contemporary life. It is this reality with which contemporary education must deal. The central issue is this: What are the values by which modern man can live most nobly, and what are the ways in which life must be organized in order to make this possible? The central task, therefore, for all of us who teach, is to plunge our students into the middle of their time, and to help them gain knowledge and make judgments about matters affecting the future of life on this planet.[a]

If we look at American education with these things in mind, we are condemned to disappointment. Throughout the school system, we find that we have deliberately trained our teachers to care desperately about only the little bits of knowledge by which they make their meager living. We make it almost a professional obligation on their part never to say anything about anybody else's bit of knowledge, nor to make any statement or take any action about life, politics, or pleasure, for fear they might be misconstrued by the community.

We find that in the practice of education, people have lost their desire to experiment, to try new things, and have found, instead, that it is wise to talk about the need for discipline, compulsion, the required curriculum, and the necessity of producing no controversy. We find that school superintendents who are socially conscious have been replaced by men who are safe and who can be relied upon to keep the buildings and the public relations program in order. There is little deep sense of urgency, of an important time passing, of the need for fresh social action, or of the enormous social possibilities which lie in American education.

Nor has there been very much radical thinking in our colleges and universities about the aims and practices of education. There has, instead, been a national obsession with the rearrangement of old courses in new clusters. Professors in every university have developed guilt feelings about the courses they have been giving harmlessly enough for years, and have added a great many facts and books from other fields, and seem bound to give the same courses next year under new and more complicated titles. Or, as an alternative, professors sometimes volunteer to give each other's courses, or to appear together in groups of three

[a]Comment by I. L. Kandel:

Dr. Taylor, dissatisfied with all other programs, would like "to plunge the students into the middle of their time and to help them gain knowledge and make judgments about matters affecting the future life on this planet." The question that this statement raises is how the students would know what the issues of their time are and with what tools would they begin to make judgments on them, and will the issues be the same ten or fifteen or thirty years after the students graduate?

[Cf. the discussion of education for contemporary problems in Chapter III by T. V. Smith and Chapter IX by Howard Mumford Jones.]

and four to conduct a single course. The whole operation is directed and inspired by curriculum committees chosen as representing each area in the curriculum, each group in the faculty, and every viewpoint in the philosophy of education. In this way, it has been possible to do a great deal of shifting around without actually changing anything, except that, because of the voting power of various departments, an enormous number of courses previously without very large enrollment have suddenly become required. In the absence of a genuine unifying philosophy which could make discriminating selections throughout the field of human knowledge, there is tacit agreement amongst the representatives of various subjects that, in all fairness to the interests of the faculty, something of everything should be required of the students.

As a result, most colleges in America now find themselves with a new curriculum. The new curriculum faces each student in his first two years with a survey of the things a young person should know, although opinion varies from college to college as to what these things are. The difficulties in performing all this rearranging are not to be underrated, however, since the new curriculum must look sufficiently different from the old one to justify all the meetings held and the number of mimeographed statements issued, yet not be different enough from the old to lose the traditional values which faculty members associate with their own work in their own institution, and which they are quite likely to call the tradition of Western culture. The fact that this feat has been accomplished by the members of the colleges and universities all the way from Boston to Los Angeles is a tribute to the ingenuity of the American academic mind.

The origin of the current mode of thinking has two major parts—the failure of the elective system to educate in breadth and in depth, and the success of the departmental system in educating narrowly. The efforts of professional educators have been directed toward the correction of these twin evils, and the name for the kind of system which is proposed as a modern reform is, general education. The effort has been diligent enough, and the elective system has been largely replaced, but in replacing it, most of the evils, of which the principle of election was only a part, have been preserved intact. That is to say, we have now a system of higher learning which continues to use most of the worn equipment of nineteenth century education—including the premise that the higher learning is a verbal process, that the mind is fully trained when it grasps generalizations, that knowledge is virtue, that lectures, notebooks, examinations, rote learning, credits, grades are essentials of method, and that the whole enterprise is capable of giving correct esthetic feelings about literature and art, and moral feelings about the good life to those who do not have them.

The root error of present day thinking about general education is that education is thought of as consisting of knowledge of general ideas. Yet a general idea is meaningless until filled with the specific content of personal experience, and experience is meaningless until related to other specific experiences and ideas. The learning process goes from immediate experience to the unity of general ideas, from a full study of one kind of knowledge to the understanding of its relation with other kinds.

In order to learn to believe with reason the values which are central to a good society, it is necessary to become emotionally attached to those values, and to make beliefs a source of action. If fact, beliefs, opinions, and attitudes are not united in a philosophy for personal and social use, they remain inert, they decay, they disappear from the consciousness. The way to develop meaningful beliefs leading to good action is to place each student in situations where he feels those beliefs to be true, and where there is an opportunity to explore their meanings in the practices of the college community and the society which surrounds it. This is true of esthetic values, moral values, social values, psychological values. It is thus true of youth's experience with the arts, where the creation of feelings of esthetic value in one's own life is the crucial point of education, rather than the reception of information about pictures, musical scores, or artists. It is equally true of youth's experience with moral values in personal and community relations. Unless the college community provides a place for living which extends beyond itself into the bigger society of contemporary life, and contains within itself the social atmosphere in which ideals can be tested and acted upon, it is bound to fail in its major task of developing in youth a loyalty to liberal principles.[b]

[b]Comment by John LaFarge, S.J.:

When President Taylor stresses the need of personal experience of given "situations" for their adequate intellectual understanding, one is reminded of the puzzled and sometimes bitter remarks made by young Europeans who came in contact with American students of social problems during or at the close of the recent war. As one Viennese girl

Now it is wise to try as hard as we can to prevent our educational system from concerning itself with specialists, and to try to develop young men and women whose interests are broad and whose knowledge is wide. But it is unlikely that this will be achieved by producing standard programs of general ideas, and surveys of the materials of Western culture. What we get is a set of short reports about ideas, events, science, and people. Large areas of the new curriculum have lost any close relationship with the student, and education has forgotten what we all thought had been learned, that our concern must be not so much with the formal order in which the curriculum is arranged and followed, but with the close relation of the student's life to the things he learns in college. The curriculum has become an end in itself. Rather than a means to the full growth of each person, it is likely to become a kind of ready-made coat which each person should wear if he wishes to be taken for a well educated man. The student is formally prepared with general ideas. Yet that preparation is not a prelude to abundant living, but an introduction to further academic study. Only after such formal preparation is the student considered ready to be faced with the big and controversial questions of contemporary life. In the present curriculum, these questions are often missed entirely, dealt with as phenomena in formal style, or included as a special course in the graduating year.

Such issues, in one form or another, should have been the beginning and the central concern of the student's whole education. For the primary intellectual necessity for modern living is an awareness of what are the biggest issues, and how we can go about settling them. Or, to put the matter differently, each must know his place in the world today, and each must know his responsibilities. Our youth in America live in a situation in which responsibility is easily shelved, in which the individual is not faced with continual necessities for action in order to survive. Therefore we must teach and youth must learn to know what we can believe, and to have some clear indication of the ways in which it is necessary to act in order that some hope and some future be assured to ourselves and to others.

To meet this need, proposals have often been made by educators who advocate a return by our colleges to the classical curriculum, on the assumption that study of the history and content of Western culture

---

who had been leader in an Austrian youth movement, expressed it to me, "the American boys and girls talk of these matters merely from books. For us they are a terrible reality."

through reading a number of prescribed texts will provide a sense of direction for contemporary living. This proposal is actually a narrower and more provincial form of the core curriculum movement—which it has undoubtedly influenced to some degree—and suffers from many of the same difficulties, while bringing one or two special ones of its own. Chief amongst the latter are the fact that the discoveries of contemporary science, philosophy, and art are shut away from the student, and that the distribution of practical knowledge of present international and national affairs is left to the auspices of the newspapers, radio, movies, and local gossip. The accumulated wisdom of our past, and an understanding of the history of our civilization, are both matters of great importance to modern education. However, they provide a knowledge of only one aspect of contemporary reality, the aspect of its past, at a time when the full dimensions of the past, present, and future demand thorough exploration.

While the reforms of the core curriculum and the classical education movement have been gaining ground, those reforms associated with the progressive education movement have, on the whole, been neglected. In the present situation, even to use the term progressive to describe educational views is to invite the notion of laxity, bad spelling, impertinence, *laissez-faire,* and the control of parents by their children.[c] Yet where other theories fail to deal with contemporary reality, the progressive theory has no such lack of intention. It has most frequently been blamed, rightly or wrongly, for its total concern with immediacy in the present. It has been blamed for ignoring history, for negating cultural values, for encouraging the dilettante, for pampering the egocentric, for aiding the pacifist, for creating the radical, and, in general, for developing ignorant, difficult, amoral, and unpleasant youth. A correspondent recently attributed something loose and sinister to the fact that Sarah Lawrence students often sit on the floor. Others make cynical remarks about coaxing Bennington students into the study of physiology by first luring them into a performance of the modern dance. The extent to which the response of the ordinarily level headed can be distorted by annoyance with progressivism is shown by Professor Brand Blanshard, who, in a singularly unhappy statement of the methods and aims of modern education claimed, "We do not need to take college students by their little hands and coax them into history or economics by showing

[c][Cf. Ruth Strang's comment on Chapter XIII by Mordecai M. Kaplan.]

them what fun it all is, or showing them what practical difference it will make."

Descent to this level of argument is usually found in those who become furious with modern painting, music, or sculpture, and seldom, in the past, has shown itself in the field of education. Yet this way of misconstruing modern education is common in every part of current discussion in colleges, where the organic or contextualist theory of knowledge which lies at the base of modern educational thought is either misunderstood or rejected outright in favor of rationalistic philosophies. The criticism has grown in proportion to the misunderstanding, on the part of educators and the general parent public, as to the meaning of such tired phrases as child centered school, self-discipline, interests, needs, and individual development.

The notion has been created that in thinking of the child, the adolescent, or the adult as the center of his own education, and in trying to bring to him the kind of knowledge and moral philosophy which meets his needs and will thus be useful to him in his life, we are developing a theory and practice of narcissism, egocentrism, and expediency. Actually, the distinctive contribution of the progressives in the past has been to demonstrate the ultimate importance of the individual student, and the ultimate union of psychological with moral factors. The aim of the progressive is to release energies, talents, and the intelligence of the child, without assuming that every impulse or talent of child or adult is of equal value. But in taking account of factors connected with motivation and with the psychology of learning, there is no less emphasis upon the moral structure which points the whole process to fruitful and desirable ends. It *is* to emphasize, however, the fact that the ends themselves are not fixed, and are an integral part of the process. This does not make them less morally valuable, but more so, since one must ask constantly, "What kind of young people are we developing? What kind of social, intellectual, emotional, and moral behavior do we want? What kind of life do we want, for ourselves, and for our students, sons and daughters?" These questions are raised not merely for the teacher, but for the student, who in this theory, is to be given responsibilities and disciplines as quickly as he seems able to cope with them. He thus becomes and remains the center of his own education, not in the sense that the world moves around him in a dance of approval, but in the sense that the individual learns only as much as he is willing and able to learn for himself. Among the things he learns is the basic fact that he is part of a context of individuals, with whose desires, experiences, and human rights he must concern himself.

There are, of course, educational risks in some of the forms of individualism with which progressive education has become involved. What begins as a true description of the way people learn—namely, that each person is unique, that each person does his own learning for himself, and that emotional aspects of his learning are of crucial importance—may end with some unwelcome consequences in the actual practice of education. If, in practice, the individual is considered as a kind of flower which will unfold if it receives the nourishment of a kindly and free environment, it is possible that no solid structure of social values will be built in the process. It is often considered that sheer uninhibited growth of the individual to that form which it is natural for him to assume, is the true aim of radical modern education. This reasoning has a streak of Aristotelianism in it which is badly suited to a philosophy which makes claims for contemporary relevance, and, as a kind of *laissez-faire* liberalism, is more appropriate to a stable world in which solid moral values of an enlightened and unselfish kind already exist in profusion, and have been absorbed by each child and adolescent. It is by reason of the previous existence of these values in the student that some of the most astounding successes which education has had in our experimental colleges have occurred with individuals who have come to college from conventionally rigid school situations from whose grip it has been possible to free the minds and attitudes of the student.

There is bound to be criticism of an educational philosophy which is intentionally vague about its ultimate value system. The chief criticism is that such a philosophy produces an infinite dispersion of aims, and fosters a calculated introversion, in which human conduct is explained in terms of the intricate play of unconscious forces over which one has no control and for whose social effects one cannot therefore be held responsible. In the context of the first half of this century, that philosophy represents, in education, a part of the general revolt against absolutism. As a philosophy of education, it is the counterpart of a philosophy of literature which revolted against clarity, completeness, and form; of a philosophy of art marked by the disappearance of the object; of a philosophy of morality in which, as Camus says, "no one was ever wrong because everybody could be right"; of a philosophy of truth in which propositions either refer to immediate objects and are thus obvious, or refer to non-sensed objects and are thus meaningless. In such inversion or discursiveness of all values lies the possibility of dilettantism, personal enjoyment of confusion, social irresponsibility, and philosophical nihilism.

Auden's *The Labyrinth* states the matter briefly, in conducting contemporary man through theology, metaphysics, sense experience, mathematics, history, and art, in search of firm values as guides in modern experience. Auden ends with the introvert, about whom he has this to say:

> His absolute presupposition
> Is—Man creates his own condition.
> This maze was not divinely built,
> But is secreted by my guilt.
>
> The centre that I cannot find
> Is known to my Unconscious Mind
> I have no reason to despair
> Because I am already there.
>
> My problem is how *Not* to will
> They move most quickly who stand still
> I'm only lost until I see
> I'm lost because I want to be.
>
> If this should fail, perhaps I should
> As certain educators would,
> Content myself with the conclusion,
> In theory there is no solution.[1]

As Auden suggests, there is probably no theory ultimately satisfactory. Whether there is or not, is, in my view, not an ultimately significant question, since life is much too rich in differences and new possibilities to be confined to a single theory of how growth may best occur. The fact is that the individual actually has a structure of values and a theory of truth, whether or not he is articulate or rational about them. These values make up a pattern of personality, of thought and of action. They are realized by the individual, in thought and action, but seldom form a coherent pattern which can be identified as a logic, or as an ethic or

---

[1] W. H. Auden, *Collected Works*, Random House, New York, 1945, p. 9. Quoted by courtesy of the publishers.

esthetic. The values themselves are in process, and fortunately, change in their emphasis from year to year, usually by the influence of material necessities or personal experiences—more rarely by the presentation of concepts from books or teachers. Values themselves have to be learned. But in order for values to be meaningful, and so absorbed into one's life as to have a continuing part in thought and in action, they must be learned as meaningful experience. The college community must therefore be organized so that each student is immersed in the stream of intellectual, social, and moral values which it is our intention to teach our youth. This means that we must have less of the competitive fraternity-sorority emphasis, with its cluster of snobbish and materialistic values, and more conscious effort to design a community in which each student and faculty member feels himself to be part of a total enterprise in which he has a share and an important contribution to make. It is possible to create the same loyalty and enthusiasm for liberal values as the enthusiasm now reserved for football teams and fraternities.

Accordingly, one can say that the whole matter of learning is much more complicated than is assumed by those who adopt traditional modes of thinking about education. New ways of educating students have relied upon psychological research into human development and the learning process. The direction of this research has been, in the past, toward individual psychology, with additional work of a horizontal kind in the development of a mass testing program for general intelligence, and in information testing performed by tests of general education. The latter research has now been frozen into the structure of secondary school education and colleges by the standard entrance examinations now administered, and by the credit—grade—objective examination system now in standard use in the colleges and universities. The more significant recent research in the psychology of learning has moved toward the study of the development of value structures, toward the relation of the individual to group attitudes and toward the relation of personality to intelligence. Yet little attention has been paid by educators to the material available from these sources, nor has contemporary thinking in higher education been modified or enriched by reference to contemporary research in the whole field of the social sciences. The demonstrations of the Dartmouth Eye Institute about the nature of perception, for example, would alter radically any traditional approach to questions of teaching and learning, even if there were not already available a large body of research giving similar conclusions. Yet no reference to these data and their conclusions appears in the curricular reports which represent the outcome of current thinking about educational reform in colleges and universities.

If modern theory of education is to advance from its present position, it must continue its earlier efforts to move behind verbal symbols and the imitation of reality to the direct knowledge of experience. In the beginning of the twentieth century, Bergson, Dewey, James, and others rebelled against the notion that reality was logical, rational, and intellectual, and that the part played by us when we perceive was minor, and at best automatic. What William James did was to make us see that a great system of philosophy could be built by trusting individual immediate experience as a legitimate and respectable way of knowing, and that ultimately we knew things to be true and real because we felt they were. What Dewey did was to make us see that knowledge was not real for its possessor until it was used in personal and social life, and that individual experience was socially derived and depended upon a complex of social and intellectual sanctions for its ultimate verification as truth. Modern philosophy, psychology, and social science, as it developed in different ways and by different influences, through Whitehead, Freud, Bergson, Frazer, and the cultural pluralists, has given contemporary thinking a philosophy of process, and of organism. That philosophy has influenced very deeply our contemporary art forms, in music, sculpture, architecture, painting, poetry, the dance. In education it has influenced the nursery school, the elementary school, and, to a more limited degree, secondary and higher education. The higher in conventional educational rank we go, the less modern does our thinking become.

What all this means in the practice of education is that progressive theory, at the beginning of this century, and particularly in the 1920's, turned organic philosophy into new educational forms, and accepted as true the proposition that immediate experience is the prime learning factor. Thus we had the use of the arts for learning; field work and projects in social research; creative work in music, literature, sculpture, and in other arts; discussions in place of lectures; original sources in place of commentaries; freedom and responsibility for students—all designed to return the growing person to the center of life and knowledge in his own experience of the realities. The science and art of education grew, and new methods of teaching were developed through experiment. The mood in those thirty years was one of rebellion, of liberation from inhibiting theories, of joy in new discoveries, and hope for a new generation of free and happy children.

Now we have stopped rebelling, partly because we have won victories, but perhaps more because the original impetus to liberation is gone. The rebellion gave a unifying purpose to teachers everywhere who were concerned not simply with teaching subjects, but with teaching students.

We now know a good deal about liberating student minds and talents. The philosophy of individual growth has been proven to be sound, our students do develop in desirable ways according to principles derived from twenty years of experiment, and many of these educational ideas have been absorbed into our present system.[d]

But in the meantime, the social climate in which those first experiments were made has changed. In that earlier time, we assumed that the successful First World War had brought us security and freedom for world democracy, and that if only each of us minded his own business and did not behave too badly, society would continue to develop with a kind of unavoidable progress. Even the word "progressive" contains the hidden assumption that we are all moving ahead, that our education in freedom will take us to new and better forms of human life. This happy philosophy has been refuted by events. As Stephen Spender says, "What (the Germans) destroyed, once and for all, is the modern middle-class idea that man, as a social being, does not have to choose between good and evil. . . . The world is now aghast with the realization that society has got to choose not just to be free but to be good." Education must decide not only to make free people, but must teach them the means of keeping their freedom. On this point, current American education has had nothing to say. It has done one of two things. It has made discreet remarks about the impossibility of accepting or teaching a modern philosophy,

[d]Comment by B. Othanel Smith:
A new and positive theory of education, broad in scope and deep in sequence, is what President Taylor calls for. Few of us will disagree with him, and I certainly go along with his desire to center the educational program in the study of social issues and conflicts. His emphasis upon the need for more adequate understanding of how people learn, is in line with what those who have made the study of human behavior their main interest have been telling us for sometime. One only wishes that President Taylor had indicated what these new developments might be. Enough is now known to enable us to outline them in some detail. My chief difficulty with the paper is its failure to present, at least in outline form, an intellectual method of dealing with social issues and conflicts. How we can study them in school without an intellectual discipline to guide us is a puzzle.

since to do so would be illiberal and a form of indoctrination, or it has recommended traditional values on the basis of their respectability and classical origins.

The task for modern education is to state a contemporary philosophy and to teach it.[e] That philosophy must deal with the social and personal needs of contemporary man, and must build new values and moral ideals in each. When the philosophy is stated, it must make the points of difference between its own assumptions and those of others very clear, and not fall into complacent and gentle habits of agreeing that all educators are really working toward the same goal. They are not.

In the first place, a new college curriculum must be created around the controversies, conflicts, and issues of contemporary life. This is not to say that all issues are social, or that each must deal with social questions. The issues are esthetic, personal, spiritual, psychological, and intellectual. Each student can best deal at first with the issues whose relevance to his own place in society he most readily comprehends. But he must be led from that beginning into the meaning of his knowledge for modern life, and each subject must lead beyond itself into the others, until he achieves some pattern of relation to the central matters of human destiny.[f] In

---

[e]Comment by John D. Wild:

Mr. Taylor's criticisms of the present chaotic state of higher education are both pointed and pertinent. I find that I can accept them all without serious qualification. I can also accept without any reservation the concrete constructive proposals he suggests. But from here on Mr. Taylor's argument plunges me into confusion.

A "contemporary philosophy" must be stated in verbal symbols, and taught by means of general ideas. I have some difficulty in reconciling this with Mr. Taylor's polemic against the "verbal process" and "general ideas." This would seem to imply a very radical skepticism concerning human intelligence which cannot proceed without the use of words and universal concepts. Mr. Taylor demands "a free ranging intelligence." But how can intelligence be active without the detachment, and the painstaking procedures of lectures, note taking, and all the paraphernalia of rational communication and argument which Mr. Taylor seems to deplore? It seems to me that he has sometimes confused the relevance of theory to life with life in the raw. If the only way we can learn is by "direct experience," why go to college at all?

A sound liberal program of social and educational reform demands an intelligible theoretical justification, ultimately a metaphysics. Without this, movements of reform either collapse into blind emotional surges with questionable results, or they wither away. The duty of the college teacher is not merely to present the great issues of contemporary life, and to arouse an emotional surge for "action" in real life. He must also engage in the even more formidable task of working out cooperatively a sound theoretical basis for constructive action.

[f]Comment by Max C. Otto:

Dr. Harold Taylor's discussion of "Education As Experiment" seems to me superb. It

Whitehead's language, "What education has to impart is an intimate sense for the power of ideas, for the beauty of ideas, and for the structure of ideas, together with a particular body of knowledge which has peculiar reference to the life of the being possessing it."

If this is true, then the intellectual life of the student must not be buttoned up in a tight curriculum. It is simply false to assume that each student is identical with every other student, that there is a standard set of facts, books, and ideas which will be appropriate for every life possessing them, or that a standard body of knowledge for everyone will have anything fully significant for anyone. The task for teachers is that of imparting values, and sharing knowledge, by finding ways to help the students to learn. If this is to be done with success, each student must actively draw that knowledge and those values into his own life. From the point of view of the person learning, there is no objectively valid system of knowledge by means of which he can equip himself for the company of the educated and the civilized, and for the accomplishment of the diversity of actions which the future may demand of him. Therefore, the choice among courses of study must be directly related to the ability, interests, and purposes of the individual, with the aid of teachers who can provide guidance in the making of choices. Those choices should not be made for everyone in *a priori* fashion by those who make academic curricula. The curricular judgments must be empirical, and must come as the result of careful attention by students and teachers to the kind of studies and projects which are most meaningful to the individual in the light of his purposes and talents.

This is to say flatly that life is open-ended, and that to educate is to experiment with means and ends in the satisfaction of human wants. No

---

is obvious that he knows what he is about. Anyone who fails to understand him or remains unconvinced by what he says would be no better off for anything I might add.

There is one aspect of the educational problem which I wish Dr. Taylor had been more explicit about. It is the relation of academic subject matter to needed changes in the social structure. His discussion, as it stands, leans heavily to the side of ideas, ideas vitalized by feelings, to be sure, and by their intimate association with values, yet nevertheless ideas which are to be acquired in the schools. Such ideas are of course important, but it happens that many of the ideas men live by, the ideas that dominate their lives, are acquired in what we call "the outside world." Unless that can be changed to a different world the best ideas acquired through schooling will go down in defeat before the less beautiful practices which are believed to be demanded by practical conduct. With the best will in the world, and with the most profound ideas about changes in general attitude, we still need to know what to do specifically and in the concrete. It is quite evident that Dr. Taylor would have challenging things to say along this line. He should let us have them.

matter to what degree our wants and needs may be modified in the future, we shall continue to fulfil them only if we can command a free ranging intelligence, a positive set of liberal values, and the strength and courage to carry them out.

A philosophy which is adequate for education as for life will take account of these needs and locate them in their setting in contemporary reality. It will assert the belief that human nature is not static, and that human life is what we make it. It will deny the superstition that man is sinful,[g] and affirm the fact that the causes of his fall from grace are in some sense discoverable and to some degree correctible. It will accept as valid the facts which social science gives us, and use those facts to reveal the path which we can take to make a good society. It will be a philosophy which accepts and welcomes change, and sets to us the task of participating in the changes.[h] It will recognize our situation in a world of collective industrial societies, and will recognize the intimate connection between individual modern man and the social groups which give him his rela-

[g]Comment by John LaFarge, S.J.:
I do not know exactly why Dr. Taylor says man is not sinful. Certainly he must agree that a certain number of men are sinful; else what sense would there have been in the Nuremberg trials? Also that most of us have some inclination toward doing wrong— much more, I fancy, than we really like to acknowledge. One need not accept the idea of the utter depravity of the poor old human race in order to acknowledge that something seems to have gone wrong with humanity at some stage of its historic existence; that the world bears the scars of some primal misuse of liberty, and is not going to find deliverance from it by a theory of pure optimism.

[h]Comment by Thurston N. Davis, S.J.:
Should education guide the historical process or merely reflect it? Much that Dr. Taylor has to say would lead us to think that the sole function of education is to mirror change, to surrender itself and its charges to the flux. All the traditional objectives are overthrown, and change itself becomes the one valid point of reference. Only let each thinking person have his or her theory of truth and the structure of values, and all will be well. How this philosophy of education can be other than vague about its ultimate value system, and how, therefore, Dr. Taylor escapes the nihilism he deplores in others, assuredly puzzles the present reader.

Given this initial irrationality in the fields of education and of total reality, everything else in the paper proceeds most convincingly from its first principle. For instance, "a new college curriculum must be created around the controversies, conflicts, and issues of contemporary life." Obviously, this curriculum must not concern itself with objective *solutions* for the problems and conflicts it studies. The philosophy imparted by such an education must be one that "accepts and welcomes change, and sets to us the task of participating in the changes." By no means is it to be normative or critical in its relation to change. Now, honestly, are we demanding too much of our vast educational institutions in America when we ask them, not merely to vibrate with contemporary problems, but also to attempt to formulate just and rational solutions?

tion to the modern world. It will recognize the value of each person, each culture, each race, each nation, and will call for protection and support of those who have not the power to protect and support themselves. It will accept as true the fact that education is an instrument of social transition. It will thus be a liberal philosophy, taking as its goal the development of free men in a changing social order.[1]

The teaching of this philosophy will mean certain immediate obligations and practical effects throughout large areas of higher education. Changes would occur in the curriculum. Studies would be organized to immerse each student in the adult world of contemporary ideas and events. The history and origin of such ideas will be discovered by moving outward and beyond our present concerns to the documents of the past. The test of whether a subject of knowledge is an essential part of liberal education will not be the weight of its place in the curricula of the past, but whether or not it yields an understanding of the most crucial questions in contemporary life.

The curriculum, however, will have to be conceived as a name for the total active life of each person in college. The college will therefore have to take account, as it never has before, of the kind of community life its students lead, and, in order to attain such a community, will have to take account in serious terms of the quality of its admission program. Education in cultural pluralism comes best by cultural diversity in the population of the community. Each college must therefore take active leadership in breaking down barriers to Negro, Jewish, foreign, and underprivileged students.

The ideal toward which we work will be a student body whose members form a community of diverse talents and personal qualities, with wide distribution of cultural and economic groups. We will bring students and faculty members from other countries, and will seek funds from every source to make our colleges into community centers for international living. This will also mean that the notion of field work will have to be expanded radically to include the first hand study of other countries by American students. The steps already taken by the federal government to use American funds to bring foreign students here,

---

[1]Comment by Paul L. Essert:
  It is indeed heartening to find a statement in which the writer ably stands his ground against the reactionary tide in education but at the same time challenges those who would be concerned with education as an experience with a "danger in an educational philosophy which is intentionally vague about its ultimate value system."

should be followed by further steps to send at least ten thousand American students abroad each year, to study the art, science, and life of other countries. A series of projects in student research could be established, and independent study and work in rehabilitation, not necessarily connected with universities, could be undertaken under the supervision of faculty members in this country. The year abroad in such a project would be an integral part of the college program of the selected student. It could be financed for approximately the same number of American dollars now used for a year in an American college.

There is room for expansion in many of the responsibilities we now give to students, particularly in the area of teaching. The methods of teaching used in experimental colleges are often criticized because they are expensive, in terms of teachers, time, and money. If those methods are to be extended to other institutions, we can invent and demonstrate ways in which they are adaptable to larger numbers of students, with fewer teachers and scanty facilities. One way would be to develop within each class a number of discussion leaders who could be given responsibility of preparing themselves to lead smaller groups within the class, and other groups within the college. This kind of experiment might serve as a source for the new teachers our entire educational system needs so badly. Each college must think of itself as a center of learning from which teachers will go. Any fully educated man is a teacher, whether or not he adopts teaching as his profession. The important fact for him is that he believes so deeply in the things he has learned, that he wants to share them with others.

In the matter of educational research, all colleges have duties and opportunities. Only the surface of the modern problem has been scratched by what has been done in the past in the experimental colleges. We are still learning how to evaluate student ability, whether in order to select a student body or to decide when he should graduate. We are still vague about the relation of personality to intelligence. We still have rather simple notions about how to develop self-discipline, how to control aggression, discourage frustration, and encourage the deepest kind of learning. We have no certainty that our teachers and students do not spend too much time discussing, and too little time in listening. In the absence of any formal examinations, what values have been lost which we might regain by more subtle modes of testing?

But these are practical matters which can be worked out in future planning, and by each college as it continues to meet the needs of American education.

The distinctive aim of a modern education is to create in youth such a deep attachment to humane moral values that the life of each becomes intuitively liberal and the action of each constantly helpful to the total community of human interests. Our unique responsibility as philosophers of education or as teachers is to be educational pioneers, working steadily at the outer edge of intellectual and social advance. Our particular hope is to make in each of our college communities a model of what life can be in a happy, free, and useful human society.[j]

[j]Comment by Mason W. Gross:

Dr. Taylor's paper fails to come to grips with the central problem confronting American higher education. The problem is simply this: what are we to do with the majority of our students, who have come to college with no vocational drive whatsoever, so far as the actual content of the college offering is concerned? These students are in the majority. Their presence and their behavior in college reflect the two common attitudes toward college education which I recently heard expressed as follows: first, that every American boy and girl has the right and should have the opportunity to go to college, and, second, that they will not acquire anything of real value while they are there. These students can be separated into two groups. There are those who have no vocational drive whatsoever. They are in college because the opportunity was offered, and they rather hope to graduate, because it would be a blow to their self-respect or to their standing in the community if they did not. The others have some sort of drive, but it has little or nothing to do with the content of their studies. They want the degree badly, because of the economic opportunities it seems to promise. But the lack of connection between their studies and their drives results in dissatisfaction, if not in outright failure.

We normally justify keeping such people in college on the ground that we can make better citizens of them. Dr. Taylor has explicitly joined the ranks of those who would make good democratic citizens of these students. We are to formulate a philosophy and teach it, without fear of the charge of indoctrination. But let us be perfectly clear about the nature of the task. In the first place we are to assume the responsibility for inspiring students who feel no inspiration themselves (for if we assume them to have a vocational inspiration, the task is easy and a pleasure), and we are to inspire them to the democratic life.

It seems to me quite clear that our colleges cannot give a student an education democratically or otherwise, until it can make the whole procedure meaningful by tying it onto the positive vocational demands of the student. There is a terrible temptation in sham or play democracy. You cannot make democrats by saying to the administration office or the fraternities, "thou shalt admit Negroes, Jews, and foreigners," or by telling the professors, "thou shalt not lecture but discuss." Nor can you "plunge a student into the middle of his time," if he is not there to take the plunge. All these things are the signs and symptoms of a democratic college, but they do not contain the germ. Dr. Taylor is mistaking necessary conditions for a sufficient condition. I volunteer instead the slogan: "No vocation—no education." So long as we are confronted with students whose primary purpose it is to sweat out for four years the miracle which will raise them from the level of menial tasks to something vaguely envisaged as more elevating and satisfying, as well as better paid, we will never be able to make any lasting educational impression at all.

Dr. Taylor's remedies will be just as wide of the mark as the old classical education.

The only way I can see to meet the problem is to release the vocational drives by breaking down the social inhibitions which cause the student to abdicate as an independent individual before he ever comes to college. Until this is done the most cleverly contrived curriculum will have no positive meaning for such students, and Dr. Taylor's democratic methods will produce only the hollow mockery of a pseudo-democracy. But once it is done, then the college teacher can pass the responsibility back to the student to undertake his own education in order that it may be a real education answering real demands, instead of a contrived curriculum designed to meet synthetic or *ersatz* demands.

[Cf. the discussion of vocational education in Chapter II by Lyman Bryson.]

Comment by Louis J. A. Mercier:

President Harold Taylor's paper pins down our central issue, that of values: What are the values by which man can live most nobly, and how should life be organized to make this possible? The Hebrew tradition would say: to be just to God and neighbor (The Ten Commandments); and the Christian would add: to love one's neighbor in the love of God beyond what justice requires (the doctrine of the Gospels). The Nazi would say that to live nobly is to fight ruthlessly for the triumph of the superior race and to eliminate from it other racial strains. The atheistic communist would say: to secure economic justice by the liquidation of the upper classes, the regimentation of the masses, and the elimination of religion as a fraudulent opium.

What then would President Taylor have us believe in as a basis for values? He proposes as the task for modern education: "to state a contemporary philosophy and to teach it." But what about the philosophy contemporary to yesterday? Did it have no abiding value? Why should our contemporary philosophy have more? If not, do the ways to live most nobly constantly change? Apparently so.

Professor Taylor wants us of course to live in terms of American democracy. Well, moral values are not necessarily democratic. They certainly cannot be democratically arrived at. Even a majority vote could not make murder noble; and there can be morality under an authoritarian regime, provided it respects the inalienable rights of man, which means to govern according to the law consonant with the nature of man, and the antecedents of the nature of man. That is precisely the difference between an authoritarian and a totalitarian regime. Even a democratic government is authoritarian, and the only thing that can save it from being totalitarian, that can save minority groups from the tyranny of the majority, is the recognition of a bill of rights based on the abiding nature of man. Page Thomas Jefferson.

So Professor Gross, in his comments on Professor Taylor's paper, may go as far as to say that Professor Taylor has failed to analyze the problem of higher education, and has not gone far enough in proposing a solution. Professor Gross would then have us put all our effort in developing vocational interest. However, he also says: "If you are without problems, desires, values, or vocation, democracy has no meaning for you." That sentence means a great deal more than: "if you have no vocation, democracy has no meaning for you," which is the burden of Professor Gross's rejoinder. Dr. Gross flays the average American student because he does not know what he wants to do. That is true of many, but it is not true that many have no problems, desires, or are not puzzled about values. Too many bull sessions are witness to the contrary. And is it not true that if students knew more about values, if their professors gave them a chance to know more about all the philosophies of value, they would be surer about whether life is worth living except for sensual pleasure, and they might be more easily inspired to settle on the vocation for which they are best fitted, and through which they could be saved from frustrations and best serve the community?

[Cf. the discussion of the place of vocational preparation in the goals of education in Chapter II by Lyman Bryson (including comment by George N. Shuster), Chapter III by T. V. Smith, Chapter IX by Howard Mumford Jones, Chapter XV by Dr. Shuster, Chapter XVI by Earl J. McGrath (including comment by Louis J. A. Mercier), and comment by George B. de Huszar in Appendix III.]

CHAPTER XIX

Guiding the Emotions[a]

By ROWLAND W. DUNHAM
Dean, College of Music, University of Colorado

To conceive a philosophy of living which ignores consideration of the emotions would circumscribe its area unthinkably. An educational plan lacking adequate emphasis on a comprehensive esthetic perception would be obviously incomplete. Educators have shown some concern over this phase of cultural necessities for some time. They have succeeded to a small degree in this direction. Unfortunately results have been more apparent than real.

Our college curricula generally contain elective courses in the survey of literary, artistic, and musical achievements intended to stimulate an interest and appreciation of these treasures of the imagination. Such efforts, sincere though they have been, have fallen far short of the desired objectives, as they have failed to reach but a small minority. The St. John plan is a good example of the extreme method of promoting culture through literature, in opposition to the practicality of the elective system. Such a return to the original intent of a gentleman's culture has reasonable basis. On the other hand, the exigencies of modern life are sufficiently strong in the minds of our youth to make its usefulness for them appear questionable. Then we have the General Education Program by which all students are exposed to all of the fundamental fields. They are thereby expected to emerge with a well rounded educational experience upon which their future life is expected to become full and adaptable.

In dealing with emotional guidance the best medium is musical art.[b]

---

[a] [Cf. the discussion of art in education in Chapter VII, Part V, by Charles W. Hendel.]
[b] Comment by Harry B. Friedgood:

Although few would question Dean Dunham's opening statement, one is inclined to take serious issue with this remark. Nero fiddled while Rome burned; and Nazidom's barbarians thrilled to the strains of Wagner while millions of men, women and children were murdered. The pages of history are stained with instances in which music eased the savage beast. It would be dangerously naïve to assume that the acquisition of the art of

To declare this to be the most satisfactory medium it is necessary that we determine its nature and the consequent reasons for such an assertion. It is evident that music is the purest of the arts, for it contains nothing that represents any reality outside of its own domain. Its meaning is self-contained apart from any reference to verbal description. Because of its spiritual nature music possesses a form and reality within its own domain. Its individuality precludes specific ideas, thereby permitting personal emotional reactions to each listener. If we can enjoy music physically, as a sort of panacea, without at all understanding it, we find it to be a direct esthetic adventure of the most beneficent kind. By repeated contact and skilful guidance as to its content an active participation in its revelation will add to its significance to an amazing degree.

There has never been a time more propitious for an appraisal of our educational accomplishments with a view to rehabilitation. With our campuses teeming with students of both maturity and youth there may

---

music, or of an appreciation for it, are conducive to the development of emotional stability or maturity. That the art of music, *per se,* is an important ingredient of the educational process is quite another concept, which makes up in realism for what it lacks in sentimentality. The role of education in music is concerned more particularly with an interpretation of its relevance for the contemporary culture without forfeiting its universal significance or individuality. Even this does not guarantee, however, that the practice of music, or its appreciation, cannot be perverted to the anti-social aims of an amoral psychotic or neurotic.

Dean Dunham's reply:
I deny the implications of this criticism. That old notion about Nero is entirely erroneous. That gentleman was not even in Rome at the conflagration. The violin had not been invented. The theory of the Teutonic superman is expounded in Wagner's *Nibelungen Lied* music dramas solely through the poetry. That Hitler was fond of the music is an indication of his sponsorship of the philosophy expressed in the poem. He probably had little if any musical understanding.

Music, unlike the other arts, is a suggestive rather than a concrete one. It is totally unable to make implications of specific character of itself. There is a widespread misconception in this connection especially as regards the alliance of music with words. These words may have a distinct message which may easily be closely allied with musical setting. This setting may indeed be appropriate and quite effective but it can never in itself deliver an exact meaning of the text. Richard Strauss complained at one time of the utter incapacity of music to represent something concrete. He said it was his wish that he could somehow hit upon a melodic fragment that would depict a *chair*. Just what advantage this would be is not quite clear. Composers of his school have tried in vain to make their music exact and pictorial. It cannot be done.

Of course the power of music as an educational or emotional factor is something that may be evaluated only through the opinions of experienced scholars. The bulk of the evidence seems to coincide with my thesis.

be observed a diversity of approach that presents many problems. While the older ex-service contingent dominate the scene with their juniors following their lead, this situation will soon pass but with the effects of their presence remaining. One of the phenomena of today is the general interest in music. What was once considered a rather effeminate avocation has now become a matter of unashamed concern. Students crowd our auditoriums for any and all musical performances. Choirs, bands, and orchestras find the best material in the institution, and in all departments, eager to participate in musical enterprises. Elective courses in "Music Appreciation" are popular. The boys who never had a desire or an opportunity to study voice, piano, or some other instrument, clamor for a teacher. Music departments everywhere report their utter inability to cope with this situation.

We are rapidly becoming a music conscious nation. The public is now aware of the place emotional experience in this field may assume in their lives. Radio, motion picture, and concert hall offer an ever increasing abundance of the very best in performance and repertoire. By taking advantage of such a unique situation education may succeed in making us a discriminating people. In accomplishing even a small part of such an obligation real strides will be made toward a cultural Utopia.

Philosophers through the ages have frequently recognized the power of music in human experience. Despite the rudimentary condition of music in their day, quotations of a few of the world's more important writings are still applicable to musical art as we know it today. In his enumeration of the qualifications of a gentleman Confucius says: "When courtesy and music droop, law and justice fail. And when law and justice fail them, a people can move neither hand or foot." Plato in the third book of his *Republic* advises: "Musical training is a more potent instrument than any other, because rhythm and harmony find their way into the secret places of the soul, on which they mightily fasten, imparting grace, and making the soul graceful of him who is rightly educated or ungraceful of him who is ill educated." Aristotle in the fifth book of his *Politics* elucidates his ideas concerning music: "Our first question is whether or not music should be made a branch of education, and whether its use is moral training or amusement or rational enjoyment. It may be placed under all three heads. . . . We must inquire whether it is not in its nature more honorable than merely to give recreation, whether we should not only enjoy the pleasure it affords of which the whole world is sensible, . . . or whether we should see if it has not also some power to form character and influence the soul."

Evolution of musical art from the age of Greek culture to modern methods of tonal enunciation would make a long story. When we remember that before about 1400 all music was entirely melodic, it becomes patent that its possibilities were indeed simple. Only after the acceptance of Christianity by the Roman Empire and the establishment of the state sponsorship did music become an important part of the Christian liturgy. The rise of intoned speech made necessary by the size of the Italian Basilica (which were used as places of worship) together with the antiphonal chanting of Psalms, similar to ancient synagogue practice, culminated in a rather impressive repertory of melodic church music. Then it was discovered that another melody could be combined with the principal one with added pleasure to the ear. This discovery was revolutionary, for it brought about the art of musical composition. Church music was gradually elaborated by the texture of many melodies moving simultaneously and in varied rhythms. The interweaving of melodic strands was called counterpoint and marks the beginning of musical composition. Thus was introduced the element of harmony without which music could not have advanced to its present state of complexity and interest.

So long as musical utterances were in one melodic line, there was some resemblance to natural phenomena such as the involuntary and uncontrolled songs of birds and to rhythmical occurrences of many kinds. After the invention of this man devised art, developments were rapid. As composition became more elaborate, choral groups needed artificial tonal support. This led to accompaniment, first by small instrumental bands and later by organs. A parallel secular activity among the people in connection with their dances and other occasions represented a quite independent musical style. Professionalism of an uncouth sort appeared with strolling musicians like the Troubadours. These entertainers sang their songs, romantic, comic or epic, accompanied by lutes which furnished limited harmonic effects. With the invention of opera, originally musical versions of Greek dramas (a part of the Renaissance movement), by Florentine aristocratic amateurs, secular music assumed a position of paramount importance. The opera became a tremendous popular success. Opera houses sprang up all over Italy and then in northern countries. Orchestras were used not only for harmonic purposes but to play incidental music by themselves. Violin solo pieces and fragile pieces for the harpsichord (forerunner of the piano) appeared. The wealthy nobility engaged companies of musicians to produce opera, furnish music for their private chapels, and give musical entertainment for the diversion of themselves and their guests. Concert music became a distinct part of the musical scene. As this new secular idiom was evolved, the modal polyphony of the liturgical music was modified to meet the new conditions. Thus modern musical art was born.

Musical Art, Its Materials and Esthetics

Music, child among the arts, is unique in many ways. Dr. William Pole in his *Philosophy of Music*[1] says, "Music is formed from sounds of peculiar kinds, which, after being selected from certain elementary series called scales, are combined and arranged at the will of the composer." Another definition is sometimes stated to the effect that music is language by means of which thoughts and emotions are suggested by successions or combinations of musical sounds (tones) in metrical patterns. In either case it is clear that music is a medium for conveying certain tonal impressions to the listener. Unlike literature and the fine arts certain special provisions are required for the realization of the intended effects in the way of a performer and particular accessories such as instruments or human voices. Moreover, its projection is a transitory one, for the auditor must listen to each momentary sound or sounds and by familiarity with the vernacular correlate them with sounds immediately preceding while anticipating relationship with those to come. This process is an illusive one which predicates some considerable previous experience. As has been indicated, the invention of the fundamental structure of music has been an entirely manmade device. Nothing like our complex musical system exists in nature. Neither does music attempt to reflect natural events or sounds. With this in mind, we may well marvel at the phenomenal success that musical composition has had in creating effects that possess such intriguing beauty. On the other hand, the effect of our greatest masterpieces must inevitably be completely futile, even irritating to a person with no previous musical experience.

[1] William Pole, *Philosophy of Music*, Stanley Paul & Company, Ltd., sixth edition, London, 1924.

Musical composition is the artificial assembling of tonal material according to accepted principles. These principles are exceedingly flexible. What we call a melody is but a series of successive notes moving upward and downward in pitch according to a deliberate plan. We realize that as the contour moves higher there may be more intensity of emotional effect with lessened tension as it descends. Thus it may be noted that even as simple a basis for music as a tune is by no means arrived at by accident. When musicians in the Middle Ages found the happy result of uniting two or more melodies, at once a new element was discovered in the process. From this horizontal simultaneous movement of two or more melodies there was apparent a pleasant vertical tonal result. As an outcome, it was found feasible to accompany a single melody with "chords"—masses or blocks of sound. Further exploration developed the fact that some chords seemed clearly consonant, others somewhat discordant, laying the foundation for judicious selection of both elements in harmonic variety. Following the pattern of poetry a metrical division of the flow of music corroborated our instinctive feeling for rhythm. This is most strongly apparent in dance music but must furnish the life blood of all other musical creation. Beyond these fundamentals music must have definite form, again resembling poetry. This architectural element furnishes a final constituent for the creation of an artistic product of inexhaustible resources.

The enjoyment of music demands an instinctive realization of these component parts. Even without any understanding of the art nearly everybody possesses a natural attraction toward tonal charm. With experience and some information pleasure is greatly magnified by an awareness of melodic line, harmonic color, and more especially by the phraseology and context of musical structure. It is this more active type of listening that leads us to an emotional reaction which is objective as well as subjective. Only by this means can we come to a genuine appreciation of the manifold beauties of musical art.

Musicians, psychologists, and philosophers have attempted for many years to formulate an answer to the problem of training listeners. We know that our reaction to music defies complete analysis. It seems to have some sort of meaning to us which is beyond description. Since it represents nothing external or real, it must be regarded as pure art of deep significance. There are indefinable spiritual values, there is an appeal to our sense of orderliness by the logic of its structure, there is an appeal to our imagination and idealism. Our emotional response is, therefore, highly intimate and infinite. Because there is a lack of anything concrete many persons find it possible to derive only a kind of sensuous enjoyment, largely physical and lacking coherence. Such purely sensuous pleasure in the sonorous charm of a piece of music, say by Chopin or Debussy, may well be the deliberate intention of the composer. Then there is the sheer joy which many possess from more formal types. Again, one may feel a sort of community delight in the mass enjoyment of an audience.

Esthetics as applied to musical art has been the subject of much controversy among psychologists. No attempt here will be made to discuss the many theories but some comprehension of the diversity of these ideas may be of interest. William James argues (1884–1890) that if emotion is truly a sort of subjective experience an analysis of it would reveal the presence of bodily processes. From this premise it would seem that emotions and bodily states are not identical or interchangeable. It may therefore be concluded that there is a reaction which might be termed esthetic emotion as opposed to purely physical emotion. Then again there is the term, "intellectual emotion," used by James which has caused much confusion. Some investigators have maintained that we can sum up our response to musical experiences by the words objective (non-emotional) and subjective (emotional). Carroll Pratt has summed up some of our questions in the following paragraph, "The reason for music's aloofness, its uncorporeal and ethereal character, is to be found in the fact of the relative absence of objective reference in tonal qualities. In no other art does the sensory material so greatly favor the esthetic attitude of detached contemplation, so quickly remove the mind from its customary concern over the practical consequences of incoming impressions."[2]

It is not, however, to be assumed that emotional reaction to music is an exclusive consideration. Such a response argues little for the quality of any composition. There are works of undeniable greatness which are essentially objective in nature. To comprehend these something more is necessary than a mere emotional response. This accounts for the initial indifference of certain individuals to music beyond their grasp, certain monumental contributions of Bach, for example.

Early exposure to musical art products are merely emotional experi-

[2]*The Meaning of Music,* New York, 1931. Courtesy of McGraw-Hill Book Company.

ences. The absence of any but sensory feeling is both inevitable and desirable. As musical contacts are repeated, even without any active participation, an instinctive realization of structure and other details becomes evident. It is quite possible to acquire a realization of many of the important details of music without any technical knowledge whatever. Far better is it to receive some of the proper kind of instruction to make possible a more intelligent approach to the matter of objective listening.

Just how much ought one to know about musical details for the ultimate in comprehension? The answer is obvious to the professional musician. Training the ear to discriminate and observe details is part of his apprenticeship. There is a ridiculous notion generally prevalent that the professional is immune to the emotions of musical experience because of the satiety of his vocation. Nothing could be farther from fact. Any sincere musician is of necessity tremendously thrilled by fine music. In addition he has an awareness of much that is obscured by the intricacies of the music from the layman. In tonal art beauty is not by any means skin deep. It lies hidden from the untrained ear in a profusion of enchantment that is the glory of the consummate imagination of its creator.

A large portion of our population has had some training in musical performance. This naturally accounts for much of the tremendous interest in music throughout the country. Not only have many acquired some technical skill by private and group study, but many more have obtained certain limited musical advantages offered by choirs and instrumental ensembles in our public schools. It is evident that a decided enthusiasm and a limited comprehension of artistic significance has emanated from this process. While it is true that there are benefits to be secured through abilities to sing and to play an instrument, this training has usually had as its objective a popular sort of exhibitionism. Such displays, necessary though they may be, do little to add to the performers' esthetic comprehension. No doubt students find exhilaration in their appearances in public where applause and praise seem to give a personal prestige. As a means of revealing to participants even a vestige of the meaning of the music, these projects offer little or nothing.

There is, in the realm of music, a reward far above a superficial skill of performance. When we are able to direct attention and understanding toward this vital intent we shall fulfil the important function of music in education. Until we do this the undertaking lacks justifiable purpose. Every experienced professional who has dealt with products of the average private teacher of vocal or instrumental music and public school ensembles will agree with the above criticism. Educators apart from the musical field have already begun to question the emphasis on an activity which seems to furnish students a special technique and neglect the more enduring values of its esthetics.

Music in Universities

Responsibilities in university for instruction in music at most universities are of two distinct kinds, (a) professional schools or departments; and (b) cultural advantages in liberal arts or general education programs.

I. Professional Training

Years ago the preparation for a career in the field of music was confined to conservatories of music. These were commercially maintained institutions, sometimes with endowments or partly subsidized by wealthy patrons, where the student received the necessary instruction to launch into a career. Little else was available for the aspirant to fame and fortune. These schools were often staffed with an adequate group of teachers, especially strong in vocal and instrumental subjects. Theoretical and historical (music) requirements covered the ground sufficiently to insure satisfactory background. Two things acted as deterrents to many: one was the high cost, the other was the highly specialized concentration, with little else but music. The quality of work offered at these schools was excellent as the eminence of their graduates will testify.

After years of small departments of music in the liberal arts colleges with one or two courses in "appreciation" or history of music plus the old fashioned glee club, happily demised, expansions and reorganizations began to occur with curricula based on those of the conservatories plus a generous amount of the academic element. Majors in music for the B.A. degree attracted many musically inclined young people who realized the prestige of the university sanction was a necessity in their profession. The professional parallel of a Bachelor of Music degree was a natural sequence. From an obscure fragment the music department rapidly assumed a position of importance and recognition. This competition made serious inroads on the enrollments and economics of the conservatories. In frantic efforts to maintain their very existence they, too, began to issue diplomas for the Bachelor of Music degree. By this move some success was won in the fight to prove the superiority of a specialized school. Then came the depression of the early thirties which marked the end of many but the strongest. Today, thanks partly to the help of veterans' educational aid, conditions have become once more favorable. Existing conservatories are crowded and prosperous and some of the defunct institutions have been revived.

The administration and conduct of professional musical projects in universities varies. Music may be a department under liberal arts or education. It may be combined with fine arts or drama and speech into a college of fine arts with a presiding dean and directors for each field. Less common but by far preferable is the independent, autonomous college of music.

There are two basic degrees now offered by most colleges of music. The first is known as Bachelor of Music. This degree is based on performance in advanced levels. Requirements consist of a complete four (or more) year concentration on the major applied music subject (voice or instrument) with usually at least two years of supplementary study in an applied music minor; there are two years of harmony and ear training; form and analysis, orchestration; sometimes conducting; frequently counterpoint and elementary composition. A course in musical literature is followed by one or more subjects covering historical material. To round out a cultural background at least one year of college English and electives in liberal arts up to about twenty-five per cent of the total hours fill out the schedule. A Bachelor of Music is presumed to be well advanced as a player or singer in his major subject.

Music education is the other field for the musician. This work is in preparation for a position as teacher or supervisor of music in the public schools. In most institutions the applied music major is insisted upon throughout with a diversity of applied music minors to qualify the student for possible needs in his later positions. Theory is covered adequately enough for the student to know the grammar of music, acquire a trained ear, and be able to analyze music thoroughly for the teaching responsibilities ahead. There is a considerable amount of work in the department of education including practice teaching and methods of various sorts in music.

Graduate schools, where the college of music is strong, are likely to make available Master's degrees in performance and in music education. The young musician finds it exceedingly difficult to secure a good position, particularly in the public schools unless he possesses a graduate degree. After the Master's degree the music student must either content himself with his academic guarantees or investigate the possibility of some sort of a Doctorate. Here he finds a difficult problem. If he is concerned with music education, he may find the answer in the Doctor of Education offered in many universities with concentration in music education. This degree is sometimes quite adequate and practical under sympathetic and capable direction and a well qualified music department or college. For the composer or musicologist several universities permit a Ph.D. with such majors. What about the pianist, singer, organist, or orchestral player? He is in a position of choosing one of these degrees in which he is neither interested nor concerned on one hand, or has not the peculiar creative talent and research inclination on the other. He may hope for the best and pray for eventual eminence that may lead to the award of an honorary Doctor of Music degree from a respectable college or university. There is one alternative to the latter rather remote chance that few musicians relish but occasionally accept. A Doctor of Music degree may be "bought" by contributing a modest scholarship or similar donation to certain known organizations.

Recognizing this situation as momentous, the musical profession has lately begun to take cognizance with the view of a practical remedy. The solution lies in the abolishment of the Doctor of Music degree as an honorary dispensation, transferring it to the position of an earned reward for artistic accomplishment above the requirements for a Master of Music degree. While this movement is in its infancy and finds opposition in some quarters, the practicability of such an arrangement and the elimination of discriminatory obstacles to an appropriate doctorate in applied music has begun to receive the support that it deserves. Justification may be easily found when it is revealed that many universities will not accept a person for a higher ranking position (if at all) without the blessing generally ascribed to a doctorate. Some of these institutions of higher learning are perfectly sincere in their stand and refute the charge of intellectual snobbery. Others maintain their attitude to be obligatory. One college president writes that he approves this move by musicians. He explains the specific requirement in his own case by attributing it to the accrediting association which demands a hard and fast basis for appointments to his faculty. The letter closes with the opinion that American institutions of higher learning are today afflicted with a violent case of "Ph.D.-itis."[c]

A case may be made in favor of the separate self-governing college of music as preferable to a department or a unit of a college of fine arts. Under a thoroughly competent dean such an organization has many decided advantages. In the first place a layman, regardless of his cultural virtues, is rarely qualified to decide on the many vital emergencies in this area. A wise man will properly consign most decisions to the department head or director. But many times he will reject a well considered recommendation which seems *to him* to be incorrect. He may often demand curricular details based upon personal bias. In selection of faculty members his ignorance may be cloaked by what he believes honestly enough to be sound—an appraisal of the candidate's record. This process may be entirely faulty as any experienced professional knows full well.

With a college of music a truly qualified dean possesses the technical knowledge, the special training, and experience to administer advantageously. Some executives work with faculty committees to secure cooperation and collaboration in particular questions. It certainly is not perchance that the finest institutions for professional training in the country are autonomous or that the heads of these schools are the most prominent men in the profession.

Accrediting in music is handled by regional authorities upon the

[c]Comment by Archibald Davison:
Particularly pertinent are Dean Dunham's observations on the preoccupation with degrees which now marks the attitude of so many institutions of learning in this country. There is almost an element of childlike discovery in the concentration many educational administrators bring to bear on brief euphonious combinations of letters, all of them ending with a capital D. One is tempted to wonder if contact with the alphabet is not a novel experience. Regarding the relative validity of all advanced degrees both earned and honorary, it might be suggested that a healthy regulation would require all holders of these degrees to insert after them the names of the granting institutions. That, at least, would offer a hint as to the degree holder's professional standing.

recommendation of the National Association of Schools of Music both for professional schools and departments in liberal arts giving music majors. Each member school is thoroughly examined by a reliable musician and accepted, if adequate qualification is demonstrated. By this means standards are established and maintained, individual departments and colleges are strengthened with able advice, and strong advocacy of needed improvements is submitted to the university administration.

On the whole the quality of instruction in the college professional music school is good. Possession of a charter to grant degrees presents recognized danger. The variance between institutions where a high standard is maintained and those whose faculties are mediocre and inadequate is far too great. Within the profession itself there is no little difference of opinion as to the efficiency of college music departments, with perhaps a few exceptions, as compared to that of the famous conservatories of today and yesterday. In the matter of salaries alone, colleges are usually unable to attract musicians of high attainments for what they can afford to pay. The weaker schools are consequently compelled to function with a staff of incompetents who eventually recommend their badly trained students for degrees. The situation is such that only recently the NASM wisely abrogated a rule that full credit should be given to all students transferring from one member school to another.

Another difficulty of securing effectual graduation standards is the academic custom of establishing a regular period of four years for a degree. Just why this particular number should be sacred in tradition and practice is hard to justify. Probably we are tradition bound. In artistic training four years may serve as a minimum for a performing musician only when his previous study has been of high calibre. Efforts are being made to raise standards to a level where most of the less talented will be required to spend at least one additional year in study before a degree can be expected. Yale has had a five year curriculum for some years. Most of the other colleges would do the same thing were it not that competition for gifted students is too keen to risk announcing such an extension in resident requirements. That five years should be the common expectancy is the belief of all administrators.

II. Music in Liberal Arts Programs

In this category may be included the colleges of specialization where music may be a possible elective. The discussion will be solely in reference to cultural aspects.

Concern over guidance in emotional phases of the college offerings is beginning to be in evidence. A feeling that a specific obligation exists seems to be becoming urgent. In the expanding adoption of the General Education Program there is a place allotted to required courses in music, art, and literature in the Humanities area. One might expect the St. John's plan to make some similar provision for music. As an elective, musical guidance is available only to the few. In the broader conception of higher education music becomes imperative. In considering objectives it is vital, however, that effectual goals be set up and achieved. Here is the rub—how shall this be done?

Presentation of music as a means of emotional training is a matter that is not too simple. First of all, instructors with the right qualifications are so rare as to be virtually impossible to find. To be sure we have the musicologists who appear to be made for the job. They have studied *about* music exhaustively. Their research and academic records appear irreproachable. We have with us many European refugees with high sounding doctor's degrees and a broken English diction that impresses the average American as evidence of that legendary superiority he believes to exist. Among musicologists there are many, mostly our own native sons and daughters, who are real musicians as well. This is not an attack on this specialty because our universities in this country are now graduating competent musical scholars whose training has been so extensive that they have far more than a speaking acquaintance with the art. In appointing an instructor for a survey course in music deans will need to exercise greatest caution. It is so easy to be misled by superficial display of knowledge in a subject that is strange.

One of the common issues concerning a survey course in the triumvirate of music, art, and literature is the glib insistence upon that pet of educationists—integration. In my own university the initial discussion introduced this subject immediately. Following the practice in a specified college that was reported to be a model example of the General Education Program, it was suggested that we must find a scholar who would give the proposed courses in all three subjects, successively or concurrently. The proponent of this idea was firm in his belief that a single individual could be found with expert knowledge of three such diversified fields. Immediately the professors of these subjects rose to the occasion with protests that a person with such profound comprehensive wisdom was not of this world but veritably a superman indeed. In any similar group the same reaction would indubitably occur.

As to integration here there would of necessity be only a relatively small amount. It would be of interest to make it clear that the careers of, say, Beethoven and Goethe, were within the same period. Just how much conditions of the era affected their creative output would be a matter that could be questioned in most instances. Music is particularly ill adapted to presentation in integration with other artistic movements. There have been attempts in recent textbooks on music history and on appreciation to present an integrated text. The limited references to other artistic fields are handled with discretion and give some added interest for the student. It must be repeated here, however, that music is an exposition of a peculiar type of beauty that is entirely dissimilar to the others. Its appeal is entirely to the imagination without reference to reality. Establishment of good taste is a matter of experience preferably under the kindly direction of a refined skilful musical mentor. Integration must obviously be more apparent than real. The value of an attempted relationship to those more realistic areas must be judged as dubious if not quite nil.

In college courses there is the ever present hurdle of grading. This basis for academic accomplishment is no doubt a necessary adjunct to the system. Without the accepted methods it would be quite impossible to determine such vital matters as *cum laude,* Phi Beta Kappa, and even eligibility to membership in the more erudite social fraternities. When an attempt is made to discover emotional progress, a professor is confronted with an enigma that defies solution. He may give tests to find out about certain facts and opinions—his own or the textbooks. He may ask for the student's views and reactions to certain musical works. Then he must, on such a feeble premise, assign a proper grade from what he infers from the paper. In music where we have already found words to be completely inadequate, such measurements must often be out of the question. The best the examiner can do is to guess as honestly and accurately as these impossible conditions permit. An eminent English professor stated once that he was violently opposed to giving grades to students in matters involving emotional response. His "system of guessing" was simple. All students who had followed the course intently and showed average intelligence received an A. Persistent absentees were failed. All others varied from B to C depending on their apparent indifference.

Any genuine love of music, such as we may hope to generate in students, is a process of infoldment that may be handicapped by false concepts. It is well to begin any organized program in education of musical taste with music as free as possible from complexity. Vocal music may well be the first step since its adornment of the words makes an immediate appeal. John Ruskin in *Sesame and Lilies* advises, "That the finest models are the truest, simplest, usefullest. Note these epithets; they will range through all the arts. Try them in music, where you might think they are least applicable. I say truest, that in which the notes most closely and faithfully express the meaning of the words or the character of the intended emotion; again, the simplest, that in which the meaning and melody are attained with the fewest and most significant notes possible; and finally, the usefullest, that music which makes the best words most beautiful, which enchants them in our memories each with its own glory of sound, and which applies them closest to the heart at the moment we need them."[3]

As musical intents in the more elaborated styles become familiar, a student may reach the place where he can thrill to the esthetic-emotional effect (subjective) and at the same time have his happiness greatly augmented by a comprehension of component features (objective). Schiller in his *Letters upon the Esthetic Education of Man* summarizes as follows: "Two opposing impulsions—I. Sensuous (changeable); II. Formal (imitable). From the association of these two opposite principles we have seen beauty result." Later comes the fine sentence, "Beauty alone confers happiness on all, and under its influence every being forgets he is limited."

One of the unforgivable errors in connection with music is the attempt to classify the intention of a composer in a piece of music. A composition must have not one meaning but as many as there are listeners. That quality is its glory and any attempt to label musical thoughts is as absurd as it is insulting. The practice, common with teaching music to children, of asking them to describe the music or how they felt about it is neither

[3] Macmillan Pocket Classics, The Macmillan Co., New York, 1919.

educational nor of any possible value. Some of these silly experiments if foisted on professional musicians would result in as many diverse answers. The professionals would probably refuse to be guinea pigs anyway. All music is not equally pleasurable. Only recently Benjamin Britten, best known of contemporary British composers, stated his honest though peculiar indifference to Beethoven and preference for Chopin and Tschaikowsky. Personal preferences are quite proper with even the beginners and should be respected. Really important is the ability to keep an open mind about all art, for what you dislike today may well be beloved by tomorrow.

Vast stores of musical information have also often been mistaken for musicianship. Some of the greatest men in the musical world have notoriously bad memories. The story is told of one of Schubert's friends who suddenly thrust a piece of music with the right upper corner torn off on a piano for the great song writer to play over. At the close came the remark, "It sounds pretty well, doesn't it?" Schubert did not recognize one of his own compositions. Quiz kid knowledge based on identification of bits of music means nothing at all. Such was a general procedure of the days of "appreciation" courses.

Educators should see to it that such absurdities will presently be eliminated at least in college teaching. Attempts to designate the character of a piece of music by a specific word are sometimes regarded as evidences of musical insight. Lack of such a word is no indication that character is not present. Music produces its own interest. All the prevalent amateurish endeavors to fit descriptions to masterpieces are proof of the complete misconceptions that are so common and so devastating.

Among educational advice frequently given is the need for attention on proper use of leisure. About one half of our wakeful hours may be devoted to the pleasant task of eating and to pleasure. We Americans have fun in a variety of ways. The addition of listening to music already occupies the interest of thousands. It is evident that some insight into the meaning of music will increase immeasurably the happiness that is present. There can be no doubt that the profitable use of leisure needs consideration in education.

A great many people who pretend to be music lovers are often the anathema of musicians. These are the busybodies who buzz around the foyers at intermission and gather together after concerts to "discuss" the performance. Many times these folks have a record collection which forms the basis for their expert opinions. They know exactly what is wrong with each number (and each number is indubitably wrong) and proclaim these colossal faults in a loud voice. Rarely do they know any piece actually—from memory, for example—so that wrong notes, deviations from the composers' markings, etc., are quite unnoticed. Their favorite criticism is that the "interpretation" is bad, as though they had any legitimate idea of what had happened. That the machinations of some of these musical morons do not always make the expected impression is indicated by the following letter printed in the student paper of the University of Colorado:

> At times we become wearied with the attitudes of the Boulder Association of Derogators, an organization made up of self-styled experts who patronize the Artist Series. These are the people who take it upon themselves to inform the world loudly and at great length of the deficiencies of the performing artists and companies which appear on the campus. Their opinions seem to be based on a wide knowledge of technical proficiency, tonal balance, and the many other details involved in such performances. We do not object to members of BAD saying what they please about an artist's performance, but we do object violently to their continual presentation of their limited ideas in such a manner as to imply that the gods are with them. It should be made clear at the outset that these persons are speaking only for themselves or for the small clique to which they belong, the BAD.
>
> Just what is the criterion for judging a performance? Do we go to a concert or play critically to examine every detail of scenery, costumes, technical proficiency, tonal balance, and staging; or do we go to enjoy ourselves? It seems quite obvious to us that most people go to enjoy themselves. Most of us are not so well versed in the arts and techniques of putting on a good show to recognize all the limitations of the performers. We must accept the over all view rather than a detailed one. In other words, we have to look at the forest because we can't see the trees. But isn't this just the thing that keeps us from getting lost in the great maze inside the forest?

The objective of building up a discriminating taste in students is not as difficult as some would have us believe. Patience and enthusiasm must characterize the instructor, or shall we say guide? Principles of music are best given in small allotments. By moving from the folk song to the symphony according to an intelligent plan, a gradual revelation of some of the meaning of music for each individual (and only to the individual) may be revealed. Succinctly and in four words the best advice is, "Fewer words, more music." As an instrument for promoting cooperation, music is certainly the best. Witness the paradox of an audience of one thousand men and women of all varieties of musical approach and experience finding in a symphonic composition exactly one thousand different reactions and each finding his own personal happiness increased in the sharing of beauty. A group of colleges, bitter rivals in athletics, keen rivals in proselyting prospective students away from each other, and disdainful of the academic standards of the others, may and frequently will gather together selected players from the bands of each and give magnificent concerts on each campus with friendship and pleasure. In music, animosities, prejudices of all kinds, and artificial loyalties to false premises, evaporate completely.

Conclusions

Any statements of goals in education would include the desirability of the creation of a cultured, well informed citizenry. If this description is applicable to our college graduates an indispensable quality is emotional stability. It is by an intelligent guidance in the objective realization of beauty through the arts that poise and balance may most likely be secured.[d] Education is stressing character, clear thinking, and personality. Certainly all three are impossible without the stability and integrity of emotional health. It has been the purpose of this essay to reveal elements, values, and procedures in an effective presentation of musical art in higher education. May it not be possible that Lessing had in mind the completely cultured man when he said in "The Education of the Human Race":

1. That which Education is to the Individual, Revelation is to the Race.
2. Education is Revelation coming to the Individual Man; and Revelation is Education which has come and is yet coming to the Human Race.

[d] Comment by Louis J. A. Mercier:
    Yes, music is most valuable. However, is it not going a little far to say that "it is in the objective realization of beauty through the arts that poise and balance may most likely be secured"? The school which bred Nazism was particularly fond of Wagner.
    [Cf. Dean Dunham's reply to Dr. Friedgood, note a, above.]

These are perilous days when our own men and women have finally been overcome with that most dreadful of all emotions—fear. As complications increase, our apprehension mounts. In our anxiety it is a comfort to find surcease in an emotional outlet that carries us away from dreadful realities. With adequate esthetic approach we concur with Schopenhauer that, "Music stands alone, quite cut off from all other arts. In it we do not recognize the copy or repetition of any idea of existence in the world. Yet it is such a great and exceedingly noble art, its effect on the inmost nature of man is as powerful, and it is so entirely and deeply understood by him in his inmost consciousness as a perfectly universal language, the distinctness of which surpasses even that of the perceptible world itself, that we certainly have more to look for in it than an *exercitum arithmeticae occultum nescientis se numerare animi,* which Leibnitz called it."[e]

[e]Comment by John D. Wild:

This paper is an interesting and informative account of the present situation of musical education in this country. What is of primary concern to this Conference, I suppose, is the possible use of music as guiding the emotions in certain cultural directions, and its possible place in an integrated scheme of general education. Dean Dunham's position on these questions leaves me in some doubt, and I should like to ask him the following questions.

Does he agree with the quotation from Aristotle that in addition to its power to produce pleasure music also has "some power to form character and influence the soul"? Throughout the greater part of his paper Dean Dunham would seem to be inclined to answer this question in the affirmative. But in the latter part he seems to argue that the appeal of music "is entirely to the imagination without reference to reality," and that it is ill adapted to any integration with other subjects or artistic movements.

At various points in his discussion Dean Dunham suggests that the cultivation of music may be helpful in overcoming fear, in developing an "attitude of detached contemplation," in confirming "our sense of orderliness," and in "promoting cooperation." All this would seem to indicate that music is of importance in guiding thought and emotion in certain directions, and that it can be integrated into some intelligible educational framework. I think it would be very helpful if Dean Dunham would expand his thought along these lines. Into what sort of integrating educational framework does he think the discipline of music should be fitted, by what sort of general introductory courses, and how?

Dean Dunham's reply:

Integration of all sorts seems to be a favorite emphasis of many educators today. In considering a presentation of the field of music in a general education program most of the thinking professional musicians agree that utmost discretion be exercised. That Beethoven's Third Symphony was written in the period of Napoleonic conquest may be understood by a student without having much bearing on the music itself. Contemporaneous conditions may have little or no influence on the actual composition of music. Too much is frequently made of extraneous influences in musical art.

The fact that the appeal of music "is entirely to the imagination without reference to reality," does not in the least affect its benign influence as possessing "some power to form character and influence the soul," as Aristotle puts it. My paper attempts, perhaps not always too exactly, to treat various aspects of the effect of music. We are dealing with a subject that is not easy to treat verbally because of its inherent nature. If music is "helpful in overcoming fear," developing an "attitude of detached contemplation," in "promoting cooperation," and "in confirming our sense of orderliness," the reason lies in a power to achieve serenity of mind, and to realize its unity and architectural contours.

Just how music fits into an intelligible educational framework is becoming clearer as our endeavors continue. The danger, we believe, of an attempt to make close integration with the other arts and humanities, is that we will fail to arouse the very powers of reaction to music which is our purpose. There does not seem to me to be any inconsistency in designating these as results of proper conduct in a course designed to give a correct comprehension of the glories of the realm of music. As a means to the cultivation of emotional stability, few subjects can offer better realizations.

APPENDIX I

Light on the Goals of Education from Preceding Conference Sessions and Publications

By F. ERNEST JOHNSON

Professor of Education, Teachers College, Columbia University

THE ASSIGNMENT I have accepted is to review the proceedings of this Conference since its inception and distil from them ideas and judgments that are relevant to the topic of the present session. I am assuming that whatever bears directly on the main purposes and goals of general education has significance for the present discussion although it is focused chiefly upon higher education. It would probably surprise most members of the Conference to discover how much attention has been given in our sessions during these eight years to basic questions of educational philosophy. Indeed, a broad construction of the assignment might bring under it the larger part of our philosophic questing in the realm of values, our analysis of cultural differences, our search for the roots of group tensions, and our wrestling with the essentials of communication. Every social, political, and cultural goal becomes an end of educational effort. As Dr. I. L. Kandel put it in the Sixth Symposium, *Approaches to Group Understanding,* "a study of textbooks on the various phases of the subject—history of education, philosophy of education, educational psychology, comparative education, theory and principles of education, educational sociology, and educational administration—will indicate the extent to which education draws upon other disciplines and the degree to which other disciplines contribute to a fuller and richer understanding of its scope."[1]

[1] I. L. Kandel, "Education," *Approaches to Group Understanding,* Lyman Bryson, Louis Finkelstein, R. M. MacIver, editors, Conference on Science, Philosophy and Religion in

What I am undertaking here is to glean from our previous sessions some of the more noteworthy specific contributions concerning the nature and purposes of general education and to sharpen some of the major issues that emerged in the effort to clarify that concept. The term general education as currently used denotes what is taken to be the normative educative experience for all citizens. With the rapid growth of secondary and higher education this concept inevitably subsumes what has been called liberal education, though the content of the word "liberal" is still a focus of much controversy.

The Goals of General Education

The Conference was told in its first session in 1940: "Liberal educational offerings in this country are scattered, disjunctive, unoriented. Many of them serve no commanding purpose worthy of the place they occupy on campuses. The American college is doubtfully liberal in the classical sense. It has fallen a prey to social license. On the one hand, state and independent colleges have lost sight of the idealistic aspects of secular purpose that have made them a signal innovation in nineteenth century higher education; on the other hand, church colleges have slavishly imitated the program of nonconformist institutions, departmentalized religion as a chapel exercise or an elective course of study, and thus lost their prophetic sense of service to youth. Both types need to recover their historic *raison d'être* and redefine their function in terms of the needs of a generation of youth whose democratic birthright is threatened by social softness within and aggressive totalitarianism without."[2]

A participant in the second session defended the thesis that "liberal education is (a) essential to the cultural and spiritual welfare of the individual, and (b) essential to political democracy and the democratic way of life."[3] He stressed free inquiry; avoidance of propaganda on

---

Their Relation to the Democratic Way of Life, Inc., New York, 1947, p. 22. (Hereafter listed as VI.)

[2]Steward G. Cole, " 'First Principles' in Liberal Education," *Science, Philosophy and Religion,* Conference on Science, Philosophy and Religion in Their Relation to the Democratic Way of Life, Inc., New York, 1941, p. 327. (Hereafter listed as I.)

[3]Theodore M. Greene, "Liberal Education and Democracy," *Science, Philosophy and Religion,* Lyman Bryson, Louis Finkelstein, editors, Conference on Science, Philosophy and

Appendix I. Light on the Goals of Education

the one hand and "indifferentism" on the other; catholicity in scope, so that the cultural heritage may be fully embraced and life may be seen "steadily and as a whole"; disciplined thinking; and the centrality of the individual as a socially responsible person. These goals, stated thus broadly, seem to be supported by a wide consensus.

"There is involved," said a later writer, "in the methods and goals of education, even in its approach to the youngest children, nothing less than a total philosophy of life. . . . Education is the conceptual and experimental process, properly adjusted to the capacities of each age, whereby the knowledge, the skills, the culture, the moral standards, and the religious faith of a people are passed on to the whole group."[4] This points to a controversial issue: the neo-classical emphasis now exemplified in the Great Books movement, *versus* the demand for a contemporary focus of the curriculum. "There are those," wrote one of the educators, "who advocate strongly that the best education is that which focuses attention on the great masterpieces of human achievement of earlier generations. There are others who believe that education will contribute most to effective living and intelligent handling of the problems of society if there is concentration on the personal and social problems of the present period."[5] He called for a synthesis of the two views.

Asserting that an essential goal of education is the development of a free mind, one of our scholars posed a question which might be addressed by a college president to a prospective instructor: "Young man, you have earned a good degree and have written what appears to be a decent book, but tell me honestly—if the shadow of totalitarianism took on flesh in America would you go to jail or wouldn't you?" Unless our education produces men and women who would unhesitatingly answer, "Yes," we have no guarantee that "freedom can be safeguarded for as much as one generation." For this freedom "is not normal to human life." It is a slowly acquired *habitus* that depends on

---

Religion in Their Relation to the Democratic Way of Life, Inc., 1942, New York, p. 122. (Hereafter listed as II.)

[4] E. Jerome Johanson, "Education for Global Brotherhood," *Approaches to World Peace,* Lyman Bryson, Louis Finkelstein, R. M. MacIver, editors, Conference on Science, Philosophy and Religion in Their Relation to the Democratic Way of Life, Inc., New York, 1944, pp. 317–318. (Hereafter listed as IV.)

[5] Grayson N. Kefauver, "Education an Important Factor in Achieving an Enduring Peace," IV, p. 342.

the "educability of the individual." And if "the vast majority of men, or even the great mass of college trained men, do not know how to be free, liberty will disappear."[6]

A leader in higher education offered an interesting list of qualities sought by business in hiring college graduates: "ability to attack problems of all sorts in an orderly and penetrating fashion; ability to deal understandingly with problems that require a grasp of current economic, social, and political forces and trends; ability to deal diplomatically and graciously with people; ability to apply general knowledge which coordinates material and human factors wisely in discrete workaday situations. What are needed and valued are good habits and attitudes of persistence, thoroughness, resourcefulness, personal integrity and trustworthiness, curiosity, and energetic drive."[7] The writer called for a bridging of the "gulf between liberal and vocational education."

An authority in the "fine arts" field noted three aspects of education "that of release, in the sense of discovering and providing means for growth and expression of capacities, emotional, physical, and intellectual; that of coordinating and harmonizing these capacities, by giving them their ethical and spiritual values; and that of purpose and direction, with which is bound up the whole question of vocational education."[8] This furnishes a basis for defining the role of the visual arts as a part of general education.

In the proceedings of last year (1947) an eminent psychiatrist suggested a formulation of educational goals in terms commonly used in the "depth" psychologies. It is noted here not only because it represents a significant body of professional thought but because it can hardly fail to impress the reader with the lack of any adequate integration, within the main body of contemporary educational psychology, of the findings and theories of the analytic psychologies. "The essential goal" of education was conceived as twofold:

> (1) To devise ways of nourishing and fortifying the ego, so that it can deal handily with the inevitable conflicts between the instinctual energies

[6]George N. Shuster, "Education and the Meaning of Freedom," IV, p. 409.
[7]Ordway Tead, "Bridging the Gap between Liberal and Vocational Education," VI, p. 80.
[8]William G. Constable, "Education in the Arts as an Element in the Integration of Human Culture," *Conflicts of Power in Modern Culture,* Lyman Bryson, Louis Finkelstein, R. M. MacIver, editors, Conference on Science, Philosophy and Religion in Their Relation to the Democratic Way of Life, Inc., New York, 1947, p. 291. (Hereafter listed as VII.)

Appendix I. Light on the Goals of Education

of the id and the realities of the external world, on the one hand, and the moral judgments of the superego, on the other. Since the capacity of the ego to fulfil its functions is dependent in part upon the reliability and strength of the superego, our education efforts should be directed also toward the problems of the latter. . . .

(2) To orient the current generation of adults with reference to two main objectives: (a) Education in the origin and social significance of the superego, with the intention that they will expose children to a minimum of psychic traumata and a maximum of security; (b) Awareness of the destructive, aggressive tendencies to which they are heir, as well as of their vulnerability to exploitation by propaganda that gives them the opportunity to unleash their aggressions rather than to sublimate them.[9]

This definition of goals has implications to which we shall return in the next section. Fresher in our minds than most of the foregoing statements is the vigorous address by the chairman of the Council of this Conference, Dr. Harlow Shapley, given at the session last year and provocatively entitled, "Must We Climb Steeples?" Among the pungent sentences are these:

A would-be professional scholar, half educated under our prevailing system, has many years after the Doctorate in which to carry out corrective measures. Eventually he can, if he will, educate himself broadly. But the non-professional, who stops formal education abruptly with his Bachelor's degree and his athletic letters, must live out a long life based intellectually on the nutrition provided by four or more years of undergraduate experience. Is a physics major, for instance, ready for the long pose of being an educated man? . . .

The epidemic of general education courses arises from recognition of the need for foundation education. Since this is a free country, where laymen can criticize the professional élite, I question the efficacy and adequacy of that movement. It falls short in coverage, in both space and time. The general education courses usually provide simply a little heavier foundation for sharper, more fragile steeples, built and climbed by amateur craftsmen in junior and senior years. . . .

Stretching the architectural analogy, let us question whether the vertical structure is sound in a burgeoning world society that of late has greatly

---

[9]Harry B. Friedgood, "Medical Education and the Psychodynamic Concept: In Relation to International Tensions," *Learning and World Peace,* Lyman Bryson, Louis Finkelstein, R. M. MacIver, editors, Conference on Science, Philosophy and Religion in Their Relation to the Democratic Way of Life, Inc., New York, 1948, p. 453. (Hereafter listed as VIII.)

increased its special fields of useful knowledge, its geographical mobility, and its responsibilities for the enlightened continuation of the human species. A structure composed of neighboring columns has basic instability. An occasional crosstie helps but does not cure the defect in design. Why not introduce deliberately, more horizontal members? Why not devote the whole of the four year liberal arts college to horizontal structures which will serve as a capping for the secondary education and at the same time provide an exceedingly firm flooring for the erection of vertical members, if competently desired, in the graduate school and later?[10]

Educational Problems Set by Human Nature

The way in which goals of education are conceived depends much on the way human nature is viewed. We have listened to much discussion of "aggressiveness" and "hostility," and other evidences of nonrational "drives" in human behavior. A prominent educational leader warned us that knowledge and skills must become means by which to "adjust asocial instincts to social living."[11] A primary need, he said, is "self-control of aggressive drives."

A paper on group tensions reminded us that social scientists give insufficient attention to the "irrational forces in human nature," which play so large a part in directing behavior. "Real persons do not follow the artificial rules of the game as it *'ought* to be played,' according to the utopians. At best, all such proposals overestimate the power of intellect because of their lack of insight into the social, selfish, and regressive trends in men. The underworld of human nature—envy, hostility, revenge, and lust of power—is ignored by the present philosophers of a hopeful, progressive, and increasingly belligerent world, who are slow to point out that frustration, discontent, and hopelessness are conditions which bring the untamed impulses of man to the surface in group tensions."[12] The implication of this analysis for educational goals is momentous. Can something be done about these evil drives? The psychologists do not call them evil, but they describe what the

---

[10] Harlow Shapley, VIII, pp. 646–647, 648.
[11] James Marshall, "The Relationship of Education to Peace," IV, p. 387.
[12] Joseph S. Roucek, "Group Tensions in the Modern World," *Approaches to National Unity,* Lyman Bryson, Louis Finkelstein, R. M. MacIver, editors, Conference on Science, Philosophy and Religion in Their Relation to the Democratic Way of Life, Inc., New York, 1945, p. 177. (Hereafter listed as V.)

Appendix I. Light on the Goals of Education

moralist means by evil. However, this comment came from a medical school: "We may recognize that the deep cause of intergroup tensions and conflicts rests back in human selfishness, ignorance, aggressiveness, sense of inferiority, and all the rest that may be lumped under the nontechnical term of 'human cussedness'; but unless we can analyze the event or events by which progressively the particular tensions of our day have come about, we have merely been indulging in conversation."[13]

An educational psychologist analyzed for us the several types of psychological theory applicable to this problem. "Psychoanalytic theory, in general, holds that aggression among children is an inevitable accompaniment of civilization. Aggression is 'always with us.' Aggression is essential for successful living in our society because it enables the individual to defend himself and to satisfy his needs and desires. But there is another strong basic tendency which works more constructively toward the promotion and enhancement of life. This is love. Thus an individual has within him positive potentialities, which may be developed through the right kind of education, especially in early childhood."[14] A technique—Menninger's—is outlined. The key point, so far as aggressiveness is concerned, is the finding of constructive uses for the kind of aggressiveness that is assumed to exist. The writer remarks that a change in his own goal may "lead an individual from hate to love, from hostility to good will. Both psychology and religion believe in the potency of purpose and the reality of a 'change of heart.'" A crucial point for general education, it would seem, is how the theory of a "fund" of native hostility is to be appraised. The paper here quoted cites well known anthropological data as to the marked differences between cultures in the expression of aggressiveness.

Secularist and Religious Goals

Highly relevant to the topic of the present session of the Conference is the ever recurring controversy over the nature of values and of the authority which they carry. It was early recognized that no agreement could be reached among us on this philosophical issue. The present writer attempted in 1947 to point out a certain inconsistency in current

---

[13] Earl W. Count, Comment on paper of Pitirim A. Sorokin, V, p. 206.
[14] Ruth Strang, "Education Against Aggression," VII, pp. 205 ff.

"progressive" educational philosophy, in that it stresses continual reconstruction of values while denying the validity of any permanent frame of reference: "There must be no 'fixed points'; all values must be tentatively held. Yet when guidance is attempted with reference to this reconstruction process, recourse is had to the central affirmations of democracy. The revaluation of values is to take place within an accepted framework—the work of persons, the right of participation in the decisions by which one is bound, the protection of minorities, and all the rest. These central affirmations of democracy are taken as 'givens,' and educators are now enjoined to seek enduring commitment to them as a goal of the educative process. This, I think, is precisely as it should be, but it hardly fits into the current experimentalist formula."[15]

One of the comments on that paper contained the following paragraph:

> The nature of this substructure of value cannot here be discussed. May I be permitted to say, however, that I think it must be the very process of interchange between human organisms which creates the human mind and magnifies it to whatever limit it may ever reach which transforms the newly born organism into a human being; which is the creative source of all values whatsoever in their human context. Once this basic value is established, individuals and groups can be free, intelligence can be as critical and wide searching as it pleases. But the process which enables us to be human must in all cases be protected and served, released and empowered, made sovereign and imperative over all of human life. What the nature of this process may be is the crucial and imperative problem of education as philosophy, as method, and as goal. We believe it can be known empirically.[16]

A physicist, who is perhaps the best known exponent in this Conference of the "logico-empirical analysis of science," told the fifth session: "What is analogous to the facts of science in moral, political, and religious life is the common faith of a group. This faith cannot be 'proved' by pseudo science. If the student of physics gets his instruction from the angle of integration of knowledge, he will learn that science cannot 'prove' any fact but confirms principles by deriving the description of facts which are not 'proved' either but regarded as 'observed' by agreement among the scientists. Our educational system has frequently led

---

[15]"Is There a Deficit in Our Prevailing Philosophy of Education," VIII, p. 395.
[16]Henry N. Wieman, VIII, p. 396.

Appendix I. Light on the Goals of Education 479

to the result that a student of science becomes an 'expert' in a narrow field and remains completely ignorant in all domains of life. He becomes one of the easiest victims of any impostor. Since in a democracy every sound legislation and administration is based upon the sound judgment of the citizens, this type of specialist should not be encouraged by the educational system."[17]

The proceedings of the seventh meeting contain a paper written by the same scholar, in which he said: "The principles of science are a structure of symbols accompanied by operational definition. This structure is a product of the creative ability of the human mind and consists of symbols which are a product of our imagination. But this structure can be checked for its truth by observations which can be described in everyday language. By logico-empirical analysis the creativity of the human mind emerges as the primary factor in science. Thus the student will learn that the role of this creativity in science is by no means inferior to its role in the humanities and even in art or religion. And we now can understand that the emphasis on science teaching will no longer interfere with the interest in the humanities but will rather support it."[18]

In the foregoing passages and the papers from which they are taken a door is invitingly opened to further study of the relation between religious, ethical, and scientific goals in education.

The very extensive controversy over the place of religion in public education has been but slightly reflected in Conference papers. It was argued in a paper presented at the first session that public education has a responsibility for acquainting students with the role of religion in human life, as empirical fact.[19] At the second session a professor of educational philosophy said: "If the subject matter of religion, including its historic outlooks and beliefs, is to be introduced into the program of the public school, under what precise conditions is it proposed that this be done? Are these beliefs and practices of religion to be given a favored position, or are they to be subjected to the same empirical procedures and tests which are applied to other aspects of the work of the school?"[20] If the former, the proposal was to be condemned. The pragmatic philosophy defended in that paper has often been chal-

[17] Philipp Frank, "Intercommunication Between Science and Philosophy in Higher Education," V, p. 611.
[18] "Science Teaching and the Humanities," VII, p. 166.
[19] F. Ernest Johnson, "Religion and the Philosophy of Education," I, pp. 346–347.
[20] John L. Childs, "Pragmatism, Religion and Education," II, p. 120.

lenged in our sessions, but I have found in the proceedings no proposal to introduce religious subject matter into the public school curriculum on the basis of indoctrination thus warned against.

Last year one of our religious educators said, "I happen to be among those who believe that living in terms of the highest and noblest ideals of America or of the given religious tradition requires a metaphysical basis and the buttressing of religious ritual and ceremony. But I also believe that it would be most unfortunate if instruction in the metaphysical basis or in the ceremonial buttressing were to become part of the business of the tax supported American school system."[21] He would depend on religious groups to make up the metaphysical and ritualistic deficit.

A philosopher, addressing the fifth session, expressed opposition to making religious faith subject matter for general education, but outlined an alternative approach. The key concept was "creativity," the demands of which "might be presented as the source of all created good and the end which all created good should serve, *so far as this source and this end appear in this temporal world and are open to every relevant form of rational and empirical search.*" In this way education might be "directed to a goal that had religious significance since it served a temporal and limited manifestation of a transcendent reality which in its transcendence can be reached by faith alone, but which in its temporal manifestation can be treated as an empirical fact, known, searched, and criticized like all other content in the arts and sciences."[22]

Education and the Social Order

In what sense can education be an instrument of social policy? "At all times," we were told at our seventh session, "the view that the political stability of a society depends on the adaptation of education to the form of government has been axiomatic with rulers of states and practical politicians, whether or not they were familiar with Aristotle's classical formulation of that precept. And since the days of Socrates' society, every society, rising in defense of its inherited culture, has shown concern lest a more self-seeking orientation of its educational system might estrange it from tradition." The paper maintained further that

---

[21]Simon Greenberg, "Education for World Citizenship," VIII, p. 472.
[22]Henry N. Wieman, "Education for Social Direction," V, p. 946.

Appendix I. Light on the Goals of Education

throughout the normal educational process "the scope for nonconformist as over against conformist attitudes is bound to be so small as to disqualify it as an instrument of change other than that imposed upon it by society itself."[23] The alternative envisaged was an appeal to enlightened self-interest directed toward the conditions of survival in an age of atom bombs.

A paper quoted in the previous section, written for the fifth session, took a more hopeful view of public education as a means of social direction:

> The controlling agency in education should be the educators, but at present for the most part they are shirking their responsibility. The kind of control they exercise is not control, because it refuses to attempt to reach any agreement on what is the good to which education should direct the student and direct society. Surely any control worthy of consideration is control directed to the good and away from the evil. If educators refuse to exercise this control some other agency will be compelled to do something about it, whether it directs to the good or the evil. Education cannot continue to drift under the cheery illusion that somehow when not directed to any specifiable good it will nevertheless produce good. This happy trustfulness is touching but hardly wise.[24]

The implication seems to be that society will accept from its educators a formulation of general social goals, as it accepts from its scientists a formulation of particular goals in technology, public health, or national defense. The problem here is basic and I think the Conference might well give more attention to it.

Even if the social goal of education be conservatively defined, in terms of the preservation and transmission of the culture, a philosophic problem arises when the criteria of democratic education are considered. At our third session the issue was raised and discussed at length by a professor of educational philosophy. He asked us to imagine a class undertaking in a "fair and impartial" manner the relative merits for democracy and Fascism:

> Such a class must have a geographical-time location; it cannot exist *in vacuo*. If it is situated in a Fascist country, no one would even expect a "fair and impartial" consideration of the problem. While one might ex-

[23]George F. Rohrlich, "Education, Politics and the Transformation of Culture," VII, pp. 197–198.
[24]Wieman, *op. cit.*, p. 956.

pect better treatment in a democratic country, would the ultimate result be much different? Is democracy *"im*partial"—without partiality for democracy? Democracy's partiality for its own ideology being well known, it is hardly more "fair" to compare Fascism by democratic standards than to compare democracy by Fascist ones. No, "fair and impartial" instruction is ultimately either a screen for inculcating our fundamental loyalties or a snare and a delusion because it may lure adherents of democracy into thinking they have no very positive preferences and hence no united loyalty to the system that makes freedom possible.[25]

This brings us back to the problem of a stable frame of reference, which was raised earlier. At best, democratic education seems to be involved in a paradox with respect to its transmissive and critical functions and likewise with respect to free inquiry and deliberate conditioning. Here again is subject matter worthy of more attention than the Conference has given it.

In the matter of education for peace and world order the Conference has been occupied largely with specifics evolved during the war period and resting on more or less conventional assumptions about "understanding," the overcoming of "prejudice," the relegation of national sovereignty, and the building of intercultural bridges. Many of our discussions seem now scarcely relevant to the critical situation of 1948. We were told last year, "The dangers to peace do not all arise from misunderstanding, and they will not be removed by mutual understanding of the cultures, histories, and circumstances of peoples: attitudes, emotions, fears, and insecurities have other than intellectual bases and they are sometimes based on genuine inequities: these bases, real or imagined, must be removed if the danger of war is to be obviated with any certainty or permanence."[26]

This, the writer of the paper went on to explain, is the reason for UNESCO's study of "tensions conducive to war." Another paper developed the same idea thus:

> The widely held faith, especially among scholars and educators, that lack of understanding between peoples lies at the root of international conflict, is not always justified. Correlatively, the almost universal be-

[25] John S. Brubacher, "Education Toward a Democratic World Order," *Science, Philosophy and Religion,* Lyman Bryson, Louis Finkelstein, editors, Conference on Science, Philosophy and Religion in Their Relation to the Democratic Way of Life, Inc., New York, 1943, p. 130.

[26] Richard P. McKeon, "The Program of UNESCO for 1947 and 1948," VIII, p. 587.

lief that better understanding would prevent the development of tensions or ease those that exist, may also be questioned. In retrospect it can be affirmed that the less we knew about the Nazis, the better we got along with them. Intensive contact between peoples on a universal scale may be expected to create both more understanding as well as more misunderstanding. There is a great difference between identical interests and reciprocal interests. People with identical interests may join in a common fight against a common enemy who is blocking the realization of these interests, but they may also fight one another for the same reason. The realization of mutual benefits based upon different interests may be a greater source of harmonious relations between states than the pursuit of identical objectives.[27]

The essence of this problem was stated for us at Chicago two years ago:

> The hopes of mankind are once more pinned on the successful establishment and operation of an international organization and within that organization of an international agency for education. But these hopes based on faith in constitutions and organizations may again be doomed to disappointment unless the education both of adults and of children is informed with a spirit which, because it has been forgotten, appears to be new, but is as old as are the aspirations of humanity for the realization of the brotherhood of man.[28]

[27] Louis Wirth, "International Tensions as Objects of Social Investigation," VIII, p. 52.
[28] I. L. Kandel, "The Transmission of Culture: Education as an Instrument of National Policy," VII, p. 217.

APPENDIX II

What Should Be the Goals for Education?

I

By LYMAN BRYSON

Professor of Education, Columbia University, Counsellor on Public Affairs, Columbia Broadcasting System

[These two addresses were delivered at the public meeting of the Conference, held on September 9, 1948, at the Harkness Academic Theater, Butler Library, Columbia University, Dean Harry J. Carman of Columbia College presiding.]

MY FIRST TASK is to defend our Conference against the accusation that in devoting our discussions to education we were ignoring or neglecting the critical problems of the present world. One of our most eminent scientific members said at an early session, "Your detachment amazes me and fills me with foreboding. How can you come together again in a year like this and discuss things that seem so remote from a world that may blow up at any moment."

In the first place, we are not detached in our general activities as citizens and all of us are ready to be of service in any way possible. But we must resist the danger of being bullied by imminent events, the danger of ruining the life we are living by fears that it will come to an end. Wise men have always lived under the shadow of their own mortality and we cannot now stop believing that it is the quality of life that counts and change to the idea that life is important because it merely continues.

This is not to admit that our deliberations have no immediate use. By devoting ourselves to education and its problems we might help to discover why the world is in its present crisis and why we reflect that world in our own present state of fear and excitement. It would be helpful to cast some light upon the reasons for our educational failures, if we could, for example, find out why it is that in this country it is still politically profitable to make a fool of yourself, why one can get votes, not only by denying, but actually interfering with the rights that democracy is supposed to ensure to its members. Our explanation might contribute to the solution of the present crisis and still more to the avoidance of the next one that may be coming along.

There is another thing, however, that needs to be said about the present crisis in world affairs. We have, in fact, two conditions that need to be described. We need to understand the world which is disturbed. We also need to understand ourselves because our own disturbance is a very important factor in the present situation. I believe that there is very little reason for thinking that the world is now in a worse state than it was after the First World War. In fact, we may be somewhat better off than we were a generation ago. But we are ourselves much more disturbed and that requires explanation. The explanation is that we educators, especially those of us who have devoted our time to adult education, have done our job altogether too well. What we asked for we got; now that we have it we do not like it. We asked that the American people become aware of what was currently going on in the world, that the man in the street when he went home at night, should lie awake as diplomats and statesmen have always lain awake at night, listening for the next explosion. We have demanded participation by the whole population of our country in the anxieties, the strains, the dangers and difficulties of running the world. Naturally, there is a deep emotional and spiritual disturbance among our people.

When an animal has made a great expenditure of energy, in a desperate fight, for example, it goes back to its lair where it thinks it is safe and lies down and regains its force in quiet somnolence. So far after previous great wars, we have been able to retreat into unawareness, to retire into a kind of blessed ignorance and recover our moral force. But ignorance is no longer possible.

From now on we are going to be aware incessantly and continuously and no strength giving retreat is open to us. We have to get our strength some other way and this puts a greater burden than ever upon education, because we now have to have far more mature adults facing more difficult lives. It is not that the problems of the world are necessarily more difficult than they were in the past. There seems to be no way to

Appendix II. What Should Be the Goals for Education?

compare different degrees of danger. But it is certain that the amount of anxiety that the problems of the world produce in all our people is greater than ever before. Our awareness is not comfortable and we should not have expected that it would be. In these circumstances the problem of education is not remote. We cannot save the world first and then begin to talk about education. We have to begin at once to decide what kind of personality is needed in the world as it is now.

In our deliberations, we have been discussing the aims of education and I have been struck by the fact that two words came up over and over again. Our members have spoken eloquently and wisely of two ideas, service and unity. The word freedom has been infrequent in our talks. No one should jump to the conclusion that our members have not been interested in freedom. It is still necessary to point out, however, that an interest in freedom that takes its value and its attainment for granted is dangerous, especially among intellectuals and those who have charge of education.

If you have studied the analyses of what happened to the intellectuals of Germany when the Nazis were coming into power, you will have noticed that even well trained minds often tricked themselves into subservience to false ideals by giving them nice new labels and allowing themselves to be diverted to other things. We are not going to make that mistake but it is nevertheless a present danger and we have to go on reminding ourselves that you could establish in this country, as in any other country, an intolerable police state following ideals of service and unity. Neither word would ever plague you afterward. After you had got your police state, your rulers would still call for service and unity. These are ideals that dictators believe in. These are ideals to which we can give part of our allegiance, but they are only part of the aims of education and of our culture and they need examination.

Let us take first this word, "service." We can begin by stating complete agreement with the view that to turn from seeking power or any material ambition to the service of others is turning from a low standard to a high ideal. But what kind of service? Service to what? Service at whose behest? Can we be content with service to the mere community, to the time and place in which one happens to be born? That is the kind of service that gets the most immediate acclaim and external satisfaction. It is not enough. The ideal of service must transcend, at times, even the ideals of the community that nurtured us and gave us our sense of ideal purposes. As our members have often said in discussing both service and unity, these terms must have a worldwide, or what we call a universal meaning. It must be service to humanity as a whole. Or still better, service to the best things that are in all men.

In trying to fix the aim of service we have specifically rejected power as an ideal, even the development of personal power. I have been struck by the fact, however, that we have never discussed at length at any of our meetings the precise nature of the corruption that power brings. It may be that we are not yet quite clear in our own minds as to our reasons for rejecting power as an aim. Perhaps we can get closer to precise meanings if we admit that when we train the young for the full use of their gifts and the full development of their personal endowment, we are giving them power. We have responsibility for the way they use it. On the other hand, when we give the young man and the young woman high ideals and do nothing to help them develop the powers by which those ideals are to be made actual, we betray both them and the future.

I would insist that effectiveness is a proper ideal in service. Some of my old philosophic friends in this Conference are ready at this point to accuse me of materialism, of believing that no ideal is any good unless it can win in the practical battles of life. This is not what I mean. An ideal that is nothing but a conviction in one human mind still counts. It is part of the nature of the universe and it may affect man's destiny. But we can also insist that we are finite human beings living finite lives, short term lives, and personal success has some importance.

It is a proper demand that any young person makes upon life that he be given a fair chance to put ideals into action, to produce changes somewhere for the good. What we are in danger of doing, what in fact we have done too much, is to substitute stimulation for training. We all know how many young people are filled with admirable, honest and appropriate ambition to change the world for the better. But they have no practical plans, no practical usefulness. Many of them see no connection between any possible way of making a living and any one of the ideals they are so hot about. This is the fault of bad teaching, not of youth itself and it is a proper aim of education to make people effective as well as inspired. We could even go further and say that for most of the young men and women who come out of our educational systems, those who lack special gifts or special chances, the only way

Appendix II. What Should Be the Goals for Education?

to count much for the betterment of the world is to win an ordinary worldly success without ever succumbing to the world's low standards, hoping in the end to use the prestige of success as a help to betterment. There is, of course, the incessant danger that the ideal will be lost in the struggle and that power once attained will be badly used. This is defeat. Ideals without effectiveness are futility. Education should teach men to avoid both evils.

The second word much talked about in our discussions was "unity." To me it is a less appealing ideal than service, needing more drastic qualification. My objection to the indiscriminate acceptance of unity as an ideal is not only that this word, like the word, "service," fits too well into the slogans by which totalitarian states are organized, but I am not at all sure how far my colleagues would agree with me when I extend my qualifications beyond this point. They are all convinced, too much perhaps, of the truth that unity in action is essential to success. Many forms of collective action are necessary, more so now in this country than ever before because of the scale on which our institutions are organized. However, one can believe in collective action when circumstances require it without admitting that it is good in itself. In fact, one can still insist that the tendency, always latent in the practices of government, to draw all forms of collective action into the state is dangerous. Some of my colleagues have spoken as if there were no choice between making the state the only center of collective action and having nothing but individual initiatives. There are many other alternatives. Man has proved over and over again that he can form voluntary associations independent of the state and it has been heretofore one of the characteristics of American life that we have trusted mostly to voluntary committees. For myself, I think it is healthy to resist the tendency to absorb all collective action into the one association from which you cannot resign—your citizenship.

But, in any case, in action we need unity. In thought, unity has a different value. In dogmatic moments, one is inclined to say that unity in thought is the death of the mind. There is always a possibility that unity in thought in large social groups is not a mere appearance; it is possible that all the members really do agree. But this is a miracle and too much to hope for, even if one could believe that it would be beneficent. Most appearances of unity have been, in fact, merely the evidence of imposition, either by force or by keeping people in such ignorance that they have no choice. You can impose an opinion by negation, by denying access to the knowledge of other possible choices. Ignorance is the strongest of all the chains upon men's minds. Ignorance is the kind of slavery that teachers always have to fight.

This is not to say that diversity is an end to be sought for in itself, although I am convinced that differences among men are naturally creative and are absolutely essential to progress. Perhaps it would not be over subtle to say that a social struggle for unity is good, but achievement of it would be bad. The struggle for unity that is actually an attempt to understand what other men think and to appreciate their reasons is a healthful exercise of the mind as well as of our moral nature. But the essential value of democracy as a social system lies not in its struggle toward unity nor in its slavery to majority opinion but in its generosity toward difference. Our Conference was set up nearly ten years ago to discuss science, philosophy and religion in their relation to the democratic way of life. I hope that we have not failed to learn from each other that free men can afford to nurture differences for their creative power. Mere tolerance is not enough. What many of us believe to be the greatest virtue of democracy is that it summons from each citizen all that his unique experience has given him a chance to learn and that it welcomes and harmonizes the uniquely different personalities that freedom brings into being.

There may be members of our Conference who would disagree with me at this point although they might hesitate to avow disagreement in a general discussion. We doubtless have members who believe that democratic pluralism is creative only in the sense that it sets up a kind of arena where all ideas, good and bad, compete until finally one, the right idea, triumphs. After that, the others are to be suppressed. This is not to me acceptable. I do not believe that democracy is, as one member said, only a moratorium. Diversity is instrumental in the continuing process arriving at the higher good. On this point, I should like to read what one of our most eminent members, not here this year, said in his address as chairman of the opening session of the Mexican City meeting of UNESCO about a year ago. He is a philosopher whose words are always interesting and he is considered by many people to be the most eminent Roman Catholic thinker of the present time. I mean, of course, Mr. Jacques Maritain. I have here the official translation of what Mr. Maritain said. He was facing the dilemma that we are trying to solve here in our own way, seeking to find the principles by which men

Appendix II. What Should Be the Goals for Education?

of different beliefs, men whose ultimate sanctions are actually different, can get together in a world order. In what terms do you create a world situation where the world is so diverse as it is?

Mr. Maritain said:

> I am quite certain that my way of justifying belief in the rights of men and the ideal of liberty, equality and fraternity, is the only way with a firm foundation in truth. This does not prevent me from being in agreement on those practical convictions with people who are certain that their way of justifying them, entirely different from mine or opposed to mine in its theoretical dynamism, is equally the only way founded on truth. If both believed in a democratic charter a Christian and a rationalist would still give mutually incompatible justifications for their belief. If their hearts and minds and blood were involved, then they would fight each other for them. And God forbid that I should say it doesn't matter which of the two is right. It matters essentially. The fact remains that on the practical expression of this charter, they are in agreement and can formulate common principles of action.

This would seem to me a satisfactory formulation of what might be called a spiritual democracy, the most stable possible basis for satisfactory democratic community at home and much more than that, the only conceivable basis on which we could ever create a world community or a world civilization.

The problem of Unity is subtle and immensely difficult. We live in a world in which men must get to some kind of practical agreement, no matter how far apart their sanctions may be, and we also live in a world in which every man's experience especially in our advanced technologies is bewilderingly pluralistic. In the first few years of a child's life we create his character in adjustment to a close knit simple community of which the family is the center. But as this child, trained to a single set of loyalties and without experience in choosing among institutions, gets out into the actual world, he finds that it is essentially pluralistic. He has to associate with different people for different purposes. He has to learn to choose and even sometimes to deny some loyalties because they are in conflict with deeper spiritual commitments. He cannot sink himself into a single integrated external pattern. He has to find his mature integration in himself. This is a task of great difficulty that our modern life imposes upon every grown person. The basic aim of all education is, I think, to enable us in this way, to create our own effective personality.

2

By R. M. MacIVER

Lieber Professor of Political Philosophy and Sociology, Columbia University

THE SUBJECT assigned to me has the title, "What are the goals of education?" As soon as you hear that you ought to pity me. Education is one of the most intriguing and one of the most challenging, but also it can be one of the most boring of all subjects.

Since I do not read anything about education—actually, it is a fact I never read books about education—how can I speak about it? In fact I am driven to speak very simply. I am driven to ask a very simple question: *What is it important that a man should know?* What is it important that we teach, we who teach those who are going to be the men and women of tomorrow? What is it important that they should learn if they are going to enjoy, shall we say, the inalienable rights of life, liberty, and the pursuit of happiness? Or, to put it in other words, if they are going to live effective lives while at the same time they serve their fellow men, what is it important that men should know?

I am not asking what a business man should know. Nor a working man, and not any other specialized kind of man. What is it important that *a man* should know? Not a churchman. Not a Roman Catholic, or a Protestant, or a Jew, or a Hindu, or a Mohammedan, or anything else. A man. Not an engineer, or a physician, or a carpenter, or a lawyer, or a plumber—but a man. And when I say man, I include, needless to say, woman.

We have to face that kind of question, because we live in this multi-group order of life, this multigroup society, where in our system of public education you cannot, you dare not, and you should not teach men to be an X-ist or a Y-ist, a Methodist or a Roman Catholic or a Unitarian or an Orthodox Jew. We have to teach them something else. We have to seek something that we can hope to call the universality of man.

In simpler societies people did not need to face that problem, because

Appendix II. What Should Be the Goals for Education?

they were all brought up in the same customs, and they all shared the same faith. So they could evade that half of the problem of education. They often evaded the other half by having no formal education at all.

However, we have to face the full brunt of the question and look at man in his full universality, because we cannot teach the mores of one group, or the religion of one group, or the values of one group, if we are going to be true to education for the democratic society in which we live.

It is said that we need more drive in our education. The suggestion has been made that the way to get it was to give a vocationalism to teaching, even in the liberal arts colleges. I myself completely reject that answer. I think it is one of the many sidetracks we take because we fail to find the main track.

After all, the problems we have to face, the problems of the kind of families we live in, and the kind of cities we live in, and the kind of world we live in, and the kind of half-peace we live in, and all the rest of it, are not going to be solved by teaching us to be more professional and more vocational. We are not so bad at that job, anyway. There is something else we are not so good at.

It is no answer to say we ought to teach this-ism or that. To say, for example, we ought to teach democracy. I do not want to say we should teach people "democracy." We should teach them so that they will be democratic, so that their way of living, their responsiveness to our teaching will make them so.

What then is it important that a man should know and should be taught to know in his youth?

We can, of course, at once mention certain obvious things that are important. I am going to leave these things out. For example, it is important that all men and all women should know how to be healthy, physically healthy, and should know the conditions of living in a physically healthy way, should know that thoroughly, straightly, and honestly. It is important that people should know the various things that will save them from the many pitfalls of ignorance, as they go about their daily lives. But beyond that, beyond those things? We will accept all that but we know the main issue lies elsewhere. Beyond that.

To go beyond that, let us get back to the beginning. In saying that, I feel somewhat like a business gentleman who once addressed a group of my students in some kind of seminar. He was going to tell them about his own field. He began by saying that he had no use for economists, no use for economic theories or economic theorists, no use for academicians, no use for people who talked about economics from their ivory tower; in fact, he did not believe theories were any good. The only way you could get there was to learn the hard bottom facts of economic life, and that was experience and not theory.

This he kept on saying for some time. He kept knocking down those poor academic gentlemen. When he got well launched, he finally came out with this, "I have a little theory of my own."

That is somewhat how I feel. I do not read any books on education, and I do not have any knowledge on education, and I am afraid I am going to give myself away and, without knowing it, show that I have a little theory of my own.

I said let us get back to the beginning. Educating means imparting the knowing of something, by those who already know, to those who do not yet know. In other words, the focus of education is the communication of knowing. You know. Somebody does not know. You pretend, at any rate, to know more, and the other knows less. The imparting of that more, the equalizing of knowledge, so to speak, is what educating means. You see, I lay the stress on knowing.

Next I would like to distinguish four kinds of knowing. I am not dividing knowing into four kinds. I am just saying I would like to distinguish four kinds of knowing.

1. There is knowing how to do.
2. There is knowing what to do.
3. There is knowing how to think.
4. There is knowing what to think.

Let us not ask for any more kinds of knowing, for the moment. These four satisfy my purpose. I want to suggest that for our problem here, we are merely concerned with the third and the fourth of those kinds of knowing—knowing how to think and knowing what to think.

I say this because knowing how to do, which is extremely important, at least as important as knowing what to do—at any rate, a fairly large part of knowing how to do—is a matter of learning techniques, and we are not too bad about that. We are reasonably good. There are some techniques we are not so good at, but most techniques we are pretty competent about. We stand up well in the history of time, and among the

Appendix II. What Should Be the Goals for Education? 495

peoples of the world, in that area. So I shall leave out, roughly speaking, knowing how to do.

Then, as for knowing what to do, I do not need to discuss that because if you know the answer to No. 4, knowing what to think, you know the answer to No. 2. What to *do,* obviously, depends on what to *think*. So we can leave out Nos. 1 and 2. That simplifies things, and we are down to Nos. 3 and 4—how to think and what to think.

By the way, you notice I defined education in terms of knowing. I said the crucial thing is the process of knowing, the relation between the more knowing and the less knowing, and the equalization of the two. That is education. I lay stress on knowing, anyway.

Hence I am not talking about things like remembering, which is often, unfortunately, used as if it were an equivalent of knowing. Remembering is a refuge often taken. If we do not know how to teach, we teach people to remember, or, at least, we drill them in remembering.

That recourse is to be found not only on the lower levels of what we call education, but right up on the highest levels. For example, I have a recollection of being at a doctoral examination, a Ph.D. examination, where questions like this were hurled at the candidate who was thereby qualifying to be called a doctor of philosophy: "Who was the postmaster general at the time of President Coolidge?"

That is remembering. The practice is common enough, and I ask you: Is it not a poor substitute for knowing? If there is something that you can find by looking it up in *The World Almanac,* why trouble anybody's brain by making the remembrance of it a condition of getting a Ph.D.? These detachable items of remembrance you remember only to forget. A lot of education in the school, in the college and in the university, unfortunately, amounts to this business of remembering in order to forget. You have to forget because, otherwise, your brain gets clogged with formless matter.

You know the lines of Wordsworth:

>Getting and spending we lay waste our powers,
>Little we see in Nature that is ours.

In the academic circle we change it to:

>Getting and forgetting we lay waste our powers,

So we come to Nos. 3 and 4, where the crucial issues of the goals of education lie in these questions: What about teaching people how to think and what about teaching people what to think? The first of these two questions might rather be: *Can* we teach people how to think? If we can, we should do it. When we come to the second issue, the question is more likely to be: *Should* we teach people what to think? Anyhow, let us look at the first. My "little theory" will be my answer to that problem.

Now as to teaching people how to think, I claim in all seriousness that this is one of the things we do least well. We do a lot of things quite decently; but one thing we badly neglect or ignore—and a very essential thing, too, a primary thing—is teaching people how to think to the limit of their capacity. As with every other capacity this one is limited, and the limit differs widely for different people. But we do not seek to teach people nearly as far as they could go.

For example, take such a thing as speech. Speech is the most wonderful, flexible, rich, variegated instrument in the world, and we do not teach our people to appreciate the significance of speech. If somebody played a fiddle badly, we would all know it is being played badly. However, when somebody speaks or writes books, or otherwise, badly, we do not even know that it is bad.

We do not read right. Many college graduates have never learned to do it. We do not know how to read the more rewarding, more difficult books, the greater books. We shirk the task: it does not challenge us. We use textbooks as substitutes for that reading. The meat of the great books is chewed into a sort of baby cud by pedagogues for students.

We do not know how to read because we are not taught how to think. When I say "how to think," I do not mean to think abstractly. I mean to *think*—an universal operation—what we do all the time in every area, but which we are not trained to do well in any area.

To think means to distinguish, and then to relate, then to comprehend, and then to appreciate. We are called to do so in every relation of life all the time. We are not trained to do it and it does not come to us by custom or by a kind of social instinct.

To think is to see things in their relationship, to see a meaning in its context, to see a star in its constellation, to see an event in its setting, to see an action in a complex of a personality, to see a person in the light

Appendix II. What Should Be the Goals for Education?

of his group, and to see a group in the light of its community, and the community in the light of the world of men.

To distinguish and relate, and then comprehend, and by comprehending or understanding, to appreciate—that is thinking. If we could follow through on that, we would know it is the way to save ourselves from a lot of the propagandistic perils that beset us. After all, what is propaganda? In a sense, we resist it. Too often it is an attempt to befuddle our thinking. We are too easily befuddled. We are not trained to distinguish and to relate.

We can do better. Here is a test of what I mean. Ask anyone who is a teacher to try this out. Give some quite good students a few simple fallacies, not the abstract form, but give good examples of fallacious connections of meaning you can pick out in people's arguments, and ask them to point out the fallacies. You will be surprised how often they will fail to do to it—people you think are good. They are not trained to think, in other words, to distinguish and then to relate, to see things properly in their setting, truly in their context.

We need to follow this line to avoid many of the perils of ignorance, of prejudice and of propagandistic persuasion, and even of the passions that beset our lives. To think, to see things in their relationship, to see the near and the far, to see the small and the great, to see the part and the whole, to see things steadily and in their relationships. It is hard, but, surely, there are ways of trying it.

We can well begin the learning of how to think by learning to use more aptly the common instrument of speech. First, to distinguish; then to relate; and last, to appreciate; and thereby to avoid false unities and false separations; thereby to get to the appreciation of unity in diversity; never to see one as though detached from the other.

I set out from the question: Can we teach people *how* to think? I suggested we can do more, far more, than we do, and that in doing so we teach people not only to be better thinkers, but also better citizens. I come lastly to the question: Can we teach them or *should* we teach them what to think? In other words, should we indoctrinate our students? Actually, we need not worry about that question. The answer is so simple.

All education indoctrinates. I can conceive of no education that does not. But two kinds of indoctrinations must be ruled out. One is the indoctrination that denies or takes liberties with scientific truth. The other is the indoctrination that indoctrinates one group, either directly or indirectly, against another. The latter is particularly pernicious in a democracy. In our general education we must not teach the values of one group over against the values of other groups.

Of course, if we can teach people how to think as I have suggested, we need no better prophylactic. Indoctrinations beset us on every side. They are bred in the home, in the group, the street, the church, all the settings of life. However, if we teach people how to think, we are giving them the best safeguard against dangerous indoctrinations.

We can then go boldly on to educational indoctrination. In what ways? I shall mention very briefly four kinds of indoctrination that I think are eminently honorable and proper. First, we ought to indoctrinate people because we want them to have a sense of belonging, a sense of home, an equilibrium which too many lack in our world today. Therefore, we must begin by indoctrinating people in the sense of place, their homeland I mean; in the sense of their homeland, of its traditions, of its services, of its unity, of what binds them to it and what binds it to them, of what binds it to the past and the future—the sense of that continuity—to give them the wider home feeling that in our multigroup society tends to be so lacking.

We should therefore teach them history in a certain way, not the minutiae of history, but history in the sense of the living, continuing context of the community as it passes through time. They are at a particular point of time and they are part and parcel of that great movement. They belong there. That sense should come to them from history.

Secondly, they should also be indoctrinated in the relation of their homeland to other homelands; in other words, the relation between them, their people and humanity. In this connection it is very important to teach what human beings are really like, so far as we know it ourselves. That is an open question. However, we know a good deal. They should be taught, and pretty thoroughly and freely, what we do know. Thus we learn that other people are not so different from ourselves. Thus we learn that it does not make so much difference as we thought, with respect to the human quality of people, whether they live in Peiping or in Boston, whether they live in Atlanta or in Timbuctoo. We have learned that people are human beings, and we have learned something about what human beings are, their faults and, I hope, their potentialities, too.

Appendix II. What Should Be the Goals for Education?

Thirdly, it is important that we should be oriented to nature. The sense of the world around and outside us is what we are concerned about, not the dissection of it. So when I speak about orientation to nature, I do not mean necessarily that they must learn physics if they are not going to be physicists, or chemistry, or geology, or biology, and so forth. I mean that they ought to know about the nature of the growth of plants and animals, the smell of trees and the flight of birds, the taste of herbs, the motions of the weather, and the feel of the earth, the circling skies, and so forth. They should be at home in the world they live in.

Now my last orientation. They ought to be oriented in greater achievements, so far as they can understand them, of man. I do not refer merely to great books that have been written, and I certainly do not mean mainly the great philosophies that have been thought; I mean the great achievements of man, as they are incarnated in various ways, incarnated in thought, in stone, in vision and dream, the great constructs of civilization.

That is orientation. That is also indoctrination. We need that kind of orientation very badly. So I want two things, you see. I want to teach people how to think, and I want to give them orientation, if I know how, and so far as they can learn.

You might say, "How are these things to be done?"—even if you agreed with me. I do not answer this question. You might say, "Where are the teachers?" I cannot answer that question. The Conference we are here representing tonight has been concerned with matters of this kind. I seemed to trace for the first time, a certain touch of convergence in the views of the most widely separated members. There seemed to be some kind of convergence in the direction that, after all, perhaps the most important thing in education is, if we know how to make it concrete, to teach people the conditions, the activities, the responsibilities and the virtues of being citizens of their country and of their world.

APPENDIX III

Comment

I

By QUINCY WRIGHT

Professor of International Law, The University of Chicago

EDUCATION HAS to do on the one hand with the adjustment of internal drives and ideals within the individual and on the other with the adjustment of the individual as a whole to his environment. The problem faced by the writers of these papers is the making of these adjustments under the conditions of the modern world. The environment to which modern people have to be fitted is in some respects unprecedented.

In the first place it is the world as a whole. No education for a national, much less a local environment will do. Some of the papers emphasized Western civilization as the environment of our students. More criticized even this as too narrow.

In the second place the environment today includes all classes of people as well as all sections of the world. The development of self-consciousness by workers and peasants makes it no longer possible for higher education to concern itself only with a limited elite as did classical, medieval, and Renaissance education.

With this broad conception of the environment it is clear that it includes a great variety of value systems. There are many religions, cultures, and nationalities, and the universal acceptance of any one is not to be anticipated. Consequently, no traditional system of values will be valid for the world. Whether a universal civilization with certain universal values is developing, and if so what are those values, present a problem considered by a number of the papers.

Finally, it is clear that the environment is changing at an accelerating rate. It can be expected to change radically in a lifetime, under the influence of inventions, technical and social, and under the impact of diverse cultures and value systems upon one another. Today skills, knowledge, and value systems all have a high rate of obsolescence. As a consequence the continued utility of the ideas and principles learned in college becomes problematical. Emphasis must be increasingly upon methods and processes for discovering or inventing ideas, principles, and standards rather than upon the ideas, principles, and standards themselves.

It seems probable that this unprecedented condition of the environment of men has produced unprecedented conditions within men. It may be, as some of the psychoanalysts insist, that maladjustments of the human personality, incompatibilities of drives and ideals, neuroses, and other psychic disorders are greater than ever before.

All or most of these considerations seem to have been in the minds of most of the writers of the papers. More concretely, the papers devoted themselves to four topics.

1. What, if any, common elements in thinking should universities seek to develop?
2. What can universities do that other institutions cannot?
3. What should be the target of the university's aim?
4. What should be the organization of the university's curriculum?

1. Most of the papers agreed that some kind of unity and some kind of continuity in the thinking of everyone is desirable, but as to the kind there was much disagreement.

The unity of a well worked out metaphysical system such as Europe enjoyed in the Middle Ages, though considered essential by a few, was rejected by most of the writers on the ground that reality was not necessarily logical, rational, and intellectual, that such a system could only be based on a type of authority inconsistent with democracy, or that no single metaphysical system had any prospect of general acceptance in the conditions of the modern world.

Some of the papers developed detailed plans of general education emphasizing minimal values which might be acceptable to people of all religious and cultural traditions or systems of thought suggested by educational experience or by recent advances in science and technology. I found Dr. Karl W. Deutsch's suggestions of new approaches to the history of human intelligence, the development of models of thought, and the investigation of key concepts particularly interesting.[a]

The idea that we ought to educate Americans or the people of Western civilization to loyalty for our democratic culture and to willingness to fight for it was expressed by a few and implied by more, though the prospect of accomplishing little beyond general destruction through such a militant faith under modern conditions was generally recognized.

The value of some kind of continuity of thought was recognized no less than the value of some kind of unity and there was frequent mention of the Chicago Great Books Course seeking to maintain the continuity of the Western tradition. Most of the writers recognized, however, that Western civilization is too narrow a base. In any case a tradition must be flexible in our rapidly changing world. While the supreme value systems of individuals or groups may be rocks of ages to which an individual may cling in the swirl of change, such systems can only be the fruit of individual reflection or of specialized religious education. They cannot be the subject matter of general education.

It is clear that unified and continuous doctrine is not to be anticipated throughout the world's population. The relativity of thought as to time, place, and circumstances, must be recognized though perhaps some common ideas (such as the value of the individual personality and of the human race as a whole, and the validity of scientific method and social tolerance as processes for understanding and controlling nature and society) can be accepted by all. The controversy in UNESCO between scientific humanism and a dialectical materialism shows the difficulties which even the most general formulations will encounter, as does the criticism of either of these theories from the point of view of particular religious and social value systems. Doubtless, demonstration of some degree of continuity of any general formulation with the living cultures, creeds, and ideologies will be necessary to give it general acceptance. Such a demonstration would, in fact, be evidence of the existence of a world civilization. Perhaps in the accumulation of such evidence a unity and continuity of modern thought can be achieved. Thought is a function of a society and a unity or continuity of thought throughout the world cannot be expected, except as the world becomes a society.

It seems to me that a world society has been developing since uni-

[a] [Cf. Chapter IV by Dr. Deutsch.]

versal regular communication among all the civilizations began with the Renaissance discoveries, but that society is loosely knit both ideologically and institutionally. Its unity of thought is no more than that expressed by Professor Robert Ulich in the following words:

> Fortunately, there can be a unity in spirit and endeavor, and a discipline of tolerance, that bind the searching individual minds more closely together and connect them all more intensely with a source of inspiration than the orthodoxy of conformism. Courage of thinking to the degree of dissension has never been an impediment to cultural vitality; such impediment has arisen much more from the intention of finite men and institutions to declare their infallibility and thus to change the idea of truth as an obligation and direction into a claim of property—which is the deepest heresy against the Spirit man can commit. The other heresy is the tendency we can observe in so many modern scholars who are proud of their "scientific" attitude, which often is nothing but a tendency to exclude from one's intellectual conscience questions which relate man to the great and universal problems of life and which, for this very reason, cannot be subjected to relatively simple experimental forms of verification.[b]

While the supreme values of individuals and groups will remain different, there is room for general understanding of these different value systems and general acknowledgment that they all spring from a common human nature subjected to varying conditions of history and environment. Furthermore, a body of common values may be detected, whether called "scientific humanism," "natural law," or "fundamental human rights," which all men can agree to observe as a practical matter even though they justify them by very different arguments and supplement them by very different systems of ultimate value.

2. There is general agreement that universities are useful though their competition with the colleges in teaching and with the industrial laboratories and technical schools in professional research is recognized.

Some thought that the university could best develop unity and continuity of thought because it combined liberal and professional faculties; others thought liberal teaching, professional training, and research antipathetic and urged a segregation.

Most agreed that the university should be an agency free to search for and teach the truth, thus emphasizing the cooperative aspects of

[b][Cf. Chapter I by Dr. Ulich.]

world society. It could not do this if it was bound to serve one side in a competitive world as do industrial or governmental institutes and laboratories. The danger to this ideal if the university is sustained by business or government patronage was recognized. Universities which become the handmaids of church or state or business cease to be strong and creative and with their collapse civilization declines. Independence of the institution and freedom of the professor is the essence of a university.

3. What should be the target of the university's aim? Who are its proper beneficiaries?

Some emphasized the individual, suggesting that he should be taught how to make a living, how to understand and get along with his fellow man, and how to sustain his morale. The latter, it was variously suggested, could be approached from the cultural point of view (appreciation of and participation in the fine arts), from the social point of view (understanding of and pride in the particular society), from the religious point of view (faith in a God who cares), or from the psychological point of view (adaptation of the ego to the drives of the id and the aspirations of the super ego).

Closely related to the individual as a target is the world as a target. Many suggested that the universities should aim to make a universal society in which all individuals can have opportunity. In the shrinking, changing, and varied world, democratic societies respecting the individual cannot exist, unless the world as a whole is a society with institutions adequate to protect them all.

A smaller number of the writers were content to consider a society less than universal as the target of education. Most of the papers recognized that if a university serves a particular civilization, a particular nation, a particular church, a particular class, or a particular corporation, it tends to stultify itself. Yet they recognize that the universities live in civilizations and cannot teach individuals to live except in a civilization or nation. They cannot ignore the demands of the state for loyalty of its citizens and of the culture for transmission of its values to the rising generation. It cannot be denied that the consensus of the group, though its values may be subordinate to those of the larger group, constitutes a source of values which the individual within the group cannot ignore.

Another approach to the problem of determining the target of education is that of classifying the functions of the university as was done by Dean Earl J. McGrath.[c] He recognized the four functions: training for a profession, service to the community, encouragement of research, and education of youth for life in society, and suggested that the first two were being done better than the last two.

4. How should the university be organized?

Opinions differed as to the desirability of separation of the functions of liberal education, professional training, practical research, and creative research. Dean McGrath urged considerable separation; Professor Ulich, less.

On the point at which secondary and higher education should be separated, there was considerable opinion favorable to the European system, adapted in part at the University of Chicago, of including "liberal education" in secondary education, thus beginning university education at the traditional junior year.

As to what should be the emphasis in education at different stages there was comparatively little discussion. T. V. Smith suggested that elementary education should be concerned with basic skills and sensory reality, secondary education with scientific principles and methods, and higher education with professional skills and values.[d] Some thought that fancy, what T. V. Smith called the "impossible," should have its part in all stages of education, but perhaps a larger number emphasized the merit of giving the child a firm foundation in an understanding of external reality and in basic skills. The distinction between what is, what is likely to be, what is desirable, and what may be, is important and it was commonly felt that a comprehension of the first was elemental.

The most basic issues discussed in these papers concerned the source and nature of the values which should integrate higher education and which, reciprocally, higher education should seek to establish. Among these issues were the following:

1. Should these values be considered absolute or relative?
2. Should values be ordered in a hierarchy or be maintained in equilibrium?
3. Should values be established by authority or grow democratically from the grass roots?
4. Should values be crusaded for or synthesized into higher values?

[c][Cf. Chapter XVI by Dean McGrath.]
[d][Cf. Chapter III by Dr. Smith.]

Appendix III. Comment

As a contribution to the goal of higher education after reading these papers, I suggest the following:

1. Better understanding of human and child development so that people will bring up children with fewer frustrations and aggressions and consequently less tendency to hunt for scapegoats upon which to project aggressive impulses or to displace animosities.

2. Better knowledge of the world, its peoples, its value systems, and the relation among them.

3. Awareness of and commitment to the common values inherent in human nature and human society.

4. Clearer understanding of the difference between objective reality and the evidences which manifest it on the one hand, and on the other, subjective wishes, and the logical systems which seek to reconcile and organize them.

Comment

2

By I. L. KANDEL

Professor of American Studies, University of Manchester, Professor Emeritus, Teachers College, Columbia University

THERE IS NOTHING that so clearly illustrates the uncertainty and instability of American education as the perennial addiction to defining its aims, objectives, and goals. This indoor pastime is justified on the ground that education must be adapted to social change, must be realistic and in touch with the current social scene, or must even go ahead and point the way to the future. Educators do not seem to be as conscious of the results of this constant tendency to pluck up the flower to see how it is growing as are the creative minds of the United States.

In *Sketches in Criticism*[1] Van Wyck Brooks wrote, "A rootless people cannot endure forever and we shall pay in the end for our superficialities in ways more terrible than we can yet conceive." Louis Bromfield discussed the same theme in *The Man Who Had Everything*[2] and concluded with this view of Americans: "When they grew roots, they were miserable. He wasn't the only American who had been practically active all his life without ever having lived at all." So, too, Santayana in *The Last Puritan*[3] wrote, "All that is American, or modern, is the absence of any tradition in which the born poet or God-intoxicated man could take root. He therefore simply evaporates or *Peters* out." When this idea is applied to education T. B. Stribling is able to write in *These Bars of Flesh* that "American education is like a man who continuously builds himself new homes and never lives in one."[4] It is true today

---

[1] Van Wyck Brooks, *Sketches in Criticism*, E. P. Dutton & Company, Inc., New York, 1932.
[2] Louis Bromfield, *The Man Who Had Everything*, Harper & Brothers, New York, 1935.
[3] George Santayana, *The Last Puritan*, Charles Scribner's Sons, New York, 1936.
[4] T. B. Stribling, *These Bars of Flesh*, Doubleday & Company, Inc., Garden City, 1938.

Appendix III. Comment 509

as when Emerson described "The Young America" as "a country of beginners, of projects, of designs, and expectations," and it is more the case with education today than it was in the days of Emerson.

There might have been some justification for the symposium on "Goals in Education," had there existed some urgent crisis in education which demanded attention. The situation in education is not new nor has it changed since the discussion of the aims and content of higher education was started in 1936 by Dr. Waldo G. Leland, then director of the American Council of Learned Societies. The discussion was continued from 1936 up to the publication a few months ago of the report of the President's Committee on Higher Education. It was sponsored through Dr. Leland by the American Council of Learned Societies and was taken up by a number of national organizations; regional conferences were created and committees appointed in colleges and universities —all of these concerned with the future of higher education and a few including secondary education in their deliberations.

Except for a few papers in this symposium practically every aspect of the problem was discussed in the six articles on "The Function of the Liberal Arts College in a Democratic Society" which appeared in *The American Scholar,* Volume 13, Number 4, Autumn, 1944, and which presented six different points of view on the subject. As the late Dr. William A. Neilson wrote in his summary, there is "a common recognition that liberal education is to be found less in a prescribed list of studies than in the spirit in which these studies are taught. But after this view has been accepted there remains the harder question of how to find teachers capable of transmitting this spirit."

Here is a challenge that has not yet been taken up except by Howard Mumford Jones, who in his *Education and World Tragedy* saw the root of one of the troubles in the kind of training given to Ph.D.'s; with this phase of the question he does not deal directly in his paper.[a] None of the contributors in fact does more than hint at the problem in criticizing specialization, fragmentation, and compartmentalization of subjects. In none of the papers is there anything that approaches the excellent discussion by John Herman Randall, Jr., in an article "Which Are the Liberating Arts?"[5]

[a] [Cf. Chapter IX by Dr. Jones.]

[5] *The American Scholar,* Volume 13, Number 3, Spring, 1944, pp. 135 ff.

One cannot resist the feeling that in all the papers, except that of Dr. Louis J. A. Mercier who still appears to be wedded too literally to tradition,[b] there is an effort to start afresh, as though there have never been any goals in education or objectives or educated men and women who have contributed something to the welfare and the progress of humanity. Some propose a complete break with the past, but it is only as the whole issue is discussed as Dr. Robert Ulich does in the light of the past and of present needs, that a real insight can be found for the difficulties that are being discussed.[c] What appears to be lacking in the discussions of "Goals in Education" Dr. Ulich supplies in his statement of the three conditions requisite to a healthy state of higher education. The question that he poses is fundamental: "Will it be possible to relate the ever expanding sphere of descriptive-experimental knowledge and research to a deeper dimension of thought from which, first, all our mental endeavor receives our inner unity, in spite of its manifoldness, which, second, allows us to link new ideas to the great chain of thought and thus gives us that feeling of historical continuity without which change becomes chaos, and which, third, gives us assurance that humanity is not just a whim of an inscrutable creator but a meaningful part of a meaningful whole?"

It is this last question that appears to have been ignored in all the papers. It is hinted at in one or two of the suggestions that higher education must develop a sense of responsibility or recognize the part that it must play as a community or an essential member of a community. The crying needs today are two: to find enough teachers at all levels who are sufficiently imbued with a sense of responsibility of their profession, and to re-emphasize the idea that education is a sociomoral process.[d] To

[b][Cf. Chapter XII by Dr. Mercier.]
[c][Cf. Chapter I by Dr. Ulich.]
[d]Dr. Kaplan's reply:
  The sum and substance of Dr. Kandel's review is that the authors seem to be unaware of the harm they are doing to American civilization by engaging in the "indoor pastime" of "plucking up the flower of education to see how it is growing." Rather inconsistently Dr. Kandel stresses the fact that "one of the two crying needs" is the need "to re-emphasize the idea that education is a sociomoral process." What are the papers concerned with, if not with the problem of integrating the sociomoral values into education, particularly higher education, where such integration is needed most and achieved least? And can there be a better way to go in search of moral values than to find out what is really wrong with our colleges and universities, from the standpoint of the sociomoral purpose of the education? That seems to be what every one of the papers, so sweepingly described as virtually superfluous, is attempting to do.

write lists of objectives is not difficult—the history of education, particularly recent American history, is paved with them; to devise new curricula is also not difficult—whether in the form of subjects, or integration, or Great Books. What is needed is not Knowledge but something that gives both knowledge and education meaning and purpose and that can be found only in a search for moral values. The Conference on Science, Philosophy and Religion might well promote that search, which was started in the discussions from 1936 to 1947 but never carried very far.

To speak for myself, I should imagine that, in attempting to reopen the problem of what constitutes maximum fulfilment of human destiny so as to know what to educate our youth for, I make bold, if not to go in search of moral values, at least to raise the problem of how to combine them.

As for the search for moral values, to which Dr. Kandel would have the Conference confine itself, they are so ubiquitous in civilizations, philosophies, and religions that they hardly require searching. Jeremiah and Diogenes went in search of moral people, not moral values. The problem with moral values is not to find them but how to translate them into politics, economics, and education. When Plato wanted to know the meaning of justice, he tried to translate it into the conception of the state. Why may not the meaning of moral values in general be arrived at by translating them into the conception of education? We would probably learn the meaning of both freedom and law, if we tried to make the teaching of them part of higher education at college. The universities would then feel called upon to teach the proper formula for combining freedom with law, as they now feel called upon to teach the proper formula for combining the various chemicals that go into the making of an atomic bomb.

Comment

3

By HARRY J. CARMAN
Dean, Columbia College, Columbia University

᙭᙭

I FIND MYSELF in virtually complete agreement with Dr. I. L. Kandel in his penetrating comment on these papers. There are four items, however, growing out of these papers and Dr. Kandel's comment on them which deserve particular emphasis: (1) The superficiality and rootlessness of most Americans including their education. (2) The gradual disappearance in American education at all levels of emphasis on moral standards and spiritual values. (3) American provincialism growing out of our failure to date to acquaint ourselves with the cultures of Russia, India, and the Orient. (4) Our failure to find a sufficient number of teachers who, on the basis of personality, interest, scholarship, and training, are competent to give instruction in our schools and colleges.

The truth of the first of these items is evident to any person acquainted with the American scene. Go wherever you will in America—to its countryside, its Main Street towns and cities, and its great metropolitan areas which boast of their cultural institutions and advantages—you are impressed that you are in the midst of people who exist but do not live, except in the most superficial way. They know little or nothing of the past and dwell on a day by day basis in the dominion of the immediate. They have no glimmering that the world of today is the result of an historical process. Few of them appreciate that that part of the past which is still alive in us must be studied in its origins before our motives and desires can be fully understood.

We boast about American Democracy and give lip service to the American way of life. But it is a safe assertion that the great majority of the American people, despite the multiplication during the past half century of schools and colleges and the coming of the radio and other rapid means of communication, are social and political illiterates. The really educated person should know why and how representative democracy was developed, under what handicaps it has labored, what theories have been held concerning it, and what obstacles must be overcome if it is to continue to function. A nation of restless, money-pleasure seeking humans, our roots—at least for most of us—are no deeper than a routine job, the movies, the bar and tavern, our favorite radio program, and commercialized sport. Most Americans accept the world as they find it and are, therefore, unaware of their latent possibilities for a fuller life.

The second item listed above is of utmost importance. Whatever else we may profess to be, we are a practical, materialistic people. The great majority of our forebears who came to these shores came to improve their social-economic status, to get on in the world. The first-comers found an unexplored virgin continent which they and succeeding generations by means of conquest, hard work, planning, and technical ingenuity proceeded to conquer and to exploit. Values were expressed in terms of money and personal material power, rather than in terms of high ethical conduct. Success in life meant getting on in a material way and it was natural that it should be so: in the past, the territorial growth of the United States, its vast stretches of fertile land, its rich stores of natural resources, the overlapping waves of immigrants continually providing a new bottom layer for the social structure, and the rise of new industries, often combined to make it relatively easy to rise from poverty to commercial prince or captain of industry.

This craze for money and material power is still very much in evidence. No one can in all fairness question the desire for material gain. But the method by which such gain is acquired is the important matter. The student of contemporary American society cannot help being impressed with certain unfortunate tendencies which are nationwide today. Among these are the tendency to get something for nothing, to be a leaner, lack of responsibility, ethical shortcomings, particularly in business and politics. "The government owes me a living" thesis widely prevails. To drive a sharp bargain is an indication of smartness. It is because of the prevalence of this state of affairs that the Conference should embark upon the search for moral values with which to furbish knowledge and education with meaning purpose. In other words, no matter how explicit and admirable our educational goals may be they must rest upon a solid ethical-moral foundation.

Those acquainted with *Education and World Tragedy* must appreciate how much we are indebted to Howard Mumford Jones. The paper which he now contributes stems from this volume.[a] Again he stresses the urgency and educational importance of broadening our educational offering at the college level by offering instruction on Russia and the Orient and other parts of the world outside the United States. To me his point of view and supporting arguments are sound. It is sheer nonsense to think and talk about world unity under American leadership, as long as the people of the United States are deeply ignorant about the Eastern and most populous half of the world. Curriculum makers confronted with the problem of finding a place for courses on cultures other than those of the Western world will perhaps be horrified that some part of the older curriculum will have to be sacrificed to make room for the new offerings. They should find comfort, however, in the thought that frequent inventory should be taken of any curriculum for the purpose of ascertaining what changes should be made for its improvement. One of the educational sins of long standing at the college level has been the homage we have rendered to things obsolescent. By permitting Western culture to monopolize our educational pattern, we have also unconsciously contributed to American provincialism. In this respect it is high time that we put our educational house in order.

All of the papers prepared for this Conference touch directly or indirectly upon the subject of finding competent teachers. Dr. Jones devoted part of his paper to this question and, as Dr. Kandel points out, is sharp in his criticism of the aridity of college teaching. Increasingly we are realizing that no matter how sound our educational goals may be their failure or success in last analysis depends upon the teacher. A course whose content should be an inspiration to any student may be made most repulsive, because the person who gives the course is incompetent in some respect—personality, scholarship, interest, training. One wonders whether the item that characterized most college instruction today is its aimlessness. A visit to many classrooms would seem to indicate that this is so. Perhaps it is more true of broadly conceived general education than of departmental courses. But even in the departmental courses one is impressed with the frequent shortcomings of many teachers. In some cases on the basis of personality alone the person should not be in the teaching profession. In others it is the lack of

[a] [Cf. Chapter IX by Dr. Jones.]

Appendix III. Comment

training. Any college administrator who serves students in an advisory capacity can testify to the complaints students make about the character of their instruction: the course is dull, the instructor seems to know the subject but does not have the art of communicating his thought to his students, the instructor uses the class period to discuss matters that have no apparent relation to the course. These and similar complaints are evidence that the finding and training of teacher personnel, especially at the college level, is one of the most pressing tasks educators face.

No one can read these papers without coming to the conclusion that while most of their content covers areas that have been pretty fully explored previously, this fresh summary is valuable.

Comment

4

By GEORGE B. de HUSZAR
History Editor, "American People's Encyclopaedia"

I AM STRUCK by the fact that several papers stress the need for providing a sound vocational education.[a] It seems to me that the effort of some educators to provide an overly idealistic liberal education is a reaction to the so-called materialism and philistinism of every day life in particular and practical life in general. But such a reaction does great disservice, for it widens the gulf between ideals and reality. One of the greatest problems of our age is the split between "intellectuals" and "practical men." Nowadays it is very rare to find a person who is properly educated and at the same time is able to handle practical affairs. In the past there were a number of philosophers, who were obviously more "intellectual" than those who today talk *about* being "intellectual," who were able to handle practical matters. The pre-Socratics, Chinese philosophers from Kwan-tsi to Confucius, were politicians, statesmen, and lawgivers. More recent examples are Leibnitz and Goethe. Formal education cannot create such persons, but perhaps its ideal man should be fashioned along the model provided by such figures.

I believe that most serious educators agree that liberal education must be supplemented by vocational education. To create the impression that we must choose between a "pure" college and a vocational one, is to produce a pseudo-problem and a disservice to education. Perhaps I am simplifying the problem, but in my opinion it is possible and desirable to offer *simultaneously* a liberal education which stresses the theoretical matters, and a vocational education which prepares for practical life.

[a] [Cf. the discussion of the place of vocational preparation in the goals of education in Chapter II by Lyman Bryson (including comment by George N. Shuster), Chapter III by T. V. Smith, Chapter IX by Howard Mumford Jones, Chapter XV by Dr. Shuster, Chapter XVI by Earl J. McGrath (including comment by Louis J. A. Mercier), Chapter XVIII by Harold Taylor (including comments by Mason W. Gross and Dr. Mercier).]

The plan to offer first liberal education and then vocational training seems to me to be undesirable for a variety of reasons, one of which is that at the end of a purely theoretical education, the student is likely to be confused and insecure and it is too late to train him vocationally and for practical matters.

I was also interested in the fact that several papers pay attention to the great books. But there is disagreement as to the purpose of their study. Dr. Shuster believes that their main value lies in learning rhetoric in the true sense; Dr. Jones maintains that they have meaning in the cultural context which produced them, not as moral absolutes in college courses. It is regrettable that the purposes of the study of the great books have never been made clear by those who promote them. Such clarification would undoubtedly be useful. It can be assumed that the great books are offered because they provide information and knowledge about the Western intellectual tradition. Those who promote the great books sometimes maintain that their study is the basis of liberal education, or that it trains the mind by making people think, or that the "best thinking of all ages may be useful in this age, too." By any of these aims, the great books program is a failure.

a. The great books program cannot offer even a superficial knowledge of the Western intellectual tradition, because the list of the Great Books Foundation leaves out the entire Protestant tradition, since no book by Calvin, Luther, or Kierkegaard is included. It also ignores the entire tradition of Spanish and French dramatists. It furthermore almost entirely ignores the nineteenth century "vitalist" tradition, for it includes only one book by Nietzsche and none by Schopenhauer. The modern scientific and philosophical tradition is also represented in an inadequate way, for none of the works of Leibnitz, none of the most important modern scientists and philosophers, is included.

b. For the above reason the great books program is also an inadequate basis for liberal education. But there are also other deficiencies if this is the aim of the great books program. There cannot be any doubt that the reading and study of great books is an important *part* of liberal education. But it cannot be repeated enough that books themselves, no matter how great, are insufficient for any serious conception of liberal education.

c. If it is the purpose of the great books program to train the mind of the participant, then one would like to know how this happens. Is the mind something like a muscle, that can be trained by exercise? Perhaps this is so, but the assumption is made that those who participate in the program all have minds that can be trained in metaphysics, theology, science, etc. Although there can be no question that a number of people can profit from reading good books, it is also true that a number of them became merely pretentious by participating in the program. It is absurd to claim that by reading in a week or two, a great book which took the author, who was a man of exceptional mental powers, some years to write, a great deal can be learned. The undiscriminating and amateurish great books program has brought into existence a number of culture-eunuchs who edify themselves from time to time by reading classics, instead of seeking to create in the same spirit and with the same imagination as their authors did.

d. It is, of course, ridiculous to claim that the great books program represents the "best thinking of all ages," for the simple reason that the entire Oriental tradition is ignored. Inasmuch as I have elaborated this point in my Eighth Conference paper I shall not comment on it here.[b]

Confusion also reigns in regard to the standards by which a great book is to be judged. It has never been made clear whether the selection of a classic is made by the criterion of intrinsic excellence or historical originality and influence of a work. To answer this question is important, for it will determine the kind of works which will be selected. Literary and philosophical works of the past are likely to be classics according to both criteria. But scientific works are bound to become outmoded and meet only the second criterion. The great books program includes such a work as Gilbert's *On the Magnet*. It can be questioned whether this work today has any significance other than a historical one.

It is my belief that due to the fact that those who promote the great books never seriously thought about the purpose of the program, and failed to establish proper criteria of selecting the great books, the list of the classics to be published by the *Encyclopaedia Britannica* is inadequate. Those who set themselves up to publish a selection of classics should observe the highest standards of a scholarship and editorial objectivity. Mr. Hutchins maintains that "there is agreement on about

[b][Cf. "The Classics and International Understanding," Chapter XLII in *Learning and World Peace*, Lyman Bryson, Louis Finkelstein, R. M. MacIver, editors, Conference on Science, Philosophy and Religion in Their Relation to the Democratic Way of Life, Inc., New York, 1948.]

Appendix III. Comment

eighty-five per cent among all lists" of great books. One wonders whether eighty-five per cent of the scholars will agree that a book of Lessing, Calvin, Leibnitz, Kierkegaard, Nietzsche, Stendhal, Molière, Calderon, etc., should be excluded from the Britannica set of great books.[c]

[c][For further discussion of the "Chicago Plan" and the "great books," see Chapter II by Lyman Bryson, Chapter III by T. V. Smith, Chapter VIII by Alain L. Locke, Chapter IX by Howard Mumford Jones, Chapter XI by John U. Nef, Chapter XIII by Mordecai M. Kaplan, Chapter XV by George N. Shuster, Chapter XVI by Earl J. McGrath, and Chapter XVII by Ordway Tead.]

Comment

5

By LOUIS J. A. MERCIER
Professor of Comparative Philosophy and Literature, Georgetown University

⁂

IN GENERAL, there seems to be a reluctance in the Conference papers to take completely into consideration the whole philosophical and religious, social, and political background of the present conflicts in education.

Yet, it is only within a full consciousness of that background that our discussions can have any value, and that the relative importance of the questions discussed may be pinned down.

We are living in an age of transition for two reasons:

1. The Greco-Roman dualistic concept of man (man distinct in nature), reinforced by the Judeo-Christian tradition of man in relation with God as his ultimate supernatural end, has been put on the defensive not only by the Deists' rejection of Christianity, but by the rejection of Deism by the naturalists who have elaborated, out of idealistic and materialistic monism, the concept of a self-existing universe in constant evolution, with man wholly continuous with nature, and the happiness of man in the present life his highest end. This is the secularism of humanitarian naturalism.

2. The social evolution is going on from a hierarchical to an equalitarian society. It began in the West as far back as the twelfth century when the bourgeoisie emerged against the aristocracy. The French Revolution insured the triumph of the first, the nineteenth century saw its reign, till the challenge of socialism and eventually of communism, for economic, as well as political, equality.

Parallel with this, the sons of European immigrants in the American Middle West, all restarting at zero economically, developed an example of equalitarian ways, though still without much planned government supervision, though this has been rapidly accelerating in our day. The American experiment raised hopes throughout the world of the possibility of an equalitarian society through the democratic process; the Russian experiment has done the same in many quarters through a totalitarian process, particularly where there had been a lag in the evolution from feudalism.

Education followed suit: In the Middle Ages, the study of Roman law by the bourgeoisie gave them arguments for the power of the king or state over the aristocracy and the church; after the Renaissance the study of antiquity gave the aristocrat-bourgeois society a culture which separated it still more from the masses, and this lasted into the nineteenth century for Europe, with the classical college an upper class school. The Middle West American college and university was bound to feel first the demand for a classless utilitarian education, an education for manual, rather than for intellectual, techniques or ornamenting culture.

We are still in the thick of these two transitions; all the papers reflect them, and we cannot appreciate fully the importance of the points they make, if we do not constantly refer back to this perspective.

Comment

6

By RUTH STRANG[a]

Professor of Education, Teachers College, Columbia University

HAVING TAUGHT every grade from the first grade through graduate school, I keep trying to translate the proposed goals into actual school practice. For example, one of my graduate students is in charge of a group of twenty obstreperous six year olds in a nursery school who are constantly snatching toys, hitting one another, saying, "Teacher, I want the blocks— Teacher, he took my hammer— Teacher, he hit me." Their previous experiences have put them on the defensive, taught them to move against people rather than to cooperate. I asked her what were her goals of education for these children, and she said, "to help them get satisfaction from being cooperative." This goal of education was stated similarly in *Little Pierre*, "I would make lovable those things that they ought to love." I would like to add this to our list of proposed goals of education: "To make lovable those things that they ought to love."

The emphasis on knowledge alone in a number of papers has bothered me. The development of kind, generous, humane feelings surely is a goal of education, for out of these feelings grows action. We need to know more about the psychological relationship between knowing, feeling, and doing. Why has the training of the mind, which has been the most commonly accepted goal of education for centuries, not been more effective in bringing peace and good will in our times?

Professor Jones[b] calls attention to the disintegrating effect of specialization and the importance of unification through a "central living idea."

---

[a][Dr. Strang's comment refers to the group of papers on the general subject, "Problems of Adaptation to Changing Conditions." See the program of the Conference, printed at the end of this volume.]
[b][See Chapter IX by Howard Mumford Jones.]

He suggested education for a vocation as a motivating factor. Vocational education, as I think Dr. Bryson conceived it in his paper,[e] is a means both of self-realization and of serving society through one's work. The conflict over the place of education for a vocation in higher institutions of learning, seems to be caused by differences in conception of one's vocation and its contribution to the welfare of all. For example, take the vocation of the farmer—that may well become a way of life rather than a specialized part of life. So it may be with other vocations. Thus instead of weakening the vocational preparation given in college, it should be broadened, humanized, if you will. There is a trend in this direction —engineers take courses in history and economics to make them more aware of the social implications of their work; they take courses in literature to obtain greater depth of understanding of people. One way of meeting the present crisis is to teach engineers and scientists to see the social, as well as the personal, significance of their work.

Professor Jones advocates "the study of personal relationships, employer and employee relationships, friendships, and even relationships to other persons not known to the individual." (For example, our relationship to the starving people of Europe and the Far East is implied by our actions, personal and collective. The abandonment of rationing as soon as the war ended said quite clearly, "We just don't care about other people—all we're interested in is having as much as we want to eat." The extravagant use of wool materials in women's dresses last winter was another indication of our indifference to human beings.) A study of personal relationships would include the study of oneself—the counseling of individual students to help each one get a clearer idea of his most acceptable self. As their understanding of themselves grows, they become more and more capable of understanding others and cooperating with others. This interpretation of the study of personal relationships is a far cry from the superficial "how to make friends and influence people" approach. It requires the development of attitudes that express themselves in techniques of living together harmoniously.

In the following up Professor Jones's emphasis on global thinking as a goal, we must consider the difficulties in realizing this goal. For example, understanding Russia involves difficulty in getting the facts, finding teachers who can present and interpret the facts to students. The idea of understanding other nations goes back to several previous Confer-

[e] [See Chapter II by Lyman Bryson.]

ences in which, I think, it was fairly well agreed that the thing to do was to look for the good in each nation. Nations, like individuals, have "much of good and much of ill" in them. We get further by recognizing and building on the good (by accentuating the positive) than by trying to correct faults. Nations need counseling. They need help in recognizing and developing their more acceptable qualities. The first Russian primer presented a hopeful constructive picture of developing its vast resources for the good of all the people. If other nations emphasized this picture—played it up—might it not affect Russia's idea of herself? Certainly to help nations gain a more acceptable idea of themselves is an important pathway to peace and a worthy goal of education.

Professor Jones quite rightly would direct the student's attention to the contemporary scene. It seems wise to start with the present situation and delve into the past, as the need arises to understand present conditions that are still being influenced by past events and ideas. History helps to explain why nations behave as they do, just as case histories throw light on an individual's present behavior. If the nation itself understands its behavior, it may be more likely to modify it. Moreover, as T. S. Eliot said in the opening lines of one of his poems:

> Time present and time past
> Are both present in time future,
> And time future contained in time past.
> If all time is eternally present
> All time is unredeemable.[1]

This emphasis on the contemporary scene is not a goal of education, but a condition necessary for realizing the goals of social welfare.

Dr. Kaplan's paper [d] builds a criterion by which to evaluate goals and procedures. Only those goals should be included in our list that include a religious sense of destiny looking forward to a more abundant life for all mankind.

[d][See Chapter XIII by Mordecai M. Kaplan.]

[1] T. S. Eliot, "Burnt Norton," *Collected Poems*, Harcourt, Brace and Company, New York, 1936, p. 213.

CONTRIBUTORS TO "GOALS FOR AMERICAN EDUCATION"

SWAMI AKHILANANDA, *Ramakrishna Vedanta Society, Boston*
DAVID BIDNEY, *The Viking Fund,* research associate; author, *Psychology and Ethics of Spinoza*
THEODORE BRAMELD, *School of Education, New York University,* professor of educational philosophy; author, *Design for America, Minority Problems in the Public Schools,* and others
LYMAN BRYSON, *Teachers College, Columbia University,* professor of education; Columbia Broadcasting System, counsellor on public affairs; Conference on Science, Philosophy and Religion, first vice president; author, *Science and Freedom,* and others; editor, *The Communication of Ideas;* co-editor, Conference on Science, Philosophy and Religion, 2nd, 3rd, 4th, 5th, 6th, 7th, 8th, and 9th symposia
SCOTT BUCHANAN, *Liberal Arts, Inc.,* director; author, *Symbolic Distance, The Doctrine of Signatures,* and others
HARRY J. CARMAN, *Columbia College, Columbia University,* dean; author, *American Husbandry, Jesse Buel, Agricultural Reformer,* and others
THURSTON N. DAVIS, S.J., *Graduate School, Fordham University,* instructor in philosophy
ARCHIBALD DAVISON, *Harvard University,* James Edward Ditson professor of music
KARL W. DEUTSCH, *Massachusetts Institute of Technology,* associate professor of history
ROWLAND W. DUNHAM, *College of Music, University of Colorado,* dean; contributor to "The Etude," and others
PAUL L. ESSERT, *Teachers College, Columbia University,* professor of education
HERMAN FINER, *The University of Chicago,* department of political science; consultant on backward economies to International Labor Organization
LOUIS FINKELSTEIN, *The Jewish Theological Seminary of America,* president—on leave, Solomon Schechter professor of theology—on leave; Conference on Science, Philosophy and Religion, president; co-editor, 2nd, 3rd, 4th, 5th, 6th, 7th, 8th, and 9th symposia.
NORMAN FOERSTER, author, *The American State University, The Future of the Liberal College, The Humanities and the Common Man,* and others
PHILIPP FRANK, *Harvard University,* lecturer on physics and mathematics and research associate in physics and philosophy; author, *Foundations of Physics, Einstein: His Life and Times,* and others
HARRY B. FRIEDGOOD, *University of California at Los Angeles,* associate clinical professor of medicine; president and chairman, Scientific Board, California Institute for Cancer Research
CHRISTIAN GAUSS, *Princeton University,* dean emeritus of the College, dean of alumni; author, *Why We Went to War, Life in College, A Primer for Tomorrow,* and others; co-author, *American Thought,* and others
MASON W. GROSS, *College of Arts and Sciences, Rutgers University,* associate professor of philosophy and assistant dean
CARYL P. HASKINS, *Haskins Laboratories,* president; Union College, research professor; Massachusetts Institute of Technology, research associate; author, *Of Ants and Men, The Amazon,* and others
CHARLES W. HENDEL, *Yale University,* professor of moral philosophy and metaphysics, director of graduate studies; author, *Jean Jacques Rousseau: Moralist, Citizen of Geneva,* and others
GEORGE B. DE HUSZAR, *American People's Encyclopedia,* history editor; author, *Practical Applications of Democracy, The United States as World Leader;* editor and co-author, *Persistent International Issues,* and others
F. ERNEST JOHNSON, *Teachers College, Columbia University,* professor of education; Federal Council of Churches of Christ in America, department of research and education, execu-

tive secretary, editor of *"Information Service";* author, *The Social Gospel Re-Examined;* editor, *World Order: Its Intellectual and Cultural Foundations, Foundations of Democracy, Wellsprings of the American Spirit,* and others

HOWARD MUMFORD JONES, *Harvard University,* professor of English; American Academy of Arts and Sciences, president; author, *Ideas in America, Education and World Tragedy,* and others

I. L. KANDEL, *University of Manchester,* professor of American studies; Teachers College, Columbia University, professor emeritus of education; author, *Intellectual Cooperation: National and International, U.S. Activities in International Cultural Relations,* and others

MORDECAI M. KAPLAN, *The Jewish Theological Seminary of America,* professor of the philosophies of religion; author, *Judaism in Transition, The Meaning of God in Modern Jewish Religion, The Future of the America Jew,* and others

JOHN LAFARGE, S.J., *"America,"* associate editor; author, *Interracial Justice, The Race Question and the Negro,* and others

RONALD B. LEVY, *Roosevelt College,* assistant professor of education

CLEM C. LINNENBERG, JR., *Division of Statistical Standards; United States Bureau of the Budget,* economist, author of monographs on economics and government

ALAIN L. LOCKE, *Howard University,* professor of philosophy; author, *Negro Art—Past and Present, The Negro in Art,* and others

R. M. MACIVER, *Columbia University,* Lieber professor of political philosophy and sociology; author, *Toward an Abiding Peace, The Web of Government, The More Perfect Union,* and others; editor, *Unity and Difference in American Life, Discrimination and National Welfare,* and others; co-editor, Conference on Science, Philosophy and Religion, 4th, 5th, 6th, 7th, 8th, and 9th symposia.

HENRY MARGENAU, *Yale University,* professor of physics

EARL J. MCGRATH, *College of Liberal Arts, State University of Iowa,* dean; editor, *"The Journal of General Education"*

ALEXANDER MEIKLEJOHN, *University of Wisconsin,* professor emeritus of philosophy; author, *What Does America Mean, Education Between Two Worlds,* and others

LOUIS J. A. MERCIER, *Georgetown University,* professor of comparative philosophy and literature

JOHN COURTNEY MURRAY, S.J., *Woodstock College,* professor of theology; editor, *"Theological Studies"*

JOHN U. NEF, *The University of Chicago,* professor of economic history, chairman, Committee on Social Thought; author, *The United States and Civilization, Universities Look for Unity,* and others

SWAMI NIKHILANANDA, *Ramakrishna-Vivekananda Center of New York,* founder and spiritual leader; author of several books on Hindu religion and philosophy

LOUIS W. NORRIS, *De Pauw University,* professor of philosophy and religion

MAX C. OTTO, *University of Wisconsin,* professor of philosophy; author, *Natural Laws and Human Hopes, The Human Enterprise,* and others; co-author, *Philosophy in American Education,* and others

GERALD B. PHELAN, *The Mediaeval Institute, University of Notre Dame,* director; author, *Some Illustrations of St. Thomas' Development of the Wisdom of St. Augustine,* and others

E. V. SAYERS, *University of Hawaii,* professor emeritus of education; New York University, visiting professor

GEORGE N. SHUSTER, *Hunter College of the City of New York,* president; Conference on Science, Philosophy and Religion, vice president; author, *Look Away, The English Ode from Milton to Keats, Religion and Education,* and others

Contributors to "Goals for American Education"

HARRY SLOCHOWER, *Brooklyn College,* assistant professor of German

B. OTHANEL SMITH, *College of Education, University of Illinois,* professor of education

T. V. SMITH, *Maxwell School, Syracuse University,* professor of philosophy; editor, *"International Journal of Ethics";* author, *Atomic Power and Moral Faith,* and others

DONALD C. STONE, *Economic Cooperation Administration,* director of administration; author of books and articles on government administration

RUTH STRANG, *Teachers College, Columbia University,* professor of education; author of educational books for children and adults

HAROLD TAYLOR, *Sarah Lawrence College,* president; contributor to philosophical and educational journals

ORDWAY TEAD, *Board of Higher Education, City of New York,* chairman; editor, social and economic books, Harper & Brothers; author, *Democratic Administration,* and others

ROBERT ULICH, *Graduate School of Education, Harvard University,* professor of education

JOHN D. WILD, *Harvard University,* professor of philosophy

QUINCY WRIGHT, *The University of Chicago,* professor of international law; author, *A Study of War,* and others

Program

NINTH CONFERENCE ON SCIENCE, PHILOSOPHY AND RELIGION IN THEIR RELATION TO THE DEMOCRATIC WAY OF LIFE

CONVOKED BY

Mortimer J. Adler
Michael J. Ahern, S.J.
William F. Albright
Franz Alexander
W. C. Allee
Rudolf Allers
Maxwell Anderson
Edwin E. Aubrey
Frank Aydelotte
Chester I. Barnard
Alfred H. Barr, Jr.
Gregory Bateson
Roy Battenhouse
Ruth F. Benedict
J. Seelye Bixler
Brand Blanshard
Ben Zion Bokser
Edgar S. Brightman
Van Wyck Brooks
J. Douglas Brown
Lyman Bryson
Ludlow Bull
Millar Burrows
Douglas Bush
George A. Buttrick
Robert L. Calhoun
A. J. Carlson
Harry J. Carman
Edward A. Cerny, S.S.
Joseph P. Chamberlain

Emmanuel Chapman *
Eliot D. Chapple
John M. Clark
Henry S. Coffin
Stewart G. Cole
Arthur H. Compton
Edwin G. Conklin
William G. Constable
Carleton S. Coon
John M. Cooper
Norman Cousins
Karl K. Darrow
Peter J. W. Debye
Henry S. Dennison
Karl W. Deutsch
Arnold Dresden
Curt J. Ducasse
Irwin Edman
Harrison S. Elliott
Hoxie N. Fairchild
Walter Farrell, O.P.
Enrico Fermi
Nels F. S. Ferré
Louis Finkelstein
Thomas K. Finletter
Dorothy Canfield Fisher
Hughell E.W. Fosbroke
Harry E. Fosdick
Lawrence K. Frank
Philipp Frank

E. Franklin Frazier
Horace L. Friess
A. Campbell Garnett
Christian Gauss
Ralph W. Gerard
Harry D. Gideonse
Eli Ginzberg
Erwin R. Goodenough
Frank P. Graham
Frederick C. Grant
Simon Greenberg
Theodore M. Greene
Michael J. Gruenthaner, S.J.
Waldemar Gurian
Hunter Guthrie, S.J.
Moses Hadas
E. H. Harbison
Henry M. Hart, Jr.
Charles Hartshorne
Hugh Hartshorne
Caryl P. Haskins
Robert J. Havighurst
Michael A. Heilperin
Charles W. Hendel
James M. Hendel
Karl F. Herzfeld
Victor F. Hess
Hudson Hoagland
Frank E. Horack, Jr.
Robert M. Hutchins
Raphael Isaacs
Dugald C. Jackson
Oscar I. Janowsky
E. Jerome Johanson
Charles S. Johnson
F. Ernest Johnson
Howard Mumford Jones
I. L. Kandel
Mordecai M. Kaplan
Edward Kasner
Robert W. King
Paul Klapper

Clyde Kluckhohn
Frank H. Knight
Carl H. Kraeling
Ernst Kris
Richard Kroner
Alfred C. Lane *
Harold D. Lasswell
Paul Lazarsfeld
Robert D. Leigh
David M. Levy
David E. Lilienthal
Ralph S. Lillie
Ralph Linton
Alain L. Locke
Robert H. Lowie
Eugene W. Lyman *
Mary E. Lyman
Richard P. McKeon
John T. McNeill
Douglas C. Macintosh *
R. M. MacIver
John A. Mackay
William de B. MacNider
Clarence Manion
Henry Margenau
Jacques Maritain
Alexander Marx
Kirtley F. Mather
Margaret Mead
Adolf Meyer
Conrad H. Moehlman
Charles R. Morey
Hans J. Morgenthau
Charles Morris
Forest Ray Moulton
Lewis Mumford
Arthur E. Murphy
Henry A. Murray
John C. Murray, S.J.
A. J. Muste
John U. Nef
William Stuart Nelson

Program

Allan Nevins
Allardyce Nicoll
Marjorie H. Nicolson
Reinhold Niebuhr
Justin Wroe Nixon
F. S. C. Northrop
Whitney J. Oates
William O'Meara
J. Robert Oppenheimer
Albert C. Outler
Harry A. Overstreet
Walter Pach
DeWitt Henry Parker
Talcott Parsons
Wilfrid Parsons, S.J.
Wilhelm Pauck
Linus C. Pauling
Anton C. Pegis
George B. Pegram
Ralph Barton Perry
Gerald B. Phelan
Clarence E. Pickett
Arthur Upham Pope
Liston Pope
I. I. Rabi
Warner G. Rice
Howard Chandler Robbins
Martin A. Rosanoff
Michael Rostovtzeff
Beardsley Ruml
Henry Norris Russell
George Sarton
Paul A. Schilpp

Herbert W. Schneider
Alphonse S. Schwitalla, S.J.
Roy W. Sellars
Harlow Shapley
Harry Shulman
George N. Shuster
Yves R. Simon
Robert J. Slavin, O.P.
Pitirim A. Sorokin
Shalom Spiegel
Donald C. Stone
Samuel A. Stouffer
Ruth Strang
Raymond Swing
Frank Tannenbaum
Francis H. Taylor
Hugh S. Taylor
Ordway Tead
George F. Thomas
Laura Thompson
Paul J. Tillich
Harold C. Urey
Mark Van Doren
Henry P. Van Dusen
Gerald G. Walsh, S.J.
Arnold M. Walter
Luther A. Weigle
Paul Weiss
Henry N. Wieman
Amos N. Wilder
M. L. Wilson
Louis Wirth
Quincy Wright

at

The Men's Faculty Club of Columbia University
400 West 117th Street
New York, New York

on Tuesday, Wednesday, Thursday, and Friday
September 7, 8, 9, and 10, 1948

* Deceased

WHAT SHOULD BE THE GOALS FOR EDUCATION?

TUESDAY, SEPTEMBER 7th

6:00 p.m.

Dinner meeting of Chairmen and Co-chairmen
To help integrate the Conference discussion, Professor Lyman Bryson and Professor R. M. MacIver will serve as chairmen at each session, with a co-chairman.

8:30 p.m.

GERALD B. PHELAN, *Co-chairman*

Discussion of[1]

PHILOSOPHICAL AND HISTORICAL APPROACHES

based on papers by

THEODORE BRAMELD
CHARLES W. HENDEL
T. V. SMITH
DONALD C. STONE

Prepared discussants

JOHN LaFARGE, S.J.
QUINCY WRIGHT

WEDNESDAY, SEPTEMBER 8th

10:00 a.m.

SIMON GREENBERG, *Co-chairman*

Discussion of[1]

PHILOSOPHICAL AND HISTORICAL APPROACHES

based on papers by

W. H. COWLEY
KARL W. DEUTSCH
ALAIN L. LOCKE
ROBERT ULICH

Prepared discussants

HENRY MARGENAU
ARTHUR E. MURPHY

2:30 p.m.

HARLOW SHAPLEY, *Co-chairman*

Discussion of[1]

PROBLEMS OF ADAPTATION TO CHANGING CONDITIONS

based on papers by

LYMAN BRYSON
SCOTT BUCHANAN
LOUIS J. A. MERCIER
JOHN U. NEF

Prepared discussants

FREDERICK G. HOCHWALT
CHANNING H. TOBIAS

8:30 p.m.

WILLIAM STUART NELSON, *Co-chairman*

Discussion of[1]

PROBLEMS OF ADAPTATION TO CHANGING CONDITIONS

based on papers by

HOWARD MUMFORD JONES
MORDECAI M. KAPLAN
JOHN C. MURRAY, S.J.[2]

Prepared discussants

W. G. CONSTABLE
RUTH STRANG

THURSDAY, SEPTEMBER 9th

8:30 a.m.

> Breakfast business meeting of the members of the Conference on Science, Philosophy and Religion, to transact necessary business of the corporation, including election of officers and new members.

10:00 a.m.

Harold D. Lasswell, Co-chairman

Discussion of[1]

PROBLEMS OF ADMINISTRATION

based on papers by

Rowland W. Dunham
Earl J. McGrath
George N. Shuster
Harold Taylor
Ordway Tead

Prepared discussants

Harry J. Carman
Ernest O. Melby

2:30 p.m.

GENERAL DISCUSSION OF ISSUES RAISED IN PREVIOUS CONFERENCES AND AT CURRENT SESSIONS

including consideration of paper by

F. Ernest Johnson

8:30 p.m.

Harry J. Carman, Chairman

Public Meeting

WHAT SHOULD BE THE GOALS FOR EDUCATION?

Addresses by Lyman Bryson

R. M. MacIver

(at the Harkness Academic Theater, 105 Butler Library, 535 West 114th Street)

FRIDAY, SEPTEMBER 10th

10:00 a.m.

CRITIQUE OF THE CONFERENCE ON SCIENCE, PHILOSOPHY AND RELIGION, WITH SPECIAL REFERENCE TO THE NINTH ANNUAL MEETING AND PLANS FOR THE FUTURE

PARTICIPANTS IN PROGRAM *

Swami Akhilananda, *Ramakrishna Vedanta Society*
Rudolf Allers, *School of Philosophy, Catholic University of America*
Ruth Benedict, *Columbia University*
David Bidney, *The Viking Fund*
Edward W. Blakeman, *University of Michigan*
C. P. Boner
Theodore Brameld, *School of Eduction, New York University*
William H. Bristow, *Board of Education, City of New York*
John S. Brubacher, *Graduate School, Yale University*
Lyman Bryson, *Teachers College, Columbia University*
Scott Buchanan, *Liberal Arts, Inc.*
Ludlow Bull, *Metropolitan Museum of Art*
Harry J. Carman, *Columbia College, Columbia University*
W. G. Constable, *Museum of Fine Arts, Boston*
James Francis Cooke, *"The Etude"*
Norman Cousins, *"The Saturday Review of Literature"*
W. H. Cowley, *Stanford University*
Malcolm W. Davis, *Carnegie Endowment for International Peace*
Thurston N. Davis, S.J., *Fordham University*
Archibald Davison, *Harvard University*
Karl W. Deutsch, *Massachusetts Institute of Technology*
Harl R. Douglass, *College of Education, University of Colorado*
Rowland W. Dunham, *College of Music, University of Colorado*
Paul L. Essert, *Teachers College, Columbia University*
Herman Finer, *University of Chicago*
Norman Foerster
Philipp Frank, *Harvard University*
Harry B. Friedgood, *University of California, Los Angeles*
Horace L. Friess, *Columbia University*
A. Campbell Garnett, *University of Wisconsin*
Christian Gauss, *Princeton University*
Eli Ginzberg, *Columbia University*
Erwin R. Goodenough, *Yale University*
Mark Graubard, *College of Science, Literature and the Arts, University of Minnesota*
Simon Greenberg, *The Jewish Theological Seminary of America*

[1]Papers and written discussion available in mimeographed form. All oral discussion off the record.
[2]Text not received before program in press.

Mason W. Gross, *College of Arts and Sciences, Rutgers University*
E. Harris Harbison, *Princeton University*
Caryl P. Haskins, *Union College*
Robert J. Havighurst, *University of Chicago*
Hiram Haydn, *"The American Scholar"*
Michael A. Heilperin, *Bristol-Myers Company*
Charles W. Hendel, *Yale University*
Frederick G. Hochwalt, *National Catholic Welfare Conference*
Sidney Hook, *New York University*
George B. de Huszar, *"American People's Encyclopedia"*
Antonio Iglesias
Oscar I. Janowsky, *College of the City of New York*
F. Ernest Johnson, *Teachers College, Columbia University*
Howard Mumford Jones, *Harvard University*
I. L. Kandel, *University of Manchester*
Mordecai M. Kaplan, *The Jewish Theological Seminary of America*
Edward Kasner, *Columbia University*
John LaFarge, S.J., *"America"*
Harold D. Lasswell, *School of Law, Yale University*
Robert D. Leigh, *Public Library Inquiry of the Social Science Research Council*
Ronald B. Levy, *Roosevelt College*
Clem C. Linnenberg, Jr., *United States Bureau of the Budget*
Alain L. Locke, *Howard University*
R. M. MacIver, *Columbia University*
Henry Margenau, *Yale University*
Jacques Maritain, *Princeton University*
James Marshall, *Board of Education, City of New York*
Earl J. McGrath, *College of Liberal Arts, University of Iowa*
Richard P. McKeon, *University of Chicago*
Alexander Meiklejohn, *University of Wisconsin*
Morris Meister, *Bronx High School of Science*
Ernest O. Melby, *School of Education, New York University*
Louis J. A. Mercier, *Georgetown University*
Charles E. Merriam, *University of Chicago*
Robert K. Merton, *Bureau of Applied Social Research*
Lewis Mumford
Arthur E. Murphy, *Sage School of Philosophy, Cornell University*
John C. Murray, S.J., *Woodstock College*
John U. Nef, *University of Chicago*
William Stuart Nelson, *School of Religion, Howard University*
Swami Nikhilananda, *Ramakrishna-Vivekananda Center of New York*
Justin Wroe Nixon, *Colgate-Rochester Divinity School*
Louis W. Norris, *DePauw University*
William O'Meara, *University of Chicago*
Max C. Otto, *University of Wisconsin*
Walter Pach
Anton C. Pegis, *Pontifical Institute of Mediaeval Studies, Toronto*
Houston Peterson, *Rutgers University*
Gerald B. Phelan, *The Mediaeval Institute, University of Notre Dame*
Liston Pope, *Divinity School, Yale University*
Edward B. Rooney, S.J., *Jesuit Educational Association*

Program

Malcolm Ross, *University of Miami*
Harold K. Schilling, *Pennsylvania State College*
Harlow Shapley, *Harvard University*
George N. Shuster, *Hunter College of the City of New York*
Ernst Simon, *Hebrew University*
Harry Slochower, *Brooklyn College*
B. Othanel Smith, *College of Education, University of Illinois*
Kerry Smith, *United States Office of Education*
T. V. Smith, *Maxwell School, Syracuse University*
Mark Starr, *International Ladies' Garment Workers' Union*
Douglas V. Steere, *Haverford College*
Donald C. Stone, *Economic Cooperation Administration*
Ruth Strang, *Teachers College, Columbia University*
Frank Tannenbaum, *Columbia University*
Harold Taylor, *Sarah Lawrence College*
Ordway Tead, *Board of Higher Education, City of New York*
Channing H. Tobias, *Phelps-Stokes Fund*
Robert Ulich, *Graduate School of Education, Harvard University*
Gerald G. Walsh, S.J., *"Thought"*
René Wellek, *Yale University*
Irl G. Whitchurch, *Graduate School of Religion, University of Southern California*
Henry N. Wieman, *Divinity School, University of Chicago*
John Daniel Wild, *Harvard University*
Louis Wirth, *University of Chicago*
Antoni Wojcicki, *UNESCO*
Kurt Wolff, *Pantheon Books, Inc.*
Julian L. Woodward
Quincy Wright, *University of Chicago*

*Writers of papers and comments, and those expected to attend, as of August 27th.

Index

Abelard, Peter, 2, 3
Abstraction, and symbols, 76-77
Abundance, economy of, 362
Academic freedom, 5, 12-13, 19, 74
Academy, 150
  European, 149
  of Renaissance, 5
  organization of, 145
Accounting system, educational, 221-222
Action, 32
  agreement on, 418
  collective, 489
  incentives to, 235-241
  thinking and, 260
  when and where, 360
Adams, Henry, 258
Adjustment, 345
  concept of, 114
Adler, Mortimer J., 141, 252
Adult education, 383
  extension classes, 386
  under Chicago plan, 252-253
Advertising, 237
Aggression, 476, 477
Akhilananda, Swami, comment by, 16, 29-30, 229, 230, 427
Albertus Magnus, 2
Ambition:
  dignity of, 22
  personal, 24
American Council of Learned Societies, 509
Americanism, 245
American Philosophical Association, 307
Ames, Edward Scribner, 368
Amherst College Report, on objectives, 414-415
Annihilation, alternatives to, 341-342
Anthropology, courses in, 220
Anti-intellectualism, 153
Anti-vocationalism, 49
Applied science, 220, 322-323
Appreciation, 193

Aquinas, Thomas, 2, 3, 15, 146, 223, 322
Arab learning, 64
Area studies, 207
Areopagitica, 172, 174, 175, 181
Aristotelian logic, 3
Aristotle, 4, 37, 38, 49, 145, 146, 216, 267, 311, 321-322
  on musical training, 451
Arnold, Matthew, 202, 324, 373
Artisan, contempt for, 93
Art of living, 311-313
Arts:
  and freedom, 194-195
  fine, 193, 194
  study of, 278
Atheism:
  of Marxism, 155
  scientific, 157
Athletics, intercollegiate, 248-249
Atlantic Charter, 336
Atomic energy, 30, 142, 143
Attitudes, 205
Auden, W. H., 437
Augustine, St., 98, 128
Authoritarianism, and democracy, 300-302, 304
Authority, democratic philosophy of, 335-338

Babbitt, Irving, 287
Backward nations, 220
Bacon, Francis, 215, 356, 369
Balance, as model, 104
Barbarians, 94
Barker, Ernest, 151
Barr, Stringfellow, 251
Beauty, 43, 323-325
Benedict, St., rule of, 98
Bennington College, 434
Bergson, Henri, 439
Berkeley, George, 67
Bernal, J. D., 66

Index

Bible, the, 3, 179
Bidney, David, comment by, 73, 138, 330
Bill of Rights, 146
Blackett, P. S. M., 69
Blanshard, Brand, 307, 434
Blueprints for reconstructed culture, 342, 361-365
Board of Higher Education, 375
Board of Trustees, 375
Boas, Franz, 77
Books, Great (*see* Great Books)
Boorstin, D. J., 256
Bourne, Randolph, 368, 370
Bowman, A. A., 186-187
Brameld, Theodore, 341-371
Braunschvig, Marcel, 280
Bridgman, P. W., 81
Brinton, Crane, 52
Britten, Benjamin, 465
Bromfield, Louis, 508
Brookings Institution, 219
Brooks, Van Wyck, 508
Brubacher, John S., 482
Bryson, Lyman, 19-30, 485-491, 523
Buchanan, Scott, 141-152, 251
  comment by, 30
Bureaucracies, 92
Burke, Edmund, 106
Bush, Vannevar, 67, 70
Bye, Raymond, 251
Byzantine Empire, 97

Cabot, Richard C., 317
Calculating machines, 110, 129, 130
Cambridge University, 5
Capitalism, 245
Carman, Harry J.:
  comment by, 512-515
  on acceptance of new objectives, 420-422
Castes, and spread of knowledge, 92
Cathedral schools, 64
Censorship, Milton and, 181
Change:
  acceptance of, 443
  tradition and, 6-7
Chesterton, G. K., 311
Chicago, University of, 30
Chicago Plan, 20, 203, 228, 247-260, 294-409, 503, 506, 517-519
  301, 307, 331, 335, 337, 396, 397,

Chicago Plan (*Cont.*)
  abolishment of intercollegiate football, 248-249
  adult education program, 252-253
  aim of, 247
  college curriculum, 250
  college entrance and graduation age, 249-250
  Committee on Social Thought, 255-258
    study of fundamentals, 257
  graduate school, abandonment of memory tests and course credits, 256
  reforms introduced, 248-249
    aimed at leadership, 250
Child-centered school, 435
Childs, John L., 479
Christianity, 241, 254-255, 301
  and development of music, 452
  and restoration of science, 95-99
  and the university, 4
  as myth, 366
  deists' rejection of, 520
  modern, 157
Christian revolution, in Middle Ages, 99-105
Church colleges, 472
Churches, 289-290
Church foundations, 290
Churchill, Winston, 379-380
Cicero, 380
Cincinnati public schools case, 291
Citizenship, 489
  American, 39-40
  education for, 20, 28
  function of university, 385, 401-403
City state, 85-86
Civilization:
  and university, 6-7, 8
  breakdowns of, 88, 89-91
Civil liberties, 144
Classes in Western society, 217
Classical college, 271-272, 276, 283
Classical curriculum, 433
Classical education movement, 434
Classical languages, in high school, 272, 275-278
Classless Society, Education for a, 61
Clinchy, Everett R., 300
Coherence, social, 129-132
Cohesion, education for, 72 ff.
Cole, Steward G., 472

Index

Coleridge, Samuel T., 58
Collective bargaining, 355
College:
   classical, 263
   colonial, 263
   first business of, 374
   good, definition of, 382
   graduates, of today, 21-22
   junior (*see* Junior college)
   liberal arts, smaller, 9-10
   liberal in classical sense, 472
   municipal, administration of, 373-384
   "pure," 379
   senior, 264, 265 (*see also* University)
   6-point program, 224-225
   smaller, encouragement to attend, 399
   under-graduate, 9
   specialism in, 219
Columbia College of Columbia University, 410, 420-422
Committees, voluntary, 489
"Common man," 171
Commonwealth, new, education for, 171-175
Communication:
   breakdown of, 90-92
   indoctrination or, 73-75
   theory of, research in, 75
Communications, mass, 193-194, 257-258
Communism, 46, 141, 151, 165, 245, 521
   and democracy, 244, 246
Communist cells, 383
Community:
   college as part of, 382-384
   informal educational services for, function of university, 385, 386-387
Competition, 185
Comte, Auguste, 158, 220, 299
Conant, James B., 4, 61, 66, 79
Concepts:
   for definition and explanation, 134
   reason and, 78-81
   words into, 77
Conference on Science, Philosophy and Religion in Their Relation to the Democratic Way of Life, 337, 338
Conferences on objectives, 419-420
Conformity, 14
Confucius, 451
Consciousness, 119-123
Conservatism, 38

Constable, William, 474
Constitution, American, 148
Contemplative life, 26-27
Contributors to *Goals for American Education*, 525-527
Controversial issues:
   education and, 205
   present day, 433
Cooperation:
   goal of, 522
   in application of objectives, 418-419
Core-curriculum, 202, 208
   reform of, 434
Count, Earl W., 477
Counter-revolution, 7
Counting, 81-83
Counts, George S., 410
Courses:
   correct labeling of, 286
   orientation, 202
   some specialized, 136
   unifying, in history of science and thought, 75-102
Crankshaw, Edward, 231
Cravings, human, 348
Creative activity, education for, 390-391
Credits, course, 256
   in music, 460-461
Crisis:
   culture, 201, 205
   periods of, and education, 56, 62, 64, 65
Critical relativism, 209-210
Criticism, modern, 186
Critics, social, 3
Cromwell, Oliver, 65, 177
Cromwellian era, 7
Crusades, 100, 101
Cultural design, 363
Cultural differences, 355-356
Cultural lag, 310
Cultural myth, role of, 342, 365 370
Cultural pluralism, 439
   education in, 444
Culture, 13 13, 81 83, 123
   comparison of cultures, 206
   continuity of, university and, 6-7, 8
   definition of, 121, 239
   reconstructed, blueprints for, 342, 361-365
   training for responsibility to one's, 20
Culture groups, isolation of, 359

Curriculum:
  alterations in, how forwarded, 418-423, 425
  classical, 433
  comparisons, 425-426
  contemporary focus of, 473
  core, 202, 208
  new, 431
    as end, not means, 433
    creation of, 441
    must be flexible, 442
  of present-day high school, 272
  possible results of, 137-139
  tentative, 136-139
Cybernetics, 68, 130

Dartmouth Eye Institute, 438
Darwin, Charles, 64, 113
Davis, Thurston N., comment by, 15, 16, 52-53, 326
Davison, Archibald, comment by, 460
Decentralization of higher education, 399-400
Declaration of Independence, 148
Defeatism, 342
Degrees:
  in music, 457-458
  university, 10, 11, 283-284, 287-288, 289, 393, 509
Deism, 289
  naturalists' rejection of, 520
Democracy, 481-482
  American, 165
  and authoritarianism, 300-302
  and communism, 244, 246
  and leadership, 332-335
  and present-day education, 302-304
  educating youth for, 385, 401-403
  generosity toward difference, 490
  Greek, 186
  institutional religion's and, 320-321
  spiritual, 491
  still in infancy, 320
  theistic, 339
  without philosophy of salvation, 304-305
  world, 364-365
Democratic indoctrination, 306
Denominations, and the university, 4
Departmental system, 222-223, 431
  and total educational effectiveness, 417
Dependability, 317

Depth psychology, 155, 474
Descartes, René, 58, 223
Desires, human, 346-348
Deutsch, Babette, 368
Deutsch, Karl W., 55-139, 208, 502
Dewey, John, 44, 159, 221, 408, 439
Dialectical materialism, 503
Dictatorships, 7, 236
Diderot, Denis, 146
Differences:
  cultural, 355-356
  democracy and, 490-491
Discrimination, 163-164
Dissension, 14-15
Disvalue, 313
Diversity, value of, 490-491
Doctors' degrees, 10, 11, 283-284, 287-289, 393, 509
Dogma, 209
Dollard, John, 112
Donham, Dean, 217
Don Quixote, 373, 374
Drives, 345, 346
  in human behavior, 476
  primary or secondary, 346-347
Dunham, Rowland W., 449-469
  comment by, 11, 363, 416

Eclecticism, 7
Economic groups, 360
Economic planning, 142
Economic theory, modern, 220
Edison, Thomas A., 69
Education:
  American:
    as experiment, 429-448
    overorganization of, 429
  and the social order, 480-483
  democratic, ferment in, 143
  elementary, 267, 271-272
  essential goal of, 474-475
  general (*see* General education)
  goals of (*see* Objectives of education)
  higher (*see* Higher education)
  problems set by human nature, 476-477
  scarcity economy in, 60
  secondary (*see* High schools; Secondary education)
  stimulation substituted for, 21
Educational psychology, teaching of, 379
Educational system of future, 363-364

Educative society, 190-191
Educators, responsibility of, 481
Egyptians, 82, 92
Einstein, Albert, 147
Elective system, failure of, 431
Elementary education, 267
  motivating subjects of, 271-272
Eliot, T. S., 524
Élite, higher learning as privilege of, 56
Emerson, Ralph Waldo, 217, 509
Emotional guidance, 449-469
  and grading, 463-464
  through literature, 449
  through music, 449-469 (see also Music)
Emotions:
  constructive, 236
  guiding the, 449-469
Empathy, breakdown of, 93-94
Employment:
  of educated youth, 10-11
  of learned class, problem, 3
Encyclopaedia Britannica, 253
Encyclopedism, 7
Encyclopedists, 146
Engels, Friedrich, 348, 356
Engineering devices, mobilization of, 67-69
English, as central subject, 279-281
Equality, principle of, 43, 331
Erasmus, 2, 167, 168, 170, 178
Escapism, 342
Essert, Paul L., comment by, 14, 33, 225, 259, 275, 338, 426, 444
Ethical mechanism, Huxley's, 315-316
Ethics, teaching of, 218-219
Ethnocentrism, 359
Euripides, dramas of, 373, 374
European Recovery Program, 71, 235, 241
Existentialists, 128, 158
Experience, 76
  sharing of, 91
Experiment:
  education as, 429-448
  need for, 430
Experts, 479
  technical, as leaders, 334
Extroverts, and goals, 31

Fact, definition of, 85
Faculty committees, and objectives, 416-423

Faculty members, disaffected, 423
Family life, role of, 188-190
Farley, James, 317
Fascism, 151, 245, 481-482
Fatalism, 245
Federalist Papers, 148
Federal Report, 294, 296-297, 299, 303, 305, 307, 328, 332, 336, 337
Federal Republic of the World, 331-332, 335
Federal support of education, 12
Feedback concept, 111 ff.
Fine arts, 193, 194
Finer, Herman, comment by, 23, 24, 25, 33, 43, 56, 57, 65, 72, 108, 109, 111, 131, 139, 217, 218, 219, 226, 299, 305, 306, 311, 336
Five Year Plans, 12
Flexner, Abraham, 9
Foerster, Norman, 286, 287, 291
  comment by, 392, 393
Folkschule of Scandinavian countries, 259
Football, intercollegiate, 248-249
Four Freedoms, 336
Fourier, François, 348
France, secondary education in, 261, 262
Frank, Philipp, 479
  comment by, 131, 132, 136
Frank, Waldo, 368-369
Freedom, 487
  academic, 5, 12-13, 19, 74
  and coherence in societies, 129-132
  and science, 195-197
  and the arts, 194-195
  education in, 178-182
  of the mind, 473-474
  education for, 179-183
  necessity for, 192
  problems re., in our time, 192-194
  philosophic, 182
Free will, 123, 125, 126, 128
French language, study of, 276, 281
French rationalists, 1
French Revolution, 5
French writers, 268-269
Freud, Sigmund, 348, 439
Friedgood, Harry B.:
  comment by, 341, 342
  quoted, 474-475
Friends of Soviet Russia, 231
Frustration, failure and, 319

Index

Fundamentals, study of, Chicago Plan, 257
Furer, Julius A., 70
Future:
  building for, social concensus in, 342, 351-357
  history as, 342, 343-344
  past and, 7

Galileo, 162, 181, 215
Gauss, Christian, comment by, 24, 25, 28-29
General education, 6, 202, 203, 220
  goals of, 472-476
  nature of, 431-432
General Education in a Free Society, 294, 414
General education program, 449
  music in, 462
General Electric Company, 388
General Electric Laboratories, 219
General knowledge, 382
Gentleman, cult of the, 216-218
German language, study of, 281
German universities, 4-5
  scholarship in, 394
Gestalt, 116
Gibbon, James, 1
Gifted, the, and graduate training, 249-250
"Global Federation, Preliminary Draft for," 331-332, 335
Goals (*see also* Objectives):
  meaning of, 113, 346
  shared, 355
Goal seeking, 342, 344-351
God and the Professors, 141
Goethe, Johann Wolfgang von, 114, 223
Good, the, 323-325
Good life, the, 240-241
Gorer, Geoffrey, 206
Government:
  and education, 30
  and the university, 4
  institutions, scientific research by, 12
Grading, emotional guidance and, 463-464
Graduate education, 9, 10, 249-250, 389-390
  and sponsoring, 391
  confusion of professional with, 390
  taken over by specialists, 219
Graduates, college, qualities sought by business, 474

Graduate students, University of Chicago, 256
Great Books, 20, 202, 251, 253, 258, 260, 285, 295, 327, 373, 379, 382, 396-397, 473, 503, 511, 517-519
Great Books Foundation, 253
Greece, 65
Greek, study of, 262, 268-270, 275-277
Greeks, 80, 82, 223
  civilization of, 323-324
  education and learning of, 63, 145
  tragedy of their science, 86-89, 92-95
Greenberg, Simon, 480
Greene, Theodore M., 9, 472-473
Gregory VII, Pope, 100
Gross, Mason W., comment by, 446-447
Grotius, Hugo, 169-171, 172, 174, 178, 179
Group:
  common faith of, 478
  concept of, 134
Group mind, as end and means, 342, 358-361
Group-soul, 148
Group tensions, 476-477
Group warfare, 185
Growth, 348
Guilds, teaching methods of, 64

Hamilton, Sir William, 4
Harris, Seymour E., 10
Hartlib, Samuel, 173
Hartmann, Nicolai, 46
Harvard Faculty Committee, on objectives, 414
Harvard Plan, 294, 295, 296, 298, 299, 307
Harvard Report on *General Education in a Free Society*, 294
Harvard University, typical first and second year program, 265
Harvey, William, 105
Haskins, C. P., comment by, 23, 132
Health, physical, 493
Hebraic tradition, 97, 99, 288, 301, 323-324, 520
Hebrews, ancient, 223
Hegel, Georg W. F., 64
Hendel, Charles W., 163-199
Hesse, Hermann, 383
Hellenism, heritage from, 323-324, 329
"Heuristics," 66
Hierarchy, 104

Index

Higher education:
  and unity of knowledge, 55-139
  as privilege of élite, 56
  axiological orientation of, 31-53
  control and financing of, 4-5
  decentralization of, 399-400
  in recent decades, 245
  in time of change, 19-30
  need for normative unity in, 293-339
  objectives of (*see* Objectives of education)
  opportunity for, 10
  persons with, increase in numbers of, 56
  quantitative expansion of, 60-62
  religion in, 298-300
  rise and decline of, 1-18
  the "impossible" for, 32, 33, 42-47
  university (*see* University)
Higher Education, Report of the President's Commission on, 10, 61, 164, 294, 296-297, 399, 412-413
Higher Education in the South, on objectives, 413-414
High schools (*see also* Secondary education):
  curriculum, present-day, 272
  motivating subjects of, 271, 272-285
  seniors, 282
  specialism and, 220
Historical continuity, 13
Historicism, 7
History:
  as future, 342, 343-344
  modern teaching of, 218
  of our civilization, 434
  of science and thought:
    basic course in, 75-102
    unifying course in, 75
  reason in, 75-102
  study of, 278, 281
  value of, 524
Hitler, Adolf, 5, 23, 328
Hobbes, Thomas, 105
Holiness, concept of, 43, 324-325
Holmes, Oliver Wendell, Jr., 45
Hopkins, Mark, 374
Humane order, 364
Humanism, scientific, 503, 504
Humanistic education, 169-171
Humanists, 64
Humanitarian naturalism, 520

Humanities, 12, 250, 256, 276, 278-279, 282, 307, 323, 381
Human life:
  phases of, 321-322
  transcendental significance of, 326-327
Human minds, interdependence of, 56, 57-59
Human nature, 57
  and power, wisdom, and morale, 329-330
  educational problems set by, 476-477
  education to serve, 246
  not static, 443
Human problems, research and, 388
Human relations, fundamental, breakdown of, 93-94
Human rights, fundamental, 504
Hume, David, 67
Hunter College, New York, 373-384
Hunter College Concert Series, 383
Hutchins, Robert M., 9, 30, 49, 50, 225, 247, 248, 252, 255, 256, 260, 264, 271, 305, 379, 380
  on purpose of education, 409
Huszar, George B. de, comment by, 249, 252, 516-519
Huxley, Julian, 58, 59, 315-316

I.B.M. machines, 67, 68
Ideology, 148
Ignatius of Loyola, 261
Ignorance, and evil, 63
Imagination, importance of, in education, 32
Imperialism, industrial, 220
Impossible, the, goal of, 32, 33, 42-47
Impossiblism, 368
Incentives, 36
Indifferentism, 473
Individual, rights and duties of, and democracy, 326
Individual development, 435
Individual personality, 503
Indoctrination, 497-498, 499
  democratic, 306
  or communication, 73-75
  religious, 53
  with irrationality, 92
Industrialization:
  of memory, 67-69
  research laboratories, 69

Industrial organizations, scientific research by, 12
Industrial revolution:
  in field of knowledge today, 64-72
  in production and treatment of knowledge, 56
Industry:
  investigations for, 386
  specialism and, 220
In Quest of Morals, 316
Instincts, transfer of, 60
Institute of Advanced Studies, 219
Institute of Higher Studies, 391
Institutes of Technology, 6
Instructors (*see* Teachers)
Instructorships, certification of, 287
Integration:
  knowledge and, 382
  teaching of music and, 462-463
Intellectual curiosity, 2
Intellectual meaningfulness, 14, 16
Intellectual techniques, mobilization of, 67-69
Intelligence, 345
  and applied science, 322
  and educational opportunity, 61
  contemporary devaluation of, 151-162
Intercultural education, 205
Interests, 347
Intergroup relations, 355
Intergroup tensions, 476-477
International consensus, 355
International law, 184
Intolerance, 245, 316
Introverts, 32
  and goals, 31
Intuition, 66
  and mimesis, 77-78
Investigators, education of, 393
Israel, greatness of, 80

Jacobins, 52
James, William, 221, 439
Japan, growth of technology in, 101
Jaspers, Karl, 128
Jernegan, Marcus W., 10
Jesuit students, 268
Jesus of Nazareth, 95, 97, 168, 288
Jewish groups, 360
Johanson, E. Jerome, 473
Johns Hopkins University, 219

Johnson, F. Ernest, 471-483
Jones, Howard Mumford, 9, 213-233, 509, 514, 517, 522-523
  suggested objectives, 411
Judaism, 97, 301
Judeo-Christian thought and tradition, 99, 520
Judgment, esthetic and moral, 193-194
Junior college, 264, 265
  curriculum in, 283-285
Junior high school, 264, 265
Jurisprudence, 154
Justice, concept of, 43, 154

Kandel, I. L., 471, 483, 512
  comment by, 232, 328, 370, 430, 508-511
Kant, Immanuel, 58, 192, 197
Kaplan, Mordecai M., 293-339, 524
Kefauver, Grayson N., 473
Kettering, Charles F., 69
Key concepts, research on, 75, 133-136
Knowledge, 32
  as power, 314
  both "know what" and "know how," 76
  fracturing of, 258
  functional quality of, 381, 382
  kinds of, 494-495
  monopolies of, end of, 60
  organized, monopolization of, 92
  sharing of, 91
  synthesis of, and Chicago Plan, 257
  transfer of, and transformation of society, 59-62
  unified, 141-152, 203
    technological growth and crises in, 62-64
Knowledge-subjects, 270-271, 273

Labeling of courses, 286
Labor, held in low esteem, 92
Laboratory scientist, 218
Labor education, 217-218
Labor management committees, 355
LaFarge, John, comment by, 8, 34, 50, 277, 321, 338, 432, 433, 443
Languages:
  modern, 276, 281
  motivating study of, 273, 275, 276-278
  Romance, 285
Lanz, Harry, 316

Index

Latin, study of, 262, 264, 268, 269-270, 275-277, 280-281
Law:
  development of, 85-86
  fundamental, 182-183
  international, 184
  trade and, 80-81
Law schools, and Chicago Plan, 252, 253-254
Lawyer, as political leader, 334
Leadership:
  democracy and, 332-335
  education for, 217, 395
Learned class, problem of employment, 3
Learned societies, 389
Learning:
  and purpose, 112-115
  desire for, 180, 188
  new, 202
  psychology of, 438-439
Learning net, 129-132
Lee, Umphrey, 291
Leibnitz, Gottfried Wilhelm von, 58
Leland, Waldo G., 509
Lessing, Ephraim, 467
Levy, Ronald B., comment by, 370-371
Liberal arts, 396
  preservation of, 6
Liberal arts colleges, separate, 400-401
Liberal arts programs, music in, 462-467
Liberal education, 472, 474, 516
Liberal living, training for, 20
Liberty, 474
  English, 171, 182
  Milton and, 172-182
Lilienthal, David E., 30, 376
Lincoln, Abraham, 42
Linnenberg, Clem C., Jr., comment by, 15, 225, 226, 229, 241, 336
Literature:
  motivating study of, 278
  promoting culture through, 449 (see also Chicago Plan; St. John's plan)
Living, art of, 311-313
Livingston, Sir Richard, 409-410
Llewellyn, Karl N., 154
Locke, Alain L., 201-212
  comment by, 27-28
Locke, John, 105, 192, 224
Logic, 81-83, 115, 282
  new, 203

Logic (*Cont.*)
  research and training in, 75
Logical positivists, 203
Logistics, science of, 71
Lombard cities, League of, 100
Love, 477
  and law, 317
Loyalties, on which men can agree, 73
Lyceum, organization of, 145
Lynd, Robert, 348, 368

McGrath, Earl J., 385-404, 506
Machiavelli, 101, 168
Machines:
  and learning, 67-69
  definitions of, 106, 129
  minds, and societies, 108-111
Machine tools, 66
Macintosh, D. C., 39, 40
MacIver, R. M., 492-499
Magic, 83-84, 195
Man:
  goal-seeking animal, 342, 344-351
  unity of, 56, 57-59
"Man Against Darkness," 155
Manhattan Project, 69
Mann, Thomas, 369
Marcel, Gabriel, 158
Margenau, Henry, comment by, 102, 132
Maritain, Jacques, 255, 490-491
Marshall, James, 476
Marshall Plan, 71
Marx, Karl, 64, 348, 356
Marxism, 155, 368
Mass communications, 193-194
  and Chicago Plan, 257-258
Master's degree, 287-288
Matching, and reason, 81-83
Materialism, 158
Mathematical techniques:
  new, 68
  of Arabs, 64
Mathematics:
  high school, 273-275
  power of, 84
  research and training in, 75
Mauldin, Bill, 43
Mead, Margaret, 206
Meaningfulness, intellectual, 14, 16
Meaning of Right and Wrong, The, 317
Means, concept of, 360

Measurement, concept of, 82
Mechanism:
    classical model of, 105-106
    study of role of, 75
Meiklejohn, Alexander, comment by, 147, 151
Melanchthon, 3
Melting pot, 412
Memories, concept of, 115
Memory:
    industrialization of, 67-69
    tests, 256
Men of affairs, education of, 169-171
Mental capacity, and educational opportunity, 61
Merchants, and history of education, 80
Mercier, Louis J. A., comment by, 13, 14-15, 25, 40, 46, 73, 74, 139, 232-233, 252, 339, 367, 380, 382, 386, 390, 426, 447, 467, 510, 520-522
Mercy, and law, 317
Mesopotamians, 82
Messages:
    and symbols, 115-117
    primary and secondary, 119-123
Middle Ages, 4, 5, 13, 65, 97, 145, 213, 214, 502
    Christian revolution in, 99-105
    secondary education in, 268
Mill, John Stuart, 72
Milton, John, 163, 172-175, 177, 178, 179, 180, 181, 182, 183, 188, 322
Mimesis, 77-78
Mind, definition of, 76-77
Minds, machines, societies, and, 108-111
Mind-sets, constructive, 205
Mobilization:
    of intellectual techniques, 67-69
    of personnel, 69-72
Models, role of, research on, 75, 102-132
Modern education, distinctive aim of, 446
Modern languages, in junior college, 283, 284
Mohammedanism, 301
Molotov, V. M., 61
Montague, William P., 369
Montesquieu, 105, 182
Morale, dimension of, 320
Moral education, 165-167, 188
    and education in freedom, 178-182
Moral imperatives, 238-239

Moral responsibility, 128
Morality, religion and, 164
Morals, In Quest of, 316
Moral standards, 512, 513
Morris, Charles, 117, 206
Motion pictures, 193
Mueller-Freienfels, R., 58
Municipal college:
    administration of, 373-384
    definition of, 374
    liberal arts in, 378
    practical education in, 378
    special problems of, 382-384
    students of, 376-378
Murray, John Courtney, 151-162
Music:
    accrediting in, 460-461
    and "integration," 462-463
    and leisure, 465-466
    and philosophy, 451-452
    appreciation courses, 465
    definitions of, 453
    degrees in, 457-460, 461
    emotional guidance through, 449-468
    enjoyment of, 454
    evolution of art, 452-453
    grading in, 463
    Hunter College concert series, 383
    in universities, 457-467
        in liberal arts programs, 462-467
        professional training, 457-461
    listener training, 454-457
    materials and esthetics of art, 453-457
    meaning in, 464-465
    musical "morons," 465-466
    period of study, 461
    role of, in education, 450-451
    taste in, aim of building, 466-467
Musical composition, 454
Music appreciation, courses in, 451
Mussolini, Benito, 23
Myths:
    cultural, role of, 342, 365-370
    good and bad, true and false, 366

Napoleonic dictatorship, 7
National Association of Schools of Music, 461
Nationalism, cultivated, in politics, 183-184
Nations:
    backward, 220

Index 549

Nations (*Cont.*)
 modern, 184
 prohibitions of, 125
Nature, prediction and control of events in, 83
Nazianzen, Gregory, 311
Nazi Germany, intellectuals in, 487
Nazism, 151
Necessities of life, 348
Needs, human, 347
Nef, John U., 155, 243-260
Negro groups, 359-360
Neilson, William A., 509
Neo-Thomism, 296, 299, 337, 367
New England, 177
Newton, Sir Isaac, 105
Niebuhr, Reinhold, 41
Nietzsche, Frederick, 344
Nikhilananda, Swami, comment by, 225, 229
Norris, Louis W., comment by, 51-52, 146, 148, 225, 233, 282, 291, 417, 418, 423
Northrop, F. S. C., 206
 suggested objectives, 411
Novelty, communication of, 91

Objective attitude, 288, 290, 316, 317
Objectives of education:
 abundance of, 405-406
 Amherst College report on, 414-415
 conferences on, 419-420
 application of:
  cooperation in, 418-419
  effectiveness of, 424-426
 evaluation procedures, 423-424
 extroverts and introverts and, 31
 faculty committees and, 416-423
 formulation of, methods, 416-417
 from preceding session and publications, 471-483
 F. S. C. Northrop on, 411-412
 Harvard Faculty Committee Report on, 414
 Higher Education in the South on, 413-414
 Howard Mumford Jones on, 411
 how forwarded, 418-423
 kinds of, 408-411
 long-range, 406, 407
 new, acceptance of, 420-422

Objectives of education (*Cont.*)
 Pennsylvania College for Women on, 415-416
 reasons for, 406
 Report of the President's Commission on Higher Education on, 412-413
 role of, 405-427
 samples of, 411-416
 secularist and religious, 477-480
 statements of, value in diversity of, 407-408
Obligations, social, 108
Office of Scientific Research and Development, 69
One world, education and, 213-233
Opera, 452
Opinion polls, 237
Opinions, variety of, 373-374
Opportunity, 505
 educational, abundance of, 60-61
Ordeal, 83
Organism:
 classical concept of, 106-108
 definitions of, 107, 129
 study of role of, 75
Organizations:
 large-scale collective, 186-187
 national, 184-185
Orient:
 instruction on, 512, 514
 study of, in college curriculum, 225, 228-231
Oriental civilizations, 296
Orientation, 498-499
 courses, 202
Oropesa, Juan, criticism of objectives, 412
Ortega y Gasset, 395
Otto, Max C., comment by, 441, 442
Oxford University, 5

Paine, Thomas, 105
Panslavism, 245
Parents, responsibilities of, 192-193
Paris, University of, 5, 213
Parker, Francis W., 266
Particularism, 245
Pascal, Blaise, 244, 318
Patriotism, 39, 51
Patronage, and university, 4, 8, 12-13
Paul, Saint, 95, 97, 100, 173
Peace, education for, 482

Pelagius, 160
Pennsylvania College for Women, 415-416
Perfection, goal of education, 51
Personality, 318, 326, 503
Personal relationships:
 in college curriculum, 224
 study of, 523
Personal responsibility, 166-167
Personnel, mobilization of, 69-72
Ph.D. degree (*see* Doctor's degrees)
Phelan, Gerald B., comment by, 47, 53, 300, 301, 302, 365
Philology, 218
Philosophers, 47-50
Philosophical faculty, 6
Philosophy, 219
 and music, 451-452
 central responsibility of, 341
 contemporary, 161, 441
 in secondary school, 279, 281
 of leadership, 335
 of life, 307, 308
 study of, 307
Philosophy in American Education, 307
Planning, 71, 72
 economic, 142
Plato, 40, 44, 47, 145, 146, 150, 151, 168, 179, 193, 223, 224
 on musical training, 451
Platonism, 366
Pleasure principle, 345
Pluralism, 439, 444, 490, 491
Poetry, 368
Pole, William, 453
Political leaders, 334
Politics, 147-151, 153-154
 education and, 163-199
 power, 185
Polls, opinion, 237
Polya, G., 66
Polybius, 93
Pope, Alexander, 179
Positivists, logical, 203
Possible, goal of the, 32, 33, 38-42
Power, 489
 dimension of, 313-315
Power politics, 185
Practical, the, goal of, 32, 33, 35-38
Practical absolute, 368
Practicality, 51
Practical minded, the, 341

Prehension, concept of, 349-351
Prejudice, 163-164, 166
 overcoming, 482
 racial, 163
President's Commission on Higher Education, Report of the, 10, 61, 164, 294, 296-297, 399, 412-413
Press, 193
 university, 219
Primary education, the "practical" for, 32, 33, 35-38
Princeton Plan, 298
Problem solving, history of, 102
Process understanding, 204
Professional education, 72, 224, 226, 249-250, 391-392
 confusion of graduate with, 390
 function of university, 385-386
 schools, early, 5
Professional work, preparation for, 1
Professors (*see also* Faculty members):
 attitude toward, 12
 German university, 5
Progressive education, 282, 283, 302-303
 aims of, 435-436
 and ends, goals, outcomes, 345
 background of, 439-440
 criticisms of, 434-435, 436
 early, 266
 in secondary school, 267
 risks in, 436
Progressive schools, 271
Prometheus, 159
Proof, 81-83
Propaganda:
 avoidance of, 472
 non-susceptibility to, 236
Propaganda analysis, 209
Protestantism, 3
Provincialism, American, 512, 514
Psychiatry, 220
Psychological research, and new educational methods, 438
Psychology, 219
 and change of heart, 477
 depth, 155, 474
 laboratory technique employed by, 219
 of learning, 438-439
 social, 220
Public activity, function and purpose differentiated, 24

Index

Public opinion:
  study of, 209
  surveys, 386
Puritan revolution, 175-177
Purpose, 318, 348 (*see also* Goals):
  learning and, 112-115
Purposelessness of nature and man, 157, 160, 161
Pyramid, Egyptian, 104

Quintilian, 268

Racial differences, in education opportunities, 61
Racial groups, social consensus and, 354
Racial myth, 365
Racial prejudice, 163
Radar, 110
Radicalism, 38
Radio, 194
Randall, John H., Jr., 509
Rationalist idealism, 7
Rationalization, 316
Ratio Studiorum, 261, 262
Reaction, 38
  danger of, 7
Reading, 496
Readjustments, 345
Reason:
  and pure science, 322
  concepts, rules, trails, 78-81
  in education, 32
  matching, logic, proof, culture, 81-83
  to science, 83-85
Reasoning, abstract, of Greeks, 88
Recognition, 81
Rehabilitation, music and, 450-451
Relativism, 7
  critical, 209 210
Religion, 46, 197-199
  and change of heart, 477
  and morality, 164
  and the holy, 324-325
  departmentalized, 472
  ideological use of, 366
  in elementary education, 267
  in higher education, 298-300
  in public education, 479-480
    state education laws, 376
  in secondary school, 279, 281

Religion (*Cont.*)
  institutional, 326, 330
  and democracy, 320-321
  great terms of, 327, 328
  teaching of, 288-290
Religious consensus, 355
Religious goals, secularist goals and, 477-480
Remembering, 495
Renaissance, education in, 214, 215
Report of the Federal Commission on Higher Education for American Democracy, 294
Report of the President's Commission on Higher Education, 10, 61, 164, 294, 296-297, 399, 412-413
Representative process:
  and democracy, 332-335
  knowledge of, 225, 227
Republic, Plato's, 47, 93, 94, 150, 168
Research:
  educational, 445
  encouraging, 385, 387-401
  on key concepts, 133-136
  on role of models, 102-132
  purpose of university, 3
  scientific, 12
  subsidation of, 219
  training in, function of university, 385, 387-401
Research laboratories, industrialization, 69
Responsibility:
  democratic, 182
  moral, 128
  of mass communications, 194
  personal, 166-167
  social, 187-188
  to one's culture, training for, 20
Rewards, concept of, 114
Rights, and interests, 154
Rohrlich, George F., 481
Roman Catholic Church, 300, 321
Roman Empire, 97, 98, 145
Roosevelt, Franklin D., 217
Rootlessness, 508, 512-513
Rosenstock-Huessy, Eugene, 99
Roucek, Joseph S., 476
Rousseau, Jean Jacques, 106, 193
Rules, reason and, 78-81
Ruskin, John, 464
Russell, Bertrand, 83, 159

Russia, 71
  government and education in, 144
  instruction on, 512, 514
    in college curriculum, 225, 228-231
  understanding, 523, 524
Russia and the Russians, 231
Russian Institute, 230

St. John's College, 20, 251, 285, 286, 295, 449, 462
Salisbury, Mr., 231
Salvation:
  mundane, 337-338, 339
  philosophy of, and democracy, 304-305, 306, 308-313
Santayana, George, 34, 46-47, 48, 51, 52, 53, 508
Sarah Lawrence College, 410, 434
Sayers, E. V., comment by, 364, 370
Scandinavian countries, *folkschule* of, 259
Schiller, Johann von, 105, 464
Scholarship:
  and the university, 2, 8, 11-12
  German university, 394
  education for, function of university, 385, 387-401
Scholasticism, 1, 2, 3, 4, 64
  Christian, 7
Scholastics, 145
School of Classical Studies, Rome, 219
Schopenhauer, Arthur, 468
Science:
  and abdication of intelligence, 157
  and life, 32
  applied, 220, 322-323
  Christianity and restoration of, 95-99
  from reason to, 83-85
  Greek, tragedy of, 86-89
  high school, 273-275
  implications of, 84-85
  intuition and, 78
  logico-empirical analysis of, 478-479
  modern, 142-143
  natural, 75-102
  not a likely cure, 159
  pure:
    and applied, 220
    purpose of, 322
  reason and, 78-81
  rise of, 82, 84
  science of, search for, 65-66

Science (*Cont.*)
  social, 75-102
  study of, 224
  wartime organization of, 69
  what it needs to live, 89-95
"Science, Strategy of," 66
Science Talent Search, 220
Scientific attitude, pride in, 15
Scientific management, 71
Scientific method:
  and fact of man's existence, 162
  techniques for reaching, 160
  validity of, 503
Scientific optimism, 7
Scientific research, by big industrial organizations and government institutions, 12
Scientific society, 363
Scientist, laboratory, 218
Secondary education:
  development of, 267-285
  goals of, 261-266
  in Europe, Canada, South America, 261-263, 264, 265
  in United States, 263-266
  progressive education and, 267
  the "possible" for, 32, 33, 38-42
Secularist goals, and religious goals, 477-480
Self-control, of aggressive drives, 476
Self-discipline, 435
Self-government, 183, 184
Self-preservation, 308
Self-support, 36
Semanticists, 203
Semantics, 66
Senior college, 264, 265
  curriculum in, 285-286
Service:
  as motto, 221
  concept of, 487-488
  humble, day-to-day, 21-22
  on job, ideal of, and education, 25-26
Services, informal, for community, function of university, 385, 386-387
Service state, 362-363
Shakespeare, William, 223
Shapley, Harlow, 475-476
Shuster, George N., 373-384, 474, 517
  comment by, 21, 22
Simson, G. O. von, 256

Singer, Charles, 84
Size, evils of, in education and modern world, 258
Skill, 36-37
Skills, new, 71
Skill-subjects, 270-271, 273, 278
Slavery, plantation, 92-93
Slochower, Harry, comment by, 369
Smith, Adam, 220
Smith, B. Othanel, 16-17
 comment by, 9, 347, 358, 402, 424, 440
Smith, T. V., 31-53, 72, 506
Smuts, Jan Christiaan, 59
Social change, worldwide pressure for, 62
Social consensus:
 and racial groups or associations, 354
 as practical device, 353-357
 definition of, 351
 implications of, 352-353
 in future building, 342, 351-357
 utopian, 360
Social critics, 3
Social education, 205
Socialism, 245
Social living, education for, 24, 25
Social order, education and, 480-483
Social psychology, 220
Social sciences, 387-388
 concept of, 220
 departments of, 221
Social Thought, Committee on, University of Chicago, 255-258
Societies:
 collective industrial, 443
 differentiated from organisms or machines, 130
 freedom and coherence in, 129-132
 machines, minds and, 108-111
 present-day, 429
Society, 318-319
 educative, 190-191
 free, 240-241
 scientific, 363
 transformation of, transfer of knowledge and, 59-62
Sociology, modern, foundation of, 220
Socrates, 63, 150, 178, 179, 180, 198-199, 317
Sophocles, 223
Soul:
 concept of, 318

Soul (*Cont.*)
 loss of knowledge of, 158
Soviet Union (*see* Russia)
Spaulding, F. T., 61
Specialism, 245
 concept of, 218
Specialists, 6, 12, 433
 education of, 72
 training of, 60-61
 triumph of, 218-222
Specialization, 259, 285
Specialized courses, 136
Speech, 496
Spencer, Herbert, 220
Spender, Stephen, 440
Spengler, Oswald, 1
Spinoza, 49, 50, 53, 192, 197
Spirit, and social science, 57
Spiritual values, 512, 513
Sponsoring of graduate students, 391
Spontaneous impulse, 127, 128
Stace, W. T., 155-157, 159, 160
Standardization, by social usage, 78
State, service, 362-363
State education laws, 375-376
State institutions, research in, 387
States, prohibitions of, 125
State universities, 263, 264, 385, 386, 472
Stephens College, 410
Stimulation, substituted for education, 21
Stone, Donald C., 235-241
Strang, Ruth, 477
 comment by, 232, 259-260, 303, 522-524
Stribling, T. B., 508
Stuart kings, 171
Students:
 and curricular reorganization, 425
 foreign, 444, 445
 individual differences, 442
 responsibilities given to, 445
Subjectivity, 317
Success, 28, 489, 513
 educational, estimations of, 425-426
 emphasis on, 237, 255
 old way of, 22-23
 youth of today and, 21-22
Sumerians, 82
Superficiality, 508, 512-513
Supernaturalism, 326
Superstition, 92

Sutherland, Justice, 39, 40
Switchboards, and values, 117-119
Symbols:
  abstraction and, 76-77
  messages and, 115-117

Talent Search, Science, 220
Taylor, Harold, 429-448
  comment by, 21, 29, 260
Teachers:
  academic, 2
  college, need for, 394
  competency of, 512, 514-515
  education of, 393, 394
  in smaller liberal arts colleges, 9-10
  task of, 442
Teaching, quality of, 512, 514-515
Tead, Ordway, 405-427, 474
Technical experts, as leaders, 334
Technical schools, 6
Technocracy, 334
Technological growth, and recurrent crises in unity of knowledge, 56
Tensions:
  conducive to war, 482-483
  group, 476-477
Tests, memory, 256
Textbooks, study of, 471
Theism, 289, 339
Theology, 33-34, 141, 147-151
  "queen of the sciences," 301
  schools of, and Chicago Plan, 252, 254
Theologians, 46-47
Thinking:
  global, 204, 523
  methodical, 3
  training in, 496-499, 502
  ways of, 75
Thirty Years War, 65
Thomas's four wishes, 348
Thomism, 366
Tolerance, 490, 503
Totalitarianism, 5, 149, 239, 240, 291, 302, 473
Total war, 185
Toynbee, A. J., 1, 59, 89-91, 131, 142, 206
Trade, and law, 80-81
Trade unions, 360
Tradition:
  and change, 6-7
  common, of man, 58

Tradition (*Cont.*)
  Milton on, 181
Trails, reason and, 78-81
Troubadours, 452
Trustees, university, choice of, 334
Truth, 43, 323-325
  accessible to man, 160
  beliefs and, 73
  love of, 316
  seeking, through social consensus, 357
Tutoring, 286

Ulich, Robert, 1-18, 408, 504, 506, 510
Un-American Activities, Committee on, 230
Undergraduate college, 9
  specialism in, 219
Understanding, process of, 204
UNESCO, 164
Unified knowledge, 203
United Nations, 164
United States, quality of scholarly production in, 10
Unity, concept of, 487, 489-491, 504
Universality of knowledge, 6, 8
University, 64
  and civilization it serves, 6
  and continuity of culture, 6-7, 8
  contributions of, 237
  control and financing of, 4-5
  curriculum, organization of, 502, 506
  function of, 235-241, 385, 506
  German, 4-5
  heritage of, 213 ff.
  historical survey of, 1-8
  inception of, 1
  intellectual leadership of, 8-11
  organization of, 101
  Protestant, 3
  purposes of, 1, 3, 4, 8
  scholarship and, 3, 8, 11-12
  Scholastic, 1, 2, 3, 4
  state, 263, 264
  target of its aim, 502
  tasks for, 72 ff.
  uniqueness of, 502, 504
University press, 219
Unlearned behavior, transfer of, 60
Utopian thinker, practical role of, 356
Utopian thought, 341, 342, 356
  need for mythical element in, 365-370

Index

Vagantes, the, 3
Value judgments, 205, 206, 207, 209
Values, 205, 206, 313, 314, 477-478, 502, 504, 506
   and progressive education, 436-437
   agreement on, enforcement of, 73-74
   central to good society, 432
   seeking, through social consensus, 357
   study of, in secondary education, 267
   switchboards and, 117-119
   truth and, 73
Van Doren, Mark, 305, 308, 324
Veblen, Thorstein, 91
Vertical movement of thought, 13
Virtue, can it be taught? 188
Vision (or intuition), 77-78
Visual arts, 474
Vives, Louis, 2
Vocational education, 5, 19, 20, 23-24, 28, 224, 226, 474, 516, 523
   a function of university, 385-386
   glorification of, 395
   liberalization of, 25-27
Vocational experiences, 380
Vocational inlays, 380
Vocational schools, 16
Voluntary committees, 489

Wants, human, 347
Warfare:
   group, 185
   international, 336
   tensions conducive to, 482-483
Watkin, E. I., 161
Wealth of Nations, 220
Weaver, Richard M., 298
Weber, Max, 97
Welfare state, and education, 24, 25, 29
Weltanschauung, 7, 13

Western civilization, 100
Western Europe, 97-98, 99
Western man, 158
Westinghouse, 388
Wheel, as model, 104
White collar jobs, 216
Whitehead, Alfred North, 350, 439, 442
Wieman, Henry N., 478, 480, 481
Wiener, Norbert, 68, 116, 130
Wild, John D., comment by, 40, 48, 148, 150, 227, 231-232, 254, 255, 278, 279, 325, 327, 357, 358, 363, 381, 441, 468
Will, 123-128
   definition of, 124
   free, 123, 125, 128
   in education, 32
Willkie, Wendell, 397-398
Wirth, Louis, 483
Wisdom, dimension of, 315-318
Wishes, Thomas's four, 348
Words, extensional definition of, 136
Wordsworth, William, 107
Work, 25-26
   Christians' attitude toward, 97
   estrangement from, 93
   experiences, 380
   function and purpose differentiated, 24
World, the, 319
World democracy, 364-365
World government, 141-142
World order, education for, 482
World War II:
   operational research of, 69-70
   soldiers of, on education, 166
Wright, Quincy, comment by, 40, 52, 238, 344, 346, 368, 501-507

Yale Plan, 298